Human Development Report **2006**

Beyond scarcity:
Power, poverty and the global water crisis

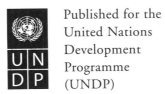

Published for the
United Nations
Development
Programme
(UNDP)

ISBN 0-230-50058-7

Palgrave Macmillan
Houndmills, Basingstoke, Hampshire RG21 6XS and
175 Fifth Avenue, New York, NY 10010

Companies and representatives throughout the world

Palgrave Macmillan is the global academic imprint of the Palgrave Macmillan division of
St. Martin's Press LLC and of Palgrave Macmillan Ltd.

Macmillan is a registered trademark in the United States, United Kingdom, and other countries.
Palgrave is a registered trademark in the European Union and other countries.

9   8   7   6   5   4   3   2   1
Printed by Hoechstetter Printing Co. on chlorine-free paper with vegetable inks and the
use of environmentally compatible technology.

Cover and layout design: Grundy & Northedge Information Designers, London
Maps and graphics: Philippe Rekacewicz, Narestø, Norway
Technical editing, layout and production management: Communications Development
Incorporated, Washington, D.C.
Editors: Bruce Ross-Larson, Meta de Coquereaumont and Christopher Trott

For a list of any errors or omissions found subsequent to printing, please visit our
website at http://hdr.undp.org

Team for the preparation of
Human Development Report 2006

Director and lead author
Kevin Watkins

Research, writing and statistics
Liliana Carvajal, Daniel Coppard, Ricardo Fuentes, Arunabha Ghosh, Chiara Giamberardini, Claes Johansson (Acting Chief of Statistics), Papa Seck, Cecilia Ugaz (Senior Policy Advisor) and Shahin Yaqub.

Statistical adviser: Tom Griffin
Production management and translation coordination: Carlotta Aiello and Marta Jaksona
Editors: Bruce Ross-Larson, Meta de Coquereaumont and Christopher Trott
Cover and layout design: Peter Grundy and Tilly Northedge
Maps and graphics: Philippe Rekacewicz

The Human Development Report Office (HDRO)
The *Human Development Report* is the product of a collective effort. Members of the National Human Development Report (NHDR) team provide detailed comments and advice throughout the research process. They also link the Report to a global HDR network in developing countries. The NHDR team, led by Sarah Burd-Sharps (Deputy Director), comprises Amie Gaye, Sharmila Kurukulasuriya, Hanna Schmitt and Timothy Scott. The HDRO administrative team makes the office function and includes Oscar Bernal, Mamaye Gebretsadik, Melissa Hernandez, Fe Juarez and Mary Ann Mwangi. Operations are managed by Sarantuya Mend. HDRO's outreach and advocacy programme is managed by Marisol Sanjines.

Foreword

Human development is first and foremost about allowing people to lead a life that they value and enabling them to realize their potential as human beings. The normative framework for human development is today reflected in the broad vision set out in the Millennium Development Goals, the internationally agreed set of time-bound goals for reducing extreme poverty, extending gender equality and advancing opportunities for health and education. Progress towards these objectives provides a benchmark for assessing the international community's resolve in translating commitments into action. More than that, it is a condition for building shared prosperity and collective security in our increasingly interdependent world.

This year's *Human Development Report* looks at an issue that profoundly influences human potential and progress towards the Millennium Development Goals. Throughout history human progress has depended on access to clean water and on the ability of societies to harness the potential of water as a productive resource. Water for life in the household and water for livelihoods through production are two of the foundations for human development. Yet for a large section of humanity these foundations are not in place.

The word *crisis* is sometimes overused in development. But when it comes to water, there is a growing recognition that the world faces a crisis that, left unchecked, will derail progress towards the Millennium Development Goals and hold back human development. For some, the global water crisis is about absolute shortages of physical supply. This Report rejects this view. It argues that the roots of the crisis in water can be traced to poverty, inequality and unequal power relationships, as well as flawed water management policies that exacerbate scarcity.

Access to water for life is a basic human need and a fundamental human right. Yet in our increasingly prosperous world, more than 1 billion people are denied the right to clean water and 2.6 billion people lack access to adequate sanitation. These headline numbers capture only one dimension of the problem. Every year some 1.8 million children die as a result of diarrhoea and other diseases caused by unclean water and poor sanitation. At the start of the 21st century unclean water is the world's second biggest killer of children. Every day millions of women and young girls collect water for their families—a ritual that reinforces gender inequalities in employment and education. Meanwhile, the ill health associated with deficits in water and sanitation undermines productivity and economic growth, reinforcing the deep inequalities that characterize current patterns of globalization and trapping vulnerable households in cycles of poverty.

As this Report shows, the sources of the problem vary by country, but several themes emerge. First, few countries treat water and sanitation as a political priority, as witnessed by limited budget allocations. Second, some of the world's poorest people are paying some of the world's highest prices for water, reflecting the limited coverage of water utilities in the slums and informal settlements where poor people live. Third, the international community has failed to prioritize water and sanitation in the partnerships for development that have coalesced around the Millennium Development Goals. Underlying each of these problems is the fact that the people suffering the most from the water and sanitation crisis—poor people in general and poor women in particular—often lack the political voice needed to assert their claims to water.

These and other issues are carefully examined in the Report. The challenges it sets out are daunting. But the authors do not offer a counsel of despair. As the evidence makes clear, this is a battle that we can win. Many countries have made extraordinary progress in providing clean water and sanitation. Across the developing world people living in slums and rural villages are providing leadership by example, mobilizing resources and displaying energy and innovation in tackling their problems. At the start of the 21st century we have the finance, technology and capacity to consign the water and sanitation crisis to history just as surely as today's rich countries did a century ago. What has been lacking is a concerted drive to extend access to water and sanitation for all through well designed and properly financed national plans, backed by a global plan of action to galvanize political will and mobilize resources.

Water for livelihoods poses a different set of challenges. The world is not running out of water, but many millions of its most vulnerable people live in areas subject to mounting water stress. Some 1.4 billion people live in river basins in which water use exceeds recharge rates. The symptoms of overuse are disturbingly clear: rivers are drying up, groundwater tables are falling and water-based ecosystems are being rapidly degraded. Put bluntly, the world is running down one of its most precious natural resources and running up an unsustainable ecological debt that will be inherited by future generations.

Far more also needs to be done in the face of the threats to human development posed by climate change. As the Report stresses, this is not a future threat. Global warming is already happening—and it has the potential in many countries to roll back human development gains achieved over generations. Reduced water supplies in areas already marked by chronic water stress, more extreme weather patterns and the melting of glaciers are part of the looming challenge. Multilateral action to mitigate climate change by reducing carbon emissions is one leg of the public policy response for meeting that challenge. The other is a far stronger focus on supporting adaptation strategies.

It is already clear that competition for water will intensify in the decades ahead. Population growth, urbanization, industrial development and the needs of agriculture are driving up demand for a finite resource. Meanwhile, the recognition is growing that the needs of the environment must also be factored in to future water use patterns. Two obvious dangers emerge. First, as national competition for water intensifies, people with the weakest rights—small farmers and women among them—will see their entitlements to water eroded by more powerful constituencies. Second, water is the ultimate fugitive resource, traversing borders through rivers, lakes and aquifers—a fact that points to the potential for cross-border tensions in water-stressed regions. Both dangers can be addressed and averted through public policies and international cooperation—but the warning signs are clearly visible on both fronts.

This Report, a product of research and analysis by international experts and staff across the UN system, is intended to stimulate debate and dialogue around a set of issues that will have a profound bearing on progress towards achieving the Millennium Development Goals and human development.

Kemal Derviş
Administrator
United Nations Development Programme

The analysis and policy recommendations of this Report do not necessarily reflect the views of the United Nations Development Programme, its Executive Board or its Member States. The Report is an independent publication commissioned by UNDP. It is the fruit of a collaborative effort by a team of eminent consultants and advisers and the *Human Development Report* team. Kevin Watkins, Director of the Human Development Report Office, led the effort.

Acknowledgements

This Report could not have been prepared without the generous contribution of many individuals and organizations. The authors wish to acknowledge their special debt to Amartya Sen, whose work has shaped the evolution of the *Human Development Report* over the years. Kemal Derviş, the Administrator of the United Nations Development Programme (UNDP), has provided consistent support and encouragement. His personal commitment is deeply appreciated. Errors of commission and omission are the sole responsibility of the authors.

Contributors

Background studies, papers and notes were prepared on a wide range of thematic issues relating to the Report. Contributors were: Martin Adams, José Albiac, Rajindra Ariyabandu, Jacob Assa, Karen Bakker, Bernard Barraqué, James Bartram, Jeremy Berkoff, Anders Berntell, Helen Bryer, Stephanie Buechler, Ximing Cai, Belinda Calaguas, Lorenzo Cotula, Elizabeth Daley, Andre DeGeorges, Malin Falkenmark, Matthew Gandy, Leonardo Gasparini, Toni German, Micheal Grimm, Alejandro Guevara-Sanginés, Laurence Haller, Ken Harttgen, Léo Heller, Juan Emilio Hernández Mazariegos, Caroline Hunt, Guy Hutton, Anders Jägerskog, Marion W. Jenkins, Stephan Klasen, Michelle Kooy, Jakub Landovsky, Jan Lundqvist, Boris Marañón, Richard R. Marcus, Ernst-Jan Martijn, Gordon McGranahan, Lyla Mehta, Ruth Meinzen-Dick, Mark Misselhorn, Erik Mostert, Synne Movik, Sobona Mtisi, Arnold Michael Muller, Sunita Narain, Alan Nicol, Tobias Pfütze, David Phillips, Brian Kevin Reilly, Claudia Ringler, Vicente Sánchez Munguía, Juan J. Sánchez-Meza, David Sattherthwaite, Christopher Scott, Dajun Shen, Nur Endah Shofiani, Steven Sugden, Erik Swyngedouw, Oumar Sylla, Sahnaz Tigrek, Leopoldo Tornarolli, Cecilia Tortajada, Håkan Tropp, Erika Weinthal, Dale Whittington and Aaron T. Wolf.

Several organizations generously shared their data and other research materials: Carbon Dioxide Information and Analysis Center, Caribbean Community Secretariat, Center for International Comparisons at the University of Pennsylvania, Development Initiatives, Economic and Social Commission for Asia and the Pacific, Economic and Social Commission for Latin America and the Caribbean, European Commission, Food and Agriculture Organization, Institute of Development Studies, Internal Displacement Monitoring Centre, International Food Policy Research Institute, International Institute for Environment and Development, International Institute for Strategic Studies, International Labour Organization, International Monetary Fund, International Organization for Migration, International Telecommunication Union, Inter-Parliamentary Union, Joint United Nations Programme on HIV/AIDS, Luxembourg Income Study, Office of the United Nations High Commissioner for Refugees, Organisation for Economic Co-operation and Development, Practical Action Consulting, Stockholm International Peace Research Institute, Stockholm International Water Institute,

United Nations Children's Fund, United Nations Conference on Trade and Development, United Nations Department of Economic and Social Affairs Statistics Division and Population Division, United Nations Development Fund for Women, United Nations Educational, Scientific and Cultural Organization Institute for Statistics, United Nations Office on Drugs and Crime Treaty Section, United Nations Office of Legal Affairs, WaterAid, World Bank, World Health Organization, World Intellectual Property Organization and World Trade Organization.

Advisory Panel

The Report benefited greatly from intellectual advice and guidance provided by an external advisory panel of experts. The panel comprised Karen Assaf, Michel Camdessus, Margaret Catley-Carlson, Leonid Dmitriev, Jan Eliasson, David Grey, Wang Hao, Sylvy Jaglin, Sir Richard Jolly, Inge Kaul, Roberto Lenton, Bindeshwar Pathak, Gérard Payen, Riccardo Petrella, Claudia W. Sadoff, Miguel Solanes, Olinda Sousa, Sandra Suarez Perez, Anna Kajumulo Tibaijuka, Klaus Toepfer, HRH Prince Willem-Alexander of the Netherlands, Ngaire Woods and Gordon Young. An advisory panel on statistics made an invaluable contribution. The panel members were Carla Abou-Zahr, Tony Atkinson, Hubert Escaith, Haishan Fu, Gareth Jones, Ian D. Macredie, Anna N. Majelantle, John Male-Mukasa, Marion McEwin, Saeed Ordoubadi, Francesca Perucci, Tim Smeeding, Eric Swanson, Pervez Tahir and Michael Ward. The team is grateful to Karen Frenken, Angela Me and David Pearce, the statistical peer reviewers who scrutinized the data in the Report and lent their statistical expertise.

Consultations

Many individuals consulted during the preparation of the Report provided invaluable advice, information and material. The Report team thanks Nigel Adderley, Wondu Alemayehu, Serge Allegrezza, Juan Carlos Alurralde, Paul Appasamy, Glauco Arbix, Togzhan Assan, Kaisha Atakhanova, Dan Banik, Michelle Barron, Aparna Basnyat, Ivar A. Baste, Charles Batchelor, Sylvia Beales, Rosangela Berman Bieler, Åsa Blomström, Rutgerd Boelens, Anne Bousquet, Benedito Braga, Marcia M. Brewster, Tony Burton, Eva Busza, Fernando Calderon, Ken Caplan, Markela Castro, Tarek Abou Chabake, Lekha Chakraborty, Mary Chamie, Jacques Charmes, Declan Conway, Esteve Corbera, Priti Darooka, Raj Kumar Daw, Partha Deb, Manuel Dengo, Catalina Devandas Aguilar, Philip Dobie, Moez Doraid, Kassym Duskayev, Arne Eide, Melissa Eisdell, Pauline Eizema, Elin Enge, Janique Etienne, Merle Douglas Faminow, Jean-Marc Faurès, Kimberly Fisher, Richard Franceys, Sakiko Fukuda-Parr, Ludmila Funso, Oscar Garcia, Maria Genina, Uladzimir Gerus, Peter Ghys, Donna L. Goodman, Maurizio Guadagni, Irene Guimarães Altafin, HRH Crown Prince Haakon, Brian Hammond, Bente Herstad, Hans Olav Ibrekk, Artemy Izmestiev, Kareen Jabre, S. Janakarajan, David Jones, Hazel Jones, Andrei Jouravlev, Tim Kasten, Ashfaq Khalfan, Nariman Kipshakbayev, Aloysius Kiribaki, Karoly Kovacs, Radhika Lal, Jean Langers, Christopher Langton, Bruce Lankford, James Lenahan, Michael Lipton, Edilberto Loaiza, Mitchell Loeb, Jan Lundqvist, Nora Lustig, Rolf Luyendijk, Howard Mann, Sebastien Martin, Wariara Mbugua, Charlotte McClain-Nhlapo, Patrick McCully, David Molden, Daniel Mont, Federico Montero, Trevor Mulaudzi, Carlos Muñoz, Teresa Munzi, Naison Mutizwa-Mangiza, Ngila Mwase, Rohini Nayyar, Gunhild Oerstavik, Siddiq Osmani, P. Sainath, Richard Palmer-Jones, Eric Patrick, David Pearce, Agueda Perez, Chris Perry, Henrik Pilgaard, Will Prince, Shammy Puri, Eva Quintana Mourelle, Xavi Ramos, Kalyan Ray, Chris Reij, Nils Rosemann, Shea Rutstein, Steven Sabey, Bharati Sadasivam, Zhanara Sagimbaeva, Julio Sanjines, Lisa Schipper, Janet Seeley, Sharda Sekaran, Yuriko Shoji, Yuriy Shokamanov, Vladimir Smakhtin, David Smith, Petter Stålenheim, Ashok Subramanian, Morten Svelle, Michel Thieren, Håkan Tropp, Tuong To Phuc, Vanessa Tobin, Kerry Turner, Sriti Vadera, Imraan Valodia, Henk van Norden, Veronique Verdeil, Saïd Ould A. Voffal, Charles Vorosmarty, Bill Walker, Tessa Wardlaw, Dominic Waughray, Siemon

Wezeman, Peter Whalley, Howard White, Florian Wieneke, Lars Wirkus, Albert M. Wright, Nancy Yanez Fuenzalida, Bulat Yessekin, Elizabeth Zaniewski and Windy Zhang.

UNDP Readers

A Readers Group, made up of colleagues in UNDP, provided extremely useful comments, suggestions and inputs during the writing of the Report. The Report team is especially grateful to Nada Al-Nashif, Amat Al Aleem Ali Alsoswa, Johan Arvling, Walid Badawi, Michel Balima, Mohamed Bayoumi, Robert G. Bernardo, Razina Bilgrami, Aeneas C. Chuma, Niamh Collier-Smith, Pedro Conceição, Philip Dobie, Jafet Enriquez, Sergio Feld, Emilie Filmer-Wilson, Bjoern Foerde, Edith Gassana, Prema Gera, Tegegnework Gettu, Rebeca Grynspan, Tim Hannan, Joakim Harlin, Gilbert Fossoun Houngbo, Andrew Hudson, Ragnhild Imerslund, Abdoulie Janneh, Bruce Jenks, Gordon Eric Johnson, Nanak Kakwani, Douglas Keh, Rima Khalaf Hunaidi, Olav Kjorven, Elie Kodsi, Oksana Leshchenko, Carlos Linares, Metsi Makhetha, Lamin Manneh, Elena Martinez, Pratibha Mehta, Kalman Mizsei, Cielo Morales, David Morrison, Abdoulaye Ndiaye, Shoji Nishimoto, Joseph Opio-Odongo, William Orme, Hafiz Pasha, Stefano Pettinato, Gonzalo Pizarro, Martin Santiago, Susanne Schmidt, Guido Schmidt-Traub, Salil Shetty, Moustapha Soumare, Juerg Staudenmann, Mounir Tabet, Sarah Timpson and Louisa Vinton.

Editing, Production and Translation

The Report benefited enormously from the advice and contribution of the editorial team at Communications Development Incorporated. Bruce Ross-Larson provided advice on structure and presentation of the argument. Technical and production editing was carried out by Meta de Coquereaumont, Elizabeth Collins and Christopher Trott. Layout and proofreading were also done by Communications Development Incorporated. The Report (including cover) was designed by Grundy & Northedge Information Designers. Maps and graphics for the Report were designed by Philippe Rekacewicz, with the assistance of Laura Margueritte.

The production, translation, distribution and promotion of the Report benefited from the help and support of the UNDP Office of Communications: Niamh Collier-Smith, Maureen Lynch, David Morrison and William Orme. Translations were reviewed by Yu Gao, Cecile Molinier, Vladimir Scherbov, Rosine Sori Coulibaly, Mounir Tabet and Oscar Yujnovsky.

Susana Franco (who managed the project on gender indicators) and Jonathan Morse made valuable contributions to the statistical team. The Report also benefited from the dedicated work of interns: Paola Adriazola, Carolina Aragon, Nurit Bodemann-Ostow, Torsten Henricson-Bell, Roshni Menon, Sarai Nuñez Ceron and Min Zhang.

Gloria Wightman and Juan Arbelaez of the UN Office of Project Services provided critical administrative support and management services.

Kevin Watkins
Director
Human Development Report 2006

Contents

Tables

Figures

Human development indicators

Beyond scarcity
Power, poverty and the global water crisis

The global crisis in water consigns large segments of humanity to lives of poverty, vulnerability and insecurity

The water is not good in this pond. We collect it because we have no alternative. All the animals drink from the pond as well as the community. Because of the water we are also getting different diseases.

Zenebech Jemel, Chobare Meno, Ethiopia

Of course I wish I were in school. I want to learn to read and write.... But how can I? My mother needs me to get water.

Yeni Bazan, age 10, El Alto, Bolivia

The conditions here are terrible. There is sewage everywhere. It pollutes our water. Most people use buckets and plastic bags for toilets. Our children suffer all the time from diarrhoea and other diseases because it is so filthy.

Mary Akinyi, Kibera, Nairobi, Kenya

They [the factories] use so much water while we barely have enough for our basic needs, let alone to water our crops.

Gopal Gujur, farmer, Rajasthan, India

Four voices from four countries united by a single theme: deprivation in access to water. That deprivation can be measured by statistics, but behind the numbers are the human faces of the millions of people denied an opportunity to realize their potential. Water, the stuff of life and a basic human right, is at the heart of a daily crisis faced by countless millions of the world's most vulnerable people—a crisis that threatens life and destroys livelihoods on a devastating scale.

Unlike wars and natural disasters, the global crisis in water does not make media headlines. Nor does it galvanize concerted international action. Like hunger, deprivation in access to water is a silent crisis experienced by the poor and tolerated by those with the resources, the technology and the political power to end it. Yet this is a crisis that is holding back human progress, consigning large segments of humanity to lives of poverty, vulnerability and insecurity. This crisis claims more lives through disease than any war claims through guns. It also reinforces the obscene inequalities in life chances that divide rich and poor nations in an increasingly prosperous and interconnected world and that divide people within countries on the basis of wealth, gender and other markers for disadvantage.

Overcoming the crisis in water and sanitation is one of the great human development challenges of the early 21st century. Success in addressing that challenge through a concerted national and international response would act as a catalyst for progress in public health, education and poverty reduction and as a source of economic dynamism. It would give a decisive impetus to the Millennium Development Goals—the targets adopted by governments as part of a global partnership for poverty reduction. The business as usual alternative is to tolerate a level of avoidable suffering and loss of human potential that all governments should regard as ethically indefensible and economically wasteful.

Water for life, water for livelihoods

"By means of water", says the Koran, "we give life to everything." That simple teaching captures a deeper wisdom. People need water as surely as they need oxygen: without it life could not exist. But water also gives life in a far broader sense. People need clean water and sanitation to sustain their health and maintain their dignity. But beyond the household water also sustains ecological systems and provides an input into the production systems that maintain livelihoods.

Ultimately, human development is about the realization of potential. It is about what people can do and what they can become—their capabilities—and about the freedom they have to exercise real choices in their lives. Water pervades all aspects of human development. When people are denied access to clean water at home or when they lack access to water as a productive resource their choices and freedoms are constrained by ill health, poverty and vulnerability. Water gives life to everything, including human development and human freedom.

In this year's *Human Development Report* we look at two distinct themes in the global water crisis. The first, explored in chapters 1–3, is water for life. Delivering clean water, removing wastewater and providing sanitation are three of the most basic foundations for human progress. We look at the costs of not putting in place these foundations and set out some of the strategies needed to bring universal access to water and sanitation within reach. The second theme, water for livelihoods, is the subject of chapters 4–6. Here we focus on water as a productive resource shared within countries and across borders, highlighting the immense challenges now facing many governments to manage water equitably and efficiently.

Some commentators trace the global challenge in water to a problem of scarcity. The spirit of Thomas Malthus, who in the 19th century disconcerted political leaders by predicting a future of food shortages, increasingly pervades international debates on water. With population rising and demands on the world's water expanding, so the argument runs, the future points to a "gloomy arithmetic" of shortage. We reject this starting point. The availability of water is a concern for some countries. But the scarcity at the heart of the global water crisis is rooted in power, poverty and inequality, not in physical availability.

Nowhere is this more apparent than in the area of water for life. Today, some 1.1 billion people in developing countries have inadequate access to water, and 2.6 billion lack basic sanitation. Those twin deficits are rooted in institutions and political choices, not in water's availability. Household water requirements represent a tiny fraction of water use, usually less than 5% of the total, but there is tremendous inequality in access to clean water and to sanitation at a household level. In high-income areas of cities in Asia, Latin America and Sub-Saharan Africa people enjoy access to several hundred litres of water a day delivered into their homes at low prices by public utilities. Meanwhile, slum dwellers and poor households in rural areas of the same countries have access to much less than the 20 litres of water a day per person required to meet the most basic human needs. Women and young girls carry a double burden of disadvantage, since they are the ones who sacrifice their time and their education to collect water.

Much the same applies to water for livelihoods. Across the world agriculture and industry are adjusting to tightening hydrological constraints. But while scarcity is a widespread problem, it is not experienced by all. In water-stressed parts of India irrigation pumps extract water from aquifers 24 hours a day for wealthy farmers, while neighbouring smallholders depend on the vagaries of rain. Here, too, the underlying cause of scarcity in the large majority of cases is institutional and political, not a physical deficiency of supplies. In many countries scarcity is the product of public policies that have encouraged overuse of water through subsidies and underpricing.

There is more than enough water in the world for domestic purposes, for agriculture and for industry. The problem is that some people—notably the poor—are systematically excluded from access by their poverty, by their limited legal rights or by public policies that limit access to the infrastructures that provide water for life and for livelihoods. In short, scarcity is manufactured through political processes and institutions that disadvantage the poor. When it comes to clean water, the pattern in many countries is that the poor get less, pay more and bear the brunt of the human development costs associated with scarcity.

Human security, citizenship and social justice

Just over a decade ago *Human Development Report 1994* introduced the idea of human security to the wider debate on development. The aim was to look beyond narrow perceptions of national security, defined in terms of military threats and the protection of strategic foreign policy goals, and towards a vision of security rooted in the lives of people.

Water security is an integral part of this broader conception of human security. In broad terms water security is about ensuring that every person has reliable access to enough safe water at an affordable price to lead a healthy, dignified and productive life, while maintaining the ecological systems that provide water and also depend on water. When these conditions are not met, or when access to water is disrupted, people face acute human security risks transmitted through poor health and the disruption of livelihoods.

In the world of the early 21st century national security concerns loom large on the international agenda. Violent conflict, concerns over terrorist threats, the proliferation of nuclear weapons and the growth of illicit trade in arms and drugs all pose acute challenges. Against this backdrop it is easy to lose sight of some basic human security imperatives, including those linked to water. The 1.8 million child deaths each year related to unclean water

and poor sanitation dwarf the casualties associated with violent conflict. No act of terrorism generates economic devastation on the scale of the crisis in water and sanitation. Yet the issue barely registers on the international agenda.

It is not just the contrast with national security imperatives that is striking. Today, international action to tackle the crisis in HIV/AIDS has been institutionalized on the agenda of the Group of Eight countries. Threatened with a potential public health crisis in the form of avian flu, the world mobilizes rapidly to draw up a global plan of action. But the living reality of the water and sanitation crisis elicits only the most minimal and fragmented response. Why is that? One plausible explanation is that, unlike HIV/AIDS and avian flu, the water and sanitation crisis poses the most immediate and most direct threat to poor people in poor countries—a constituency that lacks a voice in shaping national and international perceptions of human security.

Apart from the highly visible destructive impacts on people, water insecurity violates some of the most basic principles of social justice. Among them:

- *Equal citizenship.* Every person is entitled to an equal set of civil, political and social rights, including the means to exercise these rights effectively. Water insecurity compromises these rights. A woman who spends long hours collecting water, or who suffers from constant water-related illness, has less capacity to participate in society, even if she can participate in electing her government.
- *The social minimum.* All citizens should have access to resources sufficient to meet their basic needs and live a dignified life. Clean water is part of the social minimum, with 20 litres per person each day as the minimum threshold requirement.
- *Equality of opportunity.* Equality of opportunity, a key requirement for social justice, is diminished by water insecurity. Most people would accept that education is integral to equality of opportunity. For example, children unable to attend school when they are afflicted by constant bouts of sickness caused by unclean water do not,

There is more than enough water in the world for domestic purposes, for agriculture and for industry. The problem is that some people—notably the poor—are systematically excluded

in any meaningful sense, enjoy a right to education.

- *Fair distribution.* All societies set limits to the justifiable extent of inequality. Deep inequality in access to clean water in the home or productive water in the field does not meet the criterion for fair distribution, especially when linked to high levels of avoidable child death or poverty.

The idea of water as a human right reflects these underlying concerns. As the UN Secretary-General has put it, "Access to safe water is a fundamental human need and, therefore, a basic human right." Upholding the human right to water is an end in itself and a means for giving substance to the wider rights in the Universal Declaration of Human Rights and other legally binding instruments—including the right to life, to education, to health and to adequate housing. Ensuring that every person has access to at least 20 litres of clean water each day to meet basic needs is a minimum requirement for respecting the right to water—and a minimum target for governments.

Human rights are not optional extras. Nor are they a voluntary legal provision to be embraced or abandoned on the whim of individual governments. They are binding obligations that reflect universal values and entail responsibilities on the part of governments. Yet the human right to water is violated with impunity on a widespread and systematic basis—and it is the human rights of the poor that are subject to the gravest abuse.

Reaching the Millennium Development Goal target in 2015—a test of humanity

There is now less than 10 years to go to the 2015 target date for achieving the Millennium Development Goals—the time-bound targets of the international community for reducing extreme poverty and hunger, cutting child deaths, getting children an education and overcoming gender inequalities. Progress in each of these areas will be conditioned by how governments respond to the crisis in water.

The Millennium Development Goals provide a benchmark for measuring progress towards the human right to water. That is why

halving the proportion of world population without sustainable access to safe drinking water and basic sanitation—Goal 7, target 10—is a key target in its own right. But achieving that target is critical to the attainment of other goals. Clean water and sanitation would save the lives of countless children, support progress in education and liberate people from the illnesses that keep them in poverty.

The urgency of achieving the Millennium Development Goal for water and sanitation cannot be overstated. Even if the targets are achieved, there will still be more than 800 million people without water and 1.8 billion people without sanitation in 2015. Yet despite progress the world is falling short of what is needed, especially in the poorest countries. Changing this picture will require sustained action over the next decade allied to a decisive break with the current business as usual model.

The 2015 target date is important for practical and symbolic reasons. At a practical level it reminds us that time is running out—and that the deadline for the investments and policies needed to deliver results is fast approaching. Symbolically, 2015 matters in a deeper sense. The state of the world in that year will be a judgement on the state of international cooperation today. It will hold up a mirror to the generation of political leaders that signed the Millennium Development Goal pledge and deliver the verdict on whether the pledge was honoured in the breach or the observance.

Some time in 2015 another less important but no less symbolic event will take place. The US National Aeronautics and Space Administration will launch the Jupiter Icy Moons Project. Using technology now under development, a spacecraft will be dispatched to orbit three of Jupiter's moons to investigate the composition of the vast saltwater lakes beneath their ice surfaces—and to determine whether the conditions for life exist. The irony of humanity spending billions of dollars in exploring the potential for life on other planets would be powerful—and tragic—if at the same time we allow the destruction of life and human capabilities on planet Earth for want of far less demanding technologies: the infrastructure to deliver clean water and sanitation to all. Providing a glass of clean water and a toilet may be challenging, but it is not rocket science.

Mahatma Gandhi once commented that "the difference between what we do and what we are capable of doing would suffice to solve most of the world's problems." That observation has a powerful resonance for the Millennium Development Goals. The unprecedented combination of resources and technology at our disposal today makes the argument that the 2015 targets are beyond our reach both intellectually and morally indefensible. We should not be satisfied with progress that falls short of the goals set—or with half measures that leave whole sections of humanity behind.

Water for life—the global crisis in water and sanitation

Clean water and sanitation are among the most powerful drivers for human development. They extend opportunity, enhance dignity and help create a virtuous cycle of improving health and rising wealth.

People living in rich countries today are only dimly aware of how clean water fostered social progress in their own countries. Just over a hundred years ago London, New York and Paris were centres of infectious disease, with diarrhoea, dysentery and typhoid fever undermining public health. Child death rates were as high then as they are now in much of Sub-Saharan Africa. The rising wealth from industrialization boosted income, but child mortality and life expectancy barely changed.

Sweeping reforms in water and sanitation changed this picture. Clean water became the vehicle for a leap forward in human progress. Driven by coalitions for social reform, by moral concern and by economic self-interest, governments placed water and sanitation at the centre of a new social contract between states and citizens. Within a generation they put in place the finance, technology and regulations needed to bring water and sanitation for all within reach.

The new infrastructure broke the link between dirty water and infectious disease. By one estimate water purification explains almost half the mortality reduction in the United States in the first third of the 20th century. In Great Britain the expansion of sanitation contributed to a 15-year increase in life expectancy in the four decades after 1880.

The fault line between sanitation and water

In rich countries clean water is now available at the twist of a tap. Private and hygienic sanitation is taken for granted. Concern over water shortages may occasionally surface in some countries. But that concern has to be placed in perspective. Children in rich countries do not die for want of a glass of clean water. Young girls are not kept home from school to make long journeys to collect water from streams and rivers. And waterborne infectious disease is a subject for history books, not hospital wards and morgues.

The contrast with poor countries is striking. While deprivation is unequally distributed across regions, the facts of the global water crisis speak for themselves. Some 1.1 billion people in the developing world do not have access to a minimal amount of clean water. Coverage rates are lowest in Sub-Saharan Africa, but most people without clean water live in Asia. Deprivation in sanitation is even more widespread. Some 2.6 billion people—half the developing world's population—do not have access to basic sanitation. And systemic data underreporting means that these figures understate the problem.

"Not having access" to water and sanitation is a polite euphemism for a form of deprivation that threatens life, destroys opportunity and undermines human dignity. Being without access to water means that people resort to ditches, rivers and lakes polluted with human or animal excrement or used by animals. It also means not having sufficient water to meet even the most basic human needs.

While basic needs vary, the minimum threshold is about 20 litres a day. Most of the 1.1 billion people categorized as lacking access to clean water use about 5 litres a day—one-tenth of the average daily amount used in rich countries to flush toilets. On average, people in Europe use more than 200 litres—in the United States more than 400 litres. When a European

"Not having access" to water and sanitation is a polite euphemism for a form of deprivation that threatens life, destroys opportunity and undermines human dignity

person flushes a toilet or an American person showers, he or she is using more water than is available to hundreds of millions of individuals living in urban slums or arid areas of the developing world. Dripping taps in rich countries lose more water than is available each day to more than 1 billion people.

Not having access to sanitation means that people are forced to defecate in fields, ditches and buckets. The "flying toilets" of Kibera, a slum in Nairobi, Kenya, highlight what it means to be without sanitation. Lacking access to toilets, people defecate into plastic bags that they throw onto the streets. The absence of toilets poses particularly severe public health and security problems for women and young girls. In sanitation as in water, gender inequality structures the human costs of disadvantage.

Access to water and sanitation reinforces some long-standing human development lessons. On average, coverage rates in both areas rise with income: increasing wealth tends to bring with it improved access to water and sanitation. But there are very large variations around the average. Some countries—such as Bangladesh and Thailand in sanitation, and Sri Lanka and Viet Nam in water—do far better than would be expected solely on the basis of income. Others—such as India and Mexico for sanitation—do far worse. The lesson: income matters, but public policy shapes the conversion of income into human development.

The human development costs—immense

Deprivation in water and sanitation produces multiplier effects. The ledger includes the following costs for human development:

- Some 1.8 million child deaths each year as a result of diarrhoea—4,900 deaths each day or an under-five population equivalent in size to that for London and New York combined. Together, unclean water and poor sanitation are the world's second biggest killer of children. Deaths from diarrhoea in 2004 were some six times greater than the average annual deaths in armed conflict for the 1990s.
- The loss of 443 million school days each year from water-related illness.

- Close to half of all people in developing countries suffering at any given time from a health problem caused by water and sanitation deficits.
- Millions of women spending several hours a day collecting water.
- Lifecycles of disadvantage affecting millions of people, with illness and lost educational opportunities in childhood leading to poverty in adulthood.

To these human costs can be added the massive economic waste associated with the water and sanitation deficit. Measuring these costs is inherently difficult. However, new research undertaken for this year's *Human Development Report* highlights the very large losses sustained in some of the world's poorest countries. The research captures the costs associated with health spending, productivity losses and labour diversions.

Losses are greatest in some of the poorest countries. Sub-Saharan Africa loses about 5% of GDP, or some $28.4 billion annually, a figure that exceeds total aid flows and debt relief to the region in 2003. In one crucial respect these aggregate economic costs obscure the real impact of the water and sanitation deficit. Most of the losses are sustained by households below the poverty line, retarding the efforts of poor people to produce their way out of poverty.

On any measure of efficiency, investments in water and sanitation have the potential to generate a high return. Every $1 spent in the sector creates on average another $8 in costs averted and productivity gained. Beyond this static gain, improved access to water and sanitation has the potential to generate long-run dynamic effects that will boost economic efficiency.

Whether measured against the benchmark of human suffering, economic waste or extreme poverty, the water and sanitation deficit inflicts a terrifying toll. The flip-side is the potential for reducing that deficit as a means for human progress. Water and sanitation are among the most powerful preventive medicines available to governments to reduce infectious disease. Investment in this area is to killer diseases like diarrhoea what immunization is to measles—a life-saver. Research for this Report shows that access to safe water reduces child death rates by more than 20% in Cameroon and Uganda. In Egypt and Peru the presence of a flush toilet in the house reduces the risk of infant death by more than 30%.

A crisis above all for the poor

The crisis in water and sanitation is—above all—a crisis for the poor. Almost two in three people lacking access to clean water survive on less than $2 a day, with one in three living on less than $1 a day. More than 660 million people without sanitation live on less than $2 a day, and more than 385 million on less than $1 a day.

These facts have important public policy implications. They point clearly towards the limited capacity of unserved populations to finance improved access through private spending. While the private sector may have a role to play in delivery, public financing holds the key to overcoming deficits in water and sanitation.

The distribution of access to adequate water and sanitation in many countries mirrors the distribution of wealth. Access to piped water into the household averages about 85% for the wealthiest 20% of the population, compared with 25% for the poorest 20%. Inequality extends beyond access. The perverse principle that applies across much of the developing world is that the poorest people not only get access to less water, and to less clean water, but they also pay some of the world's highest prices:

- People living in the slums of Jakarta, Indonesia; Manila, the Philippines; and Nairobi, Kenya, pay 5–10 times more for water per unit than those in high-income areas of their own cities—and more than consumers pay in London or New York.
- High-income households use far more water than poor households. In Dar es Salam, Tanzania, and Mumbai, India, per capita water use is 15 times higher in high-income suburbs linked to the utility than in slum areas.
- Inequitable water pricing has perverse consequences for household poverty. The poorest 20% of households in El Salvador, Jamaica and Nicaragua spend on average more than 10% of their household income on water. In the United Kingdom a 3% threshold is seen as an indicator of hardship.

Prognosis for meeting the Millennium Development Goal target

The Millennium Development Goals are not the first set of ambitious targets embraced by governments. "Water and sanitation for all" within a decade was among the impressive set of targets adopted following high-level conferences in the 1970s and the 1980s. Performance fell far short of the promise. Will it be different this time round?

In aggregate the world is on track for the target for water largely because of strong progress in China and India, but only two regions are on track for sanitation (East Asia and Latin America). Large regional and national variations are masked by the global picture.

- On current trends Sub-Saharan Africa will reach the water target in 2040 and the sanitation target in 2076. For sanitation South Asia is 4 years off track, and for water the Arab States are 27 years off track.
- Measured on a country by country basis, the water target will be missed by 234 million people, with 55 countries off track.
- The sanitation target will be missed by 430 million people, with 74 countries off track.
- For Sub-Saharan Africa to get on track, connection rates for water will have to rise from 10 million a year in the past decade to 23 million a year in the next decade. South Asia's rate of sanitation provision will have to rise from 25 million people a year to 43 million a year.

The Millennium Development Goals should be seen as a minimum threshold of provision not as a ceiling. Even if they are achieved, there will still be a large global deficit. What is worrying about the current global trajectory is that the world is on course to finish below the floor defined by the Millennium Development Goal promise.

Closing the gaps between current trends and targets

Changing this picture is not just the right thing to do, but also the sensible thing to do. It is the right thing to do because water and sanitation are basic human rights—and no government should be willing to turn a blind eye to the current level of human rights violation or the

Almost two in three people lacking access to clean water and more than 660 million people without sanitation live on less than $2 a day

What is needed in the decade ahead is a concerted international drive starting with nationally owned strategies, but incorporating a global action plan

associated loss of human potential. And it is the sensible thing to do because access to water and sanitation equips people to get themselves out of poverty and to contribute to national prosperity.

Quantifying the potential gains for human development from progress in water and sanitation is difficult. But best estimates suggest that the benefits heavily outweigh the costs. The additional costs of achieving the Millennium Development Goal on the basis of the lowest-cost, sustainable technology option amount to about $10 billion a year. Closing the gap between current trends and target trends for achieving the Millennium Development Goal for water and sanitation would result in:

- Some 203,000 fewer child deaths in 2015 and more than 1 million children's lives saved over the next decade.
- An additional 272 million days gained in school attendance as a result of reduced episodes of diarrhoea alone.
- Total economic benefits of about $38 billion annually. The benefits for Sub-Saharan Africa—about $15 billion—would represent 60% of its 2003 aid flows. Gains for South Asia would represent almost $6 billion.

Can the world afford to meet the costs of accelerated progress towards water and sanitation provision? The more appropriate question is: can the world afford *not* to make the investments?

The $10 billion price tag for the Millennium Development Goal seems a large sum—but it has to be put in context. It represents less than five days' worth of global military spending and less than half what rich countries spend each year on mineral water. This is a small price to pay for an investment that can save millions of young lives, unlock wasted education potential, free people from diseases that rob them of their health and generate an economic return that will boost prosperity.

Four foundations for success

If high-level international conferences, encouraging statements and bold targets could deliver clean water and basic sanitation, the global crisis would have been resolved long ago.

Since the mid-1990s there has been a proliferation of international conferences dealing with water, along with a proliferation of high-level international partnerships. Meanwhile, there are 23 UN agencies dealing with water and sanitation.

So many conferences, so much activity—and so little progress. Looking back over the past decade, it is difficult to avoid the conclusion that water and sanitation have suffered from an excess of words and a deficit of action. What is needed in the decade ahead is a concerted international drive starting with nationally owned strategies, but incorporating a global action plan. There are no ready-made blueprints for reform, but four foundations are crucial for success.

- *Make water a human right—and mean it.* All governments should go beyond vague constitutional principles to enshrine the human right to water in enabling legislation. To have real meaning, the human right has to correspond to an entitlement to a secure, accessible and affordable supply of water. The appropriate entitlement will vary by country and household circumstance. But at a minimum it implies a target of at least 20 litres of clean water a day for every citizen—and at no cost for those too poor to pay. Clear benchmarks should be set for progressing towards the target, with national and local governments and water providers held accountable for progress. While private providers have a role to play in water delivery, extending the human right to water is an obligation of governments.
- *Draw up national strategies for water and sanitation.* All governments should prepare national plans for accelerating progress in water and sanitation, with ambitious targets backed by financing and clear strategies for overcoming inequalities. Water and, even more so, sanitation are the poor cousins of poverty reduction planning. They suffer from chronic underfinancing, with public spending typically less than 0.5% of GDP. Life-saving investments in water and sanitation are dwarfed by military spending. In Ethiopia the military budget is 10 times

the water and sanitation budget—in Pakistan, 47 times. Governments should aim at a minimum of 1% of GDP for water and sanitation spending. Tackling inequality will require a commitment to financing strategies—including fiscal transfers, cross-subsidies and other measures—that bring affordable water and sanitation to the poor. National strategies should incorporate benchmarks for enhanced equity including:

- *Millennium Development Goals.* Supplementing the 2015 target of halving the proportion of people without access to water and sanitation with policies to halve the gap in coverage ratios between rich and poor.
- *Poverty Reduction Strategy Papers.* Making water and sanitation key priorities, with clear goals and targets linked to medium-term financing provisions.
- *Water providers.* Ensuring that utilities, public and private, along with municipal bodies, include clear benchmarks for equity, with associated penalties for noncompliance.

- *Support national plans with international aid.* For many of the poorest countries development assistance is critical. Progress in water and sanitation requires large upfront investments with long payback periods. Constraints on government revenue limit the financing capacity of many of the poorest countries, while cost-recovery potential is limited by high levels of poverty. Most donors recognize the importance of water and sanitation. However, development assistance has fallen in real terms over the past decade, and few donors see the sector as a priority: the sector now accounts for less than 5% of development assistance. Aid flows will need to roughly double to bring the Millennium Development Goal within reach, rising by $3.6–$4 billion annually. Innovative financing strategies such as those provided for under the International Finance Facility are essential to provide upfront financing to avert the impending shortfall against the Millennium Development Goal target. Donors should act in support of nationally owned and nationally led strategies, providing predictable, long-term support. There is also scope for supporting the efforts of local governments and municipal utilities to raise money on local capital markets.

- *Develop a global action plan.* International efforts to accelerate progress in water and sanitation have been fragmented and ineffective, with a surfeit of high-level conferences and a chronic absence of practical action. In contrast to the strength of the international response for HIV/AIDS and education, water and sanitation have not figured prominently on the global development agenda. Having pledged a global action plan two years ago, the Group of Eight countries have not set water and sanitation as a priority. The development of a global action plan to mobilize aid financing, support developing country governments in drawing on local capital markets and enhance capacity-building could act as a focal point for public advocacy and political efforts in water and sanitation.

Providing water for life

"The human right to water", declares the United Nations Committee on Economic, Social and Cultural Rights, "entitles everyone to sufficient, safe, acceptable, physically accessible and affordable water for personal and domestic use." These five core attributes represent the foundations for water security. Yet they are widely violated.

Why is it that poor people get less access to clean water and pay more for it? In urban areas the cheapest, most reliable source of water is usually the utility that maintains the network. Poor households are less likely to be connected to the network—and more likely to get their water from a variety of unimproved sources. In Dar es Salaam, Tanzania, or Ouagadougou, Burkina Faso, fewer than 30% of households are connected.

When households are not connected, they have limited options. Either they collect water from untreated sources or a public source, or they purchase water from a range of

Poor people get less access to clean water and pay more for it intermediaries, including standpipe operators, water vendors and tanker truck operators. The debate on water privatization has tended to overlook the fact that the vast majority of the poor are already purchasing their water in private markets. These markets deliver water of variable quality at high prices.

High prices for the poor

Distance from the utility inflates prices. As water passes through intermediaries and each adds transport and marketing costs, prices are ratcheted up. Poor people living in slums often pay 5–10 times more per litre of water than wealthy people living in the same city.

Utility pricing policies add to the problems. Most utilities now implement rising block tariff systems. These aim to combine equity with efficiency by raising the price with the volume of water used. In practice, the effect is often to lock the poorest households into the higher tariff bands. The reason: the intermediaries serving poor households are buying water in bulk at the highest rate. In Dakar poor households using standpipes pay more than three times the price paid by households connected to the utility.

If utility prices are so much cheaper, why do poor households not connect to the utility? Often because they are unable to afford the connection fee: even in the poorest countries this can exceed $100. In Manila the cost of connecting to the utility represents about three months' income for the poorest 20% of households, rising to six months' in urban Kenya. Location is another barrier to entry. In many cities utilities refuse to connect households lacking formal property titles, thereby excluding some of the poorest households.

Rural households face distinct problems. Living beyond formal networks, rural communities typically manage their own water systems, though government agencies are involved in service provision. Most agencies have operated on a "command and control" model, often supplying inappropriate technologies to inappropriate locations with little consultation. The result has been a combination of underfinancing and low coverage, with rural women bearing the costs by collecting water from distant sources.

The key role of public providers

In recent years international debate on the human right to water has been dominated by polarized exchanges over the appropriate roles of the private and public sectors. Important issues have been raised—but the dialogue has generated more heat than light.

Some privatization programmes have produced positive results. But the overall record is not encouraging. From Argentina to Bolivia, and from the Philippines to the United States, the conviction that the private sector offers a "magic bullet" for unleashing the equity and efficiency needed to accelerate progress towards water for all has proven to be misplaced. While these past failures of water concessions do not provide evidence that the private sector has no role to play, they do point to the need for greater caution, regulation and a commitment to equity in public-private partnerships.

Two specific aspects of water provision in countries with low coverage rates caution against an undue reliance on the private sector. First, the water sector has many of the characteristics of a natural monopoly. In the absence of a strong regulatory capacity to protect the public interest through the rules on pricing and investment, there are dangers of monopolistic abuse. Second, in countries with high levels of poverty among unserved populations, public finance is a requirement for extended access regardless of whether the provider is public or private.

The debate on privatization has sometimes diverted attention from the pressing issue of public utility reform. Public providers dominate water provision, accounting for more than 90% of the water delivered through networks in developing countries. Many publicly owned utilities are failing the poor, combining inefficiency and unaccountability in management with inequity in financing and pricing. But some public utilities—Porto Alegre in Brazil is an outstanding example—have succeeded in making water affordable and accessible to all.

There are now real opportunities to learn from failures and build on successes. The criterion for assessing policy should not be public or private but performance or nonperformance for the poor.

Some countries have registered rapid progress in water provision. From Colombia to Senegal and South Africa innovative strategies have been developed for extending access to poor households in urban areas. While rural populations continue to lag behind urban populations globally, countries as diverse as Morocco and Uganda have sustained rapid increases in coverage. What are the keys to success?

Political leadership and attainable targets make the difference

As emphasized throughout this Report, there are no ready-made solutions. Policies that produce positive outcomes for the poor in one setting can fail in another. However, some broad lessons emerge from the success stories. The first, and perhaps the most important, is that political leadership matters. The second is that progress depends on setting attainable targets in national plans that are backed by financing provisions and strategies for overcoming inequality.

This does not mean uncritical support for blanket subsidies. Well designed subsidies in Chile, Colombia and South Africa do reach the poor—and do make a difference. But in many cases subsidies ostensibly designed to enhance equity in utility pricing provide large transfers to the wealthy, with few benefits for poor households that are not connected to utilities. Similarly, in much of Sub-Saharan Africa higher income households with connections to utilities derive the greatest gains from water sold at prices far below the level needed to cover operations and maintenance costs.

Regulation and sustainable cost-recovery are vital to equity and efficiency

Because water networks are natural monopolies, regulation needs to ensure that providers meet standards for efficiency and equity—in effect, protecting the interests of the user. Strong, independent regulatory bodies have been difficult to establish in many developing countries, leading to political interference and non-accountability. But efforts to build regulation through dialogue between utility providers and citizens have yielded some major advances—as in Hyderabad, India.

More broadly, it is important that governments extend the regulatory remit beyond formal network providers to the informal markets that poor people use. Regulation does not mean curtailing the activities of private providers serving the poor. But it does mean working with these providers to ensure adherence to rules on equitable pricing and water quality.

Sustainable and equitable cost-recovery is part of any reform programme. In many cases there are strong grounds for increasing water prices to more realistic levels and for improving the efficiency of water management: in many countries water losses are too high and revenue collection is too low to finance a viable system.

What is sustainable and equitable varies across countries. In many low-income countries the scope for cost-recovery is limited by poverty and low average incomes. Public spending backed by aid is critical. Middle-income countries have more scope for equitable cost-recovery if governments put in place mechanisms to limit the financial burden on poor households.

Middle-income and some low-income countries also have the potential to draw more on local capital markets. This is an area in which international support can make a difference through credit guarantees and other mechanisms that reduce interest rates and market perceptions of risk.

Building on the national and global planning framework set out in chapter 1, core strategies for overcoming national inequalities in access to water include:

- Setting clear targets for reducing inequality as part of the national poverty reduction strategy and Millennium Development Goal reporting system, including halving disparities in coverage between rich and poor.
- Establishing lifeline tariffs that provide sufficient water for basic needs free of charge or at affordable rates, as in South Africa.
- Ensuring that no household has to spend more than 3% of its income to meet its water needs.
- Targeting subsidies for connections and water use to poor households, as developed in Chile and Colombia.

Progress depends on setting attainable targets in national plans that are backed by financing provisions and strategies for overcoming inequality

- Increasing investments in standpipe provision as a transitional strategy to make clean, affordable water available to the poor.
- Enacting legislation that empowers people to hold providers to account.
- Incorporating into public-private partnership contracts clear benchmarks for equity in the extension of affordable access to poor households.
- Developing regulatory systems that are effective and politically independent, with a remit that stretches from the utility network to informal providers.

Closing the vast deficit in sanitation

"The sewer is the conscience of the city", wrote Victor Hugo in *Les Miserables*. He was describing 19th century Paris, but the state of sanitation remains a powerful indicator of the state of human development in any community.

Almost half the developing world lacks access to sanitation. Many more lack access to good quality sanitation. The deficit is widely distributed. Coverage rates are shockingly low in many of the world's very poorest countries: only about 1 person in 3 in Sub-Saharan Africa and South Asia has access—in Ethiopia the figure falls to about 1 in 7. And coverage rates understate the problem, especially in countries at higher incomes. In Jakarta and Manila old sewerage systems have been overwhelmed by a combination of rapid urbanization and chronic underinvestment, leading to the rapid spread of pit latrines. These latrines now contaminate groundwater and empty into rivers, polluting water sources and jeopardizing public health.

Access to sanitation bestows benefits at many levels. Cross-country studies show that the method of disposing of excreta is one of the strongest determinants of child survival: the transition from unimproved to improved sanitation reduces overall child mortality by about a third. Improved sanitation also brings advantages for public health, livelihoods and dignity—advantages that extend beyond households to entire communities. Toilets may seem an unlikely catalyst for human progress—but the evidence is overwhelming.

Why the deficit is so large

If sanitation is so critical to social and economic progress, why is the deficit so large—and why is the world off track for achieving the Millennium Development Goal target? Many factors contribute.

The first is political leadership or, rather, its absence. Public policies on sanitation are as relevant to the state of a nation as economic management, defence or trade, yet sanitation is accorded second or third order priority. Even more than water, sanitation suffers from a combination of institutional fragmentation, weak national planning and low political status.

Poverty is another barrier to progress: the poorest households often lack the financing capacity to purchase sanitation facilities. But other factors also constrain progress, including household demand and gender inequality. Women tend to attach more importance to sanitation than do men, but female priorities carry less weight in household budgeting.

How community-government partnerships can help

The daunting scale of the sanitation deficit and the slow progress in closing that deficit are seen by some as evidence that the Millennium Development Goal target is now unattainable. The concern is justified, but the conclusion is flawed. There are many examples of rapid progress in sanitation, some driven from below by local communities and some led by governments:

- In India and Pakistan slum dweller associations have collaborated to bring sanitation to millions of people, using the power of communities to mobilize resources. The National Slum Dwellers Federation in India and the Orangi Pilot Project in Pakistan, among many other community organizations, have shown what is possible through practical action.
- The Total Sanitation Campaign in Bangladesh has been scaled up from a community-based project to a national programme that is achieving rapid increases in access to sanitation. Cambodia, China, India and Zambia have also adopted it.

- Government programmes in Colombia, Lesotho, Morocco and Thailand have expanded access to sanitation across all wealth groups. West Bengal in India has also achieved extraordinary progress.
- In Brazil the condominial approach to sewerage has reduced costs and brought sanitation to millions of people—and it is now being adopted elsewhere.

Each of these success stories has different roots. Widely divergent public policies have been developed to respond to local problems. But in each case the emphasis has been on developing demand for sanitation, rather than applying top-down supply-side models of provision. Community initiative and involvement have been critical. But equally critical has been the interaction between government agencies and local communities.

Local solutions to local problems may be the starting point for change. But it is up to governments to create the conditions for resolving national problems through the mobilization of finance and the creation of conditions for markets to deliver appropriate technologies at an affordable price. Community-led initiatives are important—even critical. However, they are not a substitute for government action. And private financing by poor households is not a substitute for public finance and service provision.

Overcoming the stigma of human waste

One of the most important lessons from the sanitation success stories is that rapid progress is possible. With support from aid donors, even the poorest countries have the capacity to mobilize the resources to achieve change. Perhaps the biggest obstacle can be summarized in a single word: stigma.

There are some uncomfortable parallels between sanitation and HIV/AIDS. Until fairly recently the cultural and social taboos surrounding HIV/AIDS impeded development of effective national and international responses, at enormous human cost. That taboo has been weakening, partly because of the scale of the destruction—but also because HIV/AIDS afflicts all members of society without regard for distinctions based on wealth.

In sanitation the taboo remains resolutely intact. This helps to explain why the subject does not receive high-level political leadership, and it seldom figures in election campaigns or public debate. One of the reasons that the stigma has been so slow to dissolve is that the crisis in sanitation, unlike the crisis in HIV/AIDS, is more discriminating: it is overwhelmingly a crisis for the poor, not the wealthy. Tackling the crisis will require more awareness of the scale of the costs generated by the deficit in sanitation, as well as a wider recognition that sanitation is a basic right.

Among the key policy challenges in sanitation:
- Developing national and local political institutions that reflect the importance of sanitation to social and economic progress.
- Building on community-level initiatives through government interventions aimed at scaling up best practice.
- Investing in demand-led approaches through which service providers respond to the needs of communities, with women having a voice in shaping priorities.
- Extending financial support to the poorest households to ensure that sanitation is an affordable option.

Managing water scarcity, risk and vulnerability

In the early 21st century debates on water increasingly reflect a Malthusian diagnosis of the problem. Dire warnings have been posted pointing to the "gloomy arithmetic" of rising population and declining water availability. Is the world running out of water?

Not in any meaningful sense. But water insecurity does pose a threat to human development for a large—and growing—section of humanity. Competition, environmental stress and unpredictability of access to water as a productive resource are powerful drivers of water insecurity for a large proportion of the global population.

Viewed at a global level, there is more than enough water to go around and meet all of humanity's needs. So why is water scarcity

Community-led initiatives are important, but they are not a substitute for government action—and private financing by poor households is not a substitute for public finance and service provision

a problem? Partly because water, like wealth, is unequally distributed between and within countries. It does not help water-stressed countries in the Middle East that Brazil and Canada have more water than they could ever use. Nor does it help people in drought-prone areas of northeast Brazil that average water availability in the country is among the highest in the world. Another problem is that access to water as a productive resource requires access to infrastructure, and access to infrastructure is also skewed between and within countries.

Measured on conventional indicators, water stress is increasing. Today, about 700 million people in 43 countries live below the water-stress threshold of 1,700 cubic metres per person—an admittedly arbitrary dividing line. By 2025 that figure will reach 3 billion, as water stress intensifies in China, India and Sub-Saharan Africa. Based on national averages, the projection understates the current problem. The 538 million people in northern China already live in an intensely water-stressed region. Globally, some 1.4 billion people live in river basin areas where water use exceeds sustainable levels.

Water stress is reflected in ecological stress. River systems that no longer reach the sea, shrinking lakes and sinking groundwater tables are among the most noticeable symptoms of water overuse. The decline of river systems— from the Colorado River in the United States to the Yellow River in China—is a highly visible product of overuse. Less visible, but no less detrimental to human development, is rapid depletion of groundwater in South Asia. In parts of India groundwater tables are falling by more than 1 metre a year, jeopardizing future agricultural production.

These are real symptoms of scarcity, but the scarcity has been induced by policy failures. When it comes to water management, the world has been indulging in an activity analogous to a reckless and unsustainable credit-financed spending spree. Put simply, countries have been using far more water than they have, as defined by the rate of replenishment. The result: a large water-based ecological debt that will be transferred to future generations. This debt raises important questions about national accounting

systems that fail to measure the depletion of scarce and precious natural capital—and it raises important questions about cross-generational equity. Underpricing (or zero pricing in some cases) has sustained overuse: if markets delivered Porsche cars at give-away prices, they too would be in short supply.

Future water-use scenarios raise cause for serious concern. For almost a century water use has been growing almost twice as fast as population. That trend will continue. Irrigated agriculture will remain the largest user of water—it currently accounts for more than 80% of use in developing countries. But the demands of industry and urban users are growing rapidly. Over the period to 2050 the world's water will have to support the agricultural systems that will feed and create livelihoods for an additional 2.7 billion people. Meanwhile, industry, rather than agriculture, will account for most of the projected increase in water use to 2025.

Augmenting supply

In the past governments responded to water stress by seeking to augment supply. Large-scale river diversion programmes in China and India underline the continuing appeal of this approach. Other supply-side options have also grown in importance. Desalination of sea water is gaining ground, though high energy costs make this an option principally for wealthier countries and cities by the sea. "Virtual water" imports—the water used in the production of imported food—are another option. Here too, however, there are limited options for low-income countries with large food deficits—and there are food security threats from a potential loss of self-reliance.

Damping demand

Demand-side policies are likely to be more effective. Increasing the "crop per drop" ratio through new productivity-enhancing technology has the potential to reduce pressure on water systems. More broadly, water pricing policies need to better reflect the scarcity value of water. The early withdrawal of perverse subsidies that encourage overuse would mark an important step in the right direction for countries such as India and Mexico, which have inadvertently created incentives for the depletion of groundwater through electricity subsidies for large farms. In effect, governments have been subsidizing the depletion of a precious natural resource, transferring the costs to the environment—and to future generations.

Managing uncertainty

Many governments across the developing world are now faced with the need for managing acute adjustments in water. Realigning supply and demand within the frontiers of ecological sustainability and water availability—a central objective in new strategies for integrated water resources management—has the potential to create both winners and losers. And there are win-win scenarios. But the danger is that the interests of the poor will be pushed aside as large agricultural producers and industry—two constituencies with a strong political voice—assert their claims. Water is power in many societies—and inequalities in power can induce deep inequalities in access to water.

Water infrastructure is critical in reducing unpredictability and mitigating risk. Globally, the inequalities in access to infrastructure are very large. They are reflected in simple indicators for water storage capacity: the United States stores about 6,000 cubic metres of water per person; Ethiopia, 43. Even rich countries are exposed to water-related disruption, however, as evidenced by the impact of Hurricane Katrina on New Orleans. But the risks weigh most heavily on poor countries.

Droughts and floods, extreme forms of water insecurity, have devastating consequences for human development. In 2005 more than 20 million people in the Horn of Africa were affected by drought. Meanwhile, the floods that struck Mozambique reduced its GNI by an estimated 20%. Rainfall variability and extreme changes in water flow can destroy assets, undermine livelihoods and reduce the growth potential of whole economies: variability reduces Ethiopia's growth potential by about a third, according to the World Bank. Whole societies are affected. But it is the poor who bear the brunt of water-related shocks.

Dealing with climate change

Climate change is transforming the nature of global water insecurity. While the threat posed by rising temperatures is now firmly established on the international agenda, insufficient attention has been paid to the implications for vulnerable agricultural producers in developing countries. The Framework Convention on Climate Change adopted in 1992 warned governments that "where there are risks of serious and irreversible damage, lack of full scientific certainty should not be used as a reason for postponing action". Few warnings have been more perilously ignored.

Global warming will transform the hydrological patterns that determine the availability of water. Modelling exercises point to complex outcomes that will be shaped by micro-climates. But the overwhelming weight of evidence can be summarized in a simple formulation: many of the world's most water-stressed areas will get less water, and water flows will become less predictable and more subject to extreme events. Among the projected outcomes:

- Marked reductions in water availability in East Africa, the Sahel and Southern Africa as rainfall declines and temperature rises, with large productivity losses in basic food staples. Projections for rainfed areas in East Africa point to potential productivity losses of up to 33% in maize and more than 20% for sorghum and 18% for millet.
- The disruption of food production systems exposing an additional 75–125 million people to the threat of hunger.
- Accelerated glacial melt, leading to medium-term reductions in water availability across a large group of countries in East Asia, Latin America and South Asia.
- Disruptions to monsoon patterns in South Asia, with the potential for more rain but also fewer rainy days and more people affected by drought.
- Rising sea levels resulting in freshwater losses in river delta systems in countries such as Bangladesh, Egypt and Thailand.

The international response to the water security threat posed by climate change has been inadequate. Multilateral efforts have focussed

Climate change is transforming the nature of global water insecurity

on mitigating future climate change. These efforts are critical—and the negotiation of deeper carbon emission cuts after the expiration of the current Kyoto Protocol in 2012 is a priority. Restricting future global warming to an increase of no more than 2° Celsius over pre-industrial levels should be a priority. Attaining that target will require major adjustments in the energy policies of both industrial and developing countries, supported by financing for the transfer of clean technologies.

More adaptation—not just mitigation

Even with drastic reductions in carbon emissions, past emissions mean that the world now has to live with dangerous climate change. Climate change is not a future threat, but a reality to which countries and people have to adapt. Nowhere is the challenge of developing effective adaptation strategies more pressing than in rainfed agriculture, where the livelihoods of millions of the world's poorest people will become more precarious as rainfall patterns become more variable and, in some cases, water availability declines.

International aid for adaptation ought to be a cornerstone of the multilateral framework for dealing with climate change. However, aid transfers have been woefully inadequate. The Adaptation Fund attached to the Kyoto Protocol will mobilize only about $20 million by 2012 on current projections, while the Global Environmental Facility—the principal multilateral mechanism for adaptation—has allocated $50 million to support adaptation activities between 2005 and 2007.

Beyond the multilateral framework, a decline in development assistance to agriculture has limited the financing available for adaptation. Aid has fallen rapidly in both absolute and relative terms over the past decade. For developing countries as a group aid to agriculture has fallen in real terms from $4.9 billion a year to $3.2 billion, or from 12% to 3.5% of total aid since the early 1990s. All regions have been affected. Aid to agriculture in Sub-Saharan Africa is now just under $1 billion, less than half the level in 1990. Reversing these trends will be critical to successful adaptation.

The way ahead

Countries face very different challenges in water management. But some broad themes emerge—along with some broad requirements for successful strategies. Among the most important:

- Developing integrated water resources management strategies that set national water use levels *within* the limits of ecological sustainability and provide a coherent planning framework for all water resources.
- Putting equity and the interests of the poor at the centre of integrated water resources management.
- Making water management an integral part of national poverty reduction strategies.
- Recognizing the real value of water through appropriate pricing policies, revised national accounting procedures and the withdrawal of perverse subsidies encouraging overuse.
- Increasing pro-poor water supply through the provision of safe wastewater for productive use by separating industrial and domestic waste and working with farmers to reduce health risks.
- Increasing national investment and international aid for investment in water infrastructure, including storage and flood control.
- Recalibrating the response to global warming by placing greater emphasis on strategies for adaptation in national water management policies and aid efforts.
- Tripling aid to agriculture by 2010, with annual flows rising from $3 billion to $10 billion. Within this broad provision aid to Africa will need to increase from about $0.9 billion to about $2.1 billion a year, as envisaged for agricultural activities under the Comprehensive Africa Agricultural Development Programme of the African Union and the New Partnership for Africa's Development.

Managing competition for water in agriculture

One hundred years ago William Mulholland, superintendent of the Los Angeles Water Department, resolved the city's water shortage problem through a brutally effective innovation:

a "water grab". By forcibly transferring water used by farmers in the Owens Valley, more than 200 miles away, he made it possible for Los Angeles to become one of the fastest growing cities in the United States.

Times have changed. These days Californians resolve water disputes in courts of law. But across much of the developing world competition over water is intensifying at an alarming rate, giving rise to intense—and sometimes violent—conflict. The danger is that the Mulholland model will resurface in a new guise, with power, rather than a concern for poverty and human development, dictating outcomes.

Competition patterns vary across countries. But two broad trends are discernable. First, as urban centres and industry increase their demand for water, agriculture is losing out—and will continue to do so. Second, within agriculture, competition for water is intensifying. On both fronts, there is a danger that agriculture in general and poor rural households in particular will suffer in the adjustment.

Such an outcome could have grave implications for global poverty reduction efforts. Despite rapid urbanization, most of the world's extreme poor still live in rural areas—and small farmers and agricultural labourers account for the bulk of global malnutrition. As the single biggest user of water in most countries, irrigated agriculture will come under acute pressure. Given the role of these systems in increasing agricultural productivity, feeding a growing population and reducing poverty, this presents a major human development challenge.

Mediating through economic and political structures

With demands on water resources increasing, some reallocation among users and sectors is inevitable. In any process of competition for scarce resources, rival claims are mediated through economic and political structures and through systems of rights and entitlements. As competition for water intensifies, future access will increasingly reflect the strength of claims from different actors. Outcomes for the poorest, most vulnerable people in society will be determined by the way institutions mediate and manage rival claims—and by whether governments put equity concerns at the centre of national policies.

Balancing efficiency and equity

Adjustment processes are already taking place. Cities and industries are extending their hydrological reach into rural areas, giving rise to disputes and occasionally violent protests. Parallel conflicts between different parts of the same country and different users are increasingly evident.

The development of trade in water rights through private markets is seen by some as the solution to balancing efficiency and equity in the adjustments to water reallocation. By enabling agricultural producers to sell water, so the argument runs, governments can create the conditions for directing a scarce resource to more productive outlets, while compensating and generating an income for farmers.

Private water markets offer a questionable solution to a systemic problem. Even in the United States, where they are underpinned by highly developed rules and institutions, it has often been difficult to protect the interests of the poor. In Chile the introduction of private water markets in the 1970s enhanced efficiency but led to high levels of inequity and market distortions caused by concentrations of power and imperfect information. For developing countries, with weaker institutional capacity, there are distinct limits to the market.

Managing allocations and licencing

Looking beyond water markets, many governments are seeking to manage adjustment pressures through quantitative allocations and licences. This approach holds out more promise. Even here, however, formal and informal power imbalances often undermine the position of the poor. In West Java, Indonesia, textile factories have usurped the water rights of smallholder farmers. And in the Philippines farmers in irrigation schemes have lost out to municipal users. The absence or nonenforcement of regulations is another potent threat. In India unregulated groundwater extraction on the Bhavani River has meant less water and more poverty in irrigation systems.

Outcomes for the poorest, most vulnerable people in society will be determined by the way institutions mediate and manage rival claims— and by whether governments put equity concerns at the centre of national policies

Water rights are critical for human security in agricultural areas. The sudden loss or erosion of entitlements to water can undermine livelihoods, increase vulnerability and intensify poverty on a large scale. Far more than to the wealthy, water rights matter to the poor for an obvious reason: poor people lack the financial resources and political voice to protect their interests outside a rules-based system. Water rights count for little if, in implementation, they skew advantages to those with power.

Balancing formal and customary rights

Sub-Saharan Africa faces distinctive challenges. Governments there are seeking, with donor support, to expand the irrigation frontier and to establish formal systems of rights as a supplement—or replacement—for customary rights. What will this mean for human development?

Outcomes will depend on public policies. Expanding irrigation capacity is important because it has the potential to raise productivity and reduce risk. The region is overwhelmingly dependent on rainfed agriculture. But irrigation infrastructure is a scarce and contested resource. Evidence from the Sahel region of West Africa shows that smallholders can often lose out in competition for irrigation to larger scale, commercial producers.

Management of customary rights poses further problems. Contrary to some perceptions, customary rights to water incorporate detailed management and use provisions to maintain ecological sustainability. But they often disadvantage poorer households and women. Introducing formal rules and laws does not automatically change this picture. In the Senegal River Valley customary rights holders have used their power to maintain social exclusion from water. Meanwhile, in Tanzania the introduction of formal water rights has benefited commercial farmers on the Pangani River to the disadvantage of small farmers downstream.

Giving more attention to equity

One lesson from water reforms is that far more weight needs to be attached to equity. In contrast to land reform, for example, distributional concerns have not figured prominently on the integrated water resources management agenda. There are some exceptions—as in South Africa—but even here it has proven difficult to achieve redistributive outcomes.

Irrigation systems are at the centre of the adjustment. Infrastructure for irrigation has an important bearing on poverty. Cross-country research suggests that poverty prevalence is typically 20%–40% lower inside irrigation networks than outside, but with very large variations. Irrigation appears to be a far more powerful motor for poverty reduction in some countries than in others. Land inequality is a major factor. Highly unequal countries (India, Pakistan and the Philippines) do worse in efficiency *and* equity than more equal countries (China and Viet Nam).

This finding suggests that there is no inherent tradeoff between increasing productivity and reducing poverty in irrigation. There is considerable scope for managing adjustment pressures in agriculture through measures that enhance both efficiency and equity in a mutually reinforcing virtuous cycle. Equitable cost-sharing, pro-poor public investments and the participation of producers in management hold the key to successful reform.

Addressing deep-seated gender inequalities

Real empowerment in irrigation systems requires measures to address deep-rooted gender inequalities. Women are doubly disadvantaged in irrigation systems. Lacking formal rights to land in many countries, they are excluded from irrigation system management. At the same time, informal inequalities—including the household division of labour, norms on women speaking in public and other factors—militate against women having a real voice in decision-making.

Breaking down these structures has proven difficult even in the most ambitious schemes for transferring management authority from government agencies to users. In Andhra Pradesh, India, poor farmers now have a far greater say in management—but poor women farmers are still silent. Change is possible, however. In

Uganda legislation requiring female representation in water user associations is making a difference.

Reaching the poor

Looking to the future, one of the greatest challenges is to ensure that strategies for enhancing water productivity extend to the poor. Technology is not neutral in its distributional effects—and the danger is that efforts to get more crop per drop from water resources will bypass poor households.

This does not have to be the case. The revival of small-scale water harvesting programmes in India in response to the groundwater crisis has shown the potential to generate large returns to investment and at the same time to reduce risk and vulnerability. Similarly, micro-irrigation technologies do not have to be geared solely to large capital-intensive producers. Innovative new designs and low-cost technologies for drip irrigation have been taken up extensively. Here, too, the social and economic returns are large. On one estimate the extension of low-cost irrigation technologies to 100 million smallholders could generate net benefits in excess of $100 billion, with strong multiplier effects in income and employment generation.

The way developing country governments address the challenge of balancing equity and efficiency goals in water management will have an important bearing on human development. Putting the interests of the poor at the centre of integrated water resources management policies is an organizing principle. But that principle has to be backed by practical pro-poor policies. Among the most important:

- Strengthening the water and land rights of poor households.
- Respecting customary rights and integrating these rights into formal legal systems.
- Enhancing the capacity of poor people to claim and defend water rights through legal empowerment and accountable institutions.
- Increasing national investments in irrigation and reversing aid cuts for the irrigation sector, with development assistance doubling to about $4 billion annually over the next 20 years.

- Enhancing equity within irrigation systems to support poverty reduction and efficiency objectives through sustainable and equitable cost-sharing mechanisms.
- Decentralizing the management and financing of irrigation systems to empower users.
- Integrating irrigation development into wider rural development programmes to make agriculture more profitable for smallholders.
- Putting gender rights to water at the centre of national development, and implementing policies to increase the voice of women in water management decisions.
- Developing integrated water-harvesting and groundwater policies extending from small-scale to large-scale infrastructure.
- Promoting the development, distribution and adoption of pro-poor technologies.

Managing transboundary water for human development

Water is a source of human interdependence. Within any country water is a shared resource serving multiple constituencies, from the environment to agriculture, industry and households. But water is also the ultimate fugitive resource. It crosses national frontiers, linking users across borders in a system of hydrological interdependence.

As competition for water intensifies within countries, the resulting pressures will spill across national borders. Some commentators fear that transboundary competition will become a source of conflict and future water wars. That fear is exaggerated: cooperation remains a far more pervasive fact of life than conflict. However, the potential for crossboundary tensions and conflict cannot be ignored. While most countries have institutional mechanisms for allocating water and resolving conflict within countries, cross-border institutional mechanisms are far weaker. The interaction of water stress and weak institutions carries with it real risks of conflict.

Hydrological interdependence
Hydrological interdependence is not an abstract concept. Two in every five people in the

The fear that transboundary competition will become a source of conflict and future water wars is exaggerated: cooperation remains a far more pervasive fact of life than conflict

world live in international water basins shared by more than one country. International rivers are a thread that binds countries: 9 countries share the Amazon and 11 the Nile, for example. Rivers also bind the livelihoods of people. The Mekong, one of the world's great river systems, generates power in its upper reaches in China and sustains the rice production and fishery systems that support the livelihoods of more than 60 million people in the lower reaches of its basin.

With hydrological interdependence comes deeper interdependence. As a productive resource, water is unique in that it can never be managed for a single use: it flows between sectors and users. That is true within countries and between them. How an upstream country uses a river inevitably affects the quantity, timing and quality of water available to users downstream. The same interdependence applies to aquifers and lakes.

Why is transboundary water governance a human development issue? Because failure in this area can produce outcomes that generate inequity, environmental unsustainability and wider social and economic losses.

There is no shortage of illustrations. The Aral Sea, described by some as the world's worst human-caused ecological disaster, is an extreme case in point. Less widely appreciated is the damage caused to shared river systems and lakes by overuse: the shrinkage of Lake Chad in Sub-Saharan Africa is an example.

Inequitable water management can heighten inequalities and water insecurity. For example, people living in the Occupied Palestinian Territories face acute water scarcity. Limited access to surface water is one factor. More important is the unequal sharing between Israel and Palestine of the aquifers below the West Bank. Average per capita water use by Israeli settlers on the West Bank is some nine times higher than by Palestinians sharing many of the same water sources.

Benefits of cooperation for human development

Successful cooperation in the management of shared waters can produce benefits for human development at many levels. Apart from reducing the potential for conflict, cooperation can unlock benefits by improving the quality of shared water, generating prosperity and more secure livelihoods and creating the scope for wider cooperation.

Experience highlights both the potential benefits of cooperation and the costs of noncooperation. Countries of the European Union have dramatically improved river water standards through cooperation, creating gains for industry, human health and domestic users. In Southern Africa a joint infrastructure programme is generating revenue for Lesotho and improved water for South Africa. Brazil and Paraguay have unlocked benefits from shared river management through power generation. Countries in Central Asia, by contrast, are paying a high price for noncooperation, with large losses for irrigation and hydropower.

Contrary to the claims of water war pessimists, conflict over water has been the exception, not the rule. Going back over the past 50 years, there have been some 37 cases of reported violence between states over water—and most of the episodes have involved minor skirmishes. Meanwhile, more than 200 water treaties have been negotiated. Some of these treaties—such as the Indus Basin Treaty between India and Pakistan—have remained in operation even during armed conflict.

Despite the general absence of armed conflict, cooperation has often been limited. For the most part it has focussed on technical management of water flow and volumetric allocations. Some river basin initiatives—notably the Nile Basin Initiative—are starting to change this picture. Progress has been hampered, however, by limited mandates, weak institutional capacity and underfinancing. These are all areas where international cooperation and partnerships can make a difference.

*   *   *

Water flows through all aspects of human life. Throughout history water management has presented people and governments with far-reaching technical and political challenges. The story of water management is at once a story of human ingenuity and human frailty. From the aqueducts of ancient Rome to the great public works of 19th century Europe and the United States, the provision of clean water for life has been made possible through innovative technologies. At the same time, unclean water and poor sanitation have claimed more lives over the past century than any other cause—and in many developing countries they continue to do so.

The management of water for livelihoods has an even longer history. Since the dawn of civilization in the Indus Valley and Mesopotamia the management of water as a productive resource has been marked by ingenious infrastructure systems that have sought to harness the productive potential of water while limiting its potential for destruction. Human vulnerability in the face of failure in these endeavours, or as a result of shifts in the hydrological cycle, is reflected in the demise of civilizations, the collapse of agricultural systems and environmental destruction. Faced with the threat of climate change and mounting pressure on the world's freshwater resources, the 21st century water governance challenge may prove to be among the most daunting faced in human history.

Unclean water and poor sanitation have claimed more lives over the past century than any other cause

The Millennium Development Goals are the world's time-bound targets for overcoming extreme poverty and extending human freedom. Representing something more than a set of quantitative benchmarks to be attained by 2015, they encapsulate a broad vision of shared development priorities. That vision is rooted in the simple idea that extreme poverty and gross disparities of opportunity are not inescapable features of the human condition but a curable affliction whose continuation diminishes us all and threatens our collective security and prosperity.

The multifaceted targets set under the Millennium Development Goals cut across a vast array of interlinked dimensions of development, ranging from the reduction of extreme poverty to gender equality to health, education and the environment. Each dimension is linked through a complex web of interactions. Sustained progress in any one area depends critically on advances across all the other areas. A lack of progress in any one area can hold back improvements across a broad front. Water and sanitation powerfully demonstrate the linkages. Without accelerated progress in these areas many countries will miss the Millennium Development Goals. Apart from consigning millions of the world's poorest people to lives of avoidable poverty, poor health and diminished opportunities, such an outcome would perpetuate deep inequalities within and between countries. While there is more to human development than the Millennium Development Goals, the targets set provide a useful frame of reference for understanding the linkages between progress in different areas—and the critical importance of progress in water and sanitation.

Millennium Development Goal	Why governments should act	How governments should act
Goal 1 Eradicate extreme poverty and hunger	• The absence of clean water and adequate sanitation is a major cause of poverty and malnutrition: • One in five people in the developing world—1.1 billion in all—lacks access to an improved water source. • One in two people—2.6 billion in all—lacks access to adequate sanitation. • Diseases and productivity losses linked to water and sanitation in developing countries amount to 2% of GDP, rising to 5% in Sub-Saharan Africa—more than the region gets in aid. • In many of the poorest countries only 25% of the poorest households have access to piped water in their homes, compared with 85% of the richest. • The poorest households pay as much as 10 times more for water as wealthy households. • Water is a vital productive input for the smallholder farmers who account for more than half of the world's population living on less than $1 a day. • Mounting pressure to reallocate water from agriculture to industry threatens to increase rural poverty.	• Bringing water and sanitation into the mainstream of national and international strategies for achieving the Millennium Development Goals requires policies aimed at: • Making access to water a human right and legislating for the progressive implementation of that right by ensuring that all people have access to at least 20 litres of clean water a day. • Increasing public investment in extending the water network in urban areas and expanding provision in rural areas. • Introducing "lifeline tariffs", cross-subsidies and investments in standpipes to ensure that nobody is denied access to water because of poverty, with a target ceiling of 3% for the share of household income spent on water. • Regulating water utilities to improve efficiency, enhance equity and ensure accountability to the poor. • Introducing public policies that combine sustainability with equity in the development of water resources for agriculture. • Supporting the development and adoption of pro-poor irrigation technologies.
Goal 2 Achieve universal primary education	• Collecting water and carrying it over long distances keep millions of girls out of school, consigning them to a future of illiteracy and restricted choice. • Water-related diseases such as diarrhoea and parasitic infections cost 443 million school days each year—equivalent to an entire school year for all seven-year-old children in Ethiopia—and diminish learning potential. • Inadequate water and sanitation provision in schools in many countries is a threat to child health. • The absence of adequate sanitation and water in schools is a major reason that girls drop out. • Parasitic infection transmitted through water and poor sanitation retards learning potential for more than 150 million children.	• Linking targets and strategies for achieving universal primary education to strategies for ensuring that every school has adequate water and sanitation provision, with separate facilities for girls. • Making sanitation and hygiene parts of the school curriculum, equipping children with the knowledge they need to reduce health risks and enabling them to become agents of change in their communities. • Establishing public health programmes in schools and communities that prevent and treat water-related infectious diseases.

Millennium Development Goal	Why governments should act	How governments should act
Goal 3 Promote gender equality and empower women	• Deprivation in water and sanitation perpetuates gender inequality and disempowers women. • Women bear the brunt of responsibility for collecting water, often spending up to 4 hours a day walking, waiting in queues and carrying water. This is a major source of time poverty. • The time women spend caring for children made ill by waterborne diseases diminishes their opportunity to engage in productive work. • Inadequate sanitation is experienced by millions of women as a loss of dignity and source of insecurity. • Women account for the bulk of food production in many countries but experience restricted rights to water.	• Putting gender equity in water and sanitation at the centre of national poverty reduction strategies. • Enacting legislation that requires female representation on water committees and other bodies. • Supporting sanitation campaigns that give women a greater voice in shaping public investment decisions and household spending. • Reforming property rights and the rules governing irrigation and other water user associations to ensure that women enjoy equal rights.
Goal 4 Reduce child mortality	• Dirty water and poor sanitation account for the vast majority of the 1.8 million child deaths each year from diarrhoea—almost 5,000 every day—making it the second largest cause of child mortality. • Access to clean water and sanitation can reduce the risk of a child dying by as much as 50%. • Diarrhoea caused by unclean water is one of the world's greatest killers, claiming the lives of five times as many children as HIV/AIDS. • Clean water and sanitation are among the most powerful preventative measures for child mortality: achieving the Millennium Development Goal for water and sanitation at even the most basic level of provision would save more than 1 million lives in the next decade; universal provision would raise the number of lives saved to 2 million. • Waterborne diseases reinforce deep and socially unjust disparities, with children in poor households facing a risk of death some three to four times greater than children in rich households.	• Treating child deaths from water and sanitation as a national emergency—and as a violation of basic human rights. • Using international aid to strengthen basic healthcare provision in preventing and treating diarrhoea. • Establishing explicit linkages between targets for lowering child mortality and targets for expanding access to water and sanitation. • Prioritizing the needs of the poorest households in public investment and service provision strategies for water and sanitation. • Ensuring that Poverty Reduction Strategy Papers recognize the link between water and sanitation and child mortality. • Publishing annual estimates of child deaths caused by water and sanitation problems.
Goal 5 Improve maternal health	• The provision of water and sanitation reduces the incidence of diseases and afflictions—such as anaemia, vitamin deficiency and trachoma—that undermine maternal health and contribute to maternal mortality.	• Treating water and sanitation provision as a key component in strategies for gender equality. • Empowering women to shape decisions on water and sanitation at the household, local and national levels.
Goal 6 Combat HIV/AIDS, malaria and other diseases	• Inadequate access to water and sanitation restricts opportunities for hygiene and exposes people with HIV/AIDS to increased risks of infection. • HIV-infected mothers require clean water to make formula milk. • Achieving the Millennium Development Goal target for water and sanitation would reduce the costs to health systems of treating water-related infectious diseases by $1.7 billion, increasing the resources available for HIV/AIDS treatment. • Poor sanitation and drainage contribute to malaria, which claims some 1.3 million lives a year, 90% of them children under the age of five.	• Integrating water and sanitation into national and global strategies for tackling malaria and improving living conditions of HIV/AIDS patients. • Ensuring that households caring for people with HIV/AIDS have access to at least 50 litres of free water. • Investing in the drainage and sanitation facilities that reduce the presence of flies and mosquitoes.

(continued on next page)

Millennium Development Goal	Why governments should act	How governments should act
Goal 7 Ensure environmental sustainability **Halve the proportion of people without sustainable access to safe drinking water and basic sanitation**	• The goal of halving the proportion of people without access to water and sanitation will be missed on current trends by 234 million people for water and 430 million people for sanitation. • Sub-Saharan Africa will need to increase new connections for sanitation from 7 million a year for the past decade to 28 million a year by 2015. • Slow progress in water and sanitation will hold back advances in other areas.	• Putting in place practical measures that translate Millennium Development Goal commitments into practical actions. • Providing national and international political leadership to overcome the twin deficits in water and sanitation. • Supplementing the Millennium Development Goal target with the target of halving water and sanitation coverage disparities between the richest and poorest 20%. • Empowering independent regulators to hold service providers to account for delivering efficient and affordable services to the poor.
Reverse the loss of environmental resources	• The unsustainable exploitation of water resources represents a growing threat to human development, generating an unsustainable ecological debt that will be transferred to future generations. • The number of people living in water-stressed countries will increase from about 700 million today to more than 3 billion by 2025. • Over 1.4 billion people currently live in river basins where the use of water exceeds minimum recharge levels, leading to the desiccation of rivers and depletion of groundwater. • Water insecurity linked to climate change threatens to increase malnutrition by 75–125 million people by 2080, with staple food production in many Sub-Saharan African countries falling by more than 25%. • Groundwater depletion poses a grave threat to agricultural systems, food security and livelihoods across Asia and the Middle East.	• Treating water as a precious natural resource, rather than an expendable commodity to be exploited without reference to environmental sustainability. • Reforming national accounts to reflect the real economic losses associated with the depletion of water resources. • Introducing integrated water resources management policies that constrain water use within the limits of environmental sustainability, factoring in the needs of the environment. • Institutionalizing policies that create incentives for conserving water and eliminating perverse subsidies that encourage unsustainable water-use patterns. • Strengthening the provisions of the Kyoto Protocol to limit carbon emissions in line with stabilization targets of 450 parts per million, bolstering clean technology transfer mechanisms and bringing all countries under a stronger multilateral framework for emission reductions in 2012. • Developing national adaptation strategies for dealing with the impact of climate change—and increasing aid for adaptation.
Goal 8 Develop a global partnership for development	• There is no effective global partnership for water and sanitation, and successive high-level conferences have failed to create the momentum needed to push water and sanitation in the international agenda. • Many national governments are failing to put in place the policies and financing needed to accelerate progress. • Water and sanitation is weakly integrated into Poverty Reduction Strategy Papers. • Many countries with high child death rates caused by diarrhoea are spending less than 0.5% of GDP on water and sanitation, a fraction of what they are allocating to military budgets. • Rich countries have failed to prioritize water and sanitation in international aid partnerships, and spending on development assistance for the sector has been falling in real terms, now representing only 4% of total aid flows. • International aid to agriculture has fallen by a third since the early 1990s, from 12% to 3.5% of total aid.	• Putting in place a global plan of action to galvanize political action, placing water and sanitation on to the agenda of the Group of Eight, mobilizing resources and supporting nationally owned planning processes. • Developing nationally owned plans that link the Millennium Development Goal target for water and sanitation to clear medium-term financing provisions and to practical policies for overcoming inequality. • Empowering local governments and local communities through decentralization, capacity development and adequate financing, with at least 1% of GDP allocated to water and sanitation through public spending. • Increasing aid for water by $3.6–$4 billion annually by 2010, with an additional $2 billion allocated to Sub-Saharan Africa. • Increasing aid for agriculture from $3 billion to $10 billion annually by 2010, with a strengthened focus on water security.

1

**Ending the crisis in
water and sanitation**

"The human right to water entitles everyone to sufficient, safe, acceptable, physically accessible and affordable water for personal and domestic use"

U.N. General Comment No. 15 on the right to water, 2002

"Civilized man could embark on no task nobler than sanitary reform"

Boston Board of Health, 1869

CHAPTER 1

Ending the crisis in water and sanitation

The violation of the human right to clean water and sanitation is destroying human potential on an epic scale

Clean water and sanitation can make or break human development. They are fundamental to what people can do and what they can become—to their capabilities. Access to water is not just a fundamental human right and an intrinsically important indicator for human progress. It also gives substance to other human rights and is a condition for attaining wider human development goals.

At the start of the 21st century the violation of the human right to clean water and sanitation is destroying human potential on an epic scale. In today's increasingly prosperous and interconnected world more children die for want of clean water and a toilet than from almost any other cause. Exclusion from clean water and basic sanitation destroys more lives than any war or terrorist act. It also reinforces the deep inequalities in life chances that divide countries and people within countries on the basis of wealth, gender and other markers for deprivation.

Beyond the human waste and suffering, the global deficit in water and sanitation is undermining prosperity and retarding economic growth. Productivity losses linked to that deficit are blunting the efforts of millions of the world's poorest people to work their way out of poverty and holding back whole countries. Whether viewed from the perspective of human rights, social justice or economic common sense, the damage inflicted by deprivation in water and sanitation is indefensible. Overcoming that deprivation is not just a moral imperative and the right thing to do. It is also the sensible thing to do because the waste of human potential associated with unsafe water and poor sanitation ultimately hurts everybody.

This chapter documents the scale of the crisis in water and sanitation and traces its causes. It highlights the human development costs of the problem—and the potential benefits of resolving it. Better access to water and sanitation would act as the catalyst for a giant advance in human development, creating opportunities for gains in public health, education and economic growth. So why are these opportunities being squandered on such a large scale?

Partly because of insufficient awareness of the scale of the problem and partly because of insufficient efforts by national governments and the international community to address the poverty and inequality that perpetuate the crisis. In contrast to some of the other global threats to human development—such as HIV/AIDS—the crisis in water and sanitation is, above all, a crisis of the poor in general and of women in particular, two constituencies with limited bargaining power in setting national priorities. Water and sanitation are also the poor cousin of international development cooperation. While the international community has mobilized to an impressive degree in preparing to respond to the potential threat of an avian flu epidemic, it turns a blind eye to an actual epidemic that afflicts hundreds of millions of people every day.

The water and sanitation crisis facing poor households in the developing world has parallels with an earlier period in the history of today's rich countries. Few people in the industrial world reflect on the profound importance of clean water and sanitation in shaping the history of their countries or their life chances. Not too many generations ago the inhabitants of London,

The world has the technology, the finance and the human capacity to remove the blight of water insecurity from millions of lives

New York and Paris were facing the same water security threats as those of Lagos, Mumbai and Rio de Janeiro today. Water polluted with raw sewage killed children, created health crises, undermined growth and kept people in poverty. New technologies and finance made universal access to clean water possible. But the crucial change was political. Social reformers, physicians, municipal leaders and industrialists formed powerful coalitions that elevated water and sanitation to the top of the political agenda. They forced governments to acknowledge that curing diseases caused by unsafe water was inefficient and wasteful: prevention through clean water and sanitation was the better cure.

At the start of the 21st century the world has the opportunity to unleash another leap forward in human development. Within a generation the global crisis in water and sanitation could be consigned to history. The world has the technology, the finance and the human capacity to remove the blight of water insecurity from millions of lives. Lacking are the political will and vision needed to apply these resources for the public good. Progress in rich countries was made possible by a new social contract between governments and people—a contract based on the idea of common citizenship and the recognition of government responsibility. The world may be different today. But now, as then, progress depends on partnerships and political leadership. National policy is the starting point, because without strong national policies progress cannot be sustained. The challenge is for developed country governments to back credible national efforts in developing countries through a strong aid effort within a global plan of action for water and sanitation.

Lessons from history

For most of human history life has conformed to Thomas Hobbes' description as "nasty, brutish, and short". Life expectancy at birth for our hunter-gatherer ancestors was about 25 years, and in the Europe of the 1820s it was still only 40 years. From the late 19th century this picture started to change dramatically for the fortunate share of humanity living in today's rich countries.[1] New medicines, improved nutrition, better housing and increased income all contributed. But one of the most powerful forces for change was the separation of water from human excrement.

When it comes to water and sanitation, countries tend to have short memories. Today, people in the cities of Europe and the United States live free from fear of waterborne infectious diseases. At the turn of the 20th century the picture was very different. The vast expansion of wealth that followed industrialization increased incomes, but improvements in more fundamental indicators such as life expectancy, child survival and public health lagged far behind. The reason: cities exposed people to greater opportunities to amass wealth but also to water contaminated with human waste. The mundane reality of unclean water severed the link between economic growth and human development. It was not until a revolution in water and sanitation restored that link that wealth generation and human welfare started to move in tandem (box 1.1).

That revolution heralded unprecedented advances in life expectancy and child survival—and better public health fuelled economic advances. As people become healthier and wealthier with the provision of clean water and sanitation, a virtuous circle of economic growth and human development emerged. But the increasing returns generated by investment in clean water also helped to create and to progressively widen the deep cleavages in wealth, health and opportunity that characterize the world today.[2]

"Parliament was all but compelled to legislate upon the great London nuisance by the force of sheer stench." Thus commented the London *Times* on an episode known as the "Great Stink". So severe was the stench of sewage emanating from the Thames River in the long hot summer of 1858, that the "mother of parliaments" was forced to close temporarily. Beyond parliament the problems were more serious.

As industrialization and urbanization accelerated in the 19th century, fast growing cities like Birmingham, London and Manchester became centres of infectious disease. Sewage overflowed and leaked from the limited number of cesspools into neighbourhoods of the poor and ultimately into rivers like the Thames, the source of drinking water.

Parliamentary nostrils were offended—while poor people died. In the late 1890s the infant mortality rate in Great Britain was 160 deaths for every 1,000 live births (figure 1)—roughly the same as in Nigeria today. Children died mainly from diarrhoea and dysentery. They died for the same reason that so many children still die in developing countries: sewage was not separated from drinking water. Between 1840 and the mid-1890s, average income doubled while child mortality increased slightly—a powerful demonstration of the gap between wealth generation and human development.

Growing awareness of the human costs of urban industrial life forced water onto the political agenda. In 1834 the Office of the Registrar General was formed, producing a steady stream of mortality figures that generated public concern. Social investigation became another powerful tool for reform. Edwin Chadwick's *Report on the Sanitary Condition of the Labouring Population of Great Britain* provided an account of a crisis on a grand scale, documenting in graphic detail the consequences of the water and sanitation problem. Unaffordable water provided by private companies, poor drainage and overflowing cesspools figured prominently. "The annual loss of life from filth and bad ventilation", Chadwick concluded, "is greater than the loss from death or wounds from any war in which the country has been engaged in modern times" (p. 369). His recommendations: a private tap and a latrine connected to a sewer for every household and municipal responsibility for providing clean water.

Reform came in two great waves. The first focused on water and began in the 1840s with the Public Health Act (1848) and the Metropolitan Water Act (1852), which expanded public provision of clean water. The discovery by John Snow in 1854 that cholera—the greatest epidemic scourge—was a waterborne infection and that its spread could be halted by access to uncontaminated water supplies added to the impetus. By 1880 municipalities had displaced private water operators as the main providers of water in towns and cities.

The second great wave of reform shifted the locus of the public action from water to sanitation. This wave gathered momentum after 1880. It was reflected in a surge of public investment. Between the mid-1880s and mid-1890s capital spending per capita on sanitation more than doubled in constant prices (figure 2). It then doubled again over the next decade.

The gap between provision of water and provision of effective sanitation was a public health disaster. Streets and rivers became grossly polluted under the growing burden of waterborne wastes. The incidence of diseases such as cholera and typhoid fever fell, but deaths from gastrointestinal illness—especially diarrhoea among children—remained high. The outcome of the unbalanced early phase of local government intervention was an upward pressure on the incidence of waterborne disease.

Life expectancy and child mortality data highlight the problem (see figure 1). After 1840 life expectancy began to increase partly because of the first wave of reforms in water. However, the trend abruptly levelled off at the end of the 1870s. It was not until after the early 1880s, when the great sanitation reforms came into play, that the upward trend resumed, driven by a steep decline in child death. Sanitary reform cannot take all the credit. But the coincident timing between peak sanitary investment and the onset of a general decline in infant mortality suggests a causal relationship. In the space of little more than a decade from 1900 the infant mortality rate fell from 160 deaths per 1,000 live births to 100—one of the steepest declines in history. Public

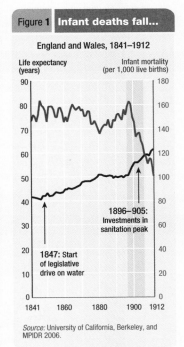

Figure 1 **Infant deaths fall...**

England and Wales, 1841–1912

Life expectancy (years) / *Infant mortality (per 1,000 live births)*

1847: Start of legislative drive on water

1896–905: Investments in sanitation peak

Source: University of California, Berkeley, and MPIDR 2006.

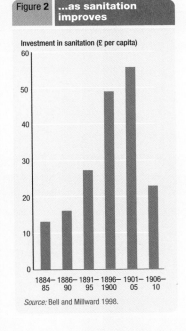

Figure 2 **...as sanitation improves**

Investment in sanitation (£ per capita)

1884–85 1886–90 1891–95 1896–1900 1901–05 1906–10

Source: Bell and Millward 1998.

(continued on next page)

Box 1.1   A great leap—from water reform to sanitation reform in 19th century Great Britain (continued)

investment in sanitation, not rising private income, was the catalyst. Average incomes rose by only 6% between 1900 and 1912.

New approaches to financing played a critical role in the second wave of reform. Mounting political pressure for public action generated an active search for new fiscal mechanisms to address a dilemma familiar in developing countries today: how to finance large upfront payments from a limited revenue base without raising taxes or charges to politically unfeasible levels. Governments developed innovative solutions. Cities supplemented low-interest loans from the central government with municipal borrowing on bond markets. Water and sanitation accounted for about a quarter of local government debt at the end of the 19th century.

This huge mobilization of public finances reflected the changing place of water and sanitation in political priorities. Sanitation reform became a rallying point for social reformers, municipal leaders and public health bodies, who increasingly viewed inadequate sanitation

as a constraint not just on human progress but on economic prosperity. The public voice of civil society played a key role in driving the sanitation reform that made advances in public health possible.

But why the lag between the two great waves of reform? One of the major reform coalition partners in the first wave was the industrialists who wanted water for factories, but who were reluctant to pay higher taxes for extending sanitation to the poor. Politically powerful segments of society remained more interested in insulating themselves from the effects of poor sanitation among the poor than in universal provision. It was not until the electoral reform that extended voting rights beyond propertied classes that the voice of the poor became a more telling factor.

This is a story from 19th century Great Britain, not the 21st century developing world. But there are marked parallels both in how water and sanitation constrains social progress and in how the forces for change emerge from coalitions for social reform.

Source: Bell and Millward 1998; Szreter 1997; Hassan 1985; Woods, Watterson and Woodward 1988, 1989; Bryer 2006.

How water insecurity decoupled economic growth and human development

At the start of the 21st century waterborne infectious diseases are a thing of the past in rich countries, accounting for a fraction of 1% of overall mortality. At the turn of the 19th century, diseases like diarrhoea, dysentery and typhoid fever posed major threats. In the late 19th century they accounted for 1 in 10 deaths in US cities, with children the primary victims. Infant mortality rates in Detroit, Pittsburgh and Washington, D.C., were more than 180 deaths for every 1,000 live births—almost twice the rate in Sub-Saharan Africa today.[3] Chicago was the typhoid capital of the country, reporting an average of 20,000 cases a year. In the United Kingdom, too, half a century after the first wave of public health reforms, water remained a potent threat. The infant mortality rate in Birmingham and Liverpool exceeded 160 deaths for every 1,000 live births, with diarrhoea and dysentery accounting for more than half the deaths.[4] High child mortality acted as a brake on increases in life expectancy. Until the last quarter of the 19th century life expectancy barely rose in the industrialized world. People were becoming wealthier but not healthier.[5]

Why in the midst of the vast expansion of wealth created by industrialization did child survival and life expectancy, two of the most basic indicators for the human condition, not advance? Partly because industrialization and urbanization were drawing poor rural migrants into urban slums that lacked water and sanitation infrastructure—a scenario played out today in many of the world's poorest countries. While cities offered employment and higher incomes, they increased exposure to lethal pathogens transmitted through overflowing cesspools, sewers and drains.[6]

Almost every major city faced the same problem. At the end of the 19th century one public health report on Paris lamented that the poor quarters of the city had become "an open-air sewer", posing a daily threat to health and life.[7] Chicago's public health crisis arose because the city used Lake Michigan both for water and for waste disposal. That worked until the population expanded after the Civil War, and the city ended up drinking its own waste, to disastrous effect: 12% of the population died from waterborne diseases in the mid-1880s. Epidemics of typhoid and cholera regularly swept through cities like New Orleans and New York.[8] Partly to combat disease, London and Paris had built sewerage systems before 1850. But the sewers drained into the Thames and the Seine, making both rivers putrid—so putrid in the case of the Thames that in the hot summer of 1858 Parliament was forced into temporary closure by an episode known as the "Great Stink".[9]

The water-sanitation disconnect— and delayed progress

Progress in water and sanitation was driven by advances in scientific knowledge, technology and—above all—by political coalitions uniting industrialists, municipalities and social reformers. But advances occurred in piecemeal fashion, with water provision fast outstripping the development of the sewers and drains needed for wastewater management. The upshot: an increase in the transmission of diseases (see box 1.1).[10]

Towards the end of the 19th century governments acted to close the gap between water and sanitation. In Great Britain public investment financed an expansion of sewerage systems. Life expectancy increased in the four decades after the 1880s by an astounding 15 years, with reduced child deaths accounting for the bulk of the gain. In the United States the New York Board of Health, a municipal body created in 1866, was given the task of breaking the cycles of cholera and other health epidemics that afflicted the city. Its creation marked the recognition that the diseases associated with water and sanitation could not be contained in the city's poorer tenements—and that public action was needed to advance private interests.[11] The example was followed elsewhere, with municipalities taking over the provision of water and then introducing filtration and chlorination systems.[12] By one estimate water purification alone explains half the mortality reduction in the United States in the first third of the 20th century (box 1.2).[13] No other period in US history has witnessed such rapid declines in mortality rates. By 1920 almost every big city in today's industrial world had purified water. Within another decade most had built large sewage treatment plants that removed, treated and disposed of human waste in areas where it would not contaminate drinking water.[14]

Progress in water and sanitation was driven by advances in scientific knowledge, technology and—above all—by political coalitions uniting industrialists, municipalities and social reformers

Today's global crisis in water and sanitation

Debates on globalization invariably focus on the large wealth gaps that separate rich and poor countries. Those gaps are highly visible (see *The state of human development*). Less attention is paid to other inequalities that shape the prosperity of countries and the well-being of their citizens. The global fault line that separates those with and those without access to water and sanitation is a case in point.

Rich world, poor world

For people in rich countries it is difficult to imagine what water insecurity means in a developing country. Concerns about a water crisis periodically generate media headlines. Falling reservoirs, declining rivers, hosepipe bans and political exhortations to use less water are becoming more common in parts of Europe. In the United States management of water shortages has long been a public policy concern in states such as Arizona and California. But almost everyone in the developed world has safe water available at the twist of a tap. Access to private and hygienic sanitation is universal. Almost nobody dies for want of clean water or sanitation—and young girls are not kept home from school to fetch water.

Contrast this with the position in the developing world. As in other areas of human

Box 1.2   **Breaking the links between race, disease and inequality in US cities**

We feel it our duty to say that high-priced water is not in the interest of public health. Pure water in abundance, at a price within the reach of all, is one of the most powerful agencies for promoting the health of any community. It is for this reason that we believe so strongly in municipal ownership.   North Carolina Board of Health, 1898

One hundred years ago people living in Chicago, Detroit and New York would have understood the public health problems of cities in the world's poorest countries today—and they understood through bitter experience the importance of clean water.

At the start of the 20th century infectious diseases accounted for 44% of mortality in US cities. Waterborne diseases like typhoid fever, cholera and diarrhoea were among the biggest killers, accounting for a quarter of deaths from infectious diseases. Only tuberculosis claimed more lives.

Two problems, both familiar to people in the slums of Lagos, Manila or Nairobi today, obstructed progress in human health. First, water supplies had been improved by private companies, but the poorest households could not afford connections. The statement above from the North Carolina Board of Health reflects the growing concern of public health agencies at the time. Second, early private and municipal water systems compounded another problem. Large amounts of human excrement and street waste washed down drains and into overburdened sewers that emptied back into the water supply system.

Although all sections of society were affected, some were more affected than others. Unable to afford either a water connection or bottled water, poor households relied on wells and surface water. They also suffered some of the worst drainage problems. Unequal access to clean water exacerbated unequal health. African Americans living in cities like New Orleans died at roughly twice the rate of whites from typhoid fever.

What brought about the breakthrough in curbing infectious disease? Municipalizing water was the main factor (figure 1). After 1900 municipal bodies gradually displaced private providers. In New Orleans, which municipalized water in 1908, public providers extended networks and lowered prices 25% below what private companies charged. In the decade to 1915 the water system, measured in pipe miles, expanded by a multiple of 4.5, with the expansion concentrated in some of the poorest districts.

Measures to protect people from harmful bacteria in water marked the other distinctive feature of the municipal revolution. Infrastructure programmes were important. Jersey City abandoned the Passaic River to seek clean water upstream. Chicago built drainage canals to carry waste down the Illinois and Mississippi Rivers rather than back into Lake Michigan, the city's water source. And Cleveland extended its water intake four miles out into Lake Erie. But it was the introduction of water filtration and chlorination systems that played the key role, as illustrated by Cincinnati (figure 2) and Detroit. Between 1880 and 1940 the share of the US population using filtered water rose from 1% to more than 50%.

Reforms in water contributed to wider public health gains. In the four decades after 1900 life expectancy at birth rose by 16 years, child death rates fell dramatically, and typhoid fever was virtually eliminated. No other period in US history has witnessed such rapidly falling mortality rates. By one estimate water and filtration systems explain almost half the mortality decline. Every life saved in this way cost about $500 (in 2002 prices). But every $1 spent generated another $23 in increased output and reduced health costs. In the early 20th century US spending on water and sanitation represented a high value for money investment—just as it does for developing countries today.

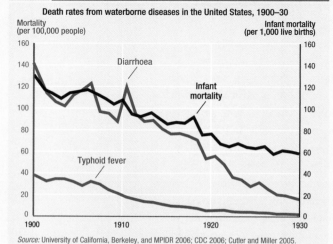

Figure 1 **Municipalizing water lowered prices, improved quality and saved lives**

Death rates from waterborne diseases in the United States, 1900–30

Source: University of California, Berkeley, and MPIDR 2006; CDC 2006; Cutler and Miller 2005.

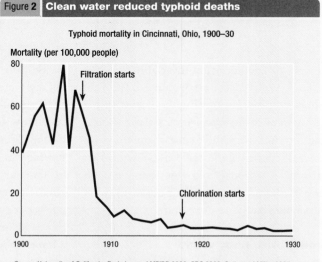

Figure 2 **Clean water reduced typhoid deaths**

Typhoid mortality in Cincinnati, Ohio, 1900–30

Source: University of California, Berkeley, and MPIDR 2006; CDC 2006; Cutler and Miller 2005.

Source: Cutler and Miller 2005; Cain and Rotella 2001; Troesken 2001; Blake 1956.

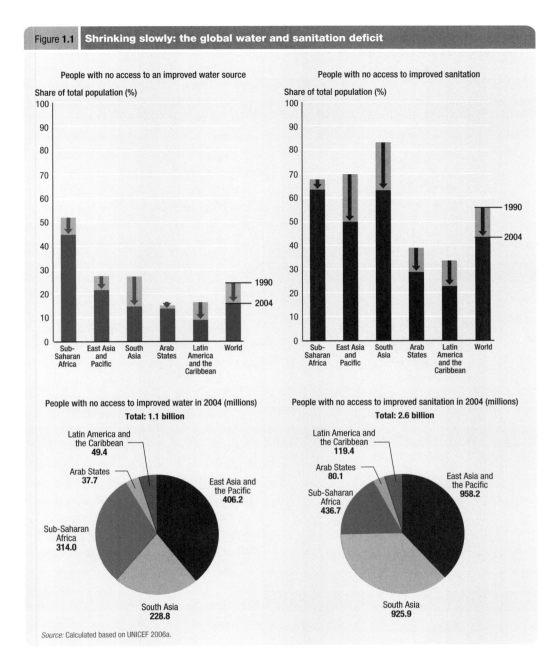

Figure 1.1 Shrinking slowly: the global water and sanitation deficit

People with no access to an improved water source

Share of total population (%)

Sub-Saharan Africa · East Asia and Pacific · South Asia · Arab States · Latin America and the Caribbean · World

1990
2004

People with no access to improved sanitation

Share of total population (%)

Sub-Saharan Africa · East Asia and Pacific · South Asia · Arab States · Latin America and the Caribbean · World

1990
2004

People with no access to improved water in 2004 (millions)
Total: 1.1 billion

Latin America and the Caribbean **49.4**
Arab States **37.7**
Sub-Saharan Africa **314.0**
South Asia **228.8**
East Asia and the Pacific **406.2**

People with no access to improved sanitation in 2004 (millions)
Total: 2.6 billion

Latin America and the Caribbean **119.4**
Arab States **80.1**
Sub-Saharan Africa **436.7**
South Asia **925.9**
East Asia and the Pacific **958.2**

Source: Calculated based on UNICEF 2006a.

development, there has been progress in water and sanitation (figure 1.1). Yet at the start of the 21st century one in five people living in the developing world—some 1.1 billion people in all—lacks access to clean water. Some 2.6 billion people, almost half the total population of developing countries, do not have access to adequate sanitation. What do these headline numbers mean?

In important respects they hide the reality experienced daily by the people behind the statistics. That reality means that people are forced to defecate in ditches, plastic bags or on road sides. "Not having access to clean water" is a euphemism for profound deprivation. It means that people live more than 1 kilometre from the nearest safe water source and that they collect water from drains, ditches or streams that might be infected with pathogens and bacteria that can cause severe illness and death. In rural Sub-Saharan Africa millions of people share their domestic water sources with animals or rely on unprotected wells that are breeding grounds for pathogens. Nor is the problem restricted to the

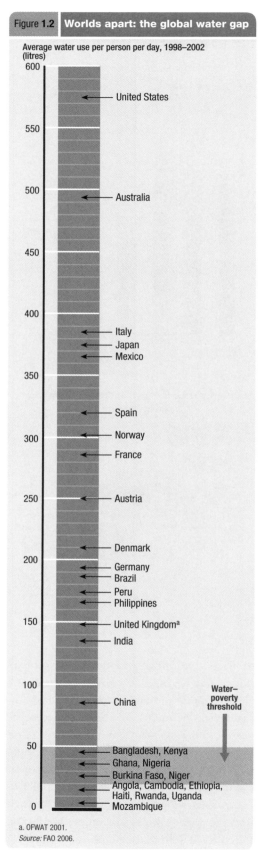

Figure **1.2** **Worlds apart: the global water gap**

Average water use per person per day, 1998–2002
(litres)

United States

Australia

Italy
Japan
Mexico

Spain

Norway

France

Austria

Denmark

Germany
Brazil
Peru
Philippines

United Kingdom[a]

India

Water–
poverty
threshold

China

Bangladesh, Kenya
Ghana, Nigeria
Burkina Faso, Niger
Angola, Cambodia, Ethiopia,
Haiti, Rwanda, Uganda
Mozambique

a. OFWAT 2001.
Source: FAO 2006.

poorest countries. In Tajikistan nearly a third of the population takes water from canals and irrigation ditches, with risks of exposure to polluted agricultural run-off.[15] The problem is not that people are unaware of the dangers—it is that they have no choice. Apart from the health risks, inadequate access to water means that women and young girls spend long hours collecting and carrying household water supplies.

Simple comparisons between rich and poor countries highlight the scale of global inequality (figure 1.2). Average water use ranges from 200–300 litres a person a day in most countries in Europe to 575 in the United States. Residents of Phoenix, Arizona, a desert city with some of the greenest lawns in the United States, use more than 1,000 litres a day. By contrast, average use in countries such as Mozambique is less than 10 litres. National averages inevitably mask very large variations. People lacking access to improved water in developing countries consume far less, partly because they have to carry it over long distances and water is heavy. The 100 litre a day minimum international norm for a family of five weighs some 100 kilograms—a heavy burden to carry for two to three hours, especially for young girls. Another problem is that poor households are often unable to afford more than a small amount of water purchased in informal markets—an issue to which we return below.

What is the basic threshold for adequate water provision? Setting a water-poverty line is difficult because of variations relating to climate—people in arid northern Kenya need more drinking water than people in London or Paris—seasonality, individual household characteristics and other factors. International norms set out by agencies such as the World Health Organization (WHO) and the United Nations Children's Fund (UNICEF) suggest a minimum requirement of 20 litres a day from a source within 1 kilometre of the household. This is sufficient for drinking and basic personal hygiene. Below this level people are constrained in their ability to maintain their physical well-being and the dignity that comes with being clean. Factoring in bathing and laundry needs would raise the personal threshold to about 50 litres a day.

Large swathes of humanity fall well below the basic needs thresholds for water either permanently or intermittently. For the 1.1 billion or so people in the world who live more than 1 kilometre from a water source, water use is often less than 5 litres a day of unsafe water.[16] To put this figure in context, the basic requirement for a lactating women engaged in even moderate physical activity is 7.5 litres a day. In other words, one in five people in the developing world lacks access to sufficient water to meet even the most basic requirements for well-being and child development. The problems are most severe in rural areas. In Uganda *average* consumption in rural areas ranges from 12 to 14 litres a day.[17] Dry season use falls sharply as the distance to water sources increases. In arid areas of western India, the Sahel and East Africa dry season water availability can fall well below 5 litres a day. But people living in urban areas also experience extreme scarcity. Water use averages 5–10 litres a day in small towns in Burkina Faso and 8 litres a day in informal settlements in Chennai, India.[18]

Beyond the extreme deprivation experienced daily by some 1.1 billion people is a far larger sphere of deprivation. For people with access to a water source within 1 kilometre, but not in their house or yard, consumption typically averages around 20 litres per day. A 2001 WHO/UNICEF study estimated that some 1.8 billion were in this position.[19]

Without downplaying the seriousness of what are perceived as water shortages in rich countries, the contrasts are striking. In the United Kingdom the average person uses more than 50 litres of water a day flushing toilets—more than 10 times the total water available to people lacking access to an improved water source in much of rural Sub-Saharan Africa. An American taking a five-minute shower uses more water than the typical person living in a developing country slum uses in a whole day. Restrictions on the use of garden sprinklers and hosepipes may doubtless cause inconvenience to households in rich countries. But parents do not lack sufficient water to keep their children clean, to meet the basic hygiene standards that ward off killer infections or to maintain their health and dignity.

Of course, water consumption in rich countries does not diminish water availability in poor countries. Global consumption is not a zero-sum game in which one country gets less if another gets more. But comparisons highlight disparities in access to clean water—and nowhere more so than in bottled mineral water.[20] The 25 billion litres of mineral water consumed annually by US households exceeds the entire clean water consumption of the 2.7 million people in Senegal lacking access to an improved water source. And Germans and Italians between them consume enough mineral water to cover the basic needs of more than 3 million people in Burkina Faso for cooking, washing and other domestic purposes. While one part of the world sustains a designer bottled-water market that generates no tangible health benefits, another part suffers acute public health risks because people have to drink water from drains or from lakes and rivers shared with animals and infected with harmful bacteria.

Wealth matters...

Global aggregates for water and sanitation coverage obscure large differences across regions. In the case of water Sub-Saharan Africa has by far the lowest coverage rates (55%), though most people without clean water live in South Asia. For sanitation the deprivation is more evenly spread. Coverage in South Asia is almost as low as in Sub-Saharan Africa, with two of every three people in both regions lacking access. Half the people in East Asia and a quarter in Latin America lack access to even the most basic sanitation. Some 40 developing countries provide clean water for fewer than 70% of their citizens, and 54 provide safe sanitation for fewer than half (figure 1.3).

The global snapshot highlights the daunting scale of the water and sanitation crisis. But it also draws attention to two wider problems. The first concerns the relation between wealth and the provision of water and sanitation. On average, coverage levels for water and sanitation rise with income: the richer the country the greater the coverage. That finding is not surprising

While one part of the world sustains a designer bottled-water market that generates no tangible health benefits, another part suffers acute public health risks because people have to drink water from drains or from lakes and rivers

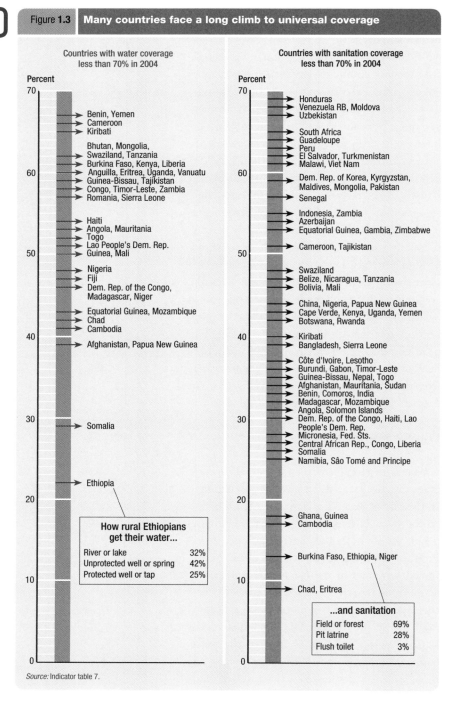

Figure 1.3 **Many countries face a long climb to universal coverage**

Countries with water coverage less than 70% in 2004

Percent

70	Benin, Yemen
	Cameroon
	Kiribati
60	Bhutan, Mongolia, Swaziland, Tanzania
	Burkina Faso, Kenya, Liberia
	Anguilla, Eritrea, Uganda, Vanuatu
	Guinea-Bissau, Tajikistan
	Congo, Timor-Leste, Zambia
	Romania, Sierra Leone
50	Haiti
	Angola, Mauritania
	Togo
	Lao People's Dem. Rep.
	Guinea, Mali
	Nigeria
	Fiji
	Dem. Rep. of the Congo, Madagascar, Niger
40	Equatorial Guinea, Mozambique
	Chad
	Cambodia
	Afghanistan, Papua New Guinea
30	Somalia
20	Ethiopia

How rural Ethiopians get their water...

River or lake	32%
Unprotected well or spring	42%
Protected well or tap	25%

Countries with sanitation coverage less than 70% in 2004

Percent

70	Honduras
	Venezuela RB, Moldova
	Uzbekistan
	South Africa
	Guadeloupe
	Peru
	El Salvador, Turkmenistan
	Malawi, Viet Nam
60	Dem. Rep. of Korea, Kyrgyzstan, Maldives, Mongolia, Pakistan
	Senegal
	Indonesia, Zambia
	Azerbaijan
	Equatorial Guinea, Gambia, Zimbabwe
50	Cameroon, Tajikistan
	Swaziland
	Belize, Nicaragua, Tanzania
	Bolivia, Mali
	China, Nigeria, Papua New Guinea
	Cape Verde, Kenya, Uganda, Yemen
	Botswana, Rwanda
40	Kiribati
	Bangladesh, Sierra Leone
	Côte d'Ivoire, Lesotho
	Burundi, Gabon, Timor-Leste
	Guinea-Bissau, Nepal, Togo
	Afghanistan, Mauritania, Sudan
	Benin, Comoros, India
	Madagascar, Mozambique
	Angola, Solomon Islands
30	Dem. Rep. of the Congo, Haiti, Lao People's Dem. Rep.
	Micronesia, Fed. Sts.
	Central African Rep., Congo, Liberia
	Somalia
	Namibia, São Tomé and Principe
20	Ghana, Guinea
	Cambodia
	Burkina Faso, Ethiopia, Niger
10	Chad, Eritrea

...and sanitation

Field or forest	69%
Pit latrine	28%
Flush toilet	3%

Source: Indicator table 7.

to sanitation. Similarly, India may outperform Bangladesh as a high growth globalization success story, but the tables are turned when the benchmark for success shifts to sanitation: despite an average income some 60% higher, India has a lower rate of sanitation coverage. Similar gaps between wealth and coverage are observed for water. With a lower average income, Egypt has higher levels of access to clean water than China, and Tanzania has higher coverage levels than Ethiopia. In water and sanitation, as in other areas of human development, countries differ widely in the rate at which they convert wealth into progress in human development—an outcome that draws attention to the importance of public policies (figure 1.4).

...and sanitation lags behind water

The second problem highlighted in global data is the gap between water and sanitation provision. In all regions and in almost all countries sanitation provision lags far behind access to water—and there is no evidence that the gap is narrowing. In South Asia access to improved sanitation is less than half that for water. Elsewhere, the gap in coverage ranges from 29% in East Asia to 18% in Sub-Saharan Africa. These gaps matter not just because access to sanitation is intrinsically important, but also because the benefits of improved access to water and to sanitation are mutually reinforcing—a point demonstrated by Europe and the United States in the 19th century (see boxes 1.1 and 1.2). In Egypt high levels of pollution from raw sewage in the Nile Delta region undermine the potential health benefits of near universal access to water. Incidence rates for diarrhoea disorders and hepatitis A are far higher in many peri-urban settlements than is predicted on the basis of income, with wastewater pollution a major factor.[21] Countries that allow sanitation coverage to lag are destined to see the benefits of progress in water diminished as a result.

The data systematically underreport the scale of the deficit

Global data on water and sanitation are provided through the Joint Monitoring Programme

because services have to be financed either out of household budgets or through public spending. More surprising is the very large variation around the average.

Many countries demonstrate the imperfect relationship between wealth and the provision of water and sanitation. The Philippines has a higher average income than Sri Lanka, but a smaller proportion of its citizens have access

of the WHO and UNICEF. That data tell a bleak story. But reality is even bleaker than the statistics show. While the data collection methodology has improved, the numbers understate the problems for a variety of reasons. Part of the problem is that the physical presence of an "improved" source—such as a pit latrine or a standpipe—is not always an accurate indicator for improved access: the technologies may not always function properly. Another difficulty relates to data coverage. When it comes to national surveys, some people—notably the poor—are undercounted because they live in areas that are not officially recognized by governments. Infrastructure deficits and decay are also unaccounted for in the statistics, as is the frequent unreliability of water services where they do exist, forcing people to rely on other sources much of the time.

Missing millions. Millions of poor people are missing from national statistics. Living in informal settlements, they simply are not counted.

- *Mumbai.* Reported data indicate that Mumbai, the world's fifth largest city, enjoys a safe water coverage rate of more than 90%. That figure is almost certainly exaggerated. By some estimates almost half the city's 18 million people now live in the *zopadpatti*—literally hut areas—appearing on city maps as amorphous grey zones clustered along railway lines and extending into creeks and old mangrove swamps. Their residents do not figure in municipal data. One such area is Dharavi, a vast slum situated between the international airport and the Mumbai financial district and home to almost 1 million people. The slum residents live in an environment that poses a daily health threat. It is estimated that there is 1 toilet for every 1,440 people. In the rainy season streets, lacking drainage, become channels for filthy water carrying human excrement. People in areas like Dharavi rely on wells, tankers or unsafe sources for their drinking water. Beyond these areas are crumbling tenements, or *chawls*, where residents make do with rusting pipes, leaking taps and badly degraded storage tanks. In a typical case 15 families share one tap that works for two hours a day.[22]

Figure **1.4** **Incomes and outcomes in water and sanitation: wealth and performance often diverge**

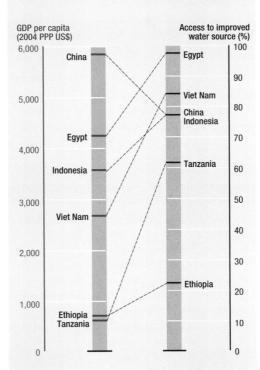

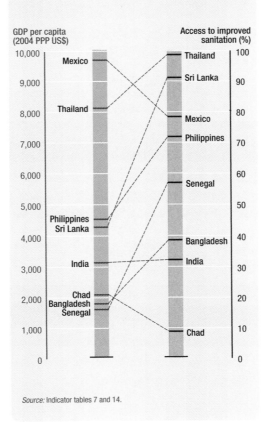

Source: Indicator tables 7 and 14.

The conditions here are terrible. You can see for yourself. There is sewage everywhere. Some people have pit latrines, but they are shallow and they overflow when it rains. Most people use buckets and plastic bags for toilets—and the children use the streets and yards. Our children suffer all the time from diarrhoea and other diseases because it is so filthy. Mary Akinyi, Mugomo-ini village, Kibera

Less than 7 kilometres from the Kenyan Parliament in central Nairobi the sprawling urban settlement of Kibera is one of Sub-Saharan Africa's largest slums. Its inhabitants experience some of the worst deprivation in water and sanitation in the world. Yet people like Mary Akinyi are largely missing from the statistics.

According to the Kenyan government report on the Millennium Development Goals, 93% of Nairobi residents have access to clean water and 99% to sanitation. Those numbers are difficult to square with life in Kibera. Somewhere between 500,000 and 1 million people live in the slum—the true figure is unknown. With 2,000–3,000 people per square hectare this is probably the most densely populated area in Sub-Saharan Africa. The average family of three to four people lives in a single-room structure of mud, timber, plastic and corrugated iron sheets.

Simple observation of Kibera's streets raises questions about data reporting. High population density, overcrowding and lack of infrastructure have created a water and sanitation nightmare. Drainage channels on the sides of roads are often blocked, pit latrines overflow in the rainy season and children scavenge in heaps of uncollected garbage.

Data on service provision are unreliable. Less than 40% of households have access to legal water connections, usually a standpipe. Of those that do, about a third receive water only once every two days. Some 80% of households purchase all or some of their water from private vendors, whose prices average $3.50 per cubic metre but rise to almost double that in the dry season. The average price is some seven times higher than that paid by people in high-income settlements served by the Nairobi Water and Sewage Company—and higher than prices in London or New York. There are almost 700 water kiosks in the slum, although sales are

concentrated in larger kiosks operated by slumlords—a fact that restricts the scope of public protest against unfair practices.

People relying on kiosks typically spend about one hour collecting water, but longer during dry periods. They also spend a large share of their limited income. For a family with two adults earning a minimum wage, average water use represents about 20% of income—a huge burden on household budgets.

Sanitation coverage is even more limited. In some areas up to 150 people share a single latrine. In many cases these latrines lack privacy and security and are unhygienic and poorly maintained, with broken walls and overflowing pits. The Nairobi City Council does not provide any sanitation services to Kibera.

One of the strongest pieces of evidence contesting data on service provision is the "flying toilet". With neither public nor private latrines available, many of Kibera's resident resort to defecating in plastic bags that they dump in ditches or throw on the roadside. Two in three people in Kibera identify the flying toilet as the primary mode of excreta disposal available to them. It is not difficult to see why. In one slum area—Laina Saba—there were 10 functioning pit latrines for 40,000 people at the end of the 1990s. To the extent that any estimate can be derived for the slum as a whole, sanitation coverage in Kibera is probably well below 20%.

Public health provides further evidence of the real state of water and sanitation in Kibera. Kiosk operators provide a lifeline. However, the pipes that they use to access the water network are often in disrepair. One consequence is that they draw in the excreta and other wastes that flow through wastewater. Inadequate water supply and the absence of infrastructure for excreta disposal and wastewater management are linked directly to the high incidence of diarrhoea, skin diseases, typhoid fever and malaria. Death rates from diarrhoea are far higher here than in the rest of Nairobi (see table).

Utilities have a weak record in meeting Kibera's needs. There are only 25 kilometres of piped water network, and the slum gets far less water than other settlements, partly because the utility diverts water to high-income areas during periods of shortage. The Nairobi Water and Sewage Company loses 40% of the

Infant and under five mortality rates and diarrhoea prevalence in Kenya

Location	Infant mortality rate (per 1,000 live births)	Under-five mortality rate (per 1,000 live births)	Prevalence of bloody diarrhoea in children under age 3 in two weeks prior to interview (%)
Kenya (rural and urban)	74	112	3.0
Rural	76	113	3.1
Nairobi	39	62	3.4
Other urban	57	84	1.7
Nairobi, informal settlements	91	151	11.3
Kibera	106	187	9.8
Embakasi	164	254	9.1

Source: APHRC 2002.

(continued on next page)

Box **1.3**   **The "flying toilets" of Kibera—the severe neglect of water and sanitation coverage in poor areas of Nairobi** (continued)

1

Ending the crisis in water and sanitation

water supplied to Kibera through leaks and illegal connections. Revenues collected by the utility are less than one-third of the amount billed, pointing to major problems in management. Residents spend an estimated $5 million a year on water purchased from kiosks—money that could be used to extend the piped network and finance connections for the poor. Why is service provision so limited? Partly because Kibera is an "illegal" settlement, municipal authorities and landlords are not obliged to provide any services.

Private markets are failing to bring down costs and improve supply for several reasons. Vendors report having to pay bribes to officials and to the water utility to make connections to the network—a cost they pass on to their customers. The private costs of connections and pipe-laying are also high since vendors

do not benefit from economies of scale. It costs an average of $1,000 to establish a kiosk—an investment amortized through water charges.

Another source of price inflation is the interaction between kiosk and utility. Because kiosks are categorized as commercial entities, they pay a block tariff twice as high as the household minimum, with costs passed on to the consumer.

The challenge in Kibera is for public authorities to acknowledge the scale of the problem—and to work with local communities to develop solutions. Formalizing property rights, regulating private sector providers, breaking water monopolies maintained by slumlords and extending public provision for the collection and disposal of sludge are all crucial. So too are legislative measures requiring landlords to improve water and sanitation provision.

Source: Kenya 2005; UN-HABITAT 2003; WSP–AF 2005c; Collignon and Vézina 2000.

- *Jakarta.* National data report improved water coverage rates of more than 90% for urban Indonesia. But surveys that factor in the large number of informal residents in Jakarta, a city of more than 12 million people, estimate that less than a quarter of the population is fully served by improved water sources. The rest rely on a variety of sources, including rivers, lakes and private water vendors. The discrepancy: some 7.2 million people.[23]
- *Nairobi.* Data for the city record access to improved water and sanitation at more than 90%. That figure is hard to square with the living experience of poor people. More than 1 million people living in slums on informal settlements in Nairobi—about a third of the city's population—depend on private vendors as a secondary water source. In sanitation the picture is even worse. The "flying toilets" of Kibera—plastic bags in which people defecate and then throw onto the street—bear testimony to the limited extent of sanitation coverage in Nairobi, as do the slums' high child mortality rates (box 1.3).

Sanitation and water pollution. Adequate sanitation coverage is defined for international reporting purposes by technology (see chapter 3). But the presence of an improved sanitation technology—such as a pit latrine—is at best a partial indicator.

In many countries the age-old problem of keeping water and excrement separate continues

to pose a formidable challenge to public policy— and to public health. Infrastructure deficits and decay are at the heart of that challenge. In Latin America less than 14% of human waste receives any form of treatment: the rest is dumped in rivers and lakes or allowed to seep through into groundwater. China has a strong record in expanding access to water in both urban and rural areas, but pollution from human and industrial waste is a serious problem. Sixteen cities with populations of more than half a million have no wastewater treatment facilities.[24] Nationally, less than 20% of municipal waste receives any treatment, forcing households to boil their water before drinking it. In 2003 the State Environmental Protection Administration reported that more than 70% of the water in five of China's seven major river systems was too polluted for human use.

An additional problem is that cities in many countries lack the infrastructure to collect waste from pit latrines, with the result that sewage enters the water systems. "Improved sanitation" for some can translate into pollution and public health threats for others—as in Manila (box 1.4).

Inadequate water infrastructure can create high levels of risk even in cities with high coverage rates. Urban improved water coverage rates for Pakistan are reported at more than 90%. But what does this mean in practice? Consider the cities of Lahore (population 5 million) and

Box 1.4 | **The water-sanitation gap in the Philippines**

*The present water closet system, with all its boasted advantages, is the worst that can be adopted....
It merely removes the bulk of our excreta from our houses to choke our rivers with foul deposits and
rot at our neighbour's door. It introduces into our homes a most deadly enemy.*

Scientific American, 24 July 1869

In 19th century Europe and the United States social reformers and engineers complained that the
spread of latrines without proper disposal facilities presented a threat to public health. Manila, the
capital of the Philippines, shows that the problem has not gone away. Sanitation coverage rates are
put at more than 80%, but that figure obscures a major public health challenge.

Since 1997, when municipal authorities privatized water and sewerage provision, there has been
a sharp focus on increasing access to clean water, both in the eastern part of the city, where the
privatized utility has improved provision, and in the western part of the city, where the privatized utility
failed. Sanitation has received far less attention, partly because of the huge scale of underprovision
and a legacy of underinvestment.

Less than 4% of Metropolitan Manila's population is connected to the sewer network. Richer
households have responded by building their own sanitation facilities. Flush toilets are widely used,
connected to private septic tanks, often serving large housing developments. Around 40% of households now have onsite latrines, which count as an improved source. There are an estimated 1 million
or more septic tanks in Manila.

The problem is that sludge treatment and disposal facilities are rare. The result: indiscriminate
disposal of inadequately treated effluents into the Pasig River—a complex network of waterways that
links the Laguna de Bay Lake to Manila Bay through a huge urban conurbation. Another 35 tons of solid
domestic waste is deposited in the Pasig annually by squatters dwelling in makeshift settlements on the
river's banks. In total, some 10 million people discharge untreated waste into the river.

This has serious consequences for public health. The Pasig is one of the world's most polluted
rivers, with human waste accounting for 70% of the pollution load. Faecal coliform levels exceed
standards set by the Department of the Environment and Natural resources by several orders of
magnitude—and around one-third of all illness in Manila is water related. The 4.4 million people living
along the river face particularly acute problems, especially during the floods in the June to October
rainy season. During the low flow season the Pasig River reverses direction and carries pollution into
Laguna Lake, creating further public health problems.

Ambitious blueprints have been drawn up for cleaning up the Pasig, but none has moved from the
drawing board, partly because of the failure of government and water providers to develop a coherent
strategy for tackling Manila's sanitation crisis.

Source: WSP–EAP 2003; AusAID 2006.

Karachi (10 million), where half the population
is estimated to live in informal slum areas. Both
cities rely on a combination of groundwater and
canal water. With more than 40% of water supply unfiltered and 60% of effluents untreated,
waterborne epidemic diseases are common. In
Lahore only some 3 industries in 100 chemi-
cally treat their wastewater. There is no sewage
treatment plant. In Karachi two of the largest
industrial estates in the country have no effluent
treatment plants. The sewerage system is in disrepair, and there are no sewage treatment facilities. Human waste and industrial pollution have
severely degraded the groundwater on which a

growing number of households depend for their
water supply.[25] Across urban Pakistan unclean
water poses a constant threat to public health.
In the first half of 2006 alone, major outbreaks
of waterborne disease epidemics have swept
Faisalabad, Karachi, Lahore and Peshawar as
a result of the leakage of sewage and industrial
waste into drinking water through damaged
pipes. So severe is the crisis that a major public
investment programme has been launched to finance more than 6,000 water filtration plants.

Mineral poisoning. Natural substances in untreated water create risks for millions of people.
The use of untreated groundwater for drinking

has exposed an estimated 60 million people to arsenic contamination, more than half of them in Bangladesh. Projected human costs over the next 50 years include 300,000 deaths from cancer and 2.5 million cases of arsenic poisoning. Concentration zones for fluoride pose an additional threat. One zone in Africa extends along the East African Rift from Eritrea to Malawi, another from Turkey through Iraq, Iran, Afghanistan, India, northern Thailand and China. The latest information shows that fluorosis is endemic in at least 25 countries across the globe. The total number of people affected is not known, but a conservative estimate would be in the tens of millions.[26]

Time, flows and availability. The presence of an improved water technology such as a tap or standpipe is another partial indicator for access. For many people taps run dry for long periods, forcing households into unsafe informal water markets. More broadly, millions of poor households use both improved and unimproved water sources on a regular basis, raising questions about the picture drawn by global data.

National statistics may indicate the physical presence of an improved water source, while households with access face problems of intermittent supply, especially in the dry season. In Delhi, Karachi and Kathmandu fewer than 10% of households with piped water receive service 24 hours a day. Two or three hours of delivery is considered standard.[27] While poor households face the greatest deprivation in access to water provided by utilities because they are less likely to be connected, poor service provision affects most people. This suggests a strong complementarity of interest in improving and expanding provision.

Living near a functioning standpipe does not guarantee easy access. The journey time might be short, but the queuing time can be long. Dhaka has a coverage rate for an improved water source of more than 90%, but this includes public taps for slum dwellers where the tap to user ratio is 1:500.[28] Problems in rural areas are even more pronounced. In Burkina Faso, Malawi and Mali research suggests that a third or more of rural water points are out of order at any one time.[29] Similar figures have been reported for South Asia. In Andhra Pradesh, where a village survey found a high level of coverage from water points, villagers reported that more than half the water points were broken at any one time.[30] The more serious problem in rural areas relates to seasonal factors, with average collection times concealing large variations between dry and rainy seasons. One study in a semi-arid region of Nigeria found that the proportion of households collecting water from a source more than 1 kilometre away increased from 4% to 23% in the dry season, while average consumption fell from 38 litres a day to 18 litres.[31] Shifts in availability were reflected in child health indicators, with the incidence of diarrhoea doubling during the dry season.

For individuals, for households and for whole societies access to clean water and sanitation is one of the foundations for progress in human development

The human development costs of the crisis

For individuals, for households and for whole societies access to clean water and sanitation is one of the foundations for progress in human development. In this section we look at the wider role of water and sanitation for:

- Reducing income poverty.
- Reducing child mortality.
- Breaking lifecycle disadvantages.
- Holding down wider health costs.

- Improving girls' education.
- Freeing girls' and women's time.
- Ensuring a sense of human dignity.

Worsening income poverty— the wealth effect of the crisis

Concern is sometimes raised about the financial costs of reducing water and sanitation deficits.

Across much of the developing world unclean water is an immeasurably greater threat to human security than violent conflict

National governments are acutely aware of the impact on scarce budget resources of multiple claims for increased expenditure. Less attention has been paid to the economic costs of the crises in water and sanitation and to the implications of these costs for poverty and prosperity.

Research carried out for this Report by the WHO used a global model to derive best estimates for the costs of the water and sanitation deficit.[32] That model asks what different regions might save if the entire population had access to basic, low-cost water and sanitation technology. Among the results:

- The overall costs of the current deficit total $170 billion, or 2.6% of developing country GDP.
- Costs for Sub-Saharan Africa total $23.5 billion, or 5% of GDP—a figure that exceeds total flows of aid and debt relief in 2003.
- Regional losses of $29 billion for Latin America, $34 billion for South Asia and $66 billion for East Asia.

These figures have to be treated with caution. Yet they highlight two important points. The first is a variation on the theme that prevention is better than cure. Achieving the Millennium Development Goal target of halving the proportion of people without access to water and sanitation would cost about $10 billion annually for low-cost, sustainable technology. Universal access would raise this figure to $20–$30 billion, depending on technology.[33] Estimating conservatively from the lower end of the cost spectrum indicates that allowing the water and sanitation deficit to continue would cost roughly nine times more than resolving it. Ultimately, the case for public action in water and sanitation is rooted in human rights and moral imperatives. At the same time, cost-benefit analysis suggests that economic common sense makes a powerful supporting case.

The second point is distributional. The estimates for economic losses associated with the water and sanitation deficit are based on regional data. However, most of the losses are absorbed by people close to or below the poverty line. They are borne disproportionately by the poor because the poor account for a large share of the population lacking access to water and

sanitation. This implies that some of the world's poorest households are seeing their efforts to mobilize resources for nutrition, health, education and—critically—production undermined by inadequate investment in water and sanitation provision. It follows that the poor stand to benefit disproportionately from investment in this area, with attendant benefits for poverty reduction efforts.

Retarding improvements in child mortality rates—the deadly link at birth

Across much of the developing world unclean water is an immeasurably greater threat to human security than violent conflict. That threat starts at birth. Unclean water and lack of sanitation are directly implicated in the huge gulf in life chances at birth that separate children born in rich countries from children born in poor countries. While life expectancy is increasing in developing countries, the rate of increase and the progress towards convergence with rich countries are being held back by the deficit in water and sanitation.

Of the 60 million deaths in the world in 2004, 10.6 million—nearly 20%—were children under the age of five. These fatalities accounted for a third of deaths in developing regions such as Sub-Saharan Africa and South Asia but for less than 1% in rich countries. Water and sanitation are directly implicated in a large share of deaths in children under five. The link: the 5 billion cases of diarrhoea in children each year in developing countries. These sickness episodes represent the second largest cause of childhood death after acute respiratory tract infection. They claim the lives of 1.8 million children under the age of five each year, or a daily death toll of about 4,900 young lives (figure 1.5). The number of deaths associated with the twin threats of unclean water and poor sanitation is not widely appreciated. Globally, diarrhoea kills more people than tuberculosis or malaria—five times as many children die of diarrhoea as of HIV/AIDS.

The human security threat of the water and sanitation crisis is growing in many countries.

Most deaths from diarrhoea—more than 1 million in 2004—are caused by shigella, or bloody diarrhoea. Unlike other forms of diarrhoea, shigella cannot be treated effectively with simple oral rehydration therapies—it requires more costly antibiotics. Even for households that can afford treatment, shigella is a growing threat because it has rapidly developed resistance to antibiotics. In northern and eastern India drug-resistant shigella has re-emerged after a hiatus of 14 years. Similarly, in rural western Kenya half of all diarrhoea cases have proved resistant to treatment.[34]

Clean water and sanitation are among the most powerful preventative medicines for reducing child mortality. They are to diarrhoea what immunization is to killer diseases such as measles or polio: a mechanism for reducing risk and averting death. In addition to saving lives, upstream investments in water and sanitation make economic sense because they would reduce the downstream costs facing health systems. Universal access to even the most basic water and sanitation facilities would reduce the financial burden on health systems in developing countries by about $1.6 billion annually—and $610 million in Sub-Saharan Africa, which represents about 7% of the region's health budget.

How much does the transition from an unimproved water and sanitation source to an improved source reduce the probability of childhood death? That question was addressed by cross-country research carried out for this report (see *Technical note 3*). Household survey data for 15 countries were used to analyze the change in the risk profile of households associated with improvements in water and sanitation. The findings underline the potential for upstream water and sanitation interventions to cut child deaths:

- *Uganda.* Access to an improved water source reduces the risk of infant mortality by 23%.
- *Egypt.* Access to a flush toilet reduces the risk of infant death by 57% compared with an infant in a household without access to sanitation (figure 1.6).
- *Peru.* Access to a flush toilet reduces the risk of infant death by 59% compared with

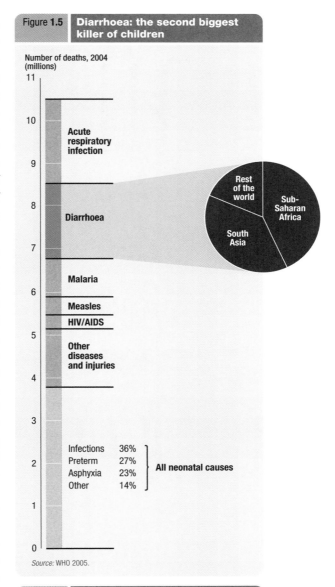

Figure 1.5 Diarrhoea: the second biggest killer of children

Number of deaths, 2004 (millions)

Acute respiratory infection

Diarrhoea

Rest of the world · Sub-Saharan Africa · South Asia

Malaria

Measles

HIV/AIDS

Other diseases and injuries

Infections	36%	
Preterm	27%	All neonatal causes
Asphyxia	23%	
Other	14%	

Source: WHO 2005.

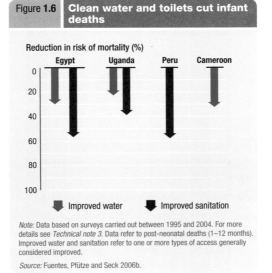

Figure 1.6 Clean water and toilets cut infant deaths

Reduction in risk of mortality (%)

Egypt   Uganda   Peru   Cameroon

Improved water   Improved sanitation

Note: Data based on surveys carried out between 1995 and 2004. For more details see *Technical note 3*. Data refer to post-neonatal deaths (1–12 months). Improved water and sanitation refer to one or more types of access generally considered improved.

Source: Fuentes, Pfütze and Seck 2006b.

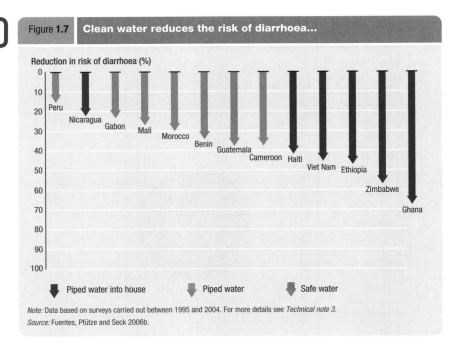

Figure 1.7 **Clean water reduces the risk of diarrhoea...**

Reduction in risk of diarrhoea (%)

Piped water into house   Piped water   Safe water

Note: Data based on surveys carried out between 1995 and 2004. For more details see *Technical note 3*.
Source: Fuentes, Pfütze and Seck 2006b.

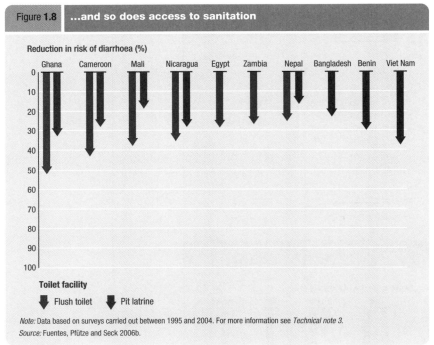

Figure 1.8 **...and so does access to sanitation**

Reduction in risk of diarrhoea (%)

Toilet facility

Flush toilet   Pit latrine

Note: Data based on surveys carried out between 1995 and 2004. For more information see *Technical note 3*.
Source: Fuentes, Pfütze and Seck 2006b.

public health gains. We used household survey data to investigate the risk profiles for diarrhoea associated with different sanitation technologies. Two important findings emerge. First, both clean water and sanitation have a major bearing on the incidence of diarrhoea. Having piped water in the house lowers the incidence by almost 70% in Ghana and more than 40% in Viet Nam (figure 1.7). Similarly, flush toilets reduce risk by more than 20% in countries such as Mali, Nicaragua and Egypt (figure 1.8). Second, there is a hierarchy of risk reduction. Pit latrines reduce risk but less than flush toilets; and access to an improved water source outside of the home reduces risk less than piped water in the home.[35]

Why are there such large variations in risk reduction by technology type and between countries? In broad terms, risk falls as households climb the technology ladder. Flush toilets and water piped into the house generate higher levels of risk reduction than pit latrines and public standpipes, for example. There are many reasons for such differences. Water quantity is one obvious consideration. Household-level research in Kenya, Tanzania and Uganda found that households with water piped into the homes used on average 16 litres a day for washing and hygiene. Households without piped water used less than 6 litres. Our research exercise did not directly ask why outcomes for similar technologies vary widely across countries. However, the findings point to the importance of factors beyond the technology deployed by the household, including the state of the community water and sanitation infrastructure (for example, even households that install a latrine and tap at home are exposed to risk from poor drainage in a street).

What our research does underline is the potential for progress in water and sanitation to cut child deaths on a large scale. That finding has a direct relevance to the Millennium Development Goals. With progress towards the target of reducing child deaths by two-thirds occurring at less than half the required rate—and a projected gap of 4 million child deaths between target and outcome in 2015—progress in water and sanitation could play a vital role in getting the world back on track.

an infant in a household without access to sanitation.

The main transmission route for risk reduction is a lower incidence of diarrhoea. Variations in risk reduction draw attention to the importance of a wide range of factors influencing risk reduction outcomes. As already noted, improved technologies cannot be considered in isolation. But they have the potential to unlock major

Spawning lifecycle disadvantages

Premature mortality may be the most disturbing product of the water and sanitation deficit. But nonfatal disease episodes can have harmful effects over an entire lifecycle. Illness in infancy can be associated with disadvantages that stretch from cradle to grave, including both cognitive and physical infirmities.

Repeat bouts of diarrhoea before age one contribute to vitamin deficiency and malnutrition. Children who are malnourished are more likely to suffer from diarrhoea—and sickness episodes last longer. In turn, diarrhoea contributes to weight loss, stunting and vitamin deficiency. Studies in The Gambia, Sudan and Uganda have shown how diarrhoea impedes infant weight gain, especially at ages 7–12 months.[36]

Children who suffer constant water-related illness carry the disadvantage into school. Poor health directly reduces cognitive potential and indirectly undermines schooling through absenteeism, attention deficits and early dropout. Water-related diseases cost 443 million school days each year—equivalent to an entire school year for all seven-year-old children in Ethiopia.

Almost half these days are lost due to intestinal parasites transmitted through water and faecal material. More than 150 million school-age children are severely affected by the main intestinal helminths such as roundworm, whipworm and hookworm. Children with infections are twice as likely to be absent from school as those without. Even when infected children attend school, they perform less well: tests point to adverse effects on memory, problem- solving skills and attention spans.[37]

The link from water insecurity to health and education stretches into adulthood. Research in many countries has found a close correlation between adult height and income. Children who suffer repeated bouts of infectious disease and diarrhoea are likely to reach adolescence and adulthood with reduced height, which is correlated with cognitive impairment and educational underattainment. So bouts of diarrhoea in childhood can pave the way to reduced earning power and poverty in adulthood.[38]

The immediate costs of lifecycle disadvantage are, of course, borne by individuals as health risks, lower incomes and increased vulnerability. But whole countries lose from the lower productivity and diminished human capital.

Raising wider health costs

Poor water and sanitation produce nonfatal chronic conditions at all stages of the lifecycle. At any given time close to half the people in the developing world are suffering from one or more of the main diseases associated with inadequate provision of water and sanitation such as diarrhoea, guinea worm, trachoma and schistosomiasis (box 1.5). These diseases fill half the hospital beds in developing countries. They probably account for an even greater share of the patients treated in primary health clinics, especially in slums and poor rural areas. Measured by conventional global health indicators, the burden of disease linked to water and sanitation is enormous: according to the WHO, it accounts for 60 million disability-adjusted life years lost each year, or 4% of the global total.[39]

What figures like this do not capture is the pain and suffering associated with water-related disease. Nor do they capture the way sickness episodes can drive already vulnerable people into destitution. Blinding trachoma provides a stark example. The disease is spread by the *musca sorbens* fly, an insect whose preferred breeding medium is human faeces. These flies burrow into the eyes of anyone from infants to the elderly, leading to decades of repeat infection. Victims liken the infection to having thorns in their eyes.

For millions of people trachoma is a passport to poverty. As the disease progresses towards blindness, people lose their ability to work and depend on care from family members (see the special contribution by US President Jimmy Carter in chapter 3). Children are most heavily infected and women are more vulnerable than men, with infection rates some three times higher, largely because they look after children. Once common in the United States, trachoma is today restricted almost entirely to the developing world, where there are 150 million

At any given time close to half the people in the developing world are suffering from one or more of the main diseases associated with inadequate provision of water and sanitation

Box 1.5 **The health costs of the water and sanitation deficit**

We asked one woman in a programme area how trichiasis [a development of trachoma] affected her ability to work. She replied: "My lids are biting like a dog and scratching like a thorn. Can you stand on a thorn? Imagine you have a thorn in your foot that you can't get out—then try talking of work."

Dr. Paul Emerson, technical director of The
Carter Center's Trachoma Control Program

If I get my health back, it means everything; I'll be able to work and support my family.

Mare Aleghan, Ethiopian trachoma sufferer, age 42

The health problems associated with inadequate water and sanitation go far beyond avoidable child deaths. Water-related illness accounts for about 5% of the global burden of disease. The anguish and suffering associated with that burden are beyond estimation.

By convention, water-related diseases are usually divided into three categories: *waterborne* (such as diarrhoeal infections transmitted though water contaminated with faeces), *water-washed* (linked to skin or eye contact with contaminated water, such as trachoma) and *water-based* (caused by parasites found in contaminated water, such as schistosomiasis and other helminths). A fourth category, not considered below, is disease caused by insect vectors, such as dengue and malaria. Some water-related diseases reach epidemic proportion in developing countries:

- *Internal helminths.* Up to 10% of the population of the developing world is infected with intestinal worms, including ascariasis, trichiasis and hookworm. Infection is strongly related to unsanitary excreta disposal and poor hygiene. It contributes to malnutrition, cognitive impairment and anaemia. Children infected with helminths are four times more likely to be underweight.
- *Cholera.* Epidemics of cholera are a major risk in areas with high population concentrations and poor sanitation. Heavy rains can flood latrines, contaminating water and exposing populations to the cholera bacteria. In 2005 West Africa suffered more than 63,000 cases of cholera, leading to 1,000 deaths. Senegal was severely affected following rainy-season flooding in Dakar. During the first half of 2006 one of the worst epidemics to sweep Sub-Saharan Africa in recent years was claiming more than 400 lives a month in Angola.

- *Trachoma. Chlamydia trachomatis,* the organism that causes trachoma, is transmitted by hands and flies that land on faces and feed from seeping eyes. Children are a favoured target. Some 6 million people have been blinded by trachoma, according to the WHO. Another 150 million need treatment, and an estimated 500 million are at risk. The disease is endemic in 55 countries, with China and India accounting for 2 million cases (see table). Ethiopia is thought to have the largest number of blind people, with trachoma implicated in a third of cases.

  Once the disease reaches an advanced stage, it can be treated only by an operation. Although relatively simple and costing just $10, the operation is nevertheless denied to many sufferers: in Ethiopia some 1 million people need the operation but only 60,000 are treated each year. Poor households are disproportionately affected since the disease is strongly related to overcrowding and the absence of safe water for washing. Productivity losses caused by trachoma are estimated at $2.9 billion a year.
- *Schistosomiasis.* Some 200 million people in 74 countries are infected with schistosomiasis, and at least 600 million risk infection. Of those infected 20 million have severe disease and 120 million have symptoms. An estimated 80% of transmission takes place in Sub-Saharan Africa, causing thousands of deaths every year. Strongly related to unsanitary excreta disposal, schistosomiasis is transmitted through human contact with contaminated water when drinking, washing, fetching water and herding animals.

Number of people with blinding trachoma by country or region, 2004

Region	Number of people with blinding trachoma
China	1,174,000
India	865,000
Other Asia and islands	1,362,000
Sub-Saharan Africa	1,380,000
Middle East	927,000
Latin America	158,000
Total	**5,866,000**

Source: Sight Savers International 2006.

Source: Sight Savers International 2006; WHO 2006a; The Carter Center 2006.

reported episodes and 2 million new cases of blindness each year.

Trachoma is one illustration of a wider interaction between water-related diseases and poverty. These diseases simultaneously reduce income, increase household spending and lead

to losses of future earnings. When people in poor households fall ill, their productivity declines and with it their ability to generate income or grow food. Because poor people are seldom insured against illness, they have to meet the costs out of their current income, sell assets or borrow. The resulting depletion of resources reinforces poverty traps and increases future vulnerability.

Hurting girls' education

For young girls the lack of basic water and sanitation services translates into lost opportunities for education and associated opportunities for empowerment. Water and sanitation deficits threaten all children. But young girls and women shoulder a disproportionate share of the costs borne by the household.

The time burden of collecting and carrying water is one explanation for the very large gender gaps in school attendance in many countries. In Tanzania school attendance levels are 12% higher for girls in homes 15 minutes or less from a water source than in homes an hour or more away. Attendance rates for boys are far less sensitive to distance to water sources.[40] For millions of poor households, there is a straight trade-off between time spent in school and time spent collecting water. These are the words of a 10-year-old girl queuing for water by a standpipe in El Alto, Bolivia:

> *Of course I wish I were in school. I want to learn to read and to write—and I want to be there with my friends. But how can I? My mother needs me to get water, and the standpipe here is only open from 10–12. You have to get in line early because so many people come here.*

Young girls, particularly after puberty, are also less likely to attend classes if the school does not have suitable hygiene facilities. Parents often withdraw girls from a school that does not offer adequate and separate toilets for girls because of concerns over security and privacy. On one estimate about half the girls in Sub-Saharan Africa who drop out of primary school do so because of poor water and sanitation facilities.[41] That helps explain why improving school sanitation can increase the demand for education among girls: between 1990 and 2000 a UNICEF school sanitation programme in Bangladesh was instrumental in increasing the number of girls enrolling by 11%.[42] Conversely, inadequate provision can retard progress

in countries striving to achieve universal education. In Uganda only 8% of schools have sufficient latrines and just one-third have separate latrines for girls—deficits that help to explain why the country has found it difficult to reduce dropout rates among girls after puberty.[43]

Disparities in education linked to water and sanitation have lifelong impacts transmitted across generations. Education can empower women to participate in decision-making in their communities. As adults, educated girls are more likely to have smaller, healthier families—and their children are less likely to die and more likely to receive an education than the children of less educated mothers. These gains are cumulative, as are the losses associated with gender inequalities linked to water and sanitation.

Exacerbating time-poverty and gender inequality

In almost all countries the gender division of labour assigns women responsibilities that men do not share. The intrahousehold division of labour interacts with problems in service provision to reinforce deep gender inequalities.

Time spent collecting water represents a heavy burden on women. In Mozambique, rural Senegal and eastern Uganda women spend on average 15–17 hours a week collecting water. It is not uncommon for women to walk more than 10 kilometres during the dry season. Research in eastern Uganda found households spending on average 660 hours a year collecting water. This represents two full months of labour, with attendant opportunity costs for education, income generation and female leisure time.[44] One estimate suggests that some 40 billion hours a year are spent collecting water in Sub-Saharan Africa[45]—a year's labour for the entire workforce in France. Reducing the time for other activities such as child care, rest or productive work, the time spent collecting water reinforces time-poverty, disempowers women and lowers income.

Research in India by the Self Employed Women's Association (SEWA) demonstrates the interaction. Women engaged in a successful microenterprise project in a semi-arid area of

For young girls the lack of basic water and sanitation services translates into lost opportunities for education and associated opportunities for empowerment

The loss of dignity associated with a lack of privacy in sanitation helps to explain why women attach more importance than men to sanitary provision

Gujarat spent three to four hours a day collecting water. During summer months, when the time to collect water increased by two hours a day, women adjusted by reducing the time spent on microenterprise work. SEWA calculated that reducing water collection to one hour a day would enable women to earn an additional $100 a year depending on the enterprise—a very large implied income loss for households in an area of high poverty. But it was not only the loss of income that was important. Women also emphasized the importance of income generation to their independence.[46]

Undermining human dignity

We feel so dirty and unclean in the summer. We do not wash our clothes for weeks. People say, these Dalits are dirty and they smell. But how can we be clean without water?[47]

Spoken by a low-caste Indian woman, these words capture the relationship between human dignity and water. Dignity is hard to measure—but it is at the heart of human development and our sense of well-being, as Adam Smith recognized. Writing in *The Wealth of Nations* he included it among the "necessities" for well-being, commodities that "the poorest creditable person of either sex would be ashamed to appear in public without".[48]

Access to safe, hygienic and private sanitation facilities is one of the strongest indicators of dignity. For millions of women across the world inadequate access is a source of shame, physical discomfort and insecurity. Cultural norms strictly control behaviour in this area, in many cases requiring that women not be seen defecating—a requirement that forces them to leave home before dawn or after nightfall to maintain privacy. As one woman in Bangladesh put it: "Men can answer the call of nature anytime they want...but women have to wait until darkness, no matter what problem she has."[49] Delaying bodily functions is a major cause of liver infection and acute constipation in many countries.

The loss of dignity associated with a lack of privacy in sanitation helps to explain why women attach more importance than men to sanitary provision. When asked in surveys about the benefits of latrines, both women and men in Cambodia, Indonesia and Viet Nam said that the main advantage was a clean home and village environment free of bad smells and flies.[50] But women were more in favour of spending on toilets, rating them far higher on a "value for cost" basis, with a strong emphasis on the benefits of privacy. They were also more likely than men to initiate the process for purchasing latrines (see chapter 3). Underfinancing of sanitation provision in the allocation of household and government resources is thus partly a product of the weak voice of women in setting priorities.

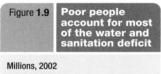

Figure **1.9** **Poor people account for most of the water and sanitation deficit**

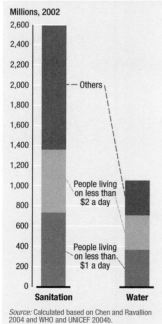

Millions, 2002

— — Others

People living on less than $2 a day

People living on less than $1 a day

Sanitation   Water

Source: Calculated based on Chen and Ravallion 2004 and WHO and UNICEF 2004b.

The crisis hits the poor hardest—by far

National average figures obscure deep structural inequalities in access to water and sanitation. In many countries these inequalities are tantamount to a system of water apartheid based on wealth, location and other markers for advantage and disadvantage. They translate into the wider inequalities in life chances that erode the basic principles of shared citizenship and equal opportunity.

The poor account for most of the deficit

How does the deficit in water and sanitation map with the distribution of global poverty?

Drawing on household survey data it is possible to develop an approximate picture of the overlap between poverty and lack of access to

1

improved water and sanitation. The association is most marked for water. About a third of people without access to an improved water source live on less than $1 a day. Twice this share live on less than $2 a day. These figures imply that 660 million people lacking access to water have, at best, a limited capacity to pay more than a small amount for a connection to water service. Of this total some 385 million people fall below the $1 a day absolute poverty threshold (figure 1.9). More than half the 1.1 billion people without access are in the poorest 40% of the income distribution.

These figures are not evidence of causation: people might lack water because they are poor, or they might be poor because they lack water. However, the statistics are strongly suggestive of a two-way relationship between income poverty and deprivation in access to water.

In sanitation, too, there is a strong association between poverty and access: the poorest two-fifths of households account for more than half the global deficit. Nearly 1.4 billion people without access live on less than $2 a day. But the coverage rates for sanitation are far lower than those for water, even in higher income groups. A quarter of the richest 20% of people in developing countries have no access to improved sanitation, rising to half for the second richest 20%.

The wealth distribution of people without access to water and sanitation has important practical implications for public policy—and for the Millennium Development Goals. The main domestic sources of financing for water and sanitation are households (from payments for tariffs, connection costs, labour inputs and capital costs) and government (taxes or aid). In any country the appropriate mix of household and public finance will depend on circumstances, including average income, poverty and the income profiles of households lacking access to water networks. In high- and middle-income countries there is scope for households to finance operating costs for provision, though governments play a critical role in financing the capital costs of creating the network. In low-income countries, and middle-income countries with low coverage rates among the poor, public finance holds the key to improving access. The 660 million people living on less than $2 a day who lack access to water and the equally poor

1.4 billion who lack access to sanitation are not well placed to finance water utility cost-recovery through household spending.

Inequality is a pervasive theme in access to water. In most rich countries people are not differentiated on the basis of where they draw their water, or what type of toilet facility they use. In many developing countries your place in the wealth distribution defines where you draw your water and what you do for sanitation.

Access to piped water is highly differentiated. An analysis of 17 developing country Demographic and Health Surveys carried out for this Report found that availability was about 85% for the richest 20% of households, compared with 25% for the poorest 20%. Across a large group of countries the top to bottom quintile coverage ratio for household connections is typically 4:1 or 5:1. In Peru access to piped water is universal for the

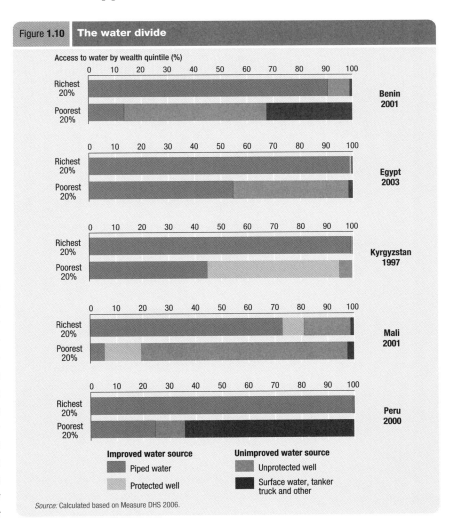

Figure 1.10 The water divide

Access to water by wealth quintile (%)

Benin 2001

Egypt 2003

Kyrgyzstan 1997

Mali 2001

Peru 2000

Improved water source
- Piped water
- Protected well

Unimproved water source
- Unprotected well
- Surface water, tanker truck and other

Source: Calculated based on Measure DHS 2006.

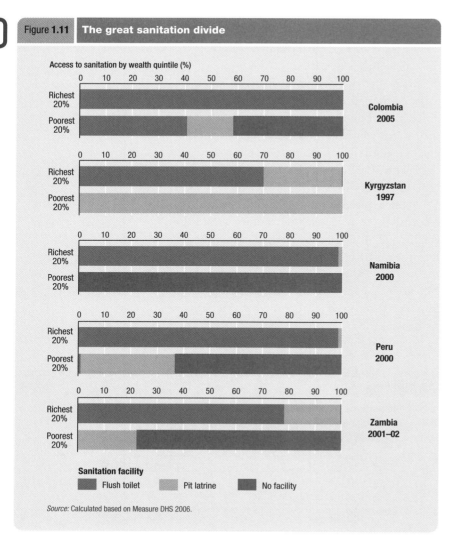

Figure **1.11** The great sanitation divide

Access to sanitation by wealth quintile (%)

Colombia
2005

Kyrgyzstan
1997

Namibia
2000

Peru
2000

Zambia
2001–02

Sanitation facility
■ Flush toilet   ■ Pit latrine   ■ No facility

Source: Calculated based on Measure DHS 2006.

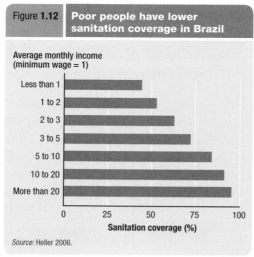

Figure **1.12** Poor people have lower sanitation coverage in Brazil

Average monthly income
(minimum wage = 1)

Less than 1
1 to 2
2 to 3
3 to 5
5 to 10
10 to 20
More than 20

Sanitation coverage (%)

Source: Heller 2006.

(figure 1.10). Disparities in access to sanitation are equally marked. These inequalities have an important bearing on human development because of their association with the distribution of opportunity for survival, education and income poverty.

Some countries register high inequality even with very low provision. In Zambia three-quarters of the richest 20% of households have access to a flush toilet. Among the poorest 20% a similar proportion use open sites—and there is no registered access to a flush toilet (figure 1.11). As incomes rise, average coverage improves. But even fairly high average national incomes provide no guarantee of high coverage rates among the poor. In Brazil the richest 20% of the population enjoy access to water and sanitation at levels broadly comparable to those in rich countries. Meanwhile, the poorest 20% have lower coverage rates for both water and sanitation than in Viet Nam, with coverage rates clearly declining with income (figure 1.12).

Inequalities in access to water and sanitation are intimately related to wider inequalities in opportunity—starting with the opportunity to stay alive. Earlier in this chapter we emphasized the importance of water and sanitation inequalities in perpetuating large health disparities that are slowing the convergence of life expectancy levels across countries. The same story plays out within countries.

Poor households are far more likely to suffer infectious diseases—and children in these households are far more likely to die. Cross-country research shows that communicable diseases cause 56% of deaths among the poorest 20% of the population compared with 8% among the richest 20%. Similarly, death rates among children under age five in the poorest 20% of the wealth distribution are often more than twice those in the richest 20%[51]—in Bolivia and Peru they are four to five times higher. And death rates among the poorest 20% are falling at less than half the average rate of decline in many countries—a problem identified in *Human Development Report 2005* as a major threat to achieving the Millennium Development Goals.

Many poverty-related factors are behind inequalities in child mortality, including poor nutrition and access to affordable health care. But

richest 20%, while two-thirds of the poorest 20% of households either purchase their water from vendors or collect it from unprotected sources increased exposure to the risk of waterborne infectious disease is a major causal link. In the Philippine city of Cebu diarrhoea is the second largest cause of infant mortality—but mortality is four times higher for children in the poorest 20% of the population than it is for those in the richest 20%. Diarrhoea accounts for 12% of deaths in the city but for 20% of inequalities in death rates between the children of the rich and the poor.[52]

Health and mortality inequalities highlight the need to look beyond aggregate figures to the specific problems facing the poorest households. Given the central role of unclean water and poor sanitation for the transmission of infectious disease, any strategy for narrowing health inequalities will have to attach considerable weight to reducing wealth-based inequalities in this area. Just as there are strong grounds for setting Millennium Development Goals–related targets that look beyond societal averages to the reduction of disparities as an explicit objective, so in water and sanitation there are grounds for setting clear equity-oriented goals. For example, halving disparities between the richest and poorest 20% of the population would help to focus public policy.

The poor pay more—and more than they can afford

Debates on water provision have given rise to polarized positions on pricing. One side calls for greater emphasis on cost sharing, with households paying more for the water they use. The other side expresses fears that cost sharing and the embrace of market principles will jeopardize poor people's access to cheap water. Both sides make important points. Yet both overlook some of the basic realities experienced by poor households. Many of these households lack the capacity to meet cost-recovery charges on a commercial basis. At the same time, the view that poor people have access to plentiful supplies of cheap water is illusory. Most are already paying far more than they can afford to pay to meet their basic water needs in water markets that reinforce their poverty. Water pricing reflects a simple perverse principle: the poorer you are, the more you pay.

There is insufficient research on how water figures in the household budgets of the poor. What is clear is that for millions of households the high price of water strains already overstretched resources. Evidence for Latin America compiled for this Report found that the poorest 20% of households in Argentina, El Salvador, Jamaica and Nicaragua allocate more than 10% of their spending to water.[53] About half of these households live below the $1 a day threshold for extreme poverty (figure 1.13).

Similar household expenditure patterns are reported for other regions. In Uganda water payments represent as much as 22% of the average income of urban households in the poorest 20% of the income distribution.[54] One household survey in Jakarta found more than 40% of households spending 5% or more of their income on water.[55] (Regulatory authorities in the United Kingdom define any expenditure on water above 3% of total household spending as an indicator of hardship.)

These figures on household spending caution against the undifferentiated adoption of greater cost recovery as a financing strategy. There is plenty of scope for more cost recovery from higher income groups, many of whom enjoy large subsidies. The same principle does not apply below the poverty line. High current spending by the poor is sometimes

Figure **1.13** **Paying the price for poverty: water takes a large share of household spending for the poorest 20%**

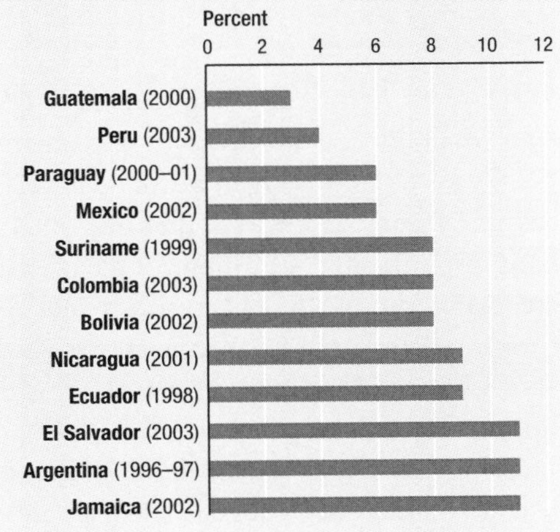

Percent
0
2
4
6
8
10
12
Guatemala (2000)
Peru (2003)
Paraguay (2000–01)
Mexico (2002)
Suriname (1999)
Colombia (2003)
Bolivia (2002)
Nicaragua (2001)
Ecuador (1998)
El Salvador (2003)
Argentina (1996–97)
Jamaica (2002)

Source: Gasparini and Tornarolli 2006.

Water pricing reflects a simple perverse principle: the poorer you are, the more you pay misinterpreted as evidence of willingness *and* ability to pay. At one level, the fact that poor households spend large amounts on water is evidence of willingness to pay. Given that the alternatives may range from using water sources that compromise health to spending large amounts of time collecting water, poor households may prefer to spend their limited resources on water.

However, willingness to pay is not the same as ability to pay—at least as that concept relates to human development. When spending on water accounts for a large share of the budget for households living on or below the income poverty line, expenditure in other areas—in health, education, nutrition and production— is compromised. Moreover, annual average payments can obscure the price spikes that cause extreme hardship during the dry season, when household budgets are most stretched.

In effect, households are balancing the benefits of spending on water against the benefits of spending in other areas that ought to be seen as a social minimum of entitlements. Reducing the financial burden of water spending on the budgets of the poor would have the effect in many cases of increasing household income, improving prospects for escaping poverty and enhancing resilience against shocks.

Inequality in water provision relates not just to access and expenditure but also to price. One of the recurrent themes in water provision across the developing world is that price is inversely related to ability to pay. Indeed, some of the poorest people living in urban slums pay some of the world's highest prices for water. In Jakarta, Lima, Manila and Nairobi households living in slums and low-income settlements typically pay 5–10 times or more for their water than high-income residents of the same city. In Manila an estimated 4 million people receive water resold through kiosks, pushcart vendors or tanker deliveries. Their average monthly water bills are $10–$20. By contrast, households directly connected to the utility pay an average of only $3–$6 a month but consume five times more water[56] (figure 1.14). There is an international dimension to the wealth divide in water prices. Poor people in urban areas

of developing countries not only pay more for their water than high-income residents of the same city—they also pay more than people in rich countries. Some of the world's poorest people living in sprawling slum areas of Accra and Manila are paying more for their water than people living in London, New York or Rome (figure 1.15).

Why are water prices inversely related to ability to pay in many countries? The reasons vary, but in urban areas a critical factor is the market distance between the water user and the utility. Formal water providers operating municipal networks typically provide the cheapest water. Households with a direct link to the network through a tap at home get access to that water. Poor households without a connection have to purchase utility water through a web of intermediaries. Prices rise steeply as water passes through intermediaries—truckers, vendors and other carriers. Securing a connection to the network would lower the unit price of water. Two major barriers restrict this option: high capital costs and prohibitions on connecting people living in informal settlements without formal property rights.

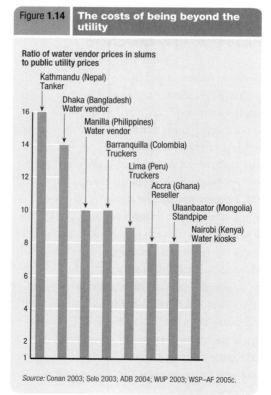

Figure **1.14** **The costs of being beyond the utility**

Ratio of water vendor prices in slums to public utility prices

Kathmandu (Nepal) Tanker
Dhaka (Bangladesh) Water vendor
Manila (Philippines) Water vendor
Barranquilla (Colombia) Truckers
Lima (Peru) Truckers
Accra (Ghana) Reseller
Ulaanbaator (Mongolia) Standpipe
Nairobi (Kenya) Water kiosks

Source: Conan 2003; Solo 2003; ADB 2004; WUP 2003; WSP–AF 2005c.

These barriers help to explain inequalities in access to the network. In Accra, Ghana, connection rates average 90% in high-income areas and 16% in low-income settlements.[57] People in Adenta and Madina, sprawling slum areas in the southeast part of the city, buy their water from intermediaries served by tanker truck associations, which in turn purchase in bulk from the water utility. The upshot: many of the 800,000 people living at or below the poverty line in Accra pay 10 times more for their water than residents in high-income areas. To add insult to injury, the volume of water available for users in slums is often reduced because of overconsumption by households in high-income areas. Water provided to slums in cities such as Accra and Nairobi is reduced during periods of shortage to maintain flows to high-income areas, where provision amounts to more than 1,000 cubic litres per person a day. Residents of the prosperous Parklands district in Nairobi receive water 24 hours a day. Residents of the Kibera slums are forced to spend an average of more than two hours a day waiting for water at standpipes that function for 4–5 hours a day or less.

The interaction of price and locational disadvantage helps explain the deep disparities in water provision that divide many cities. Absolute shortage is seldom the underlying problem: most cities have more than enough water to go around. The problem is that water is unequally distributed:[58]

- Lima produces more than 300 litres of water per capita each day, but 60% of the population receives just 12% of the water.
- In Guayaquil, Ecuador, billions of litres flow through the city each day in the Guayas River. High-income suburbs enjoy universal access to piped water. Meanwhile, some 800,000 people living in low-income and informal settlements depend on water vendors. About 40% of the population has to make do with 3% of the piped water.
- In Chennai, India, the average supply is 68 litres a day, but areas relying on tankers use as few as 8 litres. In Ahmedabad 25% of the population uses 90% of the water.

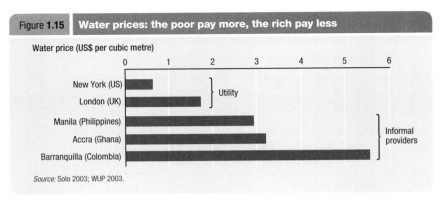

Figure 1.15 Water prices: the poor pay more, the rich pay less

Water price (US$ per cubic metre)

Source: Solo 2003; WUP 2003.

- Many countries in Sub-Saharan Africa face a national crisis in water provision—but the crisis is unequally shared. Residents of the high-income Oyster Bay settlement in Dar es Salam, Tanzania, use an average of 166 litres of water a day, while households without piped connection in Moshi use an average of 19 litres a day (figure 1.16).

Wealth-based inequalities do not operate in isolation. Within the household the gender division of labour means that women and young girls shoulder a greater burden of disadvantage than do men because they are responsible for collecting water, cooking, and caring for young, elderly and sick family members. Beyond the household, income inequality interacts with wider inequalities. Among the most important:

- *Rural-urban divides.* One of the deepest disparities in water and sanitation is between urban and rural areas. For developing countries as a group, improved water coverage is 92% for urban areas but only 72% for rural areas. Sanitation coverage is even more skewed: urban coverage is twice rural coverage (figure 1.17). Part of the rural-urban gap can be traced to differences in incomes and poverty: income deprivation is generally more marked in rural areas. But other factors are also important. Delivering services is more difficult and often more costly per capita for dispersed rural populations than for urban populations. Political factors also come into play, with people in rural areas—especially marginal areas—typically having a far weaker voice than their urban counterparts.

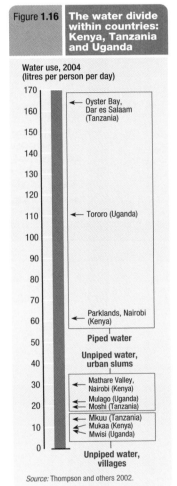

Figure 1.16 The water divide within countries: Kenya, Tanzania and Uganda

Water use, 2004
(litres per person per day)

Source: Thompson and others 2002.

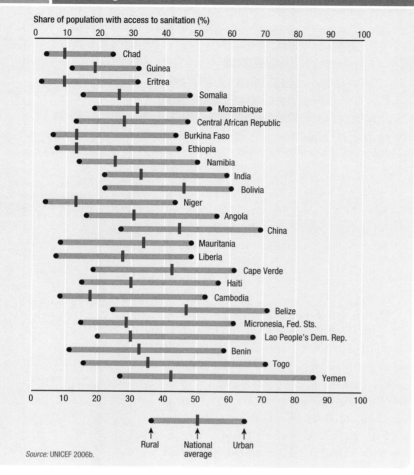

Figure 1.17 The rural-urban divide: disparities in access to sanitation remain large

Share of population with access to sanitation (%)

Chad
Guinea
Eritrea
Somalia
Mozambique
Central African Republic
Burkina Faso
Ethiopia
Namibia
India
Bolivia
Niger
Angola
China
Mauritania
Liberia
Cape Verde
Haiti
Cambodia
Belize
Micronesia, Fed. Sts.
Lao People's Dem. Rep.
Benin
Togo
Yemen

Rural   National   Urban
average

Source: UNICEF 2006b.

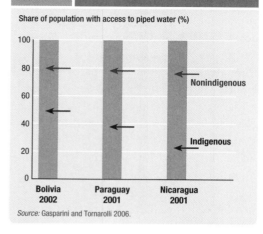

Figure 1.18 Some ethnic groups have much less access to water

Share of population with access to piped water (%)

Nonindigenous

Indigenous

Bolivia 2002   Paraguay 2001   Nicaragua 2001

Source: Gasparini and Tornarolli 2006.

dependence on cooperation from people of higher caste.[60]

- *Regional divides.* Rising average incomes create opportunities for reducing regional disparities through fiscal transfers to poor areas. But the transfers are often too limited to counter the effects of past disadvantage and local deprivation. In Mexico more than 90% of the population is connected to a safe water source—and two-thirds of households are connected to a sewer. But coverage drops sharply from more developed urban areas and more prosperous northern states through smaller towns, to more remote rural areas and the poverty-belt states of the south. The three states of Chiapas, Guerrero and Oaxaca underline the fact that physical availability of water and access to water are very different concepts: those states have the highest water availability from rainfall in Mexico and the lowest access to drinking water. Access is lower than in developing countries at far lower incomes—such as Sri Lanka and Thailand.

  Regional inequalities in access to water and sanitation are associated with wider human development inequalities. In Peru provinces such as Huancavelica and Pasco have safe water coverage rates far below the national average and child death rates far above the average. Again, association is not causation, but it is difficult to avoid the conclusion that there is an interaction at play (figure 1.19).

- *Group divides.* Group identity is a marker for disadvantage in many countries. In Latin America it is reflected in disparities between indigenous and nonindigenous people (figure 1.18). In Bolivia the average rate of access to piped water is 49% for indigenous language speakers and 80% for nonindigenous language speakers. Ethnic minorities in Viet Nam have less than a quarter of the coverage enjoyed by the majority Kinh people.[59] In South Asia caste remains an important source of inequality. In India caste rules that govern access to water have weakened—but they remain important, often in subtle ways. In Andhra Pradesh low-caste women are allowed to collect water from wells in high-caste villages, but they cannot draw the water themselves—an arrangement that leads to long waiting times and

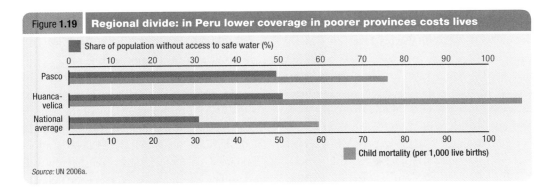

Figure 1.19 Regional divide: in Peru lower coverage in poorer provinces costs lives

Share of population without access to safe water (%)

Child mortality (per 1,000 live births)

Source: UN 2006a.

The Millennium Development Goals and beyond: getting on track

The Millennium Development Goals, set by the world's leaders at the UN Millennium Summit in 2000, aim at halving the proportion of people without access to safe water and sanitation by 2015 (target 10). This is not the first time that the international community has set ambitious targets. In the early 1980s governments enthusiastically embraced the goal of Water and Sanitation for All by 1990. At the start of the 1990s the Third Water Decade, the same goal was restated. The 1.1 billion people without access to clean water today and the 2.6 billion without access to sanitation bear testimony to the fact that high-level international conferences and impressive targets are no substitute for practical actions to provide water and toilets and sewerage systems.

Will the world in 2015 look back on another decade of missed targets? Or will this be the decade that closes the gap between international goals and outcomes on the ground? The answers will depend on national policies and international cooperation. What is clear is that success is possible and that failure will come with a very high price tag in lost human lives and wasted human potential. At the same time, the Millennium Development Goal should be seen as a floor not a ceiling—as a step on the way to universal access. It is sometimes forgotten that even if target 10 is attained, there will still be 800 million people lacking access to water and 1.8 billion people lacking access to sanitation in 2015. Population growth means that any slippage from the Millennium Development Goal target will leave the world standing still on water and sanitation coverage.

A progress report on the Millennium Development Goal target

Over the next decade the population of developing countries is projected grow by 830 million, with Sub-Saharan Africa accounting for a quarter of the increase and South Asia for another third. Taking into account this population growth, the simple version of the Millennium Development Goal challenge is that at least an additional 900 million people need access to water and 1.3 billion people need access to sanitation by 2015. These targets will not be attained if the world continues on a business as usual trajectory.

This implies several hundred thousand new connections each day in some of the world's poorest countries. For some regions the rate of new connections will need to increase sharply to bring the targets within reach (table 1.1). South Asia will need to provide sanitation coverage for 43 million people a year compared with 25 million people annually over the past decade. Sub-Saharan Africa faces an equally daunting challenge. In 1990–2004 the region increased coverage rates for clean water by an average of 10.5 million people a year. To meet the target over the next decade that figure will have to more than double to 23 million a year. For sanitation the number of people connected each year will need to increase fourfold—from 7 million to almost 28 million. Behind this regional aggregate many countries face an especially daunting challenge:

- Burkina Faso will need to provide access to sanitation for another 8 million people by 2015—almost six times the current population with coverage.
- Ethiopia will need to increase sanitation coverage by a factor of three, providing access for an additional 40 million people.
- Ghana will need to increase the rate at which coverage is increasing for water and sanitation by a factor of 9.

- Kenya will need to increase the number of people with access to water by 11.6 million and with access to sanitation by 16.5 million.

These targets are daunting but attainable. In some cases progress has accelerated in recent years, giving cause for optimism. Many of the world's poorest countries are demonstrating through practical achievements that the Millennium Development Goal target is within reach. However, the rate of progress required is far beyond that registered since 1990.

What are the prospects for the world achieving the water and sanitation Millennium Development Goal? The global aggregate picture is mixed. With strong progress in high-population countries such as China and India, the world is on track for halving the share of people without access to water, but off track on sanitation. The problem with this global aggregation is that it masks large differences between regions and countries. Disaggregation to a regional level shows less positive results

Table 1.1 The Millennium Development Goal target: past performance and future targets for water and sanitation

People with access to an improved water source (millions)

	1990	2004	Target 2015	Average annual number of people	
				Gaining access 1990–2004	Needing access to meet the target 2004–15
Sub-Saharan Africa	226.6	383.8	627.1	10.5	23.1
Arab States	180.1	231.8	335.8	4.7	6.5
East Asia and the Pacific	1,154.4	1,528.2	1,741.2	22.9	24.3
South Asia	840.6	1,296.4	1,538.1	32.5	22.1
Latin America and the Caribbean	334.3	499.0	527.8	9.0	6.1
World	2,767.7	4,266.4	5,029.5	79.5	82.4

People with access to improved sanitation (millions)

	1990	2004	Target 2015	Average annual number of people	
				Gaining access 1990–2004	Needing access to meet the target 2004–15
Sub-Saharan Africa	148.4	256.5	556.0	7.2	27.9
Arab States	120.6	196.0	267.2	4.9	6.9
East Asia and the Pacific	467.0	958.2	1,284.9	32.0	33.6
South Asia	242.9	543.8	1,083.3	24.7	42.5
Latin America and the Caribbean	279.6	423.2	492.2	8.6	8.4
World	1,456.9	2,663.9	3,994.0	77.5	120.4

Source: Calculated on the basis of WHO and UNICEF 2006 and UN 2005.

(figure 1.20). On current trends some regions will miss the water and sanitation target. Sub-Saharan Africa will miss the water target by a full generation and the sanitation target by more than two generations. South Asia will miss the sanitation target by four years, and the Arab States will miss the water target by 27 years. Looking beyond the regional picture to the national level reveals further cause for concern. Because the Millennium Development Goals are for everyone, it is country-level performance that counts—and current performance falls far short of the level required:

- Water: 55 countries are off track, and the target will be missed by about 234.5 million people, with a total of 800 million people still lacking access to water.
- Sanitation: 74 countries are off track, and the target will be missed by 430 million people, with 2.1 billion still lacking access to sanitation.

These figures understate the full extent of the shortfall. They do not factor in the problems linked to quality and continuity of provision discussed earlier, for example. Nor do they reflect the problems facing countries that need to go beyond the most basic provision. However, the projection highlights two important aspects of the Millennium Development Goal challenge. First, Sub-Saharan Africa, the world's poorest region, faces the largest prospective 2015 deficit. In water and sanitation, as in other areas of human development, Sub-Saharan Africa is falling further behind. By 2015 Sub-Saharan Africa will account for more than half of the global clean water deficit and just under half of the sanitation deficit, with South Asia accounting for the bulk of the remainder. This widening gap between Sub-Saharan Africa and the rest of the world will fuel wider inequalities in health, education and poverty reduction.

Second, the global water-sanitation gap is set to widen. The danger is that the potential benefits of progress in water will be eroded by a failure to achieve commensurate advances in sanitation. Indeed, an increased supply of water where drainage and human waste disposal provision are inadequate could exacerbate public

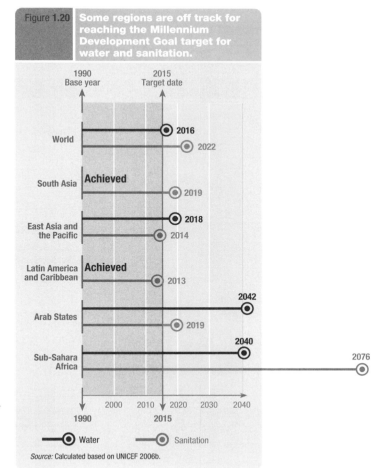

Figure 1.20 Some regions are off track for reaching the Millennium Development Goal target for water and sanitation.

Source: Calculated based on UNICEF 2006b.

health problems, especially in overcrowded cities. It would be a grave setback for human development if the world repeats in the early 21st century the mistakes made in the second half of the 19th century in Europe.

The rural-urban divide will remain important. Rural areas will continue to account for the bulk of the global deficit in 2015. However, urbanization will generate growing pressures. Over the decade to 2015 the share of the developing world's population in cities will increase from 42% to 48%, or by 675 million. Just to maintain current coverage levels cities will have to provide for this increased population. Much of the growth will occur in or around already overcrowded slums, peri-urban areas and informal settlements, with desperately poor rural migrants entering residential areas lacking basic water and sanitation infrastructure. The warning signs are already visible. Some 29 countries—China,

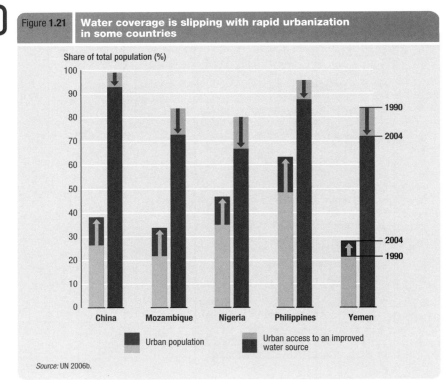

Figure 1.21 Water coverage is slipping with rapid urbanization in some countries

Share of total population (%)

Urban population

Urban access to an improved water source

Source: UN 2006b.

the most basic level of technology. Providing a higher level of service while maintaining provision at current levels to people who are already supplied would add another $15–$20 billion a year. Much larger sums would be involved if the target included costs for collecting and treating household wastewater.

These figures approximate the cost side of the equation. What of the benefits? The WHO research carried out for this year's Report addresses this question. What emerges is an overwhelming case for more investment in water and sanitation. The case extends beyond the narrow calculus of cost-benefit ratios, impressive as these figures are, to a wider case for public action. Among the core findings:

- There would be 203,000 fewer child deaths in 2015 if the Millennium Development Goal target were reached, 124,000 of them in Sub-Saharan Africa. Cumulatively, more than 1 million lives could be saved over the next decade if the world got on track.

- The economic rate of return in saved time, increased productivity and reduced health costs for each $1 invested in achieving the target is $8.

- Total economic benefits amount to $38 billion, with Sub-Saharan Africa accounting for $15 billion (just under 2% of GDP), Latin America $8 billion and South Asia $5 billion.

- The reduction in diarrhoea alone would result in a gain of 272 million days in school attendance, most of them in Sub-Saharan Africa and South Asia.

- Achieving the water and sanitation target would save about $1.7 billion a year in costs associated with the treatment of water-related infectious disease. Sub-Saharan Africa would save about $2 per capita—equivalent to about 12% of public health spending.[62] Reduced spending would release resources for other priorities, including HIV/AIDS.

- Taking into account just the impact of reduced diarrhoea, 3.2 billion working days would be gained for people ages 15–59. Annual time savings from more

Indonesia, Mozambique, Nigeria, the Philippines, Uganda and Yemen among them—have seen coverage rates slip over the past decade (figure 1.21).

Savings from meeting the Millennium Development Goal target

What would it cost to change the current global trajectory on water and sanitation and get on track for the Millennium Development Goal? The answer depends on assumptions about the level and type of technology and about the costs of delivery. Unreliable data make global estimation hazardous, but there is a surprisingly high level of agreement across various research exercises.

Current spending on water and sanitation in developing countries is estimated at $14–$16 billion annually (excluding wastewater treatment). The broad consensus on the additional financing required to achieve the Millennium Development Goal target on the basis of low-cost sustainable technologies is about $10 billion annually.[61] This is the minimum financing threshold. It reflects the cost of extending water and sanitation provision at

convenient water supplies would amount to another 20 billion working days, most of them gained by women. Coupled with the higher productivity from better health, these savings represent a large potential source of economic growth and household income.[63]

These figures provide only a very partial picture. They do not, for example, capture the benefits for education, for empowering women, for human dignity or for the reduced anguish and suffering associated with lower child death rates. But they do highlight the mutually reinforcing economic and human development case for investing in the Millennium Development Goal.

The headline numbers for achieving the Millennium Development Goal appear large. But they have to be put in context. The $10 billion required annually to get the world on track for the 2015 goal represents about eight days of global military spending. In terms of enhancing human security, as distinct from more narrowly defined notions of national security, the conversion of even small amounts of military spending into water and sanitation investments would generate very large returns.

Of course, national security is an imperative for any country. However, if protecting the lives of citizens is the objective, it is difficult to think of a public investment with the potential to safeguard more lives.

On any reasonable criteria the price tag for achieving the Millennium Development Goal is a value for money investment. That investment has the potential to save more than 1 million lives over the next decade, to end the crushing waste of lost education potential and to act as a catalyst for economic growth. From a human development perspective the real question is not whether the world can afford to achieve the Millennium Development Goal target. It is whether it can afford *not* to make the investment—and, indeed, whether we can afford not to go beyond the target. Were the world to achieve universal access to water and sanitation by 2015, it would avert 2 million deaths over the next decade. Of course, many people will argue that such a target is unrealistic. But the fact that many of the world's poorest countries have sustained a rate of progress far in excess of that required to meet the target raises the obvious counter question: does the 2015 target lack ambition?

From a human development perspective the real question is not whether the world can afford to achieve the Millennium Development Goal target. It is whether it can afford *not* to make the investment

Making progress a reality

At the start of the 10-year countdown to 2015 the international community is fast approaching a crossroad. There is an opportunity over the next decade to do for the Millennium Development Goals what the great reform movements of the 19th century did for water and sanitation in Europe and the United States. These movements have much to show us about mobilizing coalitions for change: politics, not finance, technology and economics, still holds the key to progress. Realizing the 2015 goals and progressing rapidly towards universal provision would help free millions of people from the scourge of poverty, boost economic growth and generate benefits for child survival, education and gender equity.

The Millennium Development Goal and 2015 are a first staging post, not the final destination. This is true in a dual sense. First, the ultimate goal in water and sanitation is universal access. With effective political leadership most countries have the potential to surpass the target and move rapidly towards universal provision. Second, the levels of provision required to meet the criterion for improved access should be seen as the first step on a ladder,

The unifying principle for public action in water and sanitation is the recognition that water is a basic human right

not the end of the journey. Ensuring that all people have access to the most basic technologies would make a huge difference. There would be almost 600,000 fewer child deaths in 2015. That would be a great achievement. However, it would leave more than 1 million children dying each year from diarrhoea. Bringing this number down will require sustained progress on higher levels of provision. Like their counterparts in the rich world, people in developing countries have a right to aspire to systems of provision that include piped water in their homes, access to networks for sanitation provision and a water and sanitation infrastructure that includes a capacity to process wastewater. While these aims may not be immediately achievable in many countries, it is important that public policies work progressively towards their realization.

The immediate concern at the start of the 10-year countdown to the 2015 target date is a real—and growing—threat that even the Millennium Development Goal target will be missed. Averting that outcome will require immediate action. Water and sanitation deficits are not amenable to quick fixes. Investments and policies put in place today will take several years to produce results on the scale required. Time is a luxury that developing country governments and aid donor countries cannot afford. If the policies and investments are not put in place quickly, it will be too late to catch up.

Chapters 2 and 3 look in more detail at some of the specific policies needed to bring the Millennium Development Goal target and wider water and sanitation targets within reach. Here, the focus is on some of the core policies and broad approaches needed in four areas that represent the foundations for future progress:

- Human rights.
- National strategies.
- International aid.
- A global action plan for water and sanitation.

Recognizing the human right to water and sanitation

The starting point and the unifying principle for public action in water and sanitation is the

recognition that water is a basic human right. In 2002 the United Nations Committee on Economic, Social and Cultural Rights adopted a General Comment on "the human right to water...for personal and domestic uses", establishing a non-legally binding normative framework for the "progressive realisation" of the human right to water and sanitation.

Giving substance to this framework is now the primary public policy challenge. A central feature of a rights-based approach is that it is premised on the principles of equality, universality and freedom from discrimination. Exclusion from water and sanitation services on the basis of poverty, ability to pay, group membership or place of habitation is a violation of the human right to water. If water is a human right that governments have a duty to uphold, the corollary is that many of the world's governments, developed as well as developing, are falling far short of their obligations. They are violating the human rights of their citizens on a large scale.

At a national level adherence to a rights-based approach requires the development of laws, policies, procedures and institutions that lead progressively to realization of the right to water. The provision of at least 20 litres of water a day to each person should be seen as the minimal goal for compliance with the right to water, with policies setting out nationally owned strategies for meeting this target and benchmarks for measuring progress. Mechanisms for redress and government accountability are also critical.

One of the features of a human right is universality. National governments bear primary duty for delivering on the obligation to provide water for all—but there are also global responsibilities. The 2002 General Comment recognized a special responsibility of the developed states to support poorer countries through "the provision of financial and technical assistance and necessary aid".

Some commentators see the application of rights language to water and other social and economic entitlements as an example of rhetorical "loose talk". That assessment is mistaken. Declaring water a human right clearly does not mean that the water crisis will be resolved in short order. Nor does a rights framework provide automatic answers to difficult policy questions about pricing, investment and service delivery. However, human rights represent a powerful moral claim. They can also act as a source of empowerment and mobilization, creating expectations and enabling poor people to expand their entitlements through legal and political channels—and through claims on the resources of national governments and the international community.

Developing strong national strategies

The obvious starting point for a drive towards universal access to water and sanitation is political will, broadly defined as the resolve to put the issue at the centre of the national agenda. It is not difficult to identify the financial, technological and institutional obstacles to progress, but these obstacles are often symptoms of a deeper malaise—a deficit in political leadership. Providing clean water and sanitation is as fundamental to human development and national prosperity as economic policy, international trade, health or education. Yet water and sanitation are widely perceived as meriting a limited claim on financial and political resources.

Water and sanitation have a weak voice in government. Bringing water and sanitation out of the political shadow and into the mainstream is a starting point for change. Responsibility for domestic water supply is typically split among several line ministries dealing with wider issues, with authority on domestic water and sanitation allocated to junior ministers as part of a wider brief (extending from the environment to housing or rural affairs). Sanitation is even more remote from the centre of political power. Establishing dedicated water and sanitation ministries led by senior cabinet ministers would create a political structure capable of overcoming the fragmentation of policy and the resultant underresourcing. As important, it would send a clear signal across government that water and sanitation are in the first tier of national policy priorities.

To political underrepresentation can be added stigmatization. Inadequate sanitation may kill large numbers of children, compromise public health, undermine human dignity and hold back economic growth, but the subject has a political stigma attached to it reminiscent in intensity to that surrounding HIV/AIDS. Overcoming that stigma and the political prudishness surrounding sanitation will require national political leadership of a high order.

Perhaps an even bigger obstacle to change is the interaction between stigma and social exclusion. For HIV/AIDS the indiscriminate nature of the disease, and its devastating impact on people across national wealth divides, has forced political leaders and high-income groups to confront their own prejudices: the disease has not respected social boundaries. For water and sanitation the picture is very different. Overwhelmingly, the costs of exclusion are borne by poor households, especially women. While it is true that some costs are transmitted to the whole of society, people living in urban slums and marginal rural areas bear the brunt. It is the children of the poor, not of the military high command and the top civil service, that face the greatest risk of premature death from diarrhoea. It is the young girls in poor households that are most likely to be kept home from school.

The water and sanitation crisis is overwhelmingly a crisis of marginalized social groups. However mistakenly, that crisis is widely viewed as a problem to be ring-fenced or dealt with on an incremental basis, rather than as a threat to the whole of society. That perspective is as big a barrier to progress as finance or technology. Changing it will require political leaders to put inequality and shared citizenship at the centre of national development strategies in a way that is seldom evident. It will also require a stronger voice for poor people and women among policymakers and water providers.

The low priority attached to water and sanitation is apparent at many levels. With a few notable exceptions, clean water has seldom been a make or break issue in national elections—and it is difficult to think of a single case where access to toilets has been a core concern. Pressure for radical reform has been conspicuous by its absence. Within government, responsibility for water provision is often a junior ministerial

Water and sanitation have a weak voice in government. Bringing water and sanitation out of the political shadow and into the mainstream is a starting point for change

National poverty reduction agendas reflect the pervasive benign neglect of water and sanitation

post, and sanitation is often not deemed to merit a ministerial position at all.

National poverty reduction agendas reflect the pervasive benign neglect of water and sanitation. The sector seldom figures with any prominence in Poverty Reduction Strategy Papers (PRSPs)—the documents that set out national plans and define the terms of cooperation between donors and aid recipients. One review of five countries found only one case—Uganda—of successful integration.[64] In most PRSPs water and sanitation, in contrast to macroeconomic reform, education and health, are treated dismissively, receiving little more than a few descriptive paragraphs and broad declarations of principle without even a semblance of a strategic reform agenda or financing provisions. The weakness of PRSPs reflect in turn the limited donor interest in water and sanitation.

Budget allocations reinforce the picture of neglect. Few public investments do more to enhance human security or build prosperity than investments in water and sanitation. Clean water and functioning toilets are among the

most potent health interventions that government can undertake, rivalling immunization in the benefits that they generate. Like expenditure on education or health, public spending on water and sanitation creates benefits for individuals and for society. It also generates wider public goods, such as enhanced gender equity and reduced inequalities in opportunity. There are always competing demands for public expenditure, but the high social and economic returns from investments in water and sanitation suggest that they ought to be a priority rather than a budgetary afterthought.

National expenditure patterns tell their own story. It is difficult to capture real public spending on water and sanitation partly because of the fragmentation of financing across ministries, partly because of decentralization and partly because donor financing is often off-budget. However, public spending in the sector as a whole typically represents less than 0.5% of GDP, falling to 0.1% in Pakistan and Zambia (figure 1.22). Within the sector expenditure on sanitation typically falls well short of that for water. Sanitation investment averages about 12%–15% of the total in Sub-Saharan Africa and Asia. Overall spending is low not just relative to national income, but also to other areas of social spending, such as public health. When measured against military spending, the gulf widens to very large proportions. For example, India spends 8 times more of its national wealth on military budgets than on water and sanitation. Pakistan spends 47 times more. In Sub-Saharan Africa low average incomes clearly constrain public spending capacity. At the same time, Ethiopia, one of the poorest countries in the world with some of the lowest coverage rates (and some of the highest child death rates from diarrhoea), still manages to mobilize almost 10 times more for military spending than for water and sanitation. South Africa is one of the few countries that spend less on military budgets than on water and sanitation.

Budget priorities raise some important questions about public spending. All countries see national security and defence as priorities. But viewed through the prism of human security, it is difficult to avoid the conclusion that

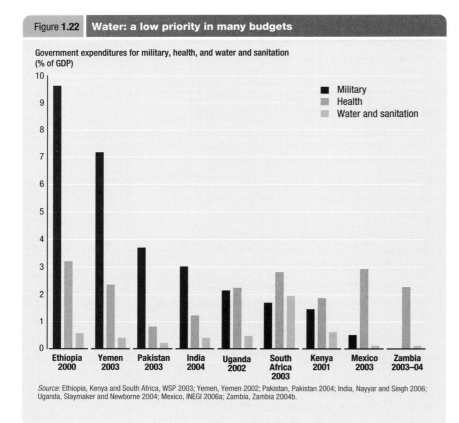

Figure 1.22   Water: a low priority in many budgets

Government expenditures for military, health, and water and sanitation (% of GDP)

Legend:
- Military
- Health
- Water and sanitation

Source: Ethiopia, Kenya and South Africa, WSP 2003; Yemen, Yemen 2002; Pakistan, Pakistan 2004; India, Nayyar and Singh 2006; Uganda, Slaymaker and Newborne 2004; Mexico, INEGI 2006a; Zambia, Zambia 2004b.

water and sanitation are underfinanced relative to military spending. Diarrhoea claims some 450,000 lives annually in India—more than in any other country—and 118,000 in Pakistan. Both countries have far higher death rates from diarrhoea than predicted on the basis of their average incomes. Pakistan ranks 28 places higher in the global league table for deaths from diarrhoea than in GDP per capita and India ranks 14 places higher. Of course, many factors are at play, but low levels of spending on water and sanitation surely contribute.

Recent years have witnessed some encouraging developments in budgets for water and sanitation. Many governments, beginning to recognize the crucial importance of progress in this area, have raised spending under national strategies to achieve—or surpass—the Millennium Development Goal. Uganda has increased public spending on water and sanitation rapidly both as a share of GNI—from 0.1% in 1997 to 0.4% in 2002 (and a projected 0.7% in 2004)—and in absolute terms because of high growth.[65] In India central government spending on rural sanitation has increased fourfold since 2002, while spending on rural water supply has doubled. Public spending has been identified as a priority for achieving broad-based growth and accelerated human development. At about 0.41% of GNI in 2005/06 spending is a third higher than in 2002/03. Most of the increase has come from the national budget, with state spending constrained by large fiscal deficits and, in some of the worst affected states, questionable allocation decisions.

National budgeting is one of the key components of any strategy for achieving progress in water and sanitation. Without predictable flows of finance, setting targets or adopting goals can degenerate into a meaningless exercise. One of the features of countries that have sustained progress is political commitment backed by real budget commitments. Political capital is every bit as important as finance. And establishing water as a human right can be seen as a form of political capital investment—but it has to mean something more than the adoption of a vague principle. All too often governments have adopted the language of human rights without adopting a policy framework for their delivery.

There are exceptions. In South Africa water was once a symbol of the inequality of apartheid. It is now treated as a basic human right. That is not unique in itself. More than 90 countries have the right to water in their constitutions.[66] For the most part, this has been a matter of profound irrelevance to their citizens. Constitutional provision has not been backed by a coherent strategy for extending access to water. But South Africa has demonstrated how the human right to water can serve as a mechanism for empowerment and a guide to policy. Rights-based water reform has enabled it to expand access and overcome the legacy of racial inequality inherited from apartheid, partly through rights-based entitlements (box 1.6). National success stories in sanitation are more thinly spread. Even here, however, there are some powerful demonstration effects. Countries as diverse as Bangladesh, Brazil, Lesotho and Thailand have overcome financial and technological constraints on progress through bold and innovative national strategies (see chapter 3).

In many countries progress in water and sanitation has been driven from below. Local and municipal governments and service providers have developed practical strategies for tackling inequalities in access. Communities have not waited passively for government help. The rural poor, women's organizations and associations of urban slum dwellers have mobilized their own resources. In some cases that mobilization has met with indifference, or even hostility. In others new partnerships have emerged between governments and people, with community initiative being scaled up.

One example comes from India. In the early 1990s the National Slum Dwellers Federation; Mahila Milan, a network of savings and credit groups formed by women slum dwellers; and the Society for the Promotion of Area Resource Centres (SPARC), a Mumbai-based nongovernmental organization, pioneered new designs for public toilet blocks to reduce excrement pollution in slums and give women more privacy. At the end of the decade, Pune, a city of more than 2 million inhabitants, adopted this

Box 1.6   South Africa—acting on the right to water

Access to water was one of the defining racial divides in apartheid South Africa. Since apartheid was brought to an end, a rights-based legislative framework and public policies aimed at extending access to water have empowered local communities and reduced inequalities. The task is not yet complete—but there are important lessons for other countries.

Surveys before the 1994 elections that marked the end of apartheid showed that access to basic services, along with employment, was the people's main expectation of the incoming government. The 1996 Constitution included a Bill of Rights enshrining "the right to adequate food and water". This constitutional right was given legislative content under the Water Services Act (1997) and the National Water Act (1998). Key provisions include:

- Clearly defined medium-term targets to provide 50–60 litres of clean water to all households, along with adequate sanitation for all urban households and 75% of rural households.
- Lifeline tariffs to ensure that all South Africans can afford sufficient water services for adequate health and hygiene. Government used its regulatory powers to require all municipalities to provide a basic minimum of 25 litres free of charge to each household. The target is to achieve free basic water for all by 2008, with no household more than 200 metres from a water source.
- Stepped tariffs to provide a cross-subsidy from high-volume users to low-volume users.
- Equitable share transfers that take into account the number of poor people in each municipality in a formula for fiscal transfers.

The new policy framework has achieved important advances. Since 1994, 10 million more people have received access to safe water, with coverage rates rising from 60% to 86%. Some 31 million people are now served by free basic water.

Empowerment has been a less tangible but important aspect of the reform. The Department of Water Affairs provides a national regulatory framework, but responsibility for implementation has been transferred to local governments. Regulation places obligations on municipal providers and elected local authorities and gives users a rights-based entitlement to demand that these obligations be met. In addition, municipal water companies are required to publish detailed information on water provision by district, disaggregated for poor and nonpoor users.

As the reforms have rolled out, they have generated a political debate over design and implementation. Some argue that the 25-litre threshold for free basic water is too low. Supplies in some areas have been erratic, forcing households to collect water from far away. Moreover, government pricing policies have led to supply cutoffs for nonpayment in some areas, raising concerns about affordability.

Progress in sanitation has been less impressive than in water. There are still 16 million people—one in three South Africans—without access to basic sanitation. The absence of a consensus on an acceptable basic level of sanitation, allied to problems in generating demand, has contributed to the failure.

The South African experience highlights three crucial policy ingredients for progress: a clear national plan with well defined targets, a strong national regulatory framework with devolution to local authorities and constant monitoring of performance and progress.

Source: Muller 2006; Sinanovic and others 2005.

model, with local authorities working with the three pioneers to identify needs and mobilize communities. Such community mobilization backed by government action is a powerful force for change.

These examples demonstrate that rapid progress is possible. However daunting the challenge may appear, governments and people have shown that poverty and low income are constraints that can be overcome. The problem is that progress

has been partial and piecemeal. Small islands of success show what is possible—but they also highlight the shortcomings that perpetuate very large deficits in water and sanitation.

Every country has to chart its own policy course for overcoming these deficits. The poorest countries with low coverage face different constraints from middle-income countries with higher coverage, more extensive infrastructure and more resources. However, it is possible to identify an indicative framework for action. That framework has five key pillars:

1. National planning. Each country should have a national water and sanitation plan, integrated in national poverty reduction strategies and reflected in medium-term financing frameworks and budget priorities. There are no global prescriptions for successful planning. However, the ingredients include clear goals backed by adequate financing and the development of structures for delivery that empower local governments, while building accountability to communities. Performance has been mixed—but there are signs of progress. Enhanced equity is critical to progress. Most countries will not achieve the Millennium Development Goal and wider goals simply by expanding infrastructure. They also need to address the inequitable distribution of access to water and sanitation linked to wealth, location, gender and other factors. Every national plan should therefore include both benchmark indicators for measuring overall progress and indicators for reducing inequalities. Among the measures for incorporating an enhanced commitment to equity in national strategies:

- *Establishing social minimum provision levels.* Every person has a human right to a minimum of about 20 litres of water each day, regardless of wealth, location, gender, or racial, ethnic or other group. All national plans should include policies for meeting the social minimum and benchmarks for measuring progress.
- *Revising Millennium Development Goal benchmarks for inequality.* Basic citizenship rights and considerations of social justice demand equity in the provision of water for basic needs. Overcoming inequality should be seen as an integral part of national water policies. The current Millennium Development Goal framework focuses on halving the share of national populations without access to water and sanitation. That target should be supplemented by targets for halving the gap in water and sanitation coverage rates between the richest 20% and the poorest 20% by 2010, with governments reporting on strategies for achieving the target and on outcomes.

- *Strengthening the treatment of inequality in Poverty Reduction Strategy Papers.* All Poverty Reduction Strategy Papers should include goals and strategies for narrowing extreme disparities in water and sanitation provision, with a special focus on inequalities based on wealth, location and gender.
- *Adopting pro-poor regulation and contracting.* All water providers should be bound by equity performance targets stipulating goals for extending access to poor households. The targets should include clear indicators for extending provision to unserved urban and rural communities, the expansion of stand-pipe provision in slums and the delivery of free or low-cost water to low-income households. Contracts drawn up within public-private partnerships should include targets in these areas, with full public disclosure, monitoring by an independent regulatory body and penalties for nonperformance (see chapter 2).

2. System financing. National plans need to include clear financing estimates for attaining their targets. All financing ultimately comes from government budgets (a category that includes aid) or users. The appropriate mix between the two varies. In low-income countries with limited coverage and high levels of poverty, a benchmark indicator is public spending on water and sanitation of about 1% of GDP (depending on per capita income and the ratio of revenue to GDP), with cost-recovery and community contributions providing an equivalent amount. Benchmarks for middle-income countries are more variable, though cost-recovery capacity rises with average income. Because water and sanitation infrastructure requires large upfront investments, with revenues coming on-stream in local currencies over a long period, strategies for mobilizing resources on local capital markets can help to spread costs.

3. Expansion of access to the unserved. The primary and immediate challenge in both water and sanitation is to extend access and improve quality for the unserved and poorly served. Later chapters set out some of strategies that have worked and delivered practical results,

Every person has a human right to a minimum of about 20 litres of water each day, regardless of wealth, location, gender, or racial, ethnic or other group

Governments have a responsibility to ensure that providers and markets deliver safe, affordable and reliable water and sanitation to the poor

though the same policies can produce different results in different environments. A pro-poor expansion package includes:

- *Lifeline tariffs* that provide free water up to a specified limit for poor households, as developed in South Africa.
- *Cross-subsidies* that transfer resources from higher income to lower income households through utility pricing or targeted fiscal transfers, as in Chile and Colombia. Where subsidies are used they should be targeted to ensure that the nonpoor pay a greater proportion of the cost of providing services than is currently the case in most countries.
- *Sustainable and equitable cost-recovery measures.* Service providers should set charges to cover recurrent costs, with public finance covering capital costs for network expansion. But affordability is one of the keys to equity. One rule of thumb is that no household should be spending more than 3% of its income on water and sanitation.
- *Strategies for supporting demand for water and sanitation among the poorest households.* Strategies have to take into account the fact that people lacking access to water overwhelmingly live below the extreme poverty line, while the sanitation deficit extends from below the extreme poverty line to higher income levels where households have a greater capacity to finance provision.

4. Scale-up of initiatives from below. The distinction between top-down and bottom-up initiatives is often overstated. Progress depends on governments doing what governments are supposed to do: creating an enabling environment, mobilize resources and setting a clear national policy framework. But in water and sanitation, as in most areas, governments work best when they work in partnerships that build on the energy, drive and innovation at a community level—and when they listen to people. Partnerships based on real participation create the potential for the rapid scaling up of local success stories.

5. Regulation for human development. Water and sanitation service delivery brings together a wide range of providers and extends across

complex markets. Governments have a responsibility to ensure that providers and markets are governed to prevent the abuse of monopolistic power and to deliver safe, affordable and reliable water and sanitation to the poor. One of the problems with current regulatory frameworks is that their remit does not extend beyond large-scale formal providers.

This is a broad agenda. It goes beyond the narrow preoccupation with private or public ownership that has dominated debates on water and sanitation. While these debates have highlighted important concerns, they have diverted attention from important public policy issues. Ultimately, water is a human right—and governments are the duty bearers for extending that right. Public agencies are also the primary providers and financers for water provision in most countries. However, the financing, delivery and regulation of water and sanitation services pose tough public policy challenges that cannot be resolved simply by claiming that water is a human right or by debating over public and private operators, issues returned to in chapters 2 and 3.

Increasing international aid for water and sanitation

International development discussions are often trapped in an unhelpful debate over whether money or policy reform is more critical for progress in human development.[67] The reality is that both are essential. Of course, money alone cannot resolve problems in service provision, especially problems that are the product of bad policies, but it can help to relieve constraints and support good policies. In water and sanitation, as in other areas, progress ultimately depends on the actions of developing countries themselves—but aid has a critical role. For a large group of low-income countries, domestic resource mobilization is too limited by poverty and low average incomes to finance investments on the scale required. Investments financed by aid can help unlock the high returns to human development by reducing the financing constraints on governments and poor households.

Sub-Saharan Africa most forcefully demonstrates the importance of aid to the realization of the water and sanitation Millennium Development Goal and wider targets. Cross-country estimates suggest that reaching target 10 will require annual investments over the next decade of about 2.7% of GDP, or $7 billion annually.[68] Cross-country budget analysis indicates that current spending is about 0.3% of GDP, or some $800 million annually. There are no reliable cross-country estimates for revenues from household and utility sources. But cost-recovery by service providers and financial resource mobilization by communities to finance water delivery would probably increase total current spending to 1% of GDP, or $2.5 billion.

Working on the optimistic assumption that public spending on water and sanitation and cost-sharing could be increased to 1.6% of GDP, this would still leave a financing gap of $2.9 billion annually. Aid flows currently cover part of the financing gap, providing an average of about $830 million annually. But the financing shortfall for meeting minimal Millennium Development Goal access requirements still amounts to about $2 billion a year. Attempting to close this gap through cost-recovery would put water and sanitation services beyond the reach of precisely the people who need to be served to achieve the target. Recent estimates for the Millennium Development Goals point to a large gap between financing requirements and current provision for many countries in Sub-Saharan Africa (figure 1.23). With less than a decade to the 2015 target date, closure of that gap is an urgent priority because of the lag between investment and increased coverage.

Most donors acknowledge the crucial importance of water and sanitation to human development. But aid flows tell a less encouraging story. Taking out the large spike in development assistance for Iraq, total development assistance for water amounted to $3.4 billion in 2004.[69] In real terms aid levels today are lower than in 1997, a marked contrast to education, where aid commitments doubled over the same period, or in health. Aid to water and sanitation has also fallen as a share of overall development assistance—from 8% to 5%. And international aid flows for the sector have been marked by large variations, pointing to the unpredictability

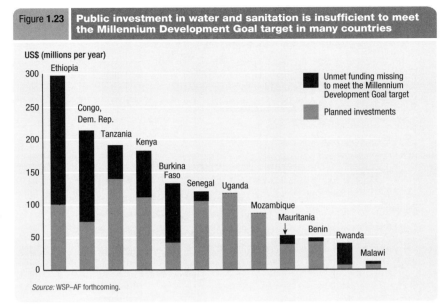

Figure **1.23**   **Public investment in water and sanitation is insufficient to meet the Millennium Development Goal target in many countries**

Source: WSP–AF forthcoming.

of financing. True, there are many competing demands for aid. But the donor community has long recognized the importance of water and sanitation for a wide range of development goals, so these are worrying trends.

Donors vary widely in commitments to water and sanitation. Japan is by far the largest bilateral donor, allocating an average of $850 million in 2003–04 (figure 1.24). That figure represents more than a fifth of all aid to water and sanitation. Multilateral donors now account for about a third of aid flows, up from 20% five years ago, with the World Bank's soft-loan International Development Association and the European Union dominating. The shift towards multilateral aid has been important for Millennium Development Goal financing because it is more focussed than bilateral aid on low-income countries and Sub-Saharan Africa.

Behind the headline figures donors vary widely in the share of aid allocated to water and sanitation. Within the Group of Eight, for example, Germany and Japan invest more than 6% of total aid to the sector, while Italy, the United Kingdom and the United States invest 3% or less (figure 1.25).

For overcoming financing constraints, the distribution of aid flows is important. Here, too, there is cause for concern. Aid flows are heavily concentrated: just 20 countries account for about three-quarters of total aid. The 10 largest

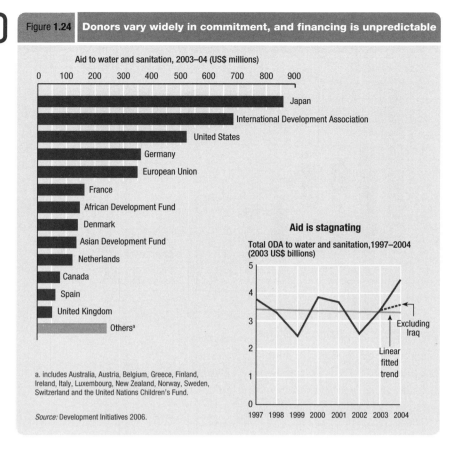

Figure **1.24** | **Donors vary widely in commitment, and financing is unpredictable**

Aid to water and sanitation, 2003–04 (US$ millions)

Japan
International Development Association
United States
Germany
European Union
France
African Development Fund
Denmark
Asian Development Fund
Netherlands
Canada
Spain
United Kingdom
Others[a]

Aid is stagnating

Total ODA to water and sanitation,1997–2004
(2003 US$ billions)

Excluding Iraq

Linear fitted trend

a. includes Australia, Austria, Belgium, Greece, Finland, Ireland, Italy, Luxembourg, New Zealand, Norway, Sweden, Switzerland and the United Nations Children's Fund.

Source: Development Initiatives 2006.

recipients of bilateral aid receive two-thirds of total disbursements. Four of these countries are lower middle income. Sub-Saharan Africa, the region facing the largest financing gap and the greatest deficits in water and sanitation, receives only about a fifth of aid. Like government spending on water and sanitation, aid flows are skewed towards urban populations. Large-scale water and sanitation infrastructure financing accounts for about half of all aid to the sector, indicating a strong urban bias.

Caution is required in assessing current aid allocations. Viewed from a human development perspective, simple associations between aid and low-income countries can be misleading. Lower middle-income countries such as Morocco, South Africa and Tunisia are all large aid recipients in water and sanitation—and each has major problems and a claim to external support. The same is true for low-income countries such as China, India and Viet Nam, all of which figure prominently in bilateral aid allocations. Increasing aid for Sub-Saharan Africa should not be at the expense of legitimate

claims from other sources. Similarly, it is important to avoid simplistic distinctions between large-scale and small-scale infrastructure. There are strong development grounds for supporting large-scale water and sanitation infrastructure as part of an overall sector strategy: the development of wastewater treatment facilities and water and sanitation networks are not development luxuries.

Nor can the small share of aid allocated to Sub-Saharan Africa be attributed solely to donor bias. Many African governments have failed to make the sector a priority or to tackle long-standing problems in institutional fragmentation. In many countries an unhealthy interaction between governments and donors acts to marginalize water and sanitation. Donors often express their preferences by prioritizing spending in areas with strong sectoral plans or sectorwide approaches. These are chronically underdeveloped in water and sanitation, creating disincentives for donor engagement. In turn, limited donor support restricts the potential for the development of sectorwide approaches, creating a vicious circle of weak planning and underfinancing

For the global financing of the Millennium Development Goal, current development assistance patterns suffer from two shortcomings. The most visible is the large aid deficit relative to financing requirements. On a rule of thumb indicator, aid flows to water and sanitation will have to increase by about $3.6–$4 billion a year to bring the target within reach, with an additional $2 billion allocated to Sub-Saharan Africa. This is an immediate priority. Without more aid, many governments will lack the revenue base to make the upfront investments needed to bring the Millennium Development Goal within reach. And policy reforms and investments in water and sanitation take considerable time to yield results.

The second problem is that aid resources are inevitably skewed towards countries with a strong donor presence—more specifically, towards countries with a critical mass of donors that prioritize aid to water and sanitation. That outcome is at once unsurprising and important. Countries in which Japan is a major partner are

1

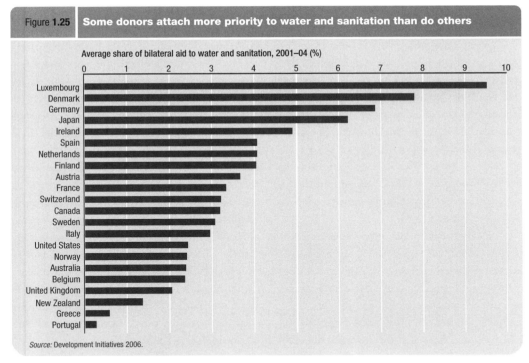

Figure 1.25 **Some donors attach more priority to water and sanitation than do others**

Average share of bilateral aid to water and sanitation, 2001–04 (%)

Luxembourg
Denmark
Germany
Japan
Ireland
Spain
Netherlands
Finland
Austria
France
Switzerland
Canada
Sweden
Italy
United States
Norway
Australia
Belgium
United Kingdom
New Zealand
Greece
Portugal

Source: Development Initiatives 2006.

more likely to secure aid for water and sanitation. The upshot is that good policies are not always backed by sufficient aid for water and sanitation in countries where donors display a weak commitment to the sector. While many factors determine aid allocations, it is difficult to avoid the conclusion that there is a mismatch in many countries between national financing needs and aid flows. In 2004 Ghana and Tunisia both received $88 in aid for every person without access to an improved water source; Burkina Faso and Mozambique received $2 per person. South Africa received $11; Chad and Nigeria received between $3 and $4.

Aid pessimists question the role of development assistance in fostering human development. That pessimism is unfounded. International development assistance has been pivotal in supporting progress in access to water in countries such as Ghana, South Africa and Uganda—and it continues to support progress towards sanitation for all in Bangladesh and Lesotho. For millions of people in the world's poorest countries aid has made a difference. That does not mean that more cannot be done by both donors and aid recipients to increase the effectiveness of development assistance. Weak coordination among donors, a preference in some cases for operating through projects rather than government programmes, and tied aid—all diminish the impact of development assistance and raise transaction costs for developing country governments. At the same time, the failure of some governments to ensure that budget outcomes reflect planned commitments has left many donors hesitant to increase programme aid. But across a large group of countries the quality of aid is improving as national policies become more effective.

Another cause for optimism is the momentum behind international aid partnerships developed since the Millennium Development Goals were launched. The Gleneagles summit of the Group of Eight (G-8) in 2005 pledged a doubling of aid by 2010—a commitment that translates into an extra $50 billion, with half the total earmarked for Sub-Saharan Africa. Innovative mechanisms have been developed to frontload development assistance through prefinanced disbursements budgeted against future aid flows. In view of the capital intensity of water investments, the need to frontload aid and the long timeframe over which water and sanitation plans have to be implemented, it is important to mobilize an early increase in aid disbursements—and to prefinance disbursements budgeted for later periods.

Strong national planning is the foundation for an accelerated drive towards the Millennium Development Goal target and—ultimately—to universal access to water and sanitation

Rich countries financed their revolution in water and sanitation more than a century ago by drawing on a wide range of new financing mechanisms, including municipal bonds that spread costs over a long period. In the globalized world of the early 21st century, it is important that the new aid partnerships developed around the Millennium Development Goals extend the same opportunities to the world's poorest countries. The International Finance Facility proposed by UK Chancellor of the Exchequer Gordon Brown is one example (see special contribution).

Looking beyond aid, many countries will need to mobilize large amounts of finance on domestic capital markets. In some cases these markets are limited and the perceived risks associated with bonds issued by municipalities or service providers can raise interest rates to prohibitive levels. This is an area in which domestic policies and effective capital market regulation are critical. Developed countries and multilateral financial institutions can support national efforts through measures aimed at reducing risk and lowering the costs of borrowing, such as credit guarantees (see chapter 2).

Building the global partnership— the case for an international water and sanitation global action plan

Strong national planning is the foundation for an accelerated drive towards the Millennium Development Goal target and—ultimately—to universal access to water and sanitation. Mobilization of domestic resources, development of efficient, accountable and responsive institutions and implementation of strategies for overcoming inequalities are foundations for progress in all countries. But in some countries they are not enough. That is why aid is so important. More generally, national planning and international aid efforts could benefit from a broader global plan of action for water and sanitation.

The case for such a plan is rooted partly in the peripheral status of water and sanitation on the international development agenda and partly in the lessons from international efforts in other areas, such as HIV/AIDS and education.

Beyond water and sanitation, it is difficult to think of any other area of comparable importance for human development that suffers from such limited global leadership. The problem is not a shortage of high-level conferences or ambitious communiqués. These have been a standard feature of international conference calendars for the more than three decades since the first UN conference on water, held in Mar del Plata, Argentina, in 1977. That event led to the adoption of an action plan that gave rise to the first International Drinking Water and Safe Sanitation Decade. To this day, that conference remains a milestone in terms of its influence. But the impressive target of "water and sanitation for all" by 1990 and the subsequent reaffirmation of the same unachieved goal for 2000 at yet another high-level conference revealed a large gap between target setting and strategic planning to attain the targets.

Since the mid-1990s there has been a proliferation of conferences dedicated to water. Two large international partnerships—the World Water Council and the Global Water Partnership—have emerged and overseen an impressive succession of global meetings, such as the triennial World Water Forum, held in Mexico City in 2006, and reports. Water has also figured prominently in wider UN meetings, such as the World Summit on Sustainable Development.

Yet it is difficult to avoid the conclusion that today, as in the 1970s, there is a very large gap between ministerial declarations and conference communiqués and practical strategies to achieve water and sanitation for all. None of this is to diminish the critical role of international conferences in informing opinion and increasing awareness of problems among policy-makers and the public. But if the ultimate objective is to improve the access of poor women and men to water, the record is less impressive—and the case for more international conferences that lack a clear agenda for achieving change is limited.

Stated in blunt terms, when it comes to water and sanitation, the world suffers from a surplus of conference activity and a deficit of action. It also suffers from fragmentation. There are no fewer than 23 UN agencies dealing with water and sanitation. Apart from problems of coordination and transaction costs within countries, the diversity of actors has militated against the development of strong international champions for water and sanitation.

The agenda of the G-8 countries bears testimony to the problem. Three years ago, at its summit in Evian, Switzerland, the G-8 adopted a Water Action Plan to achieve a wide range of goals, "assisting as a priority, countries that make a political commitment to prioritize safe drinking water and basic sanitation".[70] Since then, nothing meriting the description of an action plan has emerged. Aid levels have stagnated, and no credible attempt has been made to translate into practical global strategies capable of delivering results the commitments made at such international conferences as the Third and Fourth World Water Forms held in 2003 and 2006.

If evidence were needed of the low profile of water and sanitation on the G-8 agenda, it was provided at the 2005 Gleneagles Summit. Not only was there no reference to what was agreed at Evian, but the issue was not mentioned in the G-8 strategy set out for Sub-Saharan Africa.

With a decade to go to 2015, it is time to act on the commitment to develop a global action plan for water and sanitation. That does not mean the creation of complex, bureaucratic, top-down planning processes. Rather, the aim would be to provide an institutional point for international efforts to mobilize resources, build capacity and—above all—galvanize political action by putting water and sanitation in a more central position on the development agenda.

For any global framework to produce results, it has to be grounded at the country level and embedded in national planning processes. It also has to be rooted in a genuine development partnership. Ultimately, it is the responsibility of national governments to deliver credible national plans and to develop transparent and accountable institutions for implementation. But the core principle that underpins the Millennium Development Goals is that governments committed to progress will not be held back for want of international support and financial resources. The development of a global action plan would help to translate this commitment from words into action.

Current initiatives provide a useful point of reference. Both the Global Fund to Fight AIDS, Tuberculosis and Malaria and, on a less impressive but nonetheless important scale, the Fast Track Initiative in education have delivered real results.[71] Neither involves large organizational structures. The Global Fund has a small bureaucracy, with no in-country staff, and acts only as an instrument for financing and capacity building. It relies on government strategies and facilitates a strong role for civil society. The added value of the Global Fund has been as a focal point for political action, leveraging resources to support good policies, and building capacity. Similarly, the Fast Track Initiative has helped to reduce financing gaps and coordinate donor support for education in about a dozen countries.[72]

How would a global plan of action work for water and sanitation? And what difference would a global action plan make to the lives of poor people? In operations terms, a global plan would bring donors together under a single multilateral umbrella organized under the auspices of relevant UN agencies, the European Union and the World Bank. The emphasis would be on delivering resources and support for capacity building and on coordination and coherence, rather than on the creation of new bureaucracies.

A global framework, grounded at the country level and embedded in Poverty Reduction Strategy Papers and national development plans, could provide a platform for tackling the policy, institutional and financing issues as countries seek to scale up water and sanitation strategies and accelerate progress. Going global is not a substitute for starting locally. But it can build on the basic Millennium Development Goals compact: that good policies and serious intent to deliver at a national level will attract the support of the international community. Such a plan could bring interlocking benefits to countries with governments committed to action:

- *Galvanize international commitment and raise the profile of water and sanitation.* Adoption of an action plan by the G-8 and the wider donor community would highlight the central importance of progress in water

With a decade to go to 2015, it is time to act on the commitment to develop a global action plan for water and sanitation

1

Ending the crisis in water and sanitation

From Japan to the European Union and to the United States people in the developed world take clean water and basic sanitation for granted. But across the world too many people are still denied access to these basic human rights. This Report powerfully documents the social and economic costs of a crisis in water and sanitation.

Not only are water and sanitation essential for human life but they are also the building blocks for development in any country. That is why one of the eight Millennium Development Goals has a specific target to halve the proportion of people without sustainable access to safe drinking water and sanitation by 2015.

The lack of clean water and sanitation disproportionately affects women and girls, who are traditionally responsible for fetching water for the family. For school-age girls the time spent travelling—sometimes hours—to the nearest source of water is time lost in education, denying them the opportunity to get work and to improve the health and living standards of their families and themselves. Schools with no access to clean water or sanitation are powerful evidence of the interconnectedness of human development and the Millennium Development Goals: you cannot build effective education systems when children are constantly sick and absent from school. And you cannot achieve education for all when girls are kept at home because their parents are worried by the absence of separate toilet facilities.

Today the link between clean water, improved health and increased prosperity is well understood. We have the knowledge, the technology and the financial resources to make clean water and sanitation a reality for all. We must now match these resources with the political will to act.

The infrastructure for an effective nationwide water and sanitation system—from water pipes to pumping stations to sewerage works—requires investment on a scale beyond what the poorest countries can begin to afford. Moreover, it requires large upfront investments as well as longer term maintenance costs. Given the high proportion of people in developing countries that lack access to water and sanitation and survive on less than $1 a day, it is not feasible to meet these upfront costs through user fees.

In 2005 developed country governments promised to increase the overall amount of aid for development. The European Union has committed to increasing aid to 0.7% of its income by 2015. The G-8 has committed to doubling aid to Africa by 2010. In making that promise, the G-8 recognized that one of the purposes of this aid was ensuring that developing country populations would have access to safe water and sanitation. However, traditional increases in donor aid budgets will not be enough to provide the additional resources and meet the aid targets that have been set. Innovative financing mechanisms are needed to deliver and bring forward the financing urgently needed to achieve the Millennium Development Goals— and nowhere is this more evident than in water and sanitation.

Bluntly stated, the world cannot wait for the incremental flows of finance to come on-stream before tackling the water and sanitation crisis. That crisis is killing children and holding back development today—and we have to act now. That is why a range of innovative financing mechanisms have been considered and implemented with a view to mobilizing development finance upfront. The International Finance Facility (IFF) is one example.

The IFF mobilizes resources from international capital markets by issuing long-term bonds that are repaid by donor countries over 20–30 years. A critical mass of resources can thus be made available immediately for investment in development, while repayment is made over a longer period from the aid budgets of developed countries.

The frontloading principles have already been applied to the IFF for Immunization, which by immediately investing an extra $4 billion in vaccinations for preventable disease will save an astonishing 5 million lives between now and 2015 and a further 5 million thereafter.

These principles may also be very relevant for water. The rates of return from upfront investment in water and sanitation would significantly outweigh the costs of borrowing from bond markets, even taking into account the interest costs. Indeed, the WHO has estimated that the return on a $1 investment in sanitation and hygiene in low-income countries averages about $8. That is a good investment by any system of accounting.

The mobilization of resources from capital markets for investment in water and sanitation is not new. Industrial countries used bond issuances and capital markets to provide financing for investment in water and sanitation infrastructure at the start of the last century. And just recently countries such as South Africa issued municipal bonds to rapidly raise the critical mass of resources to make such investment.

Of course, we have to recognize that the new aid partnerships underpinning the Millennium Development Goals are a two-way contract. There are obligations and responsibilities on both sides. Developing countries should be judged on their ability to use aid resources efficiently and transparently to reach the poorest with clean water and sanitation. But they and their citizens are entitled to expect good policies to be backed by a predictable flow of aid financing commensurate with the scale of the challenge.

Developed countries should be judged not just on willing the Millennium Development Goals but on delivering the resources to achieve them. Helping provide clean water and basic sanitation will show that these promises are more than just a passing fashion— that they are a commitment for our generation.

Gordon Brown

Gordon Brown, MP, Chancellor of the
Exchequer, United Kingdom

Ngozi Okonjo-Iweala

Ngozi Okonjo-Iweala, Former Minister of Finance, Nigeria

and sanitation to the Millennium Development Goals. Properly designed and implemented, such a plan could do for water and sanitation what the Global Fund has done for HIV/AIDS—provide an institutional focal point that raises the profile of the water and sanitation problem. It could send a strong signal to national governments that the sector will be a growing priority, creating incentives for stronger national planning. On the policy front the global plan could identify broad best practice strategies for overcoming inequalities and accelerating progress, creating a global indicative framework as a basis for assessing policy. Monitoring the implementation and progress of these strategies would become a focal point for water and sanitation at International Monetary Fund–World Bank meetings and at the G-8.

- *Monitor performance.* Aid donors justifiably demand a high level of accountability and transparency by aid recipients. Far weaker standards are applied to the donor community. There are no mechanisms for holding developed countries to account for the delivery of aid against their commitments, or for the quality of aid. The global water and sanitation action plan would create such a mechanism. It would include an annual assessment of donor performance. The annual evaluation exercise would have two parts. It would include a review by aid recipients of the degree to which donors are complying in water and sanitation with wider Organisation for Economic Co-operation and Development guidelines and targets adopted in 2005 for enhancing aid effectiveness through increased budget support, greater predictability in aid flows and lower transaction costs through improved harmonization and coordination. It would also include independent evaluation of aid programmes against the targets set out in the Millennium Development Goal and in national strategies, helping to improve both donor and aid recipient understanding of what works and what does not.
- *Mobilize additional aid resources.* The global action plan would provide a focal point for

international efforts to align the external resources needed for achieving the Millennium Development Goal with the financing gaps in individual countries. With this in mind, the first key ingredient is the creation of a reliable, long-term commitment of resources contingent on countries adopting and implementing credible reform plans. The strength of prior commitments of donors can provide countries the assurance that, if they fulfil their commitments, donors will deliver funding.

Because expansion of access to water and sanitation calls for major upfront investments but delivers returns over a long period, the sector often loses out to more immediate and tangible investment projects for which political leaders can more readily claim credit. Secured financing can strengthen the hand of reformers by providing the leverage that comes with commitments of external financial support. Central to the plan would be a concrete timetable to increase aid to water and sanitation by $3.4–$4 billion annually over the next decade, with provisions for frontloading. Sub-Saharan Africa would be a focal point for the global action plan, not only in mobilizing $1.5–$2 billion in additional aid but also in putting water and sanitation at the heart of the Africa strategy adopted by the G-8 at Gleneagles. The global plan would provide a framework for performance-based aid, with aid recipients setting clear benchmarks for performance under national plans and donors adhering to benchmarks for delivering on their aid commitments (see special contribution by Gordon Brown and Ngozi Okonjo-Iweala).

- *Mobilize domestic resources.* The global action plan would support and complement domestic resource mobilization. For most middle-income countries and some low-income countries national capital markets represent a potential source of long-term financing. Because revenues from water and sanitation investments are in national currency, it is important that borrowing to support that investment be in national rather

While the precise shape of any global plan is obviously an issue for dialogue and debate, business as usual should no longer be viewed as an option

than foreign currency—one of the hard lessons of the failed privatization episodes. The problem is that market perceptions of risk and the weakness of local capital markets can both raise the cost of borrowing and diminish the flow of resources available. International support through multilateral and bilateral institutions can mitigate these effects by providing credit guarantees to utilities or municipal entities, enabling them to secure a AAA rating. This is an area that has witnessed rapid growth in recent years (see chapter 2). While a global action plan would not institutionalize credit provision, it could offer a framework for coordinating and supporting public-private partnerships, developing best practices and offering technical advice.

- *Support capacity development and national planning.* Overcoming the deficit in water and sanitation presents many of the poorest countries with acute planning problems. The legacy of fragmentation, weak institutional development and underinvestment in technical capacity building is itself a barrier to progress. In HIV/AIDS and education global initiatives have provided technical and capacity-building support as a mechanism for enhancing eligibility for development assistance. In water and sanitation the global plan framework would support sectorwide planning and mobilize resources for capacity building. As in HIV/AIDS and education, a strong vertical programme would facilitate the diffusion of best practice, accountability, performance measurements and communication to political stakeholders and civil society. It would also help to ensure that aid resources actually expand overall financing rather than substitute for government resources.

- *Improve donor coherence and coordination.* At the national level a credible global planning framework would provide an instrument for donors to align their separate programmes behind a national strategy, supporting current efforts to harmonize donor procedures and reporting requirements. It would establish a common set of

standards, reducing the transaction costs associated with multiple donor-reporting requirements—and ensuring that donors are not duplicating projects and efforts in support of their pet programmes. The global planning framework would also help to identify mismatches between aid allocation and government commitment. It would provide a multilateral vehicle to close financing gaps for countries inadequately covered by bilateral aid—as with the Global Fund and the Fast Track Initiative.

Recent developments in Sub-Saharan Africa highlight the potential for a compact on water and sanitation. Recognizing that the water and sanitation deficit is holding back advances in health, education and economic growth, the African Development Bank has established a Special Water Fund to support progress towards the Millennium Development Goal and universal provision by 2025. An indicative medium-term action plan has been developed through the African Ministers Council on Water and the New Partnership for Africa's Development for 2005–09. Through separate negotiations with eight donors the African Development Bank has secured pledges of some $50 million over periods varying from one year to three years against a target of $615 million.[73] A global framework backed by major donors would help both to reduce transaction costs and to secure financing on the scale required.

A global plan of action for water and sanitation is not an end in itself. It is a means to enhance the effectiveness of international cooperation and to build aid partnerships that can get the world on track for achieving the Millennium Development Goal and progressing towards universal access to water and sanitation. With less than a decade to go to the target date of 2015, a global plan of action could provide the predictable long-term framework for aid partnerships that could act as a catalyst for human progress, with the benefits spreading from water and sanitation to other areas of human development. While the precise shape of any global plan is obviously an issue for dialogue and debate, business as usual should no longer be viewed as an option.

2 **Water for human consumption**

"We feel it our duty to say that high-priced water is not in the interest of public health. Pure water in abundance, at a price within the reach of all, is one of the most powerful agencies for promoting the health of any community"

North Carolina Board of Health, 1898

Water for human consumption

The debate over the relative merits of public and private sector performance has been a distraction from the inadequate performance of both public and private water providers in overcoming the global water deficit

"The human right to water", declares the United Nations Committee on Economic, Social and Cultural Rights, "entitles everyone to sufficient, safe, acceptable, physically accessible and affordable water for personal and domestic use."[1] These five core attributes represent the foundations for water security. They also represent the benchmarks for a human right that is widely and systematically violated for a large section of humanity. For some 1.1 billion people, sufficient, safe, acceptable, accessible and affordable water for life is a hope for the future, not a reality for the present.

Providing universal access to water is one of the greatest development challenges facing the international community in the early 21st century. Restricted access is a brake on economic growth, a source of deep inequalities based on wealth and gender and one of the main barriers to accelerated progress towards the Millennium Development Goals (see special contribution by United Nations Secretary-General Kofi Annan). Whole countries are being held back by the lethal interaction between water insecurity and poverty. The moral, ethical and normative case for changing this picture is rooted in the recognition that clean water is a human right—and an enabling condition for attaining other rights enshrined in the Universal Declaration of Human Rights and wider international provisions. Why has progress towards water for all been so uneven and so slow?

For years the debate on that question has been dominated by exchanges about the relative merits of public and private provision. During the 1990s privatization was widely advocated as a solution to the failures of public provision. Private utilities, so the argument ran, would create efficiency gains, generate new flows of finance and provide greater accountability. While experience has been mixed, private provision did not turn out to be the magic bullet solution. In many cases the efficiency, finance and governance advantages expected of the private sector failed to materialize. At the same time, the problems in public provision are undeniable in many countries. All too often public providers combine inefficiency with unaccountability and inequity, delivering low-cost water to high-income groups and low quality service—or no service—to the poor. From the perspective of poor households, the debate over the relative merits of public and private sector performance has been a distraction from a more fundamental concern: the inadequate performance of both public and private water providers in overcoming the global water deficit.

Ultimately, it is the responsibility of national governments to secure the progressive realization of the right to water through a legislative and regulatory framework that applies to all service providers, public and private. That framework has to address two obstacles, identified in chapter 1, that have been obscured by the public-private debate.

The first obstacle is inequality. Poor households are invariably less likely to be connected to a safe water source, either because they cannot afford it or because they live beyond the

Special contribution | **Access to safe water is a fundamental human need and a basic human right**

Many people take water for granted: they turn on the tap and the water flows. Or they go to the supermarket, where they can pick from among dozens of brands of bottled water. But for more than a billion people on our planet, clean water is out of reach. And some 2.6 billion people have no access to proper sanitation. The consequences are devastating. Nearly 2 million children die every year of illnesses related to unclean water and poor sanitation—far more than the number killed as a result of violent conflict. Meanwhile, all over the world pollution, overconsumption and poor water management are decreasing the quality and quantity of water.

It was with this in mind that on World Water Day in 2004, I established an Advisory Board on Water and Sanitation. The 20-member board is composed of technical experts, eminent individuals and others with proven track records in moving the machinery of government. It was led with great skill by the late Prime Minister of Japan, Ryotaro Hashimoto, until his untimely death in July 2006. Despite that tragic loss, the board continues its efforts, working closely with the UN system, international and regional institutions, national governments, the media, the private sector and civil society at large to raise awareness, mobilize resources and promote capacity-building. The water crisis—like many issues confronting our world—can be addressed fully only through partnerships that combine national commitment with international action.

The enormous numbers we use to discuss today's water and sanitation challenges must not be allowed to obscure the individual plight faced by ordinary people. This year's *Human Development Report* provides a powerful and timely reminder that the global water crisis has a human face: a child threatened with deadly bouts of diarrhoea, a girl kept out of school to collect water or a mother denied opportunities to develop her potential by the demands of caring for relatives made sick by polluted water. The United Nations is deeply committed to this struggle. Access to safe water is a fundamental human need and a basic human right. And water and sanitation are at the heart of our quest to enable all the world's people, not just a fortunate few, to live in dignity, prosperity and peace.

Kofi A. Annan
Secretary-General
United Nations

reach of the utility network. There is also an inverse relationship between price and ability to pay: millions of the world's poorest people pay some of the world's highest prices for water, to the detriment of their productive potential and well-being. If water is a human right, it has to be a right of citizenship that is protected for all, regardless of wealth, ability to pay, gender or location.

The second obstacle is empowerment. Human rights can be a powerful vehicle for change. However, they have to be enshrined not just in normative statements, but in legislation, regulatory systems and governance systems that make governments and water providers accountable to all citizens, including the poor. Too often, the language of human rights serves as a smokescreen behind which the rights of poor people are violated by institutions that have little or no accountability.

Accelerated progress towards universal water provision is possible. Many countries have made rapid strides towards water for all, in both urban and rural areas. Innovative public-private-community partnerships have extended access to water in some of the world's most deprived areas. But advances have been piecemeal. There is an urgent need for more governments to acknowledge the water security *crisis*—and a parallel need to develop national strategies to end that crisis.

Extending water infrastructure to people without "sufficient, safe, acceptable, physically accessible and affordable" water raises difficult financing questions. Water may be a human right, but someone has to pay the capital investments and cover the operating costs—either users or taxpayers and government. Moreover, the investment needed is "lumpy", requiring upfront financing with payback periods of 20 years or more. In countries where a large part of the unserved population lives below the poverty line and where government finances are constrained, this raises issues beyond public or private provision. So, too, does the development of accountable and transparent regulatory systems that empower the poor and hold service providers to account.

With less than 10 years to go to the 2015 deadline for the Millennium Development Goals, the challenge of accelerating progress takes on a new urgency. One decade is a long time in politics. But it is a short time to develop and implement strategies to halve the number of people in the world lacking access to water. The danger is that delay will put the Millennium Development Goal target out of reach, derailing progress in other areas and perpetuating a form of deprivation that is retarding human progress in fighting extreme poverty, inequality and threats to public health (see the special contribution by Brazilian President Luiz Inácio Lula da Silva).

This chapter looks at some of the governance and financing issues that have to be addressed if the human right to water is to be extended to all. It first asks a question that goes to the heart of the violation of the human right to water: why do the poor pay more? Understanding where poor people get their water from and what market structures they operate in holds the key to answering that question—and to developing public policies that tackle the underlying inequity. The chapter turns next to the wider water governance debate and to service providers. We argue that both the private and the public sector have roles to play in delivering on the right to water, though ultimate responsibility rests with government. The final section shows that experience does not have to be a guide to future outcomes. Good policies work, and rapid progress is possible not just in urban areas but also in the rural regions that are being left behind.

Special contribution	Clean, accessible and affordable water is a human right and a foundation for economic and social development

The adoption of the Millennium Development Goals represented a victory for international cooperation and the triumph of the values of human solidarity over the doctrine of moral indifference. However, we shall be judged on the outcomes that we deliver, not on the promises that we made. And with less than a decade to go to 2015, we have to face up to an uncomfortable truth: the global community is still far from achieving the Millennium Development Goals.

Nowhere do we see this more powerfully demonstrated than in access to clean water and sanitation. None of us should be willing to tolerate a world in which 1.8 million children die each year of diarrhoea, many for want of clean water and a toilet; a world in which children are denied basic education and in which millions of people are victims of poverty and ill health.

In Brazil we have been attempting to address the water and sanitation problem as part of our broader drive to create a more just, less divided and more humane society. We have been making progress. Coverage rates for clean water have been improving in the country—and new legislation will make the utilities that provide water service more accountable to the people they serve. In sanitation the system developed in Brazil is being taken up more widely, and investments in the sector have been growing significantly.

I make these points not to hold up Brazil as a model for others to follow, or with any pretence that our problems are fully resolved. We are well aware that we need to do more to expand access to both water and sanitation among the very poor, particularly in rural areas. But the point that I want to make is that, as President, I see the Millennium Development Goal for water and sanitation as an integral part of strategies for reducing inequality, tackling poverty and ensuring wider distribution of the benefits of growth. That is why we have adopted the Millennium Development Goals as mandatory benchmarks for all government policies—including those in water and sanitation.

Human Development Report 2006 powerfully captures the costs of the global water and sanitation deficit. That deficit has to be closed more rapidly if we are to deliver on our Millennium Development Goal commitment for 2015. National governments have to do more. And the international community also has to do much more, through aid, technology transfer, capacity building and partnerships. I endorse the call to place water and sanitation at the centre of the global development agenda, within a global plan of action to meet the Millennium Development Goals. Such a measure would help to mobilize resources and focus minds on the challenge that we all have to face.

Clean, accessible and affordable water is a human right. It is also one of the foundations for economic and social development. Strengthening these foundations is not always easy: it takes political leadership and it costs money. But failing to invest political and financial capital today will carry the high price of lost opportunities for social progress and economic growth tomorrow.

Luiz Inácio Lula da Silva
President of the Federative Republic of Brazil

Why the poor pay more—and get less water

Why are some 1.1 billion people denied access to sufficient clean water to meet their basic needs? And why are so many people forced to turn to water sources that jeopardize their health and sometimes their lives?

National water scarcity metrics are an unhelpful starting point for addressing these questions. For households national per capita availability indicators are largely meaningless. Across the developing world the daily struggle to access water is a constant drain on the human, financial and physical assets of poor households, regardless of whether the country—or locality—in which they live is water scarce. As chapter 1 showed, people in the slums of Jakarta, Mumbai and Nairobi face shortages of clean water, while their neighbours in high-income suburbs have enough water not only to meet household needs but to keep their lawns green and their swimming pools topped up.

There are some obvious parallels between water insecurity and food insecurity for households. Hunger continues to afflict a large share of the world's population. Yet it is seldom an absence of food in local markets that causes famine or the more widespread problem of malnutrition. Some of the worst famines in human history have taken place without any marked change in food supply. And some of the world's highest levels of malnutrition occur today in countries that are well endowed with food: one in five people in food "self-sufficient" India is undernourished, for example (see indicator table 7). People go malnourished amidst abundant food for the same reasons that they go without access to clean water when there is more than enough to go round: unequal distribution and poverty.[2]

The concept of entitlements can help unlock the apparent paradox of scarcity amid abundance. Developed by Amartya Sen to explain the apparent paradox of hunger in the midst of plenty, entitlements can be thought of as "the set of alternative commodity bundles that can be acquired through the use of various legal channels".[3] They refer not to rights or moral claims in a normative sense but to the ability of people to secure a good or service through purchase (an exchange entitlement) or through a legally recognized and enforceable claim on a provider (a service entitlement).

The entitlements approach offers useful insights on water insecurity because it draws attention to the market structures, institutional rules and patterns of service provision that exclude the poor. It also highlights the underlying market structures that result in poor people paying far more for their water than the wealthy. People get access to water through exchange in the form of payments (to utilities, informal providers or water associations), legal claims on providers and their own labour (collecting and carrying water from streams and rivers or digging wells, for example). Whether households can meet their basic need for clean water depends partly on their own resources and partly on how public policy shapes access to infrastructure and water through investment decisions, pricing policies and legislation governing providers.

"Improved" and "unimproved" water—an illusory border between clean and dirty

In most rich countries the phrase "access to water" has a simple and widely understood meaning. Almost everybody has access to a tap in their house that is connected to a network maintained by a utility. Utilities are charged with maintaining the network and meeting water quality standards—and they are authorized to charge a stipulated price for the service that they provide. In the world's poorest countries "access to water" means something very different.

The language of international data gathering can sometimes obscure the way poor households access water. International statistics draw a distinction between "improved" and "unimproved" access. Improved encompasses three dimensions of water security: quality, proximity and quantity. For international reporting purposes people are classified as enjoying access to water if they have available at least 20 litres a day of clean water from a source less than 1 kilometre from their home. Technology broadly defines whether the source meets the criteria of being improved. In-house connections, standpipes, pumps and protected wells are all defined as improved. Water acquired from vendors and water trucks, along with water drawn from streams or unprotected wells, is not.

The distinction between improved and un-improved is clear-cut and convenient for international reporting purposes. It is also a deeply misleading guide to reality on the ground. In the real world of water-insecure households the simple border between improved and unimproved water is illusory. For millions of poor households, daily water use patterns combine recourse to improved and unimproved water. Women living in slums in the Indian city of Pune report using water from public taps (an improved source) for drinking but going to a canal for washing. Research in Cebu, Philippines, found five patterns of water use among households not connected to the main water network (table 2.1). In urban slums and rural villages poor households might draw water from a protected well or standpipe for part of the year but then be forced to draw water from rivers or streams during the dry season. The configuration of water used in any one day will depend on factors ranging from price to availability to perceptions of quality.

While the global reporting system may provide useful insights, it is something of a statistical artefact. Consider Jakarta. Global reporting systems indicate that almost 90% of urban residents in Indonesia have access to improved water. However, household surveys show that almost two in every three people in Jakarta use multiple sources of water, including shallow and deep wells (both protected and unprotected), standpipes (improved) and water vendors (unimproved). The three most frequently cited combinations were groundwater and vendors, utility and groundwater, and utility and vendors (figure 2.1).

Why this diversity of demand? Use of water sources varies temporally and seasonally, due to changes in water quality and pressure. Low pressure and irregularity of supply in the piped

network mean that households in Jakarta seek a backup source—usually a shallow well. But in many urban areas groundwater cannot be used for drinking because of salination or pollution. Groundwater is used only for cleaning or washing or to reduce water costs to more affordable levels.

What emerges from research across a large group of countries is that patterns of water use are far more complex and dynamic than the static picture presented in global reporting systems. Real-life patterns constantly adjust to take into account concerns of water quality, proximity, price and reliability. In Bangalore, India, close to a

Table 2.1	Cebu, Philippines: patterns of water use among households not connected to the main water network		
Main source of water	**Share of population (%)**	**Main use**	**Comments**
Type 1 Vendors	4	All purposes (drinking, cooking, washing)	Most of these users live in isolated areas and have no other choice available
Type 2 Public well	34	All purposes	—
Type 3 Well	15	About half use it for all purposes	About half use it for nonpotable purposes only and get drinking water from a neighbour connected to the water system
Type 4 Public standpipe	8	Two-thirds use it for all purposes	One-third reserve it for drinking, using water from a public well for washing and laundry. A few occasionally buy water from a neighbour connected to the water system.
Type 5 Neighbour connected to water system	38	About half use it for all purposes	About half use it only for drinking and cooking, relying on a public well for other purposes.

Source: Verdeil 2003a.

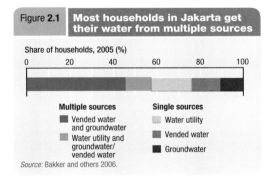

Figure 2.1   Most households in Jakarta get their water from multiple sources

Share of households, 2005 (%)

0   20   40   60   80   100

Multiple sources
- Vended water and groundwater
- Water utility and groundwater/ vended water

Single sources
- Water utility
- Vended water
- Groundwater

Source: Bakker and others 2006.

Inequalities based on
wealth and location
play a central role in
structuring water markets

third of households within the area served by the Bangalore Water Supply and Sewerage Board use public taps. Within this group 7% have no other source of water. The remainder use water from public taps and groundwater along with the water piped into the household. More than half of these households report having access to network water only three days a week on average. Daily supply is about seven hours during the rainy season and four hours during the dry season.[4]

Beneath the complex patterns of water use in most cities in the developing world, inequalities based on wealth and location play a central role in structuring water markets. As chapter 1 showed, there are deep divisions within countries in access to water sources categorized as improved. Being poor dramatically increases the likelihood of dependence on an unimproved water source—and the associated health risks attached to that dependence. More than 70% of people lacking access to improved water survive on less than $2 a day, and about half of this group survive on less than $1 a day. In many countries income is a strong predictor both of access to improved water and of the type of technology used to collect water.

Getting water from multiple providers

In the developed world people usually get their water from a single provider. In most of the developing world people get water from a bewildering array of service providers. The primary network, usually operated by a single citywide utility, functions alongside a wide variety of providers, many of them intermediaries between the utility and the household. Any consideration of water access has to start by looking at the patchwork quilt of provision.

Water utilities are authorized by governments to deliver water through the network of pumps and pipes that constitute the city's formal water system. The main market for these utilities is usually household users with pipes in their homes, and businesses. But connection rates vary widely—and are heavily skewed towards high-income neighbourhoods. In cities such as Dar es Salam, Tanzania, and Ougadougou, Burkina Faso, fewer than 30% of households are connected.

For many poor households the point of contact with the utility network is not a private household tap but a standpipe. Since most standpipe users are from low-income households, this source is a water lifeline for poor urban households across the cities of the developing world. Some 30% of households report collecting water from standpipes in Nouakachott, Mauritania, and 49% in Bamako, Mali. In Dakar, Senegal, standpipes serve half the population without private piped water.[5] Similarly, in Ougadougou utility provision covers an estimated 80% of households, with standpipes accounting for two-thirds of the total.

Similar patterns emerge in other regions. When poor people in South Asia have access to piped water, it is far more likely to mean access to a public tap or standpipe than to water piped into the home. For instance, in the Indian city of Bangalore the Water Supply and Sewerage Board reaches about 80% of the population, about 73% of which have private taps. However, the poorest households use public taps on a regular basis. For the richest households that share falls to 3%.[6] In Kathmandu, Nepal, the municipal water utility reaches about three-quarters of the population, but half of the poor depend on public taps.[7]

Standpipes can be thought of as a resale outlet for utility water. These outlets can be managed by neighbourhood committees or other local organizations or by individuals under contract with a municipal provider. But in almost all cases standpipes are just the tip of a resale iceberg. In many cities they do not reach all areas, with peri-urban locations, slums and more remote districts often underserved. Even in areas that are reached, supplies are sometimes insufficient and erratic, with rationing applied during dry seasons. Water vendors are an important link between poor households and the network. Some vendors operate from kiosks, reselling water acquired from truckers, who have access to piped water or utility standpipes. In the Ghanaian capital, Accra, and in Guayaquil, Ecuador, large water tanker fleets set off every morning for low-income settlements, where they sell to households and intermediaries. Other vendors deliver water from bicycles or donkey-drawn carts to areas that have no connection to the utility network. Precise figures are hard to come by, but for Sub-Saharan African cities an estimated 10%–30% of low-income households purchase water from neighbours and water kiosks.[8]

In sum, poor urban households with limited or no access to the formal network get their water from several sources. Apart from rivers and streams, these sources include a variety of vendors such as water truckers, private standpipe operators, water kiosk operators and agents delivering water. While the debate continues over public or private water provision, in the real world poor households are already operating in highly commercialized private water markets—markets that deliver (often poor quality) water at exceptionally high prices.

Climbing the price ladder in urban slums

Water resellers extend the coverage of the piped network. By bringing water to people they provide a service that produces important benefits for households—but they do so at a price. That price rises with distance from the utility, as defined by the number of intermediaries between the network and the end consumer.

Having a regular supply of clean water piped into the household is the optimal type of provision for human development. Cross-country experience suggests that households with water delivered through one tap on a household plot (or within 100 metres) typically use about 50 litres of water a day, rising to 100 litres or more for households with multiple taps.[9] Household-level research in urban areas of Kenya, Tanzania and Uganda found that families with piped water in the home used an average of three times as much water as families without piped water.[10] Water in the home also eliminates the need for women and young girls to collect water.

Household connections to a utility also offer financial benefits. In unit price terms, utility water is by far the lowest cost option. Because of economies of scale once the network is in place, the marginal cost of delivering each additional unit of water falls sharply. Subsidies are another important price-reducing mechanism: utilities are usually the gatekeeper for a wide range of direct and indirect subsidies that keep the price of water well below cost.

Every step removed from the household tap option adds a twist to the price spiral (figure 2.2). Water vendors often act as a link between unconnected households and the utility. In some cases water is purchased from the utility and sold on to households. Private standpipe operators are an example. In other cases water is purchased from the utility and sold to intermediaries, who in turn sell to households. In Accra, for example, private water tanker companies purchase utility water and sell it on to a wide range of intermediaries who deliver water to slum neighbourhoods.

As water passes through the marketing chain, prices ratchet up. Water delivered through vendors and carters is often 10–20 times more costly than water provided through a utility (table 2.2). In Barranquilla, Colombia, the average price of water is $0.55 per cubic metre from the utility and $5.50 from truckers. Similarly, in the slums of Accra and Nairobi people buying water from vendors typically spend 8 times as much per litre as households with piped water supplied by utilities.

Large price differences are sometimes interpreted as evidence of profiteering, but that interpretation is flawed. In some cases large-scale water trucking companies or kiosk operators might be in a position to generate excessive profits. But the underlying causes of water

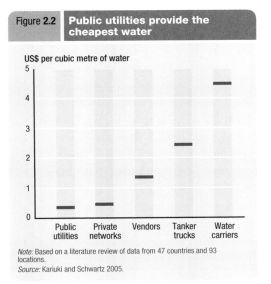

Figure **2.2** Public utilities provide the cheapest water

US$ per cubic metre of water

Note: Based on a literature review of data from 47 countries and 93 locations.
Source: Kariuki and Schwartz 2005.

In the real world poor households are already operating in highly commercialized private water markets—markets that deliver (often poor quality) water at exceptionally high prices

| Table **2.2** | Independent water providers: important but expensive actors in Latin American cities | | | |

City	Households served by independent providers (%)	Average price (US$ per cubic metre)		Type of provider
		Independent providers	Utility	
Cordoba, Argentina	15–20	1.25–2.50	0.54	Network
Asuncion, Paraguay	30	0.30–0.40	0.40	Small network
Barranquilla, Colombia	20–25	5.50–6.40	0.55	Truckers
Guatemala City	>32	2.70–4.50	0.42	Truckers
Lima, Peru	26–30	2.4	0.28	Truckers

Source: Solo 2003.

price inflation between the utility and poor households can be traced to wider structural causes. Resale prices rise with distance, because transport costs are high for informal slums and peri-urban areas that are far from resale points or located in hard to reach places. They also rise with the number of transfers between intermediaries, as each agent adds its profit margin.

Standpipe users are not immune to the price spiral. While standpipes may be used overwhelmingly by poor households with the least ability to pay, prices are usually a multiple of those charged for water piped into households. In Dakar, one study found that users of a standpipe were paying 3.5 times the social tariff rate applied to low-income families connected to the network.[11] This is not uncommon. Evidence from other countries—including Benin, Kenya, Mali and Uganda—shows that people who buy water at standpipes typically face the same prices as those paid by high-volume consumers. These are twice those for basic domestic water use in Benin, three times in Mali and five times in Côte d'Ivoire and Mauritania.[12]

Concern over transforming water into a commodity has been a powerful reaction to privatization and, more broadly, to the commercialization of water utilities. At one level, that concern is justified. As a source of life, water should not be treated as a commodity. Nor should it be traded in markets governed by the same principles as, say, markets for luxury cars or toys. Yet the hard fact remains that millions of the world's poorest and most vulnerable people are already operating in markets that treat water as a commodity and that skew prices against them.

Why tariffs matter

Water tariffs shape the access to water of poor households. Most governments regulate tariffs to achieve a range of equity and efficiency objectives. They are designed to provide water that is affordable to households and to generate enough revenues to cover part or all of the costs of delivery. The problem in many cases is that tariff structures intended to enhance equity have the opposite effect.

There are important variations across countries in tariff design (figure 2.3). In some cases—Dhaka, Bangladesh, is an example—a *flat rate* is applied to all users, whatever volume of water they use. Such structures, which provide no incentives for water conservation, are commonly applied where utilities have little capacity to monitor use through meters. More typical is the *block tariff* system, in which prices rise on a tiered basis along with the volume of water used. Both the number of tiers and the steepness of the price increases across tariff blocks can vary.

Rising block tariffs aim to achieve several public policy goals. A low or zero tariff applied to the first block can enhance affordability. For example, Durban, South Africa, provides 25 litres of water a day free of charge[13]—the lifeline or social tariff—with a steep increase above this level. This is an important part of the legislative framework for acting on the right to water discussed in chapter 1. Higher tiers aim at enabling utilities to increase efficiency, by creating disincentives for overuse, and at mobilizing revenues to cover costs. Block tariffs thus create the potential for aligning revenues with the costs of service provision, facilitating a sustainable financing model, while at the same time providing water for basic needs at below the cost of operations and maintenance.

Many countries apply a low tariff for an initial volume of water, though few countries follow South Africa's policy of free water. The size of the baseline tariff and of the increments between blocks varies across countries. Increments are particularly high in countries such as Burkina Faso and Senegal, while Bangalore, India, has limited price increases up to a high level of use.

Under the right conditions rising block tariffs can enhance water access and equity. But outcomes depend on a range of factors. In many utilities tariffs are set far below the levels needed to meet the overall costs of operation and maintenance. In effect, this delivers a subsidy to all households with private tap connections. On the other side of the balance sheet, the shortfall between revenue and cost will be reflected in transfers from government, rising debt, reduced spending on maintenance or a combination of the three.

Whether utility subsidies are progressive depends on the profile of households connected to the utilities: the lower the proportion of poor households connected, the less progressive the subsidy. Providing a subsidized social tier is an effective strategy for reaching low-income households only if they are connected. And cross-subsidies from high-consumption (and high-income) to low-consumption (low-income) households are effective only if a sufficient number of customers use the higher blocks. An obvious danger is that excessively high prices will drive users to alternative sources of provision.

Block tariffs can create structural disadvantages for the poor. This is because the private operators and intermediaries that supply households without private connections typically purchase water in bulk at the top price tiers. Standpipe operators, water vendors and truckers are thus reselling the highest cost water sold by utilities. Similarly, when poor households group together to share a metered connection, a common arrangement in many countries, their aggregate consumption level pushes them into the higher price tiers.

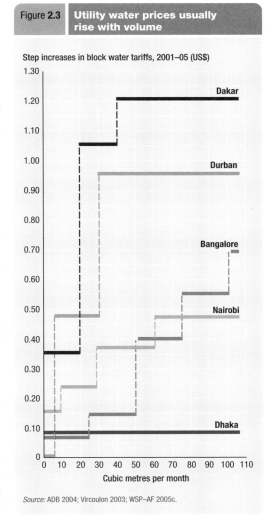

Figure **2.3** **Utility water prices usually rise with volume**

Step increases in block water tariffs, 2001–05 (US$)

Cubic metres per month

Source: ADB 2004; Vircoulon 2003; WSP–AF 2005c.

If informal water markets are so unfavourable to the poor, why not switch demand from intermediaries to formal network providers? Connection fees provide one part of the explanation. These vary widely but average about $41 in South Asia and $128 in Latin America. In Sub-Saharan African countries such as Benin, Kenya and Uganda connection fees exceed $100.[14] And the fees generally rise with distance from the network. For poor households without access to credit markets, costs on this scale present an impenetrable barrier. The average cost of connection for households in the poorest 20% of the population ranges from about three months' income in Manila to six months in Kenya and more than a year in Uganda.

Legal barriers are often added to the financial ones. Many utilities, to secure returns on their

Water is a sector in which the poor and the nonpoor have a shared interest in investment to expand the network and improve efficiency to ensure regular supply

investments to expand the network, will provide water only to households with formal property titles. Yet more than a billion people live in formally unauthorized urban and peri-urban areas in developing countries. With 80%–90% of population growth expected in urban areas in developing countries, this is a service delivery constraint that will tighten over time. Abidjan, Côte d'Ivoire, the most prosperous city in West Africa, has more than 80 unauthorized residential areas. An estimated quarter of the population of Ouagadougou resides in unauthorized areas, making them ineligible to receive basic water services.[15] As urbanization draws more people from the countryside into informal settlements, failure to recognize residency rights could become an increasingly important barrier to the realization of the Millennium Development Goal for water. Indeed, this problem is already implicated in the falling urban coverage rates for some cities (see chapter 1).

Beyond the immediate barriers stand more fundamental constraints. Compared with rich countries, in many developing countries the formal water network has limited reach. Water and sewerage networks were not created to reach

the poorest parts of cities or to provide universal access (box 2.1). Rather, they were designed to cater to the interests of elites.

Efforts to break out of the enclave model inherited from the colonial period have met with varying degrees of success. But there are some recurrent problems. Many utilities have been locked in a cycle of underfinancing, undermaintenance and underexpansion. With tariff revenues falling far short of the level needed to maintain the network, there is no money to finance expansion to unserved households on the scale required. Many developing countries also face an acute form of the dilemma faced by rich countries more than a century ago: how to extend access to poor households without raising tariffs to prohibitive levels. Unlike rich countries during the crucial phase of their development, most developing countries lack financial resources to resolve the dilemma through public finance, even if they have the political will to do it.

While this section has focussed on the specific problems facing poor households, they are not the only constituency affected. In many developing countries households connected to utilities may have access to nominally cheap water, but they face acute problems in the regularity of supply. Shortages have pushed a growing number of middle-income households into informal water markets and self-provision. Perhaps more than in any other area, water is a sector in which the poor and the nonpoor have a shared interest in investment to expand the network and improve efficiency to ensure regular supply.

Rural poor—the last in line

As in urban areas, so in rural areas, safe, accessible and affordable water brings a wide range of benefits for health, education and livelihoods. Gains for gender equity tend to be even more pronounced in rural areas because women and young girls spend more time collecting water, especially during the dry season. For gains in human development, and improvements in the lives of the poor, investments in rural water have few rivals. Yet in most developing countries rural areas have far lower rates of coverage. Why

---

Box 2.1	The burden of history: many networks were not designed to reach the poor

Historical legacy does not determine the state of today's water and sanitation infrastructure in developing countries—but it weighs heavily. In Europe and North America the political goal was to achieve rapid progress towards universal access. That goal drove financing and technology. Not so in much of the developing world.

Consider Lagos, Nigeria. At the beginning of the 20th century the European business and political elite in the city invested in an urban water and sanitation infrastructure. But this was concentrated in wealthy enclaves. Early efforts to extend the infrastructure to poorer districts were swiftly abandoned in the face of rising costs and in favour of a strategy of segregation. Similar patterns of inclusion and exclusion characterized cities from Puebla to Jakarta and Algiers. This development model failed to achieve universal access for the public good and instead generated segregation and elite havens of water security.

Financing followed a similar model. In Latin America elites financed investments in water and sanitation through taxes, with tariffs set below operating costs. As one author describes it, it was a "system running structural deficits, operat[ing] on ad hoc, piecemeal and emergency interventions, loans and subsidies from the national, state or international lending bodies. From the very beginning, the high cost of urban engineering works required high levels of (usually external) financing, while the political and economic forces demanded low water prices" (Swyngedouw, p. 37).

Source: Gandy 2006; Bakker and others 2006; Swyngedouw 2006; Chikhr Saïdi 2001.

has the rural-urban divide outlined in chapter 1 been so difficult to bridge?

Financial cost is not the most obvious barrier. The per capita costs of providing clean water are highest in urban areas and in sparsely populated rural areas, but on average expanding coverage costs less in rural areas than in high-density urban areas. Three distinctive features of rural water provision help to explain the low coverage:

- *Local scarcity.* At a national level water scarcity is seldom a problem, but the rural poor often live in dry areas subject to seasonal shortages. In northern Kenya, the Sahel region and drought-prone areas of Gujarat in India wells run dry for long periods. In semi-arid areas of western Nigeria water collection times increase from four to seven hours in the dry season. Time-poverty is one consequence of seasonal scarcity (box 2.2).

- *Communities and providers.* In most rural areas communities provide, maintain and expand water systems. Especially in arid or semi-arid areas, this requires high levels of community mobilization. Local government bodies, rather than large municipal providers, are often gatekeepers for boreholes and handpumps. The accountability of these bodies, and the strength of community water user associations, influence coverage.

- *Politics and poverty.* Beyond financing and technical questions, rural communities carry the twin burden of high poverty and low political influence. Highly dispersed rural populations, especially in marginal areas, have little influence over the institutional choices that shape decisions and set priorities for resource allocation.

Most poor rural households get their water from a variety of sources. Unimproved sources—lakes, streams, rivers—figure prominently. Protected village wells are the most common improved water sources. Efforts to expand coverage

---

| Box 2.2 | Water, gender and time-poverty |

One of the greatest returns to improved access to water is in the time savings for women and girls and the expansion of their choices. Water collection is part of a gender division of labour that reinforces inequality within households, contributes to time-poverty and retards the human development prospects for a large section of the world's people.

Social and cultural norms influence the household division of labour. In developing countries looking after children, caring for the sick and elderly, preparing food and collecting water and firewood are tasks dominated by women. Norms in this case translate into unequal working hours between men and women: time surveys in Benin, Madagascar, Mauritius and South Africa point to weekly differences ranging from five to seven hours.

Fetching water is part of the gender inequality. In rural Benin girls ages 6–14 spend an average of one hour a day collecting water compared with 25 minutes for their brothers. In Malawi there are large variations in the amount of time allocated for water collection based on seasonal factors, but women consistently spend four to five times longer than men on this task.

Why does this matter for human development? Time is an important asset for the development of capabilities. Excessive time demands for essential labour lead to exhaustion, reduce the time available for rest and child care and limit choice—they reduce the substantive freedoms that women enjoy. They also pose no-win choice dilemmas. Should a woman care for a sick child or spend two hours collecting water? Should girls be kept home from school to collect water, freeing time for mothers to grow food or generate income? Or should they be sent to school to gain the skills and assets to escape poverty?

Time-poverty also contributes to income poverty. It reduces the time available for participation in income generation, limits the scope for women to take advantage of market opportunities and impedes their ability to expand capabilities and skills, reducing future economic returns.

| Women face a heavier time burden collecting water, particularly in rural areas (minutes per day) |

	Benin, 1998		Ghana, 1998/99		Guinea, 2002/03		Madagascar, 2001	
	Women	Men	Women	Men	Women	Men	Women	Men
Urban	16	6	33	31	10	3	16	10
Rural	62	16	44	34	28	6	32	8
National	45	12	41	33	23	5	27	9

Source: Wodon and Blackden 2006.

Easier access to safe
water reduces demands
on women's time and
opens up income-
generating opportunities

have focussed on boreholes and pumps. More than in urban areas, success depends on the willingness and capacity of communities to contribute labour and finance for maintenance—and on the responsiveness of service providers to demands for appropriate technology.

As in urban areas, data on improved technologies can overstate real coverage by a considerable margin. Inadequate maintenance of infrastructure, insufficient training for repair works and inadequate financial resources for operation have eroded the rural water supply systems in many countries. A survey in Ethiopia, to take just one example, found that 29% of handpumps and 33% of mechanized boreholes in rural areas were not functioning because of maintenance problems.[16] In Rwanda an estimated one-third of the rural water infrastructure requires urgent rehabilitation. Beyond mechanical factors the main source of breakdown in rural areas has been the failure to involve rural communities—especially women—in selecting, siting and managing improved technologies.

If safe water is often scarce in rural areas, free safe water is an even rarer commodity. The use of village water points and water committees requires contributions of labour (digging wells) and cash to cover the maintenance and capital costs of pumps and well materials. In a typical cycle a village water committee raises funds to

construct a borehole and purchase a handpump. Rights to draw water require payment of an initial membership fee and a monthly fee to cover the costs of operations and maintenance.

The human and economic costs of inadequate coverage in rural areas are high, reflecting the importance of water to human development. The health benefits from improving coverage include reductions in the incidence of diarrhoea and other diseases. In the Indian state of Kerala research following implementation of seven rural water projects found that the incidence of waterborne diseases fell by half in the five years after the construction of deep wells, with no change in nonproject areas.[17] The same survey also reported a decrease in household expenditure on water purchased from vendors. About half the families covered by the programme were spending on average 12% of a poverty-threshold income to purchase water from vendors. Following implementation, the average fell to 4%, releasing resources for expenditure in other areas.

Apart from direct financial gains, easier access to safe water reduces demands on women's time and opens up income-generating opportunities. In Sri Lanka rural households in one donor-supported programme reported saving 30 hours a month—three days' work in a typical village.[18]

Managing the network for efficiency and equity

Water networks are among any country's most precious assets. How those assets are managed and operated is critical to human development, especially in countries facing grave water security challenges. In many of the world's poorest countries utility networks reach only a small fraction of the very poorest people. Chronic underfinancing, low efficiency and a limited capital base for expanding the network ensure that the system remains an enclave.

In recent years the balance of private and public sector involvement in water has been vigourously debated. Some argue that increased private sector involvement is an automatic route to more and better services per dollar, along with greater accountability and transparency. Others claim that water is an essential public good and that the human right to water is fundamentally at odds with market principles.

Evidence points to some more prosaic conclusions. Private involvement is not the bright line between success and failure in water provision. Nor is it a guarantor of market efficiency. Water provision through a network is a natural monopoly, reducing the scope for efficiency gains through competition and making effective regulation to secure consumer interests an imperative. The key role of regulation in this context is to create competitive pressures, set prices and quality standards, establish targets for investment and maintenance and ensure that the benefits of efficiency gains are passed on to consumers. Under the right institutional conditions the private sector can provide the technologies, skills and resources to enhance access to water. But creating these conditions through effective regulatory institutions is a complex affair that goes beyond passing laws and adopting models from other countries.

Decisions about the appropriate public-private mix have to be taken case by case on local values and conditions. The challenge for all providers, public and private, is to extend access and overcome the price disadvantage faced by poor households.

Public providers—key to provision and financing

Current debates on water provision have a long history. At the start of the 19th century in Europe and the United States, private companies were the major providers of water. The idea that the state should stay out of service provision in the interests of keeping taxes low was widely accepted. By the end of the century private operators had been displaced by municipal providers or were subject to stringent regulation.[19] Water was seen as too important to public health, national prosperity and human progress to be left to companies whose objective was to maximize profit rather than to optimize social returns.

More recently, the roles of public and private providers have been a source of much heat in public debate, but considerably less light. In some respects the intensity of the debate has been curiously out of step with reality. While

the number of people served by private water companies has grown—from about 51 million in 1990 to nearly 300 million in 2002—public water companies account for more than 70% of total investment globally, and fewer than 3% of people in developing countries receive water or sanitation services that are fully or partially private.[20] In Brazil 25 of 27 state capitals are served by public companies, and only 2 by partially privatized companies.[21]

The weakness of public providers in many countries is clearly part of the problem in water provision. The source of that weakness varies, though poor governance and the infrastructure decay caused by underinvestment are recurrent themes. Governance structures have a central role. Many public utilities operate a top-down service provision model that is neither transparent nor responsive to the needs of users. To the extent that any accountability operates, it is towards political power brokers, not the communities being served (or bypassed) by the utility. Operations, in many cases, combine inequity with inefficiency. Much of the water that public utilities provide is unaccounted for, either because it leaks out of pipes that have not been maintained or because of defective billing systems.

Low revenue in turn fuels a vicious cycle of deteriorating assets, water losses, low revenue collection, low investment and further infrastructure deterioration. In cities such as Delhi, Dhaka[22] and Mexico City[23] about 40% of the water pumped into the system leaks out of corroded pipes or is sold illegally. Lost water translates into lost revenues for maintaining or expanding the network. However, none of these problems are confined to the public sector. Private utilities in the United Kingdom, for example, have been repeatedly fined by regulators for failing to reduce leakage levels. Nor is underinvestment a source of inefficiency only in poor countries. The US Environmental Protection Agency estimates that $68 billion will be needed over the next two decades just to restore and maintain existing water utility assets in major US cities.[24]

Utility pricing is a central part of the financing problem in many developing countries. Tariffs are often set to cover only a small part of

The challenge for all providers, public and private, is to extend access and overcome the price disadvantage faced by poor households

operating costs. A study of Asian water utilities at the end of the 1990s found that operating income in 35 of 49 providers did not meet operations and maintenance requirements.[25] Without public investment to fill the gap, this is a prescription for decay. Increased cost-recovery from households with the capacity to pay would mobilize revenue for maintenance and associated efficiency gains, while generating funds to support demand among households that are unable to pay. But all too often public utilities are more concerned with providing cheap water to the wealthy than affordable water to the poor.

Water utilities cannot be considered in isolation. How well public providers meet standards for efficiency, equity and accountability is conditioned by the wider political culture of service provision—and by wider public investment policies. In most rich countries the capital investment for infrastructure in water comes from public investment or from private investment backed by government guarantees. In many developing countries inefficiencies in the water sectors can be traced in part to chronic underfinancing of the network over a very long period.

Acknowledging the failures of some public utilities does not imply that success requires private sector provision. Some public utilities in developing countries meet or surpass the operating standards of the best performing private companies. Public utilities in Singapore lose less water than private utilities in the United Kingdom. In Porto Alegre, Brazil, utility reform produced gains in efficiency and democratic accountability (box 2.3). The city's municipally owned water department provides households with universal access to safe, affordable water—and dramatically improved revenue collection rates and reduced water losses. Political and financial autonomy and transparency have contributed critically to success.

As Porto Alegre demonstrates, utility reform can enhance performance without changes in ownership. This is not an isolated example. In Sri Lanka the National Water Supply and Drainage Board emerged as an efficient provider

---

Box 2.3 **Public services can work—Porto Alegre's Department of Water and Sewerage shows how**

With 1.4 million people Porto Alegre, the capital of the state of Rio Grande do Sul in Brazil, has one of the lowest infant mortality rates in the country (14 deaths per 1,000 live births in a country where the national average is 65) and a human development index comparable to that in rich countries. Effective municipal governance in water supply and sanitation has played a big part in this success story.

Municipal water providers have achieved universal access to water. Prices for water—$0.30 a litre—are among the lowest in the country. Meanwhile, wastewater treatment has increased from 2% in 1990 to almost 30% today, with a target of 77% in five years. Efficiency indicators are similar to those in the world's best performing private companies. The ratio of employees to household connections, one widely used efficiency indicator, is 3:1,000. That ratio is 20 for Delhi and 5 for private companies in Manila.

The operating conditions of the Municipal Department of Water and Sewerage (DMAE), wholly owned by the municipality of Porto Alegre, help to explain the success:

- A separate legal entity, it enjoys operational and financial autonomy.
- Ring-fenced, it receives no subsidies and is financially self-reliant.
- Financially independent, it can borrow for investment without municipal support.

The operating mandate combines social and commercial objectives. The utility pursues a no-dividend policy: all profits are reinvested into the system. Its tax exemption allows it to keep water rates low. And it is required to invest at least a quarter of its annual revenue in water infrastructure.

Why has Porto Alegre achieved universal access despite a high concentration of poverty among its customers? Partly because prices are low on average and partly because low-income households, welfare institutions and residents of state and municipal housing projects for the disadvantaged are charged a social rate less than half the basic rate. The utility's governance structure combines regulatory oversight with a high level of public participation. The general director is appointed by the mayor, but a deliberative council—made up of engineers, medical staff, environmentalists and representatives of a wide range of civil society organizations—exercises management oversight and has the power to rule on all major decisions.

Porto Alegre's participatory budget process provides a form of direct democracy with 44 public meetings each year in 16 areas of the city. Participants vote on their priorities and hear submissions from managers in six core areas, one of them water. As a prelude billboards are placed in public places showing actual spending against planned spending, as well as the investment plan that follows the process. The public scrutiny of the municipal budget and the priority attached to water create strong incentives for high quality service delivery.

Source: Viero 2003; Maltz 2005.

following governance reforms that improved coordination among agencies and enhanced financial performance.[26] Water utilities in India are sometimes uniformly characterized as inefficient. But in Hyderabad the water utility has increased coverage and improved performance in revenue collection, repairs and service provision.[27] In many countries there are large variations in efficiency within the public sector. In Colombia, for example, the utilities serving Bogota and Medellin meet high standards of efficiency, while public municipal companies serving towns on the Caribbean coast operate at the other end of the efficiency spectrum.

What then are the key requirements for utility reform? While circumstances vary, successful public utilities typically operate in a public policy environment that meets four key conditions:

- Ring-fencing and financial autonomy to guard against political interference in the allocation of resources.
- Participatory and transparent policymaking to support accountability.
- Separation of the regulator and the service provider, with the regulator overseeing and publishing well defined performance standards.

- Adequate public financing for the expansion of the network, along with a national strategy for progressing towards water for all.

These conditions are as relevant to the governance framework for private companies as they are for public utilities. As argued below, creating these conditions is difficult, though the empowerment of citizens through a legislative framework for reform can play a critical role.

Private providers—beyond concessions

Introducing competition for the right to operate the main water network has been central to reform in many developing countries. The creation of concessions has been at the core of the debate. However, private involvement stretches across a far broader spectrum.

The diversity in public-private partnerships cautions against lumping all private sector involvement under the general heading of "privatization".

The terms on which the private sector enters water markets are important on several levels. A complex array of market arrangements are possible (table 2.3). These arrangements have implications for ownership only in the case of

The diversity in public-private partnerships cautions against lumping all private sector involvement under the general heading of "privatization"

2

Water for human consumption

Table 2.3 | **Private participation in water networks takes many forms...**

Option	Ownership	Management	Investment	Risk	Duration (years)	Examples
Service contract	Public	Shared	Public	Public	1–2	Finland, Maharashtra (India)
Management contract	Public	Private	Public	Public	3–5	Johannesburg (South Africa), Monagas (Venezuela), Atlanta (United States)
Lease (affermage)	Public	Private	Public	Shared	8–15	Abidjan (Côte d'Ivoire), Dakar (Senegal)
Concession	Public	Private	Private	Private	20–30	Manila (Philippines), Buenos Aires (Argentina), Durban (South Africa), La Paz-El Alto (Bolivia), Jakarta (Indonesia)
Privatization (state divestiture)	Private	Private	Private	Private	Unlimited	Chile, United Kingdom

Source: Jaglin 2005.

In developing countries a narrow and often dilapidated infrastructure, low levels of connection and high levels of poverty heighten tensions between commercial viability and delivery of affordable water to all

full privatization. More broadly, the terms on which governments contract with the private sector influence management structures, investment patterns and the distribution of risk. Concessions transfer management, risk and responsibility for investment to the private sector, while other public-private arrangements involve contracting-out some aspects of management or operations of water networks.

Privatization (full state divestiture) is rare

Few countries—France is one—have a long history of private water management. Chile privatized in the 1980s, but only after access to water was almost universal. Since then, the country has been a strong performer in both efficiency and equity. The United Kingdom was a late privatizer, with public utilities sold off at the end of the 1980s—ushering in an interest in water privatization in many developing countries.

The record since then has been mixed. Over the decade following privatization water companies in the United Kingdom made profits well in excess of predictions, paying dividends to shareholders well above average stock market returns. This drained an undervalued asset of scarce capital resources needed for development. The absence of any explicit mechanism for sharing the benefits of performance gains between shareholders and consumers—and what were seen as excessive profit margins—brought criticism. It also led to the development of a strong, independent regulatory body to protect consumer interests, establish investment targets and monitor efficiency gains.[28] However, serious problems remain as a result of inadequate investment and high levels of water losses. The UK experience shows that the design and sequencing of regulatory reform are difficult, even in countries with a highly developed institutional capacity. In the rush to sell off public assets the public interest suffered as a result of privatization, though enhanced regulation has addressed some of the failures.

Concessions have been widely tried and tested, with mixed results

In the 1990s concessions were the main conduit for private investment in water, with foreign and domestic private companies assuming

responsibility for financing and running the systems. Some concessions improved efficiency, reduced water losses, increased supply, extended meters and revenue collection and enlarged coverage. In Morocco, which created four concessions between 1997 and 2002, coverage increased (the concessions now serve about half the population), as did consumer satisfaction scores.[29] The East Manila concession expanded the proportion of population receiving 24-hour supply from about 15%–20% in 1997 to more than 60% in 2000 and expanded overall coverage from 65% to 88%. As part of a national strategy of water for all South Africa transferred a water utility in Durban to a concession. Despite concerns about equity, there has been marked improvement in access among poor households.

Set against these cases are some spectacularly high profile failures.[30] In Cochabamba, Bolivia, a concession agreement failed in 2000 in the face of political protests. In Argentina a 30-year concession agreement collapsed with the country's economy in 2001. The same fate befell the concession granted for West Manila, which was terminated in 2003. In 2004 a concession in Jakarta ended in a court dispute between municipal authorities and the company. Enthusiasm for concessions has now cooled to the point of reluctance by the private sector to enter into any deals. Major international companies such as Suez, the world's biggest water company, Veolia Environnement and Thames Water are pulling back from concessions in developing countries, sometimes in the face of pressure from government and regulators. For example, Thames Water withdrew from the operation of a plant in China in 2004, two years after the Chinese government ruled that the rate of return was too high.[31]

So what went wrong? When private companies enter developed country markets as providers, they inherit a large infrastructure (paid for by past public investments) that provides universal access in a market defined by fairly high average incomes. In developing countries a narrow and often dilapidated infrastructure, low levels of connection and high levels of poverty heighten tensions between commercial viability and delivery of affordable water to all. Three common failures, linked to regulation, financial sustainability and transparency in contracting, can be traced to these constraints (box 2.4):

- *Network expansion.* A primary objective for governments entering concessions has been to expand networks. In the Buenos Aires concession the number of connections increased but at rates lower than stipulated in the contract. Progress was slowest in the poorest areas of the city.[32] In Jakarta three-quarters of new connections under the concession were for middle- and upper-income households and government and commercial enterprises.
- *Tariff renegotiation.* Water tariffs are intensely political. From a commercial perspective revenues from tariffs generate profits for shareholders and capital for future investment. But tariff policies designed to optimize profits can minimize social

welfare and generate political unrest. In Cochabamba the concessionaire increased tariffs to transfer part of the cost of expanding the infrastructure to current water users, with explosive consequences. In Buenos Aires tariffs were first reduced and then increased six times between 1993 and 2002, almost doubling in real terms as the private operator sought to combine profitability and delivery of targets.

- *Financing.* The lumpiness of capital investments in water makes credit critical for network expansion. Large external debts were a feature of the concession operations in West Manila and Buenos Aires. In Buenos Aires investments were financed mainly through borrowing and accumulated earnings, with the equity stake accounting for less than 5%. With external borrowing in dollars and

---

Box 2.4   What went wrong with concessions? Three failures and three lessons

The domino effect of collapsing concessions has fuelled a heated debate about the past, present and future role of the private sector in water provision. While the factors behind the collapses have varied, there are instructive lessons to be derived from three key cases:

- *Cochabamba.* The 1999 agreement under which the Bolivian government awarded a 40-year concession to a consortium of foreign companies remains a point of reference. Under the 1999 Drinking Water and Sanitation Law the government authorized privatization of water provision and ended subsidies. Not only did customers have to pay more for their water, but peasants in surrounding areas had to start paying for water that had previously been available for free from public standpipes. The price increases were supposed to contribute to the capital costs of building a new dam and purification plant. Protests led to the repeal of the 1999 law, the collapse of the concession and a court case initiated by one of the companies against the Bolivian government.
- *Manila.* The 25-year concessions granted in 1997 for West Manila collapsed in 2003. Foreign debt was a key catalyst. During the first five years of the concession Maynilad, a joint venture between Ondeo, a transnational company, and a Philippine business group, had operating losses and ran up debt of $800 million to finance expansion. Coverage increased from 58% to 84%, but the East Asian financial crisis boosted debt liabilities. When the Metropolitan Waterworks and Sewerage System refused to sanction a tariff rate adjustment to cover the company's losses, the concession was terminated.

- *Buenos Aires.* The 30-year concession granted in 1993 to a consortium of foreign companies and local business groups ended with the Argentine economic collapse. During the bidding the consortium had indicated an intention to cut tariffs by 29%, but operational losses led to price increases and contract renegotiations. No provisions were made to adjust for exchange rate collapses, exposing the consortium to the risks associated with heavy external borrowing.

At least three important lessons emerge. The first lesson, most powerfully demonstrated in Cochabamba, is that transparency matters. No credible attempt was made by the government, the companies or the donors and international financial institutions that supported the deals to gauge public opinion or consider the views of the poor. One consequence was that there were no provisions for protecting the customary rights of highly vulnerable indigenous people—a factor that became politically explosive.

The second lesson concerns the tension between commercial and social imperatives. Companies undertake concessions to generate profits for shareholders. But raising tariffs to finance profits and investments can damage water security for poor households. It also raises the probability of a political backlash that reflects the critical importance of water in the community. Efforts to protect profits by raising tariffs to cover the debt liabilities created by hard-currency borrowing and currency depreciation were socially and politically unsustainable.

The third lesson is arguably the most important. The complexity of increasing access by the poor was hugely underestimated. If the problem had been properly assessed, public finance and subsidized connections would have figured more prominently.

Source: Slattery 2003; Castro 2004.

Leasing has produced
positive results for human
development in environments
where governments
have established well
defined goals backed by
regulatory capacity

a revenue stream in local currency, the result was high exposure to foreign exchange fluctuations. The East Asian and Argentine financial crises created unsustainable debt burdens for the West Manila and Buenos Aires concessions. The net loss of $1.6 billion recorded by the concessionaire in Buenos Aires in 2002 was almost entirely the product of a devaluation that tripled the company's foreign debt liability.

Other forms of private sector involvement

While private companies are pulling back from concessions, they remain heavily involved in a wide range of service delivery operations in water. Public-private management remains a central theme in debates on water governance.

Leasing (or affermage) is one common form of public-private partnership. Under this model, the government delegates management of a public service to a company in return for a specified fee, commonly based on the volume of water sold, while ownership of assets remains with a holding company operating for the government. Burkina Faso's National Office for Water and Sanitation (ONEA) operates through leasing arrangements that cover 36 towns and cities

across the country. The *affermage* model is also used in Abidjan, Côte d'Ivoire, and in Senegal, where urban water is managed through the Senegalese National Water Company (SONES), an asset holding company, and Senegalese Water (SDE), a private contractor leased to operate the system.

Leasing has produced positive results for human development in environments where governments have established well defined goals backed by regulatory capacity. ONEA is one of the few utilities in Sub-Saharan Africa to develop a strategy for ensuring that standpipes become a source of affordable water for the poor. Rates at standpipes are well below the maximum tariff (although they are still above the minimum tariff). In Senegal the leasing contract sets incremental targets for the provision of standpipe water. The aim is to have standpipes account for 30% of connections in Dakar and 50% in other towns and to provide 20 litres per person. In Abidjan the leasing arrangement has increased coverage rates with a system administered through a clear regulatory framework (box 2.5). There have been serious problems in implementation in each of these cases. For example, social pricing and subsidies

---

Box 2.5   Pro-poor water pricing practices in Côte d'Ivoire

The pricing policies applied by utilities can have a marked effect on access to water. While performance has been mixed, the private utility serving Abidjan, the Water Society of Côte d'Ivoire (SODECI), has developed some innovative strategies for expanding access. Coverage has increased steadily for the last 10 years in Abidjan and in other parts of the country.

SODECI applies three mechanisms to expand access for the poor: subsidized household connections, a rising block tariff and licensed water resellers in informal settlements. The subsidy for household connections comes from a surtax on water bills administered by the Water Development Fund (FDE), a public body. SODECI charges poor households $40 per connection instead of $150. This subsidy, financed from internal resources, reduces the dependency on donor contributions and increases sustainability in the long run.

The rising block tariff subsidizes those with lower consumption (the poor) and discourages water waste. The unit price applied to large consumers is moderate, to encourage them to remain in the

system. To solve the problem of water provision in illegal settlements, where SODECI is not permitted to operate, the utility licenses water resellers. These resellers buy the water at normal tariffs and pay a deposit ($300) to reduce the risk of nonpayment. Resellers are responsible for investments in extending the network within their area and are allowed to recover costs through water sales. Although this practice effectively increases coverage, the poor families who are the clients of water resellers have to pay twice for the investment costs of the network: once on the tariff charged to the reseller to obtain the water and again on the final price paid to the resellers, who also charge for their investment to supply the neighbourhood.

Four main lessons emerge from SODECI's experience:
- Pro-poor strategies need to be well coordinated.
- Cross-subsidies can serve the poor.
- The managerial and financial strength of the utility is more important than its public or private ownership.
- Good regulation makes the best use of the relative strengths of public and private actors.

Source: Collignon 2002.

in Côte d'Ivoire and Senegal have a mixed record in benefiting the poorest households. Even so, they demonstrate some of the strategies that governments can adopt in putting the right to water within a practical framework.

Management contracts represent another form of public-private partnerships. These are arrangements in which a municipality or local government purchases management services from a company. Ghana adopted a new water law in 2005 that commits the government to expand the role of private operators in delivering services through management contracts. As part of the policy reform, a private operator was selected in late 2005 for a five-year management contract covering Accra and other major towns. Because of a combination of underfinancing, inefficiency and inequitable pricing the publicly owned utility, the Ghana Water Company, had been failing to provide water to urban areas throughout the country, and management contracts are now seen as part of the solution.

Will the new arrangement deliver? Some of the targets set are encouraging. For Accra they include establishing 50,000 new household connections and restoring regular water supply to existing customers. The programme also envisages the creation of 350 public standpipes a year for unserved urban areas.[33] Outcomes will depend on the clarity of contracts and on regulation. One concern is the inadequacy of financing and delivery strategies for reaching the poorest households. Moreover, details about pricing for standpipes and the targeting of poor areas remain vague.

What is clear is that management contracts are not a simple solution for deep-rooted problems in water provision. For example, since 1998 Mauritania has introduced a wave of bold reforms. Four new institutions for water and sanitation management were created in 2001 alone. In rural areas and small towns the new strategy envisages a major increase in the role of the private sector. More than 350 contracts have been signed for networked service provision, with private operators involved in two-thirds of them. However, not until 2005 was a new national body created to oversee management and financing of facilities and to monitor

progress—the National Agency for Drinking Water and Sanitation. Even now, the targets and pricing strategies for leasing arrangements are not well defined, and sectoral plans are heavily underfinanced. Estimates for achieving the Millennium Development Goal indicate a financing requirement of $65 million for public spending—current spending is about $5 million. Management contracts cannot be effective without adequate financing and clearly defined targets.

Creating the institutional conditions for successful management contracts is inherently difficult. Research into management contract arrangements in Johannesburg, South Africa, and Monagas, Venezuela, has highlighted two difficulties. First, double delegation—the transfer of operating authority from local government to utility and from utility to third companies—can obscure accountability and delivery. This can disempower users by making it difficult to identify the institutional locus for holding providers to account. Second, local authorities are often both utility shareholder and regulator. Reconciling this dual identity is difficult, not least because it can enmesh the utility in local government politics. International evidence makes a strong case for an independent regulator.[34]

Complexity is another problem in management contracts, especially in countries lacking strong administrative capacity. Negotiating contracts, responsibilities, delivery targets and penalties for nondelivery is an enormous challenge. That is true even in rich countries with highly developed administrative capacity. In 1999 the US city of Atlanta awarded a 20-year management contract for operations and maintenance to a business consortium—a move prompted partly by fines from the Environmental Protection Agency for violations of water quality standards because of deteriorating infrastructure. The contract was terminated after four years, with city authorities claiming that the company failed to meet performance standards. But the process of termination involved extensive litigation on both sides.

Another way municipal providers can try to tap the efficiency gains offered by the private sector is through service contracts. Under

Management contracts cannot be effective without adequate financing and clearly defined targets

Without a coherent national plan and financing strategy for achieving water for all, neither the public sector nor the private sector will break out of the current enclave model

this arrangement, providers buy a service from a company not substantively involved in the utility's management or financing. These are increasingly common in both developed and developing countries. Service contracts have proven very effective in some cases. Research in Maharashtra, India, shows that contracting out billing, repairs, water treatment and infrastructure upgrades can improve performance. Customer surveys show increased satisfaction.[35] However, success depends on strong regulatory capacity.

Finland has extensive outsourcing of non-core water services, accounting for as much as 60%–80% of the cash flow of municipal water companies.[36] The most commonly outsourced water services are detailed design, construction, wastewater sludge treatment, equipment and material supply, workshop repairs and laboratory services. A small group of private companies and a public utility, Helsinki Water, have recently started offering management services. The market is still limited, however, with only three private operators providing services, mainly for wastewater treatment.

Public or private—some problems stay the same

Perhaps the most obvious lesson from any review of public and private provision is that there are no hard and fast cross-country blueprints for success. Some publicly owned providers (Porto Alegre) are world class performers, as are some privatized companies (Chile). Many publicly owned utilities are, by any reasonable criteria, failing the poor—and that failure is linked to underfinancing and poor governance. But the idea that public sector failures can be swiftly corrected through the presumed efficiency, accountability and financing advantages of the private concessions is flawed, as witnessed by developments in Cochabamba, Buenos Aires and West Manila. Without a coherent national plan and financing strategy for achieving water for all, neither the public sector nor the private sector will break out of the current enclave model.

Delivering the outcomes—the policies

Water is a human right. But human rights count for little if they are divorced from practical policies to protect and extend them—or from mechanisms for accountability that empower the poor to demand their rights. If access to clean and affordable water is a human right, who has the duty to deliver water services? And how should the infrastructure that water provision depends on be financed? Water has been described as a "gift from God"—but somebody has to pay to put the pipes in the ground, maintain the pumps and purify the water. Financing and delivering water services that are affordable to the poor through providers who are transparent and accountable continue to pose tough public policy challenges. The way those challenges are addressed in the years ahead will

have an enormous bearing on water security and human development.

The starting point for accelerated progress in water can be summarized in two words: national strategy. As chapter 1 suggested, each country should produce a national water and sanitation plan. National plans will vary, but there are four basic ingredients for success:

- Establishing clear goals and benchmarks for measuring progress through a national water policy.
- Ensuring that policies in the water sector are backed by secure financing provisions in annual budgets and a medium-term expenditure framework.
- Developing clear strategies for overcoming structural inequalities based on

wealth, location and other markers for disadvantage.

- Creating governance systems that make governments and water providers accountable for achieving the goals set under national policies.

Within this broad framework water policy reform should be seen as an integral part of national poverty reduction strategies. In chapter 1, we set out some of the institutional requirements for this framework. Here we turn to specific policies within the water sector.

Public financing and access for the urban poor

The financing of water services is key to expanding access. From a commercial perspective the aim is for water providers to generate enough revenue to cover their recurrent costs, with the capital costs of expanding infrastructure covered through a mix of public spending and investment from the service provider. From a human development perspective there is a limit to cost-recovery through tariffs. That limit is the point at which water becomes unaffordable to poor households.

Sustainable and equitable cost-recovery

Targeting full cost-recovery would put water security beyond the reach of millions of people now lacking access to water. Recall that more than 363 million people without clean water live on less than $1 a day. And 729 million live on less than $2 a day. Poverty sets natural limits to water charges. Research in Latin America indicates that full cost-recovery tariffs would present affordability problems for one in five households in the region. For some countries—including Bolivia, Honduras, Nicaragua and Paraguay—reaching cost-recovery would imply affordability problems for nearly half the population. Affordability is an equally serious problem in Sub-Saharan Africa, where about 70% of households could face problems paying bills if providers were to seek full cost-recovery.[37]

Apart from the strain on households, full cost-recovery would set back poverty reduction efforts in a very immediate sense. With full cost-recovery for water the incidence of poverty would increase by about 1% for middle-income countries in Latin America and by 2% for low-income countries in the region. The impact would be even more severe in Asia and in Africa, where tariffs would have to rise from a far lower base. For Mauritania and Mozambique poverty could increase by 7% if water tariffs were increased to full cost-recovery levels.[38]

These figures point to a central role for public spending in financing the extension of water systems to poor households. They also highlight the potentially important role of cross-subsidies, or transfers from higher income to lower income users, in utility pricing. For financing expansion of the network, different countries face different constraints. In some countries, especially middle-income countries, the challenge is to mobilize additional revenue through taxation or the restructuring of current spending priorities. In others aid has a critical role. But the starting point has to be an assessment of what is affordable to the poor. While there is scope for debate, a ceiling of 3% of household income might be an approximate benchmark.

Enhanced equity through pricing and subsidies

Water is one of a bundle of goods that define social justice and citizenship. One way to express social solidarity and a commitment to shared citizenship is through pricing policies and financial transfers that make water available and affordable to all. A combination of pricing and access policies, including targeted subsidies, is needed to achieve equitable outcomes.

Connection subsidies. Subsidizing connections for poor households can remove an important barrier to the network. So can innovative payment strategies. Installment payments have been proposed by utilities in Jakarta. In Côte d'Ivoire a Water Development Fund surtax is included in bills, with about 40% of the proceeds used for connection subsidies. However, the subsidy does not specifically target the poor. Elsewhere, utilities have adopted tiered pricing systems. In El Alto, Bolivia, only 20% of

One way of enhancing affordability for poor households is by providing an amount of water sufficient to cover basic needs at a low price or for free

households receiving connections in the first year of the city's concession programme paid full fees. One important innovation allowed households to provide their own labour to dig trenches for connections, with the utility treating this as a form of payment in kind.[39] Here too, though, the rules were not developed as part of an integrated strategy for reaching specified connection targets for the very poor.

Targeted subsidies. Some countries finance consumption for low-income groups through targeted subsidies. In Chile water prices have been raised to full cost-recovery levels without sacrificing distributional goals. Subsidies cover 25%–85% of household water costs, on a sliding scale for eligible low-income households (box 2.6). One of the conditions for the success of Chile's model is the capacity of state agencies to identify poor households and transfer subsidies without high levels of leakage to the nonpoor, a capacity developed over a long period of experience with a comprehensive social welfare system.

Lifeline tariffs. Another way of enhancing affordability for poor households is by providing an amount of water sufficient to cover basic needs at a low price or for free. Most countries now apply block tariffs, but progressivity varies. South Africa's lifeline tariff provides 25 litres free—a practice that could be applied far more widely. The lifeline tariff model comes with two caveats. First, in countries with low rates of connection lifeline tariffs cannot reach poor households that are not connected to the network. This is a concern even in South Africa, where coverage rates among the poor vary. Unconnected households often have to purchase water from bulk resellers, who purchase water from the utility at the highest block. Second, the lifeline or social tariff arrangement requires metering, which is not widespread in many poor settlements.

Targeting informal settlements. In many countries the majority of urban households without access to a household connection live in informal settlements. The millions of people living in these areas have shown extraordinary initiative to gain access to water services, laying kilometres of pipes, digging trenches and cooperating for mutual benefit. However, community effort alone cannot solve the problem. Utilities have been unwilling to extend networks to households lacking legal title, fearing that this could jeopardize revenue collection. New approaches are needed. Authorities can provide full or intermediate residency rights to established informal settlements. They can also require that utilities supply water to everyone regardless of location, if necessary by providing financial guarantees or investment incentive. Utilities can also make a difference. One company in Manila has extended underground water lines to the perimeter of slums and allowed households to make above ground connections through small plastic pipes linked to meters that are maintained by residents associations and nongovernment agencies. Such arrangements can be good for equity (in Manila it has reduced water costs by 25% in the slums areas now being served) and for efficiency (it reduces the revenue losses associated with illegal connections).

Box 2.6   Water consumption subsidies in Chile—greater efficiency and equity

Water provision in Chile is privatized under a strong regulatory regime that combines high levels of efficiency in provision with equally high levels of equity in access. Many factors have contributed. Initial advantages included near-universal coverage before privatization and a highly developed network. Strong economic growth has also been important. So too have targeted water subsidies.

Chile introduced means-tested water consumption subsidies in the early 1990s to guarantee affordability for low-income households. The subsidy covers 25%–85% of a household's monthly bill for up to 15 cubic metres of water a month. The government reimburses the company on the basis of the actual amount of water consumed. The subsidy is financed entirely from the central government budget. Households have to apply for the subsidy to the municipality, which determines eligibility. The subsidy can be thought of as an increasing block tariff, with subsidies inversely related to household income: support declines as incomes rise above the means-tested minimum threshold.

In 1998 about 13% of Chilean households—nearly 450,000 people—received subsidies at a cost of $33.6 million. The scheme has made it possible to increase tariffs, mobilize resources for maintenance and network expansion and minimize adverse effects on poor people.

There are two basic ingredients for the success of this model in Chile. Neither of them is easy to replicate in other developing countries. First, the scheme requires a capacity to identify, target and deliver support to low-income households. Second, every household must have a meter for monitoring water use.

Source: Alegría Calvo and Celedón Cariola 2004; Gómez-Lobo and Contreras 2003; Paredes 2001; Serra 2000.

Cross-subsidies. Cross-subsidies from higher income water users is another way to make water more affordable for poor households. In Colombia cross-subsidies are written into the Public Residential Services Law of 1994 and targeted geographically.[40] The scheme has increased access to water for the poorest 20% of the population, enabling the country to surpass the Millennium Development Goal target.

Subsidies can generate large public as well as private benefits. Apart from creating opportunities for improved health and well-being, they can reduce the deep inequalities in access described in chapter 1. But not all subsidies are equivalent in their effects—and some are better at enhancing equity than others.

Subsidies for water are rooted in a simple idea. If a big share of the population cannot pay the cost of service provision, yet there is a human development imperative to provide service, cross-subsidies, progressive pricing and fiscal transfers offer the means to do so. In effect, these arrangements finance the demands of households that would otherwise be excluded from provision because of poverty. But not all subsidies produce pro-poor outcomes. Côte d'Ivoire's Water Development Fund was intended to finance connections for poor households, but it bypassed the poorest areas of the city because unauthorized settlements are not eligible. Moreover, because connection fees rise sharply with distance from the main network (reflecting the higher costs of connection), some poor households were unable to afford connections even with a subsidy.

Subsidies delivered through the water tariff can produce mixed results (figure 2.4). If connection rates are low and most of the households lacking a connection are poor, the social block tariff is unlikely to produce progressive outcomes. For example, Bangalore, India, and Kathmandu, Nepal, apply a rising block tariff structure, but the subsidies benefit the nonpoor more than the poor.[41] In Bangalore the wealthiest 20% of households receives 30% of the water subsidy and the poorest 20% receives 10.5%.[42] In Kathmandu the average nonpoor household receives 44% more subsidy than the average poor household.[43]

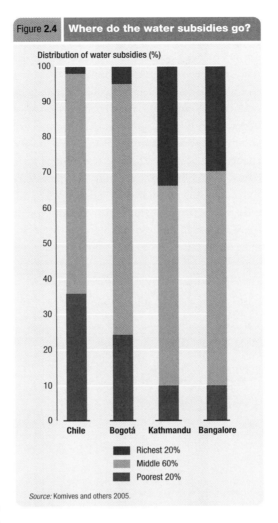

Figure **2.4** **Where do the water subsidies go?**

Distribution of water subsidies (%)

Chile   Bogotá   Kathmandu   Bangalore

■ Richest 20%
■ Middle 60%
■ Poorest 20%

Source: Komives and others 2005.

Set against these examples, some subsidy schemes have been highly effective. Chile uses means testing to identify low-income residents to receive subsidies on water and compensates the utility through government payments. Colombia uses property values and residency to identify poor households. In both cases poor households capture a large share of the subsidies linked to water use. Similarly in Durban, South Africa, the lifeline tariff results in a progressive distribution of water subsidies because 98% of poor households are connected (figure 2.5). In other areas of Kwazulu-Natal Province the subsidy produces less progressive outcomes because connection rates among the poor are lower. The lesson is that delivering subsidies through water tariffs is pro-poor only to the extent that poor people are connected to the water network.

Subsidizing the facilities used by the poor offers potentially greater equity gains. Standpipes are an obvious place to start. While the ultimate goal is private connections for all households, this is not a feasible near-term objective in many countries. Standpipes are the main source of water for millions of poor households, making standpipe subsidies among the most progressive that can be provided through the water system (box 2.7). Yet in many countries standpipe users are purchasing water at the highest price band, cross-subsidizing the domestic consumption of high-income households with access to private taps. Some countries have found ways to avoid

this. In Bangalore only 14% of standpipe subsidies do not reach the poor—for private taps that figure rises to 73%.[44] In Burkina Faso low-income urban households are able to purchase standpipe water at some of the lowest prices in Sub-Saharan Africa.

Regulation is critical

Regulation is critical to the progressive realization of the human right to water and protection of the public interest in water provision. In a market with limited competition, and for a product that is fundamental to human well-being, regulatory authorities need to ensure that providers are managed in a way that secures both equity and efficiency.

Many countries have suffered from the absence of effective regulatory institutions. In Buenos Aires a regulatory body was created to oversee the water concession. However, weaknesses were built into the system. The body was highly politicized, with membership including representatives of the presidency, the province and the municipality, bringing competing political parties into the framework. Consumer interests were not represented, however. Many aspects of the concession contract were negotiated in secret, so the regulator had limited access to information from the companies and government.

Some of the key features of the more successful regulatory bodies in Chile, the United Kingdom, the United States and elsewhere were absent in the Buenos Aires system:

- *Political independence*, with a strong culture of public interest promotion.
- *Investigative authority and penalty power*, with the regulatory body empowered to demand information from companies on a wide range of performance benchmarks, to levy penalties for nonperformance and to limit price increases. In a recent case the Chilean regulator demanded internal company tax returns to investigate transfer pricing and understatement of profit margins.
- *Information sharing* with the public on pricing, water quality and cost structures.

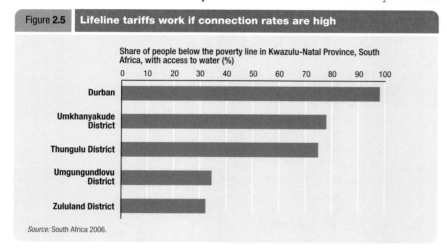

Figure **2.5** **Lifeline tariffs work if connection rates are high**

Share of people below the poverty line in Kwazulu-Natal Province, South Africa, with access to water (%)

Durban
Umkhanyakude District
Thungulu District
Umgungundlovu District
Zululand District

Source: South Africa 2006.

Box **2.7** **Standpipes—reaching the poor, but often at too high a price**

Standpipes can give poor households access to affordable water. They can also act as a conduit for targeted government support since they are used overwhelmingly by the poor, rather than the wealthy. However, experience has been mixed.

In Senegal a partnership between a private water provider, the National Water Authority and a national nongovernmental organization has extended water supply to 500,000 people in low-income areas through standpipes. Subsidies are provided for constructing public standpipes and for connecting them to the grid. This arrangement has expanded access, but because standpipe users are charged at higher rates, unit costs are still more than three times the lowest domestic tariff.

There have been similar problems in the Philippines. Private water companies in Manila have extended water connections to some 50,000 poor households in densely populated low-income areas through standpipes, with community organizations as intermediaries. Allowing households to draw water from a metered source, the contracts reduce the unit price by about a quarter. But the final price is still more than twice the lowest utility price for domestic water supply.

Shifting subsidies towards standpipes would help to improve access and enhance equity. It would also have a knock-on effect, forcing other private providers to lower their prices.

Source: WUP 2003; McIntosh 2003.

- *Public participation*, to ensure that consumer interests are represented. In the United States citizens utility boards provide a forum for customers to monitor service providers. The UK regulator, the Office of Water Services (Ofwat), provides structured access to consumer groups.

The problem in many developing countries is that there are marked limits on the capacity of regulators to regulate. The resources for effective regulation are often lacking. Legislation providing for the separation of powers between governments and regulators is often lacking. More broadly, where democratic accountability is weak, the lack of pressure on governments and companies to disclose information weakens the position of regulators.

In countries lacking the administrative capacity and institutions needed to regulate effectively, transparency and public action by citizens can create regulatory impetus from below. Social action by well organized community groups has played an important role in reducing environmental damage by companies in developing countries, forcing compliance with standards and information disclosure. Civil society has also been active, pressing for more information and publicizing underperformance by water utilities. The use of citizens report cards in Bangalore, India, gave residents associations and community groups a voice in reforming the water utility, improving accountability by evaluating and publicizing utility performance assessments (box 2.8). That model has been widely exported. Where utility managers and municipal leaders have responded with dialogue, there have been tangible improvements in service delivery.

These initiatives from below are important. But they have limits. Citizens groups, civil society and water user associations do not operate in a vacuum. Their activities and scope for achieving change are affected by government policies and institutions, especially the normative and legislative framework and the political space created by governments. In post-apartheid South Africa the adoption of a rights-based approach to water provision articulated a clear legislative

framework for utilities. As important, it created a sense of expectation and entitlement among citizens, empowering communities to hold local governments, private utilities and the national government to account. Inevitably, the human right to water remains a contested political domain in South Africa, as witnessed by high-profile disputes over supply, pricing and the appropriate threshold for free water provision. What is important though is the way in which human rights legislation has given citizens a real voice in water policy. In water, as in other areas, the effectiveness of pressure from below depends at least partly on laws that define and sustain the rights of people to hold companies and public utilities to account.[45] Activism by civil society is an important force for change in its own right—but it can be strengthened or weakened by government policy.

One problem with current approaches is that the regulatory remit extends only to formal network providers. However

---

| Box **2.8** | **Citizens report cards—voice as agency for change** |

Water utilities, public and private, are often remote, unaccountable, lacking in transparency and unresponsive to public concerns. Bringing the voice of users into the governance structure can change this picture.

Ten years ago the Public Affairs Centre, an Indian nongovernmental organization (NGO) based in Bangalore, pioneered a new approach to regulatory oversight. Using public meetings and a questionnaire-based survey, it conducted a large social audit of perceptions about the public services provided by municipal authorities, including the Bangalore Water Supply and Sewerage Board. The audit, summarized in a citizens report card, highlighted weak customer orientation, high levels of corruption and perceived high-cost, poor-quality service provision.

Following a second audit in 1999, the state government and municipal agencies embarked on a process of structured consultation. The Bangalore Water Supply and Sewerage Board initiated joint programmes with local citizens groups and residents associations to improve services, extend connection to poor households and debate reform options. New grievance procedures were established to address corruption. By 2003 the social audit was registering real improvements, with poor households reporting a sharp reduction in bribes for connections and improvements in efficiency.

Since its inception the citizen's audit has been scaled up to cover rural and urban areas in 23 Indian states. It has also been exported to the Philippines, Tanzania, Ukraine and Viet Nam. In mid-2005 three Kenyan cities—Kisumu, Mombasa and Nairobi—launched a social audit on water and sanitation, bringing together residents associations, NGOs and service providers.

Source: Paul 2005; Adikeshavalu 2004.

Community power can be a catalyst for accelerated progress—but a responsive governance system is required to make anything happen

inadequately, most governments seek to regulate the price, monitor the quality and assess the predictability of water through the network. Far less attention has gone to regulating vendors, tanker truck operators and other water suppliers. This is a serious regulatory gap, especially from the perspective of poor households in slums and informal settlements. Closing that gap through public policy interventions that regulate the quantity, quality and price of water available beyond the formal utility network is a priority. One of the most effective instruments for addressing this regulatory challenge is the public provision of water through standpipes at prices that reflect the lower tiers of the block tariff structure applied by utilities. This would force private operators, vendors and other small-scale providers to adjust to a social market price stipulated by government policy.

Reaching the poor

Slow progress in rural areas remains a threat to achieving the Millennium Development Goal for water. In many countries coverage rates for clean water are increasing far too slowly to bring the target within reach—and already-large disparities are widening. Yet experience shows that rapid progress in overcoming rural disadvantage is possible.

Community participation requires the right governance framework

Rural populations have been the experimental subjects of too many development fads. Water has often been supplied by government agencies through a top-down service delivery model using inappropriate and unaffordable technologies that have failed to meet local needs. More recently, community participation and appropriate technology have emerged as the latest answer for rural water provision. However, in many cases community participation has been used as an instrument for implementing government policies, raising finance and overcoming technological obstacles rather than as a means of empowering people or enabling them to express demand. Today, the very large number of broken water points across

rural areas in many developing countries bears testimony to the model's failure.

The governance framework for water has started to shift in a more positive direction, with growing recognition that the special problems facing rural areas and the pivotal role of local communities in service provision raise distinctive institutional challenges. Communities will not cooperate in maintaining water technologies they consider inappropriate or irrelevant to local needs. Nor, as history shows, will they act as implementation agents for policies drawn up by remote, unaccountable and opaque planning bodies. Community power can be a catalyst for accelerated progress—but a responsive governance system is required to make anything happen.

Governments and donors now stress a demand-responsive approach. At a basic level this simply means that approaches to provision should focus on what users want, on the technologies that they are willing and able to pay for and on what they are able to sustain. The starting point is for communities to participate in the design process, drawing up their own plans and collectively deciding on the type and level of services they require. Of course, this process is not without problems. Rural communities are not homogeneous, and community participation can obscure the exclusion of women and the rural poor from decision-making. But engagement with communities does provide a basis for progress.

Creating the conditions for successful demand-responsive approaches is difficult. Decentralization and devolution of authority to local levels are important—but not always successful. In Ethiopia decentralization has transferred a high level of authority to district- and village-level bodies. But financial and human capacities remain weak, and in some areas the legal status of village water supply and sanitation committees is not recognized.[46] This weakens the capacity of rural communities to pursue demands through local government. In other cases water governance and progress in coverage have benefited from a combination of decentralization and increased political and financial prioritization. The decentralization of rural water supply in Ghana is a demand-responsive approach that is working (box 2.9).

In little more than a decade Ghana transformed the structure for rural water supply, expanding coverage through more participative—and more efficient—delivery systems.

The change has been dramatic. At the start of the 1990s rural water supply was managed through the Ghana Water and Sewerage Corporation, a public utility responsible for planning, building and maintaining rural water supplies. Boreholes drilled in Ghana were among the most costly in the world, and as few as 40% of handpumps were working at any one time because of poor maintenance.

Access to water is now being extended to about 200,000 more people each year. Coverage has increased from 55% in 1990 to 75% in 2004, with rural areas figuring prominently. Ghana achieved this progress through sweeping reform of a system that was top-down, unresponsive and not delivering.

Responsibility for rural water supplies was transferred to local governments and rural communities. Authority for coordinating and facilitating the national strategy for community-managed water and sanitation was transferred to the Community Water and Sanitation Agency—a highly decentralized body with multidisciplinary staff in 10 regions of the country. The regional teams provide direct support to district assemblies in planning and managing safe water and sanitation services.

New political structures for water governance have been developed as part of a broader decentralization programme. District assemblies, an important tier of elected local government, are responsible for processing and prioritizing community applications for water supplies, awarding contracts for hand-dug wells and latrine construction and running a latrine subsidy programme. They also provide 5% of the capital costs of water facilities.

Village structures are part of the new system. To apply for capital grants, communities have to form village water committees and draw up plans detailing how they will manage their systems, contribute the cash equivalent of 5% of the capital costs and meet maintenance costs.

An assessment in 2000 identified major improvements:

- More than 90% of people were satisfied with the location, quantity and quality of the water.
- The overwhelming majority of people had contributed to the capital costs, with 85% also paying towards operation and maintenance costs. Most believed that the principle of payment was fair and intended to continue paying
- More than 90% of water and sanitation committees had received training, opened bank accounts and held regular meetings. Women played active and influential roles on these committees.

Source: Lane 2004; WSP–AF 2002e; indicator table 7.

National planning and poverty reduction strategies for water have produced mixed results

Poverty Reduction Strategy Papers (PRSPs) are important statements of policy intent and frameworks for international cooperation. Countries with a clearly defined strategy for reaching water and sanitation targets demonstrate that national political commitment backed by aid can produce dramatic results.[47] The bad news is that most PRSPs suffer from a water and sanitation blind spot—an expression of the low priority accorded to the sector.

Some countries have used the Millennium Development Goal framework and the PRSP process to bring rural water provision to the heart of national planning for poverty reduction. In Benin the National Water Council, a high-level ministerial body, has made rural areas and small towns the focal point for a national strategy for achieving the Millennium Development Goal. The Water Budget Programme, which started in 2001, provides a stable financing framework and clearly sets out the financing provisions for each district across the country. Senegal, too, has identified water and sanitation as a priority in its PRSP. It established a national programme in 2004 to coordinate the activities of different agencies under a high-level national body. Explicit targets include the extension of water supply to 3,300 settlements through a scaled-up national borehole programme. Detailed financial costing has made it possible to identify potentially large financing gaps: the projected spending requirement for rural areas is $42 million, with a financing gap of $22 million.[48] The success of Senegal's water strategy will depend critically on the response of aid donors, but the framework for success is in place.

Experience demonstrates that rapid progress is possible. The Ugandan government has a strong national strategy with clear targets backed by financial resources (box 2.10). Critically, financing for water targets has been integrated into the government's medium-term financing framework, ensuring that political commitments find budgetary expression.

Box 2.10   **"Some for all, not all for some" in Uganda**

Uganda has been a world leader in reforming the water sector. Coherent policy and financing frameworks have been developed since the mid 1990s, with water identified as a priority in the national poverty reduction strategy. The 1999 water policy sets out a strategy and investment plan aimed at 100% coverage by 2015. The organizing principle: "Some for all, not all for some."

Political commitment has meant financing. Budget allocations to water have increased from 0.5% of public expenditure in 1997 to 2.8% in 2002. Aid support provided through the general budget has underpinned this increase. Management and resources have been devolved to district-level bodies. Coverage levels have increased from 39% in 1996 to 51% in 2003. This is equivalent to an additional 5.3 million people having access to safe water in 2003, most of them in rural areas.

Water and sanitation are established as priority areas under Uganda's Poverty Eradication Action Plan. Interim targets have been set for increasing by 3.9 million the number of people with clean water and by 4.4 million those with sanitation by 2009. District plans include provisions to extend adequate sanitation and water to 75% of schools by the same date, with sharp improvements in the ratio of latrines to pupils in rural areas. Water user associations with women making up half the membership are being established as focal points for training and management.

Uganda is rightly considered a leader in water and sanitation. The country has developed a strong planning process, including well defined coordination mechanisms with a sectorwide approach, targets backed by medium-term financing provisions and annual review of progress. But past progress does not imply that Uganda has overcome the water and sanitation deficit, and policy implementation faces a number of challenges. In rural areas coverage has been strongly correlated with socioeconomic status. National water policy states that each water point should serve 300 people, implying 3.3 water points per 1,000 people. But in Tororo District in eastern Uganda the availability of water points ranges from less than 1 per 1,000 people in two subcounties, to more than 3 in the two best served subcounties. Coverage is closely correlated with the socioeconomic status of communities, with the poor being left behind.

This inequality helps explain why average water collection times for the rural poor have not fallen significantly despite the rise in coverage. Combined with the slow progress in sanitation, it also helps to explain one of the anomalies of Uganda's human development record: the failure of child death rates to fall with declining income poverty and high economic growth. Weak coordination between local planning agencies in some of the poorest rural areas has been identified as a major bottleneck. Empowering local government and increasing the voice of poor areas are keys to removing that bottleneck.

Source: Slaymaker and Newborne 2004; Uganda 2004; AfDB 2005a,b.

Tanzania is in the early stages of reform, and developments are encouraging. An additional 2 million people have gained access since 1999, and the government has set a target of 85% rural water provision by 2010.[49] However, there are large inequalities in coverage: 76 of 113 rural districts have less than 50% coverage, with a heavy concentration in the centre and the southeast of the country. In Rufiji and Liwale Districts in the southeast, coverage rates are less than 10%.[50] Future progress will depend on creating strategies for overcoming these inequalities.

It will also require donors to review their aid strategies. Extending rural water coverage is a well defined poverty reduction priority for Tanzania. But in 2002/03 urban areas received more than 60% of the development financing budget. One reason is that aid accounts for more than half the water sector budget—and there is a marked donor preference for urban water rehabilitation programmes with a perceived higher potential for cost-recovery and self-financing.[51] In addition, political decentralization has outstripped

financial decentralization, leaving local governments in rural areas with limited control over resources. While aid donors are often highly critical of what they perceive as an urban bias in policy, they often reflect and reinforce that same bias in their programmes.

Some countries have set impressive goals for expanding rural water provision but have failed to develop the policies for achieving them. Financing provisions have been out of step with targets. Not only is water consistently underfinanced, but in some countries the gap between budget allocations and real public investment is large. In Zambia less than 5% of the budget allocation for water was spent in 1999 and 2000, before surging to more than 30% in 2001, an election year. While budget performance has improved, allocations and aid levels are less than half the financing requirements for attaining the goals set out in Zambia's national strategy.

Poor budget management can create a vicious cycle. In Malawi national policy lacks provision for coherent targets, strategies and financing, the legacy of a long history of poor governance in the water sector linked to weak budget management. Distrust between government and donors has reached the point that donors have set up parallel systems, operating independently of government programmes. The Ministry of Water Development controls less than 12% of the development budget, while donors administer the balance through their own programmes. Off-budget spending is probably three times on-budget spending. Moreover, aid flows fell from $14 million in 2003 to $2 million in 2005, reflecting donor concerns over budget management and a failure to prioritize water in the PRSP. Malawi clearly demonstrates the consequences of weak government capacity for implementation, the absence of a coherent planning framework and donor concerns about corruption.[52] There are no winners in this situation: governments face higher transaction costs (having to report to multiple donors), aid effectiveness is diminished, and the rural poor lose out from decreased water availability.

Innovative governments have combined a clear policy framework and public investment commitments with governance reforms aimed at generating demand from below. This is particularly necessary in rural areas where community management is important for maintaining water infrastructure (box 2.11).

Partnerships between governments and people can act as a powerful catalyst for change. These partnerships can build on local initiatives, rapidly scaling them up to extend coverage. In the 1980s Olavanna, a largely rural community in the Indian state of Kerala, pioneered a small village water supply system, inspiring reform of Kerala's rural water supply and sanitation programme.[53] Across four districts, state and local governments are now cooperating with villages to extend the approach. The Olavanna model provides clean drinking water for 93,000 households—60% of whom live below the poverty line. As in other successful demand-driven models the capital costs are covered by government, with maintenance and management devolved to local community organizations.

Delivering services is about more than finance, infrastructure and technology. It is also about empowerment—as the Water Supply Programme for Rural Population in Morocco (PAGER) demonstrates.

Ten years ago rural areas lagged well behind the urban areas in providing drinking water in Morocco. Fewer than 1 person in 5 had access to water in the countryside, compared with 9 in 10 living in towns. Women and children typically walked 10 kilometres or more to collect water in the dry season. Reliance on unprotected water sources such as rivers resulted in a high incidence of bilharzia, diarrhoea and cholera. National planning was fragmented, and there was no clear strategy for reaching the scattered rural settlements with the lowest coverage.

That changed with PAGER. In 1995 the new programme decentralized water provision within a strong national planning framework. Local authorities were required to carry out needs assessments, working through community organizations. Interventions are triggered by requests for infrastructure from rural populations. About 80% of the budget for provision comes from the central government, 15% from local community associations and 5% from beneficiaries. Management of infrastructure has been transferred to local communities, supported by engineers and technical experts.

In the past decade another 4 million rural people have gained access to clean water, boosting rural coverage to 50%. Apart from reducing the time burden on women, there have been strong multiplier effects. Rural primary school attendance among girls increased from 30% to 51% between 1999 and 2003. There have also been marked improvements in public health. And water has been a catalyst for wider social change. Decentralization and water user associations have transformed communities from passive recipients of government services into demanders for change, with the empowerment of women as agents for change a big part of the story.

Source: Dubreuil and Van Hofwegen 2006.

International support for local financing

Today's rich countries were able to finance the public investments to universalize access to water and sanitation through public spending and public debt. Low incomes and limited revenue restrict the scope for increased public spending in many countries—hence the case for increased aid set out in chapter 1. Access to credit is also limited in many countries because of the weakness of local capital markets and perceptions of high risk. International aid can help in mobilizing credit just as it helps in overcoming financing barriers.

As the experience of failed concessions powerfully demonstrates, it is important to mobilize credit on local capital markets, to avoid currency risk. A new revenue stream for upfront investments can provide utilities with the capital to

The Millennium Development Goals provide one set of targets for expanding coverage, but national water plans should also include explicit equity goals

install new infrastructure and improve old infrastructure against future revenue streams. International support can help to overcome constraints and improve access to capital markets for subsovereign entities—such as municipalities and publicly owned utilities—while reducing risk:[54]

- *Partial guarantees.* In 2002 municipal authorities in the City of Johannesburg issued a $153 million bond. The International Finance Corporation (IFC) and the Development Bank of South Africa provided a partial credit guarantee that raised the bond's credit rating and extended the maturity to 12 years. In Mexico in 2003 the municipality of Tlanepantla issued a 10-year bond backed by the municipality and its water company in Mexican capital markets. Partial credit guarantees from the IFC raised the bond rating to AAA. Credit enhancements improved confidence in bond issues and lowered the costs of water and sanitation financing.

- *Pooling resources.* Cooperation between municipalities and private providers can stimulate resource mobilization. The Tamil Nadu Urban Development Fund, established by state authorities in 1996, developed the Water and Sanitation Pooled Fund—a 300 million rupee facility generated through bond markets for 14 small municipalities—with a partial credit guarantee from the US Agency for International Development. Its success led the state of Karnataka to adopt it, with government of India support through a pooled finance development fund.

- *Decentralized cooperation.* Links between municipalities in rich countries and municipal providers in developing countries have generated new flows of finance. The provincial government of Drenthe, in the Netherlands, and 11 municipalities set up a nonprofit organization and entered into joint venture contracts with 12 local governments in Indonesia. The nonprofit organization operates by purchasing a majority stake in the Indonesian local water utility, improving operating efficiency and selling shares back to the local government.

Other national initiatives are emerging beyond the traditional aid framework. The decentralized international financing approach developed in France is an example. New legislation in 2005—the Oudin law—established a framework for decentralized cooperation in water and sanitation covering six French basin agencies. Local authorities can now dedicate up to 1% of their water and sanitation budgets to international development programmes. In 2005 around $37 million was committed. If other high-income countries were to adopt this type of scheme, it could generate about $3 billion a year by one estimate, an important new flow of financing for water and sanitation.[55]

*   *   *

The obligation of governments to work towards the full realization of the right of access to clean, affordable water as a basic human right and to provide their citizens with adequate services involves wide-ranging financial, institutional and technical challenges.

As argued in chapter 1, most governments need to increase the budget resources allocated to water in the context of national planning strategies that address the interlocking problems of poverty and inequality. The Millennium Development Goals provide one set of targets for expanding coverage. But national water plans should also include explicit equity goals. Supplementing the Millennium Development Goal target of halving the proportion of people without access to clean water with an equity target of halving by 2010 the gap in service provision between the richest and poorest 20%, or between urban and rural areas, might be an appropriate starting point. Such an equity target could be adopted even for countries that are on track for the 2015 goals.

Specific policies for making the human right to water a reality will vary across countries. The level of coverage, specific structure of inequalities, state of institutions and income levels all interact to define the parameters for policy design. However, some broad approaches emerge from the analysis in this chapter:

- *Legislate for water as a human right.* Having a constitutional right to water is important—but not as important as the legislative obligation of governments and water providers to give practical policy substance to that right. Setting out the investment, pricing and monitoring arrangements for progressively extending the right to a basic minimum of 20 litres of water for every citizen is the starting point.

- *Put water at the centre of poverty reduction strategies and budget planning.* Having a coherent water plan is a first step. Grounding that plan in strategies for reducing poverty and extreme inequality, and in medium-term financing provisions, is a second step—and a requirement for sustained progress. Too often, bold water plans suffer from the "targets without finance" syndrome.
- *Expand pro-poor investment.* Water is underfinanced. The biggest financing gaps are in rural areas and in informal urban settlements. Closing these gaps requires increased financing and a reorientation of public spending to rural communities, through the provision of wells and boreholes, and to urban slum areas, through the provision of standpipes.
- *Extend lifeline tariffs.* Provision of a basic needs minimum of water to all households, free of charge for the poorest, should be built into national strategies for achieving water for all.
- *Rethink and redesign cross-subsidies.* Cross-subsidies can play a critical role in delivering affordable water to the poor. Too often, they deliver large financial benefits to the nonpoor instead, while poor households using public taps face the highest tariff bands. Using cross-subsidies to support standpipe users where coverage rates are low would be a step in the right direction. Ensuring that standpipes are a source of affordable water should be the central feature of national strategies.
- *Set clear goals—and hold providers to account.* Contract arrangements under public-private management agreements should set clear goals for expanding access for poor households living in slums, stipulating the numbers to be reached, investment levels and pricing arrangements. Nonperformance should result in financial penalties. The same rules should apply to public providers, with nonperformance penalized through incentive systems.
- *Develop and expand the regulatory framework.* Creating an independent regulator to oversee water providers is vital for ensuring that water provision reflects the public interest. At the same time, regulatory reach has to be extended beyond large-scale network providers to the intermediaries serving the poor.
- *Prioritize the rural sector.* Rural water supply poses special challenges. Building on successful demand-responsive approaches, governments need to make service providers more responsive and accountable to the communities that they serve. Decentralization of water governance can play an important role, provided that decentralized bodies have the technical and financial capacity to deliver services.

International aid is critical for closing the financing gaps that threaten the Millennium Development Goal for water, especially in low-income countries. But many countries also need to mobilize new resources through private capital markets. While the institutional challenge is local, there are global partnership solutions that can assist public utilities to tap into financial flows. Developing current credit guarantee arrangements could help municipalities and utilities mobilize the capital needed for network expansion. The European Union could do much, scaling up the innovative financing models of some member states. Extending the French Oudin law model to Europe, for example, could provide a framework for building capacity in poor countries. Doubtless there would be legal and financial obstacles. Yet such a move would mark a powerful European commitment to global social justice and give a strong impetus to the Millennium Development Goals.

International aid is critical for closing the financing gaps that threaten the Millennium Development Goal for water, especially in low-income countries

3 The vast deficit in sanitation

"'Latrines for us!' they exclaimed in astonishment. 'We go and perform our functions out in the open. Latrines are for you big people'"

Mahatma Gandhi recounting untouchables' grievances, Rajkot Sanitation Committee, 1896

"Filthy water cannot be washed"

African Proverb

3 The vast deficit in sanitation

Access to basic sanitation is a crucial human development goal in its own right, but sanitation is also a means to far wider human development ends

"The history of men," wrote Victor Hugo in *Les Miserables*, "is reflected in the history of sewers.... The sewer is the conscience of a city."[1] He was using the sewers of mid-19th century Paris as a metaphor for the condition of the city. However, there is a broader sense in which the state of sanitation says something about the state of a nation—and more profoundly about the state of human development.

As a global community we face a vast deficit in sanitation—a deficit overwhelmingly concentrated in developing countries. Today, almost one in two people in the developing world lacks access to improved sanitation. Many more lack access to good quality sanitation. While the provision of sanitation for all has been a key development goal since the 1970s, progress has been glacial. Coverage rates are improving. But without a rapid increase in the scale and effectiveness of sanitation programmes, the Millennium Development Goal target for 2015 will be missed by a wide margin.

That outcome would be a grave setback for human development. Each percentage point gap between the Millennium Development Goal target and actual outcomes means tens of millions of people affected by illness and tens of thousands of avoidable child deaths. Access to basic sanitation is a crucial human development goal in its own right: for millions of people not having a safe, private and convenient toilet facility is a daily source of indignity as well as a threat to well-being. But sanitation is also a means to far wider human development ends. Without basic sanitation the benefits of access to clean water are diminished—and the health, gender and other inequalities associated with the sanitation deficit systematically undermine progress in education, poverty reduction and wealth creation.

Sanitation improvements can broaden the real choices and substantive freedoms that people enjoy, acting as a catalyst for a wide range of human development benefits. They can protect people—especially children—from ill health. They can lift people out of poverty, reducing the risks and vulnerabilities that perpetuate cycles of deprivation. They can raise productivity, boost economic growth and create employment. And they can build people's pride in their homes and communities.

This chapter highlights the scale of the global deficit in sanitation. After briefly outlining the contours of the sanitation deficit, it asks why progress in reducing that deficit has been so slow, and it identifies some of the structural factors that explain why advances in sanitation have lagged behind those in water. Failure to overcome inequalities and create choices for the poorest sections of society is a central part of the problem. The chapter explores some of the policies and strategies that have created an environment for accelerated progress. Interventions organized by slum dwellers and the rural poor show what is possible through community-led interventions under the right institutional conditions. But action from below is an insufficient condition for accelerated progress. Partnerships between communities and local governments under the umbrella of effective national strategies hold the key to scaling up.

Many obstacles need to be removed if the world is to accelerate progress in sanitation.

Simple distinctions between "improved" and "unimproved" technologies tend to understate the scale of the deficit in the provision of sanitation

Perhaps the greatest obstacle of all is stigma. Much has been written about the sense of shame experienced by people lacking access to sanitation facilities. At higher political levels there is an overwhelming tendency to treat sanitation as a problem that should be hidden from view. The reality that open defecation forces on more than half the developing world's population, and the associated costs for human and national economic development, do not prompt political leaders to appoint high-level ministers or commissions to address what is a national emergency. Instead, sanitation is relegated to the back-rooms of politics.

The parallels with HIV/AIDS are at once instructive and disconcerting. HIV/AIDS was viewed as a problem to be swept under the carpet. The world is still paying the price for the unwillingness to provide decisive leadership when it would have been possible to achieve an early reversal of the pandemic. In the case of sanitation millions of people are paying every day for the failure to confront the problem of inadequate provision, many of them—especially children in poor households—with their lives. With HIV/AIDS it was not until political leaders, civil society groups, the media and ordinary people started speaking openly about the problem that the issue climbed up the political agenda and began to generate an effective policy response. What is needed now is for advocates of sanitation to force a similar change.

The 2.6 billion people without sanitation

For sanitation, as for water, international data provide an imperfect guide to the state of provision. Technology is an important aspect of provision, but simple distinctions between "improved" and "unimproved" technologies tend to understate the scale of the deficit—and to misrepresent its nature.

Perhaps the most daunting aspect of the sanitation deficit is its scale. As chapter 1 showed, some 2.6 billion people lack access to improved sanitation—two and a half times the deficit for access to clean water. Just reaching the Millennium Development Goal target of halving the global deficit against the 1990 coverage level would require bringing improved sanitation to more than 120 million people every year between now and 2015. And even if that were accomplished, 1.8 billion people would still be without access.

When people in rich countries think about basic sanitation, their perceptions are shaped by the historical experience outlined in chapter 1. Almost everyone living in the developed world has access to a private, flush toilet served by a continuous supply of piped water—with taps and toilets in close proximity. From a health perspective, this is optimal. Human waste is channelled by pipes into sewerage systems and treatment facilities, ensuring that drinking water is separated from the pathogens carried in faecal material. Meanwhile, taps located in sanitation facilities enable people to maintain personal hygiene.

But at the other end of the sanitation spectrum are the millions of people forced to defecate in bags, buckets, fields or roadside ditches. If the developed country model were the benchmark, the number of people lacking sanitation would be far higher than that recorded by World Health Organization (WHO) and United Nations Children's Fund (UNICEF) data. The global deficit would soar from 2.6 billion people to about 4 billion.[2]

The gap in sanitation between developed and developing countries is a striking example of inequality in human development. Of course, inadequate financial resources and technical capacity, allied in some cases with water shortages, make it unrealistic to assume that a developed country model could be extended rapidly across the developing world. But it is important to look beyond the minimal levels of provision needed to meet the Millennium Development Goal target. In the 1840s social reformers in Great Britain argued for public action to ensure that every house had access to clean water and an on-site toilet. More than 150 years later, that goal remains beyond the reach of large numbers of people in the developing world.

Who is where on the sanitation ladder?

The broad category of "improved" provision can be thought of as a sanitation "ladder" extending from very basic pit latrines to improved pit latrines, pour-flush facilities using water and septic tanks, through to conventional sewers (figure 3.1). Moving up the ladder has financial implications. It costs some 20 times more to connect a household to a modern sewerage system than to purchase a basic pit latrine.

The sanitation ladder draws attention to an important, but widely neglected public policy issue. Most Millennium Development Goal costing exercises, including those in chapter 1, set out by identifying the financing requirements for getting on to the ladder at the lowest appropriate rung. The $10 billion price tag for reaching the Millennium Development Goal sanitation target is based on access to the first rung of the sanitation ladder—simple pit latrines. A similar exercise for the top rungs of the sanitation ladder, including household connections to sewerage facilities and the provision of municipal wastewater treatment, would raise the cost to $34 billion.[3] Set against these cost differences, climbing the sanitation ladder offers major health benefits. While even the most basic improved sanitation offers benefits, returns to human development rise progressively at each level. In urban areas of Peru, to take one example, having a pit latrine in the home lowers the incidence of diarrhoea by 50%, while having a flush toilet lowers the risk by 70%.

Moving from open defecation at one extreme to the safe collection, storage and disposal of human excreta and the treatment or recycling of sewage effluents poses different

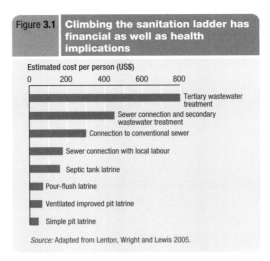

Figure 3.1 Climbing the sanitation ladder has financial as well as health implications

Estimated cost per person (US$)

- Tertiary wastewater treatment
- Sewer connection and secondary wastewater treatment
- Connection to conventional sewer
- Sewer connection with local labour
- Septic tank latrine
- Pour-flush latrine
- Ventilated improved pit latrine
- Simple pit latrine

Source: Adapted from Lenton, Wright and Lewis 2005.

challenges in different contexts. In rural areas sewerage networks are often not available. Improved sanitation usually means passing through a hierarchy of pit latrines, with pour-flush latrines and septic tank latrines the plausible options. In urban areas the picture is more mixed. For high-density urban areas sewerage systems have obvious advantages. Connections to feeder sewers and trunk sewers are the safest way to separate people and drinking water from human waste: an age-old human development challenge. But where the reach of the sewerage network is limited and the unserved population is large, the capital costs of developing a sewerage system capable of connecting all households can be prohibitive. Under these conditions on-site sanitation or public facilities may be the most viable short- to medium-run option.

Beyond the latrine

The diversity of current provision patterns cautions against universal policy prescriptions. Much of Sub-Saharan Africa has low coverage by sewerage networks, with less than 10% of the urban population connected. The same holds for countries at higher average incomes. Cities such as Jakarta and Manila have lower levels of sewerage coverage (8%–10%) than West African cities such as Dakar and Abidjan. Where coverage levels are low but cities have extensive trunk sewer systems, the costs of connecting households through feeder systems may not be prohibitive. Costs rise rapidly, however, where household connections would require large investments in trunk sewerage provision.

In some cities coverage rates are high but sewerage systems are in extreme disrepair. Delhi has many of the trappings of a developed country sanitation model—but appearances belie some serious problems. A large proportion of the city's 5,600 kilometres of feeder sewers are silted, and less than 15% of the trunk sewer is functioning. The 17 sewerage plants that serve the city have the capacity to process less than half the waste produced, and most operate far below capacity. The result: less than a fifth of the city's waste is processed before it is dumped into the Yamuna River, transmitting risks downstream.[4] In Latin America many cities have feeder and trunk sewerage systems that cover a large section of the population. But sewage treatment capacity is very limited: less than a fifth of the wastewater in Brazil and Mexico is treated.[5]

Infrastructure for sanitation extends far beyond the sewer. In cities like Jakarta and Manila the limited coverage of the sewerage system has given rise to a highly developed infrastructure of pit latrines. That infrastructure makes it possible to remove waste from households, but much of it ends in rivers. Pit latrines and septic tanks need to be emptied regularly, otherwise they overflow, block drainage channels and cause acute sanitation problems. The problem in Manila is that the pit latrine infrastructure is more developed than the waste treatment and disposal infrastructure. Many cities in Sub-Saharan Africa face the same problem. For example, an estimated 13% of latrines in Kibera, Nairobi, are unusable because they are too full.[6] Emptying latrines in densely populated urban areas requires an extensive service

| Box 3.1 | Disability and sanitation |

For people with disabilities, the physical presence of an improved sanitation facility is not the same as access. People with disabilities face special problems in households that lack improved sanitation.

Disability is not a side issue in sanitation policy. The WHO estimates that some 10% of the world's population has some impairment that restricts mobility. The overall number is on the increase, due to ageing populations and the rise in chronic illness, traffic accidents and injuries from armed conflict. The human consequences of disability are often more severe in developing countries because of widespread poverty and more limited social welfare programmes.

People with disabilities are among the most vulnerable members of society—and among the poorest. A vicious cycle links disability and chronic poverty: if you are poor you are more likely to be disabled, and if you are disabled you are more likely to be poor. In Ecuador 50% of people with disabilities belong to the lowest 40% of the income distribution. Similarly, surveys of the living conditions of people with disabilities in Malawi, Namibia and Zimbabwe show that they live in households with lower than average incomes. In Namibia 56% of households with a disabled member have no one employed in the formal sector, compared with 41% for households with no disabled members.

Some household surveys have captured the special sanitation disadvantages facing people with disabilities. In Namibia households with disabled people are less likely to have access to a private flush toilet and more likely to resort to using the bush. Inaccessible toilets in public spaces such as schools

and hospitals can affect access to education and health services. The United Nations Educational, Scientific and Cultural Organization estimates that 90% of children with disabilities in developing countries do not attend school in part because of inaccessible toilets. In Uganda the father of a disabled child who was so eager to go to school that he would not drink or eat until evening because he would otherwise need to use the toilet, reports:

My son you see here today suffers a lot. He never takes breakfast and any meal at school until he comes back home. The school toilets are filthy. The fact that he simply crawls, and does not have a wheelchair, makes him fear to enter the toilets, which are already dirty. Coupled to this is the fact that even the toilets do not have wide doors to allow our ordinary tricycle to enter. So the whole day he goes without food until he comes back home.

There is a widespread perception that addressing disability will require investments and technology beyond the capacity of households and providers. But often only minor changes are needed to give people with disabilities access to ordinary water and sanitation services. The additional costs are minimal: research indicates that incorporating "access for all" features into the design from the outset adds only 1% to the cost, compared with the far greater expense of renovating or adapting existing facilities. Five South African case studies covering a variety of applications suggest that the cost of providing accessibility can be as low as 0.5%–1% of the cost of a project. In the Ikwezi Community Centre in Gugulethu, east of Cape Town, the additional cost of providing accessible toilet facilities was 0.31%.

Source: CONADIS and others 2004; SINTEF Unimed 2002, 2003a,b; Jones and Reed 2005; Metts 2000; Metts 2000, annex I.

infrastructure. Sludge has to be removed manually or through suction pumps, transferred to trucks and delivered to waste disposal sites. If disposal sites are not properly maintained, effluents can seep into groundwater and flow into streams and rivers, creating public health hazards.

Quantifying quality and equity

Data problems loom large in dealing with sanitation. Some countries (Kenya and Tanzania to name two) register implausibly high sanitation coverage figures, while others (Brazil) have far higher rates of coverage than WHO/UNICEF data indicate.[7] Moreover, data on coverage say little about quality. Broken or poorly functioning improved pit latrines may inflate coverage rates, but they pose huge public health risks for families and communities.

While inadequate sanitation causes health risks and loses of dignity for all who are affected, people with disabilities face special problems. In most low-income countries national census data and household surveys are creating a stronger information base for understanding quality and coverage problems. However, the data sources are seldom detailed enough to identify the districts, neighbourhoods, income levels and other markers for disadvantage that governments and service providers need to build up a map of who is not served. This matters because the distribution of disadvantage has implications for the design of public policies. Data and policy responses have been found particularly wanting in relation to disability (box 3.1)

The water-sanitation-hygiene benefits loop

Climbing the sanitation ladder holds the prospect of large public health benefits. But advances in sanitation work best when associated with progress in water and hygiene.

Cross-country studies show that the method of disposing of excreta is one of the strongest determinants of child survival. On average, the transition from unimproved to improved sanitation is accompanied by a more than 30% reduction in child mortality, with flush toilets

associated with far larger reductions than pit latrines.[8]

Improved sanitation helps to break the faecal-oral transmission route that perpetuates the public health problems outlined in chapter 1. Sanitation bestows health benefits at two levels. The household that invests in a latrine secures many advantages, but a possibly greater benefit accrues to the community.

This can be illustrated by data from *favelas* in Salvador, Brazil (figure 3.2). The incidence of diarrhoea is twice as high among children in households without toilets as among children in households with sanitation, while it is three times greater for children in communities without sanitation infrastructure than in communities with drains and sewers.[9] Thus the absence of measures to promote the development of sanitation infrastructure can limit the advantages associated with household investments in sanitation.[10] Conversely, when a household installs a latrine, it not only protects them from contact with their own excreta but also helps protect their neighbors. The strong externalities associated with individual and community investments in sanitation make a solid case for public policies—such as government spending, subsidies and regulation—to promote such investments.

Hygiene is another predictor of public health. Hands transmit pathogens to foodstuffs

The transition from unimproved to improved sanitation is accompanied by a more than 30% reduction in child mortality

Figure **3.2** **The benefits of sanitation depend on household and community action**

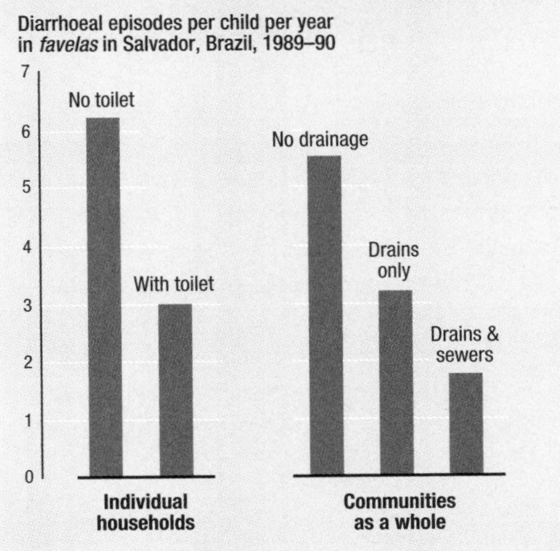

Diarrhoeal episodes per child per year in *favelas* in Salvador, Brazil, 1989–90

Source: Cairncross and others 2003.

Just a few generations ago people living in the great cities of Europe and the United States were facing grave public health threats as a result of unclean water and poor sanitation

and beverages and to the mouths of susceptible hosts. Because diarrhoeal diseases are of faecal origin, hand washing with soap and water has been identified as a major determinant of reduced child mortality, along with interventions that prevent faecal material from entering the domestic environment of children.[11]

Evidence from Burkina Faso demonstrates the interaction between sanitation and hygiene. In the mid-1990s the country's second largest city, Bobo-Dioulasso, had a well managed water supply system and most households had pit latrines, but children were still at risk from poor hygiene. The Ministry of Health and Community Groups promoted behavioural changes that reduced the incidence of diarrhoea—for example, by encouraging mothers to wash their hands with soap and water after changing diapers. Over three years the programme averted some 9,000 diarrhoea episodes, 800 outpatient visits, 300 hospital referrals and 100 deaths—at a cost of $0.30 per inhabitant.[12]

Behavioural factors may be important in hygiene, but access to clean water is essential. One study in villages in Kyrgyzstan found that few people washed their hands and that almost half of households disposed of faeces in gardens or streets.[13] The problem was not that they were ignorant of the need for hygiene; they just had few opportunities to practice it in households that lacked water supplies and could not afford soap. Hand-washing rates were three times higher in households with piped water and washstands.

Attempting to separate the effects of water, sanitation and hygiene is a popular exercise—but an unhelpful one. In today's rich countries the great public works that drove the water and sanitation revolutions—the pipes, sewers, water filtration and wastewater treatment plants—were pivotal. But so were micro-level public health changes encouraged through education. Campaigns to promote hand washing, breastfeeding and boiling water for baby bottles increased the returns on investment in public works. What is important is that public policies expand access to infrastructure and unlock the complementarities that operate across the artificial frontiers between water, hygiene and sanitation. Children are among the most effective agents for change (box 3.2).

Clean water, the sanitary removal of excreta and personal hygiene are the three foundations for any strategy to enhance public health. Collectively, these are the most potent antidotes to the parasitic diseases and other infections transmitted through flies and other vectors that blight so many lives in areas where stagnant water is the primary source for drinking, cooking and washing. While clean water and personal hygiene can make a difference on their own, the benefits for public health will be diminished without adequate sanitation, drainage and wider infrastructure for disposing of excreta. That is why public policies for water and sanitation need to be seen as part of an integrated strategy.

Box 3.2	Children as agents of change

The classroom is one of the best places for effecting positive changes in hygiene. Teaching children hand washing and other good hygiene habits protects their health and promotes transformations beyond school. In Mozambique a national campaign trained children to teach other children about hand washing and sanitation-related problems. In China and Nigeria UNICEF-supported school-based hygiene projects report increases of 75%–80% in hand washing with soap.

In some countries hygiene and sanitation have been brought into the national curriculum. In Tajikistan more than 11,000 students are engaged in an outreach programme on sanitation. In Bangladesh schools and nongovernmental organizations formed student brigades to take hygiene and sanitation messages from their schools back to their communities.

Such school-based programmes provide adequate water and sanitation and separate facilities for boys and girls.

Source: IRC International Water and Sanitation Centre 2004; International Training Network Centre 2003; UNICEF and IRC International Water and Sanitation Centre 2005; UNICEF 2005a, 2006a.

It is distressing to see a child's future threatened or diminished by preventable disease. The rights to health services and to safe, clean, affordable water are fundamental to a life of dignity and are protected by international law. Yet millions of people die of water-related diseases annually, and millions more suffer needlessly. None of us should turn a blind eye to the shocking consequences of inadequate access to clean water and to sanitation set out in this Report.

The scale of the problem in water and sanitation poses a daunting challenge, but one we can overcome. Just a few generations ago people living in the great cities of Europe and the United States were facing grave public health threats as a result of unclean water and poor sanitation. At the end of the 19th century those threats were addressed through concerted political action at a national level. At the start of the 21st century we need to extend the leadership that made progress possible in today's rich countries to the global stage.

My colleagues at The Carter Center and I are working to eradicate Guinea worm disease (dracunculiasis) and control trachoma, two horrible afflictions that can be prevented by providing access to clean water, sanitation and health services. As recently as 50 years ago trachoma, which is the world's leading cause of preventable blindness, still affected parts of the United States, including my home town of Plains, Georgia. Though today we know how to avoid such diseases, more than 1.4 million children still die each year from intestinal parasites, and millions of people throughout the developing world continue to suffer from trachoma. But there has been progress.

Guinea worm, a parasitic waterborne disease, is poised to be the first disease to be eradicated without a vaccine or medical treatment. The presence of Guinea worm disease in a geographic area indicates abject poverty, including the absence of safe drinking water. The disease is so painful and debilitating that its effects reach far beyond a single victim, crippling agricultural production and reducing school attendance. It devastates already impoverished communities and further prevents them from achieving good health and economic prosperity.

Guinea worm became the second disease in history to be targeted for eradication following the inauguration of the International Drinking Water Supply and Sanitation Decade (1981–90). In 1986 The Carter Center, the US Centers for Disease Control and Prevention, the United Nations Children's Fund, the World Health Organization and the countries plagued by Guinea worm embraced the challenge of eradicating the disease.

When the programme began, there were approximately 3.5 million cases, crippling millions of people in 20 countries in Africa and Asia. Since then, Guinea worm disease has been reduced by more than 99.7%. In 2005 only 10,674 cases of dracunculiasis were reported in nine countries—all in Africa. Today, coalition partners, in collaboration with thousands of dedicated community health workers, continue to intensify efforts as we fight the last fraction of 1% of Guinea worm disease. As an active participant in the Guinea worm campaign, my primary objective is the eradication of this terrible scourge. Our progress toward this goal gives me confidence that together we can eliminate this disease within my lifetime.

More must be done to eradicate Guinea worm, but the larger task is to provide safe drinking water and sanitation to all. Halving the number of people who lack water and sanitation by 2015 as envisaged under the Millennium Development Goals is the first step. Failure to achieve that target would set back the entire Millennium Development Goal project. Without progress in water and sanitation, we cannot accelerate social progress in other areas, such as child survival, access to education and reduction of extreme poverty.

It is fitting that as we approach the eradication of Guinea worm disease another major international effort is under way to provide safe water to 1.1 billion people and adequate sanitation to 2.6 billon people. These noble efforts will help alleviate the greatest challenge of our time—to bridge the widening chasm between the rich and the poor in our world.

Jimmy Carter

Jimmy Carter, 39th President, United States;
Founder, The Carter Center; Nobel Peace Prize Laureate 2002

Effective national policies are even more conspicuously absent for sanitation than for water

The daunting scale of human suffering rooted in the global sanitation deficit can create the impression of an insurmountable problem. That impression is wrong. One of the lessons of the past decade is that concerted national and international action can make a difference. Twenty years ago Guinea worm was a major cause of suffering and poverty in a large swathe of countries across Sub-Saharan Africa. In the mid-1980s some 3.5 million people were infected with dracunculiasis, the Guinea worm parasite that enters the body when people drink water from stagnant pools containing Guinea worm larvae. Inside the body the parasite can grow up to three feet in length. When they leave the body, they cause intense blistering and often crippling effects. Today, following the intervention of a global partnership involving UNICEF, the WHO and the Carter Center, Guinea worm has almost been consigned to the history books (see special contribution by former US President Jimmy Carter). The disease has been eradicated from 11 countries, eight of them in Africa. While major pockets of infection remain—notably in Sudan—this battle against diseases caused by stagnant water and poor sanitation has almost been won.

Success in the battle against Guinea worm disease has extended the human capabilities of countless millions of people. Further, more urgent action is needed to tackle problems such as trachoma and other parasitic infections.

Ultimately, however, for global initiatives to achieve optimal effects they have to be backed by the development of an infrastructure that provides households with clean water and sanitation. National strategies backed by a global plan of action to mobilize the resources needed to bring clean water and sanitation to all hold the key to success.

Why does sanitation lag so far behind water?

Toilets may be an unlikely catalyst for human progress—but the evidence that they are is overwhelming. Adequate sanitation has the potential to produce cumulative benefits in public health, employment and economic growth. So why is it that at the start of the 21st century so much human potential is being wasted for want of some fairly simple technologies? And why does sanitation lag so far behind water in public provision? These questions are as germane to debates on human development today as they were in developed countries more than a century ago. Six interlocking barriers provide answers: national policy, behaviour, perception, poverty, gender and supply. None of the six barriers can be considered in isolation. But each helps to explain why progress towards the long-standing goal of sanitation for all has been so slow.

The national policy barrier

Chapter 2 highlighted national policies and national political leadership in accelerating access to water. Effective national policies are even more conspicuously absent for sanitation than for water. The state of a country's sanitation may shape its prospects for human development, and yet sanitation seldom, if ever, figures prominently on the national political agenda.

That is true even for countries that have progressed rapidly in water provision. South Africa has not matched its success in expanding access and reducing inequality in water provision with a comparable effort in sanitation. The same is true for Morocco. In this case the National Drinking Water Office has been a highly effective body in expanding access to water across many cities and in rural areas. However, progress in sanitation has been held back by a far weaker national strategy, the fragmentation of governance systems, inadequate financing, and capacity constraints in rural municipalities.

The behaviour barrier

Weak national policy frameworks and the lower priority accorded sanitation relative to water in part reflect the signals received from households. Participatory research exercises show that people tend to attach a higher priority to water than to sanitation. There are some obvious explanations. Lack of clean water is a more immediate threat to life than the absence of a toilet. Moreover, water piped into a household provides rapid and tangible benefits in time saved and health risks averted, regardless of what other households do.

The benefits of sanitation can appear more contingent on factors beyond the household. For example, the public health benefits of installing a latrine may not materialize unless other households also act: installation in one household does not provide protection against the excrement of other households in slums with poor drainage. In addition, installation of a latrine may be seen as a public good, with the community deriving benefits in the form of reduced health risks and the household deriving fewer private gains than in water. For a household the costs of not having access to clean water may appear more evident than those of long-established sanitation practices, such as defecating in fields or streams—and the benefits of improved sanitation are not as widely understood as those of access to clean water.

The perception barrier

For governments and many development organizations the case for public action in sanitation rests on the public benefits of health and wealth. Things often look different at the household level. Village research in Cambodia, Indonesia and Viet Nam consistently finds "a clean home and village environment free of bad smells and flies" as the most important benefit identified by households, followed by convenience. Health benefits rank third. In Benin,

too, rural households attach a higher weight to household status—linked to the absence of smells—and to convenience than to health.[14]

The fact that households often view better sanitation as a private amenity with private benefits rather than a public responsibility may have weakened the perceived political imperative to develop national strategies. Understanding what people value about improved sanitation and why they value it is a first step towards a demand-responsive approach. But demand cannot be treated as fixed. Education, social marketing and political campaigns can shift demand patterns by raising aspirations and creating new expectations.

The poverty barrier

The cost of improved sanitation can be prohibitive when large segments of the population lack access. The ranks of people without improved sanitation are less dominated by the very poor than is the case for water, but poverty remains a major constraint to gaining access. Nearly 1.4 billion people without access to sanitation live on less than $2 a day. For most of them, even low-cost improved technology may be beyond financial reach.

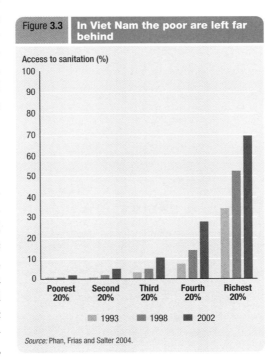

| Figure **3.3** | **In Viet Nam the poor are left far behind** |

Access to sanitation (%)

Source: Phan, Frias and Salter 2004.

1993   1998   2002

> The public health benefits of installing a latrine may not materialize unless other households also act

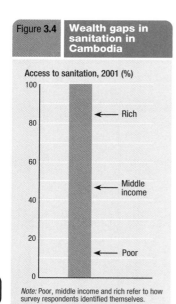

Figure 3.4 **Wealth gaps in sanitation in Cambodia**

Access to sanitation, 2001 (%)

Note: Poor, middle income and rich refer to how survey respondents identified themselves.

Source: Mukherjee 2001.

3

Consider Viet Nam, which has already achieved the Millennium Development Goal target for sanitation. Rural coverage has increased rapidly, albeit from a low base. But the poorest households have been left far behind (figure 3.3). In Cambodia the daily wage for rural labourers does not cover a family's basic nutritional requirements, leaving nothing for health, clothing and education. It would take 20 days' wages to purchase a simple pit latrine—helping to explain the very large discrepancy between coverage rates for the rich and the poor (figure 3.4). In Kibera, Nairobi, constructing a pit latrine costs about $45, or two months of income for someone earning the minimum wage. To help poor households meet the financing requirements of improved sanitation, arrangements are needed that provide subsidies or allow payments to be spread over time through microcredit.

The gender barrier

Gender inequalities help to explain the low demand for sanitation in many communities. Evidence from many countries suggests that women place a higher value on access to private sanitation facilities than do men—an outcome that reflects the greater disadvantage women face through insecurity, loss of dignity and adverse health outcomes associated with lack of access. Research in Cambodia, Indonesia and Viet Nam found that women consistently give higher value for cost scores to toilets than do men.[15]

But the weak voice of women in shaping spending priorities within the household means that the constituency with the strongest expressed demand for sanitation has little control over expenditures. For the same reason the priority that women attach to sanitation is seldom reflected in decision-making beyond the household, in political structures extending from the village through local government to national levels. Empowering women may be one of the most successful mechanisms for increasing effective demand.

The supply barrier

Turning from demand to supply shows that progress is impeded not just by the absence of affordable sanitation technology, but also by the oversupply of inappropriate technologies, leading to a mismatch between what people want and what governments have offered. For example, pour-flush latrines provided through government programmes have often had low uptake rates because communities lack secure water supplies. In other cases the technologies marketed through government agencies have been difficult or expensive to maintain. Products designed by engineers without reference to community needs and priorities and delivered through unaccountable government agencies have left a legacy of abandoned sanitation products. Time horizon is another factor. Evidence from many countries suggests that progress in sanitation, far more than in water, requires a planning frame of 10–15 years, whereas average donor cycles and national planning cycles operate over 2–3 year cycles.

Bringing sanitation for all within reach

The slow progress in sanitation has long been a source of concern. After more than three decades of high-level conferences, sweeping policy shifts and ambitious—but unrealized—targets, there is a strong undercurrent of pessimism surrounding the Millennium Development Goal for sanitation. That pessimism is as unjustified as the overweening optimism of earlier approaches.

From a distance the global sanitation picture is bleak. But a closer look reveals a striking

| Box 3.3 | **Action from below—the Orangi Project** |

Orangi is a large, low-income informal settlement—or *katchi abadi*—in Karachi, Pakistan. Home to more than a million people, it is a success story of the power of communities to expand access to sanitation.

In 1980 a local nongovernmental organization started to work through the Orangi Pilot Project with local communities to tackle the settlement's appalling sanitation situation. The focal point for mobilization was the lane. Through dialogue and education lane residents were urged to form groups to construct sewer channels to collect waste from their homes. Cooperation between lane managers then facilitated the construction of neighbourhood channels to collect the waste from multiple lanes. Initially, the channels were discharged into nearby drains. But after a period of dialogue with municipal authorities, the city agreed to finance a trunk sewer to collect the waste and transport it from the community.

Infant mortality rates in the slum have fallen from 130 deaths per 1,000 live births in the early 1980s to fewer than 40 today. Almost 100,000 families in more than 6,000 lanes representing 90% of the population have been involved. Training community workers in maintenance and labour mobilization has reduced the costs of sanitation provision to a fifth of the cost of official provision, enabling the project to recover costs without making services unaffordable.

Source: Satterthwaite 2006; Hasan 2005; Zaidi 2001.

proliferation of local and even national success stories within this larger picture. In some cases the people at the distressed end of the sanitation crisis—the slum dwellers and the rural communities lacking even basic sanitation—have driven change from below. In other cases government agencies and service providers have taken the lead or played a key role in scaling up actions initiated from below. What unites the success stories are the twin principles of shared rights and joint responsibilities, building blocks for any social contract between government and citizens. In this broad framework community demand, appropriate technology and demand-responsive and accountable service provision are recurrent themes.

Action from below makes a difference

The principles of shared rights and joint responsibilities matter in a very practical way. In urban slums with large and highly concentrated populations, the success of any community initiative depends on individual participation, especially for improved sanitation. Through mobilization from below the Orangi Pilot Project in Karachi, Pakistan, has evolved over the past two decades into a programme that brings sanitation to millions of slum dwellers.[16] Near-universal participation has been based on a collective perception of benefits and an acceptance of joint responsibility for unlocking those benefits (box 3.3).

The Orangi Project, which began as a small community-led initiative, scaled up through cooperation with local governments. Scaling up matters because small isolated projects cannot spark or sustain national progress. At the same time the energy and innovation of community actions can strengthen government capacity to deliver change.

In India in the early 1990s the National Slum Dwellers Federation (NSDF); the Society for the Promotion of Area Resource Centres (SPARC), a Mumbai-based nongovernmental organization (NGO); and Mahila Milan, a network of savings groups formed by women slum and pavement dwellers, pioneered a new approach to design and manage public toilet blocks in response to the inability of poor households to install latrines in high-density areas. Construction was preceded by slum surveys, savings mobilization and the development of organizations to manage the toilets. Design innovations included the provision of separate facilities for men and women. Initially, local authorities discouraged these efforts. But the model has since been adopted in Pune, a city of more than 2 million people, through collaboration between municipal authorities and NSDF, SPARC, and Mahila Milan. Between 1999 and 2001 more than 440 toilet blocks were constructed, with more than 10,000 new toilets. Financing has been provided through the government of Maharashtra, with NGOs taking responsibility for design and maintenance.

Community participation is probably the biggest influence on the success—or failure—of

3

The vast deficit in sanitation

But the division between household or community action and government-led public action is misleading and unhelpful. Government leadership remains vital

public sanitation facilities. Until recently facilities created by municipalities had a weak record in provision, with poor maintenance, inappropriate location and similar missteps leading to low public use. That record has started to change. City authorities in Windhoek, Namibia, recognized that government sanitation facilities were not reaching the poor because quality standards made costs prohibitive. Working with the National Shack Dwellers Federation, municipal authorities created a new legislative framework enabling neighbourhood committees to build and manage their own toilet blocks. Standards were relaxed, and regulations were applied more flexibly. In Chittagong, Bangladesh, the international NGO WaterAid, local NGOs and municipal authorities have developed cluster latrines for use by 150 households at a cost of $0.60 a month per household.[17] These latrines, maintained through community-based organizations, have brought sanitation to far more people than would have been possible through individual household purchases.

The failure of past supply-led approaches has produced a major shift in policy orientation. One of the most profound expressions of the shift is the community-led total sanitation campaign, an approach designed to build demand for improved sanitation.[18] In Bangladesh the total sanitation campaign was begun by local NGOs but has since been scaled up into a national programme. Its success has helped keep the country on track for the sanitation Millennium Development Goal target (box 3.4).

The total sanitation campaign approach begins with a community-based appraisal of current sanitation practices, which usually include open defecation.[19] Residents undertake a mapping exercise with households to identify defecation sites, the transmission routes that cause disease and the contribution of each household to the problem. The aim is to appeal to three basic drivers for change: disgust, self-interest and a sense of individual responsibility for community welfare. This approach has been widely developed and deployed with some success across such countries as Cambodia, China, India and Zambia.

Innovative design and marketing can bring improved sanitation within the reach of even the most disadvantaged. Take Sulabh in India.

Founded on Gandhian principles, it has developed products aimed at some of the poorest sections of Indian society, including low castes and migrant workers. Most striking are its scale of operation—providing improved sanitation to some 10 million people—and its business model (box 3.5).

Government leadership is vital

The central role of households in financing sanitation, the high-profile failure of some heavily subsidized government initiatives and the crucial role of household demand as a catalyst for change have spurred some people to advocate a minimalist role for government. But the division between household or community action and government-led public action is misleading and unhelpful. Government leadership remains vital.

Setting national strategies

In sanitation as in water the starting point for successful expansion of coverage is effective national planning. Many countries need to change the mindset that undervalues sanitation. That mindset is often reflected in the institutional location of responsibility for sanitation in government. One common arrangement is to assign sanitation to a technical unit within the ministry of health, an approach that limits the scope for bold political initiatives. Another problem is the fragmentation of authority. In Ghana roles and responsibilities for water are well defined within a national planning framework. That is not the case for sanitation, where authority is divided among the Ministry for Water Resources, Works and Housing and a range of other line ministries. In Niger sanitation comes under the Ministry of Water, but coordination for sanitation takes place through a national committee with limited authority. In each case, national planning would be enhanced if it were led by a senior ministerial figure coordinating the development and implementation of sanitation strategies.

Some governments have a strong track record in providing access to sanitation. Since 1990 Thailand has increased the national sanitation coverage rate from 80% to 100%. Progress

Box 3.4 **Bangladesh's total sanitation campaign**

Ten years ago Bangladesh, among the poorest countries in the world, had one of the lowest levels of coverage for rural sanitation. Today, it has ambitious plans to achieve nationwide sanitation coverage by 2010. Strongly supported by the country's aid partners, those plans target an achievable annual increase in sanitation coverage of 2.4 million households.

The total sanitation campaign is central to Bangladesh's success. Pioneered by a Bangladeshi NGO in the late 1990s, it now involves more than 600 NGOs that work with local district authorities in marketing improved sanitation messages.

The starting point is engagement with local communities in identifying the problems associated with open defecation by calculating the amount of excreta deposited in the village environment, mapping dirty zones and identifying transmission routes to diarrhoea and wider public health problems. The "walk of shame" to defecation zones and the "excreta calculation" are the two initial tools for generating shared community concern. Communities discuss and document open defecation and consider the health consequences. Once interest is ignited, there is momentum for villagers to work with government agencies, NGOs, religious organizations and others to establish sanitation forums to identify concerns.

As the campaign has developed and demand for sanitation has increased, a vibrant small business sector has emerged. Bangladesh is now a world leader in producing, marketing and maintaining low-cost latrines. At the end of 2000 there were 2,400 registered small-scale latrine production centres. That figure has since risen to 3,000, demonstrating again the capacity of small-scale providers to respond to local markets. The cost of latrines has fallen sharply. Meanwhile, village efforts have been supported by NGO-led microfinance schemes, mobilizing savings and providing loans.

While the programme has been based on demand-responsive approaches, national policy has also been important. Successive governments have made rural sanitation a priority. The National Policy for Water and Sanitation, drawn up in 1998, establishes a policy framework for partnerships of small-scale entrepreneurs and community groups and provides support for marketing and training through local and national government agencies.

To get a sense of the effectiveness of this partnership, compare Bangladesh with India. Ten years ago the two countries faced similar problems. Since then, India has enjoyed far more rapid economic growth, widening the income gap between the two countries. But in rural sanitation India has fallen behind Bangladesh (see table), even though some Indian states have made progress.

In the decade to 2015 the biggest challenges are to sustain the momentum built up over recent years and to reduce inequalities in access. While data are patchy, the Bangladeshi government is concerned that the improved national sanitation coverage rate may hide the fact that poor rural households are unable to finance even low-cost latrines. Its response has been to allocate the entire share of the annual development programme for sanitation to subsidize demand among the poorest 20% of the population.

Improvements in sanitation and infant mortality: Bangladesh and India, 1990–2004

Indicator	Bangladesh			India		
	1990	2004	Change	1990	2004	Change
Sanitation, national (%)	20	39	19	14	33	19
Rural sanitation (%)	12	35	23	3	22	19
Infant mortality (per 1,000 live births)	96	56	−40	84	62	−22

Source: Indicator table 10; WHO and UNICEF 2006.

Source: Bangladesh 1998, 2005; Kar and Pasteur 2005; Practical Action Consulting 2006a; VERC 2002; WSP–SA 2005.

in rural areas has been particularly marked: more than 13 million people in rural areas have gained access in two decades. These outcomes reflect the priority accorded to sanitation as part of national planning.[20] Under the national strategy every district has been required to identify coverage gaps from the village upwards—and to develop strategies for closing them. Government agencies in Thailand developed technologies that were affordable and accessible to the poor, provided training in maintenance and financed revolving funds to meet the capital costs. Community health programmes increased awareness of the health benefits of sanitation.

Government success in some areas can highlight public policy failures in others. Both Colombia and Morocco have expanded access to improved sanitation for some of the poorest in society. The coverage rate in Colombia—about 86% in 2005—is far higher than its national income would predict (figure 3.5). In Morocco coverage for the poorest 20% has expanded fourfold since 1992. But in both countries progress has been skewed by a distinct bias that is exacerbating inequalities between urban and rural areas.[21]

The urban bias can be traced in part to national policy planning. In Colombia responsibility for water and sanitation has been devolved to municipalities with a strong record in service provision. Fiscal transfers from the central government to municipalities account for two-thirds of investment in water and sanitation, and poorer and smaller municipalities get more per capita.[22] Other central government programmes target poor households for connection and service provision subsidies (see chapter 2) and provide smaller utilities with loans and technical assistance. This has brought tangible benefits for poor urban households. In Morocco, too, government policies have created incentives for utilities to

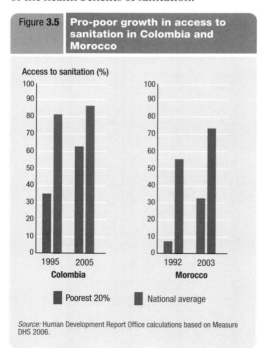

Figure 3.5   **Pro-poor growth in access to sanitation in Colombia and Morocco**

Access to sanitation (%)

Colombia: 1995, 2005
Morocco: 1992, 2003

■ Poorest 20% ■ National average

Source: Human Development Report Office calculations based on Measure DHS 2006.

The vast deficit in sanitation

3

extend provision to low-income urban house-holds. The problem in both countries is that there is no effective national sanitation strategy for rural areas. For example, Colombia's National Development Plan targets coverage in urban areas but not in rural areas. Policy goals and national standards are set for piped connections and networks, but pit latrines may be more appropriate in rural areas.

Partnering with communities

Creating an environment in which sanitation is perceived both as a household responsibility and as a community right can change the attitudes and behaviours that limit progress. Such an environment requires a dynamic interaction between government agencies and communities. It means drawing on the social capital of communities and building a sense of social solidarity and shared citizenship, with governments creating a policy environment that enables all people to progress towards improved sanitation.

Some of the most conspicuous success stories in sanitation are the product of partnerships between governments and communities, with a wide range of civil society organizations as a bridge. Public policy can create demand and scale up community-led initiatives. The Bangladesh total sanitation campaign is one example. Another is the rapid progress in rural sanitation in Lesotho, where a strong national planning process and political leadership, with a strong emphasis on community involvement, yielded real progress (box 3.6).[23]

Many government interventions have been justifiably criticized for supplying inappropriate technology, but the success stories are less widely appreciated. In Brazil municipal governments supported a shift in emphasis from conventional sewerage technology to a lower cost alternative, the condominial system. That system has facilitated a sustained increase in coverage rates.[24]

In a conventional sewerage system service is provided to each household unit. In a condominium model service is provided to blocks or groups of residences, avoiding the need for pipes in each lot or even each street of a neighbourhood. The network has two parts. The citywide

| Box 3.6 | Lesotho—progress in rural sanitation |

Twenty years ago Lesotho began a small pilot project for rural sanitation with financial assistance from the United Nations Development Programme and the United Nations Children's Fund. Since then, rural coverage has increased from 15% to 32%—higher than for many countries with higher average incomes. The current target is full coverage by 2010.

The programme has been creating demand and providing support for training in the construction of latrines. District sanitation teams work through local community structures to increase awareness of the benefits of sanitation, creating demand for improved latrines. The supply response emerged through small-scale local providers, supported through training by local government agencies.

The integration of health and hygiene education with construction and technical activities is supported through national coordination between the Ministry of the Interior (concerned mainly with hardware aspects) and the Ministry of Health. Coordination with the water supply sector has also improved.

One of the challenges looking to the 2010 target date is to reach some of the country's poorest households. The full cost-recovery and zero-subsidy policy has created incentives for innovation. But even basic latrines are still beyond the means of the very poor. Only recently have measures been put in place to reduce the costs of latrines through microcredit programmes offering extended loan repayment periods.

Source: Jenkins and Sugden 2006; World Bank 2004b.

system provides a trunk connected to parallel microsystems that receive waste from the condominial blocks. These systems take into account local topography and drainage conditions, dramatically reducing the length of the piped system. And they can be operated independently until they can be connected to a city-wide trunk.

The development of the condominial system in Brazil has been about politics as much as technology. Community participation in decision-making is widely perceived as both a right and a duty of citizenship, with the condominium providing a social unit to facilitate collective decisions. Condominium members have to agree on the appropriate location for the branch network and organize themselves to perform complementary activities, including construction and maintenance. This system is now a central part of the sewerage system serving more than 2 million people in Brasilia alone (box 3.7).

Creating conditions for progress

Government leadership in creating the conditions for progress in sanitation is vital for some obvious reasons. Communities or NGOs acting alone can

The vast deficit in sanitation

Box 3.7	The condominial approach to sewerage systems in Brasilia— politics and technology

Developed in the 1980s to bring sanitation services to low-income households, the condominial system has emerged as a solution to sewerage management for whole urban areas, irrespective of income. The Water and Sewerage Company of Brasilia demonstrates how innovative technologies can be scaled up from small projects to cover whole cities.

In the early 1990s the lack of sanitation in the peri-urban areas of Brasilia and contamination of Lake Paranoa prompted municipal authorities to embark on a major sanitation programme. The company needed to extend the sewerage network to 1.7 million people. Conventional technologies would have been unaffordable, stimulating a search for low-cost alternatives.

After initial pilot studies the condominial model was adopted both for peri-urban neighbourhoods and for more affluent areas of the capital. Funds came from the Federal Development Bank and the Inter-American Development Bank, with additional contributions from the capital and the federal district. From 1993 to 2001 an estimated 188,000 condominial sewerage connections in the federal district benefited some 680,000 people.

Community involvement was central from the outset. Households had the option of doing the connection work themselves, under the supervision of the utility, or of paying for the connection. Fees were structured to reflect costs, with lower rates applied to households willing to install pipes in their yards and to be responsible for system maintenance.

What led to the success of the Brasilia model? First, the utility made a firm policy decision about the technology, communicated this decision clearly to the public and adapted its internal structure accordingly. Second, a decentralized sanitation system with the potential for integration into a citywide network offered considerable flexibility. Demand-responsive, it lent itself to application across condominial blocks and different microsystems. Third, community participation kept down costs and improved efficiency.

Source: Melo 2005.

create islands of success, sometimes on an impressive scale. But project-led advances cannot substitute for the financial, political and administrative resources that governments can bring to bear.

Consider West Bengal in India. Since 1990 the state government has developed a strategy for expanding rural sanitation involving long-term partnerships with international agencies such as UNICEF, state-level NGOs and other groups under the umbrella of India's national total sanitation campaign.[25] The West Bengal campaign is the only one in India with a dedicated unit—the State Institute of Panchayats and Rural Development—responsible for monitoring coverage, conducting reviews and evaluations and providing support and training to local government. The campaign emphasizes hygiene education and community involvement to generate demand. But government agencies and

NGOs have also been heavily involved in supply. Local governments have supported networks of rural sanitary marts to manufacture low-cost latrine slabs, with the government also supporting the training of masons to work in villages.

The results have been impressive. In 1990 when the state government launched its rural sanitation drive in Midnapur, then the largest district in India, coverage rates were less than 5%. The district now has 100% coverage. Across the state as a whole, 2 million toilets have been constructed and installed in the last five years, increasing state coverage of sanitation from 12% in 1991 to more than 40% today. Government subsidies cover about 40% of the cost of a latrine, but most public spending has gone into social marketing campaigns and programmes for latrine construction.

West Bengal's achievements over the past five years build on more than a decade of political and institutional investment. Evidence from other states highlights the problems of achieving rapid progress without these investments. For example, Andhra Pradesh launched a huge sanitation campaign in 1997. But the focus has been on relatively high-cost, heavily subsidized latrines (with an average price five times that in West Bengal). Evaluations indicate that the campaign has reached few poor people and that many of the new latrines have been abandoned. The problem is not the use of subsidies but the failure to target them and to develop demand through community partnerships.

The high costs of connecting to a sewer mean that on-site sanitation will remain the most viable option in many low-income areas. Public toilets on the model developed by Sulabh and others illustrate one approach for use in high population density areas. However, governments could do far more to create an enabling environment for the development of services such as pit emptying and disposal that are lacking in so many cities today. In effect, poor households are bearing the cost not just of constructing latrines, but also of providing the infrastructure for excreta disposal.

Public providers or public-private partnerships can make a difference. Municipal utilities can provide services or create the conditions for their development through contracts with the private sector. In Dar es Salam municipal authorities issue licenses to small-scale companies to provide sludge removal services within a price range affordable to poor households. The companies are required to deposit the waste at authorized treatment sites. As more firms have entered the market, prices have fallen. One condition for the development of a properly regulated waste disposal infrastructure is the availability of waste disposal sites. In the Kibera slums of Nairobi small-scale providers operate on an informal basis during the rainy season, when they dump sludge to be carried away by rainwater. There are no immediate alternatives because there is no dedicated waste disposal site.

The financing problem

As with water, households wanting to connect to the formal sanitation network have to pay a connection charge and regular usage costs. For the vast majority of households without a connection installing pit latrines implies both financial costs and labour inputs. Overcoming the financing barrier is an important part of any strategy for accelerating progress.

In the past governments applied subsidies directly to sanitation hardware, attempting to increase demand by reducing price. Too often these subsidies disproportionately benefited higher income households, which were frequently the only households that could afford the sanitation facilities eligible for government support. This appears to have happened in Zimbabwe, where government subsidies supported household spending without any clear targeting to the poor. The sudden withdrawal of subsidies led to sharp reversals in toilet construction. In Mozambique a national programme for expanding urban sanitation supply built up over two decades collapsed at the end of the 1990s when a reduction in aid flows led to the withdrawal of government subsidies and a 400% increase in the price of latrine slabs.

Developing responsive markets

With new demand-responsive approaches the focus has shifted to stimulating demand. In some cases these approaches have been based on the leverage of finance within communities. Bangladesh and Lesotho have zero-subsidy policies for the nonpoor, with most government financial support going into social marketing for latrines.[26] Implicit in this approach is an assumption that increased investment in technology and production will bring latrine prices down to affordable levels as the market develops over time.

That assumption is partially supported by the evidence. In Bangladesh the total sanitation campaign fostered highly innovative small firms specializing in providing and maintaining low-cost sanitation. In Lesotho public investment in training and marketing produced a strong private sector response. Prices for latrines fell, design improved, and small firms became highly attuned to working in local markets.[27] But there are limits to what the market can achieve when poverty is widespread. Both Bangladesh and Lesotho have found it difficult to expand access among the poorest sections of society—a problem that could retard progress if it is not addressed.

The experience of Viet Nam, a country with a strong record of increasing access to sanitation, is instructive. As already noted, national figures hide large inequalities in coverage between rich and poor and between urban and rural areas. Cost factors help to explain why these inequalities exist. Aid programmes are currently marketing latrines for low-income households for $35–$90.[28] On average, these households spend 72% of their income on food. Were the remainder of their income to go to the purchase of a latrine, this would imply an enormous diversion of resources from health and education.

Some governments have developed innovative strategies for cross-subsidizing sanitation. In Burkina Faso the public utility for water and sanitation levies a small sanitation surcharge on water users, with half the proceeds financing social marketing of sanitation. Another quarter of the levy supports the construction of improved sanitation facilities in low-income areas. The surcharge has been used to finance the installation of sanitation facilities in all primary schools in Ougadougou. Households are eligible to receive financial aid for improved pit latrines and pour-flush latrines. However,

Overcoming the financing barrier is an important part of any strategy for accelerating progress in sanitation

Most countries that have achieved rapid progress have mobilized household resources on a large scale, while supporting markets that provide technologies and maintenance

households are expected to finance 70%–80% of the cost of sanitation facilities.[29] These costs are high in relation to the resources of low-income people, so the very poorest households may not be reached.

Household financing and beyond

Most countries that have achieved rapid progress have mobilized household resources on a large scale, while supporting markets that provide technologies and maintenance. Again, the critical factor is the strength of the national policy process. In China progress in sanitation in rural areas was lagging far behind that in urban areas until the mid-1990s, holding back advances in health. Since then, rural sanitation has been an integral part of the national health strategy. Provincial and county governments oversee plans for meeting targets set by government. Resources have been invested in developing and marketing sanitary latrines designed for rural areas. Uptake has been impressive, with rural sanitation coverage doubling in five years. Financing comes from a range of sources, with users meeting 70% of the cost, village associations 15% and government about 15%. These figures provide an indication of the level of household resource mobilization, though questions of affordability for poor households remain.[30]

In all developing countries household resources will remain a critical source of investment for financing sanitation. But there are limits to what the poorest households can afford. Many

governments and aid donors remain deeply averse to the use of subsidies for household sanitation. However, without subsidies adequate sanitation will likely remain beyond the reach of a large section of the developing world's population, with risks for public health as well as household poverty. While it is true that the history of subsidies in sanitation is not encouraging, that should not rule out innovative financing arrangements, like microfinance arrangements for the initial investments with payments spread over a longer period. In India Water-Aid has cooperated with local governments in developing such microfinance facilities.[31] Initiatives of this type can be scaled up into national programmes if rooted in participative community systems. As governments seek to get countries on track for the 2015 Millennium Development Goal targets, it is important to place equity squarely on the agenda. For a large part of humanity, basic sanitation is likely to remain unaffordable in the foreseeable future. Without financial support for the poorest households, overly ambitious cost-recovery measures and zero-subsidy strategies will slow progress. Some of the costs will be borne by those who are excluded. But other costs will be transmitted across whole communities. The case for subsidies in sanitation, as in water, is rooted partly in the recognition that everyone is entitled to basic human rights, regardless of ability to pay, and partly in an acknowledgement that the costs of exclusion go beyond private households into the public sphere.

The way ahead

The sheer diversity of developing country experience in sanitation cautions against universal prescription. In some areas there are obvious parallels between water and sanitation. In others sanitation poses distinctive challenges because change involves not just reform of public policies and financing but often quite radical

behavioural change. Four broad themes emerge as indicators for future success.

First, national policies and political leadership matter. Countries as diverse as Bangladesh, China and Lesotho have all registered rapid progress in sanitation—and they have followed different policy paths. But in each case national political leaders have sent a clear signal that sanitation is part of the national development policy. Colombia and Morocco have progressed in urban areas because they have strong municipal strategies for sanitation provision through utilities—but rural areas have suffered from weaker policy frameworks. Poverty Reduction Strategy Papers provide a focal point for national plans, but plans without credible and sustained political backing do not deliver optimal results. Strengthening the political and financial weight of line ministries and local government structures dealing with sanitation is a starting point for overcoming the current fragmentation.

Second, public participation has to be part of national planning—at all levels. The long history of top-down and supply-driven provision running up against demand barriers in communities is one product of weak participation. Involving local communities can identify low-cost, appropriate technology to improve coverage, as with the condominial programme in Brazil and the Orangi Pilot Project in Pakistan.

Third, accelerating progress requires identifying who is not served and why. Putting poor people at the centre of service provision by enabling them to monitor and discipline service providers, and by creating incentives for service providers to listen, is an overarching goal. Supplementing the current Millennium Development Goal target for sanitation with explicit targets for reducing inequalities based on wealth and location would help on two counts: it would sharpen the focus of public policy and raise the profile of inequality as a problem on the political agenda. Halving inequalities between the richest and poorest 20%, or between urban and rural areas, would be an obvious supplement to the Millennium Development Goal target of halving the national deficit in coverage levels. Gender inequalities are critical in holding back progress on sanitation. Increasing the voice of women in public policy debates, and in markets for sanitation technology, would strengthen incentives for better service provision. But breaking down gender inequalities goes beyond sanitation policy to deeply rooted intrahousehold power relations. Similarly, bringing the voice of slum dwellers, the rural poor and other marginalized groups to national policy debates requires fundamental political changes.

Fourth, international partnerships can make a difference. Water and sanitation remain marked by weak and fragmented aid partnerships—and by consistent underfinancing, with sanitation the poor cousin. While several donors finance sanitation infrastructure, the dialogue on extending sanitation to the poor is underdeveloped. In sanitation, as in water, effective aid partnerships built on participative national planning processes could bring the Millennium Development Goal within reach. The global action plan proposal set out in chapter 1 could play a constructive role.

Three decades ago, international conferences on water and sanitation identified technology as the major barrier to progress. The invention and development of low-cost options, so the argument ran, would create the technological impetus to resolve the problem. More recently, financing has been identified as the major constraint. What national experiences and the case studies outlined in this chapter demonstrate is that technological and financial barriers can be overcome.

The biggest barrier in sanitation is the unwillingness of national and international political leaders to put excreta and its safe disposal on the international development agenda. Until recently another taboo subject was absent from the international development agenda—HIV/AIDS. That taboo has now been challenged in many countries by political leaders and coalitions committed to tackling head on a pandemic that has eroded human well-being on an unprecedented scale. So why has the sanitation taboo been so difficult to break down? Partly because, unlike HIV/AIDS, which affects the wealthy as well as the poor, the costs of the sanitation deficit are borne overwhelmingly by the poor. And partly because the human costs are less visible. Even so, sanitation is like HIV/AIDS in one crucial respect: its potential for sustained destruction. Without strong champions to raise awareness, mobilize resources and scale up the partnerships to make a difference, inadequate sanitation will remain one of the most powerful drivers of poverty, ill health and disadvantage—and among the greatest threats to the Millennium Development Goals project.

The biggest barrier in sanitation is the unwillingness of national and international political leaders to put excreta and its safe disposal on the international development agenda

4 Water scarcity, risk
and vulnerability

"You ain't gonna miss your
water until your well runs dry"

Bob Marley

"The frog does not drink up
the pond in which he lives"

Native American saying

CHAPTER 4

Water scarcity, risk and vulnerability

Scarcity is a policy-induced outcome flowing from the predictable consequence of inexhaustible demand chasing an underpriced resource

Human security means having protection against unpredictable events that disrupt lives and livelihoods. Few resources have a more critical bearing on human security than water. As a productive resource, water is essential in maintaining the livelihoods of the world's most vulnerable people. But water also has destructive properties, as witnessed by storms and floods. Security in access to water as a productive input and protection against the vulnerabilities associated with uncertainty in water flows is one of the keys to human development.

Perceptions of water security today are heavily influenced by ideas about scarcity. Shortages of water are widely perceived as *the* defining feature of water insecurity. Concerns that the world is "running out of water" are aired with growing frequency. But scarcity is both a distorting and limiting lens for viewing water insecurity. It is distorting because much of what passes for scarcity is a policy-induced consequence of mismanaging water resources. And it is limiting because physical availability is only one dimension of water insecurity.

There is a striking similarity between perceptions of the world water crisis today and fears about an impending food crisis in an earlier era. In the early 19th century Thomas Malthus prophesied a bleak future for humanity. In his *Essay on Population* he famously—and wrongly—predicted that population growth would outstrip productivity growth in agriculture, giving rise to a growing imbalance between mouths to feed and supply of food. Food shortages, so the argument ran, would lead to recurrent cycles of hunger. "The power of population is so superior to the power of the earth to produce subsistence for many," concluded Malthus, "that premature death must in some shape or another visit the human race." [1]

That apocalyptic vision resonates with some of the more pessimistic assessments of future scenarios for water availability. The World Commission on Water has identified "the gloomy arithmetic of water" as one of the foremost threats to humanity.[2] "Water scarcity," writes another commentator, "will be the defining condition of life for many in this new century." [3] Images of shrinking lakes and disappearing rivers reinforce the perception that the world is drifting into a Malthusian crisis, with competition for an increasingly scarce resource driving conflicts within countries and causing water wars between countries.

This chapter starts out by looking at water availability. Physical water scarcity, defined as inadequate resources to satisfy demand, is a feature of water security in some countries. But absolute scarcity is the exception, not the rule. Most countries have enough water to meet household, industrial, agricultural and environmental needs. The problem is management. Until fairly recently, water has been seen as an infinitely available resource to be diverted, drained or polluted in generating wealth. Scarcity is a policy-induced outcome flowing from this deeply flawed approach, the predictable consequence of inexhaustible demand chasing an underpriced resource. As one commentator wryly notes, "If someone were selling Porsches for three thousand dollars apiece, there would be a shortage of those too." [4]

Beyond scarcity, water security is also about risk and vulnerability—themes taken up in the second part of this chapter. From the earliest civilizations to the globalizing world of today, the success—or failure—of societies in harnessing the productive potential of water while limiting its destructive potential has determined human progress. The predictability and reliability of access to water, and protection against water-related risks, are crucial to human well-being. As the images of suffering from floods in Mozambique and New Orleans and from droughts in northern Kenya powerfully demonstrate, too little or too much of a good thing like water can be a force for destruction. Progress is shaped partly by how and where nature delivers water, but more decisively by the institutions and infrastructure through which people and societies secure access to predictable flows of water and resilience against shocks.

Some shocks are more predictable than others. This chapter concludes by looking at the implication of one impending shock that, managed badly, could roll back the human development gains built up over generations for a large section of humanity. Climate change poses a profound, and profoundly predictable, threat to water security for many of the world's poorest countries and millions of its poorest households. Of course, the threat is not limited to poor countries. Rich countries will feel the impact of changing rainfall patterns, extreme weather events and rising sea levels. But poor countries—and poor people in those countries—lack the financial resources available to rich states to reduce risk on the scale required. International action to limit carbon emissions is important because it will limit the future damage caused by climate change. However, dangerous climate change will happen because current atmospheric concentrations bind us to future global warming. For millions of poor people across the world, who have played a minimal role in generating current emissions, the priority is to improve capacity to adapt. Unfortunately, strategies for adaptation are far less developed nationally and internationally than strategies for mitigation.

Rethinking scarcity in a water-stressed world

Just how scarce is the world's water? There is no simple answer. Water scarcity can be physical, economic or institutional, and—like water itself—it can fluctuate over time and space. Scarcity is ultimately a function of supply and demand. But both sides of the supply-demand equation are shaped by political choices and public policies.

Understanding scarcity

"Water, water everywhere, nor any drop to drink," laments the sailor in Samuel Coleridge's *Rime of the Ancient Mariner*. The observation remains a useful first approximation for understanding the world's supply of fresh water.

Earth may be the water planet, but 97% of its water is in oceans.[5] Most of the remainder is locked in Antarctic icecaps or deep underground, leaving less than 1% available for human use in easily accessible freshwater lakes and rivers. Unlike oil or coal, water is an infinitely renewable resource. In a natural cycle rainwater falls from the clouds, returns to the salty sea through freshwater rivers, and evaporates back to the clouds. The cycle explains why we cannot run out of water, but supply is finite. Planet Earth's hydrological system pumps and transfers about 44,000 cubic kilometres of water to the land each year, equivalent to 6,900 cubic metres for everyone on the planet. A large part of this flow is accounted for by uncontrollable floodwaters, or water too remote for effective human use. Even so, the world has far more water than the 1,700 cubic metres per person minimum threshold that hydrologists by (admittedly arbitrary) convention treat as the amount needed to grow food, support industries and maintain the environment.[6]

Unfortunately, the international average is a largely irrelevant number. At one level the world's water is like the world's wealth. Globally, there is more than enough to go round: the problem is that some countries get a lot more than others. Almost a quarter of the world's supply of fresh water is in Lake Baikal in sparsely populated Siberia.[7] Differences in availability across and within regions further highlight the distribution problem. With 31% of global freshwater resources, Latin America has 12 times more water per person than South Asia. Some places, such as Brazil and Canada, get far more water than they can use; others, such as countries in the Middle East, get much less than they need. Water-stressed Yemen (198 cubic metres per person) is not helped by Canada's overabundance of fresh water (90,000 cubic metres per person). And water-stressed regions in China and India are not relieved by Iceland's water availability of more than 300 times the 1,700 cubic metre threshold.

Within regions too there is often a large mismatch between water resources and population. As a region Sub-Saharan Africa is reasonably well endowed with water. Factoring in distribution changes the picture. The Democratic Republic of Congo has more than a quarter of the region's water with 20,000 cubic metres or more for each of its citizens, while countries like Kenya, Malawi and South Africa are already below the water-stress threshold.

Because water, unlike food or oil, is not readily transferable in bulk quantities, there is limited scope for trade to even out imbalances. What matters is local availability and access between populations through water infrastructure. This applies within countries as well. Northern China, for example, has less than a quarter of the per capita water availability of the south.[8] National data for Brazil put the country near the top of the world league for water

availability. However, millions of people living in the huge "drought polygon", a semi-arid area spanning nine states and 940,000 square kilometres in the northeast, regularly experience chronic water shortages. Ethiopia, with several major lakes and rivers, abundant groundwater and a large volume of rainfall, almost crosses the water-stress threshold. Unfortunately, rainfall is both highly seasonal and exceptionally variable over time and space. Combined with a limited infrastructure for storage and poorly protected watersheds, that variability exposes millions to the threat of drought and floods.

Time is another important part of the water availability equation. For countries that depend on monsoons or short rainy seasons, national averages provide a distorted view of real availability. Much of Asia receives almost 90% of its annual rainfall in less than 100 hours, generating risks of short, intensive flooding during some parts of the year and prolonged drought during the rest.[9] Real availability over the course of a year therefore depends not only on rainfall, but also on capacity for storage and the degree to which river flows and groundwaters are replenished.

Increasing stress and scarcity

Hydrologists typically assess scarcity by looking at the population-water equation. As noted, the convention is to treat 1,700 cubic metres per person as the national threshold for meeting water requirements for agriculture, industry, energy and the environment. Availability below 1,000 cubic metres is held to represent a state of "water scarcity"—and below 500 cubic metres, "absolute scarcity".[10]

Today, about 700 million people in 43 countries live below the water-stress threshold. With average annual availability of about 1,200 cubic metres per person the Middle East is the world's most water-stressed region; only Iraq, Iran, Lebanon and Turkey are above the threshold. Palestinians, especially in Gaza, experience some of the world's most acute water scarcity—about 320 cubic metres per person. Sub-Saharan Africa has the largest number of water-stressed countries of any region. Almost a quarter of Sub-Saharan Africa's population

Globally, there is more than enough water to go round: the problem is that some countries get a lot more than others

4

Water scarcity, risk and vulnerability

lives in a water-stressed country today—and that share is rising.

With many of the most water-stressed countries experiencing very high population growth rates, per capita availability is shrinking fast. With 1950 as a benchmark, the distribution of global population growth has dramatically reshaped the per capita availability of water. While availability stabilized in rich countries in the 1970s, the decline continued in developing countries, especially in arid developing countries (figure 4.1).

Just how rapid the decline has been becomes apparent when current trends are projected into the future. By 2025 more than 3 billion people could be living in water-stressed countries—and 14 countries will slip from water stress to water scarcity (figures 4.2 and 4.3). Developments to 2025 will include:

- Intensifying stress across Sub-Saharan Africa, with the share of the region's population in water-stressed countries rising from just above 30% to 85% by 2025.
- Deepening problems in the Middle East and North Africa, with average water availability falling by more than a quarter. By 2025 average water availability is projected to be just over 500 cubic metres per person, and more than 90% of the region's people will be living in water-scarce countries by 2025.
- High-population countries such as China and India entering the global water-stress league.

As gloomy as this projection is, it understates the problem. Consider the case of India.

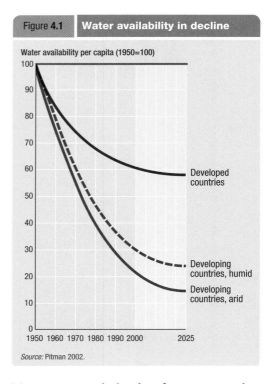

Figure 4.1 Water availability in decline

Water availability per capita (1950=100)

Developed countries

Developing countries, humid

Developing countries, arid

Source: Pitman 2002.

The country may be heading for water stress, but 224 million people already live in river basins with renewable water resources below the 1,000 cubic metres per person water-scarcity threshold. The reason: more than two-thirds of the country's renewable water is in areas that serve a third of the population. In China national per capita levels are already low, about a third of the global average. But unequal distribution within the country makes the situation far more serious: 42% of China's population—538 million people—in the northern region have access to only 14% of the country's water. If northern

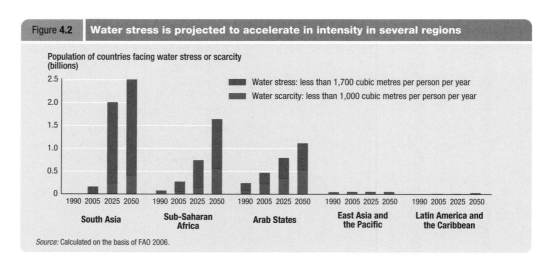

Figure 4.2 Water stress is projected to accelerate in intensity in several regions

Population of countries facing water stress or scarcity (billions)

Water stress: less than 1,700 cubic metres per person per year
Water scarcity: less than 1,000 cubic metres per person per year

South Asia   Sub-Saharan Africa   Arab States   East Asia and the Pacific   Latin America and the Caribbean

Source: Calculated on the basis of FAO 2006.

China were a country, its water availability—757 cubic metres a person[11]—would be comparable to that in parts of North Africa: it is lower than in Morocco, for example.

There are many problems associated with thresholds for water stress. As demonstrated above, national averages can mask real availability. Beyond questions of distribution, countries vary widely in the amount of water they need to produce a given volume of output, maintain their environment and meet human needs. Only the rainfall that runs off into rivers and recharges groundwater is counted as renewable water in national accounts. This "blue water" represents only 40% of total rainfall. The remainder—the "green water"—never reaches rivers but nourishes the soil, evaporates or is transpired by plants.[12] This is the resource that maintains rainfed agriculture, the livelihood for a large share of the world's poor. However, for all of these problems and omissions national water availability levels do capture some important dimensions of availability.

Growing water demand outstrips population growth

In the history of water use some things change but others remain the same. Today, as in the past, humans use water mainly for irrigation. Some of the greatest civilizations—Egyptian, Mesopotamian, Indic and Chinese—were based on control of river water for agriculture. Now, as then, irrigation and agriculture remain the dominant users of water. However, since the early 20th century, water use for industry and municipalities has been increasing. So, too, has the gap between population growth and demand for water: as the world has become richer and more industrialized, each person in it has been using more water.[13] These trends have lent a superficial credence to Malthusian concerns over future water shortages.

Water use has been growing much faster than population for at least a century—and that trend is continuing. Over the past hundred years population quadrupled, while water use grew by a factor of seven. As the world got wealthier, it also became thirstier (figure 4.4).

Water use patterns have also changed. In 1900 industry used an estimated 6% of the world's water. It now uses four times that share. Over the same period municipalities' share of water tripled, to 9%.[14]

However, while industrial and municipal demand for water grew spectacularly in the 20th century, agriculture still takes the lion's share. In developing countries agriculture still accounts for more than 80% of water consumption (figures 4.5 and 4.6).

It is not difficult to see why. Sometimes it is assumed that water scarcity is about not having enough water to meet domestic needs or the demands of cities. While some cities face problems of water stress, it is agriculture that will face the real challenge. Basic arithmetic explains the problem. People have a minimum basic water requirement of 20–50 litres each day. Compare this with the 3,500 litres to produce enough food for a daily minimum of 3,000 calories (producing food for a family of four takes the amount of water in an Olympic-size swimming pool). In other words, it takes roughly 70 times more water to produce food than people use for domestic purposes.[15] Growing a single kilo of rice takes 2,000–5,000 litres of water.[16] But some foods are thirstier than others. It takes eight times more water to grow a tonne of sugar than a tonne of wheat, for example. Producing a single hamburger takes about 11,000 litres—roughly the daily amount available to 500 people living in an urban slum without a household water connection. These facts help to explain why rising incomes and changing diets—as people get richer they consume more meat and sugar—keep the growth of water use above that of population.

Looking to the future, it is clear that the pattern of demand for water will continue to change. As urbanization and the growth of manufacturing continue to gather pace, demand for water from industry and municipalities will continue to grow (see figure 4.6).[17] At the same time population and income growth will boost demand for irrigation water to meet food production requirements. By 2025 there will be almost 8 billion people in the world, with the

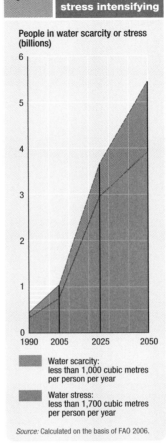

Figure 4.3 Global water stress intensifying

People in water scarcity or stress (billions)

Water scarcity: less than 1,000 cubic metres per person per year

Water stress: less than 1,700 cubic metres per person per year

Source: Calculated on the basis of FAO 2006.

4

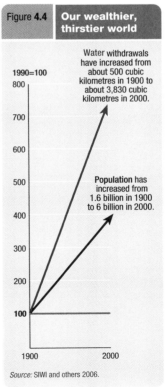

Figure 4.4 Our wealthier, thirstier world

1990=100

Water withdrawals have increased from about 500 cubic kilometres in 1900 to about 3,830 cubic kilometres in 2000.

Population has increased from 1.6 billion in 1900 to 6 billion in 2000.

Source: SIWI and others 2006.

Water scarcity, risk and vulnerability

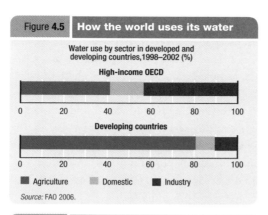

Figure 4.5 How the world uses its water

Water use by sector in developed and
developing countries,1998–2002 (%)

High-income OECD

0   20   40   60   80   100

Developing countries

0   20   40   60   80   100

■ Agriculture   ▨ Domestic   ■ Industry

Source: FAO 2006.

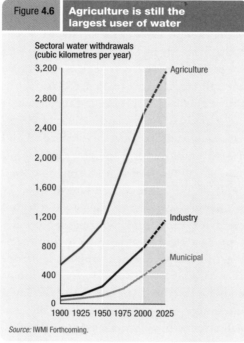

Figure 4.6 Agriculture is still the largest user of water

Sectoral water withdrawals
(cubic kilometres per year)

3,200 — Agriculture
2,800
2,400
2,000
1,600
1,200 — Industry
800
400 — Municipal
0
1900 1925 1950 1975 2000 2025

Source: IWMI Forthcoming.

developing world's share rising from 79% to 82%. By 2050 the world's agricultural systems will have to feed another 2.4 billion people.

Two important consequences flow from these broad trends. First, water withdrawals in developing countries will increase: projected withdrawals are 27% higher for developing countries in 2025 than in the mid-1990s. This is the reverse of the trend in rich countries. In the United States water use is lower today than it was three decades ago, even though population has increased by some 40 million.[18] Second, there will be a redistribution of water from agriculture to industry and municipalities. Projections point to a steady decline in the share of irrigated agriculture in global water use, to about 75% of the total by 2025.[19] But this global

figure understates the scale of the adjustment. In some parts of South Asia the share of non-agricultural users in water use will rise from less than 5% today to more than 25% by 2050 (table 4.1).

Behind these statistics are some questions with profound implications for human development. Most obviously, how will the world feed another 2.4 billion people by 2050 from a water resource base that is already under acute stress? In a world with about 800 million malnourished people, that question merits serious consideration. So, too, does a less prominent concern in international debate. As the distribution of water between sectors changes, there will be important implications for the distribution of water among people. An obvious danger is that people whose livelihoods depend on agriculture but who lack established rights, economic power and a political voice will lose out—an issue to which we return in chapter 5.

Breaching the limits of sustainable use—problems, policies and responses

Throughout history human societies have been largely river based. Historically, people had to locate near water supplies that could provide drinking water, carry off waste, supply irrigation and power industries. Over the past hundred years, industrial development came with an increased capacity to move and control water—along with a parallel increase in capacity to use more, waste more and pollute more. In many parts of the world humanity has been operating beyond the borders of ecological sustainability, creating threats to human development today and costs for generations tomorrow.

Beyond the limits of sustainability

What happens when the limits to the sustainable use of water are breached? Hydrologists address that question by reference to complex models designed to capture the functioning of river basin ecosystems. The simplified answer is that the integrity of the ecosystems that sustain flows of water—and ultimately human life—are ruptured.

	2000		2050	
Region	Volume (cubic kilometres)	Share of total (%)	Volume (cubic kilometres)	Share of total (%)
Sub-Saharan Africa	10	6	60	38
East Asia	101	6	511	35
South Asia	34	3	207	25
Central Asia and Eastern Europe	156	29	301	49
Latin America	53	15	270	53
Middle East and North Africa	24	6	93	28
OECD	518	93	774	72
World	897	18	2,216	41

Source: IWMI forthcoming.

Perceptions about water have changed slowly over time. In 1908 Winston Churchill stood near the northern shores of Lake Victoria watching the world's second largest lake flow over Owen Falls into the Nile. He later recorded his thoughts: "So much power running to waste... such a lever to control the natural forces of Africa ungripped."[20] Two decades later, Joseph Stalin famously lamented the water going to waste through the Volga, the Don and other rivers, ushering in an era of huge irrigation schemes and giant dams that shrank the Caspian Sea. By the mid-1970s the Soviet Union used eight times as much water as in 1913, most of it for irrigation.

What Churchill and Stalin had in common, along with most other political leaders in the first nine decades of the 20th century, was the idea that water was there to be exploited without reference to environmental sustainability. That approach has thrown deep roots in water governance models. For much of recent history policy-makers have focussed their attention on three great users of water: industry, agriculture and households. Lacking a vocal political constituency, the fourth great user, the environment, has been ignored. Today, we are learning the hard way that the water resources developed for agriculture and industry through infrastructure investments had not previously been "wasted". Inland water systems such as wetlands, lakes and floodplains all provide vital ecological services that depend on water.

Natural flows of water provided through rivers, or stored in lakes and aquifers, define the parameters of water availability. When those parameters are broken, water assets are depleted. An analogy with finance explains what this means. People and countries can increase consumption beyond their current income flows by borrowing and running up debt against future earnings. If incomes rise enough over time to cover repayments, the debt will remain sustainable. But water is not like income in one crucial respect. Because future flows of water (unlike income) are more or less fixed, overconsumption leads to asset depletion and an unsustainable hydrological debt.[21] In effect, we are dealing today with a hydrological debt crisis built up over several decades. That crisis is growing in scale and severity.

Hydrological debt, by its nature, is difficult to measure, but it has highly visible consequences in many regions. The International Water Management Institute uses a four-part scale to classify countries on the sustainability of water use, taking into account the water requirements of ecosystems. These requirements are not a matter of theoretical environmental accounting. If ecological requirements are not respected, the environment that sustains livelihoods is eroded, to the long-term detriment of human development. Ecological stress shows up where human water use exceeds the level required to maintain the ecological integrity of river basins (map 4.1). These are the flashpoints for the hydrological debt crisis.

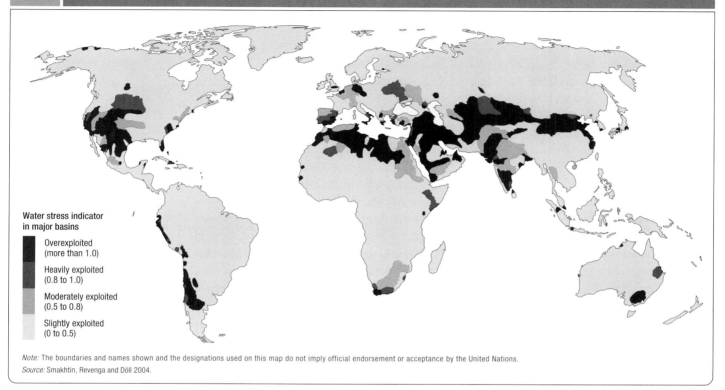

Water stress indicator
in major basins

Overexploited
(more than 1.0)

Heavily exploited
(0.8 to 1.0)

Moderately exploited
(0.5 to 0.8)

Slightly exploited
(0 to 0.5)

Note: The boundaries and names shown and the designations used on this map do not imply official endorsement or acceptance by the United Nations.

Source: Smakhtin, Revenga and Döll 2004.

High overuse tends to occur in regions heavily dependent on irrigated agriculture—such as the Indo-Gangetic Plain in South Asia, the North China Plain and the High Plains in North America—and in areas undergoing rapid urbanization and industrial development. An estimated 1.4 billion people now live in river basin areas that are "closed", in that water use exceeds minimum recharge levels, or near closure.[22] Such basins cover more than 15% of the world's land surface. Among the more prominent examples:

- In northern China an estimated quarter of the flow of the Yellow River is needed to maintain the environment. Human withdrawal currently leaves less than 10%. During the 1990s the river ran dry at its lower reaches every year and for a record 226 days in 1997, when it was dry for 600 kilometres inland.[23] The drying up of the river caused a drop in agricultural production averaging 2.7–8.5 million tonnes a year, with losses estimated at $1.7 billion for 1997.

- In Australia's Murray-Darling Basin irrigated agriculture uses almost 80% of

available water flows. With estimated environmental requirements of about 30%, the result is extensive environmental destruction, including salinity, nutrient pollution and the loss of floodplains and wetlands. The basin contains two-thirds of the country's irrigated lands. Its production of rice, cotton, wheat and cattle accounts for about 40% of the country's agricultural output—but at a high and unsustainable environmental price. In recent years virtually no Murray River water has made it to the sea.[24]

- The Orange River in southern Africa is the site of growing environmental stress. The upstream reaches of the basin have been so modified and regulated that the combined reservoir storage in the basin exceeds annual flows.[25]

As millions of people in water-stressed areas are discovering, the environment is foreclosing on unsustainable water debts on an extensive scale. For example, farmers near Sana'a in Yemen have deepened their wells by 50 metres over the past 12 years, while the amount of water they can extract has dropped by two-thirds.[26] Some people in water-stressed areas have the economic resources, skills and opportunities to leave their water problem behind. Many millions—small farmers, agricultural labourers and pastoralists in poor countries—do not.

Does a high level of ecological stress in water systems support the Malthusian thesis that the world is running out of water? Only on the most superficial reading. Take the case of the Murray-Darling Basin. Evidence of water stress is unequivocal. That stress is the product of past public policies that have decided it is worth sacrificing an entire ecosystem to grow rice, cotton and sugar—three of the thirstiest agricultural products—for export. Within the basin the country's largest reservoir—Cubbie Station—holds more water than Sydney Harbour, and loses 40% of it to evaporation.[27] Until recently, water users have been paying negligible fees for using and wasting a precious asset—and Australian taxpayers have been footing the bill for multimillion dollar engineering programmes to intercept salty drainage water. The problem in the Murray-Darling Basin is not that there is too little water. It is that there is too much cotton and rice and too many cattle.

Governments in water-stressed regions have started to acknowledge the need to tackle unsustained hydrological debt. In China demand management plays a growing role in water governance. Since 2000 the Yellow River Commission has imposed restrictions on water withdrawals by upstream provinces, increasing flows in the lower reaches of the river. Provisions have also been made along the Hei River Basin for the environment as a water user, though more stringent action will be needed in the future. The Murray-Darling Commission in Australia provides a far reaching institutional framework for rebalancing the needs of human users and the environment. That framework sets annual extraction rates at a ratio determined by the pattern of water use in 1993, even though some commentators argue that this still exceeds ecological limits. Governments in South Africa and elsewhere have enacted legislation that requires taking into account environmental needs before issuing permits for human uses (see box 4.7 later

in the chapter). Each of these examples demonstrate how governments are now being forced to respond to the consequences of past public policy mistakes. But far more radical approaches will be needed in the future.

Wider symptoms of stress

The physical symptoms of water overuse vary. Among the least visible but most pervasive problems are declining water tables, the result of using groundwater faster than the hydrological cycle replenishes it.[28] In Yemen, parts of India and northern China water tables are falling at more than 1 metre a year. In Mexico extraction rates in about a quarter of the country's 459 aquifers exceed long-term recharge by more than 20%, with most of the overdraft building up in arid parts of the country.[29]

River desiccation is another symptom of water stress. According to the UN Millennium Ecological Assessment, water-based ecosystems are now the world's most degraded natural resource—an outcome that can be traced to the breaching of ecological boundaries.[30] In China the Yangtze and Yellow Rivers are dry in their lower reaches for much of the year. The list of river systems registering major overabstraction and reduced flows includes the Colorado, the Ganges, the Jordan, the Nile and the Tigris-Euphrates.

Lakes and inland water provide another indicator for asset depletion. In 1960 the Aral Sea was the size of Belgium, sustaining a vibrant local economy. Today, it is a virtually lifeless hypersaline lake a quarter of its previous size. The reason: an earlier era of Soviet state planners determined that the great rivers of Central Asia—the Syr Darya and the Amu Darya—should be put to the service of creating a vast irrigated cotton belt. This cavalier approach to water management sealed the fate of an entire ecological system, with devastating consequences for human well-being (see chapter 6). Overexploitation has contributed to the shrinking of many of Africa's greatest lakes, including Lakes Chad, Nakivale and Nakaru. Lake Chad has shrunk to 10% of its former volume, partly as a result of climate change and partly because of overextraction.

Among the least visible but most pervasive problems are declining water tables, the result of using groundwater faster than the hydrological cycle replenishes it

Figure 1 | **Agriculture is losing out to other users**

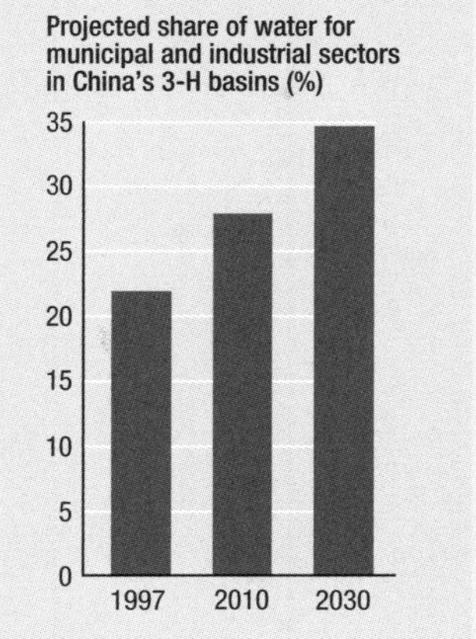

Projected share of water for municipal and industrial sectors in China's 3-H basins (%)

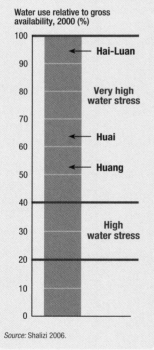

Source: Cai 2006.

Figure 2 | **China's 3-H basins are under very high water stress**

Water use relative to gross availability, 2000 (%)

Hai-Luan

Very high water stress

Huai

Huang

High water stress

Source: Shalizi 2006.

Since 1979 China has been the world's fastest growing economy. Poverty has fallen sharply, albeit with rising inequality, and education and health have improved at an impressive rate. But rapid growth has strained China's water resources. Economic success has been maintained partly through a mounting ecological overdraft, with northern China now facing a mounting crisis in water management.

Northern China is at the epicentre of that crisis. The Huai, Hai and Huang (Yellow) River Basins (3-H river basins) supply just under half the country's population, 40% of agricultural land, a large share of major grain production and a third of GDP. About half the country's rural poor live in the basin area. Yet the area accounts for less than 8% of national water resources. Thus each basin falls below 500 cubic metres of water per capita, making them areas of acute scarcity.

Rapid growth has increased demand for water. Since 1980 annual withdrawal rates in the 3-H basins have increased by 42 billion cubic metres, the total average run-off in the Hai River. There has also been a shift in demand, with agriculture losing out to industry and municipal users (figure 1). The share of industry in water use has doubled since 1980 to 21%, and the urban share has tripled.

Current projections indicate that demand will rise a further 20% by 2030. The resulting pressure threatens to exacerbate serious quality-related stress:

- *Surface water pollution*. More than 80% of the Hai and Huai basins are highly polluted. Agriculture and rural industry account for about half the pollution. High-growth industries such as textiles, chemicals and pharmaceuticals account for a quarter, and untreated human sewage the remainder. According to the State Environment Protection Administration, more than 70% of the water in the 3-H system is too polluted for human use.

- *Reduced run-off*. Flows to the ocean from the 3-H rivers have fallen by 60% since 1956–79. Water use across the three river systems now exceeds sustainability levels by very large margins. One assessment of scarcity suggests that withdrawals of more than 20% of available flow represent a threat to sustainable use, with 40% withdrawals an indicator for extreme stress (figure 2). In the 3-H system withdrawals range from more than 50% for the Huang (Yellow) River, to 65% for the Huai River and more than 90% for Hai-Luan River Basin. This is well beyond the bounds of sustainability. The transformation that has taken place over the past few decades is captured by the flow of the Huang River, once referred to as China's sorrow because high waters caused so much flooding. Today, the lower streams of the river have been reduced to a trickle that barely reaches the sea. Low-flow periods increased from 40 days in the early 1990s to more than 200 at the end of the decade.

- *Groundwater mining*. Water inputs for agriculture have been sustained by tapping groundwater, but aquifers are being depleted faster than they are being replenished. In the Hai basin sustainable groundwater supply is about 17.3 billion cubic metres a year, while withdrawals exceed 26 billion cubic metres. Water tables today are 50–90 metres lower than they were four decades ago, contributing to saline intrusion and ground subsidence of several metres in cities such as Beijing, Shanghai and Tianjin—and increasing the cost of pumping water.

These are classic symptoms of water stress. To them can be added the growing strains on water in cities across the north. The problems of Beijing are well known, but there are seven other cities in the northern region with populations over 2 million—and all of them face water shortages.

Is this a water shortage crisis? In one sense, not entirely. Current stress levels reflect past incentives for unsustainable water use patterns. Until fairly recently, water was not priced. One result has been the absence of incentives to conserve water. Low-value water-intensive cereals have dominated agricultural production. In industry Chinese companies use 4–10 times more water than their counterparts in industrial countries, partly reflecting technology but also pointing to the weakness of price incentives for reducing water use.

China has responded to the water crisis with supply- and demand-side policies. On the supply side is the South-North water transfer to divert more than 40 billion cubic metres of water—more than the total flow of the Colorado River—to industrial and urban regions in the Hai basin, a distance of more than 1,000 kilometres.

On the demand side the focus is on realigning water use with ecological capacity. Since 2000 the Yellow River Conservation Commission has been authorized to make transfers to environmental systems—a move prompted by recurrent droughts. Efficiency measures have been introduced to increase the productivity of water in agriculture, including advanced irrigation technologies and incentives for producing higher value crops. In industry water prices are rising, and new regulatory measures are in place.

Efforts to realign supply and demand through administrative reallocation under conditions of water stress present major governance challenges:

- *Social equity.* Government support for expansion of advanced irrigation systems means higher costs for water. Poor farmers may be unable to afford access because of low income and the high costs of inputs. This could force them to use less water, give up higher value crops or leave agriculture. Working through water user associations to provide support and protect vulnerable groups could address this.
- *Fragmentation and power politics.* Current water transfer policies follow the priorities of local governments, often driven by short-sighted economic concerns in order to meet national objectives. Pollution monitoring and enforcement programmes are applied selectively. To keep industries profitable, local officials often sidestep legislation and regulations to curb pollution.

- *Weak rights and entitlements.* Farmers are losing their entitlements to water, often without compensation. Water user associations, commonly supported by local government, mark an attempt to establish water rights and claims linked to transfers. But reallocation patterns reflect decisions by often fragmented water bureaucracies that come under pressure from powerful groups in industry and municipalities. An additional problem is that existing river basin commissions operate under the Ministry of Water Resources and lack authority to impose on other ministries and provinces.
- *Managing ecological claims.* For local governments the imperatives of economic growth continue to take priority over ecological considerations, perpetuating serious environmental stress.

Several provinces and municipalities are promoting reforms to merge the functions of different water management units into a single Water Affairs Bureau. These bodies could delineate secure and consistent water rights by working through water user associations to create a transfer system consistent with a commitment to social equity and ecological sustainability.

Source: World Bank 2001; Shen and Liang 2003; CAS 2005; Cai 2006; Shalizi 2006.

Water quantity is not the only benchmark indicator for scarcity. Quality also has a bearing on the volume available for use—and in many of the most stressed water basins quality has been compromised by pollution. All of India's 14 major river systems are badly polluted. In Delhi, to take one example, 200 million litres of raw sewage and 20 million litres of waste are dumped into the Yamuna River every day. In Malaysia and Thailand water pollution is so severe that rivers often contain 30–100 times the pathogen load permitted by health standards. The Tiete River flowing through São Paulo, Brazil, is chronically polluted with untreated effluent and high concentrations of lead, cadmium and other heavy metals.[31] Why does all this matter for scarcity? Because water pollution adversely affects the environment, threatens public health and reduces the flow of water available for human use.

The physical symptoms of stress and the competition between users do not operate in isolation. Northern China demonstrates starkly how different forms of stress can create a vicious cycle—the lethal interaction of dwindling river flows, falling water tables, rising demands from urban and industrial users and increasing

pollution has generated a major water crisis.[32] That crisis not only threatens to undermine future economic growth. It also poses a major threat to food security, poverty reduction and future ecological sustainability. Reversing that cycle is now a central concern of policy-makers in China (box 4.1).

Sinking aquifers—who pays the price?

Intensive development and the unsustainable depletion of water resources create winners and losers. The environment is a loser every time—while the balance sheet between human users is mixed. In some cases short-term increases in income are being generated in ways that compromise long-term livelihoods. Elsewhere, the depletion of water resources is generating profit for some while exacerbating poverty and marginalization for others. The deepening problem in groundwater highlights the difficulties.

Groundwater exploitation has done much for human development. It has given smallholder farmers—16 million of them in India alone—access to a reliable flow of water for production. In the words of one commentator groundwater has been "a great democratising force" in agricultural production.[33] One study

4

Water scarcity, risk and vulnerability

Box **4.2**   **Yemen under stress**

Water and poverty are closely linked in Yemen, which has one of the world's lowest freshwater availability levels—198 cubic metres a person—and one of the highest rates of water use for agriculture. Worsening the scarcity are spatial and temporal variations. And with a population projected to double by 2025, water availability per capita will fall by one-third.

The physical and social symptoms of acute water stress are already apparent. Groundwater extraction started to exceed recharge 20 years ago. Around the city of Sana'a aquifer extraction rates are 2.5 times the recharge rates. Growing urban demand is coming up against the barrier of agricultural use. Unregulated extraction in rural areas (of the 13,000 wells in operation, only 70 are state-owned) and the development of private markets for transferring water to urban users now pose acute threats to smallholder agriculture—heightened by uncertain customary water rights. In other cities such as Ta'iz urban tensions over water use and groundwater exploitation have led to violent confrontation.

Efforts to recharge the aquifers are being undermined by uncontrolled extraction, notably by private tanker companies delivering water to the city. About two-thirds of water in the city comes from private sources. At the current rate of depletion water stress will reduce the viability of rural livelihoods on a large scale.

Source: Molle and Berkoff 2006; Grey and Sadoff 2006; SIWI, Tropp and Jägerskog 2006.

suggests that it contributes $25–$30 billion a year to Asian agricultural economies.[34] But what happens when groundwater exploitation goes too far? Water tables sink, the costs of pumping rise and environmental problems such as soil salinization become widespread. In Pakistan groundwater depletion has gone hand in hand with soil salinity, compromising rural livelihoods by reducing productivity.[35]

The costs and benefits of unsustainable groundwater mining are not distributed equally. In some countries the depletion of groundwater is associated with processes that are marginalizing agriculture (box 4.2). Within the agricultural sector the overexploitation of groundwater can reinforce wider inequalities. As water tables fall the energy costs of pumping water rise, along with the costs of digging wells. Because wealthier farmers can dig deeper and pump more, they have developed monopolies in water markets in some areas.

The Indian state of Gujarat demonstrates the problem. In the north of the state falling water tables pose a direct threat to the smallholder dairy industry, compromising the livelihoods of hundreds of thousands of vulnerable people. In some areas large landowners with access to capital markets have financed the construction

of deep wells, depriving neighbouring villages of water. "Waterlords" now dominate an extensive market for both irrigation and drinking water—often selling water back to the same villages and neighbours whose wells they have effectively emptied. Thousands of villages have become waterless, left dependent on deliveries by water tankers.[36]

Groundwater mining highlights how the practices of private users can generate wider public costs. Water provides a vehicle for transferring environmental costs, or "externalities", distorting market signals. Individuals might be less likely to overuse or pollute water if they bore the full costs of the consequences. In Java, Indonesia, textile factories have polluted water supplies to the point where rice yields have fallen and the availability of fish in downstream ponds has been compromised.[37] The farmers, not the factories, bear the costs. Similarly, in India the Bhavani and Noyyal Rivers in Tamil Nadu are virtually unusable to downstream users in agriculture because of labour-intensive dyeing and bleaching industries in upstream Tiruppur.[38]

Policy-induced scarcity

Symptoms of scarcity appear to confirm some of the worst Malthusian fears about the interaction between people and water. The combined effects of rising population growth and increasing demand on a fixed water resource base produce water stress on an unprecedented scale. Often overlooked is the role of policy in inducing stress, through acts of commission and omission.

Acts of commission take many forms. Perverse incentives for overuse are among the most damaging. Once again, groundwater provides a good example. Groundwater extraction costs depend on the capital cost of pumps and the recurrent cost of electricity. Once a pump is installed, the only constraint on pumping is the price of electricity. In many cases electricity for agricultural users has been free or subsidized, removing incentives to conserve water. In India agriculture accounts for about a third of the sales of electricity boards but only 3% of revenue. According to the World Bank the electricity subsidies accounted for about a third of India's fiscal deficit in 2001.[39] These subsidies have created disincentives for water conservation and incentives for inappropriate cropping patterns. For instance, it is unlikely that a water-intensive crop like sugarcane would be grown on its current scale across much of Gujarat if water were sensibly priced and regulated.[40] Because electricity subsidies tend to rise with the size of holding and depth of wells, they are highly regressive: the wealthier the producer, the bigger the support (box 4.3).

Perverse subsidies are visible in many water-stressed environments. An extreme example is the past practice in Saudi Arabia of using oil revenues to pump irrigation water from a nonrenewable fossil aquifer to grow water-intensive wheat and alfalfa in the desert. In the 1980s the country embarked on a program of rapid irrigation development using a fossil aquifer. With price supports, input subsidies and state underwriting of investments in infrastructure, Saudi Arabia first attained self-sufficiency in wheat and then became an important exporter. Almost a third of arable land is still devoted to irrigated wheat production. Production costs are estimated at four to six times the world price, discounting the costs of subsidies and groundwater depletion. Every tonne of wheat is produced with about 3,000 cubic metres of water—three times the global norm. In 2004 a new water conservation strategy was launched to reduce water use and conserve the aquifer.[41]

Pricing policies often underpin perverse subsidy systems. Producer subsidies for water-intensive produce such as oilseeds, sugar, wheat and beef create incentives for investment, patterns that lead to overexploitation. Meanwhile, the underpricing of irrigation water creates disincentives for conservation. Even in the Middle East and North Africa, where the scarcity value of water is much in evidence, the cost of water is set well below cost-recovery levels. In Algeria current tariffs are estimated at only 1%–7% of the marginal cost of providing water.[42] Such pricing policies discourage efficient use and threaten sustainability. For the Middle East and North Africa as a region, it is estimated that

only 30% of the flood water used in irrigation ever reaches the crop.[43]

Would the use of pricing policies to promote efficiency and environmental sustainability damage equity by excluding poor farmers from water markets? The answer depends on the wider policy environment and a range of distributional factors. Research in Egypt suggests that a fee covering operations and maintenance costs would be equivalent to 3% of average farm revenues (double if capital costs are included). While not an insignificant amount, it is also one that commercial farms could afford. By linking charges to farm size, location and revenue, it would be possible to limit the impact on poor rural households. Governments often justify current subsidies for water on equity grounds. However, the skewed distribution of land in some countries calls that justification into question because water use rises with landholding size. In Tunisia, for example, 53% of landowners occupy only 9% of the land, suggesting that most water subsidies are captured by large producers.

Perverse subsidies are not restricted to developing countries. The United States and Europe provide generous subsidies for water mining. Farmers in the Central Valley Project in California—a centre for the production of major water-intensive export crops such as rice and wheat—use about a fifth of the state's water. They pay prices estimated at less than half the cost of water, with a total subsidy of $416 million a year. Here, too, transfers are highly regressive: the largest 10% of farms receive two-thirds of total subsidies.[44] In southern European countries such as Spain the production of water-intensive crops is a source of water stress. That production is made possible in part by subsidies under the Common Agricultural Policy.

Rich country water subsidies have implications beyond the border, especially in crops for which the European Union and the United States are major exporters. When the United States exports water-intensive crops such as rice—it is the world's third largest exporter—it is also exporting very large virtual water subsidies. Producers in other exporting countries (such as Thailand and Viet Nam) and importing

Producer subsidies for water-intensive produce such as oilseeds, sugar, wheat and beef create incentives for investment, patterns that lead to overexploitation

| Box **4.3** | **Groundwater mining subsidies in Mexico** |

Aquifers store water beneath the earth's surface. This groundwater maintains wetlands and provides water for drinking and irrigation. But in many countries the rate of use far exceeds the rate of renewal, with implications for human development prospects. That overuse has been systematically encouraged by perverse incentives.

Mexico has a good history of water management in many areas. But in the northern and central parts of the country demand for water for irrigation and industry is outstripping supply (see map). Groundwater mining has covered the gap.

Agriculture accounts for 80% of water use in Mexico. Irrigated production accounts for more than half of total agriculture production and about three-quarters of exports, dominated by such water-intensive products as fruit, vegetables and livestock. Groundwater now represents an estimated 40% of total water use in agriculture, but more than 100 of the country's 653 aquifers are overexploited, causing extensive environmental damage and undermining smallholder agriculture.

Overextraction, encouraged by electricity subsidies, threatens long-run agricultural productivity. In the state of Sonora the coastal aquifer of Hermosillo provided water at a depth of about 11 metres in the 1960s. Today, pumps extract water from a depth of 135 metres—uneconomical without electricity subsidies. Overpumping has led to saline intrusion and losses of agricultural land. Agribusiness export firms are moving inland from the worst affected coastal areas, tapping new sources.

The annual cost of electricity subsidies is $700 million a year. Because electricity use is linked to farm size, the transfers are highly regressive (see figure). What this means is that many of the largest users receive an average of $1,800 a year, while the smallest receive $94 on average. The Gini coefficient, a measure of inequality, is 0.91 (1 is perfect inequality) for subsidy distribution compared with a national Gini coefficient of 0.54.

By subsidizing consumption, electricity subsidies maintain artificially high demand for water. Econometric analysis suggests that withdrawing the subsidy would result in three-quarters of irrigators adopting more efficient practices, such as sprinkler systems. It would also give an incentive for farmers to produce crops less intensive in water use. The overall water savings would represent about one-fifth of current use—a volume equal to total urban consumption.

Source: CNA 2004; Ezcurra 1998; Guevara-Sanginés 2006; Ponce 2005; Texas Center for Policy Studies 2002; Tuinhof and Heederik 2002.

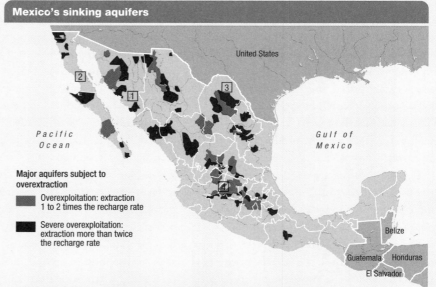

Mexico's sinking aquifers

Major aquifers subject to overextraction

- Overexploitation: extraction 1 to 2 times the recharge rate
- Severe overexploitation: extraction more than twice the recharge rate

1. Hermosillo Coast. Intensive production of agricultural exports and wheat for domestic market.
2. Baja California. Large-scale commercial production of fruit and vegetables by companies linked to US market.
3. Coahuila. One of Mexico's fastest sinking aquifers and major site for production of alfafa to supply feed to livestock sector.
4. El Bajio. Source of 90% of Mexico's frozen fruit and vegetable export. Production dominated by large-scale commercial farms and agro-industrial processing plants supplying US market.

Note: The boundaries and names shown and the designations used on this map do not imply official endorsement or acceptance by the United Nations.
Source: Guevara-Sanginés 2006.

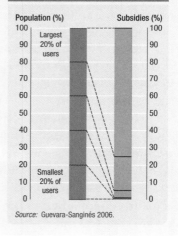

Large farmers capture most irrigation subsidies

Source: Guevara-Sanginés 2006.

countries (such as Ghana and Honduras) have to compete in markets distorted by these subsidies.

Damaging as the acts of commission of perverse subsidies can be, acts of omission are perhaps more serious. Water may be available in finite quantities—but it has been treated as an environmental resource with no scarcity value. Water-based ecosystems create the conditions and maintain the processes that sustain human life, including the provision of water for production. Yet these services are seldom traded in markets, have no price and thus are not properly valued—despite the very real

Water scarcity, risk and vulnerability

4

contribution to wealth of water-based ecosystems (box 4.4).

National accounting conventions reinforce the market blind spot for water. There is obvious asymmetry in the way that governments measure, and therefore think about, the value of financial capital and natural resource capital, such as water. The deterioration or depletion of water does not show up in the accounts as a loss, or depreciation, in natural resource assets. Perversely, in fact, the mining of groundwater, the draining of lakes and the polluting of rivers can show up in national accounts as income growth. Adjusting GDP accounts for losses of water capital would markedly change economic performance indicators for a large number of countries, while at the same time signalling a threat to future generations.[45]

At the core of the idea of sustainability in resource use is the proposition that production systems should be managed so that we live off our resources today, without eroding the asset base to be inherited by future generations. This is vital for human development. Implicit in this idea is the principle of cross-generation distributional equity—the belief that we have an obligation to future generations.[46] Governments today are widely violating that principle by running down national water assets.

The core challenge in water governance is to realign water use with demand at levels that maintain the integrity of the environment. While policies will vary across countries, five broad elements are needed:

- *Developing a national strategy.* A core aim of integrated water resources management is to adjust water use patterns to water availability, taking into account the needs of the environment. Achieving this goal requires a high level of information about water resources. It also requires a capacity on the part of national and local governments to implement pricing and allocation policies that constrain demand within the bounds of sustainability. Effective national planning has to make provisions for the environment as a water user.

| Box 4.4 | The real value of water-based ecosystems |

What is water worth? Markets provide only a very limited answer because ecosystem services are not widely traded—and because they provide public goods that are hard to price.

Ecosystems are a source of great wealth. They provide ecological services—such as water filtration—and sustain environments vital to the production of food and other products. One estimate of the economic value of wetlands in the Zambezi Basin by the World Conservation Union values their ecological services at $63 million, more than half of it in water purification and treatment services. In the Hadejia Nguru wetlands of Nigeria the traditional use of floodplains yields $12 per cubic metre of water in rice production, compared with $0.04 per cubic metre on irrigated schemes.

Wetlands are also crucial in the livelihoods of the poor. In Mali wetland areas in the Niger Delta support 550,000 people, including fisher folk, pastoralists and the producers who grow half of Mali's rice.

New York City provides one of the clearest examples of an ecoservice in operation. It derives most of its water from reservoirs in the Catskill Mountains. As this region developed, pollution threatened the city's drinking water. Faced with a choice between a $6–$8 billion filtration plant or $1.5 billion in environmental restoration, city authorities chose restoration. Using proceeds from an environmental bond issue, the city bought up land in and around the watershed and provided incentives for sustainable resource management.

As the city's environmental commissioner remarked: "All filtration does is solve a problem. Preventing the problem, through the watershed protection, is faster, cheaper and has lots of other benefits."

Source: Bos and Bergkamp 2001; Postel and Richter 2003; WRI 2005.

- *Cutting perverse subsidies and rethinking water pricing.* Eliminating state-sponsored water mining by reducing or removing electricity subsidies for irrigation would relieve some pressure on water resources. More broadly, governments can no longer treat water as a free good. Raising prices while implementing policies to protect the interests of poor farmers has the potential to advance both efficiency and environmental sustainability goals.
- *Make polluters pay.* Ensuring that industries pay for cleaning up the pollution that they cause would reduce pressure on water resources. This is partly about government regulation. By enshrining the polluter pays principle in tax provisions and enforcing strong environmental laws, government policies can enhance the water resource base. Effective regulation can also create incentives for new technologies and patterns of intervention. In India, for example, private companies have introduced

Pricing water at levels that bear no relation to scarcity, or to ecological protection, can create a hidden incentive for wasteful use and pollution. Creating the right incentives can dramatically increase water availability. India demonstrates both the problem and potential solutions.

Legislation in 2003 introducing charges to control pollution has been ineffective. The charges represent only a tiny fraction of costs for the most polluting industries. For thermal power, paper, and iron and steel the range is 0.1%–0.5% of operating costs. Tariffs have been similarly ineffective. Many industries self-provide through groundwater pumping. Even where tariffs are applied, they are usually based on average rather than marginal-cost pricing. And they ignore environmental externalities.

Water scarcity has started to generate innovative technological solutions. The operating costs of such technology have become more competitive with the higher cost of buying water in water-scarce areas. For example, the cost of treating municipal sewage water by reverse osmosis in Chennai is 25–50 rupees per cubic metre, similar to charges by the Madras Water Supply and Sewerage Board for fresh water.

Some of the best water use practices in India have emerged in water-scarce regions, exemplified by Chennai, one of the country's most water-stressed cities. Several industries there have invested in reverse osmosis water treatment and recycling technologies, effectively filtering wastewater. With an initial investment of just under $3 million, Madras Fertilisers recycles more than 80% of its daily use of 15.12 million litres of water to the plant's cooling towers. The company also supplies 3 million litres per day of fresh water to Chennai City.

Improved water efficiency has been taken up in other areas. One of the most water-efficient pulp and paper companies in the country, J K Papers, is located in the water-scarce Rayagada District of Orissa, and the most water-efficient sugar industry, Natural Sugar and Allied Industry, is in the water-scarce district of Latur in Maharastra. The first "zero-discharge" textile mill in the country, Arvind Mills, is in Santej in Gujarat, where water shortages are a recurring problem.

These success stories highlight how incentives and technology can shift the parameters of water scarcity. Most of the innovation has been driven by the private sector. Looking to the future, there is scope for tax and other incentives to encourage the spread of water-efficient technologies in the wider public interest.

Source: Bhushan 2004.

technologies that reduce water pollution and increase availability to downstream users (box 4.5).

- *Valuing ecological services.* Going beyond the polluter pays to the pollution prevention pays principle offers further benefits. As the value of water as a productive resource has increased, awareness of economic benefits linked to ecosystem trading has developed through payments for watershed services. In Costa Rica the town of Heredia uses an environmentally adjusted water tariff to finance watershed conservation upstream, paying farmers $30–$50 per hectare for good land management.[47] This is an approach that could be more widely applied.

- *Regulating groundwater extraction.* Groundwater is a strategic ecological resource. Managing that resource to meet human and environmental needs is one of the great water security challenges of the early 21st century. Countries like Jordan have embarked on a regulatory offensive in groundwater. It carried out detailed groundwater basin studies as a precursor to a range of supply-side (regulation through the use of permits) and demand-side (installation of meters and increased prices) measures. These themes could be more widely followed, combining strategies that monitor local groundwater levels and set flexible extraction limits accordingly.

Augmenting supply— options and constraints

From time immemorial governments have responded to tensions between supply and human demand for water as a productive resource by changing the supply side of the equation. The large engineering works of the 20th century bear testimony to that approach. So does supply augmentation offer a way out of 21st century water constraints?

Diverting rivers
Some governments still see the diversion of rivers, one of the great hydrological interventions of the 20th century, as a partial solution to

water stress. The south to north river diversion scheme in China is one of the world's greatest planned infrastructure programmes. With a price tag of $40–$60 billion it dwarfs even the expenditure on the Three Gorges Dam. The aim is to divert more than 40 billion cubic metres of water a year—roughly the volume of another Yellow River—from the Yangtze to the water-stressed North China plain and the megacities of the north. The Chinese plan is not an isolated case. In India the River Interlinking Project is a breathtakingly ambitious framework for redrawing the country's hydrological map, harnessing the great perennial monsoon rivers of the north, such as the Brahmaputra and the Ganges, to the perennially dry and shrinking rivers of the south, such as the Kavery and the Krishn, which have been diminished by excessive withdrawals for agriculture, industry and urban centres.

Measured in a purely quantitative sense, river diversion offers a short-term ameliorative for a long-term problem. It does not provide a panacea for overuse. Moreover, any river transfer faces the risk of creating large social and ecological costs and of running up against new environmental barriers. In Spain a scheme to divert the Ebro River from the north to commercial agricultural areas in the south has been shelved, partly because of a political reassessment of the costs and partly because the project failed to meet EU Water Directive guidelines for environmental sustainability. In China the most ambitious part of the south to north scheme envisages taking water from the glacial headwaters of the Yangtze in Tibet to the Yellow River. Yet global warming raises serious questions over the future volume and timing of glacial flows.

Desalinization

"If we could ever competitively, at a cheap rate, get fresh water from saltwater, this would be in the long-range interests of humanity [and] really dwarf any other scientific accomplishment", observed US President John F. Kennedy. Practiced since biblical times, the creation of fresh water by extracting salt from sea water is not a recent human endeavour. But does it offer a solution to problems of water stress and scarcity?

The major constraint on commercial desalinization has been energy costs. With the development of new reverse osmosis technologies, production costs have fallen sharply and output is rising. Israel, one of the world leaders, can desalinate water at costs per cubic metre comparable to those of conventional water utility plants. However, the sensitivity of production costs to energy prices, allied to the high costs of pumping water over long distances, creates restrictive conditions. For oil-rich countries and relatively wealthy cities close to the sea, desalinization holds out promise as a source of water for domestic consumption. The potential for addressing the problems of poor cities in low-income countries is more limited—and desalinization is unlikely to resolve the fundamental mismatch between supply and demand in water. It currently contributes only 0.2% to global water withdrawals and holds limited potential for agriculture or industry (box 4.6).[48]

Virtual water

Virtual water imports are another supply-side option for alleviating water stress. When countries import cereals and other agricultural products, they are also importing the water embedded in the produce. Virtual water trade generates water savings for importing countries and global water savings because of the differential in water productivity between exporters and importers.

Trade in virtual water has been rising exponentially with trade in food. Globally, the trade in 2000 was estimated at about 1,340 billion cubic metres, or three times the level in 1960. To put this figure in context, it represents about a quarter of the water required to grow food worldwide. Some analysts see virtual water trade as a way for water-scarce countries to save water by importing it from countries that face lower opportunity costs in water use and higher productivity. From this perspective virtual water trade is seen as an exercise in comparative advantage that overcomes the constraints on trading water itself.[49]

River diversion offers a short-term ameliorative for a long-term problem. It does not provide a panacea for overuse

Box 4.6 | Desalinization—and its limits

Desalinization is a technical option for creating fresh water from sea water. Distilling sea water by boiling it and collecting the vapour is an age-old activity—an activity transformed over the past 20 years through new technologies. But there are limits to its scope.

In 2002 the global market for desalinization stood at $35 billion. There are now more than 12,500 plants operating in 120 countries. Traditionally, desalinization has taken place through thermal heating, using oil and energy as the source. The most modern plants have replaced this technology with reverse osmosis—forcing water through a membrane and capturing salt molecules. The costs of producing water from this source have fallen sharply, from more than $1 per cubic metre a decade ago to less than half that today. The energy to drive the conversion is a significant part of the cost.

Israel provides the gold standard in water desalinization. Following implementation of a planning strategy launched in 2000—the Desalinization Master Plan—the country now generates about a quarter of its domestic fresh water through desalinization. The $250 million Ashkelon Plant, which began operation in 2005, is the world's largest and most advanced reverse osmosis facility, producing fresh water at a cost of $0.52 per cubic metre. It supplies about 15% of Israel's fresh water used for domestic consumption. Current plans envisage an increase in production from desalinization plants from 400 million cubic metres today to 750 million cubic metres by 2020.

Current desalinization capacity is heavily concentrated. The Gulf states account for the bulk of capacity, with Saudi Arabia accounting for one-tenth of total output. Elsewhere, Tampa Bay in Florida and Santa Cruz in California have adopted reverse osmosis plants, and China has announced plans for a plant in Tianjin, its third largest city. In Spain the new government abandoned plans to pump water across the country from the wet north to the arid south in favour of 20 reverse osmosis plants (enough to meet 1% of needs), though the costs of desalinized water may not entice farmers from their current groundwater irrigation sources. In the United Kingdom the water utility serving London has a reverse osmosis plant that will come into operation in 2007.

This pattern of distribution highlights both the potential and the limits of desalinization. While costs are falling, the capital costs of new plants are considerable and operating costs are highly sensitive to energy prices. Recent projects in Israel and other countries demonstrate this, with tenders for water supply rising to $0.80–$1.00 per cubic metre. The cost of pumping water rises sharply with distance as well, so that inland cities would face higher cost structures. These factors help to explain why oil-rich states and coastal cities in water-stressed areas will probably remain the main users.

Overall use patterns are likely to change slowly. In some countries desalinization can be expected to account for an increased share of domestic and industrial water use. Municipalities currently account for two-thirds of use and industry for a quarter. The potential in agriculture is limited by cost. That is especially so for producers of low value-added staple crops that require large volumes of water.

Source: Rosegrant and Cline 2003; Schenkeveld and others 2004; Rijsberman 2004a; BESA 2000; Water-Technology.net 2006.

Does agricultural trade offer a route out of water stress? For some countries, especially in the Middle East and North Africa, virtual water trade is already an integral element in national food security strategies.[50] Were Egypt to grow a volume of cereals equivalent to national imports, it would require one-sixth of the water in Lake Nasser, the Aswan Dam's main reservoir. For developing countries as a group virtual water imports in 2025 will represent a projected 12% of irrigation consumption. However, the case for reducing water stress by expanding virtual water trade has been overstated, not least from a human development perspective.

Consider first the argument that virtual water trade represents an exercise in comparative advantage. Rich countries account for more than 60% of agricultural exports worldwide. Considering that these countries provided more than $280 billion in agricultural support in 2005, it follows that virtual water markets suffer from the same distortions as the markets for the products that facilitate water exchange.[51] As for the opportunity costs associated with water use, it is not clear that major exporters of water-intensive products such as cotton and rice—Australia and the United States, for example—factor in environmental damage (or virtual water subsidies) to their export prices.

The complex interaction between food imports and food security is another concern. Serious food security problems can arise when food imports are the result of slow growth and declining agricultural productivity, as in much of Sub-Saharan Africa. For example, Sub-Saharan African cereal imports are projected to more than triple by 2025, to 35 million tonnes.[52] It is unlikely that the region will be in a position to finance these imports on a predictable and sustainable basis, suggesting a growing dependence on food aid. Moreover, when countries import virtual water they are also importing virtual and actual subsidies against which their own farmers will have to compete in local markets. These subsidies can lower prices and reduce market shares with damaging implications for rural poverty reduction efforts.

Recycling wastewater

Some simple water management policies allied to appropriate technology can help to alleviate the mismatch between water supply and demand. One example is the reuse of wastewater by treating sewage so that it can be safely restored to rivers, used for irrigation or deployed for industry.

Recycling wastewater for peri-urban agriculture already happens on a large-scale. Wastewater is estimated to directly or indirectly irrigate about 20 million hectares of land globally—almost 7% of total irrigated area.[53] In the Mezquital Valley in Mexico about half a million rural households are supported by irrigation systems maintained through untreated wastewater. In Ghana farmers around Kumasi use wastewater on 12,000 hectares, more than twice the area covered by formal irrigation systems across the whole country. It is estimated that dry season irrigation with wastewater raises average agricultural incomes in Kumasi by 40%–50%, with the predictability of supply and the high nutrient content of the wastewater enabling farmers to enter higher value-added vegetable markets.[54]

Expanding capacity for wastewater recycling, by increasing the supply and productivity of water, could generate multiple benefits for poor and vulnerable agricultural producers. Wastewater can also be used to replenish aquifers, alleviating problems of groundwater depletion. With urban and industrial water use projected to double by 2050, wastewater could become an expanding and dependable supply: what goes into cities has to come back out again in some form. However, using wastewater sources without adequate safeguards can expose agricultural producers and peri-urban areas to acute health risks. One study in Haroonabad,

Pakistan, found rates of diarrhoea and hookworm infection among wastewater farmers twice as high as those among irrigation canal farmers.[55]

The regulated use of treated water could significantly alleviate the adjustment pressures now facing water management in agriculture. Israel demonstrates the potential. Over two-thirds of the wastewater produced in the country every year is now treated and used for irrigation in agriculture. Most comes through the national water company, which also sets stringent rules for treatment levels: lower quality wastewater is allocated to tolerant crops such as cotton, with higher treatment standards applied to water for irrigating vegetables or replenishing groundwater.[56] Thus Tel Aviv's wastewater supports agricultural irrigation in the arid southern region. Other countries are following Israel's lead. Cities in water-scarce parts of California are investing heavily in plants that treat all domestic and industrial waste to a high standard, reusing the water for agriculture and industrial cooling. The Mexican city of San Luis Potosi recycles 60% of the city's wastewater for distribution to farmers through a modern sewerage plant.

Many developing countries start from a position of considerable disadvantage in developing wastewater resources. Most cities in low-income developing countries have either minimal or zero wastewater treatment capacity. In contrast to Israel or California they also lack the technological and wider capacity to segment wastewater into different treatment and allocation regimes. So does this rule out a substantive supply-side impetus from wastewater?

Even with severe resource constraints far more could be done. The underdevelopment of wastewater capacity in some countries is itself a product of fragmented and piecemeal planning. Many governments have seen investment in treatment plants as an unaffordable luxury, but factoring in the potentially high economic and social returns to an increased supply of water for irrigation would change the cost-benefit equation. If water and sanitation departments spoke to irrigation departments, there would almost certainly be more investment in this area. While

The regulated use of treated water could significantly alleviate the adjustment pressures now facing water management in agriculture

4

Water scarcity, risk and vulnerability

People and governments across the world are discovering the value of water and the costs of having ignored the real value of water in the past

few developing countries are in a position to duplicate Israel's wastewater allocation system, simple rules can make a difference. Mexico uses the expedient of banning wastewater for fruits and vegetables. Jordan and Tunisia have developed highly innovative public education campaigns among rural producers to communicate strategies for reducing health risks associated with the use of wastewater.

Regulating demand for a scarce resource

"When the wells dry", observed Benjamin Franklin, one of the architects of the US Declaration of Independence, "we know the value of water." Today, people and governments across the world are discovering the value of water and the costs of having ignored the real value of water in the past. Public policies today are picking up the bill for the past practice of treating water as a resource to be exploited without limit.

As awareness of the value of water has increased, there has been a growing concern for raising water productivity. What does this mean in practice? There are two broad approaches to water productivity that figure in debates on water use, though they are often confused. One approach stresses the importance of increasing physical productivity by increasing the "crop per drop" ratio. Running parallel to this approach is a focus on raising productivity as measured by value added in production: water is a scarce capital resource that should be deployed where it generates the greatest wealth.

Increasing crop per drop

What do these shifts in perspective imply for human development? The case for raising water productivity in terms of crop per drop is overwhelming. Meeting the water requirements of a growing population while protecting the natural ecosystems on which life itself depends is a critical condition for sustained human development. Addressing this challenge will involve making water management in irrigation leaner and smarter—substituting technology and knowledge for water.

Increased productivity is one route to reduced water stress—and there is great scope for generating more crop per drop. The good news is that the increase in water productivity recorded over recent decades has been spectacular. The amount of water needed to produce cereals for one person has halved since 1960. The bad news is that in many of the world's most stressed water basins productivity remains very low. Comparisons across countries amply demonstrate the scope for raising water productivity as measured on a simple crop per drop scale. In California 1 tonne of water yields 1.3 kilograms of wheat. In Pakistan it produces less than half as much.[57] Producing a tonne of maize in France takes less than half as much water as in China. Variations between irrigation systems in developing countries are equally large: China produces twice as much rice as India with the same volume of water, for example.

The benchmark for water efficiency in agriculture is drip irrigation, a method that supplies water directly to the root zone of plants.[58] In Jordan drip irrigation has reduced water use by about a third. However, Jordan is the exception. Drip technology has been adopted on less than 1% of irrigated lands worldwide—and 90% of capacity is in developed countries.[59] Global partnerships for technology transfer supported through international aid could make a difference.

From a human development perspective the problem with drip irrigation and wider technologies is distributional. New technologies have the potential to realign supply and demand at reduced water use levels. However, the technologies are seldom distribution neutral. At a global level technologies for conserving water are concentrated in rich countries partly because of the capital costs involved. Within countries, access to water-thrifty innovations requires access to capital, knowledge and wider infrastructure. Poor farmers in marginal areas are the least likely to have access to these assets, especially female farmers. The danger is that by raising productivity and reducing water use, new water technologies will help resolve one aspect of the water crisis while exacerbating wider social and economic inequalities. But that outcome is not inevitable: as we show in chapter 5, affordable drip technologies are increasingly available.

Diverting water to higher value-added uses

Diverting water use into higher value-added areas raises some analogous problems. This is one of the core recommendations of advocates for "soft-path" solutions to water stress. Rather than getting more crop per drop, the aim—crudely summarized—is to get more money per cubic metre. The underlying assumption is that water, as an increasingly scarce resource, has to be deployed where it generates high returns.[60]

At face value that assumption appears entirely reasonable. Applied to California, where water used in, say, the production of microchips, produces more income and employment than water used in heavily subsidized, capital-intensive rice and cotton farming, the policy options appear clear-cut.

In practice, though, advocates of soft-path solutions tend to overstate their case—and to suffer from an equity blind spot. The case is overstated on two counts. First, it is difficult to separate the value of water from other inputs in the production of high value-added manufactured goods. Second, and more important, there is surprisingly little evidence that the development of higher value-added industries has been held back because of competition with agriculture for water. In most cases agriculture has lost out in any competition (see chapter 5).

The equity blind spot concerns the failure to consider the range of distributional consequences that can flow from water transfer. That there are large variations in value added by water use in agricultural production is not in doubt. One cross-country study of irrigation systems covering 40 countries found a tenfold difference in the gross value of output per unit of water consumed.[61] Other things being equal, an equivalent amount of water might be expected to generate larger revenue flows when applied to the production of high

value-added fruits and vegetables or beef and dairy products than to staple foods such as rice.[62] The same is true for high value-added industry.

However, in countries where the vast majority of the population depend on agriculture for their livelihoods, and where the production of food staples represents a large share of income and employment for poor households, losses of water can translate into a major human development threat. The obvious danger is that water diversion will generate more wealth while destroying the livelihoods of some of the most vulnerable people.

Integrated water management

These distributional problems are taken up in chapter 5. The backdrop though is a new emerging consensus on water governance. At the World Summit on Sustainable Development in 2002 governments embraced integrated water resources management as the model for the future. This approach emphasizes managing water allocations within the ecological limits of availability, with a premium on the three Es: equity, efficiency and environmental sustainability (box 4.7). In practice it is difficult to balance the competing claims of different users for a resource that goes to the heart of power relationships in society—and to questions of political voice and institutional accountability.

The deeper challenge is to develop a new ethic for water management backed by a commitment to address the deep inequalities that drive water insecurity. The central question has been powerfully expressed by Sandra Postel and Brian Richter:[63]

> It would make us stop asking how we can further manipulate rivers, lakes, and streams to meet our insatiable demands, and instead ask how we can best satisfy human needs while accommodating the ecological requirements of healthy water systems. And it would inevitably lead us to deeper questions of human values—in particular, how to narrow the unacceptably wide gap between the haves and the have nots.

The deeper challenge is to develop a new ethic for water management backed by a commitment to address the deep inequalities that drive water insecurity

Box 4.7   Integrated Water Resources Management

The coordinated development and management of water, land and related resources, in order to maximise the resultant economic and social welfare in an equitable manner without compromising the sustainability of vital ecosystems.

That is the stated objective of integrated water resources management. Adopted by the World Summit on Sustainable Development in Johannesburg in 2002 as part of the wider international strategy for the Millennium Development Goals, the concept marks the latest in the evolution of water governance frameworks developed since the 1992 International Conference on Water. That conference established three key principles for good governance:

- The *ecological principle* for integrating water management around river basins rather than independent institutional users, with land and water governance integrated for environmental reasons.

- The *institutional principle* for basing resource management on dialogue among all stakeholders through transparent and accountable institutions governed by the principle of subsidiarity—the devolution of authority to the lowest appropriate level, from user groups at the base to local government and river basin bodies.

- The *economic principle* for making more use of incentives and market-based principles to improve the efficiency of water as an increasingly scarce resource.

As broad principles these are sound foundations for any water governance system. The starting point for integrated water resources management is that all water should be treated as a single environmental resource and allocated within a coherent public policy framework among the main groups of water users: agriculture, industry and households. By factoring in sustainability, the model also recognizes that there are ecological limits to water use and that the environment has to be treated as a user in its own right. Translating these principles into public policies is more problematic.

Perhaps one of the most widely cited models of good practice in integrated water resources management at the basin level is the Murray-Darling Basin Initiative in southeastern Australia, covering 20 rivers and a large number of groundwater systems extending across five states. The basin accounts for three-quarters of Australia's irrigated land area, more than a quarter of its cattle farms and half of its sheep and cropland. The initiative is a cooperative attempt at integrated water management in response to a crisis generated by severe ecological degradation and the overallocation of water for irrigation in a semi-arid region.

The scope of this cooperation is impressive. The Murray-Darling Basin Commission (MDBC), created in 1988, sets a cap on water use, taking into account the ecological requirements for maintaining the integrity of the system. Quantitative water use rights are allocated by state for distribution to different users. Disputes are settled through an established procedure, with provisions for states and individuals to trade water use rights.

Public participation in governance has evolved over time to include environmental groups, catchment committees, farmer organizations and other stakeholder representatives engaged in consultation processes. A Community Advisory Committee makes technical information on water allocations widely available. The political authority of the MDBC is rooted in an institutional structure that delegates authority from a high-level Ministerial Council.

Reproducing these conditions in developing countries is not easy. South Africa's post-apartheid water governance structure has some of the institutional features of the Murray-Darling Initiative. National planning for water is highly decentralized. A strong apex body brings together all ministries involved in water allocation. Water allocations also provide for environmental use rights that take the form of a nonnegotiable reserve set by government to ensure the quantity, quality and reliability of water required to maintain the integrity of ecological systems. In the annual planning cycle no water is licensed for use until the environmental reserve has been fixed.

Institutional development takes time, however. Brazil is sometimes cited as a model for some aspects of integrated basin management. But even in Ceará, arguably the best performing state, it has taken over a decade to develop a model of participatory water governance.

The National Water Act of 1997 revolutionized water management in Brazil. Legislation was drawn up after five years of structured national dialogue, with thousands of meetings and public hearings. Decentralization of water management emerged as a critical policy objective, with river basins identified as the appropriate unit for devolved authority. New institutions were created at all levels of governance, with an apex body bringing together representatives of all ministries with water functions, state representatives, water users and nongovernment agencies.

The state of Ceará has been among the most successful reformers. In a drought-prone, semi-arid region of the northeast, it is one of Brazil's poorest states, with more than 70% of rural households below the poverty line. Ceará has five large river basins, but no naturally perennial rivers. Conflict within these basins has intensified as growing demands from industrial users and municipalities in Fortaleza, the state capital, compete with irrigated agricultural users, who consume more than 80% of the water.

Water reform in Ceará has been part of a wider process of democratization and decentralization. The Lower Jaguaribe Basin illustrates the political process. An assembly of 180 user groups was convened by Ceará Water Resources Management Company (COGERH), the publicly owned river basin agency. The assembly, which included industry, commercial farmers, rural labour unions and cooperatives, developed an operational plan for managing water use in the river basin with technical advice from COGERH hydrologists. Implementation has been overseen by a Committee of Representatives elected by the assembly. After a year of low rainfall in 2000, the Users Commission met to draw up strategies for reducing water flows, which were voted on in the assembly.

Success was made possible by high levels of user participation and public debate within the Users Commission, which helped to

4

Water scarcity, risk and vulnerability

| Box 4.7 | **Integrated Water Resources Management** (continued) |

institutionalize the rules for managing competition. A strong technical advisory body, perceived as both competent and independent of individual user interest groups, has also been important. And cross-party support for COGERH and similar participatory policy-making processes across the state in health and education depoliticized some aspects of water management.

Experience elsewhere has been mixed. The Johannesburg Summit called on all countries to draw up integrated water resources management plans within five years, an unrealistic target since revised in the face of capacity constraints. At the end of 2005 only 20 of 95 countries surveyed by the Global Water Partnership had produced such a plan or had plans well under way. Only five were in Sub-Saharan Africa, and one (Brazil) was in Latin America.

In some cases great effort has been put into planning with no tangible outcomes. For example, Nicaragua spent more than two years drawing up a 13-volume plan, but failed to establish effective follow-up mechanisms. None of this is meant to understate the progress that has been made. From a weak base, Bangladesh, Burkina Faso, Namibia and Uganda have undertaken major institutional reforms, though implementation will prove a stern test.

Integrated water resources management requires institutions that take several years to develop, even with strong political commitment, and it offers no ready-made solutions to some of the classic problems in water management. A nominally integrated water resource management plan says little about whose interests are served or whose voice is heard. In many cases integrated water resources management has a narrow technical focus. Far more attention has gone to increasing the efficiency of water use through transfers into higher value-added areas or through new technologies than to the equity and social justice central to human development (see chapter 5).

Source: GWP 2000, 2004, 2006a; Biswas 2004; Shah 2005; Haisman 2005; Kemper, Dinar and Bloomquist 2005; Muller 2006; Lemos and de Oliveira 2005; Tortajada 2006a; Rogers 2002.

Dealing with risk, vulnerability and uncertainty

The physical availability of water is one dimension of scarcity. But in all countries the relationship between water security and water availability is mediated through the infrastructure and institutions that govern water. Countries vary enormously in their capacity in these areas, with implications for water security. Nowhere are those implications more apparent than in the threat of global warming—a threat that can be addressed only through a strong infrastructure base that facilitates adaptation.

The crucial role of infrastructure

There are large global inequalities in water infrastructure. In all industrial countries flows of rivers are regulated and managed, with water stored for multiple uses. Few people in those countries are aware of how investments in water infrastructure create the conditions for water security, economic growth and employment—or how they protect against the destructive powers of water in floods and drought. It is only during periods of crisis that water infrastructure figures prominently in public policy debates. In the United States Hurricane Katrina provided a tragically powerful reminder of the importance of infrastructure—and of human vulnerability. That event was so shocking partly because the loss of life and the destruction were so unexpected. By contrast, in much of the developing world the human costs of weak infrastructure and vulnerability to water shocks are experienced daily.

Mitigating risk in rich countries

The sheer scale of water infrastructure investment in rich countries is not widely appreciated. Investments in hydraulic infrastructure have in some cases generated great environmental damage, but they have also supported economic prosperity and social progress.

In the United States many of the largest federal investments in history were made to store water, harness it for electricity and curb the potential for floods. By one estimate the

4

Water scarcity, risk and vulnerability

US Army Corps of Engineers has spent $200 billion since 1920 on flood management and mitigation alone (yielding a benefit of about $700 billion).[64] The Tennessee Valley Authority, established in 1933 as part of the New Deal to build dams, hydropower facilities and reservoirs, transformed the Tennessee Valley from a flood-prone, impoverished part of the Dust Bowl, with some of the worst human development indicators in the United States, to an area of agricultural prosperity. The cycle of rural poverty afflicting more than 2 million people in one of the poorest regions of the United States was broken in a generation.[65]

Risk mitigation in water management through flood control systems and development of an economic infrastructure has been fundamental to human progress in many rich countries. Nowhere is this more evident than in Japan, where heavy post-war investments in infrastructure supported the rapid development of hydropower, flood control and irrigated agriculture. Until World War II flooding caused by heavy seasonal rains and typhoons had enormously detrimental effects on the Japanese economy, with losses sometimes exceeding 20% of GNI. Since the 1970s the impacts of floods have never exceeded 1% of GNI.[66] Most of Japan's population and 60% of its productive assets are on low-lying plains vulnerable to flooding, but infrastructure and water management have curtailed risk at an average cost of about $9 billion a year.

Infrastructure deficits in poor countries

The global distribution of water infrastructure is inversely related to the global distribution of water insecurity risks. Seasonal climates, variable rainfall and the risks of floods and droughts are a much greater threat in developing countries than in rich countries, while the institutions and infrastructure needed to provide water security are much weaker.[67]

Droughts provide powerful demonstration effects for the costs of weak infrastructure. Failed rains deplete watersheds, farmlands and pasture, degrading land and destroying crops. From the dustbowl of the 1930s in the United States to the Sahel in the 1970s and East Africa

today, droughts have shown an enormous capacity for destruction and the erosion of hard won human development gains. Droughts affect the rural poor through decreased production, loss of livestock and soil fertility and extreme shortages of drinking water. When livestock perish and crops fail, poor households lose income and nutrition worsens. Restoring assets can take years.

Sub-Saharan Africa is the worst affected region. In 2005 more than 20 million people were at risk from drought in the Horn of Africa alone. Across much of the Sahel, East Africa and Southern Africa droughts are endemic, with significant events occurring every 3–5 years. But Sub-Saharan Africa is not the only region affected. In South Asia about 15% of people live in areas that were affected by drought over the past two years. More frequent and longer lasting droughts have also been recorded in the Middle East. In Morocco a major drought in the mid-1990s reduced agricultural output by 45%, and rural labourers and small landholders lost an estimated 100 million days in agricultural employment.[68]

The variability of water supply is another major source of water insecurity—for people and national economies. Consider Ethiopia, better endowed with water than most drought-prone

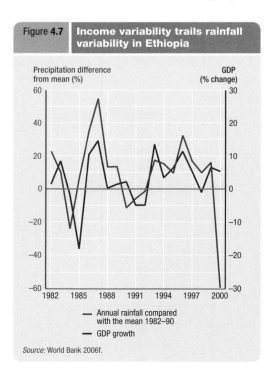

Figure 4.7 Income variability trails rainfall variability in Ethiopia

Precipitation difference from mean (%)

GDP (% change)

— Annual rainfall compared with the mean 1982–90
— GDP growth

Source: World Bank 2006f.

Box 4.8   Droughts, floods and water insecurity in Kenya

The drought in Wajir and Turkana, in northeastern Kenya, is a humanitarian catastrophe. The scale of the tragedy has attracted international media attention, but this is not an unusual event: Kenya has been affected by a succession of droughts and floods since the

Impacts of flood and drought in Kenya, 1997–2000

Impact	Amount (US$ millions)	Share of total (%)
1997–98 flood		
Transport infrastructure	777	88
Water supply infrastructure	45	5
Health sector	56	6
Total	878	
Share of GDP (%)		11
1998–2000 drought		
Hydropower losses	640	26
Industrial production losses	1,400	58
Agricultural production losses	240	10
Livestock losses	137	6
Total	2,417	
Share of GDP (%)		16

Source: World Bank 2004c, 2006e.

mid-1990s. The floods of 1997–98 were immediately followed by a drought from 1998 to 2000. Today's drought in the northeast is a continuation, and more than 3 million people risk starvation.

Beyond the human suffering, the costs have been enormous. Entire pastoral communities have seen their herds and assets depleted, increasing their vulnerability. The wider economic costs have held back the entire economy and efforts to reduce poverty.

The 1997/98 El Niño–related flood caused damage estimated at 11% of GDP (see table). Droughts in 1998–99 and 1999–2000 led to losses in excess of 16% of GDP. Industry and hydropower accounted for an estimated 80% of the losses. The full economic costs are probably much greater since the losses fail to count the effects of malnutrition, reduced investment in agriculture and a loss of investment in industry.

Crop and livestock losses represented a relatively small share of the aggregate loss, amounting to less than 16% of the total, but they have had a devastating impact on the poor, leading to extensive malnutrition, asset depletion and increased vulnerability to future risks.

---

countries. It covers 12 river basins and has just over 1,600 litres of water per person per year.[69] The problem for Ethiopia, where livelihoods for the vast majority of people depend on rainfed agriculture, is uncertainty. Rainfall variability is estimated to have pushed an additional 12 million people below the absolute poverty line in the second half of the 1990s. With more than 80% of the population living in the countryside and half of them undernourished, water holds the key to human development prospects for households. That is why poor people themselves identify variable rainfall as the greatest threat to their livelihoods. But as in other predominantly agricultural countries, failed rains in Ethiopia send shock waves beyond the household and across the entire economy (figure 4.7). A single drought event in a 12-year period will lower GDP by 7%–10% and increase poverty by 12%–14%. Economic modelling by the World Bank suggests that the inability to mitigate the effects of rainfall variability reduces Ethiopia's potential for economic growth by a third—with obvious consequences for reducing poverty.[70] Hydrological variability is estimated to increase poverty levels in 2015 by between a quarter and a third, or some 11 million people.

Water infrastructure has a major bearing on the vulnerability and capacity of households to absorb shocks. Indonesia loses an estimated 25,000 lives a year to drought-related problems—Australia, with a similar drought-risk exposure, loses none. Investments in Japan have mitigated the impact of floods so that flood damage costs seldom rise above 0.5% of GNI and losses of life are rare. But when floods struck Mozambique in 2000, they left 700 people dead and half a million homeless. Crops were destroyed, and infrastructure was damaged. Total losses amounted to an estimated 20% of GNI, with economic growth falling from 8% in 1999 to 2% in 2000. The floods also damaged or destroyed 500 primary schools and seven secondary schools.[71]

Taken as a single episode, Mozambique's experience underlines how climatic events can roll back development gains across a broad front. In many cases, though, countries have to deal with consecutive, or even simultaneous, floods and droughts (box 4.8). The poor invariably are at greatest risk from weak infrastructure. In Mozambique poor households in low-lying areas along river banks bore the brunt of the flooding. In New Orleans the devastation wrought by

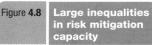

Figure **4.8** Large inequalities in risk mitigation capacity

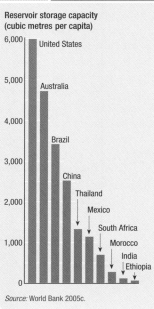

Reservoir storage capacity
(cubic metres per capita)

United States
Australia
Brazil
China
Thailand
Mexico
South Africa
Morocco
India
Ethiopia

Source: World Bank 2005c.

Hurricane Katrina affected the whole city, but poor black neighbourhoods were affected most. While the effects of extreme weather events hit all in society, poor households are more exposed to risk and less able to mitigate that risk through insurance or savings.

Inequalities in hydraulic assets show up in the human and economic costs associated with extreme weather events. Too little or too much water is the cause of most natural disasters. Cyclical factors and climate change are combining to increase the frequency of extreme weather events such as droughts and floods. All countries are affected. But rich countries can protect their citizens and their economic performance through extensive hydraulic infrastructure. Water storage capacity is one proxy indicator for comparing infrastructure capacity across counties (figure 4.8). The United States stores 6,000 cubic metres of water per person, and Australia about 5,000, compared with 43 in Ethiopia. The Colorado River has 1,400 days of storage, the Indus roughly 30 days.[72]

Cross-country water storage comparisons provide insights into one aspect of risk mitigation capacity. However, storage capacity is only one guide to the linkage between infrastructure and vulnerability. Countries such as Ghana and Zambia have very high levels of water storage per capita—higher, in fact, than the United States—but a limited capacity to mitigate risk. Most of the storage capacity is geared towards power generation, with a very limited infrastructure for smallholder producers in agriculture. There is also a flip side to large-scale water infrastructure, highlighted in the ongoing debate about the appropriate scale of interventions.

Large dams have figured prominently in that debate—and for good reason. An estimated 40–80 million people have been displaced in the last 50 years by poorly designed dam projects, many of them without adequate compensation. In the rush to develop large-scale infrastructure for irrigation or power generation, many governments have ridden roughshod over the rights and claims of communities lacking bargaining power, with indigenous people often among the worst affected.[73] In addition, many dams have caused immense social and ecological damage. Upstream effects include siltation, salinization and deforestation; downstream effects range from reduced fish stocks, damaged wetlands and lower sediment and nutrient flows. In some cases the economic benefits have been exaggerated. Offsetting the productivity gains for upstream users have been detrimental effects downstream and changes in flood ecosystems. The World Commission on Dams found a systematic bias towards underestimating the capital costs of dams (by an average of 47%) and overestimating the economic returns to large-scale irrigation.[74]

This backdrop makes clear that large infrastructure programmes should be subject to critical scrutiny for the impacts on the environment and the poor. At the same time, the contribution of large-scale infrastructure to human development should not be overlooked. In many countries such infrastructure provides water for irrigation, reducing the variability of water flows to producers and mitigating the water security risks from fluctuating rainfall. Access to irrigation is one of the most basic strategies for mitigating water insecurity.[75] In Asia the prevalence of poverty is typically 20%–40% higher outside irrigation schemes than inside (see chapter 5). Water infrastructure also offers an important source of renewable energy: it provides 22% of electricity generation in Sub-Saharan Africa.

While the contribution of large-scale infrastructure to irrigation and power generation should not be understated, neither should the potential contribution of small-scale infrastructure. Small-scale water harvesting has the potential not just to store water efficiently, thereby mitigating risk, but also to store water close to the people who need it. The fact that large volumes of water are stored in Zambia's Kariba Dam does not help small farmers in drought prone parts of the country.

Polarized debates about the relative merits of large and small infrastructure increasingly represent a diversion from the real challenge. The appropriate mix of infrastructure is best decided at national and local levels through dialogue between governments and people. But the real choice is not usually between big and small. Most developing countries do not need more of one and less of the other: they need more of both.

Global warming—the predictable emergency

In 1992 the Earth Summit in Rio de Janeiro produced a Framework Convention on Climate Change, establishing the principle that greenhouse gases should be stabilized at levels that would prevent human influence on climates. Developed countries were encouraged to stabilize emissions at 1990 levels by 2000. The convention also adopted a precautionary approach, warning that "where there are risks of serious and irreversible damage, a lack of full scientific certainty should not justify postponing action."[76]

Few warnings have been more perilously ignored. Climate change now poses what may be an unparalleled threat to human development. Much of that threat will be transmitted through shifts in hydrological cycles and rainfall patterns and the impact of higher surface temperature on water evaporation. The overall effect will be to exacerbate risk and vulnerability, threatening the livelihoods, health and security of millions of people.

Climate modelling exercises point to a complex range of possible outcomes as a result of climate change. Beyond the complexity, there are two recurrent themes. The first is that dry areas will get drier and wet areas wetter, with important consequences for the distribution of agricultural production. The second is that there will be an increase in the unpredictability of water flows, linked to more frequent and extreme weather events. While outcomes will vary across regions and within countries, some broad consequences can be predicted:

- *Agriculture and rural development will bear the brunt of climate risk.* This starting point matters because the rural sector accounts for about three-quarters of the people living on less than $1 a day and anything from a quarter to two-thirds of GNI for low-income countries. For some regions a reduction in water availability combined with a shift in rainfall could reduce yields by as much as a third by 2050, threatening millions of rural livelihoods.[77]

- *Extreme poverty and malnutrition will increase as water insecurity increases.* Attempts have been made to assess the quantitative impact of climate change on food security and nutrition. Inevitably, projections are hazardous because climate change, itself subject to considerable variation, will interact with many other variables and trends. Even so, the warning signs are clearly evident in the results of modelling exercises. Such exercises suggest that climate change could increase global malnutrition by 15%–26%, increasing the absolute number of malnourished people by 75–125 million by 2080.[78] But the systemic poverty risks will affect a far greater number. Production losses in agriculture will produce multiplier effects that spread across entire economies, transmitting poverty from rural to urban areas.

- *More extreme weather patterns will increase risk and vulnerability.* Climate change will enhance the Asian monsoon and the El Niño effect, with major implications for agricultural production. Susceptibility to drought and flood will increase over time.[79]

- *Shrinking glaciers and rising sea levels will pose new risks for human security.* The retreat of glaciers will threaten short-term flooding and long-term declines in water availability across Asia, Latin America and parts of East Africa.[80] Rising sea levels will reduce the availability of fresh water, affecting millions of people in low-lying countries and river deltas.[81]

For a large share of the world's people in developing countries climate change projections point to less secure livelihoods, greater vulnerability to hunger and poverty, worsening social inequalities and more environmental degradation. Climate change—unlike the *tsunami* in the Indian Ocean or the earthquake in Kashmir—threatens not a one-time catastrophe but a slowly unfolding disaster. While the extent of future climate change can be moderated, we are beyond the point of no return. Dangerous climate change is now inevitable. How the international community responds will

For a large share of the world's people in developing countries climate change projections point to less secure livelihoods, greater vulnerability to hunger and poverty, worsening social inequalities and more environmental degradation

4

Water scarcity, risk and vulnerability

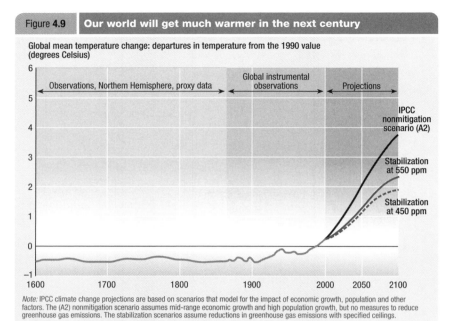

Figure 4.9 Our world will get much warmer in the next century

Global mean temperature change: departures in temperature from the 1990 value (degrees Celsius)

Observations, Northern Hemisphere, proxy data

Global instrumental observations

Projections

IPCC nonmitigation scenario (A2)

Stabilization at 550 ppm

Stabilization at 450 ppm

Note: IPCC climate change projections are based on scenarios that model for the impact of economic growth, population and other factors. The (A2) nonmitigation scenario assumes mid-range economic growth and high population growth, but no measures to reduce greenhouse gas emissions. The stabilization scenarios assume reductions in greenhouse gas emissions with specified ceilings.

Source: IPCC 2001.

warmest years on record have occurred since 1994. As a decade the 1990s were the hottest on record since the 14th century. Glaciers are shrinking and sea levels are rising far more rapidly than climate modellers anticipated even a decade ago.

Concentrations of carbon dioxide, the main greenhouse gas, are climbing steadily upwards. Currently, emissions are running at about 7 billion tonnes a year, with atmospheric concentrations reaching 380 parts per million (ppm). The exact path for future emissions will depend on many factors—including population growth, economic growth, technological change, fossil fuel prices and, above all, government actions. But the overall trajectory for carbon dioxide is clearly upwards. The *World Energy Outlook* predicts that carbon dioxide emissions will increase by 63% over 2002 levels by 2030.[82]

What does all of this mean for climate change? Even if all emissions stopped tomorrow, temperatures would continue to rise as a result of the delayed effect of past emissions. Were the trends of the past 50 years to continue, carbon dioxide concentrations would increase to 550 ppm by the middle of the 21st century and continue rising thereafter.

International bodies such as the Intergovernmental Panel on Climate Change (IPCC) have been consolidating the scientific base for understanding climate change for more than two decades.[83] Their nonmitigation scenarios suggest that emission trends could raise global temperatures by 1.4°C–5.8°C by 2100. In a more positive scenario, with stabilization of emissions at 450 ppm, the world would still be committed to an increase of about 2°C (figure 4.9 and table 4.2).[84] What these projection

determine human development prospects for current and future generations. An immediate priority is to supplement strategies to mitigate climate change with strategies to support adaptation to inevitable shifts in climate.

Our warming world

In the 20th century human activity increased the presence of greenhouse gases—mainly carbon dioxide, methane and ozone—in the atmosphere by about 30% over pre-industrial levels. That development will have momentous consequences for humanity in the 21st century and beyond.

The impact of the surge in greenhouse gases is already becoming apparent. The Earth has warmed by 0.7°C over the past century— but the pace of change is quickening. The 10

Table 4.2 Global warming thresholds and targets

Stabilization target (carbon dioxide equivalent concentration, parts per million)	Period when global emissions must fall below 1990 levels to meet stabilization target	Change in global emissions by 2050 relative to 1990 levels (%)	Temperature change based on IPCC climate models (degrees Celsius)
400	2020–30	−40% to −55%	1.2–2.5
450	2030–40	−15% to −40%	1.3–2.7
550	2045–65	−10% to +10%	1.5–3.2

Note: IPCC temperature stabilization scenarios: all major greenhouse gases included, expressed as carbon dioxide equivalent.
Source: Stern Review on the Economics of Climate Change 2006.

scenarios highlight is that current atmospheric and oceanic concentrations of greenhouse gases bind us to a certain degree of climate change.

While an analysis of the prospects for achieving stabilization at different levels is beyond the scope of this Report, two observations have a very direct bearing on water security. The first is that the current multilateral framework falls far short of what is required. The Kyoto Protocol envisages a reduction in carbon dioxide emissions of 5% against the 1990 level by 2012 on the part of signatory states. However, two major industrial countries (Australia and the United States) have not ratified the protocol, and its targets do not apply to developing countries. The upshot: it now covers less than a third of global emissions.

The second observation is that stabilization at 550 ppm or below will require an unprecedented level of international cooperation. Emissions are currently increasing: stabilization at 550 ppm will require carbon dioxide emissions to be brought back roughly to current levels by 2050 and continue to decline from that point onwards to near-zero net emissions; lowering the level to 450 ppm (still a dangerous climate change scenario) will require global emissions of carbon dioxide in 2050 to be about a half of current levels. The gap between these requirements and the IPCC development scenarios speaks volumes for the challenge now facing the international community (figure 4.10).

Meeting that challenge will require a level of ambition far beyond that reflected in the current Kyoto Protocol. Some developed country governments are pressing for the next protocol to set a stabilization limit of about 550 ppm—almost double pre-industrial levels. Others—including the European Union—have argued for a temperature-based target, with the goal of restricting temperature increases to no more than 2°C above pre-industrial levels. By one assessment this would imply a commitment by developed countries to reduce emissions to 15%–30% below 1990 levels by 2020, rising to 80% by 2050.[85] To put the scale of the challenge in context, emissions per person for the world as a whole will have to fall from about 4 tonnes of carbon dioxide today to 1.2–2.8 tonnes by 2050. The longer

the delay in arriving at a peak for emissions, the deeper the cuts that will be required.[86]

Successful mitigation of climate change will require new multilateral approaches. The current international framework recognizes a central principle of "common but differentiated responsibilities" between developed and developing countries. Rich countries manifestly have to do more to "decarbonize" their economies. At the same time the deepening environmental footprint of developing countries cannot be ignored. That is why any successor to the Kyoto Protocol will need to cover not just the entire developed world, but also major developing countries such as Brazil, China and India. Financing, technology transfer and equitable burden-sharing hold the key to bringing all countries within a multilateral framework capable of achieving effective mitigation.

Climate change and water security

Global warming may already be with us, but the much greater warming forecast for the 21st century will produce vast changes in evaporation and precipitation, allied to a more unpredictable hydrological cycle. Higher air temperatures

The much greater warming forecast for the 21st century will produce vast changes in evaporation and precipitation, allied to a more unpredictable hydrological cycle

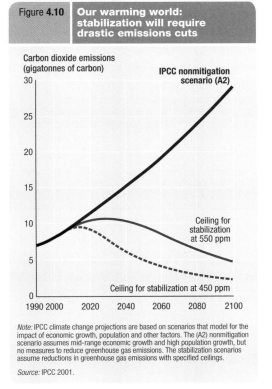

Figure **4.10** **Our warming world: stabilization will require drastic emissions cuts**

Carbon dioxide emissions
(gigatonnes of carbon)

IPCC nonmitigation scenario (A2)

Ceiling for stabilization at 550 ppm

Ceiling for stabilization at 450 ppm

Note: IPCC climate change projections are based on scenarios that model for the impact of economic growth, population and other factors. The (A2) nonmitigation scenario assumes mid-range economic growth and high population growth, but no measures to reduce greenhouse gas emissions. The stabilization scenarios assume reductions in greenhouse gas emissions with specified ceilings.

Source: IPCC 2001.

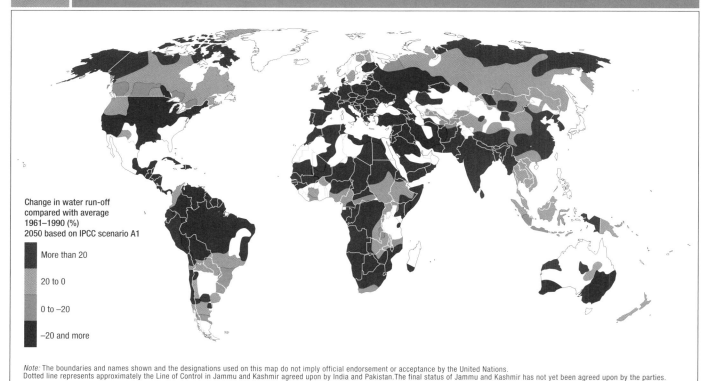

Change in water run-off
compared with average
1961–1990 (%)
2050 based on IPCC scenario A1

- More than 20
- 20 to 0
- 0 to −20
- −20 and more

Note: The boundaries and names shown and the designations used on this map do not imply official endorsement or acceptance by the United Nations.
Dotted line represents approximately the Line of Control in Jammu and Kashmir agreed upon by India and Pakistan. The final status of Jammu and Kashmir has not yet been agreed upon by the parties.

Source: Arnell 2004.

will increase evaporation from the world's oceans, intensifying the water cycle. They will also mean faster evaporation of water from land, so that less rainfall reaches rivers. These changes will be accompanied by new rainfall patterns and more extreme weather events, including floods and droughts.

What will these changes mean for water security and human development in the world's poorest countries? In any one country there may be numerous shifts in hydrological cycles linked to micro-climates. Some hydrologists also point to the potential for "tipping events" as climate change gives rise to new, less predictable cycles of change.[87] Accelerated melting of the Arctic ice sheet, for example, could set off a range of unpredictable hydrological events. What is predictable is a widespread increase in water stress for a large group of countries.

One plausible set of outcomes based on IPCC scenarios is captured in water availability projections for 2050 (map 4.2). These projections point to a decline of 30% or more in water run-off from rainfall for large swathes of the developing world, including:

- Drought-prone countries in southern Africa, including Angola, Malawi, Zambia and Zimbabwe. This region faces some of the gravest food security challenges in the world, with high levels of poverty, malnutrition and a protracted crisis in rainfed agriculture.

- A long strip from Senegal and Mauritania across much of North Africa and the Middle East. These countries include some of the world's most water-stressed nations, with high population growth and low per capita availability already at the heart of major water security challenges.

- Much of Brazil, including the semi-arid regions of the North-East, as well as parts of Venezuela, and Colombia.

In some important respects projections of run-off such as those in map 4.2 understate the problem. Water availability will also be influenced by changes in temperature and the timing of flows. Parts of Sub-Saharan Africa—including the Sahel region and East Africa—will experience more water run-off but diminished availability as a result of increased evaporation. Similarly, much of South Asia faces the prospect of an increase in average annual water flows, but with fewer rainy days. The reason: monsoons will become more intense as rising temperatures increase the volume of water pumped from the oceans through the hydrological cycle.

Extrapolating from water availability to livelihoods is difficult, but three broad conclusions can be drawn. The first is that rainfed agricultural production, the source of livelihood for most of the world's poorest people, faces grave risks in many regions. For Sub-Saharan Africa the threats are particularly acute, both because of the region's overwhelming dependence on rainfed agriculture and because of the vulnerability that comes with high levels of poverty. But the threat to rural livelihoods goes beyond Sub-Saharan Africa. For example, simulations of the impact of climate change on agricultural production in Brazil point to a decline in yields of 12%–55% for dry areas in the states of Ceará and Riaui, which have extremely high concentrations of poverty and malnutrition in rural areas.[88]

The second broad conclusion is that vulnerability and water insecurity will increase. Productivity in agricultural production, especially rainfed production, is influenced as much by the timing of water flows as the volume. And one of the clear results from a range of simulation exercises is that water flows will become more variable and uncertain. There will also be an increased incidence of extreme events in the form of droughts and floods, exacerbating the risks facing people in countries with a limited infrastructure to support adaptation.

The third conclusion to emerge from the IPCC is that, in broad terms, grain productivity will increase in developed countries while declining in many developing countries. Here too the impact of increased dependence on food imports has potentially adverse implications for food security in many countries.

Sub-Saharan Africa—a whole region at risk

Sub-Saharan Africa demonstrates both the complexity and the scale of the water security threat created by global climate change.[89]

Any evaluation of the threat posed by climate change for Sub-Saharan Africa has to start with the high level of pre-existing poverty and vulnerability. Almost half the region's population—some 300 million people—live on less than $1 a day. The majority live in rural areas, where income and employment depend almost entirely on rainfed agriculture. Sub-Saharan Africa already has a highly variable and unpredictable climate and is acutely vulnerable to floods and droughts. A third of the people in the region live in drought-prone areas, and floods are a recurrent threat in several countries. With climate change large parts of the region will become drier, increasing the number of people at risk of hunger and poverty by the tens of millions.

Climate change is already affecting the region. Reduced rainfall across the Sahel, an increase in the incidence of drought and greater volatility are among the current symptoms. But the future points to far more extreme changes: warming between 0.2°C and 0.5°C per decade, with 10% less rainfall in interior regions under intermediate global warming scenarios, and water losses increased by rising temperatures. The warming will be greatest over the semi-arid margins of the Sahara, along the Sahel and interior areas of southern Africa. Climate-induced changes to crop yields and ecosystem boundaries will dramatically affect some of the poorest people in Sub-Saharan Africa (as well as Latin America and South Asia) partly because many of them live in areas most prone to extreme climate events and partly because they have little capacity to adapt by turning to irrigated agriculture, improved seeds or alternative livelihoods.

Simulating the impact of climate change on crop yields and output is a hazardous affair. It should be emphasized at the outset that this is not an exact science. However, recent modelling has provided important insights that should serve as an early warning system. One illustration, shown on map 4.3, is based on one of the IPCC's climate change scenarios and existing

Rainfed agricultural production, the source of livelihood for most of the world's poorest people, faces grave risks in many regions

Water scarcity, risk and vulnerability

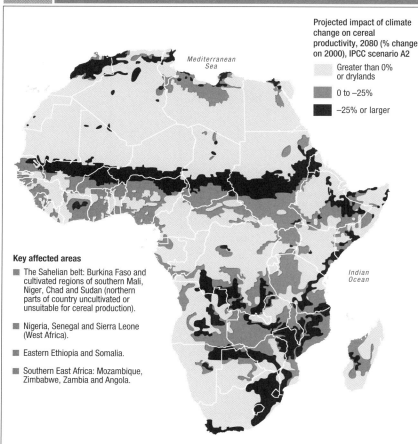

Map 4.3   Climate change threatens to reduce cereal productivity across much of Sub-Saharan Africa

Projected impact of climate change on cereal productivity, 2080 (% change on 2000), IPCC scenario A2

Greater than 0% or drylands

0 to −25%

−25% or larger

Mediterranean Sea

Indian Ocean

Key affected areas

■ The Sahelian belt: Burkina Faso and cultivated regions of southern Mali, Niger, Chad and Sudan (northern parts of country uncultivated or unsuitable for cereal production).

■ Nigeria, Senegal and Sierra Leone (West Africa).

■ Eastern Ethiopia and Somalia.

■ Southern East Africa: Mozambique, Zimbabwe, Zambia and Angola.

Note: The boundaries and names shown and the designations used on this map do not imply official endorsement or acceptance by the United Nations.

Source: Fischer and others 2005.

evidence on the relationship between water availability and productivity for the cereals sector.[90] It highlights areas of acute threat. These areas include a wide band across the Sahel region, stretching from Mauritania across Niger, Burkina Faso, Chad and Sudan. Large swathes of Southern Africa face the prospect of steep declines in yields, along with chronically food insecure countries such as Ethiopia and Somalia. Taken in conjunction with an increasing likelihood of drought, falling yields will translate into increased poverty, lower income and less secure livelihoods, and an increased threat of chronic hunger episodes.

Disconcerting as it is, even this bleak scenario may err on the side of optimism. More than 600,000 square kilometres of agricultural land now classified as moderately degraded could become severely degraded as a result of climate change, much of it in the Sahel. That outcome would intensify the pressure on cultivable land, giving rise to growing environmental strains and potential conflicts over land use. Some staple crops could be far more adversely affected than captured in the scenario outlined above. Cross-country research suggests that the productivity of maize, a staple across much of the region, is highly sensitive to variability in water availability during its flowering. Subregional scenarios for the medium-term capture some of the emerging threats:

● *East Africa.* Projections to 2030 indicate that the region will get more rain but become drier as temperatures rise. For Tanzania the predicted increase in temperature is between 2.5°C and 4.0°C. Parts of the country are projected to receive more rainfall, while the rest of the country—including the drought-prone southern areas—will receive less. Maize productivity is projected to fall on some simulations by 33%.[91] Rainfall in Kenya is projected to increase on average but to decline in semi-arid areas. Crop productivity in both countries will suffer. Yields of basic food crops, coffee and tea could fall by a third because of climatic shifts according to some IPCC scenario projections.[92]

● *Southern Africa.* Average regional temperature is projected to register a 1.5°C–3.0°C increase for intermediate global warming scenarios, with a 10%–15% decline in average annual rainfall, much of it in the growing season. The Zambezi River faces a projected drop in run-off of about a third by 2050, rising to 40% or more in the Zambezi basin. The chronic food emergencies that have afflicted Malawi, Mozambique, Zambia and Zimbabwe are set to become more frequent. Yields for maize will fall sharply, with a 1°C–2°C rise in temperature and less water.[93]

● *The Sahel.* In the past quarter century the Sahel has experienced the most substantial and sustained decline in rainfall recorded anywhere, punctuated by recurrent droughts in Burkina Faso, Mali and Niger.

In West Africa river discharge has fallen by more than 40% since the 1970s. Looking to the future, the Niger River, which provides water for 10 poor and arid countries, could lose a third of its flow. Simulations based on work in Sudan point to reduced production potential of 20%–76% for sorghum and 18%–82% for millet.[94]

Glacial melt

In many parts of the world glaciers act as water banks. They store ice and snow in the winter and release it slowly as temperatures rise, sending flows of water down to agricultural producers in lowland areas. Today, these banks are melting at an accelerating rate. And as glaciers retreat, water stocks are being depleted on a large scale.

Across much of Central Asia, Latin America and South Asia rural livelihoods depend on glaciers. The glaciers of the Himalayas and Tibet alone feed seven of the world's greatest rivers—Brahmaputra, the Ganges, Indus, Irrawady, Mekong, Salween and Yangtze—that provide water supplies for more than 2 billion people. With global warming glaciers are melting more rapidly, increasing the risk of flooding in spring, followed by water shortages in summer. Over the next 50 years glacial melt could emerge as one of the gravest threats to human progress and food security (box 4.9).

Extreme climate events

The location and timing of extreme climate events and humanitarian emergencies remain unpredictable. But their increase can now be anticipated with a degree of certainty. For many millions of people water flows will be marked by mounting uncertainty and unpredictability.

Beyond the complex variations affecting individual weather systems, some basic shifts are taking place in the forces that govern the hydrological cycle. Global warming is raising the temperature of continents while glacial melt is decreasing the temperature of the sea. The variation between the two influences the Asian monsoons. Warmer climate means that the air can hold more water vapour, so summer monsoon winds will carry more moisture. Most climate models suggest that the monsoon

rainfall patterns will change by 25%–100%. Fluctuations of just 10% are known to cause severe flooding or drought.[95] Heavier rains can have devastating consequences, as the flooding in Mumbai in 2005 demonstrated: 500 people perished.

Simple winner and loser models do not capture the real scale of the threat that climate change poses through hydrological systems. This is partly because modelling for aggregate changes can obscure large variations within countries. Some countries in Sub-Saharan Africa, such as those in the Sahel, may get more water through rain but lose even more through evaporation as temperatures rise. Reduced moisture retention in the soil can be expected to lower productivity and raise the risk of crop failure, even if average annual rainfall rises.

Projections for India highlight the complexity of climate change patterns (map 4.4). Most modelling exercises point to an increase in rainfall for the country as a whole. However, an increased proportion of rain will fall during intensive monsoon episodes in parts of the country that are already well endowed with rainfall. Meanwhile, two-thirds of the country—including semi-arid areas in Andhra Pradesh, Gujarat, Madhya Pradesh, Maharashtra and Rajasthan—will have fewer rainy days. This will translate into a net loss for water security, placing a premium on water harvesting and storage. One factor that will shape the profile of winners and losers is adaptive capacity. Irrigation systems will offer some protection, and large-scale commercial farmers are well placed to invest in technologies that raise water productivity. Risk will be skewed towards producers who depend on rainfall and lack the assets to adapt through investment.

Wider rainfall patterns will also be profoundly affected by shifting weather systems. The periodic El Niño Southern Oscillation is marked by a switching in the intensity and direction of currents and winds in the Pacific. It has been linked to droughts in East Africa, northern India, northeast Brazil and Australia and to catastrophic flooding and hurricanes from Mozambique to New Orleans. There is considerable debate about whether and how

Over the next 50 years glacial melt could emerge as one of the gravest threats to human progress and food security

4

Water scarcity, risk and vulnerability

Glaciers are water banks. They save water in the form of ice and snow during winter months, releasing it slowly into rivers and lakes as temperatures rise. Global warming has registered its main impact on glaciers. In the 1990s glacial mass fell at three times the rate of the previous decade, pointing to a global acceleration in melting. But the most profound consequences will be experienced in the decades ahead.

Pakistan. Himalayan glaciers provide about 180 billion cubic metres of water each year for Pakistan, flowing into the Indus and other river systems. Glacial water flows sustained agriculture in some of the first human settlements that flourished on the banks of the Indus in Harappa and Mohenjo-Daro. Today, they maintain the Indus irrigation system, the largest contiguous irrigation system in the world. Even with corrective action at a global level, glacial retreat will continue for at least half a century. River flows will increase, raising the likelihood of flash floods and exacerbating already acute irrigation drainage problems. In the second half of the 21st century there is likely to be a dramatic decrease in river flows, conceivably by more than 30% (see figure). This major permanent reduction in run-off will have enormous consequences for livelihoods in the Indus Basin and for Pakistan's food supplies.

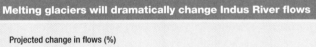

Melting glaciers will dramatically change Indus River flows

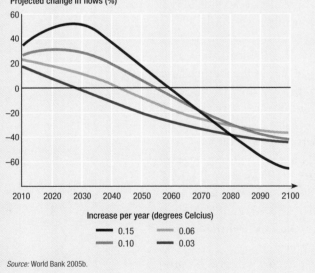

Projected change in flows (%)

Increase per year (degrees Celcius)
- 0.15
- 0.10
- 0.06
- 0.03

Source: World Bank 2005b.

Nepal. Glaciers are shrinking 30–69 metres per decade in Nepal, with more than 20 glacial lakes now identified as at risk of bursting their banks and causing flooding. Managing this threat will require huge new public investments.

China. Almost all glaciers in China have already shown substantial melting. Glacial retreat in Tibet has been described as an ecological catastrophe, and most glaciers could disappear by 2100. As the catastrophe unfolds, China is under threat. It was once argued that retreating glaciers would help overcome water stress by releasing new flows into the arid north and west. Most models now suggest that this is an illusory benefit. While glacial melt in Tibet is releasing more water, higher temperatures will lead to the evaporation of most of the additional volume. The 300 million farmers in China's arid western region are likely to see a decline in the volume of water flowing from glaciers.

The Andes. During dry seasons Andean glaciers are the main source of drinking and irrigation water for urban dwellers and farmers. These glaciers are registering some of the fastest reductions in mass in the world. Some small and medium-size glaciers are predicted to disappear by 2010. In Peru glacial coverage has fallen by a quarter in the past 30 years. In the short run water managers face the prospect of fast diminishing flows into reservoirs and irrigation systems, with costs rising for urban consumers to finance new reservoirs. Longer term effects will include a reduced flow of water for agriculture during the dry season.

Central Asia. Most of Central Asia—Kazakhstan, Kyrgyzstan, Tajikistan, Turkmenistan and Uzbekistan—is in arid and semi-arid zones, where natural evaporation significantly exceeds precipitation. Almost all fresh water originates from permanent snowfields and glaciers in the mountains of Kyrgyzstan and Tajikistan. Water from melting glaciers flows into the Amu Darya and Syr Darya Rivers and their irrigated flood plains, sustaining 22 million livelihoods in Tajikistan, Turkmenistan and Uzbekistan. Irrigated agriculture accounts for 25% of GNI in Uzbekistan and 39% in Turkmenistan. For upstream Kyrgyzstan and Tajikistan water from the same source is used to generate hydroelectric power. Glacial retreat poses a fundamental threat to livelihoods and economies across the region. The pace of that retreat is accelerating. In 1949 glaciers covered nearly 18,000 square kilometres of Tajikistan's mountainous hinterland. Satellite images from 2000 indicate that this area has shrunk to just 12,000 square kilometres—a 33% decrease in 50 years. If current trends continue, Tajikistan's glaciers will disappear within a century.

Source: Maslin 2004; UNDP 2005a; World Bank 2005c; WWF Nepal Programme 2005; World Water Assessment Programme 2006; Schneider and Lane 2006.

El Niño is linked to global warming, one of the largest—and most threatening—unknowns in climate change scenarios.

What is known is that the incidence of extreme weather events is increasing, along with the number of people affected by them. During the 1990s an average of 200 million people a year from developing countries were affected by climate-related disasters and about a million or so from developed countries. Injury, death and loss

4

Water scarcity, risk and vulnerability

of assets, income and employment from these events undermine the efforts of communities and governments to improve human development. Inevitably, the adverse impacts are greatest for people with the most limited resources. Since 2000 the growth rate in the number of people affected by climate-related disasters has doubled. Attribution may be uncertain—but there is at the very least a strong probability that global warming is implicated.[96]

Rising sea levels

Rising sea levels will be among the most powerful determinants of water security for a large share of the world's population in the 21st century. Increased salinization could dramatically reduce freshwater availability for many countries, while coastal flooding threatens millions of livelihoods.

There is a substantial group of countries that stand to be affected. Bangladesh, Egypt, Nigeria and Thailand have large populations living in delta areas threatened by saline intrusion. The low-lying regions of Bangladesh support more than 110 million people in one of the most densely populated regions of the world, and more than half of Bangladesh lies at less than 5 metres above sea level. The World Bank has estimated that by the end of the 21st century sea levels for the country could rise by as much as 1.8 metres, with worst case scenarios predicting land losses of 16%. The area affected supports 13% of the population and produces 12% of GDP. Similarly, in Egypt rising sea levels would weaken the Nile Delta's protective sand belt, with serious consequences for essential groundwater, inland freshwater fisheries and swathes of intensively cultivated agricultural land.[97]

The sheer scale of the potential adjustment pressures is not sufficiently appreciated. Some rich country governments have started to plan investment programmes to counter the effects of climate change. The Netherlands is an example. The protection of low-lying coastal areas through enhanced sea defences and measures to improve storage capacity figure increasingly prominently in national planning for developed countries. Insurance companies are adjusting risk assessments and building reserves against

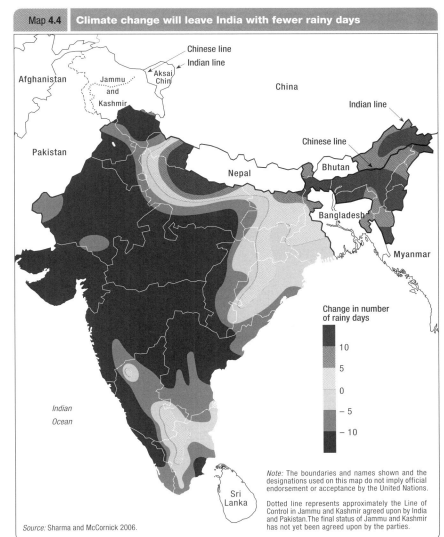

Map 4.4   Climate change will leave India with fewer rainy days

Change in number of rainy days

10
5
0
– 5
– 10

Note: The boundaries and names shown and the designations used on this map do not imply official endorsement or acceptance by the United Nations.

Dotted line represents approximately the Line of Control in Jammu and Kashmir agreed upon by India and Pakistan. The final status of Jammu and Kashmir has not yet been agreed upon by the parties.

Source: Sharma and McCornick 2006.

future claims. But poor countries face problems of a different order, both in the people affected and in the costs of controlling rising seas. People in these countries face greater risks while their governments' capacity to limit risk is constrained by financial capacity.

The international response— weak on adaptation

Mitigation and adaptation are the two strands to any strategy for tackling the threat posed by climate change. Mitigation is about minimizing future climate change by weakening the link between economic growth and carbon emissions. Adaptation is about facing up to the fact that climate change is inevitable and that many of the most threatened countries have the least capacity to adapt. The international response on both fronts has been inadequate—spectacularly so in the case of adaptation.

Recent years have seen a step change in the multilateral response to climate change mitigation. The Kyoto Protocol, which came into force in 2005 with support from 130 countries (but not Australia and the United States), represents the most comprehensive attempt to negotiate binding limits on emissions. It includes flexibility mechanisms, which allow for carbon trading between countries, and the Clean Development Mechanism (CDM), which allows developed countries to gain emissions credits by financing projects in developing countries that lower greenhouse gas emissions. Though restricted to individual projects, the number of CDM interventions has been growing.[98] Beyond Kyoto, important mitigation strategies are emerging at various levels. Linked to but independent of the Kyoto Protocol is trading among the 25 EU members through the Emissions Trading Scheme. Seven northeastern US states are also participating in a voluntary trading scheme—the Regional Greenhouse Gas Initiative, launched late in 2005. Meanwhile, 28 US states have developed action plans to reduce net greenhouse gas emissions. The state of California has introduced its own groundbreaking emissions reduction targets.

The current Kyoto Protocol suffers from a limited time horizon (which has restricted development of the carbon trading market), the absence of key developed countries and the non-inclusion of developing countries. In effect, its remit extends to a small and shrinking part of the carbon and other greenhouse gas emissions that are driving global warming. Extending that remit raises important questions for equity and burden-sharing. Industrial countries with about 12% of world population account for half of current global emissions. Their citizens also leave a far deeper carbon footprint. Average per capita emissions range from 10 tonnes of carbon dioxide equivalent in the European Union to 20 tonnes in the United States. The equivalent figures are 1.2 tonnes for India and 2.7 tonnes for China. High growth in countries such as China and India could, however, raise

the developing world's share of carbon emissions from about one half today to about two-thirds by 2050. Charting a growth path that raises living standards and reduces poverty in developing countries within a global strategy for containing global warming will require a radical shift in national policies to facilitate the spread of clean technologies, backed by international cooperation.

What is needed beyond 2012 is an ambitious set of well defined targets that provide a clear set of market signals and framework for action for national governments, industries and households. Keeping temperature increases to within 2°C above 1990 levels should be seen as a ceiling. For that to happen, global emissions in 2050 would have to be below the 1990 level (about 13% below the current level), with concentrations of greenhouse gases (measured in carbon dioxide equivalents) stabilizing at about 450 ppm. Achieving this goal will require fundamental reforms in global energy policies. Carbon taxes, the deepening of markets for tradable emission permits, incentives for the development of clean technologies, and—critically—strategies for technology transfer to developing countries are among the policy instruments for reform. Contrary to some claims the adjustment process would not jeopardize growth prospects in rich countries: the costs of reaching the 450 ppm target for developed countries represents about 0.02%–0.1% of GNI per year, compared with average annual growth rates of 2%–3% a year.[99] For developing countries the prospect for sustaining growth within a multilateral framework for limiting climate change will require financing for technology transfer on a scale far beyond that envisaged in the current arrangements under the Clean Development Mechanism.

Looking beyond mitigation, support for adaptation to climate change in developing countries is piecemeal and fragmented. The multilateral response has been woefully inadequate, highlighting wider failures in the way that global governance systems are responding to global problems. The same is true at a national level. Very few developing countries have prioritized adaptation in key planning documents such as Poverty Reduction Strategy Papers or even in integrated water resource management documents.

Provisions for financing adaptation tell their own story. Various financing mechanisms for adaptation have been put in place, but the flows involved are limited. The Kyoto Protocol includes a provision establishing an Adaptation Fund. Financing for this facility comes from a small levy (with a ceiling of 2%) on purchases of credits under the Clean Development Mechanism. On current projections by the Organisation for Economic Co-operation and Development this will generate about $20 million by 2012. The main multilateral mechanism for financing adaptation is the Global Environment Facility (GEF). But here, too, the financing parameters are modest: about $50 million has been allocated to support adaptation activities that create global environmental benefits. Under a separate Special Climate Change Fund, managed by GEF, donors contributed another $45 million. In 2001 a special Least Developed Countries Fund was created under GEF auspices for national adaptation programmes, with support from 12 donors. As of August 2006, $100 million had been contributed to this fund, but only $9 million had been spent on projects in 43 countries—a very limited response.[100]

Has bilateral aid covered for the failings of the multilateral system? Not if the benchmark is support for adaptation in agriculture, the sector that faces the gravest threats. The twin challenge in the sector is to put in place the infrastructure to mitigate risk and the poverty reduction strategies to enhance adaptive capacity at the household level. Development assistance plays a critical role, especially in Sub-Saharan Africa. However, aid flows to agriculture have fallen from an annual average of about $4.9 billion in the early 1990s to $3.2 billion today, and from 12% to 3.5% of total aid. All regions have been affected: aid to agriculture in Sub-Saharan Africa has shrunk from $1.7 billion on average during 1990–92 to just under $1 billion in real terms in 2004. The Group of Eight (G-8) countries have cut their aid to agriculture in the region by $590 million— more than half—over the same period (figure 4.11).[101] This is precisely the opposite of what needs to happen in the interests of long-run human development.

Of course, it has to be acknowledged that future climate change impacts are uncertain. But uncertainty cuts both ways: the outcome could be far more severe than indicated in current projections. Successful adaptation strategies will have to be developed in the context of wider strategies for sustainable development, including measures to reduce vulnerability to shocks and stresses. This implies that adaptation is highly context specific and that national planning based on local participation holds the key to success. But international support is a precondition for successful adaptation.

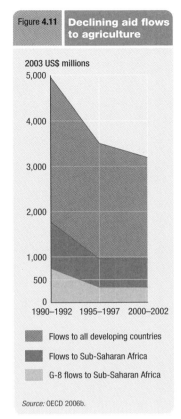

Figure 4.11 **Declining aid flows to agriculture**

2003 US$ millions

1990–1992 1995–1997 2000–2002

Flows to all developing countries

Flows to Sub-Saharan Africa

G-8 flows to Sub-Saharan Africa

Source: OECD 2006b.

The way ahead

The world is not running out of water. But many countries are running out of time to tackle the critical problems presented by water stress.

At a national level the starting point is that water has to be treated as a scarce resource, with a far stronger focus on managing demand *within* the frontiers of ecological sustainability.

Integrated water resources management provides a broad framework for governments to align water use patterns with the needs and demands of different users, including the environment (see box 4.7). Public policies that shift market signals and price incentives to assign more weight to conservation, increasing

Environmental accounting systems that value water as a natural resource asset and count its depletion as a loss would help to change the way that policy-makers view water

the crop per drop and reducing pollution, are also vital.

Environmental accounting systems that value water as a natural resource asset and count its depletion as a loss would help to change the way that policy-makers view water. The Millennium Ecosystem Assessment identified the failure of markets and national income accounts to value ecosystems as a contributory factor in environmental degradation. Nowhere is this more evident than with water, where the depletion of assets registers as an input to increased wealth. Environmental accounting that attaches real economic values to water-based ecosystems would contribute to the policy debate on water pricing, allocation and environmental needs.[102]

Integrated water resources management provides an important vehicle for wider reforms, while the policy framework will vary inevitably across countries. Core requirements include:

- Developing national water strategies that monitor water availability, assess the sustainable limits to human use and regulate withdrawals within these limits.
- Adopting pricing strategies that reflect the real scarcity value of water while maintaining equity among users.
- Cutting perverse subsidies for water overuse, ensuring that polluters pay and creating incentives for preventing pollution.
- Carrying out national audits of groundwater recharge and extraction rates and introducing pricing and regulatory systems to prevent overuse.
- Valuing ecological services provided by wetlands and other water-based systems.

Climate change presents challenges of a different order. Mitigation is an imperative. If the international community fails in this area, the prospects for human development in the 21st century will suffer a grave setback. Bold targets,

including a 450 ppm stabilization target for carbon dioxide equivalent emissions, should be backed by clear long-term strategies for carbon trading, incentives for clean technology and financing for technology transfer.

Beyond mitigation, the development of adaptation strategies should be seen as a first-order priority. That is true for both bilateral aid and multilateral initiatives. Once again, the starting point is national planning. Constrained by limited capacity and sometimes by weak governance, few developing countries have initiated country strategies for adaptation.

International aid has a central role to play in changing this picture, especially in agriculture. In practice, it is difficult to separate the effects of climate change from wider problems facing poor agricultural producers in developing countries. However, additional resources are needed to address the problems of water stress that will accompany climate change. Expanding the aid envelope for agriculture from the current level of about $3 billion a year to $10 billion by 2010 should be seen as a minimum requirement.

Sub-Saharan Africa is a priority. As in other regions aid flows need to reflect national planning estimates for financing agriculture. The Comprehensive Africa Agriculture Development Programme (CAADP) developed by the African Union and the New Partnership for Africa's Development provides a framework. CAADP is a medium-term financing strategy that aims at creating the infrastructure needed to raise productivity and reduce hunger, with an emphasis on the development of sustainable water systems. Financing provisions will require an increase in aid to primary agriculture from about $0.9 billion today to $2.1 billion by 2010. These figures are within the range of increase agreed by the G-8 countries at Gleneagles—and it is important to the well-being of millions of poor farmers that the pledge be honoured.

5 Water competition
in agriculture

"Among the many things
I learnt as a president,
was the centrality of water
in the social, political and
economic affairs of the
country, the continent
and the world"

Nelson Mandela, World Summit on Sustainable
Development, 2002

CHAPTER 5

Water competition in agriculture

An issue with important implications for human development and global poverty reduction is how to manage water resources to meet rising food needs while protecting the access of poor and vulnerable people to the water that sustains their livelihoods

One hundred years ago William Mulholland, the superintendent of the Los Angeles Water Department (LAWD), introduced California to a new concept in state politics: the water grab. Faced with meeting the water demands for a small, fast growing desert town, Mulholland quietly bought up water rights in the Owens Valley, more than 200 miles to the north, built an aqueduct across the blistering Mojave Desert and delivered the water to downtown Los Angeles. Violent protests followed. Owens Valley ranchers attempted to dynamite the aqueduct, and the LAWD responded with a massive show of armed force. The water transfer paved the way for the growth of Los Angeles. Urban users got unlimited supplies of water, and large commercial farmers got irrigation water that made the deserts bloom with cotton and other water-intensive crops. Farmers in the Owens Valley lost out.

Times change—but some things stay the same. These days southern Californians resolve their disputes over water through litigation, rather than dynamite and guns. But the Mulholland episode demonstrates two enduring features of water governance. First, water is power—and when water is in short supply, power relations figure prominently in determining who gets access to water and on what terms. Second, when water shortages intensify, people lacking a voice in allocation decisions tend to be the first in line for adjustments to reduced supplies.

Over the next few decades many developing countries face the prospect of intensified competition for water. Population growth, rising incomes, changing dietary patterns, urbanization and industrial development will increase demand for what is essentially a fixed supply of water. Where river basin systems are already overexploited, this will lead to acute adjustment pressures, even with efficiency gains. Agriculture—the major user of water and the source of food for growing populations—will be a focal point for these pressures. Power and voice will strongly influence how the adjustment process affects the poor.

As concern over scarcity has mounted, the global debate on water resource management has focussed on food security. The question commonly posed is whether the world has enough water to meet the food needs of a growing population. Less attention has been directed towards another issue with equally important implications for human development and global poverty reduction: how to manage water resources to meet rising food needs while protecting the access of poor and vulnerable people to the water that sustains their livelihoods.

This issue has a direct bearing not just on prospects for achieving a wide range of Millennium Development Goals by 2015 but also on the well-being of future generations. The world may be urbanizing, but most poor and malnourished people still live in rural areas and depend on agricultural production for employment, income and food. Water security is vital to their

Land and water are two key assets on which poor people depend for their livelihoods, usually far more than do people who are better off

livelihoods—and to their prospects for escaping poverty. The danger is that fast growing cities and industries seeking more water will extend their hydrological reach into rural areas, reducing the access of poor households to a crucial livelihood resource.

Adjustment to competition is already taking place. In many countries the dominant governance model is a path of least resistance approach, with powerful constituencies in industry, commercial agriculture and municipalities transferring water by stealth from those—including the rural poor—with the weakest political voice. Unequal outcomes in the adjustment to greater competition mirror wider inequalities based on land, wealth, gen-

der and political influence. Governance systems can redress these inequalities but all too often they exacerbate them, just as they did in Owens Valley.

This chapter looks briefly at the links between water and rural livelihoods and at the emerging scenarios for water use that can influence these links. It then focuses on three themes that will have a critical bearing on whether the governance of competition for water supports or undermines efforts to reduce poverty and inequality:

- Competition, rights and the scramble for water.
- Better governance for irrigation systems.
- Greater water productivity for the poor.

Water and human development—the livelihood links

Poor people in agriculture experience the link between water and human development as a living reality. An Indian finance minister once famously declared that his country's budget was a "gamble on the rains".[1] For millions of small farmers, pastoralists and agricultural labourers the stakes in the gamble are far higher. Variations in rainfall, or disruptions in water supply, can make the difference between adequate nutrition and hunger, health and sickness and—ultimately—life and death.

Water security in agriculture pervades all aspects of human development. Land and water are two key assets on which poor people depend for their livelihoods, usually far more than do people who are better off. Water cannot be considered in isolation from wider capabilities such as health and education, or from access to other productive assets, including land, capital and infrastructure. But water insecurity represents a powerful risk factor for poverty and vulnerability.

Livelihoods comprise the capabilities and assets that people need to make a living and maintain their well-being. In rural areas water

plays a crucial role for some obvious reasons. Like land, it is part of the natural capital base that underpins the production systems that sustain livelihoods. Access to a reliable supply of water makes it possible for people to diversify their livelihoods, increase productivity and reduce the risks associated with drought. It enables producers to enter higher value-added areas of production and creates income and employment, and it gives people the security to undertake investments (figure 5.1). The links between rural livelihoods, water and global poverty reduction efforts are immediately apparent. Some three-quarters of all people surviving on less than $1 a day live in rural areas, where their livelihoods are dependent on agriculture. Smallholder farmers and agricultural labourers also account for about two-thirds of the world's 830 million malnourished people. The water security-livelihood nexus helps to explain the widely observed relationship between water and poverty. In Ethiopia distance from a water point is one of the most accurate indicators for vulnerability and poverty.[2]

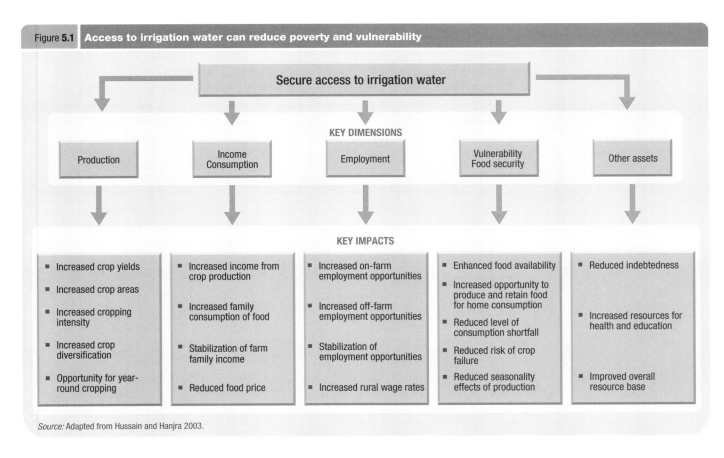

Figure **5.1** | Access to irrigation water can reduce poverty and vulnerability

Secure access to irrigation water

KEY DIMENSIONS

| Production | Income Consumption | Employment | Vulnerability Food security | Other assets |

KEY IMPACTS

- Increased crop yields
- Increased crop areas
- Increased cropping intensity
- Increased crop diversification
- Opportunity for year-round cropping

- Increased income from crop production
- Increased family consumption of food
- Stabilization of farm family income
- Reduced food price

- Increased on-farm employment opportunities
- Increased off-farm employment opportunities
- Stabilization of employment opportunities
- Increased rural wage rates

- Enhanced food availability
- Increased opportunity to produce and retain food for home consumption
- Reduced level of consumption shortfall
- Reduced risk of crop failure
- Reduced seasonality effects of production

- Reduced indebtedness
- Increased resources for health and education
- Improved overall resource base

Source: Adapted from Hussain and Hanjra 2003.

The predictability of water supply and the sustainability of water-based ecosystems are crucial dimensions of water security. Predictability helps to explain why access to irrigation is associated with a lower prevalence and reduced severity of poverty. Cross-country research shows that poverty levels are often 20%–30% lower within irrigated systems than in nonirrigated areas.[3] Irrigation provides a range of water security benefits that reduce poverty, from greater food output, higher real incomes and increased employment to lower food prices. However, the strength of the link between irrigation and poverty is conditioned by a wide range of institutional factors, including efficiency and equity in land distribution.

Agriculture under pressure—the emerging scenarios

Future water management in agriculture faces pressure from two directions. On the demand side industrialization, urbanization and changing diets will increase demand for food and the water used in its production. On the supply side the scope for expanding access to irrigation water is limited. It is this imbalance between supply and demand that is driving adjustment pressures.

The future for water management in agriculture will look very different from the past. Consider the recent history of irrigation. Over the past four decades the global area of irrigated land has doubled. Coupled with the increases in productivity that underpinned the green revolution, the expansion of the irrigation frontier enabled agriculture to feed a growing population. In South Asia annual per capita cereal availability increased from 162 kilograms in the mid-1960s to 182 kilograms in the mid-1990s.[4] Production of predominantly irrigated crops—such as rice and wheat—rose by a factor of two to four, with more than two-thirds of the gain coming from yield increases. These massive productivity gains were a key element in improving food security and reducing world hunger. Without the expansion in irrigated area, rural poverty and global food security would look very different today.

Looking to the future, prospects for extending irrigation are limited, while pressures from industry and domestic water users are rising

Contrasts with Sub-Saharan Africa, where productivity gains have barely kept pace with population growth, are instructive.

Looking to the future, prospects for extending irrigation are limited, while pressures from industry and domestic water users are rising. New sources of water for irrigation are increasingly expensive and ecologically damaging to exploit, setting limits on the potential for the type of expansion that marked the decades after 1960. The real cost of new irrigation in countries such as India, Indonesia and Pakistan has more than doubled since 1980.[5] Meanwhile, during the next four decades agriculture in many developing countries will be competing for water in basins where overuse is already resulting in closure or near closure, with water use exceeding minimum recharge levels. Large areas of China, South Asia and the Middle East are now maintaining irrigation through unsustainable mining of groundwater or overextraction from rivers. The groundwater overdraft rate is more than 25% in China and 56% in parts of India.[6] Correcting the overdraft would require cutting groundwater use from 817 billion cubic metres to 753 billion cubic metres, sharply curtailing the water for irrigation in many areas.[7] The groundwater problem now presents a risk to food production in large swathes of the developing world, with attendant risks for rural livelihoods.

Recent water-use scenario exercises developed by the International Food Policy Research Institute, the International Water Management Institute and the Food and Agriculture Organization tell slightly different stories—but with common themes. Among the core features of the scenario for the next four decades:[8]

- *Continued population growth and rapid urbanization.* Population will increase by some 80 million people a year over the next three decades, reaching 9 billion by 2050—with almost the entire increase taking place in developing countries. Population growth will go hand in hand with rapid urbanization. In 1960 two-thirds of the world's population lived in rural areas. That share has fallen to half, and by 2050 two-thirds of the world's population will live in cities. Maintaining food supplies will require large

productivity gains to ensure that fewer rural producers can meet the demands of a rising urban population.

- *Growing demand for water.* Projected water withdrawals in developing countries will be 27% higher in 2025 than in 1995. Nonirrigation water use will double, while consumption of irrigation water will increase by only 4%. As shown in chapter 4, projected use of water for irrigation will grow far more slowly than for industry, urban centres and livestock.

- *More water-intensive demand but slower expansion in irrigation.* Rising food demand in developing countries will require crop production increases of 1.4% a year on average, increasing to 2.5% for Sub-Saharan Africa. Food demand will become more water-intensive with rising incomes. Meanwhile, the rate of increase in irrigation will slow dramatically. By 2030 irrigation water withdrawals will increase by only 14%. In some regions the water constraint will be far tighter. In Asia water use for irrigation will rise by 1%, compared with 14% for other uses.

- *The imperative to raise productivity.* How will the world meet its growing demand for food? For cereals the Food and Agriculture Organization projects that irrigated yields in developing countries will need to rise by about one-third (to levels higher than in the developed world today), with production increasing by two-thirds. Rainfed agriculture will have to account for 47% of the overall increase in cereals production, highlighting the critical importance of boosting the productivity of "green water" (water absorbed by the soil and transpired by plants) through enhanced moisture retention and improved tillage practices. Rainfed production is substantial and offers considerable potential. It accounts for about two-thirds of cereals production, yet per hectare yields average only about half the 3.2 metric tons produced in irrigated areas.

These are broad global projections. They do not take into account the distributional factors that shape real food security as distinct from food availability. Nor do they capture large variations between and within regions. But they do point to intensified pressure on already overstretched water resources. India, to take just one case, will have 270 million more people living in urban areas in 2025 than in 1995. Many of these people will be employed in water-intensive—and labour-intensive—industries operating in water-stressed parts of the country.

Sub-Saharan Africa faces distinctive challenges. As the developing region most heavily dependent on rainfed agriculture (figure 5.2), green water management will remain the central priority. The region accounts for less than 5% of global irrigation (figure 5.3), and just two countries (Madagascar and South Africa) account for two-thirds of current capacity. Mozambique and Tanzania have developed just 5%–10% of their potential.[9] Increasingly, governments in the region and aid donors see the development of irrigation as a route to higher productivity and greater food security. The Commission for Africa has recommended a doubling of the area under irrigation over the next decade, adding 7 million more hectares by 2010.[10] Progress in this direction could generate important gains for human development: research on rice productivity in Tanzania suggests that irrigation could raise yields by 5% a year. However, outcomes will depend on the distribution of benefits—a governance issue to which we return below.

Immovable objects and irresistible forces

Over the next four decades water governance will be operating in the space between an immovable object and an irresistible force. The immovable object is the ecological limit to water use. The irresistible force is being brought to bear by the mounting demands from industry for water and from urban populations for food. Statistics-based scenarios hide some of the important human development questions raised by the adjustments that will have to take place.

Developed water resources are almost fully used in many countries. With the financial, environmental and political costs associated with developing new water resources rising, competition for water between uses and users is set to increase progressively. In effect, a fixed cake will be divided into unequal slices with some

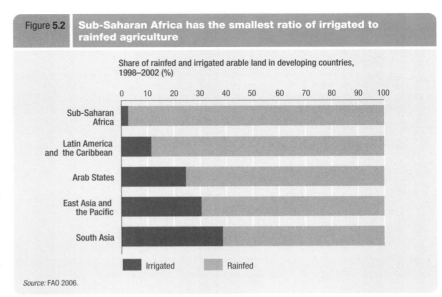

Figure 5.2 Sub-Saharan Africa has the smallest ratio of irrigated to rainfed agriculture

Share of rainfed and irrigated arable land in developing countries, 1998–2002 (%)

Source: FAO 2006.

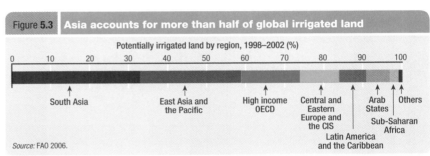

Figure 5.3 Asia accounts for more than half of global irrigated land

Potentially irrigated land by region, 1998–2002 (%)

Source: FAO 2006.

people losing out. Against this backdrop, intersectoral water transfer is likely to become one of the major human development issues of the 21st century. Much of the discussion has concentrated on economic efficiency and technology. Less attention has been directed towards equity and the consequences for vulnerable people living in rural areas, even though these are likely to be profound. As national competition for water intensifies, people with the weakest rights—small farmers and women among them—stand to see their access to water eroded by more powerful constituencies

The consequences of competition are not just theoretical outcomes of a plausible future scenario. They are already evident in the mounting conflict surrounding adjustments to water shortages in many countries. Consider these recent conflicts:[11]

- In India competition for water is escalating in many parts of the country. Chennai, in the state of Tamil Nadu, is a textbook model of a water-short city extending its

Water competition in agriculture

Secure rights to water can expand opportunities for poor people to escape poverty, while the absence of secure rights leaves people open to the risk that they will be unable to assert their claims in the face of competition

hydrological reach. It is completing a 230 kilometre pipeline to bring water from the Cauvery River basin—one of the most water-constrained basins in India and the source of a long-running dispute between Tamil Nadu and Karnataka. Competition between users is increasing in intensity. In the Pallakad district of Kerala the abstraction of groundwater by a multinational soft drink company has depleted the aquifer, dried up several wells and caused serious environmental damage.[12] In a repeat episode on the outskirts of Mumbai the same company has provoked protests by farmers against its water abstraction operations to serve the fast growing middle-class mineral water market in the city.[13] Gujarat and Rajasthan have also witnessed repeat bouts of violent conflict over water use.

- In China the government has embarked on a $2.7 billion programme to divert water from irrigated areas in Shanxi and Hebei provinces, encountering significant opposition. All along the Yellow River and across the water-stressed northern plains, authorities are mediating conflicts over water between farmers, municipalities and industry. In July 2000 violent protests followed the announcement of a plan to divert reservoir water from agriculture to industry in Shandong, the last province before the Yellow River reaches the sea.
- In Thailand agricultural producers in the Mae Teng irrigation system are protesting the transfer of water to Chiang Mai, where municipal authorities are struggling to cope with the rising demand of urban and industrial users.
- In Yemen farmers are protesting the transfer of water from agriculture to fast growing urban centres such as Ta'iz and Sana'a.
- In the Pakistan province of Sindh hundreds of "tail-end" irrigation farmers have protested against water shortages and the management of an irrigation system that favours upstream water-intensive crop production. Disputes over access to irrigation canals are increasingly common. In June 2006, 14 people were killed in the Karrum region during village disputes over irrigation channels following a decline in water availability.[14]

While international commentators reflect on the potential for water wars between countries, conflicts such as these within countries are already intensifying at a worrying rate. Violence is becoming increasingly common in many countries, and the potential for conflict will inevitably increase as competition intensifies. Adjustments to the scenarios set out earlier will create winners and losers. Who wins and who loses will be determined not through the simple calculus of supply and demand, but through institutionalized systems of rights and claims that determine entitlements to water. It is the governance of these systems that will ultimately determine human development outcomes (see chapter 6).

Competition, rights and the scramble for water

Entitlements matter in any process of competition, and entitlements are wrapped up with rights. Broadly defined, water rights represent socially accepted and enforceable claims to water. They define the terms allowing for the removal of water from its natural environment, the use of water in a natural source

and the management of water flows. As with land, secure rights to water can expand opportunities for poor people to escape poverty. Conversely, the absence of secure rights leaves people open to the risk that they will be unable to assert their claims in the face of competition.

The world's earliest legal statutes recognized the special character of water. Under Roman law in the third century, *aqua profluens* (flowing water) was a common good, neither public nor private, emphasizing equity and societywide ownership. Today, water rights vary widely across countries, often connecting a diverse array of water users. But there are three broad categories of rights common to most societies: *public water rights* held by the state, *common or customary rights* legitimized by norms and traditions and *private property rights* to use or transfer water (through, say, groundwater extraction or irrigation). These overlapping rights have an important bearing on how the claims and entitlements of rival users play out when competition increases.

As the pressure towards intersectoral resource transfer mounts and competition within agriculture grows, systems of rights and claims will become increasingly important. The transfer process for water can happen through administrative fiat, market exchange or other types of negotiation. Which stakeholders are involved in decisions, who receives compensation and who shapes the rules and norms for managing adjustment will inevitably be affected by the nature and extent of water rights and the relative power of different actors.[15]

The limits to private water markets

As competition for water has intensified, some people have argued for the development of markets based on tradable water rights to resolve competition problems. Establishing clear private water property rights, so the argument runs, will allow adjustments to increased competition to take place through the market, with the price mechanism ensuring that water flows to its most productive use. Does this represent a viable model for addressing the social and economic challenges posed by the scenarios outlined earlier?

Private water rights have a long history. In the western United States they were introduced more than a century ago, through legislation covering not just the authority to draw water but also to trade in its use.[16] Today, water trading enables cities like Los Angeles to purchase water from farmers in the Central Valley who hold the private right to irrigation water on their land. In the developing world Chile has the most highly developed system of private and tradable water rights. Introduced in the early 1980s, the system allows farmers to trade the right to draw water with other users (box 5.1).

Private water markets provide a mechanism for rebalancing supply and demand and enhancing efficiency, as measured through market pricing. However, markets do not automatically balance efficiency and equity goals—and market

| Box 5.1 | Chile—water markets and reform in a high growth economy |

Chile is often cited as a success story in incorporating water into wider strategies for sustainable resource management and accelerated economic growth. Market-based mechanisms occupy a central place in public policy. But efficiency and equity have sometimes pulled in different directions.

Tradable water rights were institutionalized under the 1981 National Water Law as part of a sweeping economic liberalization. Private markets developed, and water rights were traded as a commodity. Landowners could trade water for cash. And transfers through water markets helped sustain the rapid growth of water-intensive agricultural products, such as fruits, vegetables and wine, as well as of wood pulp and copper (mined and processed in the Atacama desert).

The reforms increased the scarcity value of water and created incentives for investment in efficiency gains. Sophisticated water management systems in the agro-export sector put Chile in the front rank of efficient water users. Between 1975 and 1992 irrigation efficiency increased by 22%–26%, the equivalent of freeing up an additional 264,000 hectares for crops and saving $400 million for developing new water supplies. Since 1980 water used in the wood pulp sector has fallen by 70%.

Beyond enterprise efficiency, however, the indicators point to a mixed balance sheet. Water scarcity prices did not reflect the costs of environmental damage related to overuse for a familiar reason: environmental externalities are not adequately priced in free markets. And government subsidies promoting forestry exports undermined the price signals from water markets, creating incentives for environmental damage.

While the 1981 law enhanced economic efficiency, it was far less successful when measured against the yardstick of equity. The allocation of water rights without limit or restriction predictably gave rise to speculation and water monopolies. And because water rights were linked to land rights in a system marked by highly unequal land distribution, the benefits were skewed against the poor. Research in the Limari Basin shows that water rights have become more concentrated in the hands of large commercial farmers and urban water traders. The poorest third of farmers have seen their share of water rights fall by more than 40% since 1981.

Reforms in 2005 aim at realigning private markets with public interest. Regulatory provisions to restrict speculative activity, dismantle monopolies and strengthen environmental protection are a central part of the new legislative framework for governing water markets.

Source: Rosegrant and Gazmuri S. 1994; Romano and Leporati 2002; Peña, Luraschi and Valenzuela 2004; GWP 2006c.

People's legal rights count for little if the institutions charged with protecting them are inaccessible or unresponsive

efficiency can be compromised by institutional failures to correct market imperfections.

Consider some of the equity issues that have arisen in US water markets. These markets have facilitated adjustments to scarcity and competition (box 5.2). The western United States, in particular, has highly developed rules and institutions governing markets and mediating claims. But equity is not always well served. One study of the distribution of gains and losses from water transfers in Mendota, California, found that the number of farms in water-exporting regions fell by 26% between 1987 and 1992. But the number of small farms fell by 70%, and labour demand fell even more as wholesale produce firms went out of business.[17] While aggregate welfare increased, the losers included a large group of poorer producers.

The US experience also demonstrates the importance of empowerment in using the law as a complement to equality before the law. People's legal rights count for little if the institutions charged with protecting them are inaccessible or unresponsive. This is true even in countries with highly developed rules and norms for the administration of justice. In New Mexico the state engineer's office is required to adjudicate the rights of small water users as well as third-party effects. Even so, small farmers from traditional farmer-managed irrigation systems (*acequias*) have found it difficult to defend their well established rights. Most of them are of Hispanic descent, socially marginalized and seldom fluent in English, the language of litigation. When it comes to implementation, empowerment matters as much as the letter of the law.[18]

Box 5.2 Water trading in the western United States

The western United States is perhaps most widely cited by reformers as a model for efficient trade in water rights. But less attention has been paid to the laws and institutions developed over a long period to govern that model.

Water transfers in the western United States have been facilitated by laws that separate water rights from land rights. It was this separation, admittedly reinforced by a disregard for other legal processes, that enabled William Mulholland to appropriate water in the Owens Valley in the 1920s and transfer it to Los Angeles. Information is critical to the water transfer regime. Extensive state records on the volumes and shares of water associated with individual rights are another feature of western US systems.

Intersectoral transfers are governed by institutional processes that differ from state to state. In Arizona, New Mexico and Utah the state engineer's office is charged with assessing the technical characteristics of all transfers and conducting hearings on third-party effects. Colorado uses water courts to rule on disputes between rival users, resulting in much higher transaction costs for those who propose and those who oppose contested actions. And only "beneficial use" rights are considered, ruling out recourse to public use complaints by people affected through reduced flows or loss of livelihoods as irrigated production falls.

In California some transfers have been conducted through a state "drought water bank" that arranges purchases from individual farmers for transfer to other uses. Most transfers take the form of temporary leases, in part because of the restrictions on water rights but also because most holders do not want to transfer rights permanently. Some municipalities secure additional water in drought years by paying farmers to install water conservation devices or by increasing recharge in wet years, with the city receiving the additional water saved or stored.

Water transfers in the western United States are a highly contested and litigated sphere of politics. What is distinctive about the system, especially when viewed from the perspective of low-income countries seeking to implement policy instruments—such as tradable permits and administrative reallocations—is the depth of institutional rules and norms. And even with these rules and norms equity in water use has been difficult to protect—an outcome that should figure prominently in public policy debate in developing countries.

Source: Meinzen-Dick and Ringler 2006; NNMLS 2000.

The evolution of private water markets in Chile has underlined the complex interaction—and the potential tensions—between efficiency and equity goals. Water efficiency has increased dramatically since the mid-1970s, reflecting the incentives and market signals that have emerged from the trading of water rights. Producers in agriculture and in water-intensive industries such as mining have responded to higher water prices by adopting new technologies, including the drip irrigation systems that have sustained an export boom in high value-added fruits and vegetables.

The development of water markets in Chile has unquestionably enhanced efficiency and helped make possible the sustained growth in high value-added agricultural exports. However, efficiency gains in water management have outpaced the management of equity. During the 1980s and 1990s the absence of effective regulatory structures led to water monopolies, market distortions and highly unequal outcomes. Small farmers were marginalized and unable to capitalize on water rights. Meanwhile, indigenous communities lost water use rights to mining companies able to assert private property claims.

The Water Code Reform adopted by Chile in 2005 marks an attempt to address these problems and fill the regulatory vacuum in water markets. The new legislation limits speculative activity, breaks up water rights monopolies and protects small farmers.[19] Indigenous groups have also mobilized to use the legal system in a bid to reassert their claims. In 2004 the Aymara and Atacemeños indigenous groups in northern Chile secured a historic ruling that customary use establishes a prior claim that overrides subsequent private water rights.[20]

Proposals for transferable water rights have generated an intense debate across the developing world. In Indonesia, Sri Lanka and Thailand such plans have generated concerns that the market power of large producers and industry will strip small farmers of their access to irrigation water. Those concerns are justified. In theory, leasing or selling water rights could offer a source of income for poor farmers—just as it has for farmers in the western United States. But there are asymmetric power relations, inequalities in access to information and disparities in capacity for legal recourse. These problems can be added to the obvious dangers of farmers being forced into "distress sales" of water rights during periods of crisis caused by drought or crop failure, with vulnerable households losing water rights in return for short-term monetary gain.

Ultimately, water rights cannot be considered in isolation from the political and institutional structures that govern them. In that respect water markets are no different from any other market. What is distinctive about water is its pivotal role in the livelihoods of people and the environment of a country. These unique properties point to the need for highly developed systems of rules and institutions to ensure that important public policy objectives of social justice and ecological sustainability are not subordinated to the pursuit of private gain.

For developing countries private property rights in water are unlikely to offer easy solutions for reallocation, especially if equity is a policy goal. Developing the institutions, rules and norms to regulate water markets in the public interest is a complex exercise, as the experience of Chile and the United States shows. In most cases rapid shifts to transferable rights systems are likely to lead to unacceptable social and political consequences in developing countries facing intense competition for water resources. The more feasible option is to gradually develop existing rights and strengthen provisions for the poor.

The water rights agenda—missing equity and empowerment

In recent years reforms based on the integrated water resources management model have brought water rights back to the front of the policy agenda. While reform paths have varied, two clear strands have emerged. In a large group of countries—including Ghana, Indonesia, South Africa, Sri Lanka, Tanzania and Thailand—new legislation has formally declared water to be state property. The aim has been to create a unified legal framework for governments to allocate

It is important that public policy objectives of social justice and ecological sustainability are not subordinated to the pursuit of private gain

Water rights, licences
and permits are intended
to facilitate adjustment
to growing competition,
but a highly visible
equity gap remains

water rights within the limits of environmental sustainability, treating water resources in an integrated fashion. The second strand involves water withdrawal permits within a formal water economy. In effect, permits and associated licensing arrangements are intended as an alternative or a supplement to pure market pricing, with allocations based on government priorities.

Like water rights, licences and permits are intended to facilitate adjustment to growing competition. However, a highly visible equity gap remains. One notable feature of the approaches that have emerged is the absence of redistributive provisions. In this respect, greater equity has been a far weaker objective in water governance reform than in land tenure rights. An exception is the 1998 South Africa Water Act (box 5.3). It provides a legislative framework for pro-poor redistribution, but outcomes have fallen short of objectives because of the slow pace of land redistribution—a key requirement for poor households to increase their share of water use in agriculture.

The failure to ensure equity has been exacerbated in implementation. Strengthened

government controls over water allocation through use permits have gone hand in hand with policies that back urban and industrial claims against agriculture. In the implementation, if not in the design of legislation, the political voices of powerful urban and industrial water users have invariably overridden the claims of rural residents. This tendency has been especially pronounced in countries seeking to balance the competing claims of rural users with high growth industries. Although China has legislated for water rights since 1993, it has managed demand through centralized policy and allocation mechanisms, sometimes without sufficiently compensating farmers.[21] This is especially pronounced in the northern plains, where agricultural water withdrawals have been falling since the mid-1990s while industrial and urban demands have risen sharply.

Another example comes from the Philippines. Manila draws almost all of its water from a single source, the Angat Reservoir, shared with farmers in one of the country's largest irrigation schemes. Both municipal and agricultural users have established rights. But adjustments to shortage are heavily skewed against the interests of farmers because of the political strength of the Metropolitan Waterworks and Sewerage System in Manila. This has made livelihoods more precarious for agricultural producers (box 5.4).

Formal licensing systems aimed at managing reallocation to enhance efficiency while protecting equity often obscure the realities of unequal power relationships. As a rule of thumb, the importance of power in shaping outcomes from legislation is inversely related to regulatory capacity. Weak regulatory capacity increases the scope for exploitation of unequal relationships. In Indonesia water for commercial purposes is governed by formal permits that limit volume. Licences cannot be traded, and water use cannot be supplemented through informal trading. By law, smallholder farmers have priority access to water. In practice, the effectiveness of these provisions depends on the capacity of governance institutions to regulate water abstraction. The textile industry in West Java has

---

Box 5.3   Water rights and redistribution in South Africa

Unlike most governments, South Africa has explicitly targeted redistribution as a policy goal in integrated water management.

Under apartheid water use was based on the English common law principle linking control and use rights to private property in land. With more than 80% of land in the hands of white farmers, who also controlled irrigation boards, this excluded the majority of rural people from groundwater, springs and dams on private property. The 1998 National Water Act declared water to be a public resource owned by all citizens.

A minimum amount of water for drinking is now guaranteed as a legally enforceable right (see chapter 1). In rural communities individuals have use rights to water for domestic purposes or small-scale gardening without payment or registration. For water for commercial purposes, individuals are required to purchase a licence. The money generated from the licensing system is intended to contribute to the costs of water management. Individuals are granted water use rights for up to 40 years.

Public regulation is intended to set controls on the volume of water used to limit overexploitation. By abolishing "riparian rights" and transferring water to public ownership for allocation through state licensing, the legislation creates a framework for the redistribution of part of the country's natural capital stock. But redistributive outcomes will be conditioned by the redistribution of the other central pillar of natural capital—land.

Source: Perret 2002; Hodgson 2004; Faysse 2004; Muller 2006.

Diverse and overlapping water rights can be managed through governance systems that mediate between different claims. The extent to which equity figures in the governance equation is determined by the politics of water management.

The Angat-Maasim River system in the Philippines serves a large irrigation area and the municipal and industrial sectors of Metropolitan Manila—a megacity with a population of more than 10 million and growing at more than 1% a year. Three different agencies hold state-recognized water rights to the reservoirs: the National Irrigation Administration (NIA), the Metropolitan Waterworks and Sewerage System and the National Power Corporation. The NIA stands at the apex of a hierarchy of rights, but the water code has emergency provisions that give priority to domestic users.

In most years there is enough water to meet the needs of all users. During periods of drought and shortage, however, agriculture loses out heavily not just to municipalities but to industry as well. With the 1997 El Niño-related drought agriculture received no water for the dry season crop while industry's allocation fell only marginally. The irrigation system lost 125 metric tons of rice production and associated income, but farmers still had to meet rental payments. Many went into debt or lost their land. Because rights to water are vested in the NIA, rather than in a water user association, farmers were not compensated. The financing capacity of the NIA was compromised by the loss of income from irrigation service fees, weakening its ability to maintain the irrigation system.

The limited rights of farmers to water, coupled with the political power of industrial lobbies in Manila, produced an inequitable distribution of adjustment costs.

Source: Meinzen-Dick and Ringler 2006.

circumvented the rules by informally purchasing water rights upstream, leading to a loss of livelihoods for downstream producers (box 5.5).[22]

As these cases suggest, formal rights offer no guarantee of equity in the face of unequal power relations. But the absence of a well defined, properly regulated and enforced rights framework is even less likely to enhance water security and opens the door to institutional "water grabs" based on power.

Groundwater management demonstrates the problem. In many developing countries private groundwater extraction has allowed rural-urban water transfers through unregulated informal markets, with devastating effects in some cases for rural poverty. An example is the irrigation systems of India's Bhavani River, whose waters have been extensively depleted by industries and urban settlements in Coimbatore, Tamil Nadu. Since 1990 water transfers have slashed farm incomes almost in half for those at the tail-end of irrigation systems. Poverty among farm households increased from 3% in 1999/2000 to 15% in 2002/03. Hardest hit have been agricultural labourers who lost employment in irrigation systems: their poverty rates increased from 15% to 34%.[23]

Customary and formal rights— evidence from Sub-Saharan Africa

Formal rights to water will play an important role in shaping outcomes related to the intersectoral transfer of water. At the same time, water use in many countries is governed by a complex interaction between customary rights and formal rights. That interaction has an important bearing not just on water transfers between sectors, but also on the allocation of water rights within agriculture. The development of irrigation potential in Sub-Saharan Africa demonstrates how the interaction between formal and customary water rights can influence human development prospects. Questions over what right is recognized by whom and with reference to what norms and laws play a pivotal role in determining the equity of outcomes.

Competition for irrigation can marginalize the poor—experience in the Sahel

Plans to develop irrigation capacity in Sub-Saharan Africa are gathering pace in many countries. The prize being sought is an increase in productivity and a reduced dependence on the

Agricultural producers in West Java have strong formal rights to water, reflecting the role of rice farmers in the country's cultural, political and economic development. But formal rights have been eroded in some areas by the competing claims of industrial users.

West Java has been the site of a fast expanding textile industry. Factories have obtained more water through three routes: government-allocated permits to draw on surface and irrigation water or groundwater, negotiations with local farmers to buy or rent land to acquire water use rights and the installation of additional pumps and pipes.

The first of these routes, the permit, is sanctioned by government. The second, purchasing or renting land, is not sanctioned by state law, but is widely accepted in local law as a legitimate means of acquiring water. The third, installing additional pumps and pipes, is sanctioned neither by state law nor by local law, but is possible because of the political power of factory owners.

How has the legislative framework shaped the pattern of winners and losers? Many companies have exploited the gap between state law and local practice to buy or rent land, thereby acquiring water rights. Because factories have purchased land and water rights from producers upstream, these farmers have been compensated, but farmers downstream have lost out from reduced water flows and illegal overpumping by factories. As a consequence of lost production and increased insecurity of supply, many downstream farmers have been forced to sell their land—and those receiving compensation are not those bearing the greatest cost. The upshot: while farmers in Indonesia have the strongest water rights in both local and state law, conflicting regulatory structures and, more important, the greater economic and political power of factory owners mean that they are often ill-equipped to defend those rights.

Source: Kurnia, Avianto and Bruns 2000.

vagaries of rainfall. However, when an asset as precious as irrigation water is introduced into a water-scarce environment, it inevitably become a focus for competing claims. The danger is that the claims of the politically and commercially powerful will take precedence over the claims of the poor and marginalized.

Developments in the Sahel demonstrate the problem. Here, large irrigation systems are comparatively rare, though they are likely to become more common in the future. The development of large systems has often gone hand in hand with the introduction of formal land rights. In one large scheme, the Office du Niger in Mali, customary systems have effectively been replaced by government regulations. Because the public investment cost of developing irrigation facilities is high—direct costs are more than three times as high per hectare in Sub-Saharan Africa as in South Asia[24]—generating high returns has been important. To attract private capital, successive governments in Mali have strengthened tenure security and created private property rights in land. An explicit objective has been to attract investment from large-scale commercial producers. One concern is that smallholders will be disadvantaged. Is this concern justified?

Large-scale producers are not inherently more efficient than small-scale producers in irrigated areas. In fact, there is evidence from several countries that smallholders can be more efficient than large commercial farmers. However, increased market orientation can strongly favour large-scale commercial producers. In 2004, for example, the Malian government decided to sell some 3,000 hectares of land in the Office du Niger to private operators, with less than 10% set aside for smallholders. At the same time some 4,000 eviction orders were served on small farmers accused of not paying water fees. As ever with water, the issues are rooted in local politics. But the Office du Niger, one of the most efficient irrigation systems in Sub-Saharan Africa, now faces the difficult challenge of managing the competing claims of smallholder farmers and politically influential large-scale producers.[25]

Similar problems have emerged in Senegal. The future of smallholder family farming is at the centre of a protracted debate in the country.

Some see the sector as a source of employment, innovation and food security in an environment marked by extreme uncertainty, financial constraints and extensive poverty. Others see a need to modernize agriculture through large-scale capital investment. The government's rural development programme seeks to develop both sectors. But in the Senegal River Valley decentralized rural councils have sought to attract large-scale foreign investors from France and Saudi Arabia, providing access to land and irrigation resources. The resulting competition for water has attracted opposition from farmers claiming customary rights to the land and water, forcing national authorities to intervene.[26]

Customary law can both enhance governance and exacerbate inequalities

Some people view customary law as an obstacle to progress and modernization in agriculture, and others view it as guarantor of equity. Both perceptions suffer from exaggeration. Customary law is often part of a highly sophisticated set of institutions for managing water as a scarce resource. It can also be a driver of inequality.

Evidence drawn from the Senegal River Valley reveals the complexity of the governance issues raised. Advocates of private property rights consider customary law as a route to the "tragedy of the commons". Lacking any formal legal binding on water use, the argument runs, individual users have no incentive to curtail demand, leading to the depletion of shared water resources by overuse. In fact, customary law often involves strict controls on water use, with water rights structured to balance claims based on inheritance, social need and sustainability. Institutional cooperation is common. One study of the Dieler Canal in Senegal found villages cooperating to finance the maintenance of canals and drainage systems and to regulate the amount of water drawn from the feeder lake. These villages are now engaged in dialogue with large-scale agro-industrial enterprises, encouraging irrigation methods that consume less water, such as drip irrigation.[27]

On the other side of the equation, customary law is not inherently more equitable than formal land rights. In many irrigation schemes customary rules that underlie social stratification tend to resurface after the renegotiation of land rights. Customary landholders are often well placed to use their position as chiefs or councillors to skew formal rules to perpetuate their privileged access to land. This has happened in the Senegal River Valley, where decentralization and the introduction of formal land laws enabled the guardians of customary law to foster inequality and social exclusion (box 5.6).

Box 5.6   Customary law and inequality in Senegal

Customary water rights are sometimes seen as inherently more equitable and democratic than formal water rights, with local institutions providing a high level of accountability within traditional structures. But evidence cautions against idealism. In many contexts customary landholders use their position in the community to circumvent formal rules and perpetuate their privileged access to land.

Towards the end of the 1980s Senegal transferred management responsibilities for irrigated lands to local governments. Since then, elected rural councils have assumed responsibility for allocating irrigated plots to user groups, which then allocate plots to individual users.

In the Fleuve Valley on the Senegal River communities are divided by rigid hierarchies that differentiate descendants of slaves and nobles. Both groups operate plots in the Senegal River Valley irrigation scheme. Democratic rural council elections give descendants of slaves the same formal opportunities for office as descendants of nobles—and all villagers are eligible for irrigated land on the basis of distribution criteria linked to family size. But social status figures in the election process. In the rural community of Bokidiawe, a typical example, 30 of 32 elected councillors are of noble origin.

Research shows how the rigid dividing line sometimes drawn between formal and customary arrangements can be illusory. Local landholding elites wear multiple hats, straddling statutory and customary institutions. In Bokidiawe the community leader is at once a village chief, a rural councillor, president of the land user group, member of a political party and a relatively large-scale rice grower.

Local elites often use their position to maintain control over irrigated land. In Senegal customary landholders have been able not only to capture a disproportionately large share of irrigated land, but to allocate and sell irrigated land to powerful outsiders (including politicians, army and government officials, and judges) despite legislation restricting access to irrigated land to local residents. Meanwhile, lower caste farmers have been forced to enter sharecropping arrangements to gain access to irrigated land, paying part of their crop as rent, even though sharecropping on irrigation schemes is illegal.

The Senegal River Valley has wider relevance. Water governance reforms typically emphasize equal access to irrigated plots for all eligible people. But while statutory laws aim to promote equity in access to water and to support greater participation and accountability, the democratic and egalitarian principles that underpin them are often at odds with customary principles that entrench social hierarchies and gender inequalities.

Source: Cotula 2006; Sylla 2006.

Water rights matter because they shape entitlements to water, both in a formal legal sense and through informal processes that empower—or disempower—people

Gender inequalities pervade both formal and informal land rights. Within most customary systems women enjoy well defined use rights but very limited decision-making authority. In Comoe Province of Burkina Faso, men have traditionally controlled the uplands used for growing groundnuts and cotton, while women cultivate rice and enjoy use rights in the lowlands. When a major infrastructure programme was launched in the early 1990s to extend irrigation to the lowlands, design and implementation were guided by traditional male chiefs and a male-biased interpretation of customary law. The outcome: improved lands were allocated to male household heads, productivity declined and gender inequality increased. The programme later corrected this male bias by involving women in land allocation.[28]

Formal rights are not a guaranteed route to equity

While formal property rights linking land and water can offer greater security, they can also conflict with customary rights. In the event of conflict formal rights often take precedence over customary rights.

Evidence of the problem is widespread in areas with pastoral systems of production. Across parts of Sub-Saharan Africa pastoralists have consistently lost out as a result of water shortages, increased pressure on land and the extension of formal land rights. Enclosing a water point, creating an irrigation scheme or attaching a legal title to land can shift the power relationship between sedentary producers and pastoralists, whose entitlements are rooted in weaker (often nonenforceable) customary claims. In northern Uganda, southern Tanzania and northeastern Kenya violent clashes between farmers and pastoralists have become increasingly common. Tensions between private and customary claims are intensifying. In Niger legislation introduced under water governance reforms allows for private water points in pastoral grazing areas. Elsewhere in West Africa, new open access wells constructed by the state have undermined traditional sharing systems. The public wells have been taken over by larger, more powerful herders, including customary

chiefs, traders and politicians, reducing access to water for other herders.[29]

Conflicts between formal and informal land rights are sometimes heightened by poor policy design and weak regulatory capacity. Managing the interface between diverse groups of users with different legal claims and interests, but linked by the same water system, is an institutional challenge. In Tanzania the Pangani River Basin has been the site of an ambitious attempt at integrated water resource management. The large majority of water users in the basin are livestock keepers and smallholders farming in wetland areas. Growing population pressure and demands from industry and irrigation have created problems of water scarcity, especially during the dry season. Formal water abstraction rights and fees failed to address these problems, and in many cases made them worse by creating unintentionally perverse incentives for large users to overextract water (box 5.7).

Water rights shape entitlements

Water rights matter because they shape entitlements to water, both in a formal legal sense and through informal processes that empower—or disempower—people. While rights are important for everyone, they matter more for some than for others. Wealthy and powerful people have many ways of protecting their interests, whether through legal or political channels. Lack of secure and enforceable rights pose a much bigger problem for the poor, especially in water. If the access of poor households to a resource as essential as water can be taken away without consultation, compensation or even advance notice, livelihoods become more precarious, and the incentives that people have to invest in improving their lives are severely compromised.

Stronger rights and enforcement mechanisms can help vulnerable producers resist the encroachments of large industry, commercial agriculture and urban users. But water rights can be a double-edged sword. The formalization of rights may also expand opportunities for those who are wealthier, more powerful and better connected, marginalizing those lacking the capacity, the confidence or the political connections to

Water policy reform in Tanzania highlights the unintended consequences of introducing new water rights into systems of customary regulation.

Over the past decade the Tanzanian government, with international support, has put in place new administrative rights systems to improve basin-level management and enhance cost-recovery for service provision. The Upper Ruaha catchment area on the Pangani River has been a centre for reform. The majority of water users there are small-scale irrigators and livestock keepers who have traditionally managed water resources through customary arrangements without state support. Competition has increased with large irrigation upstream and rising demands from urban users.

Since the reforms introduced in the mid-1990s Tanzania has devolved authority to water user associations and introduced fees. Water user groups now have to pay a minimum flat rate fee with a view to conserving water and mobilizing revenues. The fees—averaging $35–$40 for individuals and groups—are applied to all users of surface and groundwater.

Having to pay for a previously free resource has caused extreme hardship for small-scale farmers and livestock producers. Perversely, the collection costs for revenue administration have exceeded revenue flows, defeating one of the stated purposes.

Another perverse result is that a reform process designed to conserve water has instead encouraged overuse. Large-scale irrigation users have accepted the new fee structure, but they view paying the formal charge as an entitlement to use water without any limit, regardless of seasonal flows. Large producers have been expanding irrigated land area, citing payment of the water fee as justification. Overuse by upstream irrigators, previously restricted by customary rules, has increased shortages among downstream users during the dry season. Imbalances in political voice have made the problem worse: not a single water user association had been established in the downstream plains by 2003, six years after the reforms were instituted. Thus the administrative reform has also created more serious equity problems.

Fees for water use make sense for large-scale users, urban providers and industry but small-scale users managing their own water systems should be exempted. Similarly, acquisition of formal water rights should not be treated as a licence to unrestricted use: volumetric and proportional controls are needed to align supply with demand. Under a poverty-focused planning framework, volumetric and proportional allocations to large-scale modern users should take into account the needs of vulnerable small-scale users.

Source: Van Koppen and others 2004; Lankford and Mwaruvanda 2005.

act on their rights. As a group, customary rights holders may lack legal standing. An obvious danger is that narrow interpretations of water rights, based on formal state laws, will exclude groups such as women, pastoralists and smallholders.

Individual or group water rights are an important instrument for human development. The absence of secure rights can expose already vulnerable people to higher levels of risk and uncertainty, increasing their vulnerability to poverty. Much depends on local context and institutions. But one of the broad lessons is that for water rights to be meaningful for the poor, rights have to be linked to wider strategies for empowerment and equity. These strategies include legislative provisions that enshrine the rights of the marginalized and legal processes that are open to the poor.

Better governance in irrigation systems

Across much of the developing world irrigation systems will bear the brunt of increased competition from other users. That is especially the case in Asia, where irrigation is losing its privileged position as first among equals in claiming water. One challenge is how to manage transfers from agriculture to nonagricultural users. While the quantities involved may appear small when measured against water volume used in agriculture, diversion can have a profound impact on livelihoods. At the same time irrigation systems themselves will become

As irrigation systems come under pressure to produce more with less water, there is a danger that unequal rights and entitlements will widen inequalities

the locus of growing competition, as producers seek to maintain access to an increasingly scarce resource.

As irrigation systems come under pressure to produce more with less water, there is a danger that unequal rights and entitlements will widen inequalities. That outcome would have important implications for human development. Access to irrigation is associated with lower poverty levels. Even so, some one-third of people living in irrigation systems are below the income poverty line because of inequitable benefit sharing and poor performance.

Does the enhanced efficiency needed in irrigation systems to raise water productivity automatically conflict with equity objectives? Best evidence suggests that there are no inherent efficiency-equity tradeoffs. Indeed, greater equity is one of the requirements in many countries for improving basin-level efficiency. Others are increased investment, the reform of centralized top-down planning and the development of more accountable service provision.

Reducing the risk of poverty

Irrigation systems reduce the risk of poverty—but some reduce the risk more than others. Reasons vary, but the distribution of land and differences in governance are recurrent themes.

Poverty, inequality and inefficiency

Cross-country comparisons between South and East Asia demonstrate the relationship between poverty and inequality, and efficiency. The prevalence of poverty in irrigation systems in (relatively equal) Viet Nam, for example, is far lower than in (far more unequal) Pakistan and India. Indeed, Pakistan has the distinction of being one of the few countries in which poverty levels have been found to be as high inside the irrigation networks as outside (figure 5.4).

Within irrigation systems unequal access to water is a corollary of unequal access to land. In Pakistan the largest 2.5% of farms (more than 50 hectares) account for 34% of cultivated land while the smallest 55% of farms (less than 5 hectares) account for 12%.[30] Because water allocation in irrigation systems is based on

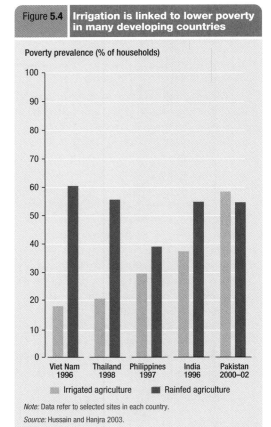

Figure 5.4   Irrigation is linked to lower poverty in many developing countries

Poverty prevalence (% of households)

- Irrigated agriculture
- Rainfed agriculture

Viet Nam 1996, Thailand 1998, Philippines 1997, India 1996, Pakistan 2000–02

Note: Data refer to selected sites in each country.
Source: Hussain and Hanjra 2003.

size of landholding, larger farms get the most water. This matters for the efficiency of water use because cropping intensity and productivity are inversely related to farm size: small farmers get more output per hectare and more crop per drop. Comparative research on different irrigation systems has found productivity per hectare to range from $230–$690 in South Asia to $665–$1,660 in East Asia. Measured on this indicator China, with relatively equitable land distribution, is the most efficient irrigator and Pakistan the least efficient (figure 5.5).[31]

Higher productivity is the link from irrigation to lower poverty through increased incomes and, in many cases, greater opportunities for employment. By one estimate Pakistan could reduce the prevalence of poverty within its irrigation systems by 20% if it were to increase its income per hectare to China's levels.[32] Such an outcome would be good for the poor and good for the country because of the benefits for growth—but it would require a commitment to land redistribution and the development of marketing and input support systems.

5

Water competition in agriculture

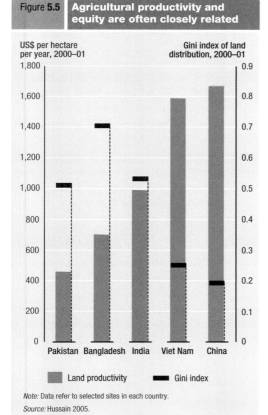

Figure 5.5 Agricultural productivity and equity are often closely related

US$ per hectare per year, 2000–01 / Gini index of land distribution, 2000–01

Land productivity
Gini index

Note: Data refer to selected sites in each country.
Source: Hussain 2005.

Tail-end disadvantage

Water scarcity is not the main cause of poverty in most irrigation systems. The underlying problem is the rules, institutions and power relationships governing access to water. Where a producer is located on an irrigation system determines the availability and reliability of water flows.

Tail-end farmers, away from the head or middle of canals, suffer a twin disadvantage: less water and more uncertainty. Farmers between the head and the middle of an irrigation canal get an abundant—often overabundant—supply of water, while those at the tail get too little (figure 5.6). In India and Pakistan it is typical for tail-end producers to receive less than a third of the water of farmers at the head of the canal.

Such inequalities erode the potential human development benefits of irrigation. Low water flows restrict the scope for adopting new varieties of seeds and new technologies to boost productivity and thus contribute to higher levels of poverty among tail-end irrigators (figure

5.7). Uncertainty and fluctuations associated with water supply increase household vulnerability and risk and create disincentives for investment. Once again, irrigation modelling has found that the reallocation from head-end to tail-end users in Pakistan can generate win-win outcomes—production and incomes at the tail can be increased with little impact at the head. Thus there is considerable scope for improving overall system productivity and enhancing efficiency.[33]

So why do governments not seize opportunities for such win-win outcomes? The answer lies in politics, not economics. Relative power, not comparative efficiency, governs water allocation systems in many countries. Rich farmers with political power can influence the timing and volume of water releases by manipulating canal managers. Meanwhile, unaccountable and sometimes corrupt governance systems harm the poor by favouring people with political connections and money for bribes. Research on an irrigation system in the Punjab in Pakistan found that a few large farmers were illegally appropriating large amounts of water from nine outlets, receiving benefits of $55 per hectare per year, while downstream losses of some $7 per hectare per year were spread across a large group of producers served by 40 outlets.[34] Small farmers at the tail-end cited their inability to afford legal costs and the corruption of local legal systems as the major barriers to contesting the illegal appropriation—a problem documented in the *Pakistan National Human Development Report 2004* and found throughout much of Asia.[35]

Financing with equity

The financing of irrigation systems raises central questions of efficiency and equity. The underfinancing of irrigation infrastructure leads to the rapid erosion of canals and drainage systems, with associated costs for efficiency and the environment. Central Asia presents an extreme case of the human development problems linked to the poor governance of large-scale irrigation systems (box 5.8). But the problem is far broader.

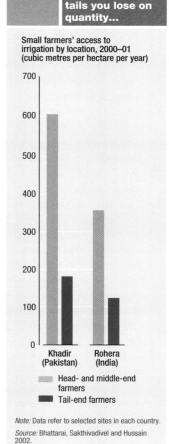

Figure 5.6 Heads you win, tails you lose on quantity...

Small farmers' access to irrigation by location, 2000–01 (cubic metres per hectare per year)

Head- and middle-end farmers
Tail-end farmers

Note: Data refer to selected sites in each country.
Source: Bhattarai, Sakthivadivel and Hussain 2002.

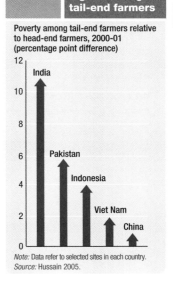

Figure 5.7 ...and poverty is higher among tail-end farmers

Poverty among tail-end farmers relative to head-end farmers, 2000-01 (percentage point difference)

Note: Data refer to selected sites in each country.
Source: Hussain 2005.

5

Water competition in agriculture

Box 5.8 | Irrigation and water management in Central Asia

Central Asia is blessed with abundant freshwater flowing down from glaciers in the Hindu Kush mountains. The region also has one of the world's most expansive irrigation systems—a legacy of a Soviet modernization model that often pushed irrigation development to generate short-term agricultural revenues at the cost of the environment. The system's collapse is now holding back human development and reinforcing poverty.

With an arid climate across much of the region, irrigation water is indispensable for agriculture—and agriculture is the mainstay of national economies and livelihoods across central Asia. Irrigated agriculture accounts for more than a quarter of GDP in Tajikistan and Turkmenistan and more than a third in Kyrgyzstan and Uzbekistan. Some 22 million livelihoods depend on irrigation. The regional inheritance from Soviet planners includes a large number of dams, canals and pumping stations, most of them on transboundary river systems. Another inheritance is the Aral Sea environmental disaster, caused by the diversion of river systems for cotton irrigation (chapter 6).

Poor management and deteriorating drainage infrastructure have led to extensive water-logging and salinization, especially in downstream states. In the Amu Darya and Syr Darya River Basins in Uzbekistan and Kazakhstan salinization has increased by more than 50% in a decade. Rising groundwater, one of the drivers of salinization, now poses a huge threat to agriculture.

The water scarcity in much of the region owes less to availability than to infrastructure decay. Measured per hectare, water use in Central Asian irrigation systems is 30% higher than in Egypt and Pakistan—themselves not the most efficient water users. Evaporation, siltation of canals and leaks from piped channels mean that less than 40% of the water diverted from rivers reaches the field. Breakdowns of pumping stations used to lift water over elevations of several hundred metres have been another source of scarcity. Inefficiency generates very large losses: Central Asian countries lose an estimated $1.7 billion annually to irrigation mismanagement.

Tajikistan illustrates the scale of the problem. Since 1991 more than a fifth of the country's irrigated land has ceased to receive water, leading to a loss of 4% of GNI by one estimate. Two-thirds of the country's 445 pumping stations are out of operation, reducing flows by 40%. And water losses through the irrigation infrastructure are increasing from already high levels. The collapse in infrastructure

has gone hand in hand with a decline in public investment. Financing for the sector in 2002 was reported at a tenth of that in 1991.

Solutions are not easy. Irrigation management in the Soviet era was highly centralized in Moscow. In the post-Soviet era some governments went to the other extreme, transferring authority to private water user associations. The lack of financing for the maintenance of the wider infrastructure, inability to afford rising electricity charges for pumping and constraints on the mobilization of local financing led to the collapse of many of these associations.

Weak regional cooperation has been another problem. Rural livelihoods across the region are linked through shared river systems. The giant Karhsi pumping cascade lifts water from the Amu Darya to irrigate 400,000 hectares of agricultural land on the steppes of southern Uzbekistan. Six of the seven pumping stations are in Turkmenistan. Differences between Turkmen and Uzbek authorities have meant underinvesting in the pumping system and shelving international aid plans to support its modernization.

Enhanced cooperation in the region and beyond is vital to recovery (see chapter 6). Downstream users such as Kazakhstan and Uzbekistan depend critically on the volume and timing of releases from upstream Kyrgyzstan. Kyrgyz authorities are exploring options for expanding hydropower generation, which would further reduce downstream flows. The costs of noncooperation will be very high: financing water self-reliance through new dams in Kazakhstan and Uzbekistan is a high-cost option. The economic benefits of cooperation are substantial, but cooperation is underdeveloped.

Central Asia's water interdependence extends to other neighbours. Failure to manage this interdependence will exacerbate water shortages in agriculture. Countries in the region depend on rivers that rise in Afghanistan, China and Russia and flow through shared river systems. For example, the Irtysh and Ili Rivers originate in China and flow into Kazakhstan. As water scarcity mounts in China, authorities have announced plans to divert water from these rivers into Xinjiang Province. If Afghanistan expands irrigation in its part of the Amu Darya Basin, it will influence flows into Tajikistan, Turkmenistan and Uzbekistan. These cases demonstrate the very real implications of water interdependence and the equally real dangers of failing to develop cooperative governance systems.

Source: UNDP 2003a, 2005a.

In South Asia the dominant model of irrigation infrastructure provision has been aptly described as "build-neglect-rebuild".[36] By an international yardstick replacement and maintenance of irrigation infrastructure require annual spending of about 3% of the value of the capital stock. In the Punjab in Pakistan actual spending is less than one-tenth of this benchmark. Financing for irrigation maintenance in

India is greater but still less than half the minimum. Chronic underinvestment in system maintenance has led to widespread problems of siltation, soil-salinization, water-logging and reduced flows in both countries.[37]

Financing for irrigation systems often reinforces the inefficiency-inequity cycle. In South Asia irrigation charges are typically very low by comparison with those in East Asia, both

Table 5.1	Irrigation charges and value of production for selected irrigation schemes in Asia	
Country	Average water charge ($ per hectare)	Average water charge as share of gross value of production (%)
Pakistan	7.4 [4.6–10.6]	2.5 [1.7–3.9]
India	10 [10]	2.8 [1.6–4.3]
China	46.5 [26–67]	3.6 [1.8–5.1]
Viet Nam	59.5 [58–61]	5.5 [4.6–6.3]

Note: Data refer to the average of selected sites in each country, with the range shown in brackets.

Source: Adapted from Hussain and Wijerathna 2004a.

in absolute terms and as a share of the value of production (table 5.1). These low charges are sometimes defended on the grounds that they are good for food security and for poverty reduction. This overlooks some serious equity problems.

How and where governments spend for irrigation are also important for equity in access to irrigation. In Latin America water is one of the assets driving extreme disparities in rural areas—and government spending sometimes widens them. The Majes project in southern Peru, to take one example, required public investment of about $1.2 billion to capture and collect water from the Colca Valley to irrigate the desert lowlands. The project irrigates about 15,000 hectares of land for 3,000 producers—at a capital investment of $400,000 per beneficiary. An evaluation by the Economic Commission for Latin America estimated that less than 1% of the public investment benefits would be realized in the upper basin, a centre of indigenous poverty in Peru. This is an extreme example of a wider pattern. In Ecuador peasants make up 60% of the rural population but receive only 13% of the benefits from state spending on irrigation. At the other end of the rural social divide, fewer than 5% of rural irrigators have more than 50% of the water rights concessions.[38]

Charging for water

Irrigation charges are typically levied as a flat rate assessed on cropped area, so that tail-end farmers pay the same even though they get less—and less reliable—water than head-end

and middle users. Moreover, poor small farmers pay more per hectare since they tend to crop a larger share of their land, with tail-end farmers also paying more, because the unreliability of irrigation water forces them to invest in groundwater extraction (some nine times more expensive than canal irrigation). Just as high-income urban consumers pay less for their domestic water than people in slums (see chapter 2), some of South Asia's poorest farmers pay more for their irrigation water than their countries' largest landowners. In China and Viet Nam charges are higher overall than in South Asia—but water is more equitably and reliably distributed across the system, enabling poor producers to finance payments through higher productivity.[39]

There are no blueprints for ensuring equity in the financing of irrigation infrastructure. The capital costs of building irrigation systems are far too high for producers to bear. That is why governments since the time of the ancient Egyptians through the Mughals to the US administrations of the 1920s and 1930s have financed capital costs out of general tax revenue. Finance for maintaining and operating systems, however, should be borne principally by users, with pricing differentiated by the ability to pay and the service provided.

This is broadly what happens in East Asia and in better performing irrigation systems worldwide—such as those in Egypt, Morocco and Turkey—and what does not happen in South Asia, where government subsidies weigh far more heavily. In Pakistan less than half the operation and maintenance costs of irrigation spending are recovered, and most of the benefits are captured by large-scale producers. In India about 13% of the population has access to irrigation. Within this group the richest one-third of farmers receive 73% of the subsidy.[40] Meanwhile, low rates of cost-recovery often lead to poor service, especially at the tail-end of irrigation canals. Low rates of cost-recovery also lead to high inequity.

Collecting revenues

Cost-recovery cannot be considered in isolation—it is part of a wider system of

Governments since the time of the ancient Egyptians have financed the capital costs of irrigation infrastructure out of general tax revenue

5

Water competition in agriculture

governance for service delivery. One of the most influential institutional changes in governance in recent years has been the introduction of participatory irrigation management and the development of water user associations. In the best cases—as in Indonesia, Mexico and Turkey—institutional reforms have transferred management to irrigation users, with marked increases in revenue collection, maintenance spending and irrigation returns. The lesson: where producers have more authority and responsibility for water management, transparency can improve pricing, cost-recovery and performance.[41]

But giving producers more authority, to be financially sustainable and bring tangible benefits to farmers, requires a combination of financial and institutional empowerment that turns on its head the top-down governance models that have dominated irrigation management. The transformation of the model underpinning state agencies—from supply and control to supporting and developing local management capacity—requires deep institutional reform, a task often more easily said than done.

Similarly, transferring management responsibility to farmers will be successful only where agriculture can be profitable. Returns to irrigation investment are the product not just of irrigation governance but of marketing infrastructure, agricultural extension services and access to information, credit and other productive resources. One of the problems documented across Sub-Saharan Africa is that transfers of irrigation management have often shifted liabilities for system maintenance without addressing market, transport and input provision problems that constrain income generation.[42] In Madagascar the transfer of a dilapidated irrigation infrastructure from regional public sector agencies to water users in the 1980s with no government budget support led to the system's collapse.[43]

Such outcomes are not inevitable. Under the right conditions, water user associations can enable members to participate in designing cost-recovery systems, improving collections and ensuring that the fees collected benefit the systems locally. The accountability of providers is critical. In Sindh, Pakistan, farmers unwill-

ing to pay for irrigation stress that the reason is not the affordability of the water but corruption in management and the failure to provide good water service.

Empowerment—the missing link

Sustainable and equitable financing is one requirement for adjustment with equity in irrigation systems. Empowerment is another. Under the emerging consensus on integrated water resources management, decentralization and devolution of authority to water user associations are seen as fast-track routes to empowerment. But empowerment is more complex than administrative reform.

Decentralization has been a core theme in water governance reforms for more than a decade. In some cases reforms have been partial and incomplete, with a primary emphasis on boosting cost-recovery and reducing pressure on government budgets. In others they have yielded noticeable benefits by improving the responsiveness of irrigation bureaucracies to water users. Decentralization can create new patterns of incentives that make service providers more accountable. Service contracts, auditing and independent water tribunals have been among the mechanisms used to promote accountability of both providers and users.

In Indonesia, following reforms in 2001, water user associations were given full control over the financial administration of irrigation facilities, including setting budgets and prices. Elected association representatives now participate in district irrigation bodies and higher level river basin councils. A more striking example of devolution is in Andhra Pradesh, where the water governance system has been transformed through the 1997 Farmer Irrigation Act (box 5.9).[44]

Having a right to be heard is not the same as having the power to influence decisions. One problem with the governance model for irrigation has been its partial approach to empowerment. Reforms have often been more about giving water users a voice than about empowering them with rights. Decentralization and the devolution of authority to the local level may en-

Box 5.9 | Devolution of water governance in Andhra Pradesh

Devolution in water governance has often meant transferring responsibility without financial capacity. The Indian state of Andhra Pradesh provides a striking exception.

The 1997 Farmer Irrigation Act followed intense political debate and consultation among national bodies, state agencies, farmer groups and village associations. More than 10,000 water user associations were created through state-level elections.

The Andhra Pradesh Irrigation Department was decentralized to provide technical support to water user associations, each empowered with decision-making authority to develop and implement service plans, enforce rules and determine spending on maintenance. Financial control and responsibility for cost-recovery were transferred to the associations, which can engage service providers and manage contracts. More than 90% of fees collected are retained locally. The better service provision financed by the fees has resulted in voluntary decisions by many farmers to increase cost-recovery, reversing the past cycle of underfinancing and deteriorating infrastructure.

High-profile public audits conducted jointly by water user associations and the irrigation department review political participation within the associations as well as water development issues. Devolution has meant a real shift in the balance of power between water users and government irrigation providers, with providers now far more responsive and accountable to local communities.

But not all community members have an equal say in how priorities are defined. Village-level research has identified large variations in formal participation—and even larger variations in how poor people and women exert their influence. An audit of 102 villages in two representative subdistricts—Dhone and Kalyandurg—found large discrepancies in participation in village meetings on water (see figure). In Kalyandurg, where a nongovernmental organization had been working with farmers for 25 years, poor people felt that they had an influence

on decisions affecting them in two-thirds of the villages covered. In Dhone participation and influence scores were far lower, with only 16% of villages registering active influence for the poor (see figure).

Devolution performed far less well in addressing the concerns of women: in only 4%–5% of the villages did women believe that they could influence decisions in village meetings. As the audit concludes: "Women, and particularly poor women, rarely participate in meetings…. Despite impressive advances towards empowerment… women still do not participate effectively in community decision-making."

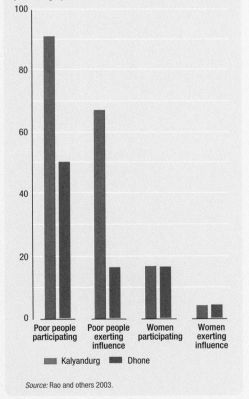

Managing water—some people have a greater voice than others

Influence and participation in water user associations by the poor and women in two subdistricts in Andhra Pradesh, 2000 (% of villages)

Legend: Kalyandurg, Dhone

Categories: Poor people participating, Poor people exerting influence, Women participating, Women exerting influence

Source: Rao and others 2003.

Source: Rao and others 2003; Vermillion 2005; Sivamohan and Scott 2005.

hance political participation and accountability. Whether that reduces inequality depends on whether disparities in access to land, water and power are addressed.

Old habits die hard…

Decentralizing water governance in irrigation is not an automatic route to enhanced equity, even where policy has an overtly redistributive

Gender inequalities in
irrigation are deeply
entrenched as a result of
formal and informal rules
that mute women's voices

design. In South Africa the 1998 water legislation institutionalized the participation of small-scale water users in what had previously been whites-only irrigation boards. Water user associations are now legally obliged to include small-scale users, including farm workers, market gardening groups and farm tenants. While the presence of small-scale users in management structures has given a greater voice to marginalized groups, old power relationships have proven highly resilient. Large-scale commercial farmers still dominate decision-making. Moreover, small-scale users often receive far less water than they are entitled to. Research in the Western Cape and other irrigation districts has found that some small-scale farmers use less than half of their entitlements. The weak political organization of small-scale users and their inability to enforce claims to land appear to be the main causes.[45]

South Africa's experience shows that old inequalities and governance habits die hard. The same is true for corruption. One of the aims of decentralization has been to establish more accountable and transparent governance structures. But progress has been mixed. Surveys of farmers on the Hakra irrigation scheme in the Punjab in Pakistan are instructive. More than half those interviewed felt that efficiency had improved with decentralization and that water theft was less prevalent. But few farmers said that bribery was not a problem, a quarter felt that office holders favoured friends and relatives, and half reported "no change" in benefits for small and poor farmers. These are signs that decentralization is not an automatic route to resolving problems of corruption and poor governance.[46]

…and so do gender inequalities

Tensions between decentralization and equity are also apparent at the household level. Gender inequalities in irrigation are deeply entrenched as a result of formal and informal rules that mute women's voices. In many countries women have use rights to irrigation water but highly restricted rights of control. Control rights are often linked to wider property rights, which are highly unequal between men and women.

Lacking rights to land, millions of women in South Asia and Sub-Saharan Africa are denied formal membership rights to participate in water user association meetings. Meanwhile, in many traditional communal irrigation systems people earn the right to use water by working on maintenance. However, cultural norms often preclude women from engaging in this activity. And even when they do, water rights do not automatically follow, as research from Kenya and Nepal documents.[47]

Public meetings on irrigation are often a male domain. Women are sometimes excluded from participation by labour demands in other areas or by a lack of confidence in speaking or a reticence about making demands. One study of women's participation in irrigated agriculture projects in Ecuador cites a woman's summary of the realities of informal gender inequality: "Meetings [of the irrigation association] are on Friday nights. At that time, after cooking for my husband and the kids, I still have a lot of work to do around the house…. Even if I go to the meeting it's only to hear what the men have to say. Men are the ones who talk and discuss".[48] In Andhra Pradesh decentralization may have empowered male water users in their relations with government agencies, but it has done little to give women a voice in management (see box 5.9).

Overcoming these gender barriers is difficult. Women are important stakeholders in food production in irrigated and nonirrigated settings: they produce an estimated two-thirds of the food in most developing countries. But low participation by women in water user associations is a systemic problem not easily amenable to resolution through decentralizing or devolving authority to water user associations. The driving force for change has to come from below. Nongovernmental organizations in Bangladesh, India and Kenya have worked with village groups to increase women's involvement, but the cultural barriers to participation remain high.

Failure to systematically empower and consult women is not just bad for social justice and equity. It is also bad for efficiency: as producers, women have skills and knowledge vital to water management. Recognizing this, some countries have undertaken bold measures to break down cultural barriers. Legislation in Uganda requires that all political and administrative agencies from the national cabinet down to village water user associations include at least 30% female representation.[49] Affirmative action may not remove cultural barriers—but it does challenge their legitimacy.

Getting more crop per drop, rather than more water to the fields, is becoming the central concern in public policy debates

Greater water productivity for the poor

For much of the past hundred years water shortages in agriculture have been countered by dams and large-scale irrigation works. In the years ahead the focus will shift decisively to demand management. Getting more crop per drop, rather than more water to the fields, is becoming the central concern in public policy debates.

Increasing the productivity of water is one obvious response to water scarcity. One powerful impetus for productivity gains will come through the market. As water becomes more scarce, prices will rise. Other things being equal, this might be expected to create incentives for investment in the development and deployment of new technologies for reducing water use. However, capacity to undertake these investments and to benefit from new technology is not equally distributed. Smallholder farmers lacking assets, tail-end irrigation producers and women are all likely to be bypassed by new technologies unless institutions and policies are put in place to avoid this outcome.

This section looks briefly at the important place occupied by water harvesting and micro-irrigation with new technologies in developing pro-poor options for water governance. Both offer benefits for water security and put water—and water storage—closer to people. They provide households with an asset that can raise productivity and reduce risk, in the same way that large dams and reservoirs can at the national level. Similarly, new pro-poor technologies offer a twin benefit. By substituting labour inputs and small amounts of capital investment for land and water, they can raise productivity and incomes.

Water harvesting and micro-irrigation

Water management is still often seen principally as a subject for large-scale projects and programmes. But small-scale water management can make smallholder agriculture more productive and less risky, with important benefits for human development. The technologies and approaches are well known. The challenge is to develop public policies that emphasize partnerships between communities and government agencies.

Water harvesting
Water harvesting experience shows how community-led initiatives can be scaled up through partnerships. Small reservoirs and rainwater harvesting structures provide an infrastructure framework that, when combined with appropriate land management practices, can increase water availability for the poor and boost the local efficiency and productivity of water use. That framework can enhance water security in rainfed areas, bringing food security and the potential for diversification into small-scale market production.

Rainwater harvesting is one of the oldest recorded hydrological activities. It was used 8,000 years ago in the first human settlements in South Asia and 4,000 years ago in Greece and Palestine. South Asia has a rich history of water harvesting, from the complex integrated

In the modern irrigation era rainwater harvesting structures have been in forced retreat

tank systems developed by the Vijayanagar kings of South India in the 14th century to the thousands of simple village ponds that support a range of local productive and domestic activities today. Across Sub-Saharan Africa too there are diverse traditional water harvesting practices, many involving the direct transfer of rainwater to recharge soil moisture. More than half of Tanzania's rice production is grown under harvesting systems built and managed by farmers. In West Africa harvesting rehabilitates land and captures nutrients washed away by the rain.[50]

In the modern irrigation era, however, rainwater harvesting structures have been in forced retreat. In India the rise of canal irrigation and, more recently, the groundwater revolution have led to systematic neglect of traditional systems (figure 5.8). Since the 1980s the number of tanks, ponds and other surface water bodies has fallen by almost a third, significantly reducing local groundwater recharge capacities—a major concern given the uptake of tubewell technology.[51]

As the groundwater crisis has deepened, state and national government bodies are revising priorities and seeking a new balance. In Gujarat, one of the epicentres of the groundwater crisis, the state government has supported community initiatives to create more than

10,000 check dams (small dams that impound excess water during monsoons and help force the water into the ground) to support irrigation and recharge groundwater. More than 40% of the investment has come from local communities in labour, material and finance. Within three years, every $1 invested has generated $1.50. Village research in Maharashtra suggests the potential for even higher economic returns over the longer term.[52]

Extending check dams across all of India's rainfed farming areas would raise the value of the monsoon crop from $36 billion a year to $180 billion, for an initial investment of $7 billion. Of course, this is a cost-benefit estimate that provides no insight into the huge governance challenges that such a programme might entail. But given the very high poverty rate in rainfed areas, it is difficult to envisage another investment with more potential to enhance human development and extend the benefits of India's economic success into rural areas.[53]

Comparisons of the relative efficiency of large- and small-scale water harvesting systems are difficult—and usually unhelpful. The two activities are complementary and should not be seen as substitutes. However, the efficiency claims offered in favour of large-scale infrastructure are sometimes overstated. Intercepting and collecting rainfall where it falls, rather than transporting it through irrigation channels, increases green water moisture in the soil, helps to replenish groundwater and provides a reserve for people to draw on as supplemental irrigation during dry periods. While some small water harvesting structures carry high unit costs relative to large reservoirs, they also offer potential efficiency gains. Recent studies in India, Arizona in the United States and the Negev Desert in Israel show that small dams retain more water per hectare than large reservoirs.[54]

Water harvesting does not make large dams obsolete. In India large-scale infrastructure has 10 times the storage capacity of small tanks—and small reservoirs depend on highly variable rainfall in their own catchments.[55] As chapter 4 argued, the large versus small debate

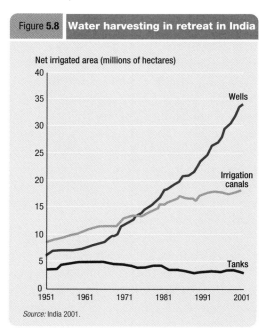

Figure 5.8   Water harvesting in retreat in India

Net irrigated area (millions of hectares)

Wells

Irrigation canals

Tanks

1951   1961   1971   1981   1991   2001

Source: India 2001.

is fast becoming anachronistic. Even so, small systems maximize the productivity of locally available water and help with groundwater recharge. They begin to address problems locally, relieving the pressure on large, central systems.

Small-scale irrigation

Raising productivity on large irrigation systems by improving maintenance and empowering water users is one response to the emerging water use scenarios outlined earlier. Expansion of the irrigation frontier through micro-level irrigation investments is also important, especially in rainfed areas.

Consider the case of Ethiopia, a water-abundant country. At the head of the Nile it covers 12 river basins and has a per capita water availability of 1,644 cubic metres—a relatively large volume. But because of large spatial and temporal variations in rainfall, farmers can produce only one crop a year. Frequent dry spells and droughts give rise to high vulnerability and poverty, with the well-being of rural populations tied to rainfall. The main problem is predictability rather than availability.

Irrigation offers a way to reduce the risk and vulnerability associated with unpredictability. Up to 2.7 million hectares of land in Ethiopia have irrigation potential, but fewer than 300,000 hectares are developed.[56] Meanwhile, the country has one of the lowest rates of artificial reservoir storage capacity in the world, less than 50 cubic metres per capita in total. Irrigation development could address the problem, but finance is a major constraint. Limited infrastructure means that Ethiopia, like most countries in Sub-Saharan Africa, faces far higher costs per hectare in large-scale irrigation schemes than does South Asia. But research by the International Water Management Institute has demonstrated the potential for expanding small-scale irrigation. Combined with low-cost drip irrigation technologies, it is estimated that with small-scale irrigation infrastructure Ethiopia could double yields over the next 10–15 years at per hectare and per capita costs lower than those required for formal irrigation investments.[57]

Low-technology solutions with high human development returns

As water scarcity constraints have tightened, industry has responded with new technologies. From Southern California to Israel and to the Murray-Darling Basin in Australia commercial producers have been pursuing more crop per drop through sophisticated, often computerized, drip irrigation systems that deliver optimal amounts of water to crops at the optimal time. Today, innovation is creating conditions in which smaller, poorer farmers can join the technological revolution in water management. Seizing the opportunity that this creates for human development will require public policies to overcome poverty-related obstacles.

Micro-level irrigation is at the cutting edge of emerging water management technologies. It has enormous potential. Drip technologies use less water than surface irrigation, deliver it directly to the crop and reduce salinization and water-logging. Unequal distribution of these technologies explains some of the marked differences in water-output rates worldwide. In France sprinklers and drips are used on 90% of irrigated area, compared with 1%–3% in China and India.[58]

Until recently, micro-irrigation technology markets were geared towards large capital-intensive producers. That picture has changed, with technologies becoming cheaper and more widely available. Drip irrigation technologies accessible to poor farmers have taken different forms. Cheap, small-scale bucket-and-drip kits have been developed for vegetable cultivation on household plots. An international nongovernmental organization, International Development Enterprises, has played a catalytic role in breaking down cost barriers to access. One model uses off-the-shelf cloth filters and plastic containers to replace sensitive metallic emitters, reducing the costs of irrigation to $250 a hectare. Field results in Andhra Pradesh, in India, and Nepal show that the area under cultivation has doubled with the same amount of water.[59]

Research by the International Water Management Institute in Kenya and Nepal points to higher productivity, with every $1 invested

5

Water competition in agriculture

generating $2 after subtracting all other costs except labour. In India low-cost micro-irrigation kits—known as Pepsee kits—have been developed and extensively taken up by farmers in semi-arid areas of Madhya Pradesh and Maharashtra, raising yields and increasing the area under cultivation. Studies show that drip techniques cut water use by 30%–60% and boost yields by 5%–50%.[60] Farmers in Burkina Faso, Kenya and Sudan claim three-fold to fourfold yield increases using drip irrigation and hand-watering from water-harvesting tanks.[61]

Another innovation is the treadle pump. This cheap and affordable technology ($12–$30) draws water from groundwater sources close to the surface to irrigate up to 0.5 hect-ares. It has been widely adopted in Bangladesh and eastern India, where groundwater tables are very high. More than 1 million pumps are now being used in Asia, and adopted pump technologies are spreading rapidly across Sub-Saharan Africa.[62] Production costs in Sub-Saharan Africa, at $50–$150 per unit, are still higher than in South Asia, but with documented annual returns to investment of 130%–850% when combined with market-oriented production, their potential for poverty alleviation is great.[63]

Combining micro-irrigation and new technology has the potential to distribute the benefits of irrigation far more widely. It also holds out the promise of facilitating the entry of small farmers into higher value-added markets, both domestic and export. Realizing this promise will require public investment to support the spread of new irrigation technologies and—more important—build marketing infrastructure in more marginal areas. But many countries will first need to review current approaches to agricultural growth. While many governments extol the virtues of small-holder farming, most concentrate scarce public investment on relatively large-scale, capital-intensive commercial farming areas. That approach may be bad for long-run growth and for poverty reduction.

The untapped potential for scaling up is considerable. Micro-irrigation may be expanding rapidly, but it still covers only about 1% of the world's irrigated area. While outcomes vary with location and technology, on-farm water productivity generally doubles with drip irrigation. Working on observed returns to current investment, it has been estimated that the adoption of new technologies by 100 million smallholder farmers could generate net benefits of $100 billion or more.[64] This is one-quarter higher than current aid. Perhaps more important, the returns would be captured directly by communities with a high concentration of poverty. Including the multiplier effects of increased demand, investment and employment, total net benefits could rise threefold, increasing annual incomes by up to $500 for those living on less than $1 a day.[65]

So why are investments in micro-irrigation not taking place on a larger scale? Demand and supply factors come into play. In Jordan volumetric water metering helped to expand drip irrigation rapidly. Farmers were given a strong market incentive to adopt the new technology. But irrigation systems in Jordan are dominated by large producers growing high value-added crops. Extending volumetric metering to hundreds of millions of small-scale farmers in Asia using groundwater and surface irrigation, many of them producing low value-added crops for home consumption, would pose formidable difficulties.

Incentives for developing and disbursing new technologies have been inadequately developed. Responsive market-based supply systems present the most efficient source of outreach to smallholder producers. But governments could do far more to promote research, support social marketing and develop the extension systems that could help markets reach poor people. Rethinking subsidies would help. Instead of providing incentives for groundwater mining through electricity subsidies, governments could offer targeted support for water conservation through micro-irrigation. This is what has happened under the National Water Conservation Programme in Tunisia, where producers can apply for grants structured to reflect farm size and the type of technology adopted.[66]

The way ahead

Governments should look beyond the scarcity equation to wider human development issues, giving equity and empowerment more prominence

As concern over global water supply and food availability increases, governments should look beyond the scarcity equation to wider human development issues. Giving equity and empowerment more prominence in the governance framework is a starting point.

There are three main requirements for addressing the challenge. The first is to prepare a transparent national strategy setting out how water resources will be allocated in the years ahead, to provide predictability. The second is to integrate that framework into national poverty reduction planning exercises, such as the Poverty Reduction Strategy Paper, to ensure that water policy is aligned with wider human development goals. The third is to recognize the rights to water of poor households with customary entitlements and to enforce rights provision by creating institutions that empower the poor. Protecting and extending the water rights of women farmers should be a central priority in all countries.

Irrigation poses special challenges. Devolution with empowerment provides the framework for reform. Recognizing the rights of women in irrigation systems and promoting meaningful female participation in management are vital for translating the rhetoric of empowerment into practical outcomes. At the same time, financing has to be placed on a footing that facilitates, rather than hinders, mutually reinforcing equity and efficiency gains. Sustainable and equitable cost-recovery to finance the operation and maintenance of irrigation systems is important. This has to start with transparent decisions on what costs should be recovered from whom, taking into account the ability to pay. Applying tiered block systems of payment, with low rates for a basic quantity and higher rates linked to volume of use or area is one option. As the International Commission on Irrigation and Drainage has argued, the key principles for cost-recovery are really the same as the principles for irrigation management: transparency, empowerment, sustainability and economic incentives for good practice.

Institutional and legal reforms to empower rural water users are a first step. The initial challenge is to develop legal systems that clarify and strengthen existing rights rather than to introduce sweeping tradable private property rights. This would provide a basis for the development of equitable transfer mechanisms. Such mechanisms, used voluntarily and with provisions for compensation, are better for enhancing water security than arbitrary administrative transfers or imperfect markets. Recognizing customary rights by empowering local institutions is also part of the process. But customary law should not override recourse to formal legal processes to defend such principles as gender equity and nondiscrimination.

Current approaches to irrigation development often neglect opportunities to enhance water security through mutually reinforcing reforms towards efficiency and equity. Putting in place efficient systems of cost-recovery linked to the benefits from irrigation systems would help to rationalize use and to finance maintenance.

Almost all countries recognize the public goods element in irrigation provision. That is why construction and capital costs are heavily subsidized. But these subsidies create a responsibility to ensure that the benefits are spread as widely as possible. In far too many cases this does not happen. For countries where unequal land ownership compromises the efficiency and equity benefits of irrigation, mechanisms for redistribution have to be part of the reform strategy. More widely, irrigation rules can require equitable water shares for the poor and equitable pricing. Policies targeted to the poor can help, such as allocating water on preferential terms at the tail end of irrigation systems, where poverty prevalence is high.

Pro-poor policies will not produce optimal outcomes where poor people are disempowered. Devolving authority and financial capacity to

5

Water competition in agriculture

water user associations can change the power balance between users and government agencies, creating more responsive and more accountable governance structures. But empowering poor people and women within water user associations is more challenging. Affirmative action can help. So can the clarification of water use rights and entitlements. Ultimately, however, empowerment requires challenging the norms and power structures that entrench disadvantage based on gender and wealth. Explicitly targeting female farmers in water development and giving women a voice in management is essential for the social and economic success of irrigation programmes.

Public spending on irrigation and water management in many countries has fallen below levels needed to maintain infrastructure. Current national spending on irrigation financing is estimated at $30–$35 billion but is on a steep downward trend.[67] The same trend applies to development assistance. Although international statistics are unreliable, lending for irrigation and drainage by multilateral agencies fell from about $3 billion annually in the mid-1980s to about $2 billion in the mid-1990s, with no recovery since then.[68] In view of the growing pressure on water systems and the threats of global climate change, it is important to reverse this trend. Private finance and public spending by governments will have to provide the primary impetus. But aid also has a role. The World Bank estimates that donor support over the next 20 years will need to double, to around $4 billion annually.[69]

Sub-Saharan Africa should be a priority for donor support. As part of a wider set of measures to support agriculture and rural development, the Commission for Africa has proposed that Africa double the area under irrigation by 2010, with emphasis on small-scale provision. This would cost about $2 billion a year, with donors covering half the costs.[70]

As governments develop water management strategies for dealing with scarcity, it is important that pro-poor technologies and other interventions figure prominently. In technology the focus for governments should not be on production but on social marketing, support for microfinance and public investments in infrastructure needed to support uptake. Micro-irrigation technology and strategies for developing markets should be an integral part of all rural development and national poverty reduction strategies.

The time to abandon the age-old dichotomy between large-scale and small-scale approaches is long overdue. In South Asia and parts of East Asia small-scale water harvesting is a vital part of the response to local groundwater crises. More widely, scaled-up programmes in this area have the potential to improve water security by increasing availability and by bringing water closer to people. Small-scale water harvesting should be a central part of water management from the local to the national level—and an element in wider efforts to empower the poor.

6 **Managing transboundary waters**

"War over water would be an ultimate obscenity"

Queen Noor of Jordan

"Whisky is for drinking, water is for fighting over"

Mark Twain

6 Managing transboundary waters

Managing shared water can be a force for peace or for conflict, but it is politics that will decide which course is chosen

For any country water is at the core of human interdependence—a shared resource that serves agriculture, industry, households and the environment. National water governance is about striking a balance among these competing users. But water is also the ultimate fugitive resource. Countries may legislate for water as a national asset, but the resource itself crosses political boundaries without a passport in the form of rivers, lakes and aquifers. Transboundary waters extend hydrological interdependence across national frontiers, linking users in different countries within a shared system. Managing that interdependence is one of the great human development challenges facing the international community.

The challenge is partly institutional. Competition for water within a country can create conflicting demands, confronting policy-makers with choices that have ramifications for equity, human development and poverty reduction. National institutions and legislative bodies provide mechanisms for addressing these choices. For water that flows across borders, there is no equivalent institutional structure. This has implications. As water becomes scarce relative to demand, transboundary competition for shared rivers and other water resources will grow. Without institutional mechanisms to respond to these transboundary problems, competition has the potential to lead to disruptive conflicts.

The spectre of growing competition for water between states has generated a sometimes polarized public debate. Some predict a future of "water wars" as states assert rival claims to water. Others point out that there have been no wars over water since an event some 4,000 years ago in what is now southern Iraq—and that countries have usually responded to transboundary water competition through cooperation rather than conflict. From this more optimistic perspective, rising competition is seen as a catalyst for deeper cooperation in the future.

This Report argues that water has the potential to fuel wider conflicts but also to act as a bridge for cooperation. Throughout history governments have found innovative and cooperative solutions to transboundary water management tensions, even in the most difficult political environments. From the Indus to the Jordan and the Mekong Rivers states in political and even military conflict have found ways of maintaining cooperation over water. When states go to war it is usually over something far less important than water. But complacency is not the appropriate antidote to water war pessimism. Cross-border waters almost always create some tension between the societies they bind. These tensions cannot be considered in isolation. They are tied up in wider factors than relations between states, including concerns over national security, economic opportunity, environmental sustainability and fairness. Managing shared water can be a force for peace or for conflict, but it is politics that will decide which course is chosen.

One problem with the polarized debate generated by water war rhetoric is that it has diverted attention from more pressing and more relevant human security concerns. Cooperative approaches to transboundary water management can yield real gains for human development. They can strengthen water security for vulnerable people on both sides of a border, enhancing the quality, quantity and predictability of flows across countries. Water sharing is not a zero sum game: one country's gain is not another's loss. Just as interdependence through trade can expand the economic benefits for all, so can cooperative interdependence in water. That is true not just in the economic sphere, where trade in hydropower or environmental services offers a potential win-win strategy—but also in wider political, social and environmental policy.

The opposite is also true. Where cooperation fails to develop or breaks down, all countries stand to lose—and the poor stand to lose the most. Failures in cooperation can cause social and ecological disasters, as in Lake Chad and the Aral Sea. They also expose smaller, vulnerable countries to the threat of unilateral actions by larger, more powerful neighbours. Above all, the absence of cooperation makes it impossible for countries to manage shared water resources to optimize conditions for human progress.

Two overarching challenges define transboundary water governance strategies at the start of the 21st century. The first is to move beyond inward-looking national strategies and unilateral action to shared strategies for multilateral cooperation. To some degree, this is already happening, but the governance response has been fragmented and inadequate. The second is to put human development at the centre of transboundary cooperation and governance.

This chapter looks first at what hydrological interdependence means in the lives of nations and people. It then considers the ecological, economic and wider human costs of failure to cooperate in transboundary water management and looks at the corollary of these costs: the case for cooperation.

Hydrological interdependence

Water is unlike other scarce resources in important respects. It underpins all aspects of human society, from ecology to agriculture to industry—and it has no known substitutes. Like air, it is fundamental to life. It is also an integral part of the production systems that generate wealth and well-being. Because water is a flowing resource rather than a static entity, its use in any one place is affected by its use in other places, including other countries. Unlike oil or coal, water can never be managed for a single purpose—or in the case of transboundary water, for a single country.

The way any one country uses water transmits effects to other countries, usually through one of three mechanisms:

- *Competition for a finite supply of water.* When countries rely on the same source of water to support their environments, sustain livelihoods and generate growth, transboundary water becomes a link between their citizens and their environments. Use in one place restricts availability in another. For example, the retention of water upstream for irrigation or power generation in one country restricts flows downstream for farmers and the environment.
- *Impacts on water quality.* The way an upstream country uses water affects the environment and the quality of water that arrives in a downstream country.

Uncoordinated dam development can cause silting in reservoirs, preventing the rich sediment from reaching low-lying plains. Similarly, industrial or human pollution can be transported through rivers to people in other countries. In November 2005, when an industrial accident caused an 80-kilometre-long chemical slick in China's Songhua River, it threatened not only the 3 million citizens of Harbin but also the residents of the Russian city of Khabarovsk across the border.

- *Timing of water flows*. When and how much water is released by upstream users has crucial implications downstream. For example, agricultural users in a downstream country may need water for irrigation at the same time as an upstream country needs it for hydropower generation—a common problem today in Central Asia (see below).

Just as tensions in each of these areas can generate competition and conflict within countries (see chapter 5), so interdependence transmits consequences of different patterns of water use across borders.

Sharing the world's water

Shared water is an increasingly important part of human geography and the political landscape. International rivers, lakes, aquifers and wetlands bind people separated by international borders, some of which follow the course of waterways. This shared water is what supports the hydrological interdependence of millions of people.

International water basins—catchments or watersheds, including lakes and shallow groundwater, shared by more than one country—cover almost half of Earth's land surface. Two in every five people in the world today live in these basins, which also account for 60% of global river flows. The number of shared basins has been growing, largely because of the breakup of the former Soviet Union and former Yugoslavia. In 1978 there were 214 international basins. Today there are 263.

The depth of interdependence implied by these figures is revealed by the number of countries in shared basins—145, accounting for more than 90% of the world's population.[1] More than 30 countries are located entirely within transboundary basins.

The depth of interdependence is illustrated by the number of countries that share some international basins (table 6.1). For example, 14 countries share the Danube (another 5 have marginal shares), 11 the Nile and the Niger and 9 the Amazon. No region better demonstrates the realities of hydrological interdependence than Africa. The political maps drawn up at conferences in Berlin, Lisbon, London and Paris more than a century ago have left more than 90% of all surface water in the region in transboundary river basins, which harbour more than three-quarters of its people.[2] Some 61 basins cover about two-thirds of the land area (map 6.1).

Governments can choose whether or not to cooperate in managing transboundary waters. Whatever the decision, rivers and other transboundary water systems bind countries into environmental resource-sharing arrangements that shape livelihood opportunities.

Upstream use determines downstream options in water management, setting the stage for dispute or cooperation. Nowhere is this more apparent than in irrigation. Among countries with highly developed irrigation systems, Egypt, Iraq, Syria, Turkmenistan and Uzbekistan depend on rivers flowing from their neighbours for two-thirds or more of their water. Changed water use patterns in upstream countries can seriously affect agricultural systems and rural livelihoods downstream. The Tigris-Euphrates Basin, to take one illustration, serves Iraq, Syria and Turkey, with a combined population of 103 million. Turkey's Southeast Anatolia Project, which encompasses the creation of 21 dams and 1.7 million hectares of irrigated land, could reduce flows in Syria by about a third, creating winners and losers within the basin area.[3]

In any country allocating water among users is a politically challenging task. Adding national borders to the equation complicates

International rivers, lakes, aquifers and wetlands bind people separated by international borders

Table **6.1**	International basins link many countries	
River basin	Number of basin countries	Basin countries
Danube	19	Albania, Austria, Bosnia and Herzegovina, Bulgaria, Croatia, Czech Republic, Germany, Hungary, Italy, Macedonia, Moldova, Montenegro, Poland, Romania, Serbia, Slovakia, Slovenia, Switzerland, Ukraine
Congo	13	Angola, Burundi, Cameroon, Central African Republic, Congo, Democratic Republic of the Congo, Gabon, Malawi, Rwanda, Sudan, Tanzania, Uganda, Zambia
Nile	11	Burundi, Central African Republic, Democratic Republic of the Congo, Egypt, Eritrea, Ethiopia, Kenya, Rwanda, Sudan, Tanzania, Uganda
Niger	11	Algeria, Benin, Burkina Faso, Cameroon, Chad, Côte d'Ivoire, Guinea, Mali, Niger, Nigeria, Sierra Leone
Amazon	9	Bolivia, Brazil, Colombia, Ecuador, Guyana, Peru, Suriname, Venezuela and French Guiana
Rhine	9	Austria, Belgium, France, Germany, Italy, Liechtenstein, Luxembourg, Netherlands, Switzerland
Zambezi	9	Angola, Botswana, Democratic Republic of the Congo, Malawi, Mozambique, Namibia, Tanzania, Zambia, Zimbabwe
Lake Chad	8	Algeria, Cameroon, Central Africa Republic, Chad, Libya, Niger, Nigeria, Sudan
Aral Sea	8	Afghanistan, China, Kazakhstan, Kyrgyzstan, Pakistan, Tajikistan, Turkmenistan, Uzbekistan
Jordan	6	Egypt, Israel, Jordan, Lebanon, Occupied Palestinian Territories, Syria
Mekong	6	Cambodia, China, Lao People's Democratic Republic, Myanmar, Thailand, Viet Nam
Volta	6	Benin, Burkina Faso, Côte d'Ivoire, Ghana, Mali, Togo
Ganges-Brahmaputra-Meghna	6	Bangladesh, Bhutan, China, India, Myanmar, Nepal
Tigris-Euphrates	6	Iran, Iraq, Jordan, Saudi Arabia, Syria, Turkey
Tarim	5 (+1)	Afghanistan, China, Chinese control claimed by India, Kyrgyzstan, Pakistan, Tajikistan
Indus	5	Afghanistan, China, India, Nepal, Pakistan
Neman	5	Belarus, Latvia, Lithuania, Poland, Russia
Vistula	5	Belarus, Czech Republic, Poland, Slovakia, Ukraine
La Plata	5	Argentina, Bolivia, Brazil, Paraguay, Uruguay

Source: Adapted from Wolf and others 1999.

governance, especially when competition for water is intensifying. In theory the optimal approach is to manage water in an integrated way across the whole basin, with countries trading agricultural resources, hydropower and other services according to their comparative advantage in water use. To take an obvious example, hydropower is more cost-effective in sloping mountainous upper reaches, while irrigation produces better results in valleys and plains: trading hydropower for agricultural goods is one way of tapping into this comparative advantage. In practice most river basins lack institutions for resolving differences and coordinating resource sharing, and factors such as trust and strategic concerns weigh heavily in government policy.

Basin-sharing gives only a partial picture of hydrological interdependence. Countries vary in their dependence on shared systems. In some cases states that represent a small part of a basin in geographic terms are highly dependent in hydrological terms, while the opposite is also true. For example, Bangladesh accounts for only 6% of the Ganges-Brahmaputra-Meghna Basin, yet the basin occupies three-quarters of the country.[4] And while one-fifth of the Mekong Basin lies in China, the basin represents less than 2% of China's territory. Farther downstream, more than four-fifths of Lao People's Democratic Republic and nearly 90% of Cambodia are within the basin.

Following the river

Most people are unaware of the human consequences of the hydrological interdependence that binds countries. Yet this is part of a reality that shapes lives and opportunities.

The Nile is one example of this reality. Some 150 million people live in the Nile Basin—a water system that links the 96% of Egyptians who live in the Nile Valley and Delta with

Map **6.1** | **Africa's rivers and lake basins cross many borders**

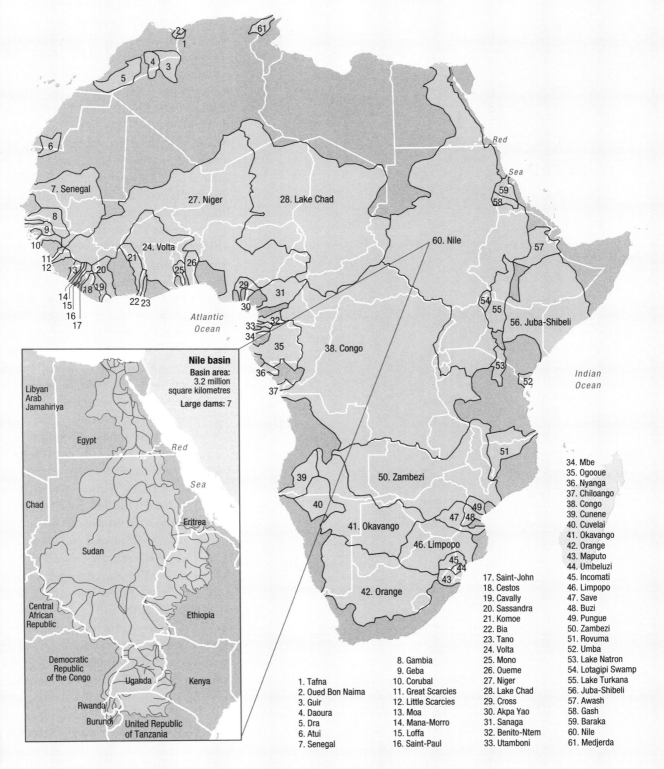

Nile basin

Basin area:
3.2 million
square kilometres

Large dams: 7

Atlantic
Ocean

Indian
Ocean

Red

Sea

1. Tafna
2. Oued Bon Naima
3. Guir
4. Daoura
5. Dra
6. Atui
7. Senegal

8. Gambia
9. Geba
10. Corubal
11. Great Scarcies
12. Little Scarcies
13. Moa
14. Mana-Morro
15. Loffa
16. Saint-Paul

17. Saint-John
18. Cestos
19. Cavally
20. Sassandra
21. Komoe
22. Bia
23. Tano
24. Volta
25. Mono
26. Oueme
27. Niger
28. Lake Chad
29. Cross
30. Akpa Yao
31. Sanaga
32. Benito-Ntem
33. Utamboni

34. Mbe
35. Ogooue
36. Nyanga
37. Chiloango
38. Congo
39. Cunene
40. Cuvelai
41. Okavango
42. Orange
43. Maputo
44. Umbeluzi
45. Incomati
46. Limpopo
47. Save
48. Buzi
49. Pungue
50. Zambezi
51. Rovuma
52. Umba
53. Lake Natron
54. Lotagipi Swamp
55. Lake Turkana
56. Juba-Shibeli
57. Awash
58. Gash
59. Baraka
60. Nile
61. Medjerda

Note: The boundaries and names shown and the designations used on this map do not imply official endorsement or acceptance by the United Nations.

Source: Wolf and others 1999; Revenga and others 1998; Rekacewicz 2006; Jägerskog and Phillips 2006.

6

Managing transboundary waters

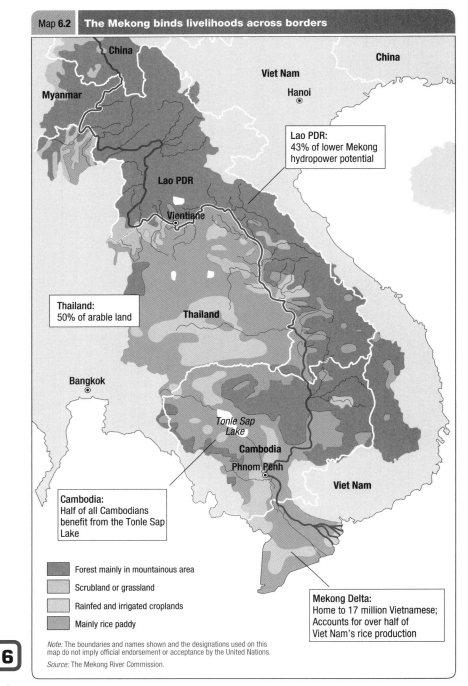

Map 6.2   The Mekong binds livelihoods across borders

China

Viet Nam

China

Myanmar

Hanoi ⊙

Lao PDR:
43% of lower Mekong
hydropower potential

Lao PDR

Vientiane ⊙

Thailand:
50% of arable land

Thailand

Bangkok ⊙

Tonle Sap
Lake

Cambodia

Phnom Penh ⊙

Viet Nam

Cambodia:
Half of all Cambodians
benefit from the Tonle Sap
Lake

☐ Forest mainly in mountainous area
☐ Scrubland or grassland
☐ Rainfed and irrigated croplands
☐ Mainly rice paddy

Mekong Delta:
Home to 17 million Vietnamese;
Accounts for over half of
Viet Nam's rice production

Note: The boundaries and names shown and the designations used on this map do not imply official endorsement or acceptance by the United Nations.

Source: The Mekong River Commission.

Perhaps the easiest way to understand what hydrological interdependence means at a human level is to follow the course of a river. Consider the Mekong, one of the world's major water systems (map 6.2). From its source on the Tibetan Plateau it drops 5,000 metres and flows across six countries before reaching its delta. More than a third of the population of Cambodia, Lao PDR, Thailand and Viet Nam—some 60 million people—live in the Lower Mekong Basin,[6] using the river for drinking water, food, irrigation, hydropower, transportation and commerce. Millions more in China and Myanmar and beyond the boundaries of the basin benefit from the river.

In the plains the river basin accounts for half the arable land in Thailand. Further downstream in Cambodia the Tonle Sap Lake, one of the world's largest freshwater fisheries, is replenished by the Mekong. Nearly half of Cambodia's people benefit directly or indirectly from the lake's resources.[7] As the river approaches the sea, the Mekong Delta yields more than half of Viet Nam's rice production and a third of its GDP.[8] Some 17 million people live in the Mekong Delta in Viet Nam. Beyond these human connections the river also powerfully demonstrates the scope for shared interest—and competition.

Rivers are just one of the webs of water interdependence. In many countries shared lakes are crucial for water security—and livelihoods. An estimated 30 million people depend on Lake Victoria—one-third of the combined population of Kenya, Tanzania and Uganda.[9] Another 37 million live in the Lake Chad Basin.[10] Although Lake Victoria is the world's most productive freshwater fishery and Lake Chad yields three-quarters of the fish in the entire region, poverty rates among these populations are exceptionally high.[11] It follows that lake management has important implications for poverty reduction efforts. The same holds true for the Lake Titicaca Basin in Latin America. More than 2 million people live in the basin which spans Bolivia and Peru. Poverty levels there are estimated at more the 70%. Two Bolivian cities in the basin—El Alto and Oruro, with a quarter of the country's population—depend on the lake for their water needs.[12]

people living on the Ethiopian highlands and in northern Uganda, among other countires.[5] Water and silt, mainly from Ethiopia, have made a long ribbon of desert habitable and have sustained the Nile Delta. In a similar way the Jordan River links the people, livelihoods and ecosystems of Israel, Jordan and the Occupied Palestinian Territories through a common water source.

Lakes pose specific challenges for cooperation. They are less renewable than rivers, adding to competitive pressures. As "closed" but interdependent ecosystems they are even more sensitive to pollution and water withdrawals than rivers, with implications for the transmission of poor water quality. Other difficulties arise from classification disputes. The five states that share the Caspian cannot agree whether it is a sea or a lake. This legal dispute has implications for the management of the shared resource because of the different rules that apply.

Unlike rivers and lakes, aquifers are invisible. They are also the repositories for more than 90% of the world's fresh water—and like rivers and lakes they span borders.[13] Europe alone has more than 100 transboundary aquifers. South America's Guaraní aquifer is shared by Argentina, Brazil, Paraguay and Uruguay. Highly water-stressed Chad, Egypt, Libya and Sudan share the Nubian Sandstone aquifer. The Great Man-Made River, a system of two major pipelines buried under the sands of the Sahara, transfers water from this fossil aquifer to the Libyan coast to irrigate fields around Benghazi and Tripoli. The Mountain Aquifer that traverses Israel and the Occupied Palestinian Territories is critical to the water security of both sets of users. It is the main source of water for irrigation on the West Bank and an important source of water for Israel.

Cooperation over groundwater confronts governments with some obvious challenges. Measurement problems make it difficult to monitor withdrawal rates for aquifers. Even when governments cooperate, groundwater can be exploited through private pumps, as witnessed by the rapid depletion of water tables in South Asia. The ecological footprint of unregulated extraction of groundwater has implications for people across national boundaries. Excessive extraction by individual users can lead to a "tragedy of the commons", the overexploitation of a common resource past the point of sustainability.

Within any country the overuse of groundwater by one set of users can undermine the resource base for all. Overextraction of groundwater in the Indian state of Gujarat, for example, has posed a twin threat to agricultural producers by reducing water availability and increasing soil salinity (see chapter 4). Similar problems can emerge across borders. As aquifers sink because of overextraction on one side of a border, the gradual intrusion of sea water and arsenic, nitrates and sulphates, if left unchecked, can make groundwater unusable in neighbouring countries. This is what has happened to large parts of the aquifer in the Gaza Strip, where pollution exacerbates already extreme problems of water scarcity.

Much of what is perceived as "national water" is in fact shared water

The costs of not cooperating

Why is transboundary water governance a human development issue? The answer to that question mirrors the answer to the same question applied at a national level. How any one country navigates through competing interests in the management of scarce water resources has profound implications for poverty, for the distribution of opportunity and for human development within its frontiers. Those implications are no less profound beyond the frontier.

Transmitting tensions down the river

Dependence on external flows is one obvious link between water and human development. Governments and most people think of the water that flows through their countries as a national resource. Legally and constitutionally, that may be accurate. But much of what is perceived as "national water" is in fact shared water.

6

Managing transboundary waters

Table **6.2**	Thirty-nine countries receive most of their water from outside their borders	
Region	**Countries receiving between 50% and 75% of their water from external sources**	**Countries receiving more than 75% of their water from external sources**
Arab States	Iraq, Somalia, Sudan, Syrian Arab Republic	Bahrain, Egypt, Kuwait
East Asia and the Pacific	Cambodia, Viet Nam	
Latin America and the Caribbean	Argentina, Bolivia, Paraguay, Uruguay	
South Asia		Bangladesh, Pakistan
Sub-Saharan Africa	Benin, Chad, Congo, Eritrea, Gambia, Mozambique, Namibia	Botswana, Mauritania, Niger
Central and Eastern Europe and CIS	Azerbaijan, Croatia, Latvia, Slovakia, Ukraine, Uzbekistan	Hungary, Moldova, Romania, Serbia and Montenegro[a], Turkmenistan
High-income OECD	Luxembourg	Netherlands
Others	Israel	

a. While Serbia and Montenegro separated into independent states in June 2006, disaggregated data on external water resources were not available for the two countries at the time of printing.
Source: FAO 2006.

For some 39 countries, with a population of 800 million people, at least half their water resources originate beyond their borders (table 6.2). Iraq and Syria rely for most of their water on the Tigris and Euphrates Rivers flowing out of Turkey. Bangladesh depends for 91% of its water on flows from India—to irrigate its crops and replenish its aquifers. The country's farmers and agricultural labourers living in the Ganges-Brahmaputra-Meghna Basin are the end users

Table **6.3**	Countries are withdrawing water faster than it is replenished	
Country	**Total water withdrawal as a share of total renewable water resources (%)**	**Total external water resources as a share of total renewable water resources (%)**
Kuwait	2,200	100
United Arab Emirates	1,553	0
Saudi Arabia	722	0
Libyan Arab Jamahiriya	711	0
Qatar	547	4
Bahrain	259	97
Yemen	162	0
Oman	138	0
Israel	123	55
Egypt	117	97
Uzbekistan	116	68
Jordan	115	23
Barbados	113	0
Malta	100	0
Turkmenistan	100	94

Source: FAO 2006.

of water that has traversed thousands of miles and the borders of five countries. Similarly, Egypt depends almost entirely on external water sources delivered through the Nile but originating in Ethiopia.

In all these cases even modest changes in water use upstream can profoundly affect all aspects of human development. Water priorities can look very different from different sides of the border. One-fifth of Turkey's irrigable land is in the eight southeastern provinces where the Tigris and Euphrates Rivers originate. Against this backdrop it is not difficult to appreciate the Southeast Anatolia Project's importance to Turkey. But one in five Syrians also live in the area surrounding the Euphrates, and the two rivers flow past Iraq's two most populous cities, Baghdad and Basra. Managing rival claims in a way that balances national interests with wider responsibilities requires a high order of political leadership.

Growing demands on shared rivers have clear spillover effects. When the Ili and Irtysh Rivers that flow from China to Kazakhstan shrink because of diversions to agriculture and industry in China, downstream Kazakhstan sees a threat to its national interests. That threat was partly addressed through an agreement on the Irtysh between the two countries signed in 2001. However, the agreement is weak and does not address the core problem of how to manage annual variations in water flow.

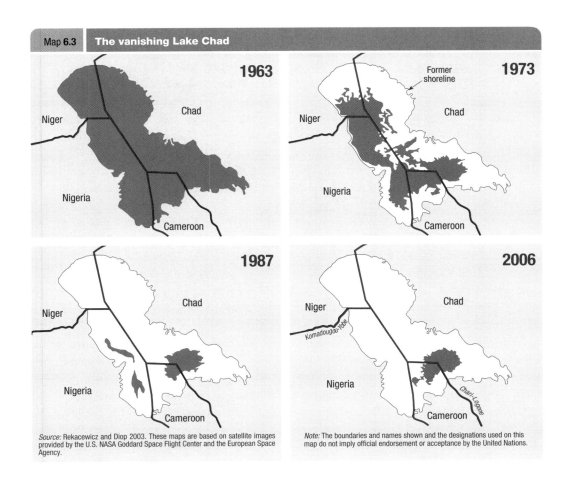

Map 6.3 The vanishing Lake Chad

1963

Niger — Chad — Nigeria — Cameroon

1973

Former shoreline

Niger — Chad — Nigeria — Cameroon

1987

Niger — Chad — Nigeria — Cameroon

2006

Niger — Komadougou-Yobe — Chad — Nigeria — Chari-Logone — Cameroon

Source: Rekacewicz and Diop 2003. These maps are based on satellite images provided by the U.S. NASA Goddard Space Flight Center and the European Space Agency.

Note: The boundaries and names shown and the designations used on this map do not imply official endorsement or acceptance by the United Nations.

Competition is not restricted to developing countries. As the Colorado and Rio Grande Rivers have shrivelled in their lower reaches through diversions for industry, agriculture and towns, Mexico receives almost none of their water. This has been a long-running source of tension in negotiations between Mexico and the United States.

Nowhere is the problem of transboundary water management as evident as in countries facing scarcity. Fifteen countries, most in the Middle East, annually consume more than 100% of their total renewable water resources. Groundwater and lake depletion cover the deficit, often placing pressure on transboundary water resources (table 6.3). Some of the most densely populated transboundary basins—in South Asia, parts of Central Asia and the Middle East—also encounter water stress. In these cases greater recourse to shared water to cover deficits can have major ramifications for human

development elsewhere—and for political relations between states.

Shrinking lakes, drying rivers

Mismanagement of international water basins threatens human security in some very direct ways. Shrinking lakes and drying rivers affect livelihoods in agriculture and fisheries, deteriorating water quality has harmful consequences for health, and unpredictable disruptions in water flows can exacerbate the effects of droughts and floods.

Some of the world's most visible environmental disasters bear testimony to the human development costs of noncooperation in transboundary water management. Lake Chad is one such case (map 6.3). Today the lake is one-tenth the size it was 40 years ago. Failed rains and drought have been major factors—but so has human agency.[14] Between 1966 and 1975, when the lake shrank by a third, low rainfall

6

Managing transboundary waters

Some of the world's most
visible environmental
disasters bear testimony
to the human development
costs of noncooperation
in transboundary
water management

was almost entirely to blame. But between 1983 and 1994 irrigation demands quadrupled, rapidly depleting an already shrinking resource and setting in train rapid losses of water.

Weak cooperation among the Lake Chad basin countries offers part of the explanation. Environmental decline and the erosion of livelihoods and productive potential have gone hand in hand. Overfishing is now institutionalized, with scant regard to rules meant to regulate use among Chad, Cameroon, Niger and Nigeria.[15] Badly planned irrigation projects have also contributed to the crisis. Dams on the Hadejia River in Nigeria have threatened downstream communities dependent on fishing, grazing and flood recession farming, and agreements to guarantee water flows have lagged in implementation.[16] The Komadougou-Yobe River system shared by Niger and Nigeria used to contribute 7 cubic kilometres to Lake Chad. Today, with water impounded in reservoirs, the system provides less than half a cubic kilometre, severely affecting the northern part of the lake basin.[17] Elsewhere, dykes built in the late 1970s on the Logone River in Cameroon disrupted small farmers' livelihoods in the downstream wetlands: within two decades cotton yields had fallen by a third and rice yields by three-fourths.[18]

The environmental consequences of unsustainable water use can eventually feed back to disrupt infrastructure investments. The Southern Chad Irrigation Project, an ambitious scheme started in 1974, barely accomplished a tenth of its target of irrigating 67,000 hectares in Nigeria. Over time, as water flows in the rivers declined, the drying canals became clogged with *typha australis* plants, the preferred nesting ground of the quelea, a bird that now destroys vast quantities of rice and other foodgrain crops. As the lake shrank competition intensified between nomadic herders and settled farmers, large-scale and small-scale users and upstream and downstream communities. Riparian communities have relocated closer to the water, crossing into areas formerly covered by the lake where national boundaries were unmarked, leading to further territorial disputes.

Dwarfing Lake Chad on the scale of human-caused environmental disasters is the Aral Sea. Half a century ago technological ingenuity, ideological zeal and political ambition persuaded Soviet planners that the Syr Darya and the Amu Darya, the great rivers of Central Asia, were being wasted. These rivers were carrying the snowmelt from high mountains into the closed basin of the Aral Sea, then the world's fourth largest lake. Diverting the water into production was seen as a route to greater wealth, with the loss of the Aral Sea a small price to pay. As one contemporary authority put it: "The drying up of the Aral Sea is far more advantageous than preserving it.... Cultivation of cotton alone will pay for the existing Aral Sea [and] the disappearance of the Sea will not affect the region's landscape."[19]

The diversion of water to support cotton through an inefficient irrigation system strangled the Aral Sea. By the 1990s it was receiving less than one-tenth of its previous flow—and sometimes no water at all. At the end of the decade it was some 15 metres below its 1960 level and had become two small, highly saline seas separated by a land bridge. The demise of the sea has been a social and environmental disaster (map 6.4).[20]

The independence of the Central Asian states has failed to stem the crisis. In fact, their noncooperation has sustained a steady deterioration in indicators of livelihoods, health and well-being. Cotton yields have fallen by a fifth since the early 1990s, but the overuse of water continues. The loss of four-fifths of all fish species has ruined the once vibrant fishing industry in downstream provinces.

The consequences for health have been just as bad. People in Qyzlorda in Kazakhstan, Dashhowuz in Turkmenistan and Karakalpakstan in Uzbekistan receive water contaminated with fertilizers and chemicals, unsuitable for human consumption or agriculture. Infant mortality rates have reached 100 per 1,000 live births in some regions—higher than the average for South Asia. Some 70% of the 1.1 million people in Karakalpakstan suffer from chronic maladies—respiratory illnesses, typhoid fever, hepatitis and oesophageal

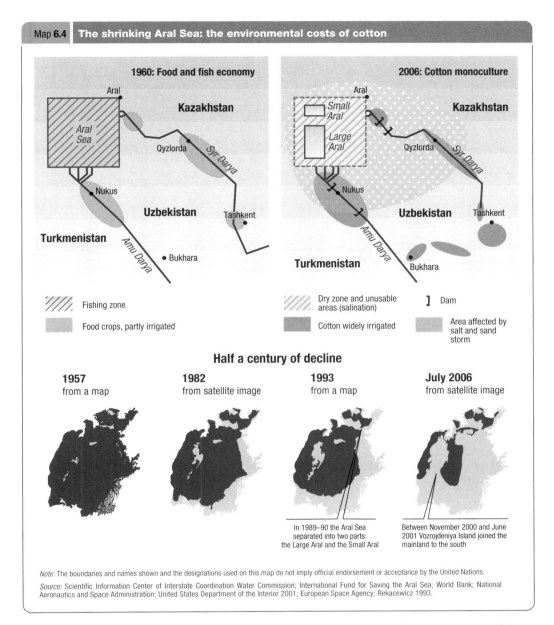

Map 6.4 The shrinking Aral Sea: the environmental costs of cotton

1960: Food and fish economy

Aral
Kazakhstan
Aral Sea
Qyzlorda
Syr Darya
Nukus
Uzbekistan
Tashkent
Turkmenistan
Amu Darya
• Bukhara

//// Fishing zone

▓ Food crops, partly irrigated

2006: Cotton monoculture

Aral
Small Aral
Large Aral
Kazakhstan
Qyzlorda
Syr Darya
Nukus
Uzbekistan
Tashkent
Turkmenistan
Amu Darya
Bukhara

//// Dry zone and unusable areas (salination)

▓ Cotton widely irrigated

] Dam

▓ Area affected by salt and sand storm

Half a century of decline

1957
from a map

1982
from satellite image

1993
from a map

July 2006
from satellite image

In 1989–90 the Aral Sea separated into two parts: the Large Aral and the Small Aral

Between November 2000 and June 2001 Vozrojdeniya Island joined the mainland to the south

Note: The boundaries and names shown and the designations used on this map do not imply official endorsement or acceptance by the United Nations.

Source: Scientific Information Center of Interstate Coordination Water Commission; International Fund for Saving the Aral Sea; World Bank; National Aeronautics and Space Administration; United States Department of the Interior 2001; European Space Agency; Rekacewicz 1993.

cancers. The Aral Sea is a stark reminder of how ecosystems can wreak revenge for human folly—rising wealth was a catalyst not for human progress but for a setback in regional human development.

But even here there is an embryonic good news story. Since 2001 in a joint project with the World Bank, Kazakhstan has built the Kok-Aral Dam and a series of dykes and canals to rehabilitate water levels in the northern (and eventually southern) parts of the Aral Sea. The project is already yielding benefits: the northern sea's area has expanded by a third, and water levels have risen from 98 feet to 125.[21] If progress continues, prospects for rehabilitating fishing communities and restoring sustainability are promising. If other basin countries also get involved, the scope for basinwide rehabilitation would increase greatly.

Lake Chad and the Aral Sea illustrate in an extreme way what happens when water flows are radically changed. In both cases water shortages have been a central part of the problem. However, water scarcity has been engineered—literally in the Aral Sea—through human intervention and diversion, highlighting the role of policies in fostering unsustainable water use patterns.

6

Managing transboundary waters

Box **6.1**   **Beyond the river—the costs of noncooperation in Central Asia**

Central Asian countries are locked in a web of hydrological interdependence. The Syr Darya and Amu Darya basins link Kazakhstan, Kyrgyzstan, Tajikistan and Uzbekistan in a water-energy nexus vital to their human development prospects—prospects severely undermined by weak cooperation.

That nexus can best be understood by following the flow of the rivers. The water in the Syr Darya's upper reaches flows rapidly down steep elevations. The huge Toktogul Reservoir in Kyrgyzstan was used in the 1970s to store water and even out flows of irrigation water between dry and wet seasons in Uzbekistan and southern Kazakhstan. In the Soviet era some three-quarters of the water would be released in the summer months and one-quarter in the winter. Electricity generated by releases in the summer months was also exported, with Kyrgyzstan receiving gas in exchange from Kazakhstan and Uzbekistan to help meet winter energy demands.

Since independence this structure of cooperation has broken down. After the liberalization of markets energy trade was put on a commercial footing, with Kyrgyz authorities having to pay world prices for fuel imports. The authorities began to increase winter releases from the Toktogul Reservoir to generate electricity, reducing the flow available for irrigation in Kazakhstan and Uzbekistan in the summer months. During the 1990s summer releases declined by half, leading to acute irrigation water shortages.

Negotiations for sharing water and energy began in 1992 but have achieved little. While downstream and upstream states acknowledge that upstream storage is an economic service and that a barter exchange of water for electricity and fossil fuels has to be developed, it has proven difficult to reach agreement on volumes and prices. In 2003 and 2004 governments were unable to agree even on minimal annual plans.

What has noncooperation meant for national policies? In Uzbekistan it has led to policies to increase self-reliance and reduce dependence on the Toktogul Reservoir. The construction of reservoirs capable of storing 2.5 billion cubic metres of water is part of the strategy. Kazakhstan has also developed a national response to

a regional problem and is exploring the option of building a 3 billion cubic metre reservoir at Koserai.

With abundant water Kyrgyzstan is pursuing self-sufficiency in energy. Authorities are exploring the construction of two new dams and hydropower plants that would generate enough electricity for national self-reliance plus a surplus for export, but the $2.3 billion price tag is 1.2 times the country's GNI. An alternative is to develop a lower cost thermal power plant to meet winter energy needs. A more economic option, it cuts against the grain of national policies for energy self-sufficiency. The plant would increase Kyrgyz dependence on natural gas supplies from Uzbekistan, which are periodically suspended unilaterally. Weak cooperation in this case is a barrier to enhanced efficiency through trade.

The inability to agree on cooperative solutions has created a "lose-lose" scenario for all parties. It has forced countries into suboptimal strategies for developing alternative infrastructure, with potentially large economic losses. The World Bank estimates that Uzbekistan would gain $36 million and Kazakhstan $31 million from operating the Toktogul Reservoir for irrigation instead of power. The incremental costs borne by Kyrgyzstan would amount to $35 million. The simple cost-benefit story is that the basin as a whole would gain $32 million from cooperation, with all countries gaining if the downstream states compensate Kyrgyzstan.

Elsewhere, Tajikistan has the potential to become the world's third largest producer of hydropower. But it is held back because lack of cooperation between countries makes international financial institutions reluctant to lend for hydropower projects.

So, if the drive for self-sufficiency is inflicting heavy economic costs across the basin, and if the economic benefits of cooperation are so substantial, what is holding back the Central Asian countries? In a word, politics. Effective transboundary water management requires constructive dialogue and negotiations to identify "win-win" scenarios and to develop the financing and wider cooperative strategies to achieve them. That dialogue has been conspicuously absent in the region.

Source: Greenberg 2006; Micklin 1991, 1992, 2000; Peachey 2004; UNDP 2005a; Weinthal 2002, 2006.

Like lakes, rivers are a source of life. But they can also export pollution to other countries. The dumping of effluents from metal and chemical plants in the Ili and Irtysh Rivers has made the waters almost unfit for human consumption in large parts of Kazakhstan. Similarly, problems have emerged in the Kura-Araks Basin, within the territories of Armenia, Azerbaijan and Georgia. The basin supports 6.2 million people in the densest concentration of municipal and industrial areas in the Trans-

Caucasus region. Underdeveloped legislation at a regional level, fragmented water monitoring and the lack of regional cooperation mechanisms—none of which can be resolved independently—make water pollution a severe problem for all three countries.[22]

Disaster can be a catalyst for cooperation. Ukraine occupies more than half the Dnieper Basin, which it shares with Belarus and Russia. Rapid industrialization has brought the third largest river in Europe under intense pressure:

less than a fifth of the water flow entering Ukraine now reaches the Black Sea. Pollution is endemic, with excessive use of fertilizers, unregulated waste dumping from uranium mining and wastewater all contributing. It was not until the Chernobyl disaster, which led to radioactive caesium deposits in reservoirs and increased risk of exposure to radioactivity all the way down to the Black Sea, that governments responded to the challenge of improving river quality.[23] In both the Dnieper and Kura-Araks Basins steps have been taken to promote cooperation, starting with environmental diagnoses and action programmes, but rehabilitating the rivers will take a long time.

The timing of water flows is another transboundary issue for human development. Secure livelihoods depend on a predictable supply of water. The use of water in one country can affect the timing of delivery for downstream users, even if the volume of water is unchanged. Upstream hydropower is an example. In Central Asia Kyrgyzstan can control the timing and availability of water downstream, while Uzbekistan and Kazakhstan depend on releases for irrigation. The breakdown of an old Soviet system for transferring gas from Kazakhstan and Uzbekistan led Kyrgyzstan to pursue self-sufficiency in winter electricity generation. To generate hydropower it now restricts the flow of water from the Toktogul Reservoir in the summer months but causes floods downstream in the winter—a central concern in regional water negotiations (box 6.1).

Transboundary water management can influence water availability in other ways. Israel, Jordan and the Occupied Palestinian Territories are located in one of the world's most water-scarce areas—and share a large proportion of their water. The Palestinian population relies almost totally on transboundary water, most of it shared with Israel (box 6.2). But the common resources are unequally shared. The Palestinian population is half the size of Israel's, but consumes only 10%–15% as much water. On the West Bank Israeli settlers consume an average of 620 cubic metres per person annually and Palestinians less than 100 cubic metres. Water shortages in the Occupied Palestinian Territories, a major constraint on agricultural development and livelihoods, are also a source of perceived injustice because current water use rules lock in unequal access to shared aquifers.

The starting point for any consideration of the scope for cooperation has to be a recognition that sovereign countries have obvious, rational and legitimate agendas for deriving maximum benefits from water

The case for cooperation

Shared water always has potential for competition. The English language reflects this: the word *rival* comes from the Latin *rivalis*, meaning one using the same river as another. Riparian countries are often rivals for the water they share. Considering the importance of water to national development, each country will have its own national agenda for using an international river. The starting point for any consideration of the scope for cooperation has to be a recognition that sovereign countries have obvious, rational and legitimate agendas for deriving maximum benefits from water.

The rules of the game

Within countries water use is governed through institutions, laws and norms developed through political processes of varying degrees of transparency. The institutions, laws and norms for governing water that crosses borders are less well defined.

One of the most important facets of transboundary water management is state sovereignty. In disputes over shared rivers with Mexico the United States adopted the Harmon Doctrine in 1895. An absolutist

Managing transboundary waters

Box **6.2** | **Water rights in the Occupied Palestinian Territories**

Nowhere are the problems of water governance as starkly demonstrated as in the Occupied Palestinian Territories. Palestinians experience one of the highest levels of water scarcity in the world. Physical availability and political governance of shared water both contribute to scarcity.

On a per capita basis people living in the Occupied Palestinian Territories have access to 320 cubic metres of water annually, one of the lowest levels of water availability in the world and well below the threshold for absolute scarcity. The unequal distribution of water from aquifers shared with Israel, a reflection of asymmetric power relations in water management, is part of the problem. With rapid population growth declining water availability is a tightening constraint on agriculture and human use.

Unequal sharing is reflected in very large discrepancies in water use between Israelis and Palestinians. The Israeli population is not quite twice the size of the Palestinian population, but its total water use is seven and a half times higher (figure 1). In the West Bank Israeli settlers use far more water per capita than Palestinians and more than Israelis in Israel (figure 2): nearly nine times as much water per person as Palestinians. By any standards, these are large disparities.

What explains the inequalities? Palestinians do not have established rights to the waters of the Jordan River—the main surface water source. This means that nearly all of the water needs in the Occupied Palestinian Territories are met by groundwater aquifers. The rules governing extraction from these aquifers have a major influence on access to water.

Management of the western and coastal aquifers demonstrates the problem. Part of the Jordan Basin, the western aquifer is the single most important source of renewable water for the Occupied Palestinian Territories. Nearly three-quarters of the aquifer is recharged within the West Bank and flows from the West Bank towards the coast of Israel. Much of this water is unused by the Palestinians. One reason: Israeli representatives on the Joint Water Committee stringently regulate the quantity and depth of wells operated by Palestinians. Less stringent rules are applied to Israeli settlers, enabling them to sink deeper wells. With only 13% of all wells in the West Bank settlers account for about 53% of groundwater extraction. Water not used in the Occupied Palestinian Territories eventually flows under Israeli territory and is extracted by wells on the Israeli side (see map).

There are similar problems with the waters of the Coastal Basin. These barely reach the Gaza Strip because of high rates of extraction on the Israeli side. The result: extraction rates from shallow aquifers within the Gaza Strip far exceed the recharge rates, leading to increasing salinization of water resources.

Limitations on access to water are holding back development of Palestinian agriculture. Although the sector represents a shrinking share of the Palestinian economy—estimated at roughly 15% for income and employment in 2002—it is nonetheless crucial to the livelihoods of some of the poorest people. Irrigation

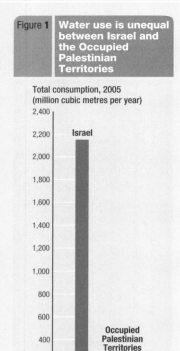

Figure 1 | Water use is unequal between Israel and the Occupied Palestinian Territories

Total consumption, 2005
(million cubic metres per year)

Source: Jägerskog and Phillips 2006.

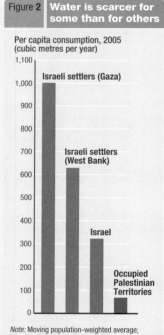

Figure 2 | Water is scarcer for some than for others

Per capita consumption, 2005
(cubic metres per year)

Note: Moving population-weighted average; Israeli settlements in the Gaza Strip were evacuated in August and September 2005.

Source: Jägerskog and Phillips 2006.

is currently underdeveloped, with less than a third of potential area covered because of the lack of water.

The underdevelopment of water resources means that many Palestinians depend on water deliveries from Israeli companies. This is a source of vulnerability and uncertainty because supplies are frequently interrupted during periods of tension.

The construction of the controversial Separation Wall threatens to exacerbate water insecurity. Construction of the wall has resulted in the loss of some Palestinian wells and the separation of farmers from their fields, especially in highly productive rainfed areas around the Bethlehem, Jenin, Nablus, Qalqilya, Ramallah and Tulkarem governorates.

Conditions in the Occupied Palestinian Territories stand in contrast to the more cooperative arrangements that have emerged elsewhere. Since the peace agreement of 1994 Israel and Jordan have collaborated to build water storage facilities in Lake Tiberias, which has improved water allocation for Jordanian farmers. The institutional structure has also helped in arbitrating disputes arising over seasonal and annual variations in water flow, even though this was not originally covered by the agreement. Elsewhere, the Middle East Desalinization Research Centre, based in Muscat, Oman, has been successfully promoting multilateral research into effective desalinization techniques for more than a decade. Its council has representatives from the European Commission, Israel, Japan, Jordan, the Republic of Korea, the Netherlands, the Palestinian National Authority and the United States.

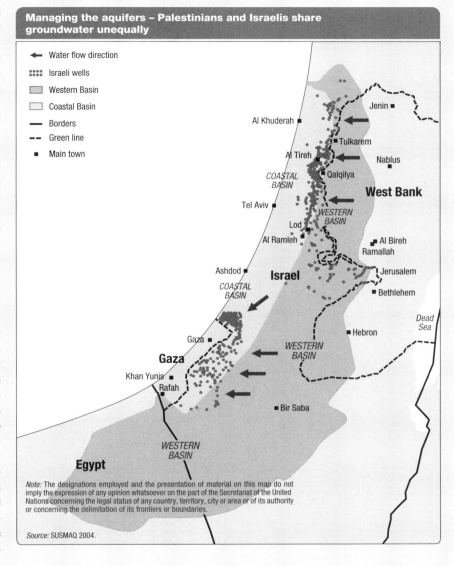

Managing the aquifers – Palestinians and Israelis share groundwater unequally

- ← Water flow direction
- ⠿ Israeli wells
- ▨ Western Basin
- ▢ Coastal Basin
- — Borders
- -- Green line
- ■ Main town

Note: The designations employed and the presentation of material on this map do not imply the expression of any opinion whatsoever on the part of the Secretariat of the United Nations concerning the legal status of any country, territory, city or area or of its authority or concerning the delimitation of its frontiers or boundaries.

Source: SUSMAQ 2004.

Perhaps more than in any other setting, water security in relations between Israel and the Occupied Palestinian Territories is bound up in wider problems of conflict and perceptions of national security. Yet water is also a powerful symbol of the wider system of hydrological interdependence that links all parties. Managing that interdependence to enhance equity could do much for human security.

Source: Elmusa 1996; Feitelson 2002; Jägerskog and Phillips 2006; MEDRC 2005; Nicol, Ariyabandu and Mtisi 2006; Phillips and others 2004; Rinat 2005; SUSMAQ 2004; SIWI, Tropp and Jägerskog 2006; Weinthal and others 2005.

sovereignty model, the Harmon Doctrine advocated that, in the absence of contrary legislation, states should be free to use the water resources in their jurisdiction without regard to effects beyond their borders. Variants of this approach survive in the national legislation of many countries. The 2001 Parliamentary Law in Kazakhstan declares that all water resources originating within its territory are its property.

The essentially competing principle of absolute territorial integrity suggests that downstream riparians have the right to receive the natural flow of a river from upstream riparians. Downstream states sometimes cite the allied principle of "prior appropriation", or the idea

One helpful framework
for thinking about
transboundary water
governance identifies four
layers of potential gains from
cooperation: benefits to the
river, benefits from the river,
benefits because of the river
and benefits beyond the river

that past use establishes a right to future use of the same amount of water, to contest absolute sovereignty approaches.[24]

In practice most governments accept that absolutist approaches to water rights are an unhelpful guide to policy design. After decades of consideration principles for sharing water were codified in the 1997 UN Convention for the Non-Navigational Use of Shared Watercourses, building on the 1966 Helsinki Rules. The core principles are "equitable and reasonable utilisation", "no significant harm" and "prior notification of works". The broad idea is that governance of international watercourses should be developed by taking into account the effects of use on other countries, the availability of alternative water sources, the size of the population affected, the social and economic needs of the watercourse states concerned, and the conservation, protection and development of the watercourse itself.

The application of these principles is fraught with difficulty, partly for the obvious reason that they do not provide tools for resolving competing claims. Upstream users can cite social and economic needs as grounds for constructing dams for hydropower, for example. Downstream states can oppose these measures, citing their own social and economic needs and existing use. The difficulty associated with competing principles and the concern over national sovereignty help explain why only 14 countries are party to the UN convention. Nor is there a practical enforcement mechanism—in 55 years the International Court of Justice has decided only one case on international rivers.

Yet for all its limitations the 1997 convention does set out principles central to human development. It provides a framework for putting people at the centre of transboundary water governance. Equally important is the 1992 UN Economic Commission for Europe Convention on Protection and Use of Transboundary Watercourses and International Lakes (ECPUTW). This convention focuses more on water quality, explicitly considering the river basin as a single ecological unit. The 1992 convention also emphasizes member states' responsibilities based on current water needs rather than historical water use—an important human development principle. The ECPUTW is already in force and has the potential to become global if 23 countries that are not members of the Economic Commission for Europe sign up: 4 have already done so. Yet for all the intuitive appeal of both conventions the political challenge is to operationalize these frameworks amid the real world problems of water governance.

On the river and beyond the river

The case for cooperation, along with the mechanisms for achieving it, will inevitably vary across international shared water systems. At its most basic level cooperation implies acting in a manner that minimizes the adverse consequences of competing claims while maximizing the potential benefits of shared solutions. Taking the principle that states seek to pursue rational and legitimate self-interest as a starting point, cooperation will occur only if the anticipated benefits exceed the costs of noncooperation. Enlightened self-interest can help identify and broaden the range of potential benefits.

One helpful framework for thinking about transboundary water governance has identified four layers of potential gains from cooperation:[25]

- Benefits *to* the river.
- Benefits *from* the river.
- Benefits *because* of the river.
- Benefits *beyond* the river.

Benefits to the river

Conserving, protecting and developing rivers can generate benefits for all users. In Europe the Rhine Action Plan, launched in 1987, marks the latest phase in cooperation to enhance the quality of the river in the interests of all users. The plan marks the culmination of more than half a century of incremental change, with France, Germany, the Netherlands and Switzerland gradually developing a response commensurate with the scale of the threat to their shared interests (box 6.3).

In poorer regions of the world maintaining the integrity of river systems can generate profound benefits for livelihoods. One illustration

Rivers connect people and livelihoods across national borders. Clean rivers are a public good—polluted rivers are vehicles for the transfer of public bads across borders. European history shows the benefits of investing in rivers as regional public goods.

The Rhine. The Rhine River, one of Europe's great river systems, flows down from the Swiss Alps and tracks through eastern France into Germany's Ruhr Valley and the Netherlands. Even in the early 19th century the river was a byword for pollution. In 1828 a visit to the city of Cologne prompted Samuel Coleridge to write:

The river Rhine, it is well known

Doth wash your city of Cologne

But tell me, Nymphs, what power divine

Shall henceforth wash the river Rhine?

No power, divine or terrestrial, washed the river. As industrialization developed, the Rhine became a vast sink for pollution. It carried off the wastes from Switzerland's chemical industries, France's potash industry and Germany's metallurgical and coal industries, transferring them to the Netherlands. Between 1900 and 1977 concentrations of chromium, copper, nickel and zinc rose to toxic levels. Fish almost disappeared from the middle and upper Rhine by the 1950s. Apart from poisoning the river, pollution from French and German industry was threatening drinking water and the flower industry in the Netherlands.

The clean-up began after the Second World War. In 1950 France, Germany, Luxembourg, the Netherlands and Switzerland established the International Commission for the Protection of the Rhine (ICPR). It focussed initially on research and data collection, but in the mid-1970s two agreements were concluded on chemical pollution and chlorides. These were aimed at reducing pollution in France and Germany, though early cooperation was difficult. Germany, the Netherlands and Switzerland agreed to contribute 70% of the costs of reducing chloride emissions in France. But facing strong domestic opposition, the French government refused to place the convention before Parliament for ratification.

An environmental crisis in late 1986—a fire in a Swiss chemical plant—spurred the next round of cooperation. By May 1987 the Rhine Action Plan had been developed. Targets were set for deep cuts in pollution. When floods occurred in 1993 ICPR activities expanded to include flood protection. The following year a new Rhine Treaty was signed, and in 2001 the 2020 Programme for Sustainable Development of the Rhine was adopted.

The ICPR is now an effective intergovernmental body to which member states must report their actions. It has a plenary assembly, secretariat and technical bodies—and considerable political authority through a ministers conference, which can make politically binding decisions. Nongovernmental organizations have observer status, which facilitates public participation. Such cooperative structures and institutions take time to develop, and they work best with high-level political leadership.

The Danube. Perhaps more than any other river the Danube reflects the turbulent history of 20th century Europe. On the eve of the First World War the major basin country was the Austro-Hungarian Empire. At the end of the Second World War most of the Danube riparians became part of the Soviet bloc. With the breakups of Czechoslovakia, the Soviet Union and Yugoslavia the Danube became the most internationalized basin in the world.

The end of the cold war and the later accession of several basin countries to the European Union made possible a basinwide approach to international cooperation. In February 1991 all the basin states agreed to develop the Convention on the Protection and Management of the River. In 1994 the Danube Convention was signed, and the International Commission for the Protection of the Danube River (ICPDR) was established, coming into force in October 1998. Serbia and Montenegro acceded to the treaty in 2002, Bosnia and Herzegovina in 2004.

The institutional foundation for the ICPDR is a conference of all involved countries, a plenary commission, nine expert and working groups and a permanent secretariat in Vienna. The commission's 11 observers include several professional organizations, the Danube Environment Forum, the Worldwide Fund for Nature and the International Association of Water Supply Companies in the Danube River Catchment Area.

Since 2001, when the Danube-Black Sea Strategic Partnership for Nutrient Reduction commenced, the Global Environment Facility's investment of about $100 million has leveraged nearly $500 million in cofinance with additional investments in nutrient reduction by the European Union, the European Bank for Reconstruction and Development and others totaling $3.3 billion. The Black Sea and Danube River ecosystems are already showing signs of recovery from the serious eutrophication of the 1970s and 1980s. Oxygen depletion has been almost nonexistent in recent years. And the diversity of species has roughly doubled from 1980 levels. The Black Sea ecosystem is well on its way to conditions observed during the 1960s.

The Danube shows how deep institutional cooperation can unlock a wide range of mutually reinforcing benefits across borders. As governments and the public in riparian countries have seen the benefits of cooperation emerging, so the authority and legitimacy of these institutions have strengthened. But successful cooperation has taken large investments of both financial and political capital.

Source: Barraqué and Mostert 2006.

is the prevention or reversal of problems such as the degradation of upstream watersheds and the mining of groundwater that expose downstream users to risks of floods or water shortages. The 2000 and 2001 flooding of the Limpopo and Save Rivers had harsh impacts on poor people living in the most vulnerable parts of the floodplains in Mozambique. Soil

6

Managing transboundary waters

Increasing the benefits from
the river and decreasing
the costs arising because
of the river can unlock
a wider potential for
human development,
economic growth and
regional cooperation

erosion, the loss of tree cover on slopes and excessive water use upstream contributed to the severity of the floods. Cooperation between states to address these problems reflects the perception of shared risk and mutual benefits offered by river systems.

Benefits from the river

The fact that water is a finite resource gives rise to a general perception that sharing is a zero sum game. That perception is flawed in important respects. The management of water in river basins can be developed to expand the size of the overall benefit, with water use optimized to increase irrigated land, power generation and environmental benefits.

Cooperation at the basin level can promote efficient techniques for water storage and distribution, expanding irrigation acreage. The Indus Waters Treaty of 1960 was the precursor to the massive expansion of irrigation works in India, which in turn played an important role in the green revolution. On the Senegal River Mali, Mauritania and Senegal are cooperating to regulate river flows and generate hydropower through co-owned infrastructure. In Southern Africa Lesotho and South Africa are cooperating in the construction of infrastructure on the Orange River in the Lesotho Highlands Project, providing South Africa with low-cost water and Lesotho with a flow of finance to maintain watersheds.[26] In South Asia India financed the Tala hydroelectric plant in Bhutan, gaining a source of energy while Bhutan gained guaranteed access to the Indian energy market.

Brazil and Paraguay provide an example of the potential benefits to be unlocked through trade and cooperation. The Itaipu Accord of 1973 ended a 100-year long boundary dispute with an agreement to jointly build the giant Guairá-Itaipu hydroelectric complex. Financed largely by Brazilian public investment, the Itaipu Dam in the Paraná-La Plata Basin has 18 generators with a capacity of 700 megawatts each, making it one of the largest hydropower plants in the world. Managed through Itaipu Binacional, a company jointly owned by the two governments, the plant meets almost all of

Paraguay's energy needs, maintains an industry that is now the single largest source of foreign exchange earnings and accounts for a quarter of Brazil's electricity consumption.[27] Both countries have gained through cooperation. The contrast with Central Asia, where a failure to cooperate has generated large losses, is striking.

Benefits because of the river

Gains from cooperation can include the costs averted by reducing tensions and disputes between neighbours. Strained interstate relations linked to water management can inhibit regional cooperation across a broad front, including trade, transport, telecommunications and labour markets. As two commentators put it, "in some international river basins, little flows between the basin countries except the river itself."[28] It is always difficult to distinguish the effects of water governance from the wider dynamics shaping relations between states, but in some cases the costs of noncooperation can be high, especially in environments marked by overlapping concerns over water scarcity and national security. Obvious examples include the Euphrates, Indus and Jordan Basins. Benefits from cooperation because of the river are inherently difficult to quantify, but the human and financial costs of noncooperation can be very real.

Benefits beyond the river

Increasing the benefits from the river and decreasing the costs arising because of the river can unlock a wider potential for human development, economic growth and regional cooperation. To some degree this is happening through river basin initiatives.

Cooperative approaches to river systems can also generate less tangible political benefits. The Nile Basin Initiative links Egypt politically and economically to poor countries in Sub-Saharan Africa. These links have the potential to create spillover benefits. For example, the political standing that Egypt has acquired through the Nile Basin Initiative could reinforce its emergence as a partner and champion of African interests at the World Trade Organization. Apart from the economic and security benefits of cooperation, the international standing of countries can be affected by perceptions of how equitably and fairly they govern water with weaker neighbours.

No single institutional framework offers a blueprint for unlocking the benefits of transboundary cooperation. At a minimal level cooperation aimed at bringing benefits to the river can range from defensive actions to more proactive measures. A disastrous fire in a chemical warehouse near Basel, Switzerland, set the scene for deeper cooperation on the Rhine. But as riparians seek to move from minimal to optimal cooperation strategies, inevitably a dynamic political interaction develops between water governance and political cooperation.

Within the European Union political and economic integration has facilitated ambitious new approaches to river basin management. The European Water Framework Directive of 2000 is one of the boldest shared water management frameworks. Its key objective is to achieve a "good status" for all European waters by 2015: meeting water quality standards, preventing overexploitation of groundwater and preserving aquatic ecosystems. As part of the directive states are required to designate "river basin districts" for the development of management plans and programmes covering a six-year period. For international basins it is even stipulated that EU members should coordinate with non-EU members. And while all these occur, the active participation of community representatives must be ensured.

The state of cooperation

In stark contrast to the steady stream of predictions of water warfare, the historical record tells a different story. Conflicts over water do emerge and give rise to political tensions, but most disputes are resolved peacefully. The absence of conflict is, however, at best only a partial indicator of the depth of cooperation.

Measuring the level of conflict between governments over water is inherently difficult. As already noted, water is seldom a stand-alone foreign policy issue. Oregon State University has attempted to compile a data set covering every reported interaction on water going back 50 years. What is striking in its data set is that there have

been only 37 cases of reported violence between states over water (all but 7 in the Middle East). Over the same period more than 200 treaties on water were negotiated between countries. In all, 1,228 cooperative events were recorded, compared with 507 conflictive events, more than two-thirds of which involved only low-level verbal hostility.[29] Most of the conflictive events were related to changes in the volume of water flows and the creation of new infrastructure, itself a proxy for the future volume and timing of flows (figure 6.1).

Looking back over the past half-century, perhaps the most extraordinary water governance outcome has been the level of conflict resolution—and the durability of water governance institutions. The Permanent Indus Water Commission, which oversees a treaty on water sharing and a mechanism for dispute resolution, survived and functioned during two major wars between India and Pakistan. The Mekong Committee, a joint body including Cambodia, Lao PDR, Thailand and Viet Nam, continued to exchange data and information during the Viet Nam War. Low-level water cooperation

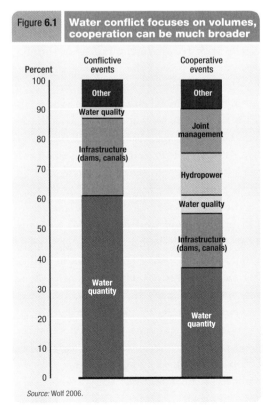

Figure **6.1** Water conflict focuses on volumes, cooperation can be much broader

Source: Wolf 2006.

Looking back over the past half-century, perhaps the most extraordinary water governance outcome has been the level of conflict resolution—and the durability of water governance institutions

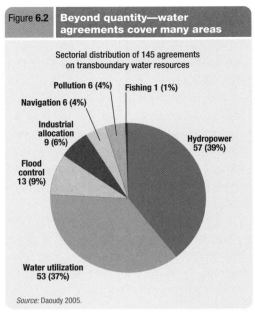

Figure **6.2** **Beyond quantity—water agreements cover many areas**

Sectorial distribution of 145 agreements
on transboundary water resources

Pollution 6 (4%)
Fishing 1 (1%)
Navigation 6 (4%)
Industrial allocation 9 (6%)
Flood control 13 (9%)
Hydropower 57 (39%)
Water utilization 53 (37%)

Source: Daoudy 2005.

between Israel and Jordan began under UN auspices in the early 1950s, when the countries were formally at war. In 1994 they created a Joint Water Committee for coordination, sharing and dispute settlement—an arrangement that has survived some acute tensions.

One clear message from the record is that even the most hostile enemies have a capacity for cooperation on water. Most governments recognize that violence over water is seldom a strategically workable or economically viable option. The institutions that they create to avert conflict have shown extraordinary resilience. The considerable time taken to negotiate the establishment of these institutions—10 years for the Indus Treaty, 20 years for the Nile Basin Initiative, 40 years for the Jordan agreement—bears testimony to the sensitivity of the issues.

If conflict is the exception to the rule, how do countries cooperate? Extensive analysis of 145 international treaties provides some insights (figure 6.2). Perhaps surprisingly, in only about a third of cases does cooperation include volumetric allocations. Hydroelectricity, flood and pollution control and navigation are more common.[30] In recent years benefit-sharing has received greater emphasis, perhaps because the requirements for negotiating volumetric allocations are so challenging. And from a future water security perspective, there are problems in not dealing with volumetric flow.

One of the most serious is that it creates the potential for conflict over the adjustment of claims on rivers and other shared water resources when availability declines, whether from seasonal factors or long-run depletion. The 1994 Israel-Jordan accord allows Jordan to store winter runoff in Israel's Lake Tiberias. The accord also allows Israel to lease from Jordan a specified number of wells to draw water for agricultural land. As part of the agreement a Joint Water Committee was created to manage shared resources. But the accord did not detail what would happen to the prescribed allocations in a drought. In early 1999 the worst drought on record led to tensions as water deliveries to Jordan fell. But the agreement itself remained intact—an outcome that demonstrated the commitment of both sides to cooperate.

While conflict is rare and cooperation common, most cooperation is quite shallow. Governments tend to negotiate agreements on very specific benefit-sharing projects, such as hydropower or information sharing. In many cases external factors served to push governments into minimalist cooperation strategies. A 1999 EU ban on Lake Victoria fish, with severe implications for foreign exchange earnings, persuaded the basin countries to begin regulating commercial fishing through the Lake Victoria Fisheries Organization. But the response was designed principally to restore commercial revenues, rather than to deal with the wider impacts of pollution and overfishing on livelihoods.

To date, there has been little in-depth cooperation to achieve the wider ranging human development goals set out in the Helsinki Rules or the 1997 UN Convention for the Non-Navigable Use of Shared Watercourses. And the geographical scope of cooperation is also limited: of 263 international water basins, 157 have no cooperative framework at all.[31]

Where such frameworks do exist they tend to be bilateral rather than multilateral. Of the 106 basins with water institutions about two-thirds have three or more riparian states, yet fewer than a fifth of the accompanying agreements are multilateral. Often even multilateral basins are managed through sets of bilateral agreements. In the Jordan basin, for example, agreements exist between Syria and Jordan, Jordan and Israel, and Israel and the Occupied Palestinian Territories.

What are the obstacles to deeper cooperation? Four stand out:

- *Competing claims and perceived national sovereignty imperatives.* Many countries remain deeply divided in the way they view shared water. India sees the flows of the Brahmaputra and Ganges Rivers as a national resource. Bangladesh sees the same water as a resource that it has claim to on the grounds of prior use patterns and needs. The differences are more than doctrinal: they relate directly to claims that both countries see as legitimate and necessary to their national development strategies. Elsewhere, the reality of water sharing has little impact on national strategies. The countries of Central Asia are heavily dependent on shared water. Since independence each country in the region has developed national economic plans that will draw on the same water resources. Yet national plans, drawn up outside of any coherent regional strategy for resource-sharing, take no account of real water availability. Were the plans themselves to be aggregated, the combined demands for irrigation and power generation would reflect an unsustainable resource use path. An obvious danger is that rival national plans could become a source of tension and a barrier to cooperation on shared ecological problems, such as restoration of the Aral Sea.
- *Weak political leadership.* Political leaders are accountable to domestic constituencies, not to basin-sharing communities and the governments that represent them. In countries where water figures prominently on the political agenda, domestic factors can create disincentives for water sharing and associated benefits: more equitable water sharing might be good for human development in a basin, but it might be a vote loser at home. There are also time-horizon problems: the domestic benefits of sharing are unlikely to come onstream during the term of office of any one government. Incentives for cooperation are strengthened when leaders can see some immediate political gain (for example, side payments to finance irrigation projects in Pakistan) or when there is a crisis (such as the chemical spill in the Rhine).
- *Asymmetries of power.* Rivers flow through countries marked by large disparities in wealth, power and negotiating capacity. It would be unrealistic to assume that these disparities do not shape the willingness to cooperate, negotiate and share benefits. There is also stark asymmetry across many shared water sources, in some cases with one overwhelmingly dominant actor: Egypt in the Nile Basin, India in the Ganges catchment area, Israel on the Jordan River, South Africa in the Incomati Basin and Turkey in the Tigris-Euphrates watershed are all examples. Unequal power relationships can have the effect of undermining trust.
- *Nonparticipation in basin initiatives.* Perceptions of the benefits of participating in multilateral basinwide initiatives are influenced by membership. That China is not a party to the Mekong River Commission is seen by some parties as a source of potential weakness of the commission. Downstream countries such as Cambodia and Viet Nam see upstream dams constructed by China as a threat to the "flood pulse" of the river and the livelihoods it sustains. The Mekong Commission is not a useful forum for negotiating on the problem because of China's absence.

More equitable water sharing might be good for human development in a basin, but it might be a vote loser at home

River basin cooperation for human development

Each river system, from its headwaters in the forest to its mouth on the coast, is a single unit and should be treated as such.

—Theodore Roosevelt[32]

Given the acute political sensitivities surrounding water, it would be unrealistic to assume that a new internationalist ethos will transform water governance in the years ahead. Perceptions of national interest will continue to weigh heavily. But national interest can be pursued in more—or less—enlightened terms. As more governments now recognize, the realities of hydrological independence require basinwide and broader multilateral governance frameworks. Recognition of two principles should guide future efforts in transboundary water management.

- *Human security in shared water management is part of national security.* Water can be a national security concern, especially for countries that rely on cross-border sources for a significant proportion of their water needs. But human security provides a powerful rationale for new approaches to governance. Shared water management can reduce the unpredictable risks and vulnerabilities created by dependence on a shared water resource. Cooperation offers a route to greater predictability and reduced risks and vulnerabilities, with wide-ranging benefits for livelihoods, the environment and the economy. Moreover, shared water governance can open up a wider set of benefits to enhance human security through expanded opportunities for cross-border cooperation.

- *Basins matter as much as borders.* Most governments now embrace the principle of integrated water resources management and recognize the need for planning strategies that cover all uses. However, integrated planning cannot stop at the border. River and lake basins are ecosystems that stretch across national frontiers, and the integrity of any part of these systems depends on the integrity of the whole. So the logical step is to manage water at the basin level, even when it crosses borders.

Basin-level cooperation

Basin-level cooperation is now well established in many regions. The range of cooperation stretches from coordination (such as sharing information) to collaboration (developing adaptable national plans) to joint action (which includes joint ownership of infrastructure assets). In some cases cooperation has resulted in the establishment of standing institutional structures through which governments can interact regularly (box 6.4).

One way of thinking about cooperation is as the exchange of baskets of benefits that add to the aggregate welfare of both sides. This approach goes beyond bargaining over volumetric allocations to identifying multiple benefits for all sides. An example is the dialogue between India and Nepal on the Bagmati, Gandak and Kosi Rivers (all tributaries of the Ganges). The treaties that emerged included provisions for a variety of water-related projects, including irrigation, hydropower, navigation, fishing and even afforestation, with India supporting the planting of trees in Nepal to contain downstream sedimentation. Although the treaties have been amended to take account of Nepalese concerns, their broad structures are good examples of how large baskets of benefits can be part of creative solutions.

Cooperative management powerfully demonstrates the potential to open up benefits beyond the river. More than 40% of transboundary water treaties include provisions that go beyond narrowly defined shared water management.[33] Some examples:

- *Financial resource flows.* Several agreements include investment provisions, such as Thailand's financing of a hydroelectric project

Box 6.4 River basin cooperation takes many forms

Cooperative institutions exist in numerous river basins, although their impact has varied greatly. The examples here illustrate that governments can come together in many different contexts to manage shared water resources. The challenge is to strengthen and deepen the sense of shared interests that underpins cooperation and to develop effective, transparent and accountable institutions to meet the challenges of the future.

Mekong River Commission. The Mekong River Commission was formed in 1995 as an intergovernmental agency of the four countries of the lower Mekong Basin: Cambodia, Lao PDR, Thailand and Viet Nam. The commission replaced the Mekong Committee (1957–76) and the Interim Mekong Committee (1978–92), setting a new stage for cooperation in the Mekong Basin. It has three permanent bodies: the secretariat, the technical joint committee and the ministerial-level council. National Mekong committees have been established in each member country to coordinate national ministries and line agencies and to liaise with the commission secretariat. Since 2002 selected civil society representatives have also been invited to attend joint committee and council meetings.

Nile Basin Initiative. The Nile Basin Initiative has a similar structure: a council of ministers, a technical advisory committee and a secretariat. But the initiative is much more recent and has little experience in joint programmes. Until recently, water issues were limited to volumetric allocations between Egypt and Sudan. But the initiative now focuses on a range of benefits that can be reaped across the entire basin, from hydropower to flood control to environmental sustainability, and a Strategic Action Programme is under way to identify cooperative projects. Some donors are trying to promote the participation of civil society groups through the Nile International Discourse Desk.

Senegal River Development Organization. The Senegal River Basin has witnessed a steady progression in integrated water management among Mali, Mauritania and Senegal. Guinea has joined recently. Cooperation started soon after the riparians gained independence, when in 1964 the river was declared an international

waterway. By 1972 the Senegal River Development Organization had been established with a conference of heads of state, a council of ministers, a high commissioner, three advisory bodies and respective national offices. Strong political leadership ensured that funds were raised in time to finance the construction of two jointly owned dams, which were managed by separate companies.

Alongside the infrastructure and institutional development, plans for basinwide integrated water resources management schemes have been scaled up. A Permanent Water Commission meets thrice a year to determine the best use of water from the two dams. The dams supply electricity to all three countries and irrigation water to farmers in areas where there is greatest fluctuation of rainfall. Efforts are also made to control floods in the upper valley and delta regions. Programmes have begun to address adverse environmental impacts such as the spread of water hyacinth and increasing soil salinity.

The Lesotho Highlands Water Project in the Orange River Basin. The 1986 arrangement transfers water from the Senqu River in water-rich Lesotho to the Vaal River in South Africa. Lesotho receives hydropower and royalties in return. In line with integrated water resources management principles the water project is also linked to the Orange-Senqu River Basin Commission, established in 2000.

Limpopo River Basin Commission. The first multilateral agreement between Botswana, Mozambique, South Africa and Zimbabwe created the Limpopo Basin Permanent Technical Committee in 1986 to advise on improving water quantity and quality. But political tensions hampered close cooperation. After the end of apartheid negotiations were renewed, starting with the 1997 permanent commission for cooperation between Botswana and South Africa. In 2003 a Limpopo Watercourse Commission was created, with the objective of implementing the Southern African Development Committee protocol on water. That same year the Limpopo River Basin Commission was established to manage the entire basin holistically.

Source: Amaaral and Sommerhalder 2004; Lindemann 2005.

---

in Lao PDR, India's contribution to Pakistan for irrigation infrastructure under the Indus Waters Treaty and South Africa's role in developing water resources in the Lesotho highlands.

- *Trade in energy resources.* The creation of markets in hydropower can create benefits for importers and exporters. Illustrations include Brazil's purchasing of electricity from Paraguay's Itaipu Dam in the Paraná-La Plata Basin and India's purchasing of hydropower from the Tala Dam in Bhutan.

- *Data sharing.* Information is a critical part of integrated water resources management at the basin level. The Mekong Committee's first five-year plan consisted almost entirely of data-gathering projects aimed at creating the conditions for more effective basin management.

- *Political linkages as part of general peace talks.* Agreements on water can contribute to wider political negotiations. The Israel-Jordan water accord was part of the peace agreement between the two countries in 1994. A final political settlement between

Table **6.4**	**Potential benefits in the Kagera subbasin**

Geographic extent of benefit	Benefit
Region	• Stability and "peace dividend" • Economic integration (East African Community, Burundi, Rwanda and the Democratic Republic of Congo) • Regional infrastructure assets
Riparian countries	• Sediment control • Watershed management • Energy supply and rural electrification • Irrigation and agribusiness • River regulation • Biodiversity conservation • Commercial development • Private sector development
Downstream riparians	• Water quality control • Water hyacinth control • Sediment reduction • Regional stability • Growing trade markets

Source: Jägerskog and Phillips 2006; World Bank 2005f.

Israel and the Occupied Palestinian Territories would also need to include an agreement on their shared water resources.

Some river basin initiatives could generate significant benefits for human development across a large group of countries. Consider the Nile Basin Initiative. Five of the 11 countries that share the Nile are among the poorest countries in the world. All 11 see Nile resources as central to their survival. In a noncooperative environment this could be a source of conflict and insecurity. But cooperative management helps in sharing benefits throughout the basin and averting risks. Cooperation can identify pathways to reduce losses due to floods, tap hydropower and irrigation potential and conserve an ecosystem stretching from Lake Victoria to the Mediterranean.

Looking beyond national borders to the subbasin level offers a wider lens to view options for cooperation. The Kagera subbasin in the Nile system, shared by Burundi, Rwanda, Tanzania and Uganda, is the main contributor of water to Lake Victoria and the source of the White Nile.[34] The basin's alluvial deposits, swamps, forests and fauna constitute an ecosystem that has come under pressure from increasingly dense human settlements. Attempts at institutional cooperation through the 1970s and 1980s suffered from severe financial and capacity con-

straints. In its first five years the Kagera Basin Organization raised only a tenth of its budgeted finances.[35] By the 1990s civil wars in Burundi and Rwanda rendered the cooperative process almost defunct. Only recently, under the aegis of the Nile Basin Initiative and the Nile Equatorial Lakes Subsidiary Action Programme, have a number of more sustainable projects been launched. If successful, Kagera could become a model for more integrated cooperation throughout the Nile Basin (table 6.4).

Southern Africa provides another striking example of regional cooperation. Water is a major area of cooperation and integration in the Southern African Development Community. During the apartheid era few countries in the region were willing to cooperate with South Africa. Since the end of apartheid shared water management has been on an integral part of regional cooperation, with political leaders playing an important role in defining new rules and developing new institutions. The high level of cooperation reflects the fact that all countries in the region stand to gain together or lose together (box 6.5). Taking a cue from this initiative, the African Union adopted the Sirte Declaration in February 2005, encouraging member states to enter into appropriate regional protocols to promote integrated water management and sustainable development of agriculture in Africa.

The basket of benefits approach to cooperation is more than an analytical framework. It can help countries look beyond narrowly focussed goals of self-reliance, and it presents political leaders with options that they can "sell" to their constituencies. It allows smaller countries to negotiate with a stronger hand, offering concessions but also getting a range of benefits in return. It can also help generate financial resource flows, expand the scope of cooperation and open up new linkages beyond water. Towards these ends, however, strong institutions are needed.

Weak institutional structures for water management

International water institutions have multiple uses. They can serve as neutral forums for discussion, undertake fact-finding missions and

Southern Africa has 15 major international rivers. In the decade since the end of apartheid South Africa has used water to support regional integration. Improved political relations are a factor: past attempts to cooperate on the Zambezi River were unsuccessful without South Africa's involvement. So is the size of the South African economy, which drives the economic incentives for cooperation in the region. The process of forming basin partnerships was triggered by an operational requirement to augment water supply to the economic heartland of South Africa. Since then, however, basin cooperation has been consolidated by improved political relations among the basin states.

Legislative innovation. The Southern African Development Community (SADC) protocol signed in August 1995 drew on the Helsinki Rules, which had a strong focus on state sovereignty. When both Mozambique and South Africa signed the 1997 UN Convention for the Non-Navigable Use of Shared Watercourses, Mozambique pushed for further revisions. A revised protocol, signed in 2000, gave greater influence to downstream states and to environmental needs. It also established formal procedures for notification, negotiation and conflict resolution. The stronger protocol also had a basis in national legislation. The South African Water Act of 1998 states that one of its purposes is to meet international obligations in regional water management. South Africa's credibility in the process increased as a result.

Strengthening the institutional framework. The objective of the revised protocol was to promote the SADC agenda of regional integration and poverty alleviation. The member states adopted watercourse agreements and institutions, encouraging coordination and harmonization of legislation and policies and promoting research and information exchange. Several programmes were initiated towards these aims such as professional training in integrated water resources management, joint work on data collection and changes since 2001 to centralize management.

Regional strategic action plan. A 2005–10 regional strategic action plan for water management is under way. It focuses on water resource development through monitoring and data collection, infrastructure development (to increase energy and food security as well as water supply schemes to small border towns and villages), capacity building (to strengthen river basin organizations) and water governance. Each area has its own projects, involving SADC national committees, a technical committee, river basin organizations and implementing agencies.

Several challenges remain. There is no long-term regional water policy, so projects are implemented basin-by-basin. Seasonal variations continue to put competitive pressure on water availability. There are also lags in implementing the progressive national laws and uncertainties about conflict resolution procedures.

Source: Lamoree and Nilsson 2000; Leestemaker 2001; Nakayama 1998; SADC 2000, 2005a,b; UNEP 2001; van der Zaag and Savenije 1999; Conley and van Niekerk 2000.

research on behalf of member states, monitor compliance with treaties and enforce sanctions on erring states. Given the weakness of treaties as stand-alone documents, investing energy in creating sustainable institutions is deeply beneficial. Sustainability is a critical need because basins are regularly subject to stresses, whether biophysical, geopolitical or socioeconomic. Institutions are thus the shock absorbers that increase a basin's resilience to sudden changes.

There is no dearth of river basin initiatives or of institutions. Most have two things in common. Their day-to-day operation is dominated by technical experts doing critically important work, and they lack high-level political engagement. The upshot is an institutional structure for river basin cooperation with a focus on discrete projects rather than the bigger picture of gains on and beyond the river. Among the symptoms:

- *Limited mandates.* In most cases river basin organizations are expected to work on narrow technical areas, such as collecting data or monitoring flows across the border. This limits their ability to cope with basinwide socioeconomic and environmental challenges—or to develop broader systems of benefit sharing to promote human development.

- *Constrained autonomy.* Most river basin cooperation takes place within highly circumscribed institutional autonomy. This is a weakness, because a degree of autonomy can increase both the objectivity and legitimacy of institutions. The Binational Autonomous Authority of Lake Titicaca set up by Bolivia and Peru in 1996 shows how full autonomy over technical, administrative and financial decisions can make institutions more effective. The authority has prepared a 20-year strategy to manage water availability and monitor water quality. While not independent of the governments, the institution looks beyond competing national inter-

6

Managing transboundary waters

Given the different strategic, political and economic contexts in international basins, it makes sense to promote and support cooperation of any sort, no matter how slight

ests and is seen by both parties as a source of credible advice on lake management. By contrast, the Interstate Coordination Water Commission in the Aral Sea Basin and the International Fund for the Aral Sea, with limited capacity and autonomy, have become a locus for interstate rivalry, reflected in disputes about staffing patterns and country representation.

- *Weak institutional capacity.* River basin organizations often suffer from a lack of technical expertise, poor staffing and poor executive direction in programme objectives and project design. The Niger Basin Authority, created in 1980, remained largely ineffective through several rounds of restructuring. Lacking financial or political support, it was unable to develop strategies for integrated socioeconomic development and environmental conservation, as envisaged in its remit. Only recently have basin countries begun to acknowledge their interdependence in the basin and to contribute their financial shares to the authority.

- *Insufficient financing.* The process of negotiation in the development of river basin institutions can be as important as the outcome. Balanced negotiations are costly because they often stretch over long periods and because of the need for technical data and legal expertise. Initiatives in Sub-Saharan Africa in particular have suffered from inadequate funding, holding back institutional cooperation. For the past 15 years the Lake Chad Basin Commission has been talking about diverting water from the Ubangi River to the Chari River, which feeds into the lake. This is an urgent priority in view of the lake's rapid shrinkage. To date, however, the five member countries have only managed to raise $6 million for a feasibility study. On current trends, the scheme itself could take another 10–20 years to achieve, which might be too late.[36] Similarly, the International Fund for the Aral Sea, meant to serve as a funding mechanism for Aral Sea programmes, failed to elicit adequate contributions from the five Central Asian states.

- *Lack of enforcement.* The ability of institutions to enforce agreements is important, not least because enforcement failures weaken credibility and incentives for compliance with negotiated agreements. Weak enforcement can undermine even the most imaginative treaties. In 1996 and 1997, after years of dispute, two treaties were signed to find equitable water-sharing solutions on the Syr Darya and to exploit energy resources. Implementation has suffered from noncompliance and the absence of enforcement. By contrast, the Israel-Jordan experience during the drought of 1999 shows how institutions can resolve conflicts that might otherwise have major political repercussions. The difference: the Jordan-Israel agreement included enforcement mechanisms.

Creating the conditions for cooperation

A wide range of cases have included cooperation. Cooperation need not always be deep—in the sense of agreeing to share all resources and engaging in all types of cooperative ventures—for states to derive benefits from rivers and lakes. Indeed, given the different strategic, political and economic contexts in international basins, it makes sense to promote and support cooperation of any sort, no matter how slight. There are, however, a few clear steps that states, civil society bodies and international organizations can take to create the conditions for initial cooperation and to move towards wider benefit-sharing systems. Among the requirements:

- Assessing human development needs and goals.
- Building trust and increasing legitimacy.
- Strengthening institutional capacity.
- Financing transboundary water management.

Assessing human development needs and shared goals. The management of cross-border water cannot be separated from wider international development goals, including the Millennium Development Goals. Most river basin initiatives focus on river sharing arrangements

Set up in 1991 and receiving strong support at the 1992 Earth Summit, the Global Environment Facility (GEF) has become the largest source of multilateral aid for global environmental issues. The GEF was established as a partnership of the United Nations Development Programme, with its strength in capacity-building projects; the United Nations Environment Programme, with its strength in identifying regional priorities and action plans; and the World Bank, with its strength in financing.

On international waters, one of six focal areas, the GEF sees itself as a facilitator for ecosystem-based action programmes for transboundary water bodies. Their growing importance can be gauged by the various roles in promoting cooperation.

- *Setting priorities and building partnerships.* In each international basin the GEF supports a multicountry fact-finding process to prepare a transboundary diagnostic analysis as the basis for a strategic action programme, adopted at a high level and implemented over several years. The process has several benefits: producing scientific knowledge, building trust, analysing root causes, harmonizing policy, breaking down complex water resource and environmental concerns into manageable problems and promoting water resource management at the regional level. It also draws attention to the links between social, economic and environmental concerns. For instance, in Lake Victoria connections were drawn between invasive species, deforestation, biodiversity, navigation, hydropower, migration and disease.

- *Promoting regional water governance.* Almost two-thirds of GEF projects have helped create or strengthen treaties, legislations and institutions. Since 2000 as many as 10 new regional water treaties have been adopted or are in an advanced stage of development. Perhaps the most successful examples are the International Commission for the Protection of the Danube River and the Black Sea Commission. In 2000 a cyanide spill was reported to the International Alarm Centre for the Danube in time to avert a potentially tragic environmental disaster.

- *Building national capacity.* A key to ensuring sustainable programmes is building the capacity to respond to local demands and concerns. Although there are numerous training workshops, financial constraints impose limits on the participation of local stakeholders. In the Mekong Basin nongovernmental organizations are active in Thailand but not in Cambodia, Lao PDR or Viet Nam. In Lake Victoria, poverty and illiteracy are barriers to the effective spread of environmental knowledge.

- *Catalysing investment.* Over the last 15 years the GEF has provided more than $900 million in grants, leveraged by more than $3.1 billion in cofinance, for transboundary water management programmes in more than 35 water bodies involving 134 countries. About three-quarters of its funding is directed towards regional (rather than country) projects.

Source: Gerlak 2004; Sklarew and Duda 2002; Uitto 2004; Uitto and Duda 2002.

negotiated by technical experts. That process provides a foundation for cooperation. But political leaders could build on this foundation by identifying at a basin level shared goals for human development—in poverty reduction, employment creation and risk management—and make this an integral part of river basin planning.

The first step towards effective cooperation for human development is to create a common pool of information. Information is necessary for riparian countries to recognize the inefficiencies in unilateral programmes that fail to account for interdependencies. It can also help to identify shared interests. Many instances of conflict arise more from mistrust and poor information about the use and abuse of water resources than from substantive differences. Joint research and information exchanges can provide timely notification of infrastructure initiatives, identification of shared interests and development potential, increased chances of reaching

agreements and, most important, the foundations of long-term trust.

This is one area where international support can make a difference. The Global Environment Facility (GEF) has taken the lead in assisting legal and institutional reform in water governance (box 6.6). Since 1991 the GEF has supported fact-finding missions in more than 30 transboundary basins, achieving successes to varying degrees in the Aral Sea, Lake Victoria, Lake Tanganyika, the Danube (including the Black Sea) and the Mekong. Alongside the GEF, the Global International Waters Programme has identified 66 subregions for evaluating the causes and effects of environmental problems in transboundary water bodies.

But it is also important that fact-finding studies go beyond the technical. Community-based data collection and survey activities are one vehicle for identifying human development problems. River basin communities derive direct benefits from shared water resources and are directly in the line of risks. They are thus an important source of information on environmental hazards and livelihood impacts. Here, too, aid can help build institutional capacity. Communities in the Rio Bermejo Basin, shared by Argentina and Bolivia, face high levels of poverty. Excessive deforestation has created acute environmental problems, prompting the governments of the two countries to develop a binational strategy for basin management. As part of that strategy more than 1,300 civil society participants were consulted in a GEF project to identify problems and solutions in areas such as soil erosion, land reclamation and sediment control. Community voices ensured that a project to build several dams was scaled down and required to adopt environmentally sustainable practices.

As river basin cooperation evolves, political leaders must raise the bar to an appropriate level of ambition. The Helsinki Rules and the 1997 UN Convention for the Non-Navigable Use of Shared Watercourses identify social and economic needs as a priority. Yet current approaches have evolved out of negotiating approaches aimed at increasing economic exchanges, sharing information or resolving conflicts. All these tasks are critical—a foundation for success. But river basin bodies also provide political leaders with an opportunity to look to human development beyond their borders. To some degree, this is starting to happen in the Nile Basin Initiative and in Southern Africa. But far more could be done, including a human development needs assessment for each river basin.

Building trust and increasing legitimacy. Misinformation or a lack of information is an obstacle to close cooperation in many river basins. Cross-border cooperation on water depends on the willingness of riparian states to share governance. Here too international support can help create an environment for successful cooperation.

As in any process of mediation, parties perceived as impartial can build trust and legitimacy. The World Bank has supported basin management processes over a long period, from the Indus Treaty negotiations in the

1950s to the current Nile Basin Initiative. The World Bank also brings political weight and capacity to the formulation of objectives and development of institutions. The United Nations Development Programme (UNDP) has provided capacity-building inputs to the Nile River Basin Cooperative Framework Agreement. To fill this type of role, third parties must be perceived as neutral facilitators without any geopolitical ambition linked to water governance.

One requirement for successful cooperation is long-term political engagement. Negotiations over shared waters are invariably lengthy, requiring support from donors over the long haul. In 1993 the World Bank and other donors launched the Aral Sea Basin Programme to stabilize the environment, rehabilitate the disaster zone and improve management capacity. A year later the European Union's Technical Assistance for the Commonwealth of Independent States initiated the Water Resources Management and Agricultural Production project to support the International Commission for the Aral Sea. The UNDP has since launched the Aral Sea Basin Capacity Development project. The US Agency for International Development was crucial in linking water and energy concerns in the Syr Darya agreements. Despite the persisting problems in the Aral Sea Basin, interventions by international organizations since the early 1990s have averted a potentially acute conflict over water resources.

Strengthening institutional capacity. Strengthened river basin organizations must chart a practical course for the future. Although the design of institutions will differ by region and circumstances, the problem of inadequate technical capacity is common to many of them. Cooperation in this area could be scaled up through the transfer of institutional knowledge. The European Union, with its extensive experience in transboundary water management, for example, could do far more to support institutional development in poor countries, working with agencies such as the World Bank and UNDP to develop programmes for training and capacity building.

There is also scope for working towards regional legislation. The absence of harmonized or structured water policies in riparian countries can undermine efforts at integrated water management across borders. However, harmonization of legislation on water is technically challenging and often politically difficult. Given its experience in the area, the United Nations Environment Programme could take the lead in assessing national legislative frameworks and identifying overlaps. These could become the basis for developing regional water policies, as happened in the Southern African Development Community.

Financing transboundary water management. Transboundary water management generates important international public goods. With more than 40% of the world's people now living within transboundary basins, managing these basins has implications for regional peace and security, as well as for poverty reduction and environmental sustainability. Some of the public bads that flow from mismanagement include environmental refugees, pollution and poverty, all of which cross national boundaries—like water itself. This context provides a strong case for financing through development assistance programmes.

Transboundary management has attracted very little international aid financing. Of total development assistance spending on water and sanitation of about $3.5 billion, less than $350 million is allocated for transboundary water resources.[37] Donors should aim to substantially increase aid for transboundary waters. Running costs for water management institutions are fairly modest. Trust funds could provide a predictable source of financing and support the participation of poor member states; they are also a useful funding source for project implementation. Experience shows that this type of financial support could be especially useful in Sub-Saharan Africa and Central Asia. Relative to the number of countries that share international water basins and the large environmental costs and development losses, financial support to effective river basin institutions would be a high-yield investment. But creating an environment for cooperation and sustaining a dialogue over many years can be expensive—an area for innovative international financing.

In the interests of ownership the riparian countries have to bear a substantial part of the financial burden for managing transboundary institutions and approaches. A danger of aid financing is that it can create a supply-led approach to setting priorities, with donor priorities defining the agenda. Where aid is critical is in financing start-up costs, training and capacity development. Financing aid is best done through grants rather than loans, because the costs of coordination between countries are high and attributing responsibility for loan repayments is difficult. The GEF remains one of the main financing instruments for directing aid towards transboundary resources. In the past 15 years it has committed $900 million in grant financing, with three times that amount leveraged in cofinancing. Similar financing models could tap into financial markets to fund large infrastructure projects, for example. Risk financing and contractual arrangements that tie in river basin organizations can attract private capital while adding to the stability of transboundary cooperation.

* * *

Beyond the rhetoric on the threat of water wars two things are certain. First, for a large group of countries, transboundary water management will figure as an increasingly important issue in bilateral and regional dialogue. Second, increasing competition for water will have marked human development consequences that spill across borders.

Beyond these givens much is uncertain. Will water become an increasing source of tension between neighbours? That will depend partly on wider peace and security issues that have nothing to do with water, and partly on whether governments choose to resolve differences through cooperation. What is clear is that people living in areas marked by water stress will continue to have a strong human security interest in more ambitious and less fragmented approaches to water governance.

Donors should aim to substantially increase aid for transboundary waters but in the interests of ownership the riparian countries have to bear a substantial part of the financial burden for managing transboundary institutions and approaches

6

Managing transboundary waters

Notes

Chapter 1

1   Deaton 2004.
2   McNeill 2000.
3   Cain and Rotella 2001.
4   Woods, Watterson and Woodward 1988; Szreter and Mooney 1998.
5   Cutler, Deaton and Lleras-Muney 2005.
6   Hassan 1985; Szreter and Mooney 1998.
7   Cited in Bryer 2006.
8   Troesken 2001.
9   Halliday 1999.
10 Hassan 1985.
11 Rosenberg 1962.
12 Cutler and Miller 2005.
13 Cutler and Miller 2005; Cain and Rotella 2001.
14 McNeill 2000.
15 UNDP 2003a.
16 WHO and UNICEF 2005.
17 Uganda 2004.
18 Molle and Berkoff 2006.
19 Howard and Bartram 2003.
20 Earth Policy Institute 2006.
21 Allen, Davila and Hoffman 2006.
22 Gandy 2006.
23 Bakker and others 2006.
24 Ito 2005; Shalizi 2006; Cai 2006.
25 On Lahore and Karachi see World Bank 2005c; Urban Resource Centre 2004; Molle and Berkoff 2006.
26 WHO and UNICEF 2005; WHO 2001.
27 ADB 2004.
28 UN-HABITAT 2003.
29 Redhouse 2005.
30 Rao and others 2003.
31 Nyong and Kanaroglou 2001.
32 WHO and others 2006.
33 Smets 2004; Van Hofwegen 2006.
34 Dutta and others 2003; Sang and others 1997.
35 These findings are consistent with wider micro-level research into other indicators for ill-health. One study in northern Ghana, for example, found that infection rates from worms were eight times higher among households collecting water from streams and rivers than for those using piped water. It also found that the incidence of illness reported by households rose from 5% to 24% during periods of water scarcity. Buor 2004.
36 Commission on Macroeconomics and Health 2001.

37 Kremer and Miguel 1999.
38 Strauss and Thomas 1998.
39 Hutton and Haller 2004.
40 Tanzania 2002.
41 UNICEF 2005b.
42 UNICEF 1999.
43 Uganda 2005.
44 Uganda 2004.
45 Lenton, Wright and Lewis 2005.
46 James and others 2002.
47 Joshi 2005.
48 Smith [1776] 1976.
49 Redhouse 2005.
50 Mukherjee 2001.
51 Wagstaff 2000.
52 Wagstaff 2001.
53 Gasparini and Tornarolli 2006.
54 Uganda 2004.
55 Bakker and others 2006.
56 McIntosh 2003.
57 Collignon and Vézina 2000.
58 Swyngedouw 2004; Molle and Berkoff 2006.
59 Phan, Frias and Salter 2004.
60 Rao and others 2003.
61 On financing estimates see Winpenny 2003; Toubkiss 2006; Smets 2004.
62 Calculated on the basis of population size from indicator table 5, GDP from indicator table 14 and health expenditure from indicator table 6.
63 Hutton and Haller 2004.
64 Slaymaker and Newborne 2004; WSP 2003.
65 WSP–AF 2004e.
66 Scanlon, Cassar and Nemes 2004.
67 This section is based on Development Initiatives 2006; Van Hofwegen 2006.
68 WSP–AF 2005a.
69 Development Initiatives 2006.
70 G-8 2003.
71 The Global Fund to Fight AIDS, Tuberculosis and Malaria 2006a; Sperling and Balu 2005.
72 World Bank 2006c; Sperling and Balu 2005; World Bank and IMF 2003; the Global Fund to Fight AIDS, Tuberculosis and Malaria 2006b; AfDB 2005b.
73 AfDB 2005b.

Chapter 2

1   CESCR 2002.
2   Sen 1982.

3   Sen 1981.
4   Connors 2005.
5   Collignon and Vézina 2000.
6   Komives and others 2005.
7   Foster, Pattanayak and Prokopy 2003.
8   Collignon and Vézina 2000.
9   Howard and Bartram 2003.
10 Thompson and others 2002.
11 WUP 2003.
12 Collignon and Vézina 2000.
13 Equivalent to 7.5 cubic metres a month.
14 Collignon and Vézina 2000.
15 Collignon and Vézina 2000.
16 WSP–AF 2004b.
17 Parker and Skytta 2000.
18 Parker and Skytta 2000.
19 Bakker 2003b.
20 Wolff and Hallstein 2005.
21 Hall and others 2002.
22 McIntosh 2003.
23 Tortajada 2006c.
24 Wolff and Hallstein 2005.
25 Komives and others 2005.
26 Franceys 1997.
27 Caseley 2003.
28 Bakker and others 2006.
29 De Miras and Le Tellier 2005; Jamati 2003.
30 Slattery 2003.
31 *The Economist* 2004.
32 Delfino, Casarin and Delfino 2005.
33 *Afrol News* 2006.
34 Coing 2003; Smith 2005.
35 Pangare, Kulkarni and Pangare 2005.
36 Pietilä and others 2004.
37 Foster and Yepes 2005. Affordability is defined within the threshold of water representing at most 5% of household income.
38 Foster and Yepes 2005.
39 Komives 1999.
40 Gómez-Lobo and Contreras 2003.
41 Komives and others 2005.
42 Based on data in Komives and others 2005. See also Raghupati and Foster 2002; Foster, Pattanayak and Prokopy 2003.
43 Foster, Pattanayak and Prokopy 2003.
44 Foster, Pattanayak and Prokopy 2003.
45 Graham and Woods 2006.
46 WSP–AF 2004b.
47 Slaymaker and Newborne 2004.
48 WSP–AF forthcoming.

49 Tanzania 2002.
50 WaterAid 2005.
51 Tanzania 2002.
52 Slaymaker and Newborne 2004.
53 WSP–SA 1999; Dhanuraj, Das Gupta and Puri 2006.
54 Van Hofwegen 2006.
55 Van Hofwegen 2006.

Chapter 3

1 Hugo [1862] 1982, book II, chapter 1.
2 Satterthwaite and McGranahan 2006; Satterthwaite 2006.
3 Winpenny 2003.
4 Briscoe 2005.
5 Ringler, Rosegrant and Paisner 2000.
6 WSP–AF 2005d.
7 Satterthwaite and McGranahan 2006; Hunt 2006.
8 Hunt 2006; Esrey and others 1991.
9 Cairncross and others 1996.
10 Cairncross and others 2003.
11 Curtis and Clarke 2002; Curtis and Cairncross 2003.
12 WSP–AF 2002b.
13 Biran, Tabyshalieva and Salmorbekova 2005.
14 WSP–AF 2004a,f.
15 Mukherjee 2001.
16 Satterthwaite 2006.
17 Hanchett and others 2003.
18 Kar and Bongartz 2006.
19 WSP–SA 2005.
20 Luong, Chanacharnmongkol and Thatsanatheb 2002.
21 Levine and the What Works Working Group 2004; WHO and UNICEF 2004a; World Bank 2004d; 2005d; 2006g.
22 World Bank 2004a; Crook and Sverrisson 2001.
23 Jenkins and Sugden 2006; Practical Action Consulting 2006a,c.
24 Melo 2005; Heller 2006.
25 WSP–SA 2005.
26 Jenkins and Sugden 2006; Practical Action Consulting 2006a,c.
27 World Bank 2004b.
28 Phan, Frias and Salter 2004.
29 WSP–AF 2004c.
30 World Bank 2004b; WSP 2002d.
31 Sakthivel and Fitzgerald 2002.

Chapter 4

1 Malthus [1798] 1826.
2 WWC 2000.
3 Brown 2003.
4 Reisner 1986.
5 This section is based on McNeill 2000; World Water Assessment Programme 2006; Postel 1992.
6 Rijsberman 2004c. Such threshold levels are, by their very nature, arbitrary. Scarcity is subject to considerable regional variation due to factors not captured by these thresholds. Such factors include the state of water storage infrastructure and influences on water demand, such as climate, the nature and extent of productive water use and the development of agricultural systems. However, a major advantage lies in their simplicity: data are readily available and their meaning is intuitive and easy to understand.
7 McNeill 2000.
8 Shalizi 2006.
9 Rijsberman 2004a.
10 Rijsberman 2004c.
11 Shalizi 2006.
12 Falkenmark and Rockström 2005; SIWI and others 2006.
13 McNeill 2000.
14 McNeill 2000.
15 Rijsberman, Manning and de Silva 2006.
16 Rijsberman, Manning and de Silva 2006.
17 Rosegrant, Cai and Cline 2002a; Meinzen-Dick and Rosegrant 2001; Alcamo, Henrichs, and Rösch 2000.
18 FAO 2006. Annual per capita water withdrawals in the United States, however, continue to remain amongst the highest in the world: 1,650 cubic metres against a world average of just over 600 cubic metres.
19 IWMI 2006; Rosegrant and Cai 2001.
20 Quoted in Worthington 1983.
21 Ballabh 2005.
22 Smakhtin, Revenga and Döll 2004.
23 Cai 2006; Postel 1999.
24 Pearce 2006.
25 Smakhtin, Revenga and Döll 2004.
26 Shetty 2006.
27 Pearce 2006.
28 On groundwater depletion see Molden, Amarasinghe and Hussain 2001; World Bank 2004e; Buechler and Mekala 2005.
29 Guevara-Sanginés 2006.
30 WRI 2005.
31 Hinrichsen, Robey and Upadhyay 1997.
32 World Bank 2001; Cai 2006; Shalizi 2006.
33 Shah and others 2003.
34 Moench, Burke and Moench 2003.
35 World Bank 2005c.
36 Vira, Iyer and Cassen 2004.
37 Kurnia, Avianto and Bruns 2000.
38 Vira, Iyer and Cassen 2004; Saravanan and Appasamy 1999.
39 Briscoe 2005.
40 Hanchate and Dyson 2004.
41 Abderrahman 2002; Csaki and De Haan 2003; SIWI, Tropp and Jägerskog 2006.
42 Shetty 2006.
43 Shetty 2006.
44 Environmental Working Group 2005.
45 On the national accounting problem see Repetto and others 1989; Solórzano and others 1991; Daly and Cobb 1989.
46 Anand and Sen 1994.
47 Pagiola, Arcenas and Platais 2005.
48 On desalinization see World Water Assessment Programme 2006; Rijsberman 2004a.
49 World Bank 2006h.
50 Allan 1998; Rosegrant, Cai and Cline 2002b.
51 OECD 2006a.
52 Rosegrant, Cai and Cline 2002b.
53 World Water Assessment Programme 2006
54 Scott, Faruqui and Raschid-Sally 2004; IWMI 2006.
55 Scott, Faruqui and Raschid-Sally 2004; IWMI 2006.
56 BESA 2000.
57 Cai and Rosegrant 2003.
58 Shah and Keller 2002.
59 World Bank 2006h.
60 See for example Gleick 2003, 2005.
61 World Bank 2006h.
62 Gleick 2003.
63 Postel and Richter 2003.
64 Grey and Sadoff 2006.
65 Miller and Reidinger 1998.
66 Grey and Sadoff 2006.
67 Brown and Lall 2006.
68 Shetty 2006.
69 Awulachew and others 2005
70 World Bank 2006f.
71 World Bank 2006e
72 Grey and Sadoff 2006.
73 World Commission on Dams 2000.
74 World Commission on Dams 2000; Berkamp and others 2000.
75 Hussain and Hanjra 2003.
76 UN 1992.
77 Dixon, Smith and Guill 2003; Fischer and others 2005; Stern Review on the Economics of Climate Change 2006.
78 Fischer, Shah and van Velthuizen 2002.
79 IPCC 2001; Arnell and Liu 2001.
80 Briscoe 2005; World Water Assessment Programme 2006.
81 Conway 2005; Maslin 2004.
82 Stern Review on the Economics of Climate Change 2006.
83 IPCC 2001.
84 Hare and Meinhausen 2004.
85 Den Elzen and Meinhausen 2005.
86 Den Elzen and Meinhausen 2005. In order to reach a target of 450 ppm global emissions will need to decline at 2.5% a year from a peak level in 2012. Delaying the peak by 10 years doubles the required rate of reduction to 5% a year.
87 Hadley Centre 2004.
88 Bronstert and others 2005.
89 Fischer and others 2005; Parry, Rosenzweig and Livermore 2005; Nyong 2005.
90 Stern 2006. IPCC SRES A2 scenario, which corresponds to 520–640 ppm carbon dioxide levels by 2050—not an unreasonable scenario.
91 Tanzanian submission to the IPCC quoted in Murray and Orindi 2005.
92 Murray and Orindi 2005.
93 Dixon, Smith and Guill 2003; Desanker and Magadza 2001.

94 Fischer and others 2005.
95 Barnett, Adam and Lettenmaier 2005.
96 World Bank 2006a.
97 Maslin 2004.
98 Ellis, Corfee-Morlot and Winkler 2004; Ellis and Levina 2005. At the end of 2005 there were 35 registered projects under the Clean Development Mechanism (CDM), with more than 600 in the pipeline. Projected financial flows of $1 billion are estimated through the CDM for 2012. Most of the projects involved are in the energy sector, with a heavy concentration on Brazil, China, India, Republic of Korea and Mexico (which account for about 70% of CDM trading). The only Sub-Saharan country involved is Nigeria, which accounts for less than 2% of total CDM credits. Wider multilateral aid efforts on global warming have been led by the Global Environment Facility, which by 2004 had committed about $1.8 billion in grants for climate change projects, leveraging about four times more in co-financing. Around two-thirds of the total has been committed to large mitigation projects. As with the CDM, there has been a focus on larger developing countries, with 10 countries receiving more than half of the total financing.
99 Stern Review on the Economics of Climate Change 2006.
100 GEF 2006.
101 Calculated from OECD 2006b.
102 Sachs and others 2005.

Chaper 5

1   Quoted in Briscoe 2005.
2   World Bank 2006f.
3   Hussain 2005.
4   World Bank 2006h.
5   Rosegrant, Cai and Cline 2002b.
6   World Bank 2006h.
7   World Bank 2006h.
8   Seckler and others 2000; Rosegrant, Cai and Cline 2002b; FAO 2003b.
9   FAO 2005; Grey and Sadoff 2006.
10 Commission for Africa 2005
11 Molle and Berkoff 2006; Narain 2006; Cai 2006.
12 Molle and Berkoff 2006.
13 Gandy 2006.
14 *Gulf Times* 2006.
15 Meinzen-Dick and Pradhan 2005.
16 Kenney 2005; Meinzen-Dick and Ringler 2006.
17 Villarejo 1997, cited in Meinzen-Dick and Ringler 2006.
18 NNMLS 2000, cited in Meinzen-Dick and Ringler 2006.
19 Peña, Luraschi and Valenzuela 2004.
20 Miguel Solanes, personal communication.
21 Cai 2006; World Bank 2001; Shalizi 2006; Molle and Berkoff 2006.
22 Kurnia, Avianto and Bruns 2000.

23 Palanisami 1994; Palanisami and Malaisamy 2004.
24 Rosegrant and Perez 1997.
25 Cotula 2006; Sylla 2006.
26 Sylla 2006.
27 Sylla 2006.
28 Van Koppen 1998; Pander 2000.
29 Cotula 2006; Adams, Berkoff and Daley 2006.
30 World Bank 2005c.
31 Hussain and Wijerathna 2004b; Lipton 2004a. Analysis of agricultural production in India and Pakistan identified inequity in the distribution of land and canal water, poor quality of groundwater (especially at tail-end areas where the availability of canal water is less), and farm-level practices (sowing of older varieties, delay in timing of sowing and application of inputs), as the key factors explaining low agricultural productivity. See also World Bank 2002.
32 Hussain 2005; Hussain and Wijerathna 2004b.
33 Hussain and Hanjra 2003; Hussain 2005.
34 Azam and Rinaud 2000, pp. 8–10, cited in Lipton 2004a, p. 17.
35 Lipton 2004a.
36 Briscoe 2005.
37 Briscoe 2005; World Bank 2005c.
38 Boelens, Dourojeanni and Hoogendam 2005.
39 Hussain 2005.
40 Briscoe 2005.
41 Tortajada 2006b.
42 Shah and others 2002.
43 Marcus 2006.
44 Sarwan, Subijanto and Rodgers 2005; Vermillion 2005.
45 Faysse 2004.
46 Hussain 2004, cited in Lipton 2004a.
47 Meinzen-Dick and Zwarteveen 1998; van Koppen 2002.
48 Bastidas 1999, p. 16.
49 Interagency Task Force on Gender and Water 2004.
50 Oweis, Hachum and Kijne 1999; Vaidyanathan 2001.
51 Narain 2006.
52 Rijsberman 2004b.
53 Rijsberman 2004b.
54 Narain 2006.
55 Vaidyanathan 2001.
56 FAO 2005.
57 Awulachew and others 2005; Inocencio and others 2005.
58 World Bank 2006h.
59 Shah and Keller 2002.
60 Shah and others 2002.
61 Inocencio, Sally and Merrey 2003.
62 Shah and others 2000; Polak 2005a.
63 Namara 2005.
64 Rijsberman 2004b. Assumes a 10% discount rate.
65 Polak 2005b.
66 Brown 2003.

67 Cleaver and Gonzalez 2003.
68 Cleaver and Gonzalez 2003.
69 World Bank 2006h.
70 Commission for Africa 2005.

Chaper 6

1   Giordano and Wolf 2002.
2   Jägerskog and Phillips 2006.
3   Medzini and Wolf 2006; World Bank 2006h.
4   Calculated from Wolf and others 1999, table 4; CIA 2006.
5   Elhance 1999, p. 60.
6   MRC 2006; HDRO calculations.
7   Bonheur 2001; Keskinen and others 2005.
8   Nguyen and others 2000, p. 4.
9   Kayombo and Jorgensen 2006, p. 433.
10 UNEP 2004b.
11 Jolley, Béné and Neiland 2001, p. 31; Kayombo and Jorgensen 2006, p.433; Klohn and Andjelic 1997, p.1; Odada, Oyebande and Oguntola 2006, p. 77.
12 ALT 2003, p. 468.
13 Puri and Arnold 2002.
14 Coe and Foley 2001.
15 Sarch and Birkett 2000.
16 IUCN 2004.
17 Sikes 2003; UNEP 2004a, p. 19.
18 Odada, Oyebande and Oguntola 2006, p. 83.
19 Quoted in McNeill 2000.
20 Peachey 2004; Weinthal 2006.
21 Greenberg 2006.
22 UNDP 2002.
23 GEF 2002.
24 There is a certain irony in this. Historically, the "prior appropriation" doctrine was used by the United States to assert upstream claims against Mexico.
25 Sadoff and Grey 2002.
26 Wolf 2006.
27 Itaipu Binacional 2006.
28 Sadoff and Grey 2005.
29 Wolf, Yoffe and Giordano 2003.
30 Hamner and Wolf 1998.
31 Wolf 2006.
32 Quoted in Priscoli 1998, p. 633.
33 Fischhendler and Feitelson 2003, p. 563.
34 WSP International 2003; NEL-SAP 2002.
35 UNECA 2000.
36 White 2006.
37 Nicol 2002; Jägerskog and Phillips 2006, p. 20.

Bibliographic note

Chapter 1 draws on ADB 2004; AfDB 2005b; African Population and Health Research Center 2002; Allen, Davila, and Hoffman 2006; Alves and Belluzzo 2005; Amani, Kessy, and Macha 2004; APHRC 2002; AquaFed 2006; AusAID 2006; Bakker 2003b; Bakker and others 2006; Bartram and others 2005; Bell and Millward 1998; Blake 1956; Bryer 2006; Buor 2004; Cain and Rotella 2001; The Carter Center 2006; CDC 2006; Chen and Ravallion 2004; Clermont 2006; Collignon and Vézina 2000; Commission on Macroeconomics and Health 2001; CSA 2004; Curtis 2001; Cutler and Miller 2005; Cutler, Deaton, and Ileras-Muney 2005; Deaton 2002, 2003, 2004; Deaton and Paxson 2004; Development Initiatives 2006; Dubreuil and Van Hofwegen 2006; Dutta and others 2003; Earth Policy Institute 2006; Environmental Health at USAID 2004; European Regional Committee 2006; FAO 2006; Filmer-Wilson 2005; Freedman and others 2005; Fuentes, Pfütze, and Seck 2006a,b; G-8 2003; Gandy 2006; Gasparini and Tornarolli 2006; Gleick 2002; The Global Fund to Fight AIDS, Tuberculosis and Malaria 2006a,b; The Global Public-Private Partnership for Handwashing with Soap 2003; Gwatkin 2002; Halliday 1999; Hamlin 1988; Hassan 1985; Heller 2006; Hernández Mazariegos 2006; Hunt 2006; Hutton and Haller 2004; IDS 2006; INEGI 2006a,b; Ito 2005; James and others 2002; Joshi 2005; Kenya 2005; Kisima Newsletter 2005; Kremer and Miguel 1999; Larrea, Montalvo, and Ricuarte 2005; McIntosh 2003; Measure DHS 2006; Mehta 2000; Miller 2001; Milliband 2005; Miovic 2004; Mukherjee 2001; Muller 2006; Nayyar and Singh 2006; Neumayer 2004; Nyong and Kanaroglou 2001; ODI 2004; Pakistan 2004; Payen 2005; Phan, Frias, and Salter 2004; Redhouse 2005; Rosenberg 1962; Ruxin and others 2005; Salmon 2002; Sang and others 1997; Scanlon, Angela, and Nemes 2004; Schuttelar and others 2003; Shiklomanov 1993; Sight Savers International 2006; Sinanovic and others 2005; Slaymaker and Newborne 2004; Smets 2004; Smith 1976; Sperling and Balu 2005; Strauss and Thomas 1998; Swyngedouw 2004; Szreter 1997; Szreter and Mooney 1998; Tanzania 2002; Thompson and others 2002; Toubkiss 2006; Troesken 2001; UCLG Committee on the Local Management of Water and Sanitation 2006; Uganda 2004, 2005; UN 2005, 2006a,b; UNDP 2005e; UN-HABITAT 2003; UNICEF 1999, 2005b, 2006b; United Nations Secretary-General's Advisory Board on Water and Sanitation 2006; University of California, Berkeley, and MPIDR 2006; Urban Resource Centre 2004; Van Hofwegen 2006; Wagstaff 2000, 2001; Whittington, Mu, and Roche 1990; WHO 2001, 2005, 2006a,b; WHO and UNICEF 2004b, 2005, 2006; WHO and others 2006; Winpenny 2003; Woods, Watterson, and Woodward 1988, 1989; World Bank 2004b, 2005a,b,c; 2006c; World Bank and IMF 2003; WSP 2002c, 2003, 2004; WSP–AF 2003a, 2004c,e, 2005a,c, forthcoming; WSP–EAP 2003; WUP 2006; Yemen 2002; Yepes 1999; Zambia 2004a,b.

Chapter 2 draws on Abeyasekere 1987, 1989; ADB 2003, 2004, 2006; Adikeshavalu 2004; AfDB 2005a; Afrol News 2006; Alegría Calvo and Caledón Cariola 2004; Allain-El Mansouri 2001; Argo and Laquian 2004; Armstrong, Cowan, and Vickers 1995; Baker, Hern, and Bennett 1999; Bakker 2003a,b; Bakker and others 2006; Baldwin and Cave 1999; Bapat and Agarwal 2003; Bhatnagar and Dewan 2006; Black 1998; Bousquet 2004; Breuil 2004; Brown 2005; Budds and McGranahan 2003; Caseley 2003; Castro 2004; CESCR 2002; Chan 2006; Chikhr Sa di 1997, 2001; Coing 2003; Colin 1999; Collignon 2002; Collignon and Vézina 2000; Connors 2005; Corporate Europe Observatory 2003; Davis 2005; de Miras and Le Tellier 2005; Delfino, Casarin, and Delfino 2005; Dhanuraj, Gupta, and Puri 2006; Dubreuil and Van Hofwegen 2006; The Economist 2004; Elamon 2005; Esguerra 2002, 2005; Etienne 1998; Etienne and others 1998; Foster and Yepes 2005; Foster, Pattanayak, and Prokopy 2003; Fournier 2003; Franceys 1997; Gandy 2004, 2005, 2006; Gasparini and Tornarolli 2006; Gleick 2004; Gómez-Lobo and Contreras 2003; Graham and Woods 2006; Graham and Marvin 2001; Grimsey and Lewis 2002; Guasch and Spiller 1999; Guislain and Kerf 1995; Haarmeyer

and Mody 1998; Hall and Viero 2002; Heller 2006; ID21 2006d; IEG 2006a,b; Isham and Kahkonen 2002; Jaglin 1997, 2001a,b, 2002, 2003, 2004a,b,c, 2005; Jaglin and Dubresson 1999; Jamati 2003; Jouravlev 2001a,b; Juuti and Katko 2005; Kähkönen 1999; Kariuki and Schwartz 2005; Kerf 2000; Kjellén 2000; Kjellén and McGranahan 2006; Kleiman 2004; Komives 1999; Komives and others 2005; Lane 2004; Lauria, Hopkins, and Debomy 2005; Ledo 2005; Lenton, Wright, and Lewis 2005; Maltz 2005; Mapetla 2006; Marin 2002; Maronier 1929; Matthew 2005; McGranahan and others 2001; Ménard 2001; Menegat 2002; Mitlin 2004; Morel à l'Huissier, Verdeil, and Le Jallé 1998; Narayan 1995; Oxera Consulting Ltd. 2002; Pangare, Kulkarni, and Pangare 2005; Paredes 2001; Parker and Skytta 2000; Paul 2005; Pietilä and others 2004; Pitman 2002; Raghupati and Foster 2002; Rayaleh 2004; Santiago 2005; Sara and Katz 1998; Schneier-Madanes and de Gouvello 2003; Sen 1981, 1982; Serra 2000; Shen 2006; Slattery 2003; Slaymaker and Newborne 2004; Smets 2004; Smith 2005; Solo 1999, 2003; Summers 2005; Surjadi 2003; Surjadi and others 1994; Susantono 2001; Swyngedouw 2006; Taylor 1983; Tortajada 2006; Trémolet 2002; Ugaz 2003; US Agency for International Development 2005a,b; Valfrey 1997; Van Breen 1916; Van Hofwegen 2006; Van Leeuwen 1920; Verdeil 2003a,b, 2004; Vickers and Yarrow 1998; Viero 2003; Viero and Cordeiro 2006; Vircoulon 2003; WaterAid 2005, 2006; Weitz and Franceys 2002; Whittington 2006; Winpenny 2003; Wodon and Blackden 2006; World Bank 2004f, 2006e,h; World Water Assessment Programme 2003; WSP 2002, 2006; WSP–AF 2002a,b,e, 2003b, 2005c, forthcoming; WSP–LAC 2004; WSP–SA 1999; Yescombe 2002; Zérah 2000.

Chapter 3 draws on Amarasinghe and others 2006; Bangladesh 1998, 2005; Bartram and others 2005; Bhatia 2004; Biran and others 2005; Cain, Daly, and Robson 2002; Cairncross 2003; Cairncross and others 1996, 2003; Canelli 2001; Chary, Narender, and Rao 2003; Collignon and Vézina 2000; CONADIS and others 2004; Crook and Sverrisson 2001; Curtis and Cairncross 2003; Curtis and Clarke 2002; Esrey and others 1991; Fewtrell and others 2005; Foxwood 2005; Fuentes, Pfütze, and Seck 2006a,b; HABITAT 2001; Halim 2002; Hanchett and others 2003; Hasan 2005; Heller 2006; Hugo 1862; Hunt 2006; International Training Network Centre 2003; IRC International Water and Sanitation Centre 2004; Jenkins and Sugden 2006; Jensen and others 2005; Jones and Reed 2005; Kar and Bongartz 2006; Kar and Pasteur 2005; Keohane and Ostrom 1995; Kiribaki 2006; Levine and others 2004; Luong, Chanacharnmong, and Thatsanatheb 2002; Mehta 2004; Mehta and Knapp 2004; Melo 2005; Metts 2000; Mukherjee 2001; Patak 2006; Phan, Frias, and Salter 2004; Practical Action Consulting 2006a,b,c; Ringler, Rosegrant, and Paisner 2000; Sakthivel and Fitzgerald 2003; Satterthwaite 2006; Satterthwaite and McGranahan 2006; Shuchen, Yong, and Jiayi 2004; SINTEF Unimed 2002, 2003a,b; Slaymaker and Newborne 2004; UNA and WSSCC 2004; UNICEF 2005a, 2006a; UNICEF and IRC International Water and Sanitation Centre 2005; VERC 2002; WaterAid Uganda 2003; Waterkeyn and Cairncross 2005; WHO and UNICEF 2004a; Winpenny 2003; World Bank 2004a,b,d, 2005d, 2006g; WSP 2000, 2002a,d; WSP–AF 2002b,c,d, 2004a,c,d,f, 2005b,d; WSP–EAP 2003, 2005; WSP–LAC 2005; WSP–SA 2000, 2005; Zaidi 2001.

Chapter 4 draws on Abderrahman 2002; ACTS 2005a,b; Albiac 2006; Alcamo, Henrichs, and Rösch 2000; Allan 1998; Anand and Sen 1994; Arnell 2004; Arnell and Liu 2001; Assaf 2006; Ballabh 2005; Barnett, Adam, and Lettenmaier 2005; Berkamp and others 2000; BESA 2000; Bhushan 2005; Biswas 2004; Biswas and Tortajada 2005; Biswas, Ünver, and Tortajada 2004; Black and others 2003; Bos and Bergkamp 2001; Briscoe 2005; Bronstert and others 2005; Brown and Lall 2006; Brown 2003; Buechler and Mekala 2005; Buechler and Scott 2006; Cai 2006; Cai and Rosegrant 2003; CAS 2005; Cassen, Visaria, and Dyson

2004; Chenoweth and Bird 2005; CNA 2004; Conan 2003; Conway 2005; Corbera and others 2006; Csaki and De Haan 2003; CSO 2004; Cyranoski 2005; Daly and Cobb 1989; DeGeorges and Reilly 2006; den Elzen and Meinshausen 2005; Desanker and Magadza 2001; Dixon, Smith, and Guill 2003; Earth Policy Institute 2002; The Economist 2003; Ellis and Levina 2005; Ellis, Corfee-Morlot, and Winkler 2004; Environmental Working Group 2005; Esteller and Diaz-Delgado 2002; Ezcurra 1998; Falkenmark 2003; Falkenmark and Rockström 2004, 2005; FAO 2003; Feld, Prajamwong, and Sherman 2003; Fischer and others 2005; GEF 2006; Gleick 2000, 2003, 2005; Gleick and others 2002; Greenfacts.org 2006; Grey and Sadoff 2006; Guevara-Sanginés 2006; GWP 2000, 2004, 2006a,b; Hadley Centre 2004; Haile 2005; Hanchate and Dyson 2004; Hansen and Bhatia 2004; Hare and Meinhausen 2004; Hildebrandt and Turner 2005; Hinrichsen, Robey, and Upadhyay 1997; Hoanh and others 2003; Hussain and Hanjra 2003; ID21 2006b,c; IFAD 2001, 2006; IPCC 2001; IWMI 2003, 2006, forthcoming; Jewitt 2002; Jones 1998; Jones 1995; Kemper, Dinar, and Bloomquist 2005; Kibreab and Nicol 2002; Kijne, Barker, and Molden 2003a,b; Krol and Bronstert forthcoming; Kumar 2005; Lankford 2005a; Lawrence and others 2002; Lemos and de Oliveira 2004, 2005; Lomborg 2004; Lucas and Hilderink 2004; Mace 2005; Malthus [1798] 1826; Marañón 2006; Maslin 2004; Mayer 2002; McNeill 2000; Meinzen-Dick and Rosegrant 2001; Merrey and others 2006; Miller and Reidinger 1998; Moench, Burke, and Moench 2003; Moench 2001; Moench and others 2003; Molden, Amarasinghe, and Hussain 2001; Molden and de Fraiture 2004; Molden and others 2003; Molle and Berkoff 2006; Movik and others 2005; Murray and Orindi 2005; Myers 1998; Narain 2006; Noble and others 2005; Nyong 2005, 2006; OECD 2006a,b; Ostrom, Schroeder, and Wynne 1993; Oweis and Hachum 2005; Pagiola, von Ritter, and Bishop 2004; Pagiola, Arcenas, and Platais 2005; Pander 2000; Parry, Rosenzweig, and Livermore 2005; Pearce 2006; Perry 2001; Pitman 2002; Polak 2005a; Ponce 2005; Postel 1992, 1999; Postel and Richter 2003; Rahman and Alam 2003; Raskin and others 1997; Repetto and others 1989; Reyes-Sánchez and others 2006; Rijsberman 2003, 2004a,b; Rijsberman and Molden 2001; Rijsberman, Manning, and de Silva 2006; Ringler, Rosegrant, and Paisner 2004; Rodgers, de Silva, and Bhatia 2002; Rogers 2002; Rosegrant and Cai 2001; Rosegrant and Cline 2003; Rosegrant and Perez 1997; Rosegrant and Ringler 2000; Rosegrant and Sohail 1995; Rosegrant, Cai, and Cline 2002a,b; Sachs and others 2005; Sánchez Munguía 2006; Sanctuary and Tropp 2005; Saravanan and Appasamy 1999; Schenkeveld and others 2004; Schneider and Lane 2006; Scott, Faruqui, and Raschid-Sally 2004; Seckler and others 2000; Shah 2005; Shah and Keller 2002; Shah and others 2003; Shalizi 2006; Sharma and McCornick 2006; Shen and Liang 2003; Shetty 2006; Shiklomanov 2000; SIWI, Tropp, and Jägerskog 2006; SIWI and others 2005, 2006; Smakhtin, Revenga, and Döll 2004; Solórzano and others 1991; Soussan 2003, 2004; Stern 2006; Stern Review on the Economics of Climate Change 2006; Texas Center for Policy Studies 2002; Tortajada 2006; Tuinhof and Heederik 2002; Turner and Hildebrandt 2005; Turner and others 2004; UN 1992; UNDP 2003b; UNEP-FI 2004; Université Catholique de Louvain 2006; Vira, Iyer, and Cassen 2004; Vogel and Nyong 2005; Vörösmarty and others 2000; Water-Technology.net 2006; Wax 2006; WBCSD 2005; Wolff and Hallstein 2005; Wolfowitz 2005; World Bank 2001, 2004c,e, 2005c, 2006a,b,e,f,h; World Commission on Dams 2000; Worthington 1983; WRI 2005; WRI and others 2005; WWC 2000; WWF Nepal Programme 2005.

Chapter 5 draws on Adams 2000; Adams, Berkoff, and Daley 2006; Agarwal and Narain 1997; Agarwal, Narain, and Khurana 2001; Albiac and Martinez 2004; Al-Ibrahim 1991; Araral 2005; Awulachew and others 2005; Azam and Rinaud 2000; Bakker and others 1999; Bastidas 1999; Batchelor and others 2002; Bhattarai and Narayanamoorthy 2003; Bhattarai, Sakthivadivel, and Hussain 2002; Bird, Haas, and Mehta 2005; Black and others 2005; Boelens, Dourojeanni, and Hoogendam 2005; Briscoe 2005; Bruns 1997; Bruns and Meinzen-Dick 2000; Bruns, Ringler, and Meinzen-Dick 2005; Cai 2006; Cai and Rosegrant 2003; Chenoweth and Bird 2005; Commission for Africa 2005; Cotula 2006; DeGeorges and Reilly 2006; Development Initiatives 2006; Dubash 2000; Dubreuil and Van Hofwegen 2006; Ebarvia 1997; Environmental Justice Coalition for Water 2005; FAO 2002, 2003a,b, 2004a,b, 2005; Faysse 2004; Figuères, Tortajada, and Rockström 2003; Garduño 2005; Gleick 2000; Gleick and others 2002; Grey and Sadoff 2006; Guerquin and others 2003; Guevara-Sanginés 2006; Gulf Times 2006; GWA 2003; GWP 2004, 2006c; Haisman 2005; Hildebrandt and Turner 2005; Hoanh and others 2003; Hodgson 2004; Hussain 2004, 2005; Hussain and Hanjra 2003; Hussain and Wijerathna 2004a,b; ID21 2006a; IFAD 2001, 2006; India 2001; Inocencio, Sally, and Merrey 2003; Inocencio and

others 2005; Interagency Task Force on Gender and Water 2004; IWMI forthcoming; Iyer 2003; Jones 1998; Jones 1995; Kemper 2005; Kenney 2005; Kerr 2002; Kibreab and Nicol 2002; Kurian and Dietz 2005; Kurnia, Avianto, and Bruns 2000; Lankford 2005a,b; Lankford and Mwaruvanda 2005; Lipton 2004a,b; Lipton and others 2003; Liu 2005; Marcus 2006; Mayer 2002; McCully 2006; Meinzen-Dick and Nkonya 2005; Meinzen-Dick and Pradhan 2005; Meinzen-Dick and Ringler 2006; Meinzen-Dick and Zwartevenn 1998; Meinzen-Dick, Zwartevenn, and Zwartevenn 1998; Moench 1998; Moench and others 2003; Molden and de Fraiture 2004; Molden and others 2003; Molle 2005; Molle and Berkoff 2006; Moriarty and Butterworth 2005; Muller 2006; Namara 2005; Narain 2006; Nicol, Ariyabandu, and Mtisi 2006; NNMLS 2000; ODI 1999, 2004; OECD 2006b; Ostrom, Schroeder, and Wynne 1993; Oweis, Hachum and Kijne 1999; Palanisami 1994; Palanisami and Malaisamy 2004; Pander 2000; Peña and Valenzuela 2004; Perret 2002; Perry 2001; Pitman 2002; Polak 2005a,b; Postel 1999; Postel and Richter 2003; Rao and others 2003; Rathgeber 2003; Ravallion and van de Walle 2003; Reij 2004; Reisner 1986; Rijsberman 2003; Rijsberman and Manning 2006; Rijsberman and Molden 2001; Rodgers, de Silva, and Bhatia 2002; Rogers 2002; Romano and Leporati 2002; Rosegrant and Perez 1997; Rosegrant and Ringler 2000; Rosegrant and Gazmuri S. 1994; Roy and Crow 2004; Saleth and others 2003; Sanctuary and Tropp 2005; Sánchez Munguía 2006; Sarwan, Subijanto, and Rodgers 2005; Schreiner and van Koppen 2003; Schuttelar and others 2003; Scoones 1998; Shah and Keller 2002; Shah and others 2000, 2003; Shivakoti and others 2005; Sivamohan and Scott 2005; SIWI, Tropp and Jägerskog 2006; SIWI and others 2006; Solanes 2006; Soussan 2003, 2004; Sylla 2006; Thébaud, Vogt, and Vogt 2006; Tortajada 2006a,b; Turner and Hildebrandt 2005; Turner and others 2004; UNDP 2003a,b, 2005a,b; Upadhyay 2003; Vaidyanathan 2001; van der Hoeck 2001; Van Hofwegen 2006; van Koppen 1998, 2002; van Koppen and others 2004; van Koppen, Namara, and Safilios-Rothschild 2005; van Koppen, Parthasarathy, and Safiliou 2002; Vermillion 2005; Water Policy Briefing 2002; Wax 2006; WBCSD 2005; Wolff and Hallstein 2005; World Bank 2001, 2002, 2004e, 2006b,f,h; World Commission on Dams 2000; WRI and others 2005.

Chapter 6 draws on AAAS 2002a,b; Abu-Zeid 1998; Allan 1996; Allan 1999; Allouche 2004; ALT 2003; Amaaral and Sommerhalder 2004; Aspinall and Pearson 2000; Assaf 2004; Barraqué and Mostert 2006; Beaumont 2000; Bell, Stewart, and Nagy 2002; Bonetto and Wais 1990; Bonheur 2001; Bonn International Center for Conversion 2006; Carlisle 1998; CIA 2006; Clarke and King 2004; Coe and Foley 2001; Commission on Human Security 2003; Conley and van Niekerk 2000; Crow and Singh 2000; Daoudy 2005; de Mora and Turner 2004; Elhance 1999; Elmusa 1996; FAO 2006; Feitelson 2000, 2002; Fischhendler and Feitelson 2003; Formas 2005; Frisvold and Caswell 2000; Fürst 2003; GEF 2002; Gerlak 2004; Giordano and Wolf 2002; Gleick 1993; Greenberg 2006; Grover 1998; GWP 2001a,b; Haftendorn 1999; Hamner and Wolf 1998; Hirsch and others 2006; Homer-Dixon 1994; Itaipu Binacional 2006; IUCN 2004; Jacobs 1998; Jägerskog and Phillips 2006; Jansky, Pchova, and Murakami 2004; Jolley, Béné, and Neiland 2001; Kamara and Sally 2003; Karaev 2005; Kayombo and Jorgensen 2006; Kemelova and Zhalkubaev 2003; Keohane and Ostrom 1995; Keskinen and others 2005; Kliot 1994; Klohn and Andjelic 1997; Lamoree and Nilsson 2000; Landovsky 2006; Lankford 2005a; Leestemaker 2001; Lindemann 2005; Lonergan 2000; Matsumoto 2002; Matthews 2000; McKinney 2003; MEDRC 2005; Medzini and Wolf 2006; Micklin 1991, 1992, 2000; Mostert 1999, 2005; MRC 2006; Murphy and Sabadell 1986; Nakayama 1998; NEL-SAP 2002; Nguyen and others 2000; Nicol 2002; Nicol, Ariyabandu, and Mtisi 2006; Nishat 2001; O'Lear 2004; Odada, Oyebande, and Oguntola 2006; Peachey 2004; Phillips and others 2004; Priscoli 1998; Puri 2001; Puri and Arnold 2002; Puri and Aureli 2005; PWA 2005; Rekacewicz 1993, 2006; Rekacewicz and Diop 2003; Revenga and others 1998; Rinat 2005; Russell and Morris 2006; SADC 2000, 2005a,b; Sadoff and Grey 2002, 2005; Sánchez Munguía 2006; Sarch and Birkett 2000; Shmueli 1999; Sievers 2002; Sikes 2003; SIWI, Tropp, and Jägerskog 2006; Sklarew and Duda 2002; Sneddon and Fox 2006; Struckmeier, Rubin, and Jones 2005; SUSMAQ 2004; Thébaud and Batterbury 2001; Toset, Gleditsch, and Hegre 2000; Uitto 2004; Uitto and Duda 2002; UNDP 2002, 2005a; UN-DPI 2002; UNECA 2000; UNEP 2001, 2004a,b,c; United States Department of the Interior 2001; van der Zaag and Savenije 1999; VanDeveer 2002; Vinogradov and Langford 2001; Waterbury 1979; Weinthal 2002, 2006; Weinthal and others 2005; White 2006; Wolf 1998, 2000, 2006; Wolf, Yoffe, and Giordano 2003; Wolf and others 1999, 2005; World Bank 2005f, 2006; WSP International 2003; Yang and Zehnder 2002; Yetim 2002; Yoffe and Wolf 1999.

Bibliography

Commissioned research

Background Papers

Bakker, Karen, Michelle Kooy, Nur Endah Shofiani, and Ernst-Jan Martijn. 2006. "Disconnected: Poverty, Water Supply and Development in Jakarta, Indonesia."

Cotula, Lorenzo. 2006. "Water Rights, Poverty and Inequality: The Case of Dryland Africa."

Development Initiatives. 2006. "Development Assistance for Water and Sanitation."

Fuentes, Ricardo, Tobias Pfütze, and Papa Seck. 2006a. "Does Access to Water and Sanitation Affect Child Survival? A Five Country Analysis."

———. 2006b. "A Logistic Analysis of Diarrhea Incidence and Access to Water and Sanitation."

Gandy, Matthew. 2006. "Water, Sanitation and the Modern City: Colonial and Post-colonial Experiences in Lagos and Mumbai."

Grimm, Michael, Kenneth Harttgen, Stephan Klasen, and Mark Misselhorn. 2006. "A Human Development Index by Income Groups."

IDS (Institute of Development Studies). 2006. "Water and Human Development: Capabilities, Entitlements and Power."

Jägerskog, Anders, and David Phillips. 2006. "Managing Transboundary Waters for Human Development."

Narain, Sunita. 2006. "Community-led Alternatives to Water Management: India Case Study."

Nicol, Alan, Rajindra Ariyabandu, and Sobona Mtisi. 2006. "Water as a Productive Resource: Governance for Equity and Poverty Reduction."

Satterthwaite, David, and Gordon McGranahan. 2006. "Overview of the Global Sanitation Problem."

SIWI (Stockholm International Water Institute), Håkan Tropp, Malin Falkenmark and Jan Lundqvist. 2006. "Water Governance Challenges: Managing Competition and Scarcity for Hunger and Poverty Reduction and Environmental Sustainability."

Swyngedouw, Erik. 2006. "Power, Water and Money: Exploring the Nexus."

Tortajada, Cecilia. 2006b. "Water Governance with Equity: Is Decentralisation the Answer? Decentralisation of the Water Sector in Mexico and Intercomparison with Practices from Turkey and Brazil." With Sahnaz Tigrek and Juan J. Sánchez-Meza.

———. 2006c. "Who Has Access to Water? Case Study of Mexico City Metropolitan Area."

WaterAid. 2006. "Getting the 'Off Track' on Target."

Whittington, Dale. 2006. "Pricing Water and Sanitation Services."

Wolf, Aaron T. 2006. "Conflict and Cooperation Over Transboundary Waters."

Thematic Papers

Adams, Martin, Jeremy Berkoff, and Elizabeth Daley. 2006. "Land-Water Interactions: Opportunities and Threats to Water Entitlements of the Poor in Africa for Productive Use."

Barraqué, Bernard, and Erik Mostert. 2006. "Transboundary River Basin Management in Europe."

Gasparini, Leonardo, and Leopoldo Tornarolli. 2006. "Disparities in Water Pricing in Latin America and the Caribbean."

Guevara-Sanginés, Alejandro. 2006. "Water Subsidies and Aquifer Depletion in Mexico's Arid Regions."

Heller, Léo. 2006. "Access to Water Supply and Sanitation in Brazil: Historical and Current Reflections; Future Perspectives."

Hernández Mazariegos, Juan Emilio. 2006. "Water and Basic Sanitation in Latin America and the Caribbean."

Hunt, Caroline. 2006. "Sanitation and Human Development."

Jenkins, Marion W., and Steven Sugden. 2006. "Rethinking Sanitation: Lessons and Innovation for Sustainability and Success in the New Millennium."

Marcus, Richard R. 2006. "Local Responses to State Water Policy Changes in Kenya and Madagascar."

Muller, Arnold Michael. 2006. "Sustaining the Right to Water in South Africa."

Satterthwaite, David. 2006. "Appropriate Sanitation Technologies for Addressing Deficiencies in Provision in Low- and Middle-Income Nations." With Arif Hassan, Perween Rahman, Sheela Patel and Allan Cain.

SIWI (Stockholm International Water Institute), Håkan Tropp and Anders Jägerskog. 2006. "Water Scarcity Challenges in the Middle East and North Africa (MENA)."

Weinthal, Erika. 2006. "Water Conflict and Cooperation in Central Asia."

WHO (World Health Organization), Guy Hutton, Laurence Haller and Jamie Bartram. 2006. "Economic and Health Effects of Increasing Coverage of Low Cost Water and Sanitation Interventions."

Issue Notes

Albiac, José. 2006. "The Case of the Water Framework Directive and Irrigation in Mediterranean Agriculture."

Bryer, Helen. 2006. "England and France in the Nineteenth Century."

Buechler, Stephanie, and Christopher Scott. 2006. "Wastewater as a Controversial, Contaminated yet Coveted Resource in South Asia."

Cai, Ximing. 2006. "Water Stress, Water Transfer and Social Equity in Northern China: Implications for Policy Reforms."

DeGeorges, Andre, and B. K. Reilly. 2006. "Dams and Large Scale Irrigation on the Senegal River. Impacts on Man and the Environment."

Landovsky, Jakub. 2006. "Institutional Assessment of Transboundary Water Resources Management."

Marañón, Boris. 2006. "Tension Between Agricultural Growth and Sustainability: The El Bajio Case, Mexico."

Meinzen-Dick, R. S., and Claudia Ringler. 2006. "Water Reallocation: Challenges, Threats, and Solutions for the Poor."

Patak, Bindeshwar. 2006. "Operation, Impact and Financing of Sulabh."

Practical Action Consulting. 2006a. "Bangladesh Rural Sanitation Supply Chain and Employment Impact."

———. 2006b. "Peru SANBASUR Rural Sanitation Financing Mechanisms."

———. 2006c. "Rural Sanitation in Southern Africa: A Focus on Institutions and Actors."

Sánchez Munguía, Vicente. 2006. "Water Conflict Between the US and Mexico: Lining of the All-American Canal."

Shen, Dajun. 2006. "Access to Water and Sanitation in China: History, Current Situation and Challenges."

Sylla, Oumar. 2006. "Decentralized Management of Irrigation Areas in the Sahel: Water User Associations in the Senegal River Valley."

Tortajada, Cecilia. 2006a. "São Francisco Water Transfer."

UNICEF (United Nations Children's Fund). 2006a. "Children and Water, Sanitation and Hygiene: The Evidence."

References

AAAS (American Association for the Advancement of Science). 2002a. "Mekong Exploratory Mission: Trip Report. Thailand, Cambodia, Vietnam, and the Lao People's Democratic Republic. January 4–22, 2002." Summary. [www.aaas.org/international/ssd/mekong/trip_report.shtml]. July 2006.

———. 2002b. "Mekong River Basin Project." [www.aaas.org/international/ssd/mekong/]. May 2006.

Abderrahman, Walid. 2002. "Policy Analysis of Water, Food Security and Agriculture in Saudi Arabia." Review paper prepared for the World Bank for the Third World Water Forum, 16–23 March 2003, Kyoto. King Fahd University of Petroleum and Minerals, Dhahran, Saudi Arabia.

Abeyasekere, Susan. 1987. "Death and Disease in 19th Century Batavia." In Norman G. Owen, ed., Death and Disease in Southeast Asia: Explorations in Social, Medical and Demographic History. Singapore: Oxford University Press.

———. 1989. Jakarta: A History. Singapore: Oxford University Press.

Abu-Zeid, Mahmoud A. 1998. "Water and Sustainable Development: The Vision for World Water, Life and the Environment." Water Policy 1 (1): 9–19.

ACTS (African Centre for Technology Studies). 2005a. "Climate Change and Development in East Africa: A Regional Report." Nairobi.

———. 2005b. "Climate Change and Development in Kenya." Nairobi.

Adams, A. 2000. "Social Impacts of an African Dam: Equity and Distributional Issues in the Senegal River Valley." Contributing Paper, Thematic Review I.1: Social Impacts of Large Dams Equity and Distributional Issues. World Commission on Dams, Cape Town. [www.dams.org/docs/kbase/contrib/soc193.pdf]. July 2006.

ADB (Asian Development Bank). 2003. "Water in Asian Cities. Summary of Findings of the Study and a Regional Consultation Workshop." Manila.

———. 2004. "Water in Asian Cities. Utilities' Performance and Civil Society Views." Manila.

———. 2006. "Water in Asian Cities. Utility Profile." Manila.

Adikeshavalu, Ravindra. 2004. "An Assessment of the Impact of Bangalore Citizen Report Cards on the Performance of Public Agencies." ECD Working Paper Series 12. World Bank, Washington, DC.

AfDB (African Development Bank). 2005a. "Appraisal Report. Rural Water Supply and Sanitation Program: Uganda." Infrastructure Department, North, East and South Region. Tunis Belvedere. [www.afdb.org/pls/portal/url/ITEM/084B449D5E817267E040C00A0C3D4328]. July 2006.

———. 2005b. "The Rural Water Supply and Sanitation Initiative." New York.

Afrol News. 2006. "Ghana Goes Ahead with Controversial Water Privatisation." 13 January. [www.afrol.com/articles/15312]. July 2006.

Agarwal, A., and Sunita Narain. 1997. "Dying Wisdom: The Rise, Fall and Potential of India's Traditional Water Harvesting Systems." Centre for Science and the Environment, New Delhi.

Agarwal, A., Sunita Narain, and I. Khurana. 2001. "Making Water Everybody's Business: Practice and Policy of Water Harvesting." Centre for Science and Environment, New Delhi.

Albiac, José, and Yolanda Martinez. 2004. "Agricultural Pollution Control Under Spanish and European Environmental Policies." Water Resources Research 40 (10).

Alcamo, J., T. Henrichs, and T. Rösch. 2000. "World Water in 2025: Global Modeling and Scenario Analysis for the World Commission on Water for the 21st Century." Report A0002, Center for Environmental Systems Research, University of Kassel. Kassel, Germany.

Alegría Calvo, María Angélica, and Eugenio Celedón Cariola. 2004. "Analysis of the Privatization Process of the Water and Sanitation Sector in Chile." United Nations Research Institute for Social Development, Geneva.

Al-Ibrahim, Abdulla Ali. 1991. "Excessive Use of Groundwater Resources in Saudi Arabia: Impacts and Policy Options." Ambio 20 (1): 34–37.

Allain-El Mansouri, Béatrice. 2001. L'eau et la ville au Maroc. Rabat-Salé et sa périphérie. Paris: L'Harmattan.

Allan, J. Anthony, ed. 1996. Water, Peace and the Middle East: Negotiating Resources in the Jordan Basin. London: I.B. Tauris.

Allan, T. 1998. "Moving Water to Satisfy Uneven Global Needs: 'Trading Water' as an Alternative to Engineering it." ICID Journal 47 (2): 1–8.

Allan, Tony. 1999. "Israel and Water in the Framework of the Arab-Israeli Conflict." Occasional Paper 15. School of Oriental and African Studies Water Issues Group, Conference on Water and the Arab-Israeli Conflict, 29 April–1 May, Center of Law, Bir Zeit University. [www.soas.ac.uk/waterissues/occasionalpapers/OCC15.PDF]. March 2006.

Allen, Adriana, Julio Davila, and Pascale Hoffman. 2006. "Governance of Water and Sanitation Services for the Peri-Urban Poor: A Framework for Understanding and Action in Metropolitan Regions." University College London, Development Planning Unit, London.

Allouche, Jeremy. 2004. "A Source of Regional Tension in Central Asia: The Case of Water." CIMERA, Geneva. [www.cimera.org/sources/92_104.pdf]. March 2006.

ALT (The Binational Autonomous Authority of Lake Titicaca). 2003. "Lake Titicaca Basin, Bolivia and Peru." In Water for People, Water for Life: The United Nations World Water Development Report. Paris: United Nations Educational, Scientific and Cultural Organization and Berghahn Books.

Alves, Denisard, and Walter Belluzzo. 2005. "Child Health and Infant Mortality in Brazil." Research Network Working Paper R-493. Inter-American Development Bank, Washington, DC.

Amaaral, Helena, and Rubik Sommerhalder. 2004. "The Limpopo River Basin: Case Study on Science and Politics of International Water Management." ETH, Zurich.

Amani, Haidari K. R., Flora Lucas Kessy, and Deogratias Macha. 2004. "Tanzania Country Study. Millennium Development Goals Needs Assessment." Dar es Salaam, Tanzania.

Amarasinghe, Upali A., Bharat R. Sharma, Noel Aloysius, Christopher Scott, Vladimir Smakhtin, and Charlotte de Fraiture. 2006. "Spatial Variation in Water Supply and Demand Across River Basins of India." Research Report 83. International Water Management Institute, Colombo.

Anand, Sudhir, and Amartya Sen. 1994. "Sustainable Human Development: Concepts and Priorities." United Nations Development Programme, New York.

APHRC (African Population and Health Research Center). 2002. Population and Health Dynamics in Nairobi's Informal Settlements. Nairobi.

AquaFed (The International Federation of Private Water Operators). 2006. "Private Water Operators Call to Turn the Right to Water into a Reality for All People." Press Release. [www.

aquafed.org/pdf/Operators_Right-to-Water_PR_Pc_2006-03-19.pdf]. June 2006.

Araral, Eduardo. 2005. "Water User Associations and Irrigation Management Transfer: Understanding Impacts and Challenges." In Priya Shyamsundar, Eduardo Araral and Suranjan Weeraratne, eds., *Devolution of Resource Rights, Poverty and Natural Resource Management: A Review.* Environmental Economics Series Paper 104. Washington, DC: World Bank.

Argo, Teti, and Aprodicio Laquian. 2004. "Privatization of Water Utilities and Its Effects on the Urban Poor in Jakarta Raya and Metro Manila." Forum on Urban Infrastructure and Public Service Delivery for the Urban Poor. Regional Focus: Asia, 24–25 June, New Delhi. [www.wilsoncenter.org/topics/docs/Argo.doc]. May 2006.

Armstrong, Mark, Simon Cowan, and John Vickers. 1995. *Regulatory Reform: Economic Analysis and British Experience.* Cambridge, Mass.: MIT Press.

Arnell, Nigel W. 2004. "Climate Change and Global Water Resources: SRES Emissions and Socio-economic Scenarios." *Global Environmental Change* 14 (1): 31–52.

Arnell, Nigel W., and Chunzhen Liu. 2001. "Hydrology and Water Resources." In James J. McCarthy, Osvaldo F. Canziani, Neil A. Leary, David J. Dokken and Kasey S. White, eds., *Climate Change 2001: Impacts, Adaptation and Vulnerability.* Cambridge, UK: Cambridge University Press for the Intergovernmental Panel on Climate Change.

Aspinall, Richard, and Diane Pearson. 2000. "Integrated Geographical Assessment of Environmental Condition in Water Catchments; Linking Landscape Ecology, Environmental Modelling and GIS." *Journal of Environmental Management* 59 (4): 299–319.

Assaf, Karen. 2004. "Joint Projects and Programs Promoting Middle East Cooperation and Knowledge in the Water Sector." Second Israeli-Palestinian International Conference on Water for Life in the Middle East, October 10–14, Antalya, Turkey.

———. **2006.** Personal correspondence. "The Water Usage Cycle—The Key Management Concept for the Protection of Water and the Environment." Water Studies Center, Arab Scientific Institute. 12 April. New York.

AusAID. 2006. "The Pasig River—Life after Death." Canberra. [www.ausaid.gov.au/publications/pdf/pasigriver.pdf]. July 2006.

Awulachew, S. B., D.J. Merrey, A. B. Kamara, B. van Koppen, F. Penning de Vries, and E. Boelee. 2005. "Experiences and Opportunities for Promoting Small-Scale/Micro Irrigation and Rainwater Harvesting for Food Security in Ethiopia." Working Paper 98. International Water Management Institute, Colombo.

Azam, Jean-Paul, and Jean-Daniel Rinaud. 2000. "Encroached Entitlements: Corruption and Appropriation of Irrigation Water in Southern Pun jab (Pakistan)." Development Studies Working Paper 144. Centro Studi Luca D'Agliano, Milano, Italy. [www.qeh.ox.ac.uk/pdf/lda/lda144.pdf]. June 2006.

Baker, William, Richard Hern, and Matthew Bennett. 1999. *Capital Structure, Interest Coverage and Optimal Credit Ratings.* London: National Economic Research Associates.

Bakker, Karen. 2003a. "Gouvernance urbaine et services de l'eau: la participation du secteur privé à Djakarta (Indonésie)." In Graciela Schneier-Madanes and Bernard de Gouvello, eds., *Eaux et réseaux. Les défis de la mondialisation.* Paris: IHEAL-CREDAL.

———. **2003b.** *An Uncooperative Commodity: Privatizing Water in England and Wales.* New York: Oxford University Press.

Bakker, Margaretha, Randolph Barker, Ruth Meinzen-Dick, and Flemming Konradsen. 1999. "Multiple Uses of Water in Irrigated Areas: A Case Study from Sri Lanka." SWIM Paper 8. Colombo.

Baldwin, Robert, and Martin Cave. 1999. *Understanding Regulation. Theory, Strategy, and Practice.* New York: Oxford University Press.

Ballabh, Vishna. 2005. "Emerging Water Crisis and Political Economy of Irrigation Reform in India." In Ganesh P. Shivakoti, Douglas L. Vermillion, Wai-Fung Lam, Elinor Ostrom, Ujjwal Pradhan and

Robert Yoder, eds., *Asian Irrigation in Transition: Responding To Challenges.* New Delhi and London: Sage.

Bangladesh, Government of. 1998. *Country Strategy Paper for Community Led Total Sanitation.* Dhaka.

———. **2005.** *National Sanitation Strategy.* Ministry of Local Government, Rural Development and Cooperatives. Dhaka. [www.buet.ac.bd/itn/publications/NSS_2005.pdf]. July 2006.

Bapat, Meera, and Indu Agarwal. 2003. "Our Needs, Our Priorities; Women and Men from the Slums in Mumbai and Pune Talk about Their Needs for Water and Sanitation." *Environment and Urbanization* 15 (2): 71–86.

Barnett, T. P., J. C. Adam, and D. P. Lettenmaier. 2005. "Potential Impacts of a Warming Climate on Water Availability in Snow-dominated Regions." *Nature* 438: 303–09.

Bartram, Jamie, Kristen Lewis, Roberto Lenton, and Albert Wright. 2005. "Millennium Project: Focusing on Improved Water and Sanitation for Health." *Lancet* 365 (9461): 810–12.

Bastidas, Elena P. 1999. "Gender Issues and Women's Participation in Irrigated Agriculture: The Case of Two Private Irrigation Canals in Carchi, Ecuador." Research Report 31. International Water Management Institute, Colombo.

Batchelor, Charles, Ashok Singh, M. S. Rama Mohan Rao, and John Butterworth. 2002. "Mitigating the Potential Unintended Impacts of Water Harvesting." IWRA International Regional Symposium "Water for Human Survival," 26–29 November, New Delhi.

Beaumont, Peter. 2000. "Conflict, Coexistence, and Cooperation: A Study of Water Use in the Jordan Basin." In Hussein A. Amery and Aaron T. Wolf, eds., *Water in the Middle East: A Geography of Peace.* Austin: University of Texas Press.

Bell, Frances, and Robert Millward. 1998. "Public Health Expenditures and Mortality in England and Wales, 1870-1914." *Continuity and Change* 13 (2): 221–49.

Bell, Ruth Greenspan, Jane Bloom Stewart, and Magda Toth Nagy. 2002. "Fostering a Culture of Environmental Compliance through Greater Public Involvement." *Environment* 44 (8): 34–44.

Berkamp, G., M. McCartney, P. Dugan, J. McNeely, and M. Acreman. 2000. "Dams, Ecosystem Functions and Environmental Restoration." Thematic Review II.1, Background study for the World Commission on Dams, Cape Town.

BESA (The Begin-Sadat Center for Strategic Studies). 2000. "Efficient Use of Limited Water Resources: Making Israel a Model State." Israel. [www.biu.ac.il/SOC/besa/water/project.html]. July 2006.

Bhatia, Ramesh. 2004. "Community-Managed Sanitation Services for the Urban Poor in Asia, Africa and Latin America: Constraints to Scaling-up of 'Islands of Success.'" Oslo.

Bhatnagar, Deepti, and Ankita Dewan. 2006. "Citizens' Report Cards on Public Services: Bangalore, India." [http://povlibrary.worldbank.org/files/14832_Bangalore-web.pdf]. June 2006.

Bhattarai, Madhusudan, and A. Narayanamoorthy. 2003. "Impact of Irrigation on Rural Poverty in India: An Aggregate Panel-data Analysis." *Water Policy* 5 (5): 443–58.

Bhattarai, Madhusudan, R. Sakthivadivel, and Intizar Hussain. 2002. "Irrigation Impacts on Income Inequality and Poverty Alleviation: Policy Issues and Options for Improved Management of Irrigation Systems." IWMI Working Paper 39. International Water Management Institute, Colombo.

Bhushan, Chandra. 2004. "Water Use in Industry." A *Down to Earth* Supplement, Centre for Science and the Environment. [www.cseindia.org/dte-supplement/industry20040215/non-issue.htm]. December 2005.

Biran, Adam, Anara Tabyshalieva, and Zumrat Salmorbekova. 2005. "Formative Research for Hygiene Promotion in Kyrgyzstan." *Health Policy and Planning* 20 (4): 213–21.

Bird, Jeremy, Larry Haas, and Lyla Mehta. 2005. "'Rights, Risks and Responsibilities' Approach to Implementing Stakeholder

Participation. Scoping Report." [www.accountability21.net/default.
aspx?id=61]. July 2006.

Biswas, Asit K. 2004. "Integrated Water Resources Management: A
Reassessment." *Water International* 29 (2): 248–56.

Biswas, Asit K., and Cecilia Tortajada, eds. 2005. *Water Pricing and
Public-Private Partnership*. Oxon, UK: Routledge.

Biswas, Asit K., Olcay Ünver, and Cecilia Tortajada, eds. 2004.
Water as a Focus for Regional Development. New Delhi: Oxford
University Press.

Black, Maggie. 1998. "1978-1998 Learning What Works. A 20
Year Retrospective View on International Water and Sanitation
Cooperation." Water and Sanitation Program, Washington, DC.

Black, Maggie, Ramesh Bhatia, Kumbulani Murenga, and the
Global Water Partnership Technical Committee. 2003. "Poverty
Reduction and IWRM." GWP TEC Background Paper 8. Stockholm.

Blake, Nelson M. 1956. *Water for the Cities: A History of the Urban
Water Supply Problem in the United States*. New York: Oxford
University Press.

Boelens, Rutgerd. 2003. "Local Rights and Legal Recognition: The
Struggle for Indigenous Water Rights and the Cultural Politics of
Participation." Paper presented at the Third World Water Forum,
16–23 March, Kyoto, Japan.

Boelens, Rutgerd, Axel Dourojeanni, and Paul Hoogendam. 2005.
"Improving Water Allocation for User Communities and Platforms
in the Andes." In Bryan Randolph Bruns, Claudia Ringler, and R. S.
Meinzen-Dick, eds., *Water Rights Reform: Lessons for Institutional
Design*. Washington, DC: International Food Policy Research Institute.

Bonetto, A. A., and I. R. Wais. 1990. "Powerful Paraná." *Geographical
Magazine* 62 (3): 1–3.

Bonheur, Neou. 2001. "Tonle Sap Ecosystem and Value." Technical
Coordination Unit for Tonle Sap, Ministry of Environment, Phnom Penh.

Bonn International Center for Conversion. 2006. "Transboundary
Waters and Crisis Prevention." [www.bicc.de/water/index.php].
May 2006.

Bos, Elroy, and Ger Bergkamp. 2001. "Water and the Environment."
In R. S. Meinzen-Dick and Mark W. Rosegrant, eds., *Overcoming
Water Scarcity and Quality Constraints*. 2020 Vision Publications,
Focus Brief 9, International Food Policy Research Institute,
Washington, DC.

Bousquet, Anne. 2004. "Desserte collective des quartiers pauvres en
Zambie, un long apprentissage." *Flux* 56/57: 71–86.

Breuil, Lise. 2004. *Renouveler le partenariat public-privé pour les
services d'eau dans les pays en développement*. Thèse de doctorat.
Paris: Ecole National du génie Rural, des Eaux et des Forêts.

Briscoe, John. 2005. "India's Water Economy: Bracing for a Turbulent
Future." World Bank, Washington, DC.

Bronstert, Axel, A. Gäuntner, J. C. de Araújo, A. Jaeger, and M. S.
Krol. 2005. "Possible Climate Change Impacts on Water Resources
Availability in a Large Semi-arid Catchment in Northeast Brazil."
IAHS-Publications 295. Wallingford, UK.

Brown, Casey, and Upmanu Lall. 2006. "Water and Economic
Development: The Role of Interannual Variability and a Framework
for Resilience." Working Paper. International Research Institute for
Climate and Society, New York.

Brown, Julia. 2005. "Water Service Subsidies and the Poor: A Case
Study of Greater Nelspruit Utility Company, Mbombela Municipality,
South Africa." Working Paper 112. Centre on Regulation and
Competition, Institute for Development Policy and Management,
Manchester. [www.competition-regulation.org.uk/publications/
working_papers/WP112.pdf]. May 2006.

Brown, Lester R. 2003. *Plan B: Rescuing a Planet Under Stress and a
Civilization in Trouble*. New York and London: W.W. Norton & Company.

Bruns, Bryan Randolph. 1997. "Participatory Management
for Agricultural Water Control in Vietnam: Challenges and
Opportunities." National Seminar on Participatory Irrigation
Management, 7–11 April, Vinh City, Nghe An Province, Viet Nam.

Bruns, Bryan Randolph, and Ruth S. Meinzen-Dick, eds. 2000.
Negotiating Water Rights. London: ITDG Publishing.

Bruns, Bryan Randolph, Claudia Ringler, and R. S. Meinzen-Dick.
2005. "Water Rights Reform: Lessons for Institutional Design."
International Food Policy Research Institute, Washington, DC.

Budds, Jessica, and Gordon McGranahan. 2003. "Privatization and
the Provision of Urban Water and Sanitation in Africa, Asia and Latin
America." Human Settlements Discussion Paper Series, Theme:
Water-1. International Institute for Environment and Development,
London.

Buechler, Stephanie, and Gayathri Devi Mekala. 2005. "Local
Responses to Water Resource Degradation in India: Groundwater
Farmer Innovations and the Reversal of Knowledge Flows." *Journal
of Environment and Development* 14 (4): 410–38.

Buor, Daniel. 2004. "Water Needs and Women's Health in the Kumasi
Metropolitan Area, Ghana." *Health & Place* 10 (1): 85–103.

Cai, Ximing, and Mark W. Rosegrant. 2003. "World Water
Productivity: Current Situation and Future Options." In Jacob
W. Kijne, Randolph Barker, and David Molden, eds., *Water
Productivity in Agriculture: Limits and Opportunities for Improvement*.
Comprehensive Assessment of Water Management in Agriculture
Series, No. 1. Colombo: International Water Management Institute.

Cain, Allan, Mary Daly, and Paul Robson. 2002. "Basic Service
Provision for the Urban Poor: The Experience of Development
Workshop in Angola." Working Paper 8. International Institute for
Environment and Development, London.

Cain, Louis P., and Elyce J. Rotella. 2001. "Death and Spending:
Urban Mortality and Municipal Expenditure on Sanitation." *Annales
de Démographie Historique* 2001/1 (101): 139–54.

Cairncross, Sandy. 2003. "Sanitation in the Developing World: Current
Status and Future Solutions." *International Journal of Environmental
Health Research* 13 (Supplement 1): 123–31.

Cairncross, Sandy, Dominic O'Neill, Anne McCoy, and Dinesh Sethi.
2003. "Health, Environment and the Burden of Disease; a Guidance
Note." UK Department for International Development, London.

Cairncross, Sandy, Ursula Blumenthal, Peter Kolsky, Luiz Moraes,
and Ahmed Tayeh. 1996. "The Public and Domestic Domains in
the Transmission of Disease." *Tropical Medicine and International
Health* 1 (1): 27–34.

Canelli, N. 2001. "El Alto Condominial Pilot Project Impact Assessment.
A Summary." Water and Sanitation Program Andean Region, Lima.

Carlisle, H. L. 1998. "Hydropolitics in Post-Soviet Central Asia:
International Environmental Institutions and Water Resource
Control." Institute on Global Conflict and Cooperation, University
of California, San Diego. [www.ciaonet.org/wps/ria01/igcc29ad.
html.]. May 2006.

The Carter Center. 2006. "Carter Center's Trachoma Control Program."
Atlanta, Ga. [www.cartercenter.org]. July 2006.

CAS (Chinese Academy of Science). 2005. "The Impacts of Human
Activities on Droughts in Arid Regions." Beijing. [http://pd973.tea.
ac.cn/download/middle/kt4.pdf]. December 2005.

Caseley, J. 2003. "Blocked Drains and Open Minds: Multiple
Accountability Relationship and Improved Service Delivery
Performance in an Indian City." IDS Working Paper 211. Institute of
Development Studies, Brighton, UK.

Cassen, Robert, Leela Visaria, and Tim Dyson, eds. 2004. *Twenty-
first Century India: Population, Economy, Human Development, and
the Environment*. New York: Oxford University Press.

Castro, José Esteban. 2004. "Barriers to and Conditions for the
Involvement of Private Capital and Enterprise in Water Supply and
Sanitation in Latin America and Africa: Seeking Economic, Social,
and Environmental Sustainability." Final Project Report (draft
version). In J. E. Castro, coordinator, *PRINWASS Project (European
Commission, Framework V – INCO-DEV Project Contract: PL ICA4-
2001-10041)*. Oxford, University of Oxford. [http://users.ox.ac.
uk/~prinwass/documents.shtml]. July 2006.

CDC (Center for Disease Control and Prevention). 2006. "National Center for Health Statistics." Hyattsville, Md. [www.cdc.gov/nchs/products/pubs/pubd/vsus/historical/historical.htm]. June 2006.

CESCR (Committee on Economic, Social and Cultural Rights). 2002. "The Right to Water." Twenty-Ninth Session, General Comment No. 15 (E/C.12/2002/11), 11–29 November, Geneva. [www.unhchr.ch/html/menu2/6/gc15.doc]. July 2006.

Chan, Ngai Weng. 2005. "Some Comments on Water Privatisation in Malaysia." The Second Southeast Asia Water Forum, Global Water Partnership Southeast Asia, 29 August–3 September, Bali. [www.gwpsea.org/web/Proceedings%20-%202nd%20SEA%20Water%20Forum,%20Bali%202005/Water-Privatisation.pdf]. July 2006.

Chary, Srtinivas V., A. Narender, and K. Rajeswara Rao. 2003. "Serving the Poor with Sanitation: The Sulabh Approach." Third World Water Forum, 19 March, Osaka.

Chen, Shaohua, and Martin Ravallion. 2004. "How Have the World's Poorest Fared Since the Early 1980s?" World Bank Research Observer 19 (2): 141–69.

Chenoweth, Jonathan, and Juliet Bird. 2005. The Business of Water and Sustainable Development: Making Environmental Product Information Systems Effective. Sheffield, UK: Greenleaf Publishing.

Chikhr Saïdi, Fatiha. 1997. La crise de l'eau à Alger: une gestion conflictuelle. Paris: L'Harmattan.

———. 2001. "Alger: des inégalités dans l'accès à l'eau." Nouvelles Politiques de l'eau. Enjeux urbains, ruraux, régionaux, Revue Tiers Monde 32 (166): 305–15.

CIA (Central Intelligence Agency). 2006. "The World Factbook." Washington, DC. [www.cia.gov/cia/publications/factbook/index.html]. May 2006.

Clarke, Robin, and Jannet King. 2004. The Water Atlas: A Unique Visual Analysis of the World's Most Critical Resource. New York: The New Press.

Cleaver, K., and F. Gonzalez. 2003. "Challenges for Financing Irrigation and Drainage." World Bank, Agriculture and Rural Development Department, Washington, DC.

Clermont, Florence. 2006. "Official Development Assistance for Water from 1990 to 2004." [www.worldwatercouncil.org/]. June 2006.

CNA (Comisión Nacional del Agua). 2004. "Statistics on Water in Mexico." Mexico. [www.cna.gob.mx/eCNA/Espaniol/Estadisticas/Central/Estadisticas_Agua_2004/SWM_2004.htm]. July 2006.

Coe, Michael T., and Jonathan A. Foley. 2001. "Human and Natural Impacts on the Water Resources of the Lake Chad Basin." Journal of Geophysical Research (Atmospheres) 106 (D4): 3349–56.

Coing, Henri. 2003. "Décentralisation et gérance privée à Monagas (Venezuela): A quoi servent les contrats?" In Graciela Schneier-Madanes and Bernard de Gouvello, eds., Eaux et réseaux. Les défis de la mondialisation. Paris: IHEAL-CREDAL.

Colin, Jeremy. 1999. "VLOM for Rural Water Supply: Lessons from Experience." Task 162. WELL, Water, Engineering and Development Center, Loughborough University, Loughborough, UK.

Collignon, Bernard. 2002. "Urban Water Supply Innovations in Côte d'Ivoire: How Cross-Subsidies Help the Poor." Field Note 11. Water and Sanitation Program–Africa, Nairobi.

Collignon, Bernard, and Marc Vézina. 2000. "Independent Water and Sanitation Providers in African Cities. Full Report of a Ten-Country Study." Water and Sanitation Program, Washington, DC.

Commission for Africa. 2005. "Our Common Interest: Report of the Commission for Africa." London.

Commission on Human Security. 2003. "Human Security Now: Protecting and Empowering People." New York.

Commission on Macroeconomics and Health. 2001. "Macroeconomics and Health: Investing in Health for Economic Development." World Health Organization, Geneva.

CONADIS, BID, INEC and World Bank. 2004. Ecuador: la Discapacidad en cifras. Análisis de resultados de la Encuesta Nacional de Discapacidades. CD-ROM. Quito, Ecuador

Conan, Hervé. 2003. "Small Piped Water Networks: Helping Local Entrepreneurs to Invest." Water for All Series 13. Asian Development Bank, Manila.

Conley, Alan H., and van Niekerk, Peter H. 2000. "Sustainable Management of International Waters: The Orange River Case." Water Policy 2 (1–2): 131–49.

Connors, Genevieve. 2005. "When Utilities Muddle Through: Pro-poor Governance in Bangalore's Public Water Sector." Environment and Urbanization 17 (1): 201–18.

Conway, Declan. 2005. "From Headwater Tributaries to International River Basin: Adaptation to Climate Variability and Change in the Nile River Basin." Global Environmental Change 15 (2): 99–114.

Corbera, Esteve, Declan Conway, Marisa Goulden, and Katharine Vincent 2006. "Climate Change in Africa: Linking Science and Policy for Adaptation." Workshop Report. London.

Corporate Europe Observatory. 2003. "Alternatives to Privatization: The Power of Participation." [www.tni.org/altreg-docs/participation.pdf#search='porto%20alegre%20brazil%20water']. July 2006.

Crook, Richard C., and Alan Sturla Sverrisson. 2001. "Decentralisation and Poverty Alleviation in Developing Countries." Working Paper 130. Institute of Development Studies, University of Sussex, Brighton, UK.

Crow, Ben, and Nirvikar Singh. 2000. "Impediments and Innovation in International Rivers: The Waters of South Asia." World Development 28 (11): 1907–25.

CSA (Central Statistical Agency of Ethiopia). 2004. "Indicators on Living Standard, Accessibility, Household Assets, Food Security and HIV/AIDS." In Ethiopia Welfare Monitoring Survey 2004, Addis Ababa.

Csaki, Csaba, and C. De Haan. 2003. Reaching the Rural Poor: A Renewed Strategy for Rural Development. Washington, DC: World Bank.

CSO (Central Statistical Organization of India). 2004. Statistical Abstract India, 2003. Ministry of Statistics and Programme Implementation, Government of India. New Delhi: Controller of Publications.

Curtis, Val. 2001. "The Hand Wash Initiative: Third Quarterly Progress Report. Sept 15th–Dec 15th 2001." World Bank and London School of Hygiene and Tropical Medicine. [http://globalhandwashing.org/Global%20activities/Attachments/ppphw_3rdrpt.pdf]. July 2006.

Curtis, Val, and Sandy Cairncross. 2003. "Effect of Washing Hands with Soap on Diarrhoea Risk in the Community: A Systematic Review." Lancet Infectious Diseases 3 (5): 275–81.

Curtis, Val, and Rachel Clarke. 2002. "Hygene: the Art of Public Health." London School of Hygiene and Tropical Medicine, Environmental Health Group, London. [www.lshtm.ac.uk/art/hygiene/danger.html]. June 2006.

Cutler, David, and Grant Miller. 2005. "The Role of Public Health Improvements in Health Advances: The Twentieth-Century United States." Demography 42 (1): 1–22.

Cutler, David, Angus Deaton, and Adriana Lleras-Muney. 2005. "The Determinants of Mortality." NBER Working Paper 11963. National Bureau of Economic Research, Cambridge, Mass.

Cyranoski, David. 2005. "The Long-range Forecast." Nature 438 (17): 275–76.

Daly, Herman, and J. Cobb. 1989. Of the Common Good: Redirecting the Economy Toward Community, the Environment, and a Sustainable Future. Boston, Mass.: Beacon Press.

Daoudy, Marwa. 2005. Le Partage des Eaux Entre la Syrie, l'Irak et la Turquie: Négociation, Sécurité et Asymétrie des Pouvoirs. Paris: CNRS Éditions.

Davis, Jennifer. 2005. "Private Sector Participation in the Water and Sanitation Sector." Annual Review of Environment and Resources 30: 145–83.

de Miras, Claude, and Julien Le Tellier. 2005. Gouvernance urbaine et accès à l'eau potable au Maroc. Partenariat Public-Privé à Casablanca et Tanger-Tétouan. Paris: L'Harmattan.

de Mora, Stephen J., and Tim Turner. 2004. "The Caspian Sea: A Microcosm for Environment Science and International Cooperation." *Marine Pollution Bulletin* 48 (1–2): 26–29.

Deaton, Angus. 2002. "Policy Implications of the Gradient of Health and Wealth." *Health Affairs* 21 (2): 13–30.

———. 2003. "Health, Inequality and Economic Development." *Journal of Economic Literature* 41 (1): 113–58.

———. 2004. "Health in an Age of Globalization." NBER Working Paper 10669. National Bureau of Economic Research, Cambridge, Mass.

Deaton, Angus, and Christina Paxson. 2004. "Mortality, Income and Income Inequality Over Time in Britain and the United States." In David Wise, ed., *Perspectives on the Economics of Aging.* Chicago, Ill.: University of Chicago Press.

Delfino, José, Ariel Casarin, and María Eugenia Delfino. 2005. "How Far Does it Go? The Buenos Aires Water Concession a Decade after the Reform." United Nations Research Institute for Social Development, Geneva.

den Elzen, M. G. J., and M. Meinshausen. 2005. "Meeting the EU 2°C Climate Target: Global and Regional Emission Implications." Netherlands Environmental Assessment Agency. Bilthoven, Netherlands.

Desanker, P. V., and C. Magadza. 2001. "Africa." In James J. McCarthy, Osvaldo F. Canziani, Neil A. Leary, David J. Dokken and Kasey S. White, eds., *Climate Change 2001: Impacts, Adaptation, and Vulnerability.* Intergovernmental Panel on Climate Change, Geneva.

Dhanuraj, D., Prateep Das Gupta, and Swati Puri. 2006. "Community Innovations in Water Delivery: Case Studies of Olavanna and Sangam Vihar." Alternative Reality Series 1. Centre for Civil Society, New Delhi.

Dixon, Robert K., Joel Smith, and Sandra Guill. 2003. "Life on the Edge: Vulnerability and Adaptation of African Ecosystems to Global Climate Change." *Mitigation and Adaptation Strategies for Global Change* 8 (2): 93–113.

Drèze, Jean, and Amartya Sen. 1989. *Hunger and Public Action.* New York: Oxford University Press.

Dubash, N. K. 2000. "Ecologically and Socially Embedded Exchange: The 'Gujarat Model' of Water Markets." *Economic and Political Weekly.* 15 April.

Dubreuil, Céline, and Paul Van Hofwegen. 2006. "The Right to Water: From Concept to Implementation." World Water Council, Marseille, France. [www.worldwatercouncil.org/]. June 2006.

Dutta, S., D. Dutta, P. Dutta, S. Matsushita, S. K. Bhattacharya, and S. Yoshida. 2003. "*Shigella dysenteriae* Serotype 1, Kolkata, India." *Emerging Infectious Diseases* 9 (11): 1471–74. [www.cdc.gov/ncidod/EID/vol9no11/02-0652.htm]. July 2006.

Earth Policy Institute. 2002. "Water Scarcity Spreading." Washington, DC. [www.earth-policy.org/Indicators/indicator7.htm]. June 2006.

———. 2006. "Bottled Water: Pouring Resources Down the Drain." Washington, DC. [www.earth-policy.org/Updates/2006/Update51.htm]. July 2006.

Ebarvia, M. C. M. 1997. "Pricing for Groundwater Use of Industries in Metro Manila, Philippines." Economy and Environment Program for Southeast Asia, Singapore.

The Economist. 2003. "Priceless. A Survey of Water." 19 July.

———. 2004. "The Flood Dries Up." 28 August.

Elamon, Joy. 2005. "People's Initiative in Water-Olavanna Village in Kerala, India Shows the Way." In Belén Balanyá, Brid Brennan, Olivier Hoedeman, Satoko Kishimoto, and Philipp Terhorst, eds., *Reclaiming Public Water: Achievements, Struggles and Visions from Around the World.* Amsterdam: Transnational Institute and Corporate Europe Observatory.

Elhance, Arun P. 1999. *Hydropolitics in the Third World: Conflict and Cooperation in International River Basins.* Washington, DC: United States Institute of Peace Press.

Ellis, Jane, and Ellina Levina. 2005. "The Developing CDM Market." Organisation for Economic Co-operation and Development, Paris.

Ellis, Jane, Jan Corfee-Morlot, and Harald Winkler. 2004. "Taking Stock of Progress Under the Clean Development Mechanism (CDM)." Organisation for Economic Co-operation and Development, Paris.

Elmusa, Sharif S. 1996. "Negotiating Water: Israel and the Palestinians." Institute for Palestine Studies Working Paper. [www.ciaonet.org/wps/els01/]. July 2006.

Environmental Health at USAID. 2004. "Water, Sanitation, Hygiene, and Diarrheal Diseases Bibliography." EHProject Information Center. Arlington, Va. [www.ehproject.org/PDF/Others/WSDD-Bibliography%202004.pdf]. June 2006.

Environmental Justice Coalition for Water. 2005. "Thirsty for Justice: A People's Blueprint for California Water." Oakland, Calif.

Environmental Working Group. 2005. "California Water Subsidies." Oakland, Calif. [www.ewg.org/reports/watersubsidies/]. November 2005.

Esguerra, Jude. 2002. "The Corporate Muddle of Manila's Water Concessions: How the World's Biggest and Most Successful Privatisation Turned Into a Failure." WaterAid, London.

———. 2005. "Manila Water Privatization: Universal Service Coverage after the Crisis?" United Nations Research Institute for Social Development, Geneva.

Esrey, S. A., J. B. Potash, L. Roberts, and C. Shiff. 1991. "Effects of Improved Water Supply and Sanitation on Ascariasis, Diarrhoea, Dracunculiasis, Hookworm Infection, Schistosomiasis, and Trachoma." *Bulletin of the World Health Organization* 69 (5): 609–21.

Esteller, Maria Vicenta, and Carlos Diaz-Delgado. 2002. "Environmental Effects of Aquifer Overexploitation: A Case Study in the Highlands of Mexico." *Environmental Management* 29 (2): 266–78.

Etienne, Janique. 1998. *Formes de la demande et modes de gestion des services d'eau potable en Afrique subsaharienne: spécificité des milieux semi-urbains.* Thèse de doctorat. Marne-la-Vallée: Ecole Nationale des Ponts et Chaussées.

Etienne, Janique, Henri Coing, Hervé Conan, Sylvy Jaglin, Alain Morel à l'Huissier, Michel Tamiatto, and Yves Vailleux. 1998. "Analyse comparative des performances de divers systèmes de gestion déléguée des points d'eau collectif. Bénin, Burkina Faso, Guinée, Mali, Namibie, Niger, Sénégal." BURGEAP, Boulogne, France.

The European Regional Committee. 2006. "Europe, Water and the World." European Regional Document. Prepared for the Fourth World Water Forum, 16–22 March, Mexico City. [www.worldwatercouncil.org/fileadmin/wwc/World_Water_Forum/WWF4/Regional_process/EUROPE.pdf]. June 2006.

Ezcurra, Exequiel M. 1998. "Conservation and Sustainable Use of Natural Resources in Baja California: An Overview." Briefing paper prepared for San Diego Dialogue. San Diego, Calif. [http://sandiegodialogue.org/pdfs/Baja%20Natural%20Resources%20doc.pdf]. July 2006.

Falkenmark, Malin. 2003. "Freshwater as Shared between Society and Ecosystems: From Divided Approaches to Integrated Challenges." *Philosophical Transactions of the Royal Society B* 358 (1440): 2037–50.

Falkenmark, Malin, and Johan Rockström. 2004. *Balancing Water for Humans and Nature.* Earthscan: London.

———. 2005. "Rain: The Neglected Resource. Embracing Green Water Management Solutions." Swedish Water House Policy Brief 2. Stockholm International Water Institute, Stockholm.

FAO (Food and Agriculture Organization of the United Nations). 2002. "The State of Food and Agriculture 2002." Rome.

———. 2003a. "Groundwater Management. The Search for Practical Approaches." Water Report 25. Rome.

———. 2003b. "Projections Largely Vary by the Extent to Which It Is Estimated Productivity of Rainfed Agriculture Will Increase." Rome.

———. 2004a. "Gender and Food Security." [www.fao.org/Gender/en/agri-e.htm]. April 2006.

———. 2004b. "The State of Food Insecurity in the World (SOFI)." Rome.

———. 2005. "Irrigation in Africa in Figures: AQUASTAT Survey–2005." Water Report 29. Rome.

———. 2006. The AQUASTAT Database. Rome. [www.fao.org/ag/agl/aglw/aquastat/dbase/index.stm]. July 2006.

FAO (Food and Agriculture Organization of the United Nations) and Jelle Bruinsma, eds. 2003. *World Agriculture: Towards 2015/2030—An FAO Perspective*. London: Earthscan.

Faysse, Nicolas. 2004. "An Assessment of Small-Scale Users' Inclusion in Large-Scale Water User Associations of South Africa." IWMI Research Report 84. International Water Management Institute, Colombo.

Feitelson, Eran. 2000. "The Ebb and Flow of Arab-Israeli Water Conflicts: Are Past Confrontations Likely to Resurface?" *Water Policy* 2 (4): 343–63.

———. 2002. "Implications of Shifts in the Israeli Water Discourse for Israeli-Palestinian Water Negotiations." *Political Geography* 21 (3): 293–318.

Feld, Sergio, Somkiat Prajamwong, and Susan Sherman. 2003. "Proposed Integrated Land and Water Resources Management System (ILWRMS) for the Bang Pakong River Basin: Lessons from a User Needs Assessment." *Journal of Water Supply Research and Technology - AQUA* 52 (6): 435–42.

Fewtrell, Lorna, Rachel B. Kaufmann, David Kay, Wayne Enanoria, Laurence Haller, and John M. Colford, Jr. 2005. "Water, Sanitation, and Hygiene Interventions to Reduce Diarrhoea in Less Developed Countries: A Systematic Review and Meta-Analysis." Lancet Infectious Diseases 5 (1): 42–52.

Figuères, Caroline M., Cecilia Tortajada, and Johan Rockström, eds. 2003. *Rethinking Water Management: Innovative Approaches to Contemporary Issues*. London and Sterling, Va.: Earthscan.

Filmer-Wilson, Emilie. 2005. "The Human Rights-Based Approach to Development: The Right to Water." *Netherlands Quarterly of Human Rights* 23 (2): 213–41.

Fischer, Günther, Mahendra Shah, and Harrij van Velthuizen. 2002. "Climate Change and Agricultural Vulnerability." Report prepared for the World Summit on Sustainable Development, Johannesburg, 26 August–4 September. International Institute for Applied Systems Analysis, Laxenburg, Austria.

Fischer, Günther, Mahendra Shah, Francesco N. Tubiello, and Harrij van Velthuizen. 2005. "Socio-economic and Climate Change Impacts on Agriculture: An Integrated Assessment, 1990-2080." *Philosophical Transactions of the Royal Society B: Biological Sciences* 360 (1463): 2067–83.

Fischhendler, Itay, and Eran Feitelson. 2003. "Spatial Adjustment as a Mechanism for Resolving River Basin Conflicts: the US-Mexico Case." *Political Geography* 22 (5): 557–83.

Formas (Swedish Research Council for Environment, Agricultural Sciences and Spatial Planning). 2005. "Groundwater under Threat." Stockholm. [www.formas.se/upload/dokument/PDF%20filer/groundwater_under_threat.pdf]. May 2006.

Foster, Vivien, and Tito Yepes. 2005. "Latin America Regional Study on Infrastructure. Is Cost Recovery a Feasible Objective for Water and Electricity?" World Bank, Washington, DC.

Foster, Vivien, Subhrendu Pattanayak, and Linda Stalker Prokopy. 2003. "Do Current Water Subsidies Reach the Poor?" Water Tariffs and Subsidies in South Asia, Paper 4. Water and Sanitation Program and Public-Private Infrastructure Advisory Facility, Washington, DC.

Fournier, Jean-Marc. 2003. "Service de l'eau, inégalités socials et heritage colonial à Puebla, (Mexique)." In Graciela Schneier-Madanes and Bernard de Gouvello, eds., *Eaux et réseaux. Les défis de la mondialisation*. Paris: IHEAL-CREDAL.

Foxwood, Naomi. 2005. "Making Every Drop Count. Financing Water, Sanitation and Hygiene in Sierra Leone." Water Supply and Sanitation Collaborative Council and Tearfund, Geneva and Teddington, UK.

Franceys, R. 1997. "Sri Lanka: Urban Water Supply. Role of Government in Adjusting Economies." Paper 17. Development Administration, University of Birmingham, UK.

Freedman, Lynn P., Ronald J. Waldman, Helen de Pinho, Meg E. Wirth, A. Mushtaque R. Chowdhury, and Allen Rosenfield. 2005. "Transforming Health Systems to Improve the Lives of Women and Children." *Lancet* 365 (9463): 997–1000.

Friedman, Thomas L. 2005. *The World is Flat*. New York: Farrar, Straus and Giroux.

Frisvold, George B., and Margriet F. Caswell. 2000. "Transboundary Water Management: Game-Theoretic Lessons for Projects on the U.S.-Mexico Border." *Agricultural Economics* 24 (1): 101–11.

Fürst, Heiko. 2003. "The Hungarian-Slovakian Conflict over the Gabcikovo-Nagymaros Dams: An Analysis." Institute for Peace Research and Security Policy. University of Hamburg, Hamburg, Germany. [www.columbia.edu/cu/sipa/REGIONAL/ECE/furst3.pdf]. July 2006.

G-8 (Group of Eight). 2003. "G-8 Evian 2003." [www.g8.fr/evian/]. July 2006.

Gandhi, Mohandas Karamchand. [1927–29] 1993. *An Autobiography: The Story of My Experiments with Truth*, trans. Mahadev Desai. Boston, Mass.: Beacon Press.

Gandy, Matthew. 2004. "Rethinking Urban Metabolism: Water, Space and the Modern City." *City* 8 (3): 363–79.

———. 2005. "Learning from Lagos." *New Left Review* 33 (May/June): 37–52.

Garduño, Héctor. 2005. "Making Water Rights Administration Work." International Workshop on African Water Laws: Plural Legislative Frameworks for Rural Water Management in Africa, Johannesburg, South Africa.

GEF (Global Environment Facility). 2002. "UNDP-GEF Dnipro Basin Environment Program." Washington, DC. [www.dnipro-gef.net/about/summary.php]. July 2006.

———. 2006. Correspondence on adaptation funds. September. New York.

Gerlak, Andrea K. 2004. "One Basin at a Time: The Global Environment Facility and Governance of Transboundary Waters." *Global Environmental Politics* 4 (4): 108–41.

Giordano, Meredith A., and Aaron T. Wolf. 2002. "The World's International Freshwater Agreements." In *The Atlas of International Freshwater Agreements*. United Nations Environment Programme. Nairobi. [www.transboundarywaters.orst.edu/publications/atlas/atlas_html/foreword/internationalAgreements.html]. May 2006.

Gleick, Peter H. 1993. "Water and Conflict: Fresh Water Resources and International Security." *International Security* 18 (1): 79–112.

———. 2000. "The Changing Water Paradigm: A Look at Twenty-First Century Water Resources Development." *Water International* 25 (1): 127–38.

———. 2002. "Dirty Water: Estimated Deaths from Water-Related Diseases 2000-2020." Pacific Institute for Studies in Development, Environment, and Security. [www.pacinst.org/]. June 2006.

———. 2003. "Global Freshwater Resources: Soft-Path Solutions for the 21st Century." *Science* 302 (5650): 1524–28.

———. 2004. *The World's Water 2004-2005: The Biennial Report on Freshwater Resources*. Washington, DC: Island Press.

———. 2005. "Water for Our Future." Testimony to a Joint Hearing of the California Senate and Assembly Committees on "The State of California's Environment: Obstacles and Opportunities," 2 March. Sacramento, Calif.

Gleick, Peter H., Gary Wolff, Elizabeth L. Chalecki, and Rachel Reyes. 2002. "The New Economy of Water: The Risks and Benefits of Globalization and Privatization of Fresh Water." Pacific Institute, Oakland, Calif.

The Global Fund to Fight AIDS, Tuberculosis and Malaria. 2006a. "How the Fund Works." Geneva. [www.theglobalfund.org/en/about/how/]. July 2006.

———. 2006b. "Investing in Impact. Mid-Year Result Report." Geneva. [www.theglobalfund.org/en/files/about/replenishment/progress_report_midyear_2006.pdf]. July 2006.

The Global Public-Private Partnership for Handwashing with Soap. 2003. "First Public-Private Handwashing Initiative." Country-Sharing and Orientation Workshop, 14–17 May, Accra.

Gómez-Lobo, Andrés, and Dante Contreras. 2003. "Water Subsidy Policies: A Comparison of the Chilean and Colombian Schemes." The World Bank Economic Review 17 (3): 391–407.

Graham, David, and Ngaire Woods. 2006. "Making Corporate Self-Regulation Effective in Developing Countries." World Development 34 (5): 868–83.

Graham, Stephen, and Simon Marvin. 2001. Splintering Urbanism: Networked Infrastructures, Technological Mobilities and the Urban Condition. London: Routledge.

Greenberg, Ilan. 2006. "As a Sea Rises, So Do Hopes for Fish, Jobs and Riches." New York Times. 6 April.

Greenfacts.org. 2006. "Scientific Facts on Ecosystem Change." Brussels. [www.greenfacts.org]. June 2006.

Grey, David, and Claudia W. Sadoff. 2006. "Water for Growth and Development: A Framework for Analysis. A Baseline Document for the 4th World Water Forum. Theme 1: Water for Growth and Development." [www.worldwaterforum4.org.mx/uploads/TBL_DOCS_46_55.pdf]. June 2006.

Grimsey, Darrin, and Mervyn K. Lewis. 2002. "Evaluating the Risks of Public-Private Partnerships for Infrastructure Projects." International Journal of Project Management 20 (2): 107–18.

Grover, Brian. 1998. "Twenty-five Years of International Cooperation in Water-related Development Assistance, 1972-1997." Water Policy 1 (1): 29–43.

Guasch, J. Luis, and Pablo Spiller. 1999. "Managing the Regulatory Process: Design, Concepts, Issues, and the Latin America and Caribbean Story." Latin American and Caribbean Studies, Viewpoints. Washington, DC: World Bank.

Guislain, Pier, and Michel Kerf. 1995. "Concessions—The Way to Privatize Infrastructure Sector Monopolies." Public Policy for the PRIVATE Sector Note 59. World Bank, Washington, DC.

Gulf Times. 2006. "Clashes Over Water Claims 14 Lives." 21st June.

GWA (Gender and Water Alliance). 2003. "The Gender and Water Development Report 2003: Gender Perspectives on Policies in the Water Sector." Delft, Netherlands.

Gwatkin, Davidson. 2002. "Who Would Gain Most from Efforts to Reach the Millennium Development Goals for Health? An Inquiry into the Possibility of Progress that Fails to Reach the Poor." Health, Nutrition and Population Discussion Paper. World Bank, Washington, DC.

Gwatkin, Davidson, Shea Rutstein, Kiersten Johnson, Eldaw Abdalla Suliman, Adam Wagstaff, and Agbessi Amouzou. 2005. "Socioeconomic Differences in Health, Nutrition, and Population. Second edition." World Bank, Washington, D.C.

GWP (Global Water Partnership). 2000. "Integrated Water Resources Management." TEC Background Paper 4. Technical Committee. Stockholm.

———. 2001a. "Senegal—Establishing a Transboundary Organisation for IWRM in the Senegal River Basin." GWP Toolbox Case 45. Stockholm. [www.gwptoolbox.org/ZappEngine/objects/ACFA73.pdf]. May 2006.

———. 2001b. "West Africa—IWRM in the Niger River Basin." GWP Toolbox Case 46. Stockholm. [www.gwptoolbox.org/ZappEngine/objects/ACFA76.pdf]. May 2006.

———. 2004. "Catalyzing Change: A Handbook for Developing Integrated Water Resources Management (IWRM) and Water Efficiency Strategies." Stockholm.

———. 2006a. "Setting the Stage for Change." Stockholm. [www.gwpforum.org]. June 2006.

———. 2006b. "Setting the Stage for Change: Second Informal Survey by the GWP Network Giving the Status of the 2005 WSSD Target on National Integrated Water Resources Management and Water Efficiency Plans." Stockholm. [www.gwpforum.org/gwp/library/IWRMSurvey-final.pdf]. April 2006.

———. 2006c. "Water and Sustainable Development: Lessons from Chile." Stockholm. [www.gwpforum.org/gwp/library/Policybrief2Chile.pdf]. June 2006.

Haarmeyer, David, and Ashoka Mody. 1998. "Financing Water and Sanitation Projects—The Unique Risks." Public Policy for the Private Sector Note 151 (September). World Bank, Washington, DC.

HABITAT (United Nations Centre for Human Settlements). 2001. Cities in a Globalizing World. Global Report on Human Settlements 2001. London and Sterling, Va.: Earthscan.

Hadley Centre. 2004. "Uncertainty, Risk and Dangerous Climate Change." Exeter, UK. [www.metoffice.com/research/hadleycentre/pubs/brochures/B2004/global.pdf]. July 2006.

Haftendorn, Helga. 1999. "Water and International Conflict." International Studies Association. 40th Annual Convention, 16–20 February, Washington, DC.

Haile, Menghestab. 2005. "Weather Patterns, Food Security and Humanitarian Response in sub-Saharan Africa." Philosophical Transactions of the Royal Society B 360 (1463): 2169–82.

Haisman, Brian. 2005. "Impacts of Water Rights Reform in Australia." In Bryan Randolph Bruns, Claudia Ringler, and R. S. Meinzen-Dick, eds., Water Rights Reform: Lessons for Institutional Design. Washington, DC: International Food Policy Research Institute.

Halim, Shaikh A. 2002. "Shifting Millions from Open Defecation to Hygienic Latrines." Village Education Resource Center, Dhaka.

Hall, David, Emanuele Lobina, Odete Maria Viero, and Hélio Maltz. 2002. "Water in Porto Alegre, Brazil - Accountable, Effective, Sustainable and Democratic." A Public Services International Research Unit and Municipal Department of Water and Sanitary Sewage paper for the World Summit on Sustainable Development, 26 August–4 September, Johannesburg. [www.psiru.org/reports/2002-08-W-dmae.pdf]. July 2006.

Halliday, Stephen. 1999. The Great Stink of London. Sir Joseph Bazalgette and the Cleansing of the Victorian Metropolis. Phoenix Mill: Sutton Publishing.

Hamlin, Christopher. 1988. "Muddling in Bumbledom: On the Enormity of Large Sanitary Improvements in Four British Towns, 1855-1885." Victorian Studies 32 (1): 55–83.

Hamner, Jesse, and Aaron T. Wolf. 1998. "Patterns in International Water Resource Treaties: The Transboundary Freshwater Dispute Database." Colorado Journal of International Environmental Law and Policy. 1997 Yearbook. University of Colorado at Boulder.

Hanchate, Amresh, and Tim Dyson. 2004. "Prospects for Food Demand and Supply." In Robert Cassen, Leela Visaria, and Tim Dyson, eds., Twenty-first Century India: Population, Economy, Human Development, and the Environment. New York: Oxford University Press.

Hanchett, Suzanne, Shireen Akhter, Mohidul Hoque Khan, Stephen Mezulianik, and Vicky Blagbrough. 2003. "Water, Sanitation and Hygiene in Bangladeshi Slums: An Evaluation of the WaterAid-Bangladesh Urban Programme." Environment and Urbanization 15 (2): 43–55.

Hansen, S., and R. Bhatia. 2004. "Water and Poverty in a Macro-economic Context." Paper commissioned by the Norwegian Ministry of the Environment in preparation for the United Nations Commission on Sustainable Development 12, 19–30 April, New York.

Hare, Bill, and Malte Meinhausen. 2004. "How Much Warming Are We Committed to and How Much Can Be Avoided?" Potsdam Institute for Climate Impact Research, Potsdam, Germany.

Hasan, Arif. 2005. "The Orangi Pilot Project: Research and Training Institute's Mapping Process and Its Repercussions." Orangi Pilot Project, International Institute for Environment and Development, Karachi.

Hassan, J. A. 1985. "The Growth and Impact of the British Water Industry in the Nineteenth Century." *The Economic History Review* New Series, 38 (4): 531–47.

Hildebrandt, Timothy, and Jennifer L. Turner. 2005. "Water Conflict Resolution in China." *China Environment Series* 7: 99–103.

Hinrichsen, D., B. Robey and U. D. Upadhyay. 1997. "Solutions for a Water-Short World." Population Reports, Series M, No. 14. Johns Hopkins School of Public Health, Population Information Program, Baltimore, Md.

Hirsch, Philip, and Kurt Mørck Jensen. 2006. "National Interests and Transboundary Water Governance in the Mekong." With Ben Boer, Naomi Carrard, Stephen FitzGerald, and Rosemary Lyster. Australian Mekong Resource Center and Danish International Development Assistance. [www.mekong.es.usyd.edu.au/projects/mekong_water_governance2.htm]. July 2006.

Hoanh, C. T., T. P. Tuong, K. M. Gallop, J. W. Gowing, S. P. Kam, N. T. Khiem, and N. D. Phong. 2003. "Livelihood Impacts of Water Policy Changes: Evidence from a Coastal Area of the Mekong River Delta." *Water Policy* 5 (5): 475–88.

Hodgson, S. 2004. "Land and Water—The Rights Interface." LSP Working Paper. Food and Agriculture Organization of the United Nations, Rome.

Homer-Dixon, Thomas F. 1994. "Environmental Scarcities and Violent Conflict: Evidence from Cases." *International Security* 19 (1): 5–40.

Howard, Guy, and Jamie Bartram. 2003. "Domestic Water Quantity, Service Level and Health." WHO/SDE/WSH/03.02. World Health Organization, Geneva.

Hugo, Victor. [1862] 1982. *Les Misérables*, trans. Norman Denny. New York: Penguin Classics.

Hussain, Intizar. 2004. "Pakistan Country Report: Pro-poor Intervention Strategies in Irrigated Agriculture in Asia: Issues and Options." With Waqar A. Jehangir, Muhammad Ashfaq, Intizar Hussain, Muhammad Mudasser, and Aamir Nazir. International Water Management Institute and Asian Development Bank, Colombo.

———. 2005. "Pro-poor Intervention Strategies in Irrigated Agriculture in Asia. Final Synthesis Report." International Water Management Institute, Colombo.

Hussain, Intizar, and Munir Hanjra. 2003. "Does Irrigation Water Matter for Rural Poverty Alleviation? Evidence from South and South-East Asia." *Water Policy* 5 (5): 429–42.

Hussain, Intizar, and Deeptha Wijerathna. 2004a. "Implications of Alternate Irrigation Water Charging Policies for the Poor Farmers in Developing Asia: A Comparative Analysis." International Water Management Institute, Colombo.

———. 2004b. "Irrigation and Income-Poverty Alleviation: A Comparative Analysis of Irrigation Systems in Developing Asia." International Water Management Institute, Colombo.

Hutton, Guy, and Laurence Haller. 2004. "Evaluation of the Costs and Benefits of Water and Sanitation Improvements at the Global Level." World Health Organization, Geneva.

ID21. 2006a. "Can Targeting Family Farms Help to Reduce Poverty?" Brighton, UK. [www.id21.org/nr/n1ml1g1.html]. June 2006.

———. 2006b. "Is Trade in Virtual Water a Solution for Water-Scarce Countries?" Brighton, UK. [www.id21.org/nr/r2cd1g1.html]. June 2006.

———. 2006c. "Managing the Business Costs of Water Scarcity." Brighton, UK. [www.id21.org/urban/u3ac1g1.html]. June 2006.

———. 2006d. "The Role of Water Security in Poverty Reduction." Brighton, UK. [www.id21.org/nr/n6js1g1.html]. June 2006.

IEG (Independent Evaluation Group). 2006a. "India—Comparative Review of Rural Water Systems Experience: The Rajastan Water Supply and Sewerage Project, and the Rural Water Supply and Environmental Sanitation Projects for Maharastra and Karnataka." World Bank, Washington, DC.

———. 2006b. "Irrigation: Operation, Maintenance, and System Performance in Southeast Asia: An OED Impact Study." World Bank, Washington, DC.

IFAD (International Fund for Agricultural Development). 2001. "Rural Poverty Report 2001. The Challenge of Ending Rural Poverty." Rome.

———. 2006. "Plan to Cut Global Poverty by 50% is Failing: Needs of Rural Majority Neglected." Rome. [www.ifad.org/poverty/pr.htm]. June 2006.

India, Government of. 2001. "Land Use Statistics at a Glance (1998–99 and 1999–2000)." Department of Agriculture and Cooperation, Ministry of Agriculture. [http://agricoop.nic.in/statistics/st3.htm]. May 2006.

INEGI (Instituto Nacional de Estadística, Geografía e Informática). 2006a. "Gasto programable ejercido del sector público presupuestal por clasificación funcional." Aguascalientes, Mexico. [www.inegi.gob.mx/est/contenidos/espanol/rutinas/ept.asp?t=fipu05&c=5031]. June 2006.

———. 2006b. "Porcentaje de la población con servicios de agua potable por entidad federativa, 1990 a 2003." Aguascalientes, Mexico. [www.inegi.gob.mx/est/contenidos/espanol/rutinas/ept.asp?t=mamb105&c=5850]. June 2006.

Inocencio, A., H. Sally, and Douglas J. Merrey. 2003. "Innovative Approaches to Agricultural Water Use for Improving Food Security in Sub-Saharan Africa." International Water Management Institute, Colombo.

Inocencio, A., M. Kikuchi, D. Merrey, M. Tonosaki, A. Maruyama, I. de Jong, H. Sally, and F. Penning de Vries. 2005. "Lessons from Irrigation Investment Experiences: Cost-Reducing and Performance-Enhancing Options for Sub-Saharan Africa." International Water Management Institute, Colombo.

Interagency Task Force on Gender and Water. 2004. "A Gender Perspective on Water Resources and Sanitation." Background Paper submitted to the Commission on Sustainable Development, United Nations Department of Economic And Social Affairs, New York.

International Training Network Centre. 2003. "Chapter 5: Thematic Presentations and Discussions." South Asian Conference on Sanitation, 21–23 October, Bangladesh University of Engineering and Technology, Dhaka.

IPCC (Intergovernmental Panel on Climate Change). 2001. "Climate Change 2001: Synthesis Report. A Contribution of Working Groups I, II, and III to the Third Assessment Report of the Intergovernmental Panel on Climate Change." R. T. Watson and the Core Writing Team, eds., Cambridge University Press, Cambridge, UK, and New York.

IRC International Water and Sanitation Centre. 2004. "School Sanitation and Hygiene Education: Symposium Proceedings & Framework for Action." The Way Forward: Construction is Not Enough, Symposium, 8–10 June, Delft, Netherlands.

Isham, Jonathan, and Satu Kahkonen. 2002. "Institutional Determinants of the Impact of Community-Based Water Services: Evidence from Sri Lanka and India." Middlebury College Working Paper Series 0220. Middlebury College, Department of Economics, Middlebury, Ind.

Itaipu Binacional. 2006. "Itaipu Binacional Technical Data: Production." [www.itaipu.gov.br/]. July 2006.

Ito, Chieko. 2005. "Urbanization and Water Pollution in China." Policy and Governance Discussion Paper 05-13. Canberra.

IUCN (World Conservation Union). 2004. "Komadugu-Yobe (Nigeria): Laying the Foundation for Joint Action." Gland, Switzerland. [www.iucn.org/themes/wani/1d.html]. July 2006.

IWMI (International Water Management Institute). 2003. "Confronting the Realities of Wastewater Use in Agriculture." Water Policy Briefing 9. Colombo.

———. 2006. "Recycling Realities: Managing Health Risks to Make Wastewater an Asset." Water Policy Briefing 17. Colombo.

———. Forthcoming. "Comprehensive Assessment of Water Management in Agriculture." Colombo.

Iyer, Ramaswamy. 2003. *Water. Perspectives, Issues, Concerns*. New Delhi: Sage.

Jacobs, Jeffrey W. 1998. "The United States and the Mekong Project." *Water Policy* 1 (6): 587-603.

Jaglin, Sylvy. 1997. "La commercialisation du service d'eau potable à Windhoek (Namibie). Inégalités urbaines et logiques marchandes." *Flux* 30: 16–29.

———. 2001a. "L'eau potable dans les villes en développement: les modèles marchands face à la pauvreté." *Nouvelles Politiques de l'eau. Enjeux urbains, ruraux, régionaux, Revue Tiers Monde* 42 (166): 275–303.

———. 2001b. "Villes disloquées? Ségrégations et fragmentation urbaine en Afrique australe." *Annales de géographie* 619: 243–65.

———. 2002. "Diversifier pour intégrer? La difficile regulation des modes d'approvisionnement en eau potable dans les villes d'Afrique subsaharienne." Rencontres scientifiques franco-africaines de l'innovation territoriale, 22–28 January, Grenoble, France. [http://iga.ujf-grenoble.fr/teo/Innovation/PDF/36%20Jaglin%20Contrib%20cor.pdf]. May 2006.

———. 2003. "Les échelles des réformes des services urbains de l'eau." In Graciela Schneier-Madanes and Bernard de Gouvello, eds., *Eaux et réseaux. Les défis de la mondialisation*. Paris: IHEAL-CREDAL.

———. 2004a. "Etre branché ou pas. Les entre-deux des villes du Sud." *Services en réseaux, services sans réseaux dans les villes du Sud. Flux* 56/57: 4–12.

———. 2004b. "Les services d'eau urbains en Afrique subsaharienne: vers une ingénierie spatiale de la diversité?" N-AERUS Annual Conference, 16–17 September, Barcelona, Spain. [www.naerus.net/sat/workshops/2004/papers/Jaglin.pdf]. May 2006.

———. 2004c. "Vingt ans de réformes dans les services d'eau urbains d'Afrique subsaharienne: une géographie de la diversité." *Cybergéo*. L'eau à la rencontre des territoires.

———. 2005. *Services d'eau en Afrique subsaharienne. La fragmentation urbaine en question*. Paris: Editions du CNRS. Collection Espaces et Milieux.

Jaglin, Sylvy, and Alain Dubresson. 1999. "Les décentralisations au risque de la fragmentation urbaine en Afrique subsaharienne." L'Europe et le sud à l'aube du XXIe siècle. Enjeux et renouvellement de la coopération. Conférence générale de l'EADI, September, Paris. [www.euforic.org/eadi/pubs/pdf/jaglin.pdf?&username=guest@eadi.org&password=9999&groups=EADI&workgroup=]. May 2006.

Jamati, Claude. 2003. "Casablanca (Morocco): An Example of Public-Private Partnership." *International Journal of Water Resources Development* 19 (2): 153–58.

James, A. J., Joep Verhagen, Christine van Wijk, Reema Nanavaty, Mita Parikh, and Mihir Bhatt. 2002. "Transforming Time into Money Using Water: A Participatory Study of Economics and Gender in Rural India." *Natural Resources Forum* 26 (3): 205–17.

Jansky, Libor, Nevelina I. Pchova, and Masahiro Murakami. 2004. "The Danube: A Case Study of Sharing International Waters." *Global Environmental Change* 14 (Supplement 1): 39–49.

Japan Water Forum. 2005. "A Study on Water Infrastructure Investment and its Contribution to Socioeconomic Development in Modern Japan." Tokyo. [www.waterforum.jp/eng/]. June 2006.

Jensen, Peter Kjær, Pham Duc Phuc, Anders Dalsgaard, and Flemming Konradsen. 2005. "Successful Sanitation Promotion Must Recognize the Use of Latrine Wastes in Agriculture: the Example of Viet Nam." *Bulletin of the World Health Organization* 83 (11): 873–74.

Jewitt, Graham. 2002. "Can Integrated Water Resources Management Sustain the Provision of Ecosystem Goods and Services?" *Physics and Chemistry of the Earth* 27 (11–22): 887–95.

Jolley, Thomas H., Christophe Béné, and Arthur E. Neiland. 2001. "Lake Chad Basin Fisheries: Policy Formation and Policy Formation Mechanisms for Sustainable Development." *Research for Sustainable Development* 14 (1–4): 31–33. [http://europa.eu.int/comm/development/body/publications/fish/120131.pdf]. May 2006.

Jones, H. E., and R. A. Reed. 2005. "Water and Sanitation for Disabled People and Other Vulnerable Groups: Designing Services to Improve Accessibility." Water, Engineering, and Development Centre, Loughborough University, Loughborough, UK.

Jones, T. 1998. "Recent Developments in the Pricing of Water Services in OECD Countries." Paper presented at the World Bank Sponsored Workshop on Political Economy of Water Pricing Implementation, 3–5 November, Washington, DC.

Jones, William. 1995. "The World Bank and Irrigation." World Bank, Washington, DC.

Joshi, Deepa. 2005. "Water Access, Poverty and Social Exclusion in India." Overseas Development Institute/Economic and Research Council "Water Governance—Challenging the Consensus." "Seminar 2: Access, Poverty and Social Exclusion." 1 March, University of Bradford, Overseas Development Institute and World Wildlife Fund, London. [www.bradford.ac.uk/acad/bcid/seminar/water].

Jouravlev, Andrei. 2001a. *Regulación de la industria de agua potable. Volumen I: Necesidades de información y regulación estructural*. Serie Recursos Naturales e Infraestructura. Santiago: Economic Commission for Latin America and the Caribbean.

———. 2001b. *Regulación de la industria de agua potable. Volumen II: Regulación de las conductas*. Serie Recursos Naturales e Infraestructura. Santiago: Economic Commission for Latin America and the Caribbean.

Juuti, Petri, and Tapio Katko, eds. 2005. *Water, Time and European Cities. History Matters for the Futures*. Tampere, Finland: Tampere University of Technology.

Kähkönen, Satu. 1999. "Does Social Capital Matter in Water and Sanitation Delivery? A Review of Literature." Social Capital Initiative Working Paper 9. World Bank, Washington, DC.

Kamara, A., and H. Sally. 2003. "Water for Food, Livelihoods and Nature: Simulations for Policy Dialogue in South Africa." *Physics and Chemistry of the Earth* 28 (20–27): 1085–94.

Kar, Kamal, and Petra Bongartz. 2006. "Update on Some Recent Developments in Community-Led Total Sanitation." University of Sussex, Institute of Development Studies, Brighton, UK.

Kar, Kamal, and Katherine Pasteur. 2005. "Subsidy or Self-respect? Community Led Total Sanitation. An Update on Recent Developments." Working Paper 257. University of Sussex, Institute of Development Studies, Brighton, UK.

Karaev, Zainiddin. 2005. "Water Diplomacy in Central Asia." *Middle East Review of International Affairs* 9 (1): 63–69.

Kariuki, Mukami, and Jordan Schwartz. 2005. "Small-Scale Private Service Providers of Water Supply and Electricity—A Review of Incidence, Structure, Pricing and Operating Characteristics." Policy Research Working Paper 3727. World Bank, Washington, DC.

Kayombo, S., and S. Jorgensen. 2006. "Lake Victoria." Experience and Lessons Learned Brief. International Lake Environment Committee, Lake Basin Management Initiative. [www.ilec.or.jp/lbmi2/reports/27_Lake_Victoria_27February2006.pdf]. May 2006.

Kemelova, Dinara, and Gennady Zhalkubaev. 2003. "Water, Conflict, and Regional Security in Central Asia Revisited." *NYU Environmental Law Journal* 11 (1): 479–502.

Kemper, Karin E. 2001. "Markets for Tradable Water Rights." Overcoming Water Scarcity and Quality Constraints. Brief 11. International Food Policy Research Institute, Washington, DC.

Kemper, Karin E., Ariel Dinar, and William Bloomquist. 2005. "Institutional and Policy Analysis of River Basin Management Decentralisation: The Principle of Managing Water Resources at the Lowest Appropriate Level—When and Why Does It (Not) Work in Practice?" World Bank, Washington, DC.

Kennedy, John F. 1962. Remarks in Pueblo, Colorado, August 17. *The Public Papers of the Presidents of the United States.*

Kenney, Douglas S. 2005. "Prior Appropriation and Water Rights Reform in the Western United States." In Bryan Randolph Bruns, Claudia Ringler, and R. S. Meinzen-Dick, eds., *Water Rights Reform: Lessons for Institutional Design.* Washington, DC: International Food Policy Research Institute.

Kenya, Government of. 2005. *MDGs Status Report for Kenya 2005.* Nairobi. [www.ke.undp.org/MDGsO5status.pdf]. July 2006.

Keohane, Robert, and Elinor Ostrom, eds. 1995. *Local Commons and Global Interdependence: Heterogeneity and Cooperation in Two Domains.* London: Sage Publications.

Kerf, Michel. 2000. "Do State Holding Companies Facilitate Private Participation in the Water Sector? Evidence from Côte d'Ivoire, The Gambia, Guinea, and Senegal." Policy Research Working Paper 2513. World Bank, Washington, DC.

Kerr, John. 2002. "Watershed Development, Environmental Services, and Poverty Alleviation in India." *World Development* 30 (8): 1387–1400.

Keskinen, Marko, Jorma Kopenen, Matti Kummu, Jussi Nikula, Juha Sarkkula, and Olli Varis. 2005. "Integration of Socio-Economic and Hydrological Information in the Tonle Sap Lake, Cambodia." International Conference on Simulation and Modeling, SimMod 2005, January 17–19, Bangkok, Thailand. [www.mssanz.org.au/simmod05/papers/C1-02.pdf]. July 2006.

Kibreab, Gaim, and Alan Nicol. 2002. "Returning Thirsty: Water, Livelihoods and Returnees in the Gash-Barka Region, Eritrea." Overseas Development Institute, London.

Kijne, Jacob W., Randolph Barker, and David Molden. 2003a. "Improving Water Productivity in Agriculture: Editors' Overview." In Jacob Kijne, Randolph Barker and David Molden, eds., *Water Productivity in Agriculture: Limits and Opportunities for Improvement.* Wallington, UK: CABI Publishing.

Kijne, Jacob W., Randolph Barker, and David Molden, eds. 2003b. Water Productivity in Agriculture: Limits and Opportunities for Improvement. Wallington, UK: CABI Publishing.

Kiribaki, Aloysius. 2006. Personal correspondence on sensitization of education authorities in Busia District. Action on Disability and Development. 20 February. Kampala, Uganda.

Kisima Newsletter. 2005. "Long Road to Regulating Water Services in Kenya." Issue 2. Nairobi.

Kjellén, Marianne. 2000. "Complementary Water Systems in Dar es Salaam, Tanzania: The Case of Water Vending." *Water Resources Development* 16 (1): 143–54.

Kjellén, Marianne and Gordon McGranahan. 2006. "Informal Water Vendors and The Urban Poor." Human Settlements Discussion Paper Series, Theme: Water-3. International Institute for Environment and Development, London.

Kleiman, Mauro. 2004. "Pratiques quotidiennes des communautés populaires mal branches aux réseaux d'eau et d'assainissement dans les métropoles brésiliennes: les cas de Rio de Janeiro et Salvador." *Services en réseaux, services sans réseaux dans les villes du Sud. Flux* 56/57: 44–56.

Kliot, Nurit. 1994. *Water Resources and Conflict in the Middle East.* London and New York: Routledge.

Klohn, Wulf, and Mihailo Andjelic. 1997. "Lake Victoria: A Case in International Cooperation." Food and Agriculture Organization of the United Nations and Water Resources, Development and Management Service. [www.fao.org/waicent/FaoInfo/Agricult/AGL/AGLW/webpub/VICPUB.HTM]. May 2006.

Komives, Kristin. 1999. "Designing Pro-Poor Water and Sewer Concessions: Early Lessons from Bolivia." Policy Research Working Paper 2243. World Bank, Washington, DC.

Komives, Kristin, Vivien Foster, Jonathan Halpern, and Quentin Wodon. 2005. *Water, Electricity, and the Poor: Who Benefits from Utility Subsidies?* With support from Roohi Abdullah. Washington, DC: World Bank.

Kremer, M., and T. Miguel. 1999. "The Educational Impact of De-Worming in Kenya." Northeast Universities Development Conference, 8–9 October, Harvard University.

Krol, Maarten S., and Axel Bronstert. Forthcoming. "Regional Integrated Modelling of Climate Change Impacts on Natural Resources and Resource Usage in Semi-arid Northeast Brazil." *Environmental Modelling & Software*, doi:10.1016/j.envsoft.2005.07.022.

Kumar, Pushpam. 2005. *Market for Ecosystem Services.* Manitoba, Canada: International Institute for Sustainable Development.

Kurian, Mathew, and Ton Dietz. 2005. "How Pro-Poor are Participatory Watershed Management Projects? An Indian Case Study." Research Report 92. International Water Management Institute, Colombo.

Kurnia, G., T. W. Avianto, and Bryan Randolph Bruns. 2000. "Farmers, Factories and the Dynamics of Water Allocation in West Java." In Bryan Randolph Bruns, Claudia Ringler, and R. S. Meinzen-Dick, eds., *Negotiating Water Rights.* London: Intermediate Technology Publications.

Lamoree, G., and A. Nilsson. 2000. "A Process Approach to the Establishment of International River Basin Management in Southern Africa." *Physics and Chemistry of the Earth, Part B: Hydrology, Oceans and Atmosphere* 25 (3): 315–23.

Lane, Jon. 2004. "Rural Water Supply and Sanitation in Africa: Global Learning Process on Scaling up Poverty Reduction." Scaling Up Poverty Reduction: A Global Learning Process, and Conference; Shanghai, May 25–27, 2004. Water and Sanitation Program–Africa, Kenya. [www.wsp.org/publications/af_globalstudy.pdf]. July 2006.

Lankford, Bruce A. 2005a. "Rural Infrastructure to Contribute to African Agricultural Development: The Case of Irrigation." Report for the Commission for Africa. Overseas Development Group, Norwich, UK. [www.uea.ac.uk/dev/faculty/lankford/cfa_irrig_may05.pdf]. July 2006.

———. **2005b.** "Water Resources Management: Finding Space in Scarcity." Scarcity and the Politics of Allocation workshop, 6–7 June, University of Sussex, Brighton, UK.

Lankford, Bruce A., and W. Mwaruvanda. 2005. "A Framework to Integrate Formal and Informal Water Rights in River Basin Management." African Water Laws: Plural Legislative Frameworks for Rural Water Management in Africa, 26–28 January, Johannesburg, South Africa.

Larrea, Carlos, Pedro Montalvo, and Ana María Ricuarte. 2005. "Child Malnutrition, Social Development and Health Services in the Andean Region." Research Network Working Paper R-495. Inter-American Development Bank, Washington, DC.

Lauria, Donald, Omar Hopkins, and Sylvie Debomy. 2005. "Pro-Poor Subsidies For Water Connections in West Africa. A Preliminary Study." Water Supply and Sanitation Sector Board Working Note 2. World Bank, Washington, DC.

Lawrence, Peter, Jeremy Meigh, and Caroline Sullivan. 2002. "The Water Poverty Index: An International Comparison." Keele Economics Research Paper 2002/19. Keele, UK.

Ledo, Carmen. 2005. "Inequality and Access to Water in the Cities of Cochabamba and La Paz-El Alto." United Nations Research Institute for Social Development, Geneva.

Leestemaker, Joanne Heyink. 2001. "An Analysis of the New National and Sub National Water Laws in Southern Africa: Gaps between the

UN-Convention, the SADC Protocol and National Legal Systems in South Africa, Swaziland and Mozambique." [www.thewaterpage. com/leestemaker.htm]. May 2006.

Lemos, Maria Carmen, and Lúcio Farias de Oliveira. 2004. "Can Water Reform Survive Politics? Institutional Change and River Basin Management in Ceará, Northeast Brazil." *World Development* 32 (12): 2121–37.

———. 2005. "Water Reform Across the State/Society Divide: The Case of Ceará, Brazil." *International Journal of Water Resources Development* 21 (1): 133–47.

Lenton, Roberto, Albert M. Wright, and Kristen Lewis. 2005. *Health, Dignity, and Development: What Will it Take?* UN Millennium Project Task Force on Water and Sanitation. London and Sterling, Va.: Earthscan.

Levine, Ruth, and the What Works Working Group. 2004. "Millions Saved: Proven Successes in Global Health." With Molly Kinder. Center for Global Development, Washington DC.

Lindemann, Stefan. 2005. "Explaining Success and Failure in International River Basin Management - Lessons from Southern Africa." Sixth Open Meeting of the Human Dimensions of Global Environmental Change Research Community, 9–13 October, Bonn, Germany.

Lipton, Michael. 2004a. "Approaches to Rural Poverty Alleviation in Developing Asia: Role of Water Resources." Plenary address at the Regional Workshop and Policy Roundtable, "Pro-Poor Intervention Strategies in Irrigated Agriculture in Asia," 25–27 August, International Water Management Institute, Colombo. [www.sussex. ac.uk/Units/PRU/iwmi_irrigation.pdf]. July 2006.

———. 2004b. "New Directions for Agriculture in Reducing Poverty: The DfID Initiative." Poverty Research Unit, University of Sussex, Brighton, UK. [http://dfid-agriculture-consultation.nri.org/ launchpapers/michaellipton.html]. July 2006.

Lipton, Michael, Julie Litchfield, and Jean-Marc Faurès. 2003. "The Effects of Irrigation on Poverty: A Framework for Analysis." *Water Policy* 5 (5): 413–27.

Liu, Bin. 2005. "Institutional Design Considerations for Water Rights Development in China." In Bryan Randolph Bruns, Claudia Ringler and R. S. Meinzen-Dick, eds., *Water Rights Reform: Lessons for Institutional Design.* Washington, DC: International Food Policy Research Institute.

Lomborg, Bjørn, ed. 2004. *Global Crises, Global Solutions.* Cambridge: Cambridge University Press.

Lonergan, Steve. 2000. "Forces of Change and the Conflict over Water in the Jordan River Basin." In Hussein A. Amery and Aaron T. Wolf, eds., *Water in the Middle East: A Geography of Peace.* Austin: University of Texas Press.

Lucas, P. L., and H. B. M. Hilderink. 2004. "The Vulnerability Concept and Its Application to Food Security." RIVM (National Institute for Public Health and the Environment), Bilthoven, Netherlands.

Luong, T. V., O. Chanacharnmongkol, and T. Thatsanatheb. 2002. "Universal Sanitation in Rural Thailand." *Waterfront* 15: 8–10.

Mace, M. J. 2005. "Funding for Adaptation to Climate Change: UNFCCC and GEF Developments Since COP-7." *Reciel* 14 (3): 225–46.

Malthus, Thomas Robert. [1798] 1826. *An Essay on the Principle of Population, As It Affects the Future Improvement of Society. With Remarks on the Speculations of Mr. Godwin, M. Condorcet, and Other Writers.* London: John Murray.

Maltz, Hélio. 2005. "Porto Alegre's Water: Public and for All." In Belén Balanyá, Brid Brennan, Olivier Hoedeman, Satoko Kishimoto, and Philipp Terhorst, eds., *Reclaiming Public Water: Achievements, Struggles and Visions from Around the World.* Amsterdam: Transnational Institute and Corporate Europe Observatory.

Mapetla, Matseliso. 2006. "Brewing and Housing Strategies in Lesotho." In Ann Schlyter, ed., *A Place to Live: Gender Research Housing in Africa.* Uppsala, Sweden: Nordiska Afrikainstitutet.

Marin, Philippe. 2002. "Output-Based Aid: Possible Applications in the Design of Water Concessions." World Bank, Washington, DC.

Maronier, V. F. C. 1929. "De Drinkwatervoorziening van Batavia. (The Drinking Water Network of Batavia)." *De Waterstaats-Ingenieur* 8: 223–39.

Maslin, Mark. 2004. *Global Warming. A Very Short Introduction.* Oxford: Oxford University Press.

Matsumoto, Kyoko. 2002. "Transboundary Ground Water and International Law: Past Practices and Current Implications." Department of Geosciences, Oregon State University, Corvallis, Ore.

Matthew, Brian. 2005. "Ensuring Sustained Beneficial Outcomes for Water and Sanitation Programmes in the Developing World." Occasional Paper Series 40. IRC International Water and Sanitation Centre, Delft, Netherlands.

Matthews, Mary M. 2000. "International Lending Agencies and Regional Environmental Cooperation in the Black and Caspian Sea." Annual Meeting of the International Association for the Study of Common Property, 31 May–4 June, Bloomington, Ind. [http://dlc. dlib.indiana.edu/archive/00000300/00/matthewsm042400.pdf]. May 2006.

Mayer, Enrique. 2002. *The Articulated Peasant: Household Economies in the Andes.* Boulder, Colo., and Oxford, UK: Westview Press.

McCully, Patrick. 2006. "Spreading the Water Wealth: Making Infrastructure Work for the Poor." IRN Dams, Rivers and People Report 2006. International Rivers Network, Berkeley, Calif.

McGranahan, Gordon, Pedro Jacobi, Jacob Songsore, Charles Surjadi, and Marianne Knellen. 2001. *The Citizens at Risk: From Urban Sanitation to Sustainable Cities.* London: Earthscan.

McIntosh, Arthur C. 2003. "Asian Water Supplies. Reaching the Urban Poor." Asian Development Bank and International Water Association, Manila.

McKinney, Daene C. 2003. "Cooperative Management of Transboundary Water Resources in Central Asia." In D. Burghart and T. Sabonis-Helf, eds., *In the Tracks of Tamerlane - Central Asia's Path into the 21st Century.* Washington, DC: National Defense University Press.

McNeill, John. 2000. *Something New Under the Sun. An Environmental History of the Twentieth Century.* London: Penguin Books.

Measure DHS. 2006. Demographic and Health Surveys Database. Calverton, Md. [www.measuredhs.com]. July 2006.

MEDRC (Middle East Desalination Research Center). 2005. "MEDRC Project Portfolio 2005." Muscat, Oman. [www.medrc. org/]. July 2006.

Medzini, Arnon, and Aaron T. Wolf. 2006. "The Euphrates River Watershed: Integration, Coordination, or Separation?" In Matthias Finger, Ludivine Tamiotti, and Jeremy Allouche, eds., *The Multi-Governance of Water: Four Case Studies.* Albany, N.Y.: SUNY Press.

Mehta, Lyla. 2000. "Water for the Twenty-First Century: Challenges and Misconceptions." Institute of Development Studies, Brighton, UK.

———. 2003. "Problems of Publicness and Access Rights: Perspectives from the Water Domain." In Inge Kaul, Pedro Conceição, Katell Le Goulven, and Ronald U. Mendoza, eds., *Providing Global Public Goods: Managing Globalization.* New York: Oxford University Press.

Mehta, Meera. 2004. "Meeting the Financing Challenge for Water Supply and Sanitation. Incentives to Promote Reforms, Leverage Resources and Improve Targeting." Summary Report. Water and Sanitation Program–Africa, Nairobi.

Mehta, Meera, and Andreas Knapp. 2004. "The Challenge of Financing Sanitation for Meeting the Millennium Development Goals." Water and Sanitation Program–Africa, Nairobi.

Meinzen-Dick, R. S., and Leticia Nkonya. 2005. "Understanding Legal Pluralism in Water Rights: Lessons from Africa and Asia." International Workshop on African Water Laws: Plural Legislative

Frameworks for Rural Water Management in Africa, 26–28 January, Johannesburg, South Africa.

Meinzen-Dick, R. S., and Rajendra Pradhan. 2005. "Recognising Multiple Water Uses in Intersectoral Water Transfers." In Ganesh P. Shivakoti, Douglas L. Vermillion, Wai-Fung Lam, Elinor Ostrom, Ujjwal Pradhan, and Robert Yoder, eds., *Asian Irrigation in Transition: Responding to Challenges*. New Delhi and London: Sage.

Meinzen-Dick, R. S., and Mark W. Rosegrant, eds. 2001. "Overcoming Water Scarcity and Quality Constraints." 2020 Vision Publications, Focus Brief 9. International Food Policy Research Institute, Washington, DC.

Meinzen-Dick, R. S., and Margreet Zwarteveen. 1998. "Gender Participation in Water Management: Issues and Illustrations from Water Users' Associations in South Asia." International Irrigation Management Institution, Colombo.

Meinzen-Dick, R. S., Ruth Zwartevenn, and Margreet Zwartevenn. 1998. "Gendered Participation in Water Management: Issues and Illustrations from Water Users' Associations in South Asia." *Agriculture and Human Values* 15 (4): 337–45.

Melo, Jose Carlos. 2005. *The Experience of Condominial Water and Sewerage Systems in Brazil: Case Studies from Brasilia, Salvador and Parauapebas*. Lima: World Bank–Bank-Netherlands Water Partnership and Water and Sanitation Program.

Ménard, Claude. 2001. "Enjeux d'eau: la dimension institutionnelle." *Nouvelles Politiques de l'eau. Enjeux urbains, ruraux, régionaux, Revue Tiers Monde* 42 (166): 259–74.

Menegat, Rualdo. 2002. "Participatory Democracy and Sustainable Development: Integrated Urban Environmental Management in Porto Alegre, Brazil." *Environment and Urbanization* 14 (2): 181–206.

Merrey, Douglas J., Ruth Meinzen-Dick, Peter P. Mollinga, and Eiman Karar. 2006. "Policy and Institutional Reform Processes for Sustainable Agricultural Water Management: The Art of the Possible." Comprehensive Assessment of Water Management in Agriculture, Colombo.

Metts, Robert. 2000. "Disability Issues, Trends and Recommendations for the World Bank." Social Protection Discussion Paper 0007. World Bank, Washington, DC.

Micklin, Philip. 1991. "The Water Management Crisis in Soviet Central Asia." Carl Beck Paper 905. University of Pittsburgh Center for Russian and East European Studies, Pittsburgh, Penn.

———. 1992. "The Aral Crisis: Introduction to the Special Issue." *Post-Soviet Geography* 33 (5): 269–82.

———. 2000. *Managing Water in Central Asia*. London: Royal Institute of International Affairs.

Miller, Barbara A., and Richard B. Reidinger. 1998. "Comprehensive River Basin Development. The Tennessee Valley Authority." World Bank Technical Paper 416. World Bank, Washington, DC.

Miller, David. 2001. *Principles of Social Justice*. Cambridge, Mass.: Harvard University Press.

Milliband, David. 2005. "Building a Modern Social Contract." Together We Can, 29 June, London. [www.neighbourhood.gov.uk/news.asp?id=1524]. June 2006.

Miovic, Peter. 2004. "Poverty Reduction Support Credits in Uganda: Results of a Stocktaking Study." World Bank, Washington, DC.

Mitlin, Diana. 2004. "Beyond Second Best: The Whys, Hows and Wherefores of Water Subsidies." Centre on Regulation and Competition, Institute for Development Policy and Management. Paper 93. Manchester, UK.

Moench, M., J. Burke, and Y. Moench. 2003. "Rethinking the Approach to Groundwater and Food Security." Food and Agriculture Organization of the United Nations, Rome.

Moench, Marcus. 1998. "Allocating the Common Heritage: Debates over Water Rights and Governance Structures in India." *Economic and Political Weekly* 33 (26): A46–A53.

———. 2001. "Groundwater: Potential and Constraints." In Ruth S. Meinzen-Dick and Mark W. Rosegrant, eds., *Overcoming Water Scarcity and Quality Constraints*. 2020 Vision Publications, Focus Brief 9, International Food Policy Research Institute, Washington, DC.

Moench, Marcus, Ajaya Dixit, S. Janakarajan, M. S. Rathore, and Srinivas Mudrakartha. 2003. "The Fluid Mosaic: Water Governance in the Context of Variability, Uncertainty and Change." Nepal Water Conservation Foundation and the Institute for Social and Environmental Transition; Kathmandu, and Boulder, Colo.

Molden, D. J., U. Amarasinghe, and I. Hussain. 2001. "Water for Rural Development." Working Paper 32. International Water Management Institute, Colombo.

Molden, David, and Charlotte de Fraiture. 2004. "Investing in Water for Food, Ecosystems and Livelihoods." Blue Paper. Comprehensive Assessment of Water Management in Agriculture. International Water Management Institute, Colombo.

Molden, David, Hammond Murray-Rust, R. Sakthivadivel, and Ian Makin. 2003. "A Water-Productivity Framework for Understanding and Action." Colombo.

Molle, François. 2005. "Irrigation and Water Policies in the Mekong Region: Current Discourses and Practices." International Water Management Institute, Colombo.

Molle, François, and Jeremy Berkoff. 2006. "Cities Versus Agriculture: Revisiting Intersectoral Water Transfers, Potential Gains and Conflicts." Comprehensive Assessment Research Report 10. Comprehensive Assessment of Water Management in Agriculture. International Water Management Institute, Colombo.

Morel à l'Huissier, Alain, Véronique Verdeil, and Christophe Le Jallé. 1998. "Modes de gestion des bornes-fontaines dans les quartiers périurbains, le cas de trios villes maliennes." Programme Solidarité Eau. Cahier Technique 11. Paris.

Moriarty, Patrick, and John Butterworth. 2005. "Water, Poverty and Productive Uses of Water at the Household Level." Background paper for PRODWAT Thematic Group Meeting, 7–8 December, Overseas Development Institute, London.

Mostert, Erik. 1999. "Perspectives on River Basin Management." *Physics and Chemistry of the Earth (B)* 24 (6): 563–69.

———. 2005. "How can International Donors Promote Transboundary Water Management?" Discussion Paper 8. German Development Institute, Bonn.

Movik, Synne, Lyla Mehta, Sobona Mtisi, and Alan Nicol. 2005. "A 'Blue Revolution' for African Agriculture?" *IDS Bulletin* 36 (2): 41–45.

MRC (Mekong River Commission). 2006. "About Mekong." Vientiane. [www.mrcmekong.org/about_mekong/people.htm]. July 2006.

Mukherjee, Nilanjana. 2001. "Achieving Sustained Sanitation for the Poor. Policy and Strategy Lessons from Participatory Assessments in Cambodia, Indonesia, Vietnam." Water and Sanitation Program–East Asia and the Pacific, Jakarta.

Murphy, Irene L., and Eleonora J. Sabadell. 1986. "International River Basins: A Policy Model for Conflict Resolution." *Resources Policy* 12 (1): 133–44.

Murray, Laurel, and Victor Orindi. 2005. "Adapting to Climate Change in East Africa: A Strategic Approach." Gatekeeper Series 117. International Institute for Environment and Development, London.

Myers, Norman. 1998. "Perverse Subsidies: Tax $s Undercutting Our Economies and Environments Alike." With Jennifer Kent. International Institute for Sustainable Development, Winnipeg, Canada.

Nakayama, Mikiyasu. 1998. "Politics behind Zambezi Action Plan." *Water Policy* 1 (4): 397–409.

Namara, Regassa. 2005. "Synthesis of Sub-Saharan African Case Study Reports by Peacock, Omilola, and Kamara et al." Part Two in "Reducing Poverty through Investments in Agricultural Water Management." International Water Management Institute and African Development Bank. [www.iwmi.cgiar.org/Africanwaterinvestment/files/Theme_Reports/5_Reducing_Poverty.pdf]. July 2006.

Narayan, Deepa. 1995. *The Contribution of People's Participation: Evidence from 121 Rural Supply Projects*. Washington, DC: World Bank.

Nayyar, Rohini, and Nagesh Singh. 2006. Personal communication. Water and Sanitation Expenditure in India. June. New Delhi.

NEL-SAP (Nile Equatorial Lakes Subsidiary Action Project). 2002. "Nile Equatorial Lakes Subsidiary Action Program ICCON1: Proposal for Preparation Phase." Project Identification Document. Program 3. [www.nilebasin.org/nelsapbackup/documents/p3-2_kagera_river_basin.pdf]. July 2006.

Neumayer, Eric. 2004. "HIV/AIDS and Its Impact on Convergence in Life Expectancy, Infant and Child Survival Rates." London.

Nguyen, Pham Thanh Nam, Phuoc Minh Hiep, Mai Van Nam, Bui Van Trinh, and Pham The Tri. 2000. "Human Resources Development in the Mekong Delta." CAS Discussion Paper 31. Centre for ASEAN Studies and the Centre for International Management and Development, Antwerp. [http://143.129.203.3/cas/PDF/CAS31.pdf]. July 2006.

Nicol, Alan. 2002. "Financing Transboundary Water Management." Water Policy Brief 2. Overseas Development Institute, London. [www.odi.org.uk/wpp/publications_pdfs/BP_2.pdf]. July 2006.

Nishat, Ainun. 2001. "Development and Management of Water Resources in Bangladesh: Post-1996 Treaty Opportunities." In Asit K. Biswas and Juha I. Uitto, eds., *Sustainable Development of the Ganges-Brahmaputra-Meghna Basins*. Tokyo: United Nations University Press.

NNMLS (Northern New Mexico Legal Services). 2000. "*Acequias* and Water Rights Adjudications in Northern New Mexico." In Bryan Randolph Bruns and R. S. Meinzen-Dick, eds., *Negotiating Water Rights*. London: Intermediate Technology Publications.

Noble, I., J. Parikh, R. Watson, R. Howarth, R. J. T. Klein, A. Abdelkader, and T. Forsyth. 2005. "Responses to Climate Change." In K. Chopra, R. Leemans, P. Kumar, and H. Simons, eds., *Ecosystems and Human Well-Being: Policy Responses*. Volume 3 of the Millennium Ecosystem Assessment. Washington, DC: Island Press.

Nyong, Anthony. 2005. "Impacts of Climate Change in the Tropics: The African Experience." Avoiding Dangerous Climate Change: A Scientific Symposium on Stabilization of Greenhouse Gases, 1–3 February, Met Office, Exeter, UK.

———. 2006. "Reducing Africa's Vulnerability to Climate Change through Adaptation." Climate Change in Africa: Linking Science and Policy for Adaptation, 30 March, Tyndall Centre, University of East Anglia, Norwich, UK.

Nyong, Anthony, and P. S. Kanaroglou. 2001. "A Survey of Household Domestic Water-Use Patterns in Rural Semi-Arid Nigeria." *Journal of Arid Environments* 49 (2): 387–400.

Odada, Eric O., Lekan Oyebande, and Johnson A. Oguntola. 2006. "Lake Chad." Experience and Lessons Learned Brief. Lake Basin Management Initiative, International Lake Environment Committee. Shiga, Japan. [www.ilec.or.jp/lbmi2/reports/06_Lake_Chad_27February2006.pdf]. May 2006.

ODI (Overseas Development Institute). 1999. "What Can We Do with a Rights-based Approach to Development?" ODI Briefing Paper. London.

———. 2004. "Right to Water: Legal Forms, Political Channels." ODI Briefing Paper. London.

OECD (Organisation for Economic Co-operation and Development). 2006a. "Agricultural Policies in OECD Countries." At a Glance. Paris.

———. 2006b. International Development Statistics (IDS) Online. Database on Aid and Other Resource Flows. Paris. [www.oecd.org/dac/stats/idsonline]. June 2006.

O'Lear, Shannon. 2004. "Resources and Conflict in the Caspian Sea." *Geopolitics* 9 (1): 161–86.

Ostrom, Elinor, Larry Schroeder, and Susan Wynne. 1993. *Institutional Incentives and Sustainable Development: Infrastructural Policies in Perspective*. Boulder, Colo.: Westview Press.

Oweis, Theib, and Ahmed Hachum. 2003. "Improving Water Productivity in the Dry Areas of West Asia and North Africa." In Jacob Kijne, ed., *Water Productivity in Agriculture: Limits and Opportunities for Improvement*. Colombo: International Water Management Institute.

Oweis, Theib, Ahmed Hachum, and Jacob Kijne. 1999. "Water Harvesting and Supplemental Irrigation for Improved Water Use Efficiency in Dry Areas." Swim Paper 7. International Water Management Institute, Colombo.

Oxera Consulting Ltd. 2002. "The Capital Structure of Water Companies." Commissioned by the UK Office of Water Services. [www.ofwat.gov.uk/aptrix/ofwat/publish.nsf/AttachmentsByTitle/oxera_report_1002.pdf/$FILE/oxera_report_1002.pdf]. July 2006.

Pagiola, Stefano, Agustin Arcenas, and Gunars Platais. 2005. "Can Payments for Environmental Services Help Reduce Poverty? An Exploration of the Issues and Evidence to Date from Latin America." *World Development* 33 (2): 237–53.

Pagiola, Stefano, Konrad von Ritter, and Joshua Bishop. 2004. "Assessing the Economic Value of Ecosystem Conservation." Environment Department Paper 101. World Bank, Washington, DC.

Pakistan, Government of. 2004. "Pakistan: Poverty Reduction Strategy Paper." IMF Country Report 04/24. International Monetary Fund, Washington, DC.

Palanisami, K. 1994. "Evolution of Agricultural and Urban Water Markets in Tamil Nadu, India." Irrigation Support Project for Asia and the Near East, United States Agency for International Development, Arlington, Va.

Palanisami, K., and A. Malaisamy. 2004. "Taking Water Out of Agriculture in Bhavani Basin: Equity, Landscape and Livelihood Consequences." Water Technology Centre. Tamil Nadu Agricultural University, Coimbatore, India.

Pander, H. 2000. "Gender and Land Tenure—Women's Access to Land and Inheritance Rights: The Cases of Burkina Faso and Lesotho." Paper written for the Food and Agriculture Organization of the United Nations and German Technical Cooperation.

Pangare, Ganesh, Neelesh Kulkarni, and Vasudha Pangare. 2005. "An Assessment of the Water Sector Reform in the Indian Context: The Case of the State of Maharashtra." United Nations Research Institute for Social Development, Geneva.

Paredes, Ricardo. 2001. "Redistributive Impact of Privatisation and Deregulation of Utilities in Chile." WIDER Discussion Paper 2001/19. United Nations University, World Institute for Development Economics, Helsinki.

Parker, Ronald, and Tauno Skytta. 2000. "Rural Water Projects. Lessons from OED Evaluations." OED Working Paper Series 3. World Bank, Washington, DC.

Parry, Martin, Cynthia Rosenzweig, and Matthew Livermore. 2005. "Climate Change, Global Food Supply and Risk of Hunger." *Philosophical Transactions of the Royal Society B* 360 (1463): 2125–38.

Paul, Samuel. 2005. "Holding the State to Account: Lessons of Bangalore's Citizen Report Cards." Public Affairs Centre, Bangalore.

Payen, Gérard. 2005. "The Right to Have Access to Drinking Water: Economic, Institutional and Practical Factors." Institut de droit d'expression et d'inspiration françaises, Lausanne Conference, 29 September, Lausanne, Switzerland.

Peachey, Everett J. 2004. "The Aral Sea Basin Crisis and Sustainable Water Resource Management in Central Asia." *Journal of Public and International Affairs* 15: 1–20.

Pearce, Fred. 2006. *When the Rivers Run Dry: What Happens When our Water Runs Out?* London: Eden Project Books.

Peña, H., M. Luraschi, and S. Valenzuela. 2004. "Water, Development, and Public Policies: Strategies for the Inclusion of Water in Sustainable Development." South American Technical Advisory Committee, Global Water Partnership, Santiago.

Perret, S. R. 2002. "Water Policies and Smallholding Irrigation Schemes in South Africa: A History and New Institutional Challenges." *Water Policy* 4 (3): 283–300.

Perry, C. J. 2001. "Charging for Irrigation Water: The Issues and Options, with a Case Study from Iran." International Water Management Institute, Colombo.

Phan, K. T., J. Frias, and D. Salter. 2004. "Lessons from Market-based Approaches to Improved Hygiene for the Rural Poor in Developing Countries." 30th WEDC International Conference. People-centered Approaches to Water and Environmental Sanitation, 25–29 October, Vientiane.

Phillips, David J. H., Shaddad Attili, Stephen McCaffrey, and John S. Murray. 2004. "Factors Relating to the Equitable Distribution of Water in Israel and Palestine." 2nd Israeli-Palestinian International Conference on Water for Life in the Middle East, 10–14 October, Antalya, Turkey. [www.ipcri.org/watconf/papers/davidp.pdf]. July 2006.

Pietilä, Pekka E., Tapio S. Katko, Jarmo J. Hukka, and Osmo T. Seppälä. 2004. "Water Services in Finland: Flexible Organizational Arrangements and Competition for Non-Core Operations." United Nations Research Institute for Social Development, Geneva.

Pitman, George Keith. 2002. "Bridging Troubled Waters: Assessing the World Bank Water Resources Strategy." World Bank, Washington, DC.

Polak, Paul. 2005a. "The Big Potential of Small Farms." *Scientific American* 293 (3): 84–91.

———. 2005b. "Water and the Other Three Revolutions Needed to End Rural Poverty." *Water Science & Technology* 51 (8): 133–43.

Ponce, Victor M. 2005. "Groundwater Utilization and Sustainability." San Diego State University, College of Engineering. San Diego, Calif. [http://groundwater.sdsu.edu/]. July 2006.

Postel, Sandra. 1992. *Last Oasis: Facing Water Scarcity.* New York and London: W.W. Norton & Company.

———. 1999. *Pillar of Sand: Can the Irrigation Miracle Last?* New York and London: Worldwatch Institute; Norton.

Postel, Sandra, and Brian Richter. 2003. *Rivers for Life: Managing Water for People and Nature.* Washington, DC: Island Press.

Priscoli, Jerome Delli. 1998. "Water and Civilization: Using History to Reframe Water Policy Debates and to Build a New Ecological Realism." *Water Policy* 1 (6): 623–36.

Puri, Shammy, ed. 2001. *Internationally Shared (Transboundary) Aquifer Resources Management: Their Significance and Sustainable Management.* Paris: United Nations Educational, Scientific and Cultural Organization. [http://unesdoc.unesco.org/images/0012/001243/124386e.pdf]. May 2006.

Puri, Shammy, and Geo Arnold. 2002. "Challenges to Management of Transboundary Aquifers: The ISARM Programme." Second International Conference on Sustainable Management of Transboundary Waters in Europe, 21–24 April, Miedzyzdroje, Poland. [www.unece.org/env/water/meetings/conf2/3-transboundaquifers_puri.pdf]. May 2006.

Puri, Shammy, and Alice Aureli. 2005. "Transboundary Aquifers: A Global Program to Assess, Evaluate, and Develop Policy." *Ground Water* 43 (5): 661–69.

PWA (Palestinian Water Authority). 2005. "Technical Data of the Palestinian Water Authority." Ramallah, Occupied Palestinian Territories.

Raghupati, Usha P., and Vivien Foster. 2002. "A Scorecard for India." Paper 2, Water Tariffs and Subsidies in South Asia. Water and Sanitation Program and Public-Private Infrastructure Advisory Facility, Washington, DC.

Rahman, Atiq, and Mazharul Alam. 2003. "Mainstreaming Adaptation to Climate Change in Least Developed Countries. Bangladesh Country Case Study." Working Paper 2. London.

Rao, M. S. Rama Mohan, C. H. Batchelor, A. J. James, R. Nagaraja, J. Seeley, and J. A. Butterworth. 2003. "Andhra Pradesh Rural Livelihoods Programme Water Audit Report." Andhra Pradesh Rural Livelihoods Programme. Rajendranagar, India.

Raskin, Paul, Peter Gleick, Paul Kirshen, Robert G. Pontius, Jr., and Kenneth Strzepek. 1997. "Water Futures: Assessment of Long-Range Patterns and Problems." In *Comprehensive Assessment of the Freshwater Resources of the World.* Stockholm: Stockholm Environment Institute.

Rathgeber, Eva. 2003. "Dry Taps...Gender and Poverty in Water Resource Management." Food and Agriculture Organization of the United Nations, Rome.

Ravallion, Martin, and Dominique van de Walle. 2003. "Land Allocation in Vietnam's Agrarian Transition Part 1: Breaking Up the Collective Farms." Centre for the Evaluation of Development Policies, Washington, DC.

Rayaleh, Hassan-Omar. 2004. *La gestion d'une pénurie: l'eau à Djibouti.* Thèse de doctorat. Orléans: Université d'Orléans.

Redhouse, David. 2005. "Getting to Boiling Point: Turning Up the Heat on Water and Sanitation." WaterAid, London.

Reij, Chris. 2004. "Indigenous Soil and Water Conservation in Africa." International Institute for Environment and Development, London.

Reisner, Marc. 1986. *Cadillac Desert. The American West and Its Disappearing Water.* New York: Viking Press.

Rekacewicz, Philippe. 1993. "An Assassinated Sea." *In Histoire-Géographie, initiation économique, Classe de Troisième.* Data updated in June 2006. Paris: Hatier.

———. 2006. "Atlas de poche." Librairie Générale Française, Paris.

Rekacewicz, Philippe, and Salif Diop. 2003. *Atlas mondial de l'eau: Une pénurie annoncée.* Paris: Éditions Autrement.

Repetto, Robert, William Magrath, Michael Wells, Christine Beer, and Fabrizio Rossini. 1989. *Wasting Assets: Natural Resources in the National Income Accounts.* Washington, DC: World Resources Institute.

Revenga, Carmen, Siobhan Murray, Janet Abramovitz, and Allen Hammond. 1998. "Watersheds of the World." World Resources Institute, Washington, DC.

Reyes-Sánchez, Laura Bertha, Alejandra Irazoque Reyes, Javier Medina Barrón, Raúl Espinoza S., and René Miranda Ruvalcaba. n.d. "The Mexican Bajío: Yesterday the Grain Growing Country; Today, Degraded Soils, Polluted Waters and Human Poverty." Torba Soil Society, Montpellier, France. [www.torba-soil-society.org/docs/Reyes_Sanchez_et_al_article.pdf]. July 2006.

Rijsberman, Frank R. 2003. "Can Development of Water Resources Reduce Poverty?" *Water Policy* 5 (5): 399–412.

———. 2004a. "Sanitation and Access to Clean Water." In Bjørn Lomborg, ed., *Global Crises, Global Solutions.* Cambridge: Cambridge University Press.

———. 2004b. "The Water Challenge." Paper prepared for the Copenhagen Consensus Project of the Environmental Assessment Institute, Copenhagen. [www.copenhagenconsensus.com]. June 2006.

———. 2004c. "Water Scarcity: Fact or Fiction?" New Directions for a Diverse Planet, Fourth International Crop Science Congress, 26 September–1 October, Brisbane, Australia. [www.cropscience.org.au]. June 2006.

Rijsberman, Frank R., and Nadia Manning. 2006. "Beyond More Crop per Drop. Water Management for Food and the Environment." Fourth World Water Forum, 16–22 March, Mexico City.

Rijsberman, Frank R., and David Molden. 2001. "Balancing Water Uses: Water for Food and Water for Nature." International Conference on Freshwater, 3–7 December, Bonn, Germany.

Rijsberman, Frank R., Nadia Manning, and Sanjiv de Silva. 2006. "Increasing Green and Blue Water Productivity to Balance Water for Food and Environment." Fourth World Water Forum, 16–22 March, Mexico City.

Rinat, Zafrir. 2005. "The Water Crisis Is Already Here in Gaza." *Haaretz*. 23 September. [www.haaretzdaily.com/hasen/pages/ShArt.jhtml?itemNo=208392&contrassID=2&subContrassID=4&sbSubContrassID=0&listSrc=Y]. May 2006.

Ringler, Claudia, Mark W. Rosegrant, and Michael S. Paisner. 2000. "Irrigation and Water Resources in Latin America and the Caribbean: Challenges and Strategies." EPTD Discussion Paper 64. International Food Policy Research Institute, Environment and Production Technology Division, Washington, DC.

Rodgers, P., R. de Silva, and R. Bhatia. 2002. "Water is an Economic Good: How to Use Prices to Promote Equity, Efficiency and Sustainability." *Water Policy* 4 (1): 1–17.

Rogers, Peter. 2002. "Water Governance in Latin America and the Caribbean." Inter-American Development Bank, Washington, DC.

Romano, Donato, and Michel Leporati. 2002. "The Distributive Impact of the Water Market in Chile: A Case Study in Limarí Province, 1981-1997." Case Study Report, United Nations Development Programme. [http://europeandcis.undp.org/WaterWiki/images/2/29/Romano_Leporati_2002.pdf]. July 2006.

Rosegrant, Mark W., and Ximing Cai. 2001. "Water for Food Production." Overcoming Water Scarcity and Quality Constraints, Brief 2. International Food Policy Research Institute, Washington, DC.

Rosegrant, Mark W., and Sarah A. Cline. 2003. "Global Food Security: Challenges and Policies." *Science* 12 (302): 1917–19.

Rosegrant, Mark W., and Renato Gazmuri S. 1994. "Reforming Water Allocation Policy through Markets in Tradable Water Rights: Lessons from Chile, Mexico, and California." Discussion Paper 6. International Food Policy Research Institute, Washington, D.C.

Rosegrant, Mark W., and Nicostrato D. Perez. 1997. "Water Resources Development in Africa: A Review and Synthesis of Issues, Potentials and Strategies for the Future." EPTD Discussion Paper 28. International Food Policy Research Institute, Environment and Production Technology Division, Washington, DC.

Rosegrant, Mark W., and Claudia Ringler. 2000. "Impact on Food Security and Rural Development of Transferring Water Out of Agriculture." *Water Policy* 1 (6): 567–86.

Rosegrant, Mark W., and Malik Sohail. 1995. "A 2020 Vision for Food, Agriculture, and the Environment in South Asia: A Synthesis." International Food Policy Research Institute, Washington, DC.

Rosegrant, Mark W., Ximing Cai, and Sarah A. Cline. 2002a. *Global Water Outlook 2025: Averting an Impending Crisis*. Washington, DC: International Food Policy Research Institute.

———. 2002b. *World Water and Food to 2025: Dealing with Scarcity*. Washington, DC: International Food Policy Research Institute.

Rosenberg, Charles E. 1962. *The Cholera Years. The United States in 1832, 1849, and 1866*. Chicago and London: University of Chicago Press.

Roy, Jessica, and Ben Crow. 2004. "Gender Relations and Access to Water: What We Want to Know About Social Relations and Women's Time Allocation." Paper CGIRS-2004-5. Center for Global, International and Regional Studies, Santa Cruz, Calif. [http://repositories.cdlib.org/cgirs/CGIRS-2004-5]. July 2006.

Russell, Ben, and Nigel Morris. 2006. "Armed Forces Are Put on Standby to Tackle Threat of Wars over Water." *The Independent*. 28 February. [http://news.independent.co.uk/environment/article348196.ece]. May 2006.

Ruxin, Josh, Joan E. Paluzzi, Paul A. Wilson, Yesim Tozan, Margaret Kruk, and Awash Teklehaimanot. 2005. "Emerging Consensus in HIV/AIDS, Malaria, Tuberculosis, and Access to Essential Medicines." *Lancet* 365 (9459): 618–21.

Sachs, Jeffrey, Glen-Marie Lange, Geoffrey Heal, and Arthur Small. 2005. "Global Initiative for Environmental Accounting. A Proposal to Build a Comprehensive System of Environmental and Economic National Accounts." Department of Economic and Social Affairs, Statistics Division, United Nations, New York.

SADC (Southern African Development Community). 2000. "Revised Protocol on Shared Watercourses in the Southern African Development Community." Windhoek. [www.internationalwaterlaw.org/RegionalDocs/SADC2.htm]. May 2006.

———. 2005a. "Regional Strategic Action Plan on Integrated Water Resources Development and Management: Annotated Strategic Action Plan." Gaborone.

———. 2005b. "Regional Water Policy." Gaborone.

Sadoff, Claudia W., and David Grey. 2002. "Beyond the River: the Benefits of Cooperation on International Rivers." *Water Policy* 4 (5): 389–403.

———. 2005. "Cooperation on International Rivers: A Continuum for Securing and Sharing Benefits." *Water International* 30 (4): 1–8.

Sakthivel, S. Ramesh, and Roger Fitzgerald. 2002. "The Soozhal Initiative: A Model for Achieving Total Sanitation in Low-Income Rural Areas." WaterAid India Fieldwork Report, London.

Saleth, Maria R., Regassa E. Namara, and Madar Samad. 2003. "Dynamics of Irrigation-poverty Linkages in Rural India: Analytical Framework and Empirical Analysis." *Water Policy* 5 (5): 459–73.

Salmon, Katy. 2002. "Nairobi's Flying Toilets—Tip of an Iceberg." *Terra Viva*. August 26. [www.ipsnews.net/riomas10/2608_3.shtml]. July 2006.

Sanctuary, Mark, and Hakån Tropp. 2005. "Making Water a Part of Economic Development: The Economic Benefits of Improved Water Management and Services." Stockholm International Water Institute, Stockholm.

Sang, W. K, J.O. Oundo, J.K. Mwituria, P.G. Waiyaki, M. Yoh, T. Iida, and T. Honda. 1997. "Multidrug-Resistant Enteroaggregative *Escherichia coli* Associated with Persistent Diarrhea in Kenyan Children." *Emerging Infectious Diseases* 3 (3): 373–74. [www.cdc.gov/ncidod/eid/vol3no3/sang.htm]. July 2006.

Santiago, Charles. 2005. "Public-Public Partnership: An Alternative Strategy in Water Management in Malaysia." In Belén Balanyá, Brid Brennan, Olivier Hoedeman, Satoko Kishimoto, and Philipp Terhorst, eds., *Reclaiming Public Water: Achievements, Struggles and Visions from Around the World*. Amsterdam: Transnational Institute and Corporate Europe Observatory.

Sara, Jennifer, and Travis Katz. 1998. "Making Rural Water Supply Sustainable: Report on the Impact of Project Rules." Water and Sanitation Program, Washington, DC.

Saravanan, V., and P. Appasamy. 1999. "Historical Perspectives on Conflicts over Domestic and Industrial Supply in the Bhavani and Noyyal River Basins, Tamil Nadu." In M. Moench, E. Caspari, and A. Dixit, eds., *Rethinking the Mosaic: Investigations into Local Water Management*. Kathmandu and Boulder, Colo.: Nepal Water Conservation Foundation and the Institute for Social and Environmental Transition.

Sarch, M. T., and C. Birkett. 2000. "Fishing and Farming at Lake Chad: Responses to Lake-level Fluctuations." *Geographic Journal* 166 (2): 156–72.

Sarwan, Suharto, Tjoek Walujo Subijanto, and Charles Rodgers. 2005. "Development of Water Rights in Indonesia." In Bryan Randolph Bruns, Claudia Ringler, and R. S. Meinzen-Dick, eds., *Water Rights Reform: Lessons for Institutional Design*. Washington, DC: International Food Policy Research Institute.

Scanlon, John, Angela Cassar, and Noémi Nemes. 2004. "Water as a Human Right?" IUCN Environmental Policy and Law Paper 51. World Conservation Union, Gland, Switzerland and Cambridge, UK.

Schenkeveld, Maarten M., Richard Morris, Bart Budding, Jan Helmer, and Sally Innanen. 2004. "Seawater and Brackish Water Desalination in the Middle East, North Africa and Central Asia: A Review of Key Issues and Experiences in Six Countries." Working Paper 33515. World Bank, Washington, DC.

Schneider, S. H., and J. Lane. 2006. "An Overview of 'Dangerous' Climate Change." In H. J. Schellnhuber, ed., *Avoiding Dangerous Climate Change*. Cambridge: Cambridge University Press.

Schneier-Madanes, Graciela, and Bernard de Gouvello, eds. 2003. *Eaux et réseaux. Les défis de la mondialisation*. Paris: IHEAL-CREDAL.

Schreiner, Barbara, and Barbara van Koppen. 2003. "Policy and Law for Addressing Poverty, Race and Gender in the Water Sector: The Case of South Africa." *Water Policy* 5 (5): 489–501.

Schuttelar, Marlies, Vedat Ozbilen, Tetsuya Ikeda, Mia Hua, François Guerquin, and Tarek Ahmed. 2003. *World Water Actions. Making Water Flow for All*. London: Earthscan.

Scoones, Ian. 1998. "Sustainable Rural Livelihoods: A Framework for Analysis." IDS Working Paper 72. University of Sussex, Institute of Development Studies, Brighton, UK.

Scott, Christopher, N. I. Faruqui, and L. Raschid-Sally. 2004. "Wastewater Use in Irrigated Agriculture: Management Challenges in Developing Countries." In C. A. Scott, ed., *Wastewater Use in Irrigated Agriculture: Confronting the Livelihood and Environmental Realities*. Ottawa, Canada: CAB International, International Water Management Institute, and International Development Research Centre.

Seckler, D., D. Molden, U. Amarasinghe, and C. de Fraiture. 2000. "Water Issues for 2025: A Research Perspective. IWMI's Contribution to the 2nd World Water Forum." International Water Management Institute, Colombo.

Sen, Amartya. 1981. *Poverty and Famines: An Essay on Entitlements and Deprivation*. Oxford: Clarendon Press.

———. 1982. "The Right Not to Be Hungry." In Guttorm Fløistad, ed., *Contemporary Philosophy: A New Survey*, Volume 2: *Philosophy of Science*. The Hague: Martinus Nijoff.

———. 1999. *Development as Freedom*. New York: Oxford University Press.

Sen, Amartya, and Jean Drèze. 1999. *The Amartya Sen and Jean Drèze Omnibus: "Poverty and Famines," "Hunger and Public Action," and "India: Economic Development and Social Opportunity."* New Delhi: Oxford University Press.

Serra, Pablo. 2000. "Subsidies in Chilean Public Utilities." Policy Research Working Paper 2445. World Bank, Washington, DC.

Shah, Tushaar. 2005. "Integrated Water Resources Management in Informal Water Economies: Fitting Reforms to Context." Presentation at the SDC Roundtable, Swiss Agency for Development and Cooperation, 29 November, Bern, Switzerland.

Shah, Tushaar, and J. Keller. 2002. "Micro-irrigation and the Poor: Livelihood Potential of Low-cost Drip and Sprinkler Irrigation in India and Nepal." In H. Sally and C. Abernethy, eds., *Private Irrigation in Sub-saharan Africa*. Colombo: Food and Agriculture Organization of the United Nations and International Water Management Institute.

Shah, Tushaar, Aditi Deb Roy, Asad S. Qureshi, and Jinxia Wang. 2003. "Sustaining Asia's Groundwater Boom: An Overview of Issues and Evidence." *Natural Resources* Forum 27 (2): 130–41.

Shah, Tushaar, M. Alam, M. Dinesh Kumar, R. K. Nagar, and Mahendra Singh. 2000. "Pedaling Out of Poverty: Social Impact of a Manual Irrigation Technology in South Asia." IWMI Research Report 45. International Water Management Institute, Colombo.

Shah, Tushaar, Barbara van Koppen, Douglas Merrey, Marna de Lange, and Madar Samad. 2002. "Institutional Alternatives in African Smallholder Irrigation: Lessons from International Experience with Irrigation Management Transfer." IWMI Research Report H30202. International Water Management Institute, Colombo.

Shalizi, Zmarak. 2006. "Addressing China's Growing Water Shortages and Associated Social and Environmental Consequences." Policy Research Working Paper 3895. World Bank, Washington, DC.

Sharma, Bharat R., and Peter G. McCornick. 2006. "India: Country Case Study on Domestic Policy Frameworks for Adaptation in the Water Sector." Paper presented at the Annex I Expert Group Seminar in Conjunction with the OECD Global Forum on Sustainable Development, "Working Together to Respond to Climate Change," 27–28 March, Paris.

Shen, Dajun, and Ruiju Liang. 2003. "State of China's Water." Research Report. Third World Centre for Water Management with the Nippon Foundation. [www.thirdworldcentre.org/epubli.html].

Shetty, Shobha. 2006. "Water, Food Security and Agricultural Policy in the Middle East and North Africa Region." MNA Working Paper 47. World Bank, Middle East and North Africa Region, Washington, DC.

Shiklomanov, I. 1993. "World Fresh Water Resources." In Peter H. Gleick, ed., *Water in Crisis: A Guide to the World's Fresh Water Resources*. New York: Oxford University Press.

———. 2000. "Appraisal and Assessment of World Water Resources." *Water International* 25 (1): 11–32.

Shivakoti, Ganesh P., Douglas L. Vermillion, Wai-Fung Lam, Elinor Ostrom, Ujjwal Pradhan, and Robert Yoder, eds. 2005. *Asian Irrigation in Transition: Responding to Challenges*. New Delhi and London: Sage.

Shmueli, Deborah. 1999. "Water Quality in International River Basins." *Political Geography* 18 (4): 437–76.

Shuchen, Meng, Tao Yong, and Liu Jiayi. 2004. "Rural Water Supply and Sanitation in China: Scaling Up Services for the Poor." World Bank, Washington, DC.

Sievers, Eric W. 2002. "Water, Conflict, and Regional Security in Central Asia." *NYU Environmental Law Journal* 10 (3): 356–402.

Sight Savers International. 2006. "Prevalence of Trachoma." [www.sightsavers.org/html/eyeconditions/trachoma_extent.htm]. Accessed in July 2006.

Sikes, S. 2003. *Lake Chad versus the Sahara Desert*. Newbury: Mirage Newbury.

Sinanovic, Edina, Sandi Mbatsha, Stephen Gundry, Jim Wright, and Clas Rehnberg. 2005. "Water and Sanitation Policies for Improving Health in South Africa: Overcoming the Institutional Legacy of Apartheid." *Water Policy* 7 (6): 627–42.

SINTEF Unimed. 2002. "Living Conditions among People with Activity Limitations in Namibia. A Representative, National Survey." Oslo.

———. 2003a. "Living Conditions among People with Activity Limitations in Malawi. A National Representative Study." Oslo.

———. 2003b. "Living Conditions among People with Activity Limitations in Zimbabwe. A Representative Regional Survey." Oslo.

Sivamohan, M. V. K., and Christopher Scott. 2005. "Coalition-Building for Participatory Irrigation Management under Changing Water Resource Trends: Reflections on Reforms in Andhra Pradesh, India." In Ganesh P. Shivakoti, Douglas L. Vermillion, Wai-Fung Lam, Elinor Ostrom, Ujjwal Pradhan, and Robert Yodereds, eds., *Asian Irrigation in Transition: Responding to Challenges*. New Delhi and London: Sage.

SIWI (Stockholm International Water Institute), IFPRI (International Food Policy Research Institute), IUCN (World Conservation Union), and IWMI (International Water Management Institute). 2005. "Let It Reign: The New Water Paradigm for Global Food Security." Stockholm International Water Institute, Stockholm.

Sklarew, Dann M., and Alfred M. Duda. 2002. "The Global Environment Facility: Forging Partnerships and Fostering Knowledge Transfer to Sustain Transboundary Waters in Europe, Central Asia and Around the World." IW:LEARN, Washington, DC. [www.iwlearn.net/publications/misc/presentation/File_112866880982]. May 2006.

Slattery, Kathleen. 2003. "What Went Wrong: Lessons from Manila, Buenos Aires and Atlanta." Institute for Public-Private Partnerships, Washington, DC.

Slaymaker, Tom, and Peter Newborne. 2004. "Implementation of Water Supply and Sanitation Programmes under PRSPs. Synthesis of Research Findings from Sub-Saharan Africa." Overseas Development Institute and WaterAid, London.

Smakhtin, Vladimir, Carmen Revenga, and Petra Döll. 2004. "Taking into Account Environmental Water Requirements in Global-scale Water Resources Assessments." Comprehensive Assessment Research Report 2. Comprehensive Assessment Secretariat, Colombo.

Smets, Henri. 2004. "The Cost of Meeting the Johannesburg Targets for Drinking Water. A Review of Various Estimates and a Discussion of the Feasibility of Burden Sharing." Académie de l'eau, Nanterre, France.

Smith, Adam. [1776] 1976. An Inquiry into the Nature and Causes of the Wealth of Nations. Oxford: Oxford University Press.

Smith, Laila. 2005. "Neither Public nor Private: Unpacking the Johannesburg Water Corporatization Model." United Nations Research Institute for Social Development, Geneva.

Sneddon, Chris, and Coleen Fox. 2006. "Rethinking Transboundary Waters: A Critical Hydropolitics of the Mekong Basin." Political Geography 25 (2): 181–202.

Solanes, Miguel. 2006. Personal email communication. "Indigenous groups in Chile." UN adviser on water law and public utilities. 7 June.

Solo, Tova Maria. 1999. "Small-scale Entrepreneurs in the Urban Water and Sanitation Market." Environment and Urbanization 11 (1): 117–32.

———. 2003. "Independent Water Entrepreneurs in Latin America: The Other Private Sector in Water Services." World Bank, Washington, DC.

Solórzano, Raúl, Ronnie de Camino, Richard Woodward, Joseph Tosi, Vicente Watson, Alexis Vásquez, Carlos Villalobos, Jorge Jiménez, Robert Repetto, and Wilfrido Cruz. 1991. Accounts Overdue: Natural Resources Depreciation in Costa Rica. Washington, DC: World Resources Institute.

Soussan, John. 2003. "Povetry, Water Security and Household Use of Water." International Symposium on Water, Poverty and Productive Uses of Water at the Household Level, 21–23 January, Muldersdrift, South Africa.

———. 2004. "Water and Poverty. Fighting Poverty through Water Management." Asian Development Bank, Manila.

South Africa, Republic of. 2006. Department of Water Affairs and Forestry. "Free Basic Services: Water." [http://www.dwaf.gov.za/FreeBasicWater/scripts/FrmImpStatus.asp?ServiceType=1&ProvID=5&Perspective=Households]. June 2006.

Sperling, Gene, and Rekha Balu. 2005. "Designing a Global Compact on Education." Finance and Development 42 (2): 38–41.

Stern, Nicholas. 2006. "Remarks by Sir Nicholas Stern." Delhi Sustainable Development Summit, 3 February, New Delhi. [www.hm-treasury.gov.uk/media/91C/23/Stern_DSMS_030206.pdf]. July 2006.

Stern Review on the Economics of Climate Change. 2006. "What is the Economics of Climate Change?" Discussion Paper. London. [www.hm-treasury.gov.uk/media/213/42/What_is_the_Economics_of_Climate_Change.pdf]. July 2006.

Strauss, John, and Duncan Thomas. 1998. "Health, Nutrition, and Economic Development." Journal of Economic Literature 36 (2): 766–817.

Struckmeier, Wilhelm, Yoram Rubin, and J. A. A. Jones. 2005. "Groundwater—Reservoir for a Thirsty Planet?" Leiden, Netherlands, Earth Sciences for Society. [www.esfs.org/downloads/Groundwater.pdf]. May 2006.

Summers, Robert James. 2005. "Indigenous Institutions of Water Point Management. A Study of Three Cases in Rural Malawi." Doctoral dissertation. Faculty of Graduate Studies of the University of Guelph: Guelph, Canada.

Surjadi, C., L. Padhmasutra, D. Wahyuningsih, G. McGranahan, and M. Kjellén. 1994. "Household Environmental Problems in Jakarta." Stockholm Environment Institute, Stockholm.

Surjadi, Charles. 2003. "Public Private Partnerships and the Poor: Case Study: Jakarta, Indonesia—Drinking Water Concessions."

Loughborough University, Water, Engineering and Development Centre, Loughborough, UK.

Susantono, Bambang. 2001. "Informal Water Services in Metropolitan Cities of Developing World: The Case of Jakarta, Indonesia." Doctoral dissertation, Department of City and Regional Planning, University of California, Berkeley, Calif.

SUSMAQ (Sustainable Management of the West Bank and Gaza Aquifers Project). 2004. Aquifer map developed by SUSMAQ, 1999-2004, and received from Dr. Karen Assaf, former water minister, Palestinian National Authority, and Dr. Amjad Aliewi, former head of SUSMAQ. Palestinian Water Authority, University of Newcastle upon Tyne, British Geological Survey, and the Department for International Development. Ramallah, Occupied Palestinian Territories.

Swyngedouw, Erik. 2004. Social Power and the Urbanization of Water: Flows of Power. New York: Oxford University Press.

Szreter, Simon. 1997. "Economic Growth, Disruption, Deprivation, Disease, and Death: On the Importance of the Politics of Public Health for Development." Population and Development Review 23 (4): 693–728.

Szreter, Simon, and Graham Mooney. 1998. "Urbanization, Mortality, and the Standard of Living Debate: New Estimates of the Expectation of Life at Birth in Nineteenth-Century British Cities." The Economic History Review New Series, 51 (1): 84–112.

Tanzania, Government of. 2002. Poverty and Human Development Report. Poverty Monitoring Service. Dar es Salaam.

Taylor, John. 1983. "An Evaluation of Selected Impacts of Jakarta's Kampung Improvement Program." Doctoral dissertation, Department of Urban Planning, University of California, Los Angeles.

Texas Center for Policy Studies. 2002. "Los efectos de la industrialización y del sector industria maquiladora de exportación en la economía, la salud y el ambiente en Aguascalientes." Austin, Tex. [www.texascenter.org/publications/aguas.pdf]. July 2006.

Thébaud, B., K. Vogt, and G. Vogt. 2006. "The Implications of Water Rights for Pastoral Land Tenure: The Case of Niger." In Lorenzo Cotula, ed., Land and Water Rights in the Sahel: Tenure Challenges of Improving Access to Water for Agriculture. London: International Institute for Environment and Development.

Thébaud, Brigitte, and Simon Batterbury. 2001. "Sahel Pastoralists: Opportunism, Struggle, Conflict and Negotiation. A Case Study from Eastern Niger." Global Environmental Change 11 (1): 69–78.

Thompson, John, Ina T. Porras, James K. Tumwine, Mark R. Mujwahuzi, Munquit Katui-Katua, Nick Johnstone, and Libby Wood. 2002. Drawers of Water II: 30 Years of Change in Domestic Water Use and Environmental Health in East Africa. London: International Institute for Environment and Development. [www.iied.org/pubs/pdf/full/9049IIED.pdf]. July 2006.

Toset, Hans Petter Wollebæk, Nils Petter Gleditsch, and Håvard Hegre. 2000. "Shared Rivers and Interstate Conflict." Political Geography 19 (8): 971–96.

Toubkiss, Jérémie. 2006. "Costing MDG Target 10 on Water Supply and Sanitation: Comparative Analysis, Obstacles and Recommendations." World Water Council, Montreal, Canada.

Trémolet, Sophie. 2002. "Rural Water Service. Is a Private National Operator a Viable Business Model?" World Bank Note 249. World Bank, Washington, DC.

Troesken, Werner. 2001. "Race, Disease, and the Provision of Water in American Cities, 1889-1921." The Journal of Economic History 61 (3): 750–76.

Tuinhof, Albert, and Jan Piet Heederik, eds. 2002. "Management of Aquifer Recharge and Subsurface Storage: Making Better Use of Our Largest Reservoir." NNC–IAH publication No. 4. Seminar, 18–19 December, Netherlands National Committee and International Association of Hydrogeologists, Wageningen. [http://siteresources.worldbank.org/INTWRD/Resources/GWMATE_Final_booklet.pdf]. July 2006.

Turner, Jennifer L., and Timothy Hildebrandt. 2005. "Navigating Peace: Forging New Water Partnerships: U.S.-China Water Conflict Resolution Water Working Group." *China Environment Series* 7: 89–98.

Turner, R. Kerry, Stavros Georgiou, Rebecca Clark, Roy Brouwer, and Jacob Burke. 2004. *Economic Valuation of Water Resources in Agriculture: From the Sectoral to a Functional Perspective of Natural Resource Management*. Rome: Food and Agriculture Organization of the United Nations.

UCLG (United Cities and Local Governments) Committee on the Local Management of Water and Sanitation. 2006. "Declaration on Water by Mayors and Local Elected Representatives." Fourth World Water Forum, 16–22 March, Mexico City.

Uganda, Government of. 2004. "Poverty Eradication Action Plan (2004/5–2007/8)." Ministry of Finance, Planning and Economic Development, Kampala.

———. 2005. "Uganda: Poverty Reduction Strategy Paper." Kampala.

Ugaz, Cecilia. 2003. "Universal Access to Water: Are There Limits to Commodification of a Basic Need?" Background Issues Paper and Project Proposal. United Nations Research Institute for Social Development, Geneva.

Uitto, Juha I. 2004. "Multi-country Cooperation around Shared Waters: Role of Monitoring and Evaluation." *Global Environmental Change* 14 (Supplement 1): 5–14.

Uitto, Juha I., and Alfred M. Duda. 2002. "Management of Transboundary Water Resources: Lessons from International Cooperation for Conflict Prevention." *The Geographical Journal* 168 (4): 365–78.

UN (United Nations). 1992. "United Nations Framework Convention on Climate Change." New York.

———. 2005. *World Population Prospects 1950–2050*. Database. New York.

———. 2006a. "Hacia el cumplimiento de los objectivos de desarollo del Milenio en el Perú. Un compromiso del país para acabar con la pobreza, la desigualdad y la exclusión." Lima.

———. 2006b. *World Urbanization Prospects: The 2005 Revision*. Department of Economic and Social Affairs. New York.

UN DPI (United Nations Department of Public Information). 2002. "Water: A Matter of Life and Death." Fact sheet. New York. [www.un.org/events/water/factsheet.pdf]. May 2006.

UNA (United Nations Association) and WSSCC (Water Supply and Sanitation Collaborative Council). 2004. "Conference Report." UNA-WSSCC Conference for World Water Day, 22 March, London.

UNAIDS (Joint United Nations Programme on HIV/AIDS). 2006. Correspondence on HIV Prevalence. May. Geneva.

UNDP (United Nations Development Programme). 2002. "Regional Partnership for Prevention of Transboundary Degradation of the Kura-Aras River Basin." New York. [www.undp.org.ge/Projects/kura.html]. July 2006.

———. 2003a. "Tapping the Potential: Improving Water Management in Tajikistan." Tajikistan Human Development Report. Dushanbe.

———. 2003b. "Water As a Key Human Development Factor. Kazakhstan Human Development Report." Almaty, Kazakhstan.

———. 2005a. "Bringing Down the Barriers: Regional Cooperation for Human Development and Human Security in Central Asia." Central Asia Human Development Report. Bratislava.

———. 2005b. "Decentralization and Human Development. Uzbekistan Human Development Report." Tashkent.

———. 2005c. "Ethnic and Cultural Diversity: Citizenship in a Plural State. National Human Development Report for Guatemala 2005." Guatemala City.

———. 2005d. "Linking Industrialisation with Human Development. National Human Development Report for Kenya 2005." Nairobi.

———. 2005e. "Poverty and the City." In Focus. International Poverty Centre, Brasilia.

———. 2005f. "Towards Human Development with Equity. National Human Development Report for China 2005." Beijing.

UNECA (United Nations Economic Commission for Africa). 2000. "Transboundary River/Lake Basin Water Development in Africa: Prospects, Problems, and Achievements." Addis Ababa. [www.uneca.org/publications/RCID/Transboundary_v2.PDF]. May 2006.

UNEP (United Nations Environment Programme). 2001. "SADC Consultative Process on Dams and Development." Dams and Development Project. Information Sheet 5. Nairobi. [http://hq.unep.org/dams/files/information_sheet_5.pdf]. May 2006.

———. 2004a. "Analyzing Environmental Trends using Satellite Data: Selected Cases." Nairobi. [http://grid2.cr.usgs.gov/publications/Analyzing_Environment.pdf]. June 2006.

———. 2004b. *Lake Chad Basin*, M. P. Fortnam and J. A. Oguntola, eds. GIWA Regional Assessment 43. Kalmar, Sweden: University of Kalmar.

———. 2004c. *Understanding Environmental Conflict and Cooperation*. Nairobi: United Nations Environment Program and Division of Early Warning and Assessment.

UNEP–FI (United Nations Environment Programme–Finance Initiative). 2004. "Challenges of Water Scarcity. A Business Case for Financial Institutions." Nairobi.

UN–HABITAT (United Nations Human Settlements Programme). 2003. *Water and Sanitation in the World's Cities. Local Action for Global Goals*. London and Sterling, Va.: Earthscan.

UNICEF (United Nations Children's Fund). 1999. "Sanitation and Hygiene: A Right for Every Child." New York.

———. 2005a. "Water, Sanitation and Hygiene Education: Children and Adolescents Leading the Way in Tajikistan." Dushanbe.

———. 2005b. "Women, Water and Hygiene Are Key to Change in Africa." Press release, 14 September, New York.

———. 2006b. *State of the World's Children 2006*. New York.

UNICEF (United Nations Children's Fund) and IRC International Water and Sanitation Centre. 2005. "Water, Sanitation and Hygiene Education for Schools: Roundtable Proceedings and Framework for Action." Roundtable Meeting, 24–26 January, Oxford, UK.

United Nations Secretary-General's Advisory Board on Water and Sanitation. 2006. "Hashimoto Action Plan: Compendium of Actions." Reported at the Fourth World Water Forum, 16–22 March, Mexico City. [www.unsgab.org/Compendium_of_Actions_en.pdf]. July 2006.

United States Department of the Interior. 2001. *Earthshots*, 8th ed. Washington, DC. [http://edcwww.cr.usgs.gov/earthshots/]. July 2006.

Université Catholique de Louvain. 2006. *EM-DAT: The International Disaster Database*. Office of U.S. Foreign Disaster Assistance and Centre for Research on the Epidemiology of Disasters. Brussels. [www.em-dat.net/]. July 2006.

University of California, Berkeley, and MPIDR (Max Planck Institute for Demographic Research). 2006. Human Mortality Database. Berkeley, Calif., and Munich. [www.mortality.org]. May 2006.

Upadhyay, Bhawana. 2003. "Water, Poverty and Gender: Review of Evidences from Nepal, India and South Africa." *Water Policy* 5 (5): 503–11.

Urban Resource Centre. 2004. Sewerage and water supply news update. [www.urckarachi.org/sewerage%20update.htm]. July 2006.

U.S. Agency for International Development. 2005a. "Case Studies of Bankable Water and Sewerage Utilities. Volume I: Overview Report." Washington, DC.

———. 2005b. "Case Studies of Bankable Water and Sewerage Utilities. Volume II: Compendium of Case Studies." Washington, DC.

Vaidyanathan, A., ed. 2001. *Tanks of South India*. New Delhi: Centre for Science and Environment.

Valfrey, Bruno. 1997. "Les opérateurs privés du service de l'eau dans les quartiers irréguliers des grandes métropoles et dans les petits centers en Afrique. Burkina Faso, Cap-Vert, Haiti, Mali, Mauritanie, Senegal." Action de recherche 9. Hydro Conseil, Paris. [http://ww3.pseau.org/outils/ouvrages/pseau_epaqppc_act_rech_9_haiti.pdf]. May 2006.

Van Breen, H. 1916. Beschouwingen: van de Technische-en Watervoorzieningscommissies betreffende de verschillende in zake de voorgenomen verbetering van de watervoorziening der Gemeente Batavia verschenen artikelen en uitgebrachte adviezen (Reviews: of the Technical and Water Supply commissions concerning the different articles and advice dealing with the intended improvement of water provision for the Municipality of Batavia). [Batavia] Jakarta, Indonesia: Ruygrok and Co.

van der Hoeck, Wim. 2001. "Water and Rural Livelihoods." Overcoming Water Scarcity and Quality Constraints Brief 5. International Food Policy Research Institute, Washington, DC.

van der Zaag, P., and H. Savenije. 1999. "The Management of International Waters in EU and SADC Compared." Physics and Chemistry of the Earth (Part B) 24 (6): 579–89.

Van Hofwegen, Paul. 2006. "Enhancing Access to Finance for Local Governments. Financing Water for Agriculture." Task Force on Financing Water for All, Report 1. Chaired by Angel Gurria. World Water Council, Marseilles, France.

van Koppen, B. 1998. "Gendered Water and Land Rights in Construction: Rice Valley Improvement in Burkina Faso." Paper presented at the 8th Biennial Conference of the International Association for the Study of Common Property, 31 May–4 June, Bloomington, Ind.

———. 2002. "A Gender Performance Indicator for Irrigation: Concepts, Tools and Applications." IWMI Research Report 59. International Water Management Institute, Colombo.

van Koppen, B., C. Sokile, N. Hatibu, B. Lankford, H. Mahoo, and P. Yanda. 2004. "Formal Water Rights in Tanzania: Deepening the Dichotomy?" Working Paper 71. International Water Management Institute, Colombo.

van Koppen, Barbara, Regassa Namara, and Constantina Safilios-Rothschild. 2005. "Reducing Poverty through Investments in Agricultural Water Management: Poverty and Gender Issues and Synthesis of Sub-Saharan Africa Case Study Reports." Working Paper 101. International Water Management Institute, Colombo.

van Koppen, Barbara, R. Parthasarathy, and Constantina Safiliou. 2002. "Poverty Dimensions of Irrigation Management Transfer in Large-Scale Canal Irrigation in Andhra Pradesh and Gujarat, India." Research Report 61. International Water Management Institute, Colombo.

Van Leeuwen, C. A. E. 1920. "Het rioleeringsvraagstuk in Nederlandsch-Indie (The question of water treatment in Netherlands Indie)." De Waterstaats-Ingenieur 5: 196–212.

VanDeveer, Stacy D. 2002. "International Environmental Cooperation at Sea: Caspian, Mediterranean and North Sea Cases." Global Environmental Politics 2 (1): 111–19.

VERC (Village Education Resource Center). 2002. "Shifting Millions from Open Defecation to Hygienic Latrines." Dhaka.

Verdeil, Véronique. 2003a. "Etudier les comportements et les demandes des usagers: Un préalable indispensable pour réduire les inégalités d'accès a l'eau." La Lettre du Programme Solidarité Eau 44. Paris.

———. 2003b. Marchés locaux de l'eau. Pratiques et territoires de l'approvisionnement en eau à Metro Cebu, Philippines. Paris: Thèse de Doctorat en Urbanisme et Aménagement, Université de Paris 8.

———. 2004. "Branchements collectives et pratiques sociales à Metro Cebu, Philippines: des services d'eau en quête de légitimation." Services en réseaux, services sans réseaux dans les villes du Sud. Flux 56/57: 57–70.

Vermillion, Douglas L. 2005. "Irrigation Sector Reform in Asia: From 'Participation with Patronage' to 'Empowerment with Accountability'." In Ganesh P. Shivakoti, Douglas L. Vermillion, Wai-Fung Lam, Elinor Ostrom, Ujjwal Pradhan, and Robert Yoder, eds., Asian Irrigation in Transition: Responding to Challenges. New Delhi and London: Sage.

Vickers, John, and George Yarrow. 1998. Privatization: An Economic Analysis. Cambridge, Mass.: MIT Press.

Viero, Odete Maria. 2003. "Water Supply and Sanitation in Porto Alegre, Brazil." Paper presented at PRINWASS Second International Conference, "Private Participation in Water and Sanitation: Tools for Exploring and Evaluating Current Policies in the Sector," Latin American Faculty of Social Sciences (FLASCO) Mexico, 2–3 April, Mexico City. [http://users.ox.ac.uk/~prinwass/PDFs/DMAE.PDF#search='porto%20alegre%20brazil%20water']. July 2006.

Viero, Odete Maria, and Andre Passos Cordeiro. 2006. "Public Interest vs. Profits: The Case of Water Supply and Sewage in Porto Alegre, Brazil." In Dynamics of Urban Change: A Collection of Resources. CD-ROM. Department for International Development, Urban Infrastructure, Services and Management, Basic Infrastructure, London. [www.ucl.ac.uk/dpu-projects/drivers_urb_change/urb_infrastructure/pdf_public_private_services/W_WaterAid-Public_Porto%20Alegre.pdf#search='porto%20alegre%20brazil%20water']. July 2006.

Vinogradov, Sergei, and Vance P. E. Langford. 2001. "Managing Transboundary Water Resources in the Aral Sea Basin: In Search of a Solution." International Journal of Global Environmental Issues 1 (3–4): 345–62.

Vira, Bhaskar, Ramaswamy Iyer, and Robert Cassen. 2004. "Water." In Robert Cassen, Leela Visaria, and Tim Dyson, eds., Twenty-first Century India: Population, Economy, Human Development, and the Environment. Oxford: Oxford University Press.

Vircoulon, Thierry. 2003. "L'eau gratuite pour tous? L'exemple de la nouvelle politique de l'eau en Afrique du Sud." Afrique contemporaine 1 (205): 135–150.

Vogel, Coleen, and Anthony Nyong. 2005. "The Economic, Developmental and Livelihood Implications of Climate Induced Depletion of Ecosystems and Biodiversity in Africa." Avoiding Dangerous Climate Change: A Scientific Symposium on Stabilization of Greenhouse Gases, 1–3 February, Met Office, Exeter, UK.

Vörösmarty, Charles J., Pamela Green, Joseph Salisbury, and Richard B. Lammers. 2000. "Global Water Resources: Vulnerability from Climate Change and Population Growth." Science 289 (5477): 284–88.

Wagstaff, Adam. 2000. "Socioeconomic Inequalities in Child Mortality: Comparisons across Nine Developing Countries." Bulletin of the World Health Organization 78 (1): 19–29.

———. 2001. "What Do Poor Children Die from? Some Evidence from Cebu, the Philippines." World Bank, Washington, DC.

Water Policy Briefing. 2002. "The Socio-Ecology of Groundwater in India." Issue 4. IWMI-TATA, Colombo.

WaterAid. 2005. "Water and Sanitation in Tanzania: An Update Based on the 2002 Population and Housing Census." London and Dar es Salaam. [www.wateraid.org/documents/2002_census_update.pdf]. July 2006.

WaterAid Uganda. 2003. "Sustainable Hygiene Behaviour Change. A Study of Key Determinants." Kampala.

Waterbury, John. 1979. Hydropolitics of the Nile Valley. Syracuse, N.Y.: Syracuse University Press.

Waterkeyn, Juliet, and Sandy Cairncross. 2005. "Creating Demand for Sanitation and Hygiene Through Community Health Clubs: A Cost-effective Intervention in two Districts in Zimbabwe." Social Science & Medicine 61 (9): 1958–70.

Water-Technology.net. 2006. "Ashkelon Desalination Plant, Seawater Reverse Osmosis (SWRO) Plant, Israel." London. [www.water-technology.net/projects/israel/]. July 2006.

Wax, Emily. 2006. "Dying for Water in Somalia's Drought: Amid Anarchy, Warlords Hold Precious Resource." Washington Post Foreign Service. 14 April.

WBCSD (World Business Council for Sustainable Development). 2005. "Collaborative Actions for Sustainable Water Management." Geneva.

Weinthal, Erika. 2002. *State Making and Environmental Cooperation: Linking Domestic and International Cooperation in Central Asia.* Cambridge, Mass., and London: MIT Press.

Weinthal, Erika, A. Vengosh, A. Marei, A. Gutirrez, and W. Kloppmann. 2005. "The Water Crisis in the Gaza Strip: Prospects for Resolution." *Ground Water* 43 (5): 653–60.

Weitz, Almud, and Richard Franceys, eds. 2002. *Beyond Boundaries. Extending Services to the Urban Poor.* Manila: Asian Development Bank.

White, David. 2006. "Local Ways Start to Change as Waters of Lake Chad Recede." *Financial Times.* 4 February.

Whittington, Dale, Xinming Mu, and Robert Roche. 1990. "Calculating the Value of Time Spent Collecting Water: Some Estimates for Ukunda, Kenya." *World Development* 18 (2): 269–80.

WHO (World Health Organization). 2001. *WHO World Water Day Report.* Geneva. [www.worldwaterday.org/wwday/2001/report/index.html]. June 2006.

———. 2005. *World Health Report 2005: Make Every Mother and Child Count.* Geneva.

———. 2006a. Water and sanitation related diseases fact sheets. Geneva. [www.who.int/water_sanitation_health/diseases/diseasefact/en/index.html]. July 2006.

———. 2006b. Water-related Disease. Geneva. [www.who.int/water_sanitation_health/diseases/en/]. June 2006.

WHO (World Health Organization) and UNICEF (United Nations Children's Fund). 2004a. "Coverage Estimates. Improved Sanitation: Morocco." Joint Monitoring Programme for Water Supply and Sanitation. Geneva and New York.

———. 2004b. "Meeting the MDG Drinking Water and Sanitation Target: A Mid-term Assessment of Progress." Joint Monitoring Programme for Water Supply and Sanitation, Geneva and New York.

———. 2005. *Water for Life: Making it Happen.* Joint Monitoring Programme for Water Supply and Sanitation, Geneva and New York.

———. 2006. Correspondence on access to improved water and sanitation. April. New York.

Winpenny, James. 2003. *Financing Water for All: Report of the World Panel on Financing Water Infrastructure.* Chaired by Michel Camdessus. 3rd World Water Forum. World Water Council and Global Water Partnership.

Wodon, Quentin, and C. Mark Blackden, eds. 2006. *Gender, Time Use, and Poverty in Sub-Saharan Africa.* Washington, DC: World Bank.

Wolf, Aaron T. 1998. "Conflict and Cooperation along International Waterways." *Water Policy* 1 (2): 251–65.

———. 2000. "'Hydrostrategic' Territory in the Jordan Basin: Water, War, and Arab-Israeli Peace Negotiations." In Hussein A. Amery and Aaron T. Wolf, eds., *Water in the Middle East: A Geography of Peace.* Austin, Tex.: University of Texas Press.

Wolf, Aaron T., Shira B. Yoffe, and Meredith Giordano. 2003. "International Waters: Identifying Basins at Risk." *Water Policy* 5 (1): 29–60.

Wolf, Aaron T., Annika Kramer, Alexander Carius, and Geoffrey D. Dabelko. 2005. "Managing Water Conflict and Cooperation." In *State of the World 2005: Redefining Global Security.* Washington, DC: Worldwatch Institute.

Wolf, Aaron T., Jeffrey A. Natharius, Jeffrey J. Danielson, Brian S. Ward, and Jan K. Pender. 1999. "International River Basins of the World." *International Journal of Water Resources Development* 15 (4): 387–427. [www.transboundarywaters.orst.edu/publications/register/]. July 2006.

Wolff, Gary, and Eric Hallstein. 2005. "Beyond Privatization: Restructuring Water Systems to Improve Performance." Pacific Institute, Oakland, Calif.

Wolfowitz, Paul. 2005. "Environment and Development: Reaching for a Double Dividend." Address to the Special Session of the Sao Paulo Forum on Climate Change, 20 December. Sao Paulo, Brazil.

Woods, R. I., P. A. Watterson, and J. H. Woodward. 1988. "The Causes of Rapid Infant Mortality Decline in England and Wales, 1861-1921. Part I." *Population Studies* 42 (3): 343–66.

———. 1989. "The Causes of Rapid Infant Mortality Decline in England and Wales, 1861-1921. Part II." *Population Studies* 43 (1): 113–32.

World Bank. 2001. "China: Agenda for Water Sector Strategy for North China." Washington, DC.

———. 2002. "Pakistan Poverty Assessment, Poverty in Pakistan, Vulnerabilities, Social Gaps and Rural Dynamics." Report 24296-PAK. Poverty Reduction and Economic Management Sector Unit, South Asia Region, Washington, DC.

———. 2004a. "Colombia Recent Economic Developments in Infrastructure." Report 20279-CO. Washington DC.

———. 2004b. "Scaling Up Poverty Reduction." The Shanghai Conference, 25–27 May, Shanghai, China.

———. 2004c. "Towards a Water-Secure Kenya: Water Resources Sector Memorandum." Washington, DC.

———. 2004d. "Water and Sanitation Sector: Morocco." Report 29634-MOR. Washington DC.

———. 2004e. *Water Resources Sector Strategy. Strategic Directions for World Bank Engagement.* Washington, DC.

———. 2004f. *World Development Report 2004: Making Services Work For Poor People.* Washington, DC.

———. 2005a. *Ethiopia: A Country Status Report on Health and Poverty. Volume II: Main Report.* Washington, DC.

———. 2005b. "Ethiopia: Risk and Vulnerability Assessment." Washington, DC.

———. 2005c. "Pakistan's Water Economy: Running Dry." Report 34081-PK. South Asia Region, Agriculture and Rural Development Unit, Washington DC.

———. 2005d. "Project Appraisal Document: Morocco." Report 33881-MOR. Washington DC.

———. 2005e. "Scaling Up Support to Water Supply and Sanitation in Ethiopia." Water Supply and Sanitation Feature Story, Washington, DC.

———. 2005f. "Support to Multi-Purpose Development of the Kagera River Basin and the Rusumo Falls Project: Approach Paper." Washington, DC.

———. 2005g. *World Development Indicators 2005.* CD-ROM. Washington, DC.

———. 2006a. "Clean Energy and Development: Towards an Investment Framework." Washington, DC.

———. 2006b. "The Diversity, Contributions, and Achievements of Agricultural Water Management." In *Reengaging in Agricultural Water Management. Challenges and Options.* Washington, DC.

———. 2006c. "Education for All—Fast Track Initiative." Informal World Bank Executive Board Briefing. Washington, DC.

———. 2006d. *Global Economic Prospects 2006: Economic Implications of Remittances and Migration.* Washington, DC.

———. 2006e. *Hazards of Nature, Risks to Development.* An IEG Evaluation of World Bank Assistance for Natural Disasters. Independent Evaluation Group, Washington, DC.

———. 2006f. "Managing Water Resources to Maximize Sustainable Growth: A Country Water Resources Assistance Strategy for Ethiopia." Washington, DC.

———. 2006g. "Promoting Rural Sanitation and Hygiene in Morocco." Water Supply and Sanitation Feature Story Number 11, Washington DC.

———. 2006h. *Reengaging in Agricultural Water Management. Challenges and Options.* Washington, DC.

World Bank and IMF (International Monetary Fund). 2003. *Progress Report and Critical Next Steps in Scaling up: Education for All, Health, HIV/AIDS, Water and Sanitation.* Washington, DC.

World Commission on Dams. 2000. *Dams and Development: A New Framework for Decision-Making.* London: Earthscan.

World Water Assessment Programme. 2003. *The United Nations World Water Development Report: Water for People, Water for Life.* Barcelona: United Nations Educational, Scientific and Cultural Organization and Berghahn Books.

———. 2006. *The United Nations World Water Development Report 2: Water, A Shared Responsibility.* Paris: United Nations Educational, Scientific and Cultural Organization.

Worthington, E. Barton. 1983. *The Ecological Century: A Personal Appraisal.* Oxford: Clarendon Press.

WRI (World Resources Institute). 2005. *Ecosystems and Human Well-Being: Wetlands and Water Synthesis: A Report of the Millennium Ecosystem Assessment.* Washington DC.

WRI (World Resources Institute), UNEP (United Nations Environment Programme) and the World Bank in collaboration with UNDP (United Nations Development Programme). 2005. *World Resources 2005: The Wealth of the Poor—Managing Ecosystems to Fight Poverty.* World Resources Institute, Washington, DC.

WSP (Water and Sanitation Program). 2000. "The Treadle Pump. An NGO Introduces a Low-Cost Irrigation Pump to Bangladesh." Washington, DC.

———. 2002a. "New Designs for Water and Sanitation Transactions. Making Private Sector Participation Work for the Poor." Washington, DC.

———. 2002b. "Taking Sustainable Rural Water Supply Services to Scale: A Discussion Paper." Washington, DC.

———. 2002c. "Water Supply and Sanitation in Social Funds. A Rapid Assessment of the Ethiopian Social Rehabilitation and Development Fund." Sector Finance Working Paper 3. Washington, DC.

———. 2002d. "Willingness to Charge and Willingness to Pay: The World Bank-assisted China Rural Water Supply and Sanitation Program." Washington, DC.

———. 2003. "Factors behind the Poor Integration of the Water Supply and Sanitation Sector in PRSPs in Sub-Saharan Africa." Sector Finance Working Paper 6. Washington, DC.

———. 2004. "The Case for Water and Sanitation. Better Water and Sanitation Make Good Fiscal and Economic Sense, and should be Prominent in PRSPs and Budget Allocations." Sector Finance Working Paper 3. Washington, DC.

———. 2006. "Featured News - Strengthening Voice of Water Consumers in Kenya." [www.wsp.org/06_FeaturedNews. asp?FeatureID=174]. June 2006.

WSP–AF (Water and Sanitation Program–Africa). 2002a. "Blue Gold: Building African Solutions for Water, Sanitation and Hygiene." Blue Gold Introductory Field Note. Nairobi.

———. 2002b. "Hygiene Promotion in Burkina Faso and Zimbabwe: New Approaches to Behaviour Change." Blue Gold Series, Field Note 7. Nairobi.

———. 2002c. "The National Sanitation Programme in Mozambique: Pioneering Peri-Urban Sanitation." Blue Gold Series, Field Note 9. Nairobi.

———. 2002d. "The National Water and Sanitation Programme in South Africa: Turning the 'Right to Water' into Reality." Blue Gold Series, Field Note 8. Nairobi.

———. 2002e. "Rural Water Sector Reform in Ghana: A Major Change in Policy and Structure." Blue Gold Series, Field Note 2. Nairobi.

———. 2003a. "Governance and Financing of Water Supply and Sanitation in Ethiopia, Kenya and South Africa. A Cross Country Synthesis." Sector Finance Working Paper 5. Nairobi.

———. 2003b. "Water Supply and Sanitation in Poverty Reduction Strategy Papers in Sub-Saharan Africa: Developing a Benchmarking Review and Exploring the Way Forward." Nairobi.

———. 2004a. "The Case for Marketing Sanitation." Nairobi.

———. 2004b. "Ethiopia Water Supply Sector. Resource Flows Assessment." Sector Finance Working Paper 10. Nairobi.

———. 2004c. "Mobilizing Resources for Sanitation." Field Note. Nairobi.

———. 2004d. "Sanitation and Hygiene in Kenya: Lessons on What Drives Demand for Improved Sanitation." Nairobi.

———. 2004e. "Strengthening Budget Mechanisms for Sanitation in Uganda." Nairobi.

———. 2004f. "Who Buys Latrines, Where and Why?" Sanitation and Hygiene Series. Nairobi.

———. 2005a. "Financing the Millennium Development Goals for Water and Sanitation: What Will It Take?" Sector Finance Working Paper 10. Nairobi.

———. 2005b. "A Review of EcoSan Experience in Eastern and Southern Africa." Nairobi.

———. 2005c. "Rogues No More? Water Kiosk Operators Achieve Credibility in Kibera." Field Note. Nairobi.

———. 2005d. "Understanding Small Scale Providers of Sanitation Services: A Case Study of Kibera." Nairobi.

———. Forthcoming. "Is Africa on Target to Meet the Millennium Development Goals on Water Supply and Sanitation? A Status Overview of Sixteen African Countries." Washington, DC.

WSP–EAP (Water and Sanitation Program—East Asia and the Pacific). 2003. "Urban Sewerage and Sanitation. Lessons Learned from Case Studies in the Philippines." Jakarta.

———. 2005. "Harnessing Market Power for Rural Sanitation. Making Sanitation Attractive and Accessible for the Rural Poor." Jakarta.

WSP International (War-torn Societies Project International). 2003. "Kagera River Basin Integrated Water Resources Management Project." [ftp://ftp.fao.org/agl/agll/kageradocs/ch3/IWRMDraftFinalReportKagera.pdf]. July 2006.

WSP–LAC (Water and Sanitation Program–Latin America and the Caribbean Region). 2004. "New Roles for Rural Water Associations and Boards in Honduras." Field Note. Lima.

———. 2005. "Delegating Water and Sanitation Services to Autonomous Operators." Field Note. Lima.

WSP–SA (Water and Sanitation Program–South Asia). 1999. "Villagers Treat Water As an Economic Good, Olavanna, Kerala, India." New Delhi.

———. 2000. "Marketing Sanitation in Rural India." New Delhi.

———. 2005. "Scaling-Up Rural Sanitation in South Asia. Lessons Learned from Bangladesh, India, and Pakistan." New Delhi.

WUP (Water Utility Partnership for Capacity Building). 2003. "Better Water and Sanitation for the Urban Poor: Good Practice from Sub-Saharan Africa." Kenya.

WWC (World Water Council). 2000. *A Water Secure World: Vision for Water, Life and the Environment.* Commission Report. Marseille, France.

WWF Nepal Programme. 2005. "An Overview of Glaciers, Glacier Retreat and Subsequent Impacts in Nepal, India and China." Kathmandu. [www.panda.org/downloads/climate_change/himalayaglaciersreport2005.pdf]. June 2005.

Yang, Hong, and Alexander J. B. Zehnder. 2002. "Water Scarcity and Food Import: A Case Study for Southern Mediterranean Countries." *World Development* 30 (8): 1413–30.

Yemen, Government of. 2002. "Poverty Reduction Strategy Paper (PRSP) 2003-2005." International Monetary Fund, Washington, DC.

Yepes, Guillermo. 1999. "Do Cross-Subsidies Help the Poor to Benefit from Water and Wastewater Services? Lessons from Guayaquil." Water and Sanitation Program, Washington, DC.

Yescombe, Edward, and E. R. Yescombe. 2002. *Principles of Project Finance.* San Diego, Calif.: Academic Press.

Yetim, Muserref. 2002. "Governing International Common Pool Resources: The International Watercourses of the Middle East." *Water Policy* 4 (4): 305–21.

Yoffe, Shira B., and Aaron T. Wolf. 1999. "Water, Conflict and Co-operation: Geographical Perspectives." *Cambridge Review of International Affairs* 12 (2): 197–213.

Zaidi, Akbar. 2001. "From the Lane to the City: The Impact of the Orangi Pilot Project's Low Cost Sanitation Model." WaterAid, London.

Zambia, Government of the Republic of. 2004a. "Water Supply and Sanitation Sector. Finance and Resource Flow Assessment." Sector Finance Working Paper 7. Water and Sanitation Program, Washington, DC.

———**2004b.** "Zambia: Poverty Reduction Strategy Paper Progress Report." IMF Country Report 04/181. International Monetary Fund, Washington, DC.

Zérah, Marie-Hélène. 2000. *Water: Unreliable Supply in Delhi*. New Delhi: Manohar.

Human development indicators

The state of human development

"The basic objective of development", wrote Mahbub ul Haq in the first *Human Development Report* in 1990, "is to create an enabling environment in which people can enjoy long, healthy and creative lives." Sixteen years on, that vision retains a powerful resonance.

People are the real wealth of nations. That simple truth is sometimes forgotten. Mesmerized by the rise and fall of national incomes (as measured by GDP), we tend to equate human welfare with material wealth. The importance of GDP growth and economic stability should not be understated: both are fundamental to sustained human progress, as is clear in the many countries that suffer from their absence. But the ultimate yardstick for measuring progress is people's quality of life. As Aristotle argued, "Wealth is evidently not the good we are seeking; for it is merely useful and for the sake of something else."[1] That "something else" is the opportunity of people to realize their potential as human beings. Real opportunity is about having real choices—the choices that come with a sufficient income, an education, good health and living in a country that is not governed by tyranny. As Amartya Sen has written: "Development can be seen... as a process of expanding the real freedoms that people enjoy."[2]

Over the past decades there have been unprecedented increases in material wealth and prosperity across the world. At the same time these increases have been very uneven, with vast numbers of people not participating in progress. Mass poverty, deeply entrenched inequality and lack of political empowerment contribute to deny a large share of the world's population the freedom to make real choices. Moreover, GDP is still measured in a way that does not take into account environmental degradation and the depletion of natural resources.

The human development index

Each year since 1990 this report has published a human development index (HDI) that looks beyond GDP to a broader definition of well-being. The HDI provides a composite measure of three dimensions of human development: living a long and healthy life (measured by life expectancy), being educated (measured by adult literacy and enrolment at the primary, secondary and tertiary level) and having a decent standard of living (measured by purchasing power parity, PPP, income). The index is not in any sense a comprehensive measure of human development. It does not, for example, include important indicators such as respect for human rights, democracy and inequality. What it does provide is a broadened prism for viewing human progress and the complex relationship between income and well-being.

This year's HDI, which refers to 2004, highlights the very large gaps in well-being and life chances that continue to divide our increasingly interconnected world. It was US President John F. Kennedy who coined the adage that "a rising tide lifts all boats."[3] But when it comes to human development, the rising tide of global prosperity has lifted some boats faster than others—and some boats are sinking fast. Enthusiasts who emphasize the positive aspects of globalization sometimes get carried away. They increasingly use the language of the global village to describe the new order. But when viewed through the lens of human development the global village appears deeply divided between the streets of the haves and those of the have-nots. The average person in Norway (at the top of the HDI league) and the average person in countries such as Niger (at the bottom) certainly live in different human development

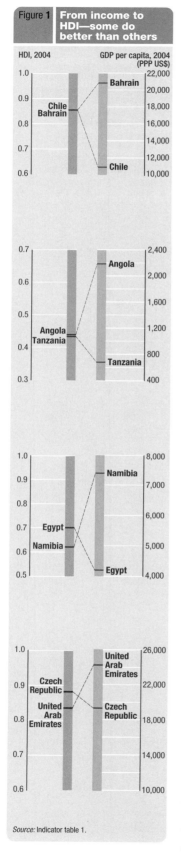

Figure 1 From income to HDI—some do better than others

HDI, 2004   GDP per capita, 2004 (PPP US$)

Source: Indicator table 1.

districts of the global village. People in Norway are more than 40 times wealthier than people in Niger. They live almost twice as long. And they enjoy near universal enrolment for primary, secondary and tertiary education, compared with an enrolment rate of 21% in Niger. For the 31 countries in the low human development category—a group with 9% of the world's people—life expectancy at birth is 46 years, or 32 years less than in high human development countries.

The HDI underlines another core theme that has run through the *Human Development Report* since its inception. On average human development indicators tend to rise and fall with income. That finding is hardly surprising. Very low average incomes and high levels of income poverty contribute to the lack of substantive freedoms in the world, robbing people of the ability to achieve adequate nutrition, treat illness or gain an education. The HDI reflects the positive association between income on one side and health and education on the other: people in richer countries tend to be healthier and to have more educational opportunities. It also draws attention to the fact that some countries are far better than others at converting wealth into opportunities for health and education.

Some countries have an HDI rank far below their income rank, while others invert this relationship. For example, Viet Nam remains quite poor but has a much higher HDI ranking than many countries with higher per capita incomes. Conversely, Bahrain has an average income almost twice the level in Chile but, despite recent progress, a lower HDI rank because it underperforms on education and literacy. In Sub-Saharan Africa Tanzania has an average income one-third that in Angola but a similar HDI rank—an outcome that reflects the high human cost of conflict in Angola (figure 1).

Governments often look at the HDI as an instrument for assessing their performance against that of neighbouring countries. Competition for human development is a healthy rivalry—more healthy, it might be argued, than competition on GDP. However, there has been something of a tendency for governments to

neglect more pressing questions, including the underlying reasons for large discrepancies between the national position in global income tables and in HDI rank. In some cases, as in Southern Africa, these discrepancies can be traced to specific problems (such as HIV/AIDS). In many others they can be traced to domestic policy failures in providing opportunities for health and education.

The HDI is a less effective measure of cross-country performance at the top end of the league table. Near universal literacy and educational enrolment, allied to upper limits on life expectancy (see *Technical note 1*), tend to equalize scores among countries. But even here the index highlights some discrepancies between income and overall HDI rank. For example, the United States, whose citizens are on average the second richest in the world after Luxembourg, stands six places lower in its HDI rank than its income rank. One reason is that average life expectancy is almost three years less than in Sweden—a country with an average income that is one-fourth lower. Within the high human development group Chile and Cuba enjoy HDI ranks far above their income ranks.

As with any index that aggregates data across several areas of achievement, the HDI is subject to constant adjustment in the light of shifts in statistical reporting systems. In some cases these shifts can affect a country's ranking in either a positive or negative direction, regardless of underlying performance. This year's HDI demonstrates the problem. Several countries have seen their HDI scores drop not because of a change in underlying performance, but because of a change in reporting systems for education. By definition the school enrolment data used in the HDI should not include adult education. However, some 32 countries have in the past included adult education when reporting school enrolment. This year these countries have changed data reporting to correct this anomaly. The new data sets are now more uniform and more accurate. But the change has had an adverse effect on the HDI rank of several countries, including Argentina, Belgium, Brazil, Paraguay, Peru and the United Kingdom. For Brazil the decline in the HDI rank—from 63 to 69—is almost entirely a result of the change in statistical reporting rather than any real deterioration in education performance. Similar outcomes can be observed for other countries in the group.

Human development trends—the HDI and beyond

Human development trends tell an important story. Since the mid-1970s almost all regions have been progressively increasing their HDI score (figure 2). East Asia and South Asia have accelerated progress since 1990. Central and Eastern Europe and the Commonwealth of Independent States (CIS), following a catastrophic decline in the first half of the 1990s, has also recovered strongly and regained the level before the reversal. The major exception is Sub-Saharan Africa. Since 1990 it has stagnated, partly because of economic reversal but principally because of the catastrophic effect of HIV/AIDS on life expectancy. Eighteen countries have a lower HDI score today than in 1990—most in Sub-Saharan Africa. Today 28 of the 31 low human development countries are in Sub-Saharan Africa. This underlines the supreme importance for the Millennium Development Goals of national efforts and global partnerships to overcome the enormous inherited disadvantage faced by people in Africa today.

Progress in human development is sometimes taken as evidence of convergence between the developed and the developing world. In broad terms, that picture is accurate: there has been a steady improvement in human development indicators for the developing world over several decades. But convergence is taking place at very different rates in different regions—and from different starting points. Inequalities in human development remain large, and for a large group of countries divergence is the order of the day. This can be illustrated by reference to some of the core indicators that underpin the HDI.

Life expectancy

Over the past three decades developing countries as a group have been converging on developed countries in life expectancy. Their average life expectancy at birth has increased by nine years, compared with seven in high-income countries (figure 3). The exception again is Sub-Saharan Africa. For the region as a whole life expectancy today is lower than it was three decades ago—and even this headline story understates the problem. Several countries in Southern Africa have suffered catastrophic reversals: 20 years in Botswana, 16 in Swaziland and 13 in Lesotho and Zambia. These demographic

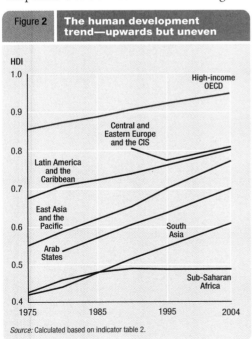

Figure 2 The human development trend—upwards but uneven

Source: Calculated based on indicator table 2.

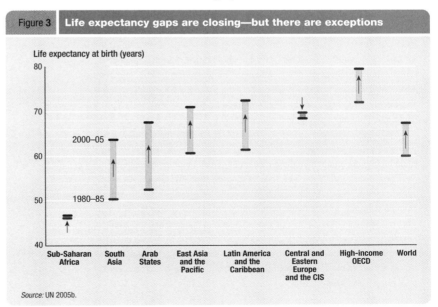

Figure 3 Life expectancy gaps are closing—but there are exceptions

Source: UN 2005b.

Box 1   The feminization of HIV/AIDS in Sub-Saharan Africa

HIV/AIDS has thrown human development into reverse gear across a large group of countries. More than 39 million people are infected with HIV, the virus that causes AIDS, and 3 million died of the disease in 2005 alone. Falling life expectancy has been one of the most visible impacts of HIV/AIDS on the human development index (HDI). Less visible has been the feminization of the disease and the consequences for gender equity.

In Sub-Saharan Africa, the epicentre of the crisis, infection rates have been growing far more rapidly for women than for men (figure 1). Women now account for 57% of HIV infections in the region, and young African women (ages 15–24) are now three times more likely to become infected than men.

The pandemic is shaping the demographic structure of many African countries. Women have a greater probability of contracting the infection—and are more likely to die from it earlier in life. In Southern Africa this is reversing the standard life expectancy pattern for men and women (figure 2). On current trends average life expectancy in Botswana, Lesotho, South Africa and Swaziland will be two years less for women than for men by 2005–10, compared with seven years more in 1990–95. Part of the gender bias in HIV/AIDS death rates can be traced to early marriage or sexual unions that increase the exposure of young women and girls to risk.

Even so, evidence from 11 countries studied in detail by the Joint United Nations Programme on HIV/AIDS shows a decline in eight countries in the proportion of people having sex before age 15 and an increase in the use of condoms. The figures for treatment are also moving in the right direction: use of antiretroviral drugs in Sub-Saharan Africa expanded from 100,000 people in 2003 to 810,000 at the end of 2005. But only about one person in every six of the 4.7 million in need of treatment now receives it. And coverage rates range broadly—from more than 80% in Botswana to 4% in Angola. South Africa alone accounts for about a quarter of those receiving treatment.

Does gender bias also skew prevention and treatment? The evidence is mixed. Unequal power relationships can disadvantage women and young girls in prevention because they are able to exercise less control over decision-making. Educational disadvantage is also a factor. Because school is an important site for education on HIV/AIDS, gender disparities in school attendance disadvantage girls. Current evidence does not point to systematic bias in treatment. In Ethiopia and Ghana women account for a smaller share of treatment than predicted on the basis of infection rates, but in South Africa and Tanzania they account for a larger share.

Like men, women in Sub-Saharan Africa suffer from the stigma, fear and weak leadership and inadequate political participation that have held back the development of an effective response to HIV/AIDS in many countries. They also stand to gain if the goal of the Global Fund to Fight AIDS, Malaria and Tuberculosis of providing 10 million people globally with antiretroviral treatment by 2010 is attained. The commitment by the Group of Seven leading industrial countries to provide as close to universal access to treatment as possible by 2010 is important. At the same time national governments should put gender and overcoming gender inequality at the centre of strategies for prevention and treatment.

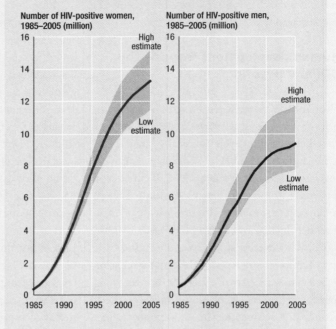

Figure 1   Sub-Saharan Africa—an increasingly female crisis

Number of HIV-positive women, 1985–2005 (million)

Number of HIV-positive men, 1985–2005 (million)

Note: Refers to adults ages 15 and older.
Source: UNAIDS 2006.

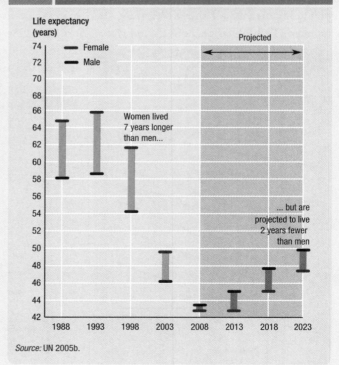

Figure 2   Life expectancy—the great gender reversal in Southern Africa

Life expectancy (years)

Women lived 7 years longer than men...

... but are projected to live 2 years fewer than men

Source: UN 2005b.

reversals are greater than France's after the First World War (see *Human Development Report 2005*). There has also been a reversal in the gender pattern of life expectancy. Across Sub-Saharan Africa women account for a rising share of HIV/AIDS infections—a trend that is dramatically lowering female relative to male life expectancy. Prevention and treatment of HIV/AIDS remain among the most important conditions for a resumption of positive human development trends across much of the region (box 1).

Child mortality

Survival rates for children are among the most sensitive indicators of human well-being. Here, too, there are some encouraging trends. Child mortality rates are falling: there were 2.1 million fewer deaths in 2004 than in 1990. Survival prospects are improving in all regions (figure 4). Yet the 10.8 million child deaths in 2004 bear testimony to the inequality in the most basic of all life chances—the chance of staying alive. Being born on the wrong street in the global village carries with it a large risk in terms of survival prospects.

For children in much of the developing world the risk differential is increasing. Child death rates in all developing regions are rising when expressed as a multiple of the rate in high-income countries. Moreover, the rate of progress in reducing child mortality has slowed for a large group of countries. Had the rate of progress registered in the 1980s been sustained since then, there would have been 1.5 million fewer child deaths in the world in 2004. The slowdown in the reduction in child mortality rates has implications for the Millennium Development Goals. On current trends the target of cutting overall death rates by two-thirds by 2015 will be missed by some 4.4 million deaths in that year. Only three Sub-Saharan African countries are on track for achieving the goal.

Perhaps more powerfully than any other indicator, child mortality demonstrates that increases in income are not equivalent to improvements in human development. Measured by wealth generation, India is one of the success stories of globalization: its GDP per capita growth has averaged 4% a year since 1990. But

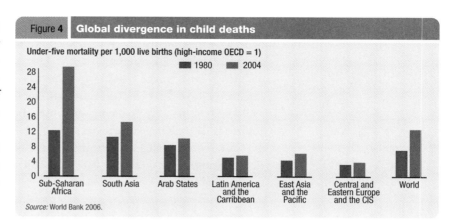

Figure 4 | **Global divergence in child deaths**

Under-five mortality per 1,000 live births (high-income OECD = 1)
■ 1980 ■ 2004

Source: World Bank 2006.

the trend rate for reducing child mortality has slowed from 2.9% a year in the 1980s to 2.2% since 1990. While India has outperformed Bangladesh in economic growth and average income, Bangladesh has outperformed India in reducing child death rates, maintaining a rate of decline of 3.45% since 1990. The contrasting fortune of children in India and Bangladesh when assessed on survival prospects points to the limits of wealth as a metric for measuring human development.

Education

Progress in education is critical for human development in its own right and because of the links to health, equity and empowerment. Here, too, the progress report is one of a glass half empty and half full. Much has been achieved—but large deficits remain.

Illiteracy patterns today are a legacy of education deficits of the past. Since 1990 adult literacy rates have risen from 75% to 82%, reducing the number of illiterate people in the world by 100 million. There has been less progress in gender equity. Women still account for about two-thirds of adult illiteracy—the same as in the 1990s. Net primary enrolment ratios have increased across the developing world, and the gender equity gap in enrolment is shrinking in all regions. Set against this good news, the bad news is that 115 million children are still out of school—and some 62 million of them are girls.

Enrolment differences at the primary level capture an important dimension of progress in education, but only one dimension. In a knowledge-based global economy a good quality primary education is just a first step on a ladder and not a destination. In this broader perspective the inequality in the distribution of global education opportunities remains daunting. On average a child in Burkina Faso can expect less than 4 years of education, compared with more than 15 in most high-income countries. These large educational inequalities of today are the income and health inequalities of tomorrow. Among the core challenges to be addressed:

- *The enrolment-completion gap.* Almost one child in five in developing countries drops out before completing primary school. In some cases high enrolment rates mask limited progress towards the acquisition of basic literacy and numeracy skills. In countries such as Chad, Malawi and Rwanda fewer than 40% of the children who enrol in school complete a full primary education cycle.
- *Low rates of transition to secondary school and beyond* (figure 5). In rich countries more than 80% of children who reach the end of primary school continue their studies at a lower secondary level. Over half go on to tertiary education. The picture is very different in Sub-Saharan Africa, where less than half of children make the transition from primary to secondary school. There

are 37 countries with net secondary enrolment rates of less than 40%, 26 of them in Sub-Saharan Africa.

- *High levels of post-primary gender inequality.* While enrolment gaps between girls and boys are narrowing, large disparities remain at secondary and tertiary levels (figure 6). The disparities reflect institutionalized gender discrimination that disadvantages women by restricting their choices and reducing their opportunities for income and employment. Because of the links between maternal education and child health, gender discrimination also holds back progress in child mortality reduction.

Income poverty and distribution

Income poverty has fallen in all regions since 1990, except in Sub-Saharan Africa. The share of the world's people living on less than $1 a day has fallen from 28% to 21%, leaving just over 1 billion people below the threshold. High economic growth in China and India has been the most powerful motor for reducing income poverty. Sub-Saharan Africa is the only region that has witnessed an increase both in the

| Figure 5 | From primary school to university— the widening gap in opportunity |

Enrolment ratio, 2004 (%)

Net primary enrolment — Net secondary enrolment — Gross tertiary enrolment

Finland, Japan, Viet Nam, Bangladesh, Mozambique

Source: Indicator table 12.

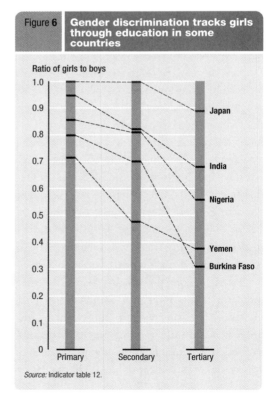

| Figure 6 | Gender discrimination tracks girls through education in some countries |

Ratio of girls to boys

Primary — Secondary — Tertiary

Japan, India, Nigeria, Yemen, Burkina Faso

Source: Indicator table 12.

incidence of poverty and in the absolute number of poor. Some 300 million people there—almost half of the region's population—live on less than $1 a day.

While the world as a whole is on track for achieving the 2015 target of halving extreme income poverty, Sub-Saharan Africa is off track, as are many countries in other regions. Country-level data indicate that the 2015 goals will be missed by about 380 million people. Such high levels of poverty in a more prosperous global economy reflect the extreme disparities in wealth and the small shares of world income captured by the poor:

- The poorest 20% of the world's people, roughly corresponding to the population living on less than $1 a day, account for 1.5% of world income. The poorest 40%, corresponding to the $2 a day poverty threshold, account for 5% of world income.

- Nine of 10 people in high-income Organisation for Economic Co-operation and Development (OECD) countries are in the top 20% of the global income distribution. At the other end of the scale one person in two in Sub-Saharan Africa is in the poorest 20%—and the region's share of people in the bottom 20% has more than doubled since 1980 (to 36% of the total).

- Average income for the world as a whole is $5,533 (PPP)—but 80% of the world lives on less than this average. Global inequality is captured in the large gap between average and median incomes ($1,700 in 2000).

- The world's 500 richest people have an income of more than $100 billion, not taking into account asset wealth. That exceeds the combined incomes of the poorest 416 million. Wealth accumulation at the top of the global income distribution has been more impressive than poverty reduction at the bottom. The 2004 World Wealth Report prepared by Merrill Lynch projects that the financial asset wealth of 7.7 million "high net worth individuals" reached $28 trillion in 2003, with projected growth to $41 trillion by 2008.

Globalization has given rise to a protracted debate over the precise direction of trends in global income distribution. What is sometimes lost sight of is the sheer depth of inequality—and the associated potential for greater equity to accelerate poverty reduction. Measured in 2000 purchasing power parity (PPP) terms, the gap between the incomes of the poorest 20% of the world's population and the $1 a day poverty line amounts to about $300 billion. That figure appears large, but it is less than 2% of the income of the world's wealthiest 10%. Achieving greater equity in world income distribution through inclusive and broad-based national growth strategies—backed by international action through aid, trade and technology transfer—is one of the keys to bringing the 2015 goals for income poverty within reach.

Inequality and human development

The HDI provides a snapshot of average national performance in human development. However, averages can obscure large disparities within countries. Inequalities based on income, wealth, gender, race and other forms of inherited disadvantage, as well as location, can make national averages a misleading indicator for human well-being.

Can the HDI be used to capture inequalities in human development within countries? Research undertaken for this year's *Human Development Report* addressed this question by attempting to disaggregate national HDI scores by income quintiles. The exercise covered 13 developing countries and two developed countries—Finland and the United States—with sufficient data available.

The construction of HDI scores for different income groups within countries poses technical challenges (see *Technical note 2*). Standardized household income surveys and Demographic and Health Surveys make it possible to generate data for the index at different points in the income distribution. But problems in data availability and comparability make it difficult to construct indexes that are comparable across countries. An added problem is that the data required for the construction of HDI scores by income group are not available for many high-income countries. Despite these problems the construction of

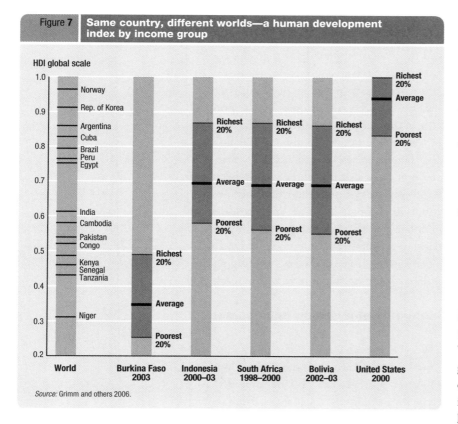

Figure 7 Same country, different worlds—a human development index by income group

HDI global scale

| World | Burkina Faso 2003 | Indonesia 2000–03 | South Africa 1998–2000 | Bolivia 2002–03 | United States 2000 |

Norway — 0.9
Rep. of Korea
Argentina — 0.85
Cuba
Brazil — 0.8
Peru
Egypt
India — 0.6
Cambodia
Pakistan — 0.55
Congo
Kenya
Senegal
Tanzania
Niger — 0.3

Richest 20%
Average
Poorest 20%

Source: Grimm and others 2006.

internationally comparable HDI scores based on national income groups has the potential to provide a powerful instrument for understanding the dimensions of capability deprivation.

The HDI by income group points to stark inequalities in human development (figure 7). For Burkina Faso, Madagascar and Zambia the HDI score for the richest 20% is about twice that for the poorest 20%. The observed gaps in Bolivia, Nicaragua and South Africa are also very large. HDI disparities by income between rich and poor in high-income countries are smaller, partly because income differentials translate less emphatically into life expectancy differences and basic education outcome. Even so, the United States displays significant HDI disparities by income group.

Beyond the domestic rankings, cross-country comparisons highlight the inequality of human development:

● The richest 20% of the people in Bolivia have a ranking that would place them in the high human development league, alongside Poland, while the poorest 20% would rank at a level comparable to the average for

Pakistan. The two groups are separated by 97 places on the global HDI ranking. For Nicaragua the HDI gap between the richest and the poorest 20% is 87 places in the global league.

● In South Africa the richest 20% have an HDI rank 101 places above the poorest 20%.

● In Indonesia human development stretches from a level comparable to that of the Czech Republic for the richest 20% to that of Cambodia for the poorest 20%.

● While the richest 20% in the United States (followed by Finland) would top the list of human development achievements, the poorest quintile in the United States achieves only a rank of 50.

Behind the HDI inequalities—child mortality and education inequalities

The HDI by income group provides an aggregate indicator of some important dimensions of well-being. Behind it are some very stark inequalities in capabilities and life chances linked to income inequalities. These can be highlighted by reference to household survey data for some of the countries covered by the research exercise.

Children born into the poorest 20% of the income distribution in countries such as Bolivia, Indonesia and South Africa face a risk of dying before their fifth birthday that is about four times higher than for children born into the richest 20% (figure 8). School completion rates also vary, with gender inequalities interacting with wealth-based disparities. Both girls and boys in the poorest 20% of the income distribution in Burkina Faso are far less likely to complete primary school than their high-income counterparts, though the disparity between girls and boys is equally marked (figure 9). These large variations in life chances based on inherited markers for advantage and disadvantage point to the need for public policies that equalize choice and opportunity by extending substantive freedoms.

Apart from the moral imperative to overcome extreme disparities in these areas, inequalities have important implications for the Millennium Development Goals. Consider the

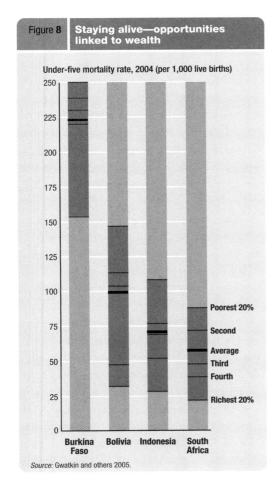

Figure 8 Staying alive—opportunities linked to wealth

Under-five mortality rate, 2004 (per 1,000 live births)

Poorest 20%
Second
Average
Third
Fourth
Richest 20%

Burkina Faso | Bolivia | Indonesia | South Africa

Source: Gwatkin and others 2005.

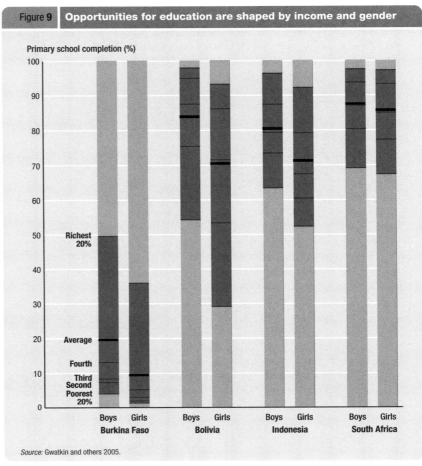

Figure 9 Opportunities for education are shaped by income and gender

Primary school completion (%)

Richest 20%
Average
Fourth
Third
Second
Poorest 20%

Boys Girls | Boys Girls | Boys Girls | Boys Girls
Burkina Faso | Bolivia | Indonesia | South Africa

Source: Gwatkin and others 2005.

target of reducing child mortality rates by two-thirds. Poor households, with child death rates that are typically two to three times the national average, account for a disproportionate share of overall child deaths. In Nicaragua and Peru, for example, about 40% of child deaths occur in the poorest 20% of households. Policies to reduce death rates among the poor have the potential to accelerate progress towards the target, though in most countries child mortality inequalities are widening: death rates among the poor are falling on average at less than half the rate among the rich.

Looking beyond household income, disaggregating the HDI can capture inequalities at various levels. In many countries it reveals large differences among regions. Kenya has an HDI that ranges from 0.75 in Nairobi (almost on par with Turkey) to 0.29 in Turkana, a pastoral area in the north of the country (figure 10). If Turkana were a country, it would be off the current HDI scale by a considerable margin, reflecting the region's

recurrent droughts, poor access to health and water infrastructure and high malnutrition rates.

Rural-urban differences interact with regional disparities. In China urban Shanghai would rank 24 in the global HDI league, just above Greece, while rural Guizhou Province would rank alongside Botswana (figure 11).

For some countries the HDI reveals very large inequalities based on group membership. An example is Guatemala, where human development opportunities are heavily skewed against indigenous groups. Q'eqchi have an HDI rank on par with Cameroon and 32 places below the rank for *ladinos* (roughly equivalent to Indonesia) (figure 12).

Income inequality

Inequality raises important questions rooted in normative ideas about social justice and fairness in all societies. Because income distribution patterns directly affect opportunities for nutrition, health and education, income inequality

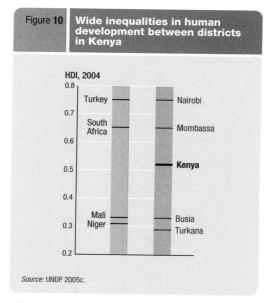

Figure 10 Wide inequalities in human development between districts in Kenya

HDI, 2004

Turkey
South Africa
Kenya
Mali
Niger

Nairobi
Mombassa
Busia
Turkana

Source: UNDP 2005c.

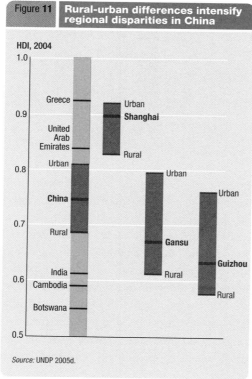

Figure 11 Rural-urban differences intensify regional disparities in China

HDI, 2004

Greece
United Arab Emirates
Urban
China
Rural
India
Cambodia
Botswana

Urban
Shanghai
Rural

Urban
Gansu
Rural

Urban
Guizhou
Rural

Source: UNDP 2005d.

is also intimately related to wider inequalities in capability and in some cases to absolute deprivation.

Regional variations in income inequality are large. The Gini coefficient, a measure of inequality calibrated on a scale from 0 (perfect equality) to 100 (perfect inequality), ranges from 33 in South Asia to 57 in Latin America and to more than 70 in Sub-Saharan Africa.

While caution has to be exercised in cross-regional comparisons, these regional differences are associated with large variations in the income shares of the richest and poorest 20%. They also reflect the gap between average income and median income, which widens with inequality. In a highly unequal country like Mexico the median income is only 51% of the average. For Viet Nam, where income distribution is more equitable, the median rises to 77% of the average.

Why does income distribution matter for poverty reduction? In a mechanical sense the rate of income poverty reduction in a country is a function of two things: the rate of economic growth and the share of any increment in growth captured by the poor. Other things being equal, the larger the share of income captured by the poor, the more efficient the country is in converting growth into poverty reduction. Holding income distribution patterns constant and projecting current growth rates into the future, it would take three decades for the median household in poverty to cross the poverty line in Mexico. Doubling the share of the poor in future income growth would cut this time horizon by half. For Kenya the time horizon would be reduced by 17 years, from 2030 to 2013—a transition that would bring the country within touching distance of an otherwise unattainable Millennium Development Goal target of halving income poverty.

As the examples show, distribution matters because it affects the rate at which economic growth converts into poverty reduction (the growth elasticity of poverty). Thus every 1% increase in growth reduces poverty by about 1.5% in Viet Nam—twice the 0.75% in Mexico. The good news is that extreme inequality is not an immutable fact of life. Over the past five years Brazil, one of the world's most unequal countries, has combined strong economic performance with a decline in income inequality (according to national sources, the Gini index has come down from 56 in 2001 to 54 in 2004) and poverty. Economic growth has created employment and increased real wages. And a large social welfare programme—Bolsa Familia—has provided financial transfers to 7 million families living in extreme or moderate poverty to support nutrition, health and education, creating benefits today and assets for the future.[4]

Income distribution is not only an issue for developing countries. As underlined by the HDI by income quintiles for the United States, it is also important in some of the world's richest countries. Over the past quarter century the gap between the bottom of the US income distribution and the middle and top has widened dramatically. Between 1980 and 2004 the income of the richest 1% of households (average incomes of more than $721,000 in 2004) rose 135%. Over the same period real manufacturing wages declined by 1%. The share of national income of the richest 1% doubled to 16% over the same period. In other words, the fruits of the productivity gains that have driven growth in the United States have been heavily skewed towards the wealthiest sections of society.

Does rising inequality restrict opportunity? One way of addressing that question is to measure the influence of the earning power of parents on the future earnings of their offspring. In countries with low inequality—such as Denmark and Norway—parental income explains about 20% of the earnings of offspring. For the United States—and for the United Kingdom—that figure rises to more than 50%.

Within any one country high levels of inequality in income and opportunity are a constraint on human development. Apart from their adverse implications for economic dynamism, growth and social cohesion, they limit the conversion of growth into human development. The same applies at a global level, where the increasingly visible divides that separate the haves and the have-nots have become a focal point for discontent. One of the central human development challenges in the decades ahead is to diminish the tolerance for extreme inequalities that have characterized globalization since the early 1990s and to ensure that the rising tide of prosperity extends opportunities for the many, and not just the privileged few.

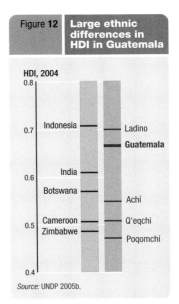

Figure 12 Large ethnic differences in HDI in Guatemala

HDI, 2004

Source: UNDP 2005b.

Notes

1 Aristotle, *Nicomachean Ethics*, book 1, chapter 5.
2 Sen 1999, p.3.
3 Kennedy 1962, p. 626.
4 IBGE 2005.

Readers guide and notes to tables

The human development indicator tables provide a global assessment of country achievements in different areas of human development. The main tables are organized thematically, as described by the running titles at the top of each table. The tables include data for 175 UN member states—those for which the human development index (HDI) could be calculated—along with Hong Kong, China (SAR), and the Occupied Palestinian Territories. Because of lack of data, an HDI could not be calculated for the remaining 17 UN member countries. Basic human development indicators for these countries are presented in table 1a.

In the tables, countries and areas are ranked by their HDI value. To locate a country in these tables, refer to *Key to countries* on the back cover flap, which lists countries alphabetically with their HDI rank. Most of the data in the tables are for 2004 and are those available to the Human Development Report Office as of 1 August 2006, unless otherwise specified.

Sources and definitions

The Human Development Report Office is primarily a user, not a producer, of statistics. It relies on international data agencies with the resources and expertise to collect and compile international data on specific statistical indicators. Sources for all data used in compiling the indicator tables are given in short citations at the end of each table. These correspond to full references in *Statistical references*. When an agency provides data that it has collected from another source, both sources are credited in the table notes. But when an agency has built on the work of many other contributors, only that agency is given as the source. The source notes also show the original data components used in

any calculations by the Human Development Report Office to ensure that all calculations can be easily replicated. Indicators for which short, meaningful definitions can be given are included in *Definitions of statistical terms*. Other relevant information appears in the notes at the end of each table. For more detailed technical information about these indicators, please consult the relevant Web sites of the source agencies through the *Human Development Report* Web site at http://hdr.undp.org/statistics/.

Inconsistencies between national and international estimates

When compiling international data series, international data agencies often apply international standards and harmonization procedures to improve comparability across countries. When international data are based on national statistics, as they usually are, national data may need to be adjusted. When data for a country are missing, an international agency may produce an estimate if other relevant information can be used. And because of the difficulties in coordination between national and international data agencies, international data series may not incorporate the most recent national data. All these factors can lead to significant inconsistencies between national and international estimates.

This Report has often brought such inconsistencies to light. When data inconsistencies have arisen, we have helped to link national and international data authorities to address those inconsistencies. In many cases this has led to better statistics in the Report. The Human Development Report Office advocates for improvements in international data, plays an active role in supporting efforts to enhance data quality and works with national agencies and international bodies to improve data consistency through more systematic reporting and monitoring of data quality.

Comparability over time

Statistics presented in different editions of the Report may not be comparable, due to revisions to data or changes in methodology. For this reason the Human Development Report Office strongly advises against trend analysis based on data from different editions. HDI values and ranks similarly are not comparable across editions of the Report. For HDI trend analysis based on consistent data and methodology, refer to table 2 (Human development index trends).

Country classifications

Countries are classified in four ways: by human development level, by income, by major world aggregates and by region (see *Classification of countries*). These designations do not necessarily express a judgement about the development stage of a particular country or area. The term *country* as used in the text and tables refers, as appropriate, to territories or areas.

Human development classifications
All countries included in the HDI are classified into one of three clusters by achievement in human development: high human development (with an HDI of 0.800 or above), medium human development (HDI of 0.500–0.799) and low human development (HDI of less than 0.500).

Income classifications
All countries are grouped by income using World Bank classifications: high income (gross national income per capita of $10,066 or more in 2004), middle income ($826–$10,065) and low income ($825 or less).

Major world classifications
The three global groups are *developing countries, Central and Eastern Europe and the CIS (Commonwealth of Independent States)* and *OECD (Organisation for Economic Co-operation and Development)*. These groups are not mutually exclusive. (Replacing the OECD group with the high-income OECD group and excluding the Republic of Korea would produce mutually exclusive groups.) Unless otherwise specified, the classification *world* represents the universe of 194 countries and areas covered—192 UN member countries plus Hong Kong, China (SAR), and the Occupied Palestinian Territories.

Regional classifications
Developing countries are further classified into regions: Arab States, East Asia and the Pacific, Latin America and the Caribbean (including Mexico), South Asia, Southern Europe and Sub-Saharan Africa. These regional classifications are consistent with the Regional Bureaux of the United Nations Development Programme. An additional classification is *least developed countries,* as defined by the United Nations (UN-OHRLLS 2006).

Aggregates and growth rates

Aggregates
Aggregates for the classifications described above are presented at the end of tables where it is analytically meaningful to do so and data are sufficient. Aggregates that are the total for the classification (such as for population) are indicated by a *T.* All other aggregates are weighted averages.

In general, an aggregate is shown for a country grouping only when data are available for half the countries and represent at least two-thirds of the available weight in that classification. The Human Development Report Office does not fill in missing data for the purpose of aggregation. Therefore, unless otherwise specified, aggregates for each classification represent only the countries for which data are available, refer to the year or period specified and refer only to data from the primary sources listed. Aggregates are not shown where appropriate weighting procedures are unavailable.

Aggregates for indices, growth rates and indicators covering more than one point in time are based only on countries for which data exist for all necessary points in time. When no aggregate is shown for one or more regions, aggregates are not always shown for the *world* classification, which refers only to the universe of 194 countries and areas.

Aggregates in this Report will not always conform to those in other publications because of differences in country classifications and methodology. Where indicated, aggregates are calculated by the statistical agency providing the data for the indicator.

Growth rates

Multiyear growth rates are expressed as average annual rates of change. In calculating growth rates, the Human Development Report Office uses only the beginning and end points. Year-to-year growth rates are expressed as annual percentage changes.

Country notes

Unless otherwise noted, data for China do not include Hong Kong, China (SAR), Macau, China (SAR), or Taiwan Province of China. In most cases data for Eritrea before 1992 are included in the data for Ethiopia. Data for Germany refer to the unified Germany, unless otherwise noted. Data for Indonesia include Timor-Leste through 1999, unless otherwise noted. Data for Jordan refer to the East Bank only. Economic data for Tanzania cover the mainland only. Data for Sudan are often based on information collected from the northern part of the country. While Serbia and Montenegro became two independent states in June 2006, the indicator tables generally report data only for the country of Serbia and Montenegro since disaggregated data were not available at the time of printing. And data for the Republic of Yemen refer to that country from 1990 onward, while data for earlier years refer to aggregated data for the former People's Democratic Republic of Yemen and the former Yemen Arab Republic.

Symbols

In the absence of the words *annual, annual rate* or *growth rate,* a dash between two years, such as in 1995–2000, indicates that the data were collected during one of the years in that period. A slash between two years, such as in 1998/2001, indicates an average for the years

shown unless otherwise specified. The following symbols are used:

- .. Data not available.
- (.) Greater (or less) than zero but small enough that the number would round to zero at the displayed number of decimal points.
- < Less than.
- — Not applicable.
- T Total.

Table 1: about the human development index

The human development index (HDI) is a composite index that measures the average achievements in a country in three basic dimensions of human development: a long and healthy life, as measured by life expectancy at birth; knowledge, as measured by the adult literacy rate and the combined gross enrolment ratio for primary, secondary and tertiary schools; and a decent standard of living, as measured by gross domestic product (GDP) per capita in purchasing power parity (PPP) US dollars. The index is constructed from indicators that are available globally using a methodology that is simple and transparent (see *Technical note 1*).

While the concept of human development is much broader than any single composite index can measure, the HDI offers a powerful alternative to income as a summary measure of human well-being. It provides a useful entry point into the rich information contained in the subsequent indicator tables on different aspects of human development.

Data availability determines HDI country coverage

The HDI in this Report refers to 2004. It covers 175 UN member countries, along with Hong Kong, China (SAR), and the Occupied Palestinian Territories. Because of a lack of comparable data, 17 UN member countries cannot be included in the HDI this year. Basic human development indicators for these countries are presented in table 1a.

To enable cross-country comparisons, the HDI is, to the extent possible, calculated based on data from leading international data agencies available at the time the Report was prepared (see *Primary international data sources* below). But for a number of countries data are missing from these agencies for one or more of the four HDI components.

In response to the desire of countries to be included in the HDI table, and in line with the goal of including as many UN member countries as possible, the Human Development Report Office has made special efforts to obtain estimates from other international, regional or national sources when the primary international data agencies lack data for one or two HDI components for a country. In a few cases the Human Development Report Office has produced an estimate. These estimates from sources other than the primary international agencies are clearly documented in the footnotes to table 1. They are of varying quality and reliability and are not presented in other indicator tables showing similar data.

Primary international data sources

Life expectancy at birth. The life expectancy at birth estimates are from the *2004 Revision* of *World Population Prospects* (UN 2005b), the official source of UN population estimates and projections. They are prepared biannually by the Population Division of the United Nations Department of Economic and Social Affairs using data from national vital registration systems, population censuses and surveys.

In the *2004 Revision* the United Nations Population Division incorporated national data available to it through the end of 2004. For assessing the impact of HIV/AIDS, the latest HIV prevalence estimates available at the time, prepared by the Joint United Nations Programme on HIV/AIDS, are combined with a series of assumptions about the demographic trends and mortality of both infected and noninfected people in each of the 60 countries for which the impact of the disease is explicitly modelled.

These life expectancy estimates are published by the United Nations Population Division with five-year intervals as the reference point. The estimates for 2004 shown in table 1 and those underlying table 2 are annual interpolations based on these five-year data (UN

2005a). For details on the *2004 Revision* of *World Population Prospects* (UN 2005b), see www.un.org/esa/population/unpop.htm.

Adult literacy rate. Data on adult literacy come from national population censuses or household surveys. This Report uses national estimates of adult literacy from the United Nations Educational, Scientific and Cultural Organization (UNESCO) Institute for Statistics (UIS) April 2006 Assessment (UNESCO Institute for Statistics 2006c) and UIS estimates from UNESCO Institute for Statistics (2003). The national estimates, made available through targeted efforts by UIS to collect recent literacy data from countries, are obtained from national censuses or surveys between 2000 and 2005 (with the exception of a few cases referring to 1995–99). The UIS estimates, produced in July 2002, were based mostly on national data collected before 1995. For details on these literacy estimates, see www.uis.unesco.org.

Many high-income countries, having attained high levels of literacy, no longer collect basic literacy statistics and thus are not included in the UIS data. In calculating the HDI, a literacy rate of 99.0% is applied for these countries.

In collecting literacy data, many countries estimate the number of literate people based on self-reported data. Some use educational attainment data as a proxy, but measures of school attendance or grade completion may differ. Because definitions and data collection methods vary across countries, literacy estimates should be used with caution.

The UIS, in collaboration with partner agencies, is actively pursuing an alternative methodology for measuring literacy, the Literacy Assessment and Monitoring Programme (LAMP). LAMP seeks to go beyond the current simple categories of literate and illiterate by providing information on a continuum of literacy skills.

Combined gross enrolment ratio for primary, secondary and tertiary schools. Gross enrolment ratios are produced by the UIS based on enrolment data collected from national governments (usually from administrative sources) and population data from the United Nations Population

Division's *2004 Revision* of *World Population Prospects* (UN 2005). The ratios are calculated by dividing the number of students enrolled in all levels of schooling (excluding adult education) by the total population in the official age group corresponding to these levels. The tertiary age group is set to five cohorts immediately following on the end of upper secondary school in all countries.

Though intended as a proxy for educational attainment, combined gross enrolment ratios do not reflect the quality of education outcomes. Even when used to capture access to education opportunities, combined gross enrolment ratios can hide important differences among countries because of differences in the age range corresponding to a level of education and in the duration of education programmes. Grade repetition and dropout rates can also distort the data. Measures such as the mean years of schooling of a population or school life expectancy could more adequately capture education attainment and should ideally supplant the gross enrolment ratio in the HDI. However, such data are not yet regularly available for a sufficient number of countries.

As currently defined, the combined gross enrolment ratio does not take into account students enrolled in other countries. Current data for many smaller countries, for which pursuit of a tertiary education abroad is common, could significantly underrepresent access to education or educational attainment of the population and thus lead to a lower HDI value.

In previous editions data for some countries included adult education, contrary to the preferred definition of the enrolment indicator. The data in this year's Report excludes adult education for these countries, bringing their data into compliance with the standard definition. As a result, enrolment ratios and HDI values for these countries are lower than if adult education had been included.

GDP per capita (PPP US$). In comparing standards of living across countries, economic statistics must be converted into PPP terms to eliminate differences in national price levels. The GDP per capita (PPP US$) data for the HDI are provided for 164 countries by the World Bank based on price data from the latest International Comparison Program (ICP) surveys and GDP in local currency from national accounts data. The latest round of ICP surveys covered 118 countries. PPPs for these countries are estimated directly by extrapolating from the latest benchmark results. For countries not included in the ICP surveys, estimates are derived through econometric regression. For countries not covered by the World Bank, PPP estimates provided by the Penn World Tables of the University of Pennsylvania (Heston, Summers and Aten 2001, 2002) are used.

Though much progress has been made in recent decades, the current PPP data set suffers from several deficiencies, including lack of universal coverage, of timeliness of the data and of uniformity in the quality of results from different regions and countries. The importance of PPPs in economic analysis underlines the need for improvement in PPP data. A new Millennium Round of the ICP has been established and promises much improved PPP data for economic policy analysis, including international poverty assessment. For details on the ICP and the PPP methodology, see the ICP Web site at www.worldbank.org/data/icp.

Comparisons over time and across editions of the Report

The HDI is an important tool for monitoring long-term trends in human development. To facilitate trend analyses across countries, the HDI is calculated at five-year intervals for the period 1975–2004. These estimates, presented in table 2, are based on a consistent methodology and on comparable trend data available when the Report is prepared.

As international data agencies continually improve their data series, including updating historical data periodically, the year to year changes in the HDI values and rankings across editions of the *Human Development Report* often reflect revisions to data—both specific to a country and relative to other countries—rather than real changes in a country. In addition, occasional changes in country coverage could also affect the HDI ranking of a country, even when consistent methodology is used to calculate the HDI. As a result, a country's HDI rank could drop considerably between two consecutive Reports. But when comparable, revised data are used to reconstruct the HDI for recent years, the HDI rank and value may actually show an improvement.

For these reasons HDI trend analysis should not be based on data from different editions of the Report. Table 2 provides up-to-date HDI trend data based on consistent data and methodology. For HDI values and ranks recalculated for 2003 (the reference year of the HDI in *Human Development Report 2005*) based on the data sources used for the HDI in this year's Report, please visit http://hdr.undp.org/statistics.

HDI for high human development countries

The HDI in this Report is constructed to compare country achievements across all levels of human development. Thus the indicators chosen are not necessarily those that best differentiate between rich countries. The indicators currently used in the index yield very small differences among the top HDI countries, and thus the top of the HDI ranking often reflects only very small differences in these underlying indicators. For these high-income countries, an alternative index—the human poverty index (shown in table 4)—can better reflect the extent of human deprivation that still exists among the populations of these countries and help direct the focus of public policies.

For further discussions on the use and limitations of the HDI and its component indicators, see http://hdr.undp.org/statistics.

Tables 24 and 25: revisiting the gender-related development index and the gender empowerment measure

In 1995 the *Human Development Report* introduced the gender-related development index (GDI) and the gender empowerment measure (GEM). These measures have since been used as advocacy and monitoring tools for gender-related human development analysis and policy discussions. To mark the 10th anniversary of the GDI and GEM, the Human Development Report Office launched an evaluation of the indices to identify areas for improvement and consider alternative measurement tools for examining gen-

der equity as a key aspect of human development. This section summarizes the main findings from this project and outlines possible changes to the indices. The papers prepared for this project as well as the proceedings of a workshop organized to discuss them were published in a special edition of the *Journal of Human Development*.[1]

(Mis)interpretation of the GDI

The review concluded that the indices have often been misinterpreted, particularly the GDI. The GDI is not a measure of *gender inequality*. Rather, it is a measure of *human development* that adjusts the human development index (HDI) to penalize for disparities between women and men in the three dimensions of the HDI: a long and healthy life, knowledge and a decent standard of living (as measured by estimated earned income) (see *Technical note 1*).

The method of calculating the GDI implies that it will always have a lower value than the HDI. But a low GDI value can result from disparities in achievements of women and men as well as from low average achievement in any of the dimensions considered in the index despite high levels of gender equity. Conversely, a country can have a relatively high GDI value despite large inequalities between men and women as long as its level of human development is high. To obtain a measure of gender inequality requires comparing the GDI with the HDI, using either the difference or the ratio between the two as an indicator rather than using the GDI alone.

In general, the differences between the HDI and GDI tend to be small. The GDI is on average about 0.6% lower than the HDI. This gives the highly misleading impression that gender gaps are largely irrelevant for human development. The reason for the problem is that the gender gaps in the three dimensions captured tend to be small—and are diminished further by the aversion to inequality formula used in calculating the GDI. As such, very large gender inequalities linked to pay and promotion in employment, and to quality of education, are often not captured in the GDI.

The GEM—a measure of agency

The GEM was intended to measure women's and men's abilities to participate actively in economic and political life and their command over economic resources.

In contrast to the GDI, which is concerned with well-being, the GEM focuses on agency. It measures three dimensions in this area: political participation and decision-making power, economic participation and decision-making power, and command over economic resources. Calculation of the GEM, also explained in *Technical note 1*, mirrors that of the GDI. The first two components are calculated using shares of female to male participation to which an inequality aversion penalty is applied. The earned income component, by contrast, incorporates inequality-adjusted income levels.

This has implications for interpreting the index. A poor country cannot achieve a high value for the GEM, even if earned income is equally distributed. Conversely, a rich country might do well in the GEM either because the gender gaps in the three dimensions are low or because the country is rich (which raises its GEM value due to the earnings component).

Issues raised in the GDI and GEM review

The GDI and GEM review addressed a wide range of analytical and methodological questions. Among the key measurement issues and proposed solutions:

- *Improving the presentation and explanation of the GDI and GEM.* Understanding the conceptual and empirical problems identified here will help readers make more informed use of the two indices. Future *Human Development Reports* will continue to refine and clarify the GDI and GEM.
- *Creating a separate HDI for men and for women to replace the GDI.* A more intuitive way of presenting gender-related differences in the human development indicators would be to create a separate HDI for men and for women. Differences between the two indices might be easier to interpret than the GDI.
- *Tackling problems linked to earned income for men and women.* Because gender disaggregated income figures are not widely available, estimating earned income for men and women is the most problematic issue in the current calculation of the GDI and the GEM. The Human Development Report Office

estimation of male and female earnings is based on the wage ratio in the nonagricultural sector and the labour force participation rate by gender. This approach has serious shortcomings. First, the underlying data are often not available. Second, income transfers within the household often mean that differences in living standards of individual household members are smaller than actual earnings would imply. There are no easy solutions to these problems, though ongoing work has the potential to refine the measurement of gender disparity.

- *Producing a GEM with income shares.* The GEM includes the absolute average level of income in a country, which means that only rich countries can achieve a high GEM score. Considering only the relative income shares of men and women rather than average income levels would remedy this problem.
- *Considering new indicators.* Current indicators do not capture some important dimensions of gender discrimination in human development. One example is care work, which is not reflected in the GDI or GEM, because the focus is exclusively on market work. This is an area in which researchers and the international statistics community could help over time to build and consolidate a more robust data base. Violence against women is another important gap in the indices. While data on violence has improved greatly in recent years, there are serious problems in making cross-country comparisons and measuring trends over time. Because reliable data still exist for only a small number of countries, it is not yet possible to include an indicator on gender-related violence, but the *Human Development Report* will encourage and monitor further development of these data.

Both the GDI and the GEM have stimulated public debate on gender equity. The *Human Development Report* is committed to maintaining that debate. The problems raised by the GDI and GEM review and outlined here will be addressed in future Reports as research progresses.

Note

1 *Journal of Human Development* 7 (2).

Human development indicators

Indicator tables

Human development index

HDI rank [a]		Human development index (HDI) value 2004	Life expectancy at birth (years) 2004	Adult literacy rate [b] (% ages 15 and older) 2004	Combined gross enrolment ratio for primary, secondary and tertiary schools (%) 2004 [c]	GDP per capita (PPP US$) 2004	Life expectancy index	Education index	GDP index	GDP per capita (PPP US$) rank minus HDI rank [d]
HIGH HUMAN DEVELOPMENT										
1	Norway	0.965	79.6	.. [e]	100 [f]	38,454	0.91	0.99	0.99	3
2	Iceland	0.960	80.9	.. [e]	96 [g]	33,051	0.93	0.98	0.97	3
3	Australia	0.957	80.5	.. [e]	113 [f]	30,331	0.92	0.99	0.95	11
4	Ireland	0.956	77.9	.. [e]	99	38,827	0.88	0.99	1.00	−1
5	Sweden	0.951	80.3	.. [e]	96	29,541	0.92	0.98	0.95	11
6	Canada	0.950	80.2	.. [e]	93 [g, h]	31,263	0.92	0.97	0.96	4
7	Japan	0.949	82.2	.. [e]	85	29,251	0.95	0.94	0.95	11
8	United States	0.948	77.5	.. [e]	93	39,676	0.88	0.97	1.00	−6
9	Switzerland	0.947	80.7	.. [e]	86	33,040	0.93	0.95	0.97	−3
10	Netherlands	0.947	78.5	.. [e]	98	31,789	0.89	0.99	0.96	−1
11	Finland	0.947	78.7	.. [e]	100 [f]	29,951	0.89	0.99	0.95	4
12	Luxembourg	0.945	78.6	.. [e]	85 [h, i]	69,961 [j]	0.89	0.94	1.00	−11
13	Belgium	0.945	79.1	.. [e]	95	31,096	0.90	0.98	0.96	−2
14	Austria	0.944	79.2	.. [e]	91	32,276	0.90	0.96	0.96	−7
15	Denmark	0.943	77.3	.. [e]	101 [f]	31,914	0.87	0.99	0.96	−7
16	France	0.942	79.6	.. [e]	93	29,300	0.91	0.97	0.95	1
17	Italy	0.940	80.2	98.4 [e]	89	28,180	0.92	0.96	0.94	3
18	United Kingdom	0.940	78.5	.. [e]	93 [g]	30,821	0.89	0.97	0.96	−5
19	Spain	0.938	79.7	98.0 [e, k]	96	25,047	0.91	0.98	0.92	3
20	New Zealand	0.936	79.3	.. [e]	100 [f]	23,413	0.90	0.99	0.91	5
21	Germany	0.932	78.9	.. [e]	89 [g]	28,303	0.90	0.96	0.94	−2
22	Hong Kong, China (SAR)	0.927	81.8	.. [l]	77	30,822	0.95	0.88	0.96	−10
23	Israel	0.927	80.0	97.1	90	24,382	0.92	0.95	0.92	0
24	Greece	0.921	78.3	96.0 [e]	93	22,205	0.89	0.97	0.90	3
25	Singapore	0.916	78.9	92.5	87 [m]	28,077	0.90	0.91	0.94	−4
26	Korea, Rep. of	0.912	77.3	98.0 [e, k]	95	20,499	0.87	0.98	0.89	5
27	Slovenia	0.910	76.6	.. [e, l]	95	20,939	0.86	0.98	0.89	1
28	Portugal	0.904	77.5	92.0 [e, k]	89	19,629	0.87	0.96	0.88	5
29	Cyprus	0.903	78.7	96.8	79 [g]	22,805	0.90	0.91	0.91	−3
30	Czech Republic	0.885	75.7	.. [e]	81	19,408	0.85	0.93	0.88	4
31	Barbados	0.879	75.3	.. [e, h, l]	89 [h]	15,720 [h, n]	0.84	0.96	0.84	10
32	Malta	0.875	78.6	87.9 [o]	81	18,879	0.89	0.86	0.87	5
33	Kuwait	0.871	77.1	93.3	73 [g]	19,384 [p]	0.87	0.87	0.88	2
34	Brunei Darussalam	0.871	76.6	92.7	77 [g]	19,210 [h, q]	0.86	0.88	0.88	2
35	Hungary	0.869	73.0	.. [e, l]	87	16,814	0.80	0.95	0.86	4
36	Argentina	0.863	74.6	97.2	89 [h]	13,298	0.83	0.95	0.82	10
37	Poland	0.862	74.6	.. [e, l]	86	12,974	0.83	0.95	0.81	11
38	Chile	0.859	78.1	95.7	81	10,874	0.89	0.91	0.78	18
39	Bahrain	0.859	74.5	86.5	85 [g]	20,758	0.82	0.86	0.89	−10
40	Estonia	0.858	71.6	99.8 [e]	92	14,555	0.78	0.97	0.83	4
41	Lithuania	0.857	72.5	99.6 [e]	92	13,107	0.79	0.97	0.81	6
42	Slovakia	0.856	74.3	100.0 [e, k]	77	14,623	0.82	0.92	0.83	1
43	Uruguay	0.851	75.6	.. [l]	89 [g, h]	9,421	0.84	0.95	0.76	19
44	Croatia	0.846	75.2	98.1	73 [h]	12,191	0.84	0.90	0.80	7
45	Latvia	0.845	71.8	99.7 [e]	90	11,653	0.78	0.96	0.79	9
46	Qatar	0.844	73.0	89.0	76	19,844 [h, r]	0.80	0.85	0.88	−14
47	Seychelles	0.842	72.7 [h, m]	91.8	80 [g]	16,652	0.80	0.88	0.85	−7
48	Costa Rica	0.841	78.3	94.9	72	9,481 [p]	0.89	0.87	0.76	13
49	United Arab Emirates	0.839	78.3	.. [l]	60 [g, h]	24,056 [p]	0.89	0.71	0.92	−25
50	Cuba	0.826	77.6	99.8 [e]	80 [h]	.. [s]	0.88	0.93	0.67	43
51	Saint Kitts and Nevis	0.825	70.0 [h, m, t]	97.8 [m]	80 [g]	12,702 [h]	0.75	0.92	0.81	−2
52	Bahamas	0.825	70.2	.. [l]	66 [g]	17,843 [h]	0.75	0.86	0.87	−14
53	Mexico	0.821	75.3	91.0	75	9,803	0.84	0.86	0.77	7

TABLE 1

Human development index

HDI rank [a]		Human development index (HDI) value 2004	Life expectancy at birth (years) 2004	Adult literacy rate [b] (% ages 15 and older) 2004	Combined gross enrolment ratio for primary, secondary and tertiary schools (%) 2004 [c]	GDP per capita (PPP US$) 2004	Life expectancy index	Education index	GDP index	GDP per capita (PPP US$) rank minus HDI rank [d]
54	Bulgaria	0.816	72.4	98.2	81	8,078	0.79	0.92	0.73	12
55	Tonga	0.815	72.4	98.9 [o]	80 [g]	7,870 [p]	0.79	0.93	0.73	13
56	Oman	0.810	74.3	81.4	68 [g]	15,259	0.82	0.77	0.84	−14
57	Trinidad and Tobago	0.809	69.8	.. [l]	67 [g]	12,182	0.75	0.88	0.80	−5
58	Panama	0.809	75.0	91.9	80	7,278	0.83	0.88	0.72	18
59	Antigua and Barbuda	0.808	73.9 [h, m, t]	85.8 [h, u]	69 [h, m]	12,586	0.82	0.80	0.81	−9
60	Romania	0.805	71.5	97.3	75	8,480	0.78	0.90	0.74	3
61	Malaysia	0.805	73.4	88.7	73 [h]	10,276	0.81	0.84	0.77	−4
62	Bosnia and Herzegovina	0.800	74.3	96.7	67 [h, v]	7,032	0.82	0.87	0.71	16
63	Mauritius	0.800	72.4	84.4	74 [g]	12,027	0.79	0.81	0.80	−10
MEDIUM HUMAN DEVELOPMENT										
64	Libyan Arab Jamahiriya	0.798	73.8	.. [l]	94 [g, h]	7,570 [h, w]	0.81	0.86	0.72	7
65	Russian Federation	0.797	65.2	99.4 [e]	88 [g]	9,902	0.67	0.95	0.77	−6
66	Macedonia, TFYR	0.796	73.9	96.1	70	6,610	0.82	0.87	0.70	16
67	Belarus	0.794	68.2	99.6 [e, o]	88	6,970	0.72	0.95	0.71	12
68	Dominica	0.793	75.6 [h, u]	88.0 [h, u]	83 [g]	5,643	0.84	0.86	0.67	27
69	Brazil	0.792	70.8	88.6	86 [h]	8,195	0.76	0.88	0.74	−5
70	Colombia	0.790	72.6	92.8	73	7,256 [p]	0.79	0.86	0.72	7
71	Saint Lucia	0.790	72.6	94.8 [h, u]	76	6,324	0.79	0.89	0.69	16
72	Venezuela, RB	0.784	73.0	93.0	74 [g, h]	6,043	0.80	0.87	0.68	17
73	Albania	0.784	73.9	98.7	68 [h]	4,978	0.82	0.88	0.65	26
74	Thailand	0.784	70.3	92.6	74	8,090	0.75	0.86	0.73	−9
75	Samoa (Western)	0.778	70.5	.. [l]	74 [g]	5,613	0.76	0.90	0.67	22
76	Saudi Arabia	0.777	72.0	79.4	59	13,825 [p]	0.78	0.72	0.82	−31
77	Ukraine	0.774	66.1	99.4 [e]	85	6,394	0.69	0.94	0.69	9
78	Lebanon	0.774	72.2	.. [l]	84	5,837	0.79	0.86	0.68	13
79	Kazakhstan	0.774	63.4	99.5 [e, o]	91	7,440	0.64	0.96	0.72	−5
80	Armenia	0.768	71.6	99.4 [e]	74	4,101	0.78	0.91	0.62	32
81	China	0.768	71.9	90.9	70	5,896 [x]	0.78	0.84	0.68	9
82	Peru	0.767	70.2	87.7	86 [g]	5,678	0.75	0.87	0.67	12
83	Ecuador	0.765	74.5	91.0	.. [y]	3,963	0.82	0.86	0.61	30
84	Philippines	0.763	70.7	92.6	82	4,614	0.76	0.89	0.64	19
85	Grenada	0.762	65.3 [h, u]	96.0 [u]	73 [g]	8,021	0.67	0.88	0.73	−18
86	Jordan	0.760	71.6	89.9	79	4,688	0.78	0.86	0.64	16
87	Tunisia	0.760	73.5	74.3	75	7,768	0.81	0.75	0.73	−18
88	Saint Vincent and the Grenadines	0.759	71.3	88.1 [u]	68	6,398	0.77	0.81	0.69	−3
89	Suriname	0.759	69.3	89.6	72 [g, h]	.. [p, z]	0.74	0.84	0.70	−5
90	Fiji	0.758	68.0	.. [l]	75 [g]	6,066	0.72	0.87	0.69	−2
91	Paraguay	0.757	71.2	.. [l]	70 [g, h]	4,813 [p]	0.77	0.86	0.65	9
92	Turkey	0.757	68.9	87.4	69	7,753	0.73	0.81	0.73	−22
93	Sri Lanka	0.755	74.3	90.7	63 [g]	4,390	0.82	0.81	0.63	13
94	Dominican Republic	0.751	67.5	87.0	74 [g]	7,449 [p]	0.71	0.83	0.72	−21
95	Belize	0.751	71.8	75.1 [h, u]	81	6,747	0.78	0.77	0.70	−15
96	Iran, Islamic Rep. of	0.746	70.7	77.0	72 [g]	7,525	0.76	0.75	0.72	−24
97	Georgia	0.743	70.6	100.0 [e, k, aa]	75	2,844	0.76	0.91	0.56	23
98	Maldives	0.739	67.0	96.3	69 [g]	.. [h, p, z]	0.70	0.87	0.65	3
99	Azerbaijan	0.736	67.0	98.8 [o]	68	4,153	0.70	0.89	0.62	12
100	Occupied Palestinian Territories	0.736	72.7	92.4	81 [g]	.. [ab]	0.80	0.89	0.53	26
101	El Salvador	0.729	71.1	.. [l]	70 [g]	5,041 [p]	0.77	0.76	0.65	−3
102	Algeria	0.728	71.4	69.9	73	6,603 [p]	0.77	0.71	0.70	−19
103	Guyana	0.725	63.6	96.5 [h, u]	76 [h]	4,439 [p]	0.64	0.90	0.63	2
104	Jamaica	0.724	70.7	79.9 [o]	77 [g]	4,163	0.76	0.79	0.62	6
105	Turkmenistan	0.724	62.5	98.8 [o]	.. [y]	4,584 [h]	0.63	0.91	0.64	−1
106	Cape Verde	0.722	70.7	.. [l]	67	5,727 [p]	0.76	0.73	0.68	−14

TABLE 1

HDI rank[a]		Human development index (HDI) value 2004	Life expectancy at birth (years) 2004	Adult literacy rate[b] (% ages 15 and older) 2004	Combined gross enrolment ratio for primary, secondary and tertiary schools (%) 2004[c]	GDP per capita (PPP US$) 2004	Life expectancy index	Education index	GDP index	GDP per capita (PPP US$) rank minus HDI rank[d]
107	Syrian Arab Republic	0.716	73.6	79.6	63 [g]	3,610	0.81	0.74	0.60	8
108	Indonesia	0.711	67.2	90.4	68	3,609	0.70	0.83	0.60	8
109	Viet Nam	0.709	70.8	90.3 [o]	63 [g]	2,745	0.76	0.81	0.55	12
110	Kyrgyzstan	0.705	67.1	98.7 [o]	78	1,935	0.70	0.92	0.49	32
111	Egypt	0.702	70.2	71.4	76 [g]	4,211	0.75	0.73	0.62	−2
112	Nicaragua	0.698	70.0	76.7	70 [g]	3,634 [p]	0.75	0.75	0.60	2
113	Uzbekistan	0.696	66.6	.. [e, l]	74 [g]	1,869	0.69	0.91	0.49	32
114	Moldova, Rep. of	0.694	68.1	98.4	70 [g]	1,729	0.72	0.89	0.48	33
115	Bolivia	0.692	64.4	86.7	87 [g]	2,720	0.66	0.87	0.55	7
116	Mongolia	0.691	64.5	97.8	77	2,056	0.66	0.91	0.50	18
117	Honduras	0.683	68.1	80.0	71 [g]	2,876 [p]	0.72	0.77	0.56	2
118	Guatemala	0.673	67.6	69.1	66 [g]	4,313 [p]	0.71	0.68	0.63	−11
119	Vanuatu	0.670	68.9	74.0 [o]	64 [g]	3,051 [p]	0.73	0.71	0.57	−1
120	Equatorial Guinea	0.653	42.8	87.0	58 [g, h]	20,510 [h, p]	0.30	0.77	0.89	−90
121	South Africa	0.653	47.0	82.4 [o]	77 [h]	11,192 [p]	0.37	0.80	0.79	−66
122	Tajikistan	0.652	63.7	99.5 [e]	71	1,202	0.65	0.90	0.41	34
123	Morocco	0.640	70.0	52.3	58	4,309	0.75	0.54	0.63	−15
124	Gabon	0.633	54.0	71.0 [k]	72 [g, h]	6,623	0.48	0.71	0.70	−43
125	Namibia	0.626	47.2	85.0	67 [h]	7,418 [p]	0.37	0.79	0.72	−50
126	India	0.611	63.6	61.0	62 [g]	3,139 [p]	0.64	0.61	0.58	−9
127	São Tomé and Principe	0.607	63.2	83.1 [h, m]	63	1,231 [h, r]	0.64	0.76	0.42	28
128	Solomon Islands	0.592	62.6	76.6 [h, m]	47 [g, h]	1,814 [p]	0.63	0.67	0.48	18
129	Cambodia	0.583	56.5	73.6	60 [h]	2,423 [p]	0.52	0.69	0.53	−4
130	Myanmar	0.581	60.5	89.9	49 [g]	1,027 [h, w]	0.59	0.76	0.39	33
131	Botswana	0.570	34.9	81.2	71 [g]	9,945	0.16	0.78	0.77	−73
132	Comoros	0.556	63.7	.. [l]	46 [g]	1,943 [p]	0.64	0.53	0.50	8
133	Lao People's Dem. Rep.	0.553	55.1	68.7	61	1,954	0.50	0.66	0.50	5
134	Pakistan	0.539	63.4	49.9	38	2,225	0.64	0.46	0.52	−6
135	Bhutan	0.538	63.4	47.0 [k]	.. [y]	1,969 [h, r]	0.64	0.48	0.50	2
136	Ghana	0.532	57.0	57.9	47 [g]	2,240 [p]	0.53	0.54	0.52	−9
137	Bangladesh	0.530	63.3	.. [l]	57 [h]	1,870	0.64	0.46	0.49	7
138	Nepal	0.527	62.1	48.6	57 [h]	1,490	0.62	0.51	0.45	13
139	Papua New Guinea	0.523	55.7	57.3	41 [g, h]	2,543 [p]	0.51	0.52	0.54	−15
140	Congo	0.520	52.3	.. [l]	52 [g]	978	0.46	0.72	0.38	25
141	Sudan [ac]	0.516	56.5	60.9	37 [g]	1,949 [p]	0.53	0.53	0.50	−2
142	Timor-Leste	0.512	56.0	58.6 [h, m]	72 [g, h]	.. [ad]	0.52	0.63	0.39	20
143	Madagascar	0.509	55.6	70.7	57 [g]	857	0.51	0.66	0.36	26
144	Cameroon	0.506	45.7	67.9	62 [g]	2,174	0.34	0.66	0.51	−13
145	Uganda	0.502	48.4	66.8	66	1,478 [p]	0.39	0.67	0.45	7
146	Swaziland	0.500	31.3	79.6	58 [g, h]	5,638	0.10	0.72	0.67	−50
LOW HUMAN DEVELOPMENT										
147	Togo	0.495	54.5	53.2	55 [g]	1,536 [p]	0.49	0.54	0.46	3
148	Djibouti	0.494	52.9	.. [l]	24	1,993 [p]	0.47	0.52	0.50	−13
149	Lesotho	0.494	35.2	82.2	66 [g]	2,619 [p]	0.17	0.77	0.54	−26
150	Yemen	0.492	61.1	.. [l]	55 [g]	879	0.60	0.51	0.36	18
151	Zimbabwe	0.491	36.6	.. [l]	52 [g, h]	2,065	0.19	0.77	0.51	−18
152	Kenya	0.491	47.5	73.6	60 [g]	1,140	0.37	0.69	0.41	7
153	Mauritania	0.486	53.1	51.2	46	1,940 [p]	0.47	0.49	0.49	−12
154	Haiti	0.482	52.0	.. [l]	.. [y]	1,892 [h, p]	0.45	0.50	0.49	−11
155	Gambia	0.479	56.1	.. [l]	50 [g]	1,991 [p]	0.52	0.42	0.50	−19
156	Senegal	0.460	56.0	39.3	38 [g]	1,713	0.52	0.39	0.47	−8
157	Eritrea	0.454	54.3	.. [l]	35	977 [p]	0.49	0.50	0.38	9
158	Rwanda	0.450	44.2	64.9	52	1,263 [p]	0.32	0.61	0.42	−5
159	Nigeria	0.448	43.4	.. [l]	55 [g]	1,154	0.31	0.63	0.41	−1

Human development indicators

TABLE 1

Human development index

HDI rank [a]	Human development index (HDI) value 2004	Life expectancy at birth (years) 2004	Adult literacy rate [b] (% ages 15 and older) 2004	Combined gross enrolment ratio for primary, secondary and tertiary schools (%) 2004 [c]	GDP per capita (PPP US$) 2004	Life expectancy index	Education index	GDP index	GDP per capita (PPP US$) rank minus HDI rank [d]
160 Guinea	0.445	53.9	29.5	42	2,180	0.48	0.34	0.51	−30
161 Angola	0.439	41.0	67.4	26 [g, h]	2,180 [p]	0.27	0.53	0.51	−32
162 Tanzania, U. Rep. of	0.430	45.9	69.4	48 [g]	674	0.35	0.62	0.32	13
163 Benin	0.428	54.3	34.7	49 [g]	1,091	0.49	0.40	0.40	−2
164 Côte d'Ivoire	0.421	45.9	48.7	40 [g, h]	1,551	0.35	0.46	0.46	−15
165 Zambia	0.407	37.7	68.0 [o]	54	943	0.21	0.63	0.37	2
166 Malawi	0.400	39.8	64.1 [o]	64 [g]	646	0.25	0.64	0.31	10
167 Congo, Dem. Rep. of the	0.391	43.5	67.2	27 [g, h]	705 [p]	0.31	0.54	0.33	6
168 Mozambique	0.390	41.6	..[l]	49	1,237 [p]	0.28	0.47	0.42	−14
169 Burundi	0.384	44.0	59.3	36	677 [p]	0.32	0.52	0.32	5
170 Ethiopia	0.371	47.8	..[l]	36	756 [p]	0.38	0.40	0.34	1
171 Chad	0.368	43.7	25.7	35 [g]	2,090 [p]	0.31	0.29	0.51	−39
172 Central African Republic	0.353	39.1	48.6	30 [g, h]	1,094 [p]	0.24	0.42	0.40	−12
173 Guinea-Bissau	0.349	44.8	..[l]	37 [g, h]	722 [p]	0.33	0.39	0.33	−1
174 Burkina Faso	0.342	47.9	21.8	26 [g]	1,169 [p]	0.38	0.23	0.41	−17
175 Mali	0.338	48.1	19.0 [o]	35	998	0.39	0.24	0.38	−11
176 Sierra Leone	0.335	41.0	35.1	65 [g]	561	0.27	0.45	0.29	1
177 Niger	0.311	44.6	28.7	21	779 [p]	0.33	0.26	0.34	−7
Developing countries	0.679	65.2	78.9	63	4,775	0.67	0.72	0.65	..
Least developed countries	0.464	52.4	63.7	45	1,350	0.46	0.50	0.43	..
Arab States	0.680	67.3	69.9	62	5,680	0.71	0.66	0.67	..
East Asia and the Pacific	0.760	70.8	90.7	69	5,872	0.76	0.84	0.68	..
Latin America and the Caribbean	0.795	72.2	90.2	81	7,964	0.79	0.87	0.73	..
South Asia	0.599	63.7	60.9	56	3,072	0.64	0.58	0.57	..
Sub-Saharan Africa	0.472	46.1	63.3	50	1,946	0.35	0.57	0.50	..
Central and Eastern Europe and the CIS	0.802	68.2	99.2	83	8,802	0.72	0.94	0.75	..
OECD	0.923	77.8	..	89	27,571	0.88	0.95	0.94	..
High-income OECD	0.946	79.0	..	95	32,003	0.90	0.98	0.96	..
High human development	0.923	78.0	..	91	26,568	0.88	0.95	0.93	..
Medium human development	0.701	67.3	80.5	66	4,901	0.71	0.75	0.65	..
Low human development	0.427	45.8	57.9	46	1,113	0.35	0.53	0.40	..
High income	0.942	78.8	..	94	31,331	0.90	0.97	0.96	..
Middle income	0.768	70.3	89.9	73	6,756	0.76	0.84	0.70	..
Low income	0.556	58.7	62.3	54	2,297	0.56	0.58	0.52	..
World	0.741	67.3	..	67	8,833	0.71	0.77	0.75	..

NOTES

a The HDI rank is determined using HDI values to the sixth decimal point.

b Data refer to national literacy estimates from censuses or surveys conducted between 2000 and 2005, unless otherwise specified. Due to differences in methodology and timeliness of underlying data, comparisons across countries and over time should be made with caution. For more details, see www.uis.unesco.org.

c In 2006 the United Nations Educational, Scientific and Cultural Organization (UNESCO) Institute for Statistics changed its convention for citing the reference year of education data to the calendar year in which the academic or financial year ends—from 2003/04, for example, to 2004. Data for some countries may refer to national or UNESCO Institute for Statistics estimates.

d A positive figure indicates that the HDI rank is higher than the GDP per capita (PPP US$) rank, a negative the opposite.

e For purposes of calculating the HDI, a value of 99.0% was applied.

f For purposes of calculating the HDI, a value of 100% was applied.

g Preliminary national or UNESCO Institute for Statistics estimate, subject to further revision.

h Data refer to a year other than that specified.

i Statec 2006. Data refer to nationals enrolled both in the country and abroad and thus differ from the standard definition.

j For purposes of calculating the HDI, a value of $40,000 (PPP US$) was applied.

k UNICEF 2004.

l In the absence of recent data, estimates from UNESCO Institute for Statistics 2003, based on outdated census or survey information, were used and should be interpreted with caution: Bahamas 95, Bangladesh 41, Barbados 100, Cape Verde 76, Comoros 56, Congo 83, Djibouti 65, El Salvador 80, Eritrea 57, Ethiopia 42, Fiji 93, Gambia 38, Guinea-Bissau 40, Haiti 52, Hong Kong, China (SAR) 94, Hungary 99, Lebanon 86, Libyan Arab Jamahiriya 82, Mozambique 46, Nigeria 67, Paraguay 93, Poland 99, Samoa (Western) 99, Slovenia 99, Trinidad and Tobago 98, United Arab Emirates 77, Uruguay 98, Uzbekistan 99, Yemen 49 and Zimbabwe 90.

m Data are from national sources.

n World Bank 2005.

o Data refer to the most recent year available between 1995 and 1999.

p Estimate is based on regression.

q World Bank 2003.

r Heston, Summers and Aten 2002. Data differ from the standard definition.

s Efforts to produce a more accurate and recent estimate are ongoing (see Readers guide and notes to tables). A preliminary estimate of $5,700 (PPP US$) was used.

t Data are from the Secretariat of the Organization of Eastern Caribbean States, based on national sources.

u Data are from the Secretariat of the Caribbean Community, based on national sources.

v UNDP 2005a.

w Heston, Summers and Aten 2001. Data differ from the standard definition.

x Estimate is based on a bilateral comparison of China and the United States (Ruoen and Kai 1995).

y Because the combined gross enrolment ratio was unavailable, the following Human Development Report Office estimates were used: Bhutan 49, Ecuador 75, Haiti 48 and Turkmenistan 75.

z In the absence of an official estimate of GDP per capita (PPP US$), the following preliminary World Bank estimates, subject to further revision, were used: Maldives $4,798 and Suriname $6,552.

aa Data refer to a year or period other than that specified, differ from the standard definition or refer to only part of a country.

ab In the absence of an estimate of GDP per capita (PPP US$), the Human Development Report Office estimate of $2,331 was used, derived from the value of GDP in US dollars and the weighted average ratio of PPP US dollars to US dollars in the Arab States.

ac Estimates are based primarily on information for Northern Sudan.

ad A national estimate of $1,033 (PPP US$) was used.

SOURCES

Column 1: calculated on the basis of data in columns 6–8; see Technical note 1 for details.

Column 2: UN 2005a, unless otherwise specified.

Column 3: UNESCO Institute for Statistics 2006a, unless otherwise specified.

Column 4: UNESCO Institute for Statistics 2006c, unless otherwise specified.

Column 5: World Bank 2006, unless otherwise specified; aggregates calculated for the Human Development Report Office by the World Bank.

Column 6: calculated on the basis of data in column 2.

Column 7: calculated on the basis of data in columns 3 and 4.

Column 8: calculated on the basis of data in column 5.

Column 9: calculated on the basis of data in columns 1 and 5.

Monitoring human development: enlarging people's choices . . .

Basic indicators for other UN member countries

| | Human development index components | | | | | | | | | | |
	Life expectancy at birth (years) 2000–05 [b]	Adult literacy rate (% ages 15 and older) 2004 [c]	Combined gross enrolment ratio for primary, secondary and tertiary schools (%) 2004 [d]	GDP per capita (PPP US$) 2004	Total population (thousands) 2004	Total fertility rate (births per woman) 2000–05 [b]	MDG Under-five mortality rate (per 1,000 live births) 2004	MDG Net primary enrolment ratio (%) 2004 [d]	HIV prevalence [a] (% ages 15–49) 2005	MDG Population under-nourished (% of total population) 2001/03 [e]	MDG Population with sustain-able access to an improved water source (%) 2004
Afghanistan	46.0	28.1	45.3	..	28,574	7.5	257	..	<0.1 [<0.2]	..	39
Andorra	..	..	66.9	..	67	..	7	89 [f]		..	100
Iraq	58.8	74.1	59.7	..	28,057	4.8	125	88	[<0.2]	..	81
Kiribati	..	..	77.2	..	97	..	65	97 [f, g]		6	65
Korea, Dem. Rep.	63.0	..	..	..	22,384	2.0	55	..	[<0.2]	35	100
Liberia	42.5	..	57.4	..	3,241	6.8	235	66 [h]	[2.0–5.0]	49	61
Liechtenstein	..	..	69.3	..	34	..	5	88 [i]	..	..	..
Marshall Islands	..	..	..	..	60	..	59	90 [f]	..	..	87
Micronesia, Fed. Sts.	67.6	..	..	..	110	4.4	23	..	..	..	94
Monaco	..	..	..	..	35	..	5	..	..	..	100
Montenegro [j]	73.2	96.4 [k]	74.5	..	.. [l]	1.7	15	96 [i, m]	0.2 [0.1–0.3]	10	93
Nauru	..	..	50.6	..	13	..	30	..	..	..	..
Palau	..	..	94.6	..	20	..	27	96 [f, h]	..	..	85
San Marino	..	..	..	..	28	..	4	..	..	..	..
Serbia [j]	73.2	96.4 [k]	74.5	..	.. [l]	1.7	15	96 [i, m]	0.2 [0.1–0.3]	10	93
Somalia	46.2	..	..	..	7,964	6.4	225	..	0.9 [0.5–1.6]	..	29
Tuvalu	..	..	69.2	..	10	..	51	..	..	..	100

NOTES

a Data refer to point and range estimates based on new estimation models developed by the Joint United Nations Programme on HIV/AIDS (UNAIDS). Range estimates are presented in square brackets.
b Data refer to estimates for the period specified.
c Data refer to national literacy estimates from censuses or surveys conducted between 2000 and 2005. Due to differences in methodology and timeliness of underlying data, comparisons across countries and over time should be made with caution.

d In 2006 the United Nations Educational, Scientific and Cultural Organization (UNESCO) Institute for Statistics changed its convention for citing the reference year of education data to the calendar year in which the academic or financial year ends—from 2003/04, for example, to 2004.
e Data refer to the average for the years specified.
f Preliminary UNESCO Institute for Statistics estimate, subject to further revision.
g Data refer to the 1999 school year.
h Data refer to the 2000 school year.

i National estimates.
j Data refer to Serbia and Montenegro prior to its separation into two independent states in June 2006.
k Excludes Kosovo and Metohia.
l The combined population for Serbia and Montenegro was 10.51 million.
m Data refer to the 2001 school year.

SOURCES

Columns 1, 5 and 6: UN 2005b.
Column 2: UNESCO Institute for Statistics 2006a.
Columns 3 and 8: UNESCO Institute for Statistics 2006c.
Column 4: World Bank 2006.
Column 7: UN 2006c, based on data from a joint effort by the United Nations Children's Fund and the World Health Organization.
Column 9: UNAIDS 2006.
Column 10: UN 2006c, based on data from the Food and Agriculture Organization.
Column 11: UN 2006c, based on a joint effort by the United Nations Children's Fund and the World Health Organization.

Human development index trends

HDI rank	1975	1980	1985	1990	1995	2000	2004
HIGH HUMAN DEVELOPMENT							
1 Norway	0.868	0.888	0.898	0.912	0.936	0.956	0.965
2 Iceland	0.865	0.888	0.897	0.916	0.921	0.945	0.960
3 Australia	0.848	0.866	0.878	0.893	0.933	0.947	0.957
4 Ireland	0.813	0.828	0.848	0.873	0.897	0.932	0.956
5 Sweden	0.868	0.878	0.890	0.901	0.933	0.949	0.951
6 Canada	0.870	0.886	0.909	0.929	0.935	..	0.950
7 Japan	0.859	0.884	0.897	0.914	0.927	0.939	0.949
8 United States	0.868	0.889	0.902	0.917	0.930	0.940	0.948
9 Switzerland	0.882	0.893	0.900	0.914	0.925	0.941	0.947
10 Netherlands	0.871	0.883	0.898	0.913	0.932	0.944	0.947
11 Finland	0.843	0.864	0.882	0.904	0.917	0.938	0.947
12 Luxembourg	0.843	0.854	0.861	0.887	0.913	0.930	0.945
13 Belgium	0.849	0.867	0.881	0.902	0.932	0.945	0.945
14 Austria	0.846	0.861	0.874	0.897	0.916	0.937	0.944
15 Denmark	0.874	0.883	0.891	0.898	0.913	0.932	0.943
16 France	0.853	0.869	0.884	0.904	0.923	0.935	0.942
17 Italy	0.844	0.859	0.868	0.890	0.908	0.924	0.940
18 United Kingdom	0.851	0.859	0.868	0.889	0.927	0.939	0.940
19 Spain	0.844	0.861	0.875	0.893	0.910	0.927	0.938
20 New Zealand	0.849	0.855	0.868	0.876	0.906	0.925	0.936
21 Germany	..	0.861	0.868	0.887	0.912	..	0.932
22 Hong Kong, China (SAR)	0.761	0.801	0.829	0.864	0.883	0.917	0.927
23 Israel	0.804	0.829	0.850	0.867	0.890	0.918	0.927
24 Greece	0.839	0.854	0.868	0.876	0.880	0.897	0.921
25 Singapore	0.727	0.763	0.786	0.823	0.862	..	0.916
26 Korea, Rep. of	0.712	0.746	0.785	0.823	0.860	0.890	0.912
27 Slovenia	..	..	..	..	0.855	0.888	0.910
28 Portugal	0.791	0.807	0.830	0.853	0.883	0.902	0.904
29 Cyprus	..	0.803	0.823	0.846	0.868	0.893	0.903
30 Czech Republic	..	..	..	..	0.850	0.865	0.885
31 Barbados	..	..	..	..	..	..	0.879
32 Malta	0.730	0.766	0.793	0.828	0.855	0.876	0.875
33 Kuwait	0.763	0.778	0.781	..	0.814	0.841	0.871
34 Brunei Darussalam	..	..	..	..	..	..	0.871
35 Hungary	0.783	0.798	0.811	0.811	0.815	0.845	0.869
36 Argentina	0.787	0.802	0.811	0.813	0.835	0.860	0.863
37 Poland	..	..	..	0.807	0.820	0.848	0.862
38 Chile	0.706	0.741	0.765	0.787	0.818	0.843	0.859
39 Bahrain	..	0.747	0.784	0.812	0.828	0.842	0.859
40 Estonia	..	..	..	0.813	0.793	0.831	0.858
41 Lithuania	..	..	..	0.825	0.789	0.830	0.857
42 Slovakia	..	..	..	..	..	..	0.856
43 Uruguay	0.761	0.781	0.788	0.806	0.819	0.841	0.851
44 Croatia	..	..	..	0.810	0.803	0.828	0.846
45 Latvia	..	0.795	0.809	0.803	0.769	0.815	0.845
46 Qatar	..	..	..	..	..	..	0.844
47 Seychelles	..	..	..	..	..	..	0.842
48 Costa Rica	0.745	0.772	0.776	0.793	0.812	0.832	0.841
49 United Arab Emirates	0.734	0.769	0.786	0.810	0.819	0.833	0.839
50 Cuba	..	..	..	..	..	..	0.826
51 Saint Kitts and Nevis	..	..	..	..	..	..	0.825
52 Bahamas	..	0.811	0.820	0.823	0.812	0.831	0.825
53 Mexico	0.691	0.737	0.757	0.766	0.784	0.811	0.821

TABLE 2

HDI rank	1975	1980	1985	1990	1995	2000	2004
54 Bulgaria	..	0.768	0.788	0.794	0.783	0.797	0.816
55 Tonga	..	..	..	..	..	..	0.815
56 Oman	0.492	0.546	0.639	0.695	0.740	0.776	0.810
57 Trinidad and Tobago	0.751	0.783	0.790	0.793	0.791	0.801	0.809
58 Panama	0.712	0.739	0.750	0.751	0.774	0.797	0.809
59 Antigua and Barbuda	..	..	..	..	..	..	0.808
60 Romania	..	..	..	0.775	0.770	0.778	0.805
61 Malaysia	0.616	0.659	0.696	0.723	0.761	0.791	0.805
62 Bosnia and Herzegovina	..	..	..	..	..	..	0.800
63 Mauritius	..	0.661	0.692	0.726	0.749	0.779	0.800
MEDIUM HUMAN DEVELOPMENT							
64 Libyan Arab Jamahiriya	..	..	..	..	..	..	0.798
65 Russian Federation	..	..	..	0.818	0.771	0.785	0.797
66 Macedonia, TFYR	..	..	..	..	..	..	0.796
67 Belarus	..	..	..	0.788	0.753	0.775	0.794
68 Dominica	..	..	..	..	..	..	0.793
69 Brazil	0.647	0.684	0.699	0.720	0.749	0.785	0.792
70 Colombia	0.664	0.693	0.710	0.730	0.754	0.775	0.790
71 Saint Lucia	..	..	..	..	..	..	0.790
72 Venezuela, RB	0.719	0.734	0.742	0.760	0.768	0.774	0.784
73 Albania	..	..	0.693	0.704	0.704	0.738	0.784
74 Thailand	0.615	0.654	0.680	0.717	0.751	0.775	0.784
75 Samoa (Western)	..	..	0.705	0.700	0.742	0.765	0.778
76 Saudi Arabia	0.606	0.661	0.674	0.708	0.742	0.765	0.777
77 Ukraine	..	..	..	0.800	0.748	0.755	0.774
78 Lebanon	..	..	..	0.682	0.729	0.748	0.774
79 Kazakhstan	..	..	..	0.768	0.723	0.736	0.774
80 Armenia	..	..	..	0.738	0.701	0.736	0.768
81 China	0.527	0.560	0.596	0.628	0.685	0.730	0.768
82 Peru	0.645	0.675	0.699	0.708	0.735	0.760	0.767
83 Ecuador	0.632	0.676	0.700	0.716	0.732	..	0.765
84 Philippines	0.655	0.689	0.695	0.722	0.738	0.759	0.763
85 Grenada	..	..	..	..	..	..	0.762
86 Jordan	..	0.643	0.665	0.685	0.710	0.744	0.760
87 Tunisia	0.516	0.572	0.623	0.659	0.700	0.739	0.760
88 Saint Vincent and the Grenadines	..	..	..	..	..	..	0.759
89 Suriname	..	..	..	..	..	..	0.759
90 Fiji	0.663	0.686	0.701	..	0.742	0.744	0.758
91 Paraguay	0.671	0.705	0.712	0.721	0.740	0.754	0.757
92 Turkey	0.591	0.614	0.650	0.682	0.713	0.743	0.757
93 Sri Lanka	0.612	0.653	0.684	0.706	0.729	0.747	0.755
94 Dominican Republic	0.622	0.652	0.674	0.682	0.703	0.733	0.751
95 Belize	..	0.709	0.719	0.748	0.770	0.780	0.751
96 Iran, Islamic Rep. of	0.567	0.571	0.612	0.651	0.695	0.723	0.746
97 Georgia	..	..	..	..	..	..	0.743
98 Maldives	..	..	..	..	..	..	0.739
99 Azerbaijan	..	..	..	..	..	..	0.736
100 Occupied Palestinian Territories	..	..	..	..	..	..	0.736
101 El Salvador	0.593	0.589	0.610	0.651	0.690	0.715	0.729
102 Algeria	0.508	0.560	0.611	0.650	0.672	0.701	0.728
103 Guyana	0.679	0.685	0.678	0.684	0.687	0.716	0.725
104 Jamaica	0.687	0.695	0.699	0.719	0.725	0.737	0.724
105 Turkmenistan	..	..	..	..	..	..	0.724
106 Cape Verde	..	..	..	0.628	0.679	0.711	0.722

TABLE 2

Human development index trends

HDI rank	1975	1980	1985	1990	1995	2000	2004
107 Syrian Arab Republic	0.543	0.589	0.625	0.646	0.673	0.690	0.716
108 Indonesia	0.469	0.532	0.585	0.626	0.665	0.682	0.711
109 Viet Nam	..	..	..	0.618	0.661	0.696	0.709
110 Kyrgyzstan	..	..	..	..	..	..	0.705
111 Egypt	0.439	0.488	0.541	0.580	0.613	0.654	0.702
112 Nicaragua	0.585	0.595	0.603	0.610	0.642	0.667	0.698
113 Uzbekistan	..	..	..	..	0.681	0.688	0.696
114 Moldova, Rep. of	..	..	..	0.740	0.683	0.679	0.694
115 Bolivia	0.514	0.550	0.582	0.605	0.637	0.675	0.692
116 Mongolia	..	..	0.642	0.646	0.634	0.659	0.691
117 Honduras	0.519	0.570	0.602	0.625	0.642	0.654	0.683
118 Guatemala	0.511	0.546	0.561	0.586	0.617	0.656	0.673
119 Vanuatu	..	..	..	..	..	..	0.670
120 Equatorial Guinea	..	..	0.484	0.501	0.519	0.643	0.653
121 South Africa	0.653	0.673	0.703	0.735	0.741	0.691	0.653
122 Tajikistan	..	..	0.700	0.697	0.631	0.627	0.652
123 Morocco	0.432	0.479	0.517	0.549	0.580	0.610	0.640
124 Gabon	..	..	..	..	..	..	0.633
125 Namibia	..	..	..	..	0.694	0.647	0.626
126 India	0.413	0.439	0.477	0.515	0.548	0.577	0.611
127 São Tomé and Principe	..	..	..	..	..	..	0.607
128 Solomon Islands	..	..	..	..	..	..	0.592
129 Cambodia	..	..	..	..	0.536	0.545	0.583
130 Myanmar	..	..	..	..	..	..	0.581
131 Botswana	0.500	0.575	0.636	0.680	0.660	0.598	0.570
132 Comoros	..	0.483	0.500	0.506	0.521	0.539	0.556
133 Lao People's Dem. Rep.	..	..	0.425	0.451	0.488	0.523	0.553
134 Pakistan	0.365	0.388	0.420	0.463	0.493	0.511	0.539
135 Bhutan	..	..	..	..	..	..	0.538
136 Ghana	0.438	0.467	0.482	0.511	0.531	0.555	0.532
137 Bangladesh	0.347	0.366	0.391	0.422	0.454	0.510	0.530
138 Nepal	0.299	0.336	0.378	0.425	0.467	0.500	0.527
139 Papua New Guinea	0.424	0.444	0.466	0.481	0.514	0.530	0.523
140 Congo	0.454	0.500	0.541	0.528	0.533	0.502	0.520
141 Sudan	0.350	0.376	0.396	0.427	0.465	0.496	0.516
142 Timor-Leste	..	..	..	..	..	..	0.512
143 Madagascar	0.404	0.440	0.438	0.448	0.459	0.482	0.509
144 Cameroon	0.417	0.464	0.506	0.515	0.495	0.502	0.506
145 Uganda	..	..	0.414	0.411	0.413	0.474	0.502
146 Swaziland	0.529	0.561	0.583	0.622	0.604	0.536	0.500
LOW HUMAN DEVELOPMENT							
147 Togo	0.424	0.475	0.472	0.498	0.507	0.504	0.495
148 Djibouti	..	..	..	..	0.479	0.485	0.494
149 Lesotho	0.463	0.511	0.535	0.572	0.573	0.524	0.494
150 Yemen	..	..	..	0.394	0.438	0.467	0.492
151 Zimbabwe	0.548	0.576	0.642	0.639	0.591	0.525	0.491
152 Kenya	0.465	0.513	0.533	0.548	0.525	0.504	0.491
153 Mauritania	0.342	0.365	0.386	0.390	0.425	0.447	0.486
154 Haiti	..	0.451	0.458	0.446	0.451	..	0.482
155 Gambia	0.286	..	..	..	0.426	0.459	0.479
156 Senegal	0.313	0.342	0.378	0.405	0.422	0.439	0.460
157 Eritrea	..	..	..	..	0.420	0.441	0.454
158 Rwanda	0.342	0.388	0.401	0.339	0.337	0.426	0.450
159 Nigeria	0.317	0.376	0.387	0.407	0.419	0.433	0.448

TABLE 2

HDI rank	1975	1980	1985	1990	1995	2000	2004
160 Guinea	..	..	..	..	..	..	0.445
161 Angola	..	..	..	..	..	..	0.439
162 Tanzania, U. Rep. of	..	..	..	0.437	0.423	0.420	0.430
163 Benin	0.310	0.341	0.365	0.372	0.397	0.416	0.428
164 Côte d'Ivoire	0.415	0.445	0.449	0.443	0.428	0.427	0.421
165 Zambia	0.470	0.477	0.486	0.464	0.425	0.409	0.407
166 Malawi	0.327	0.357	0.368	0.372	0.414	0.398	0.400
167 Congo, Dem. Rep. of the	0.414	0.423	0.431	0.422	0.392	..	0.391
168 Mozambique	..	0.302	0.290	0.316	0.330	0.364	0.390
169 Burundi	0.285	0.312	0.344	0.351	0.325	0.344	0.384
170 Ethiopia	..	..	0.293	0.314	0.322	0.349	0.371
171 Chad	0.269	0.272	0.313	0.335	0.344	0.357	0.368
172 Central African Republic	0.345	0.365	0.387	0.384	0.367	..	0.353
173 Guinea-Bissau	0.255	0.263	0.283	0.313	0.341	0.353	0.349
174 Burkina Faso	0.256	0.277	0.301	0.308	0.312	0.330	0.342
175 Mali	0.232	0.258	0.264	0.285	0.309	0.332	0.338
176 Sierra Leone	..	..	..	..	..	..	0.335
177 Niger	0.234	0.250	0.240	0.246	0.254	0.268	0.311

NOTE
The human development index values in this table were calculated using a consistent methodology and data series. They are not strictly comparable with those in earlier *Human Development Reports*. For detailed discussion, see *Readers guide and notes to tables*.

SOURCES
Columns 1–6: calculated on the basis of data on life expectancy from UN 2005a; data on adult literacy rates from UNESCO Institute for Statistics 2003, 2006a; data on combined gross enrolment ratios from UNESCO Institute for Statistics 1999, 2006c; and data on GDP per capita (2000 PPP US$) and GDP per capita (PPP US$) from World Bank 2006.
Column 7: column 1 of indicator table 1.

Human and income poverty: developing countries

HDI rank	Human poverty index (HPI-1) Rank	Human poverty index (HPI-1) Value (%)	Probability at birth of not surviving to age 40 [a],[†] (% of cohort) 2000–05	Adult illiteracy rate [b],[†] (% ages 15 and older) 2004	Population without sustainable access to an improved water source [†] (%) 2004	MDG Children under weight for age [†] (% under age 5) 1996–2004 [c]	MDG Population below income poverty line (%) $1 a day 1990–2004 [c]	$2 a day 1990–2004 [c]	National poverty line 1990–2003 [c]	HPI-1 rank minus income poverty rank [d]
HIGH HUMAN DEVELOPMENT										
22 Hong Kong, China (SAR)	..	..	1.5	..	..	..	..	..	..	..
25 Singapore	7	6.3	1.8	7.5	0	14 [e]	..	..	..	..
26 Korea, Rep. of	..	..	2.7	2.0 [e]	8	..	2.0	<2	..	..
29 Cyprus	..	..	2.8	3.2	0	..	..	..	..	..
31 Barbados	5	4.5	6.3	.. [f]	0	6 [e]	..	..	..	..
33 Kuwait	..	..	2.5	6.7	..	10	..	..	..	..
34 Brunei Darussalam	..	..	2.8	7.3	..	..	..	..	..	..
36 Argentina	3	4.3	5.0	2.8	4	5	7.0	23.0	..	−16
38 Chile	2	3.7	3.5	4.3	5	1	2.0	9.6	17.0	1
39 Bahrain	..	..	3.8	13.5	..	9 [e]	..	..	..	..
43 Uruguay	1	3.3	4.4	.. [f]	0	5 [e]	2.0	5.7	..	0
46 Qatar	13	7.9	4.7	11.0	0	6 [e]	..	..	..	..
47 Seychelles	..	..	..	8.2	12	6 [e]	..	..	..	..
48 Costa Rica	4	4.4	3.7	5.1	3	5	2.2	7.5	22.0	−7
49 United Arab Emirates	34	15.9	2.2	.. [f]	0	14 [e]	..	..	..	..
50 Cuba	6	4.7	3.2	0.2	9	4	..	..	..	..
51 Saint Kitts and Nevis	..	..	..	..	0	..	..	..	..	..
52 Bahamas	..	..	13.4	..	3	..	..	..	..	..
53 Mexico	9	7.2	6.0	9.0	3	8	4.4	20.4	20.3	−10
55 Tonga	..	..	5.0	1.1 [g]	0	..	..	..	..	..
56 Oman	..	..	3.9	18.6	..	24 [e]	..	..	..	..
57 Trinidad and Tobago	17	8.8	11.6	.. [f]	9	7 [e]	12.4	39.0	21.0	−12
58 Panama	12	7.9	6.8	8.1	10	7	6.5	17.1	37.3	−9
59 Antigua and Barbuda	..	..	..	..	9	10 [e]	..	..	..	..
61 Malaysia	15	8.3	4.3	11.3	1	11	2.0	9.3	15.5 [h]	9
63 Mauritius	24	11.3	5.0	15.6	0	15 [e]	..	..	..	..
MEDIUM HUMAN DEVELOPMENT										
64 Libyan Arab Jamahiriya	..	..	4.2	..	..	5 [e]	..	..	..	..
68 Dominica	..	..	..	12.0 [h],[i]	3	5 [e]	..	..	..	..
69 Brazil	22	10.1	10.3	11.4	10	6	7.5	21.2	22.0	−5
70 Colombia	10	7.6	8.3	7.2	7	7	7.0	17.8	64.0	−12
71 Saint Lucia	..	..	5.9	..	2	14 [e]	..	..	..	..
72 Venezuela, RB	16	8.8	8.2	7.0	17	4	8.3	27.6	31.3 [h]	−11
74 Thailand	19	9.3	9.9	7.4	1	19 [e]	2.0	25.2	13.1	13
75 Samoa (Western)	..	..	6.5	..	12	..	..	..	..	..
76 Saudi Arabia	..	..	5.8	20.6	..	14	..	..	..	..
78 Lebanon	20	9.6	5.7	.. [f]	0	3	..	..	..	..
81 China	26	11.7	6.9	9.1	23	8	16.6	46.7	4.6	−14
82 Peru	25	11.6	10.3	12.3	17	7	12.5	31.8	49.0	−8
83 Ecuador	18	8.9	8.6	9.0	6	12	15.8	37.2	46.0	−17
84 Philippines	31	15.3	7.2	7.4	15	28	15.5	47.5	36.8	−6
85 Grenada	..	..	..	4.0 [i]	5	..	..	..	..	..
86 Jordan	11	7.6	6.4	10.1	3	4	2.0	7.0	11.7	6
87 Tunisia	39	17.9	4.7	25.7	7	4	2.0	6.6	7.6	26
88 Saint Vincent and the Grenadines	..	..	6.6	11.9 [i]	..	..	..	..	..	..
89 Suriname	23	10.3	10.1	10.4	8	13	..	..	..	..
90 Fiji	45	21.3	7.0	.. [f]	53	8 [e]	..	..	..	..
91 Paraguay	14	8.3	8.1	.. [f]	14	5	16.4	33.2	21.8	−22
92 Turkey	21	9.8	8.9	12.6	4	4	3.4	18.7	27.0	1
93 Sri Lanka	38	17.7	4.3	9.3	21	29	5.6	41.6	25.0	10
94 Dominican Republic	27	11.9	14.1	13.0	5	5	2.5	11.0	28.6	7
95 Belize	..	..	10.6	..	9	6 [e]	..	..	..	..
96 Iran, Islamic Rep. of	35	16.4	7.2	23.0	6	11	2.0	7.3	..	23

Human development indicators

TABLE 3

HDI rank		Human poverty index (HPI-1) Rank	Value (%)	Probability at birth of not surviving to age 40 [a],[†] (% of cohort) 2000–05	Adult illiteracy rate [b],[†] (% ages 15 and older) 2004	Population without sustainable access to an improved water source [†] (%) 2004	MDG Children under weight for age [†] (% under age 5) 1996–2004 [c]	MDG Population below income poverty line (%) $1 a day 1990–2004 [c]	$2 a day 1990–2004 [c]	National poverty line 1990–2003 [c]	HPI-1 rank minus income poverty rank [d]
98	Maldives	36	16.9	11.4	3.7	17	30	..	..	..	..
100	Occupied Palestinian Territories	8	6.5	5.3	7.6	8	4	..	..	..	..
101	El Salvador	32	15.7	9.9	..[f]	16	10	19.0	40.6	48.3	−12
102	Algeria	46	21.5	7.8	30.1	15	10	2.0	15.1	22.6	31
103	Guyana	..	..	18.2	..	17	14	2.0	..	..	..
104	Jamaica	30	14.8	11.3	20.1 [g]	7	4	2.0	13.3	18.7	20
106	Cape Verde	43	18.7	7.6	..[f]	20	14 [e]	..	..	..	..
107	Syrian Arab Republic	29	14.4	4.6	20.4	7	7	..	..	..	..
108	Indonesia	41	18.5	11.2	9.6	23	28	7.5	52.4	27.1	9
109	Viet Nam	33	15.7	9.4	9.7 [g]	15	28	..	..	28.9	..
111	Egypt	44	20.0	7.8	28.6	2	9	3.1	43.9	16.7	18
112	Nicaragua	40	18.0	10.1	23.3	21	10	45.1	79.9	47.9	−28
115	Bolivia	28	13.9	16.0	13.3	15	8	23.2	42.2	62.7	−20
116	Mongolia	42	18.5	13.3	2.2	38	13	27.0	74.9	35.6	−15
117	Honduras	37	17.2	15.8	20.0	13	17	20.7	44.0	48.0	−11
118	Guatemala	48	22.9	15.9	30.9	5	23	13.5	31.9	56.2	7
119	Vanuatu	49	24.7	8.9	26.0 [g]	40	20 [e]	..	..	..	..
120	Equatorial Guinea	69	38.1	47.7	13.0	57	19	..	..	..	..
121	South Africa	53	30.9	43.3	17.6 [g]	12	12	10.7	34.1	..	11
123	Morocco	59	33.4	8.6	47.7	19	9	2.0	14.3	19.0	37
124	Gabon	50	27.3	32.6	..	12	12	..	..	..	..
125	Namibia	57	32.5	45.4	15.0	13	24	34.9	55.8	..	−14
126	India	55	31.3	16.6	39.0	14	47	34.7	79.9	28.6	−14
127	São Tomé and Principe	..	..	17.1	..	21	13	..	..	..	..
128	Solomon Islands	..	..	14.1	..	30	21 [e]	..	..	..	..
129	Cambodia	73	39.3	28.3	26.4	59	45	34.1	77.7	35.9	−1
130	Myanmar	47	21.6	21.2	10.1	22	32	..	..	..	..
131	Botswana	93	48.3	69.1	18.8	5	13	23.5	50.1	..	22
132	Comoros	56	31.6	15.5	..[f]	14	25	..	..	..	..
133	Lao People's Dem. Rep.	63	36.0	28.0	31.3	49	40	27.0	74.1	38.6	−3
134	Pakistan	65	36.3	16.1	50.1	9	38	17.0	73.6	32.6	10
135	Bhutan	71	39.0	18.0	..	38	19	..	..	..	..
136	Ghana	58	33.1	27.7	42.1	25	22	44.8	78.5	39.5	−18
137	Bangladesh	85	44.2	15.9	..[f]	26	48	36.0	82.8	49.8	5
138	Nepal	68	38.1	17.6	51.4	10	48	24.1	68.5	30.9	4
139	Papua New Guinea	75	40.5	22.4	42.7	61	35 [e]	..	..	37.5	..
140	Congo	51	27.9	33.6	..[f]	42	14	..	..	..	..
141	Sudan	54	31.3	27.0	39.1	30	17 [e]	..	..	..	..
142	Timor-Leste	..	..	25.5	..	42	46	..	..	..	..
143	Madagascar	66	36.3	27.8	29.3	50	42	61.0	85.1	71.3	−20
144	Cameroon	61	35.6	43.9	32.1	34	18	17.1	50.6	40.2	6
145	Uganda	62	36.0	41.6	33.2	40	23	..	..	37.7	..
146	Swaziland	97	52.5	74.3	20.4	38	10	..	..	..	..
LOW HUMAN DEVELOPMENT											
147	Togo	72	39.2	31.0	46.8	48	25	..	..	32.3 [h]	..
148	Djibouti	52	30.0	30.6	..[f]	27	18	..	..	..	..
149	Lesotho	89	47.5	67.6	17.8	21	18	36.4	56.1	..	8
150	Yemen	77	40.6	18.8	..[f]	33	46	15.7	45.2	41.8	21
151	Zimbabwe	88	46.0	65.9	..[f]	19	13	56.1	83.0	34.9	−1
152	Kenya	60	35.5	44.8	26.4	39	20	22.8	58.3	52.0	1
153	Mauritania	81	41.0	30.5	48.8	47	32	25.9	63.1	46.3	9
154	Haiti	74	39.4	34.4	..[f]	46	17	53.9	78.0	65.0 [h]	−10
155	Gambia	86	44.7	27.8	..[f]	18	17	59.3	82.9	57.6	−5
156	Senegal	84	44.0	26.6	60.7	24	23	22.3	63.0	33.4	18

Human development indicators

TABLE 3

Human and income poverty: developing countries

HDI rank	Human poverty index (HPI-1) Rank	Human poverty index (HPI-1) Value (%)	Probability at birth of not surviving to age 40 [a],† (% of cohort) 2000–05	Adult illiteracy rate [b],† (% ages 15 and older) 2004	Population without sustainable access to an improved water source † (%) 2004	MDG Children under weight for age † (% under age 5) 1996–2004 [c]	MDG Population below income poverty line (%) $1 a day 1990–2004 [c]	MDG Population below income poverty line (%) $2 a day 1990–2004 [c]	MDG Population below income poverty line (%) National poverty line 1990–2003 [c]	HPI-1 rank minus income poverty rank [d]
157 Eritrea	70	38.1	27.6	..[f]	40	40	..	..	53.0	..
158 Rwanda	67	37.3	45.5	35.1	26	27	51.7	83.7	60.3	−12
159 Nigeria	76	40.6	46.0	..[f]	52	29	70.8	92.4	34.1	−17
160 Guinea	96	52.0	30.0	70.5	50	21	..	..	40.0	..
161 Angola	79	40.9	48.1	32.6	47	31	..	..	..	..
162 Tanzania, U. Rep. of	64	36.3	44.4	30.6	38	22	57.8	89.9	35.7	−19
163 Benin	90	47.8	30.0	65.3	33	23	30.9	73.7	29.0	14
164 Côte d'Ivoire	82	41.5	42.3	51.3	16	17	14.8	48.8	..	26
165 Zambia	87	45.6	60.1	32.0[g]	42	23	75.8	94.1	72.9	−10
166 Malawi	83	43.0	56.3	35.9[g]	27	22	41.7	76.1	65.3	0
167 Congo, Dem. Rep. of the	80	40.9	45.4	32.8	54	31	..	..	..	..
168 Mozambique	94	48.9	50.9	..[f]	57	24	37.8	78.4	69.4	11
169 Burundi	78	40.7	46.3	40.7	21	45	54.6	87.6	36.4	−8
170 Ethiopia	98	55.3	39.5	..[f]	78	47	23.0	77.8	44.2	26
171 Chad	100	57.9	45.2	74.3	58	28	..	..	64.0	..
172 Central African Republic	91	47.8	56.2	51.4	25	24	66.6	84.0	..	−3
173 Guinea-Bissau	92	48.2	42.9	..[f]	41	25	..	..	..	..
174 Burkina Faso	101	58.3	38.9	78.2	39	38	27.2	71.8	46.4	21
175 Mali	102	60.2	37.3	81.0[g]	50	33	72.3	90.6	63.8	1
176 Sierra Leone	95	51.9	47.0	64.9	43	27	..	74.5	70.2	..
177 Niger	99	56.4	41.4	71.3	54	40	60.6	85.8	63.0[h]	3

NOTES

† Denotes indicators used to calculate the human poverty index (HPI-1). For further details, see *Technical note 1*.

a Data refer to the probability at birth of not surviving to age 40, multiplied by 100.

b Data refer to national literacy estimates from censuses or surveys conducted between 2000 and 2005, unless otherwise specified. Due to differences in methodology and timeliness of underlying data, comparisons across countries and over time should be made with caution. For more details, see www.uis.unesco.org.

c Data refer to the most recent year available during the period specified.

d Income poverty refers to the share of the population living on less than $1 a day. All countries with an income poverty rate of less than 2% were given equal rank. The rankings are based on countries for which data are available for both indicators. A positive figure indicates that the country performs better in income poverty than in human poverty, a negative the opposite.

e Data refer to a year or period other than that specified, differ from the standard definition or refer to only part of a country.

f Data refer to the most recent year available between 1995 and 1999.

g In the absence of recent data, estimates from UNESCO Institute for Statistics 2006a, based on outdated census or survey information, were used and should be interpreted with caution: Bangladesh 58.9, Barbados 0.3, Cape Verde 24.3, Comoros 43.8, Congo 17.2, Djibouti 34.5, El Salvador 20.3, Eritrea 43.3, Ethiopia 58.5, Fiji 7.0, Gambia 62.2, Guinea-Bissau 60.4, Haiti 48.1, Lebanon 13.5, Mozambique 53.5, Nigeria 33.2, Paraguay 7.0, Trinidad and Tobago 1.5, United Arab Emirates 22.7, Uruguay 2.3, Yemen 51.0 and Zimbabwe 10.0.

h Data refer to a period other than that specified.

i Data are from the Secretariat of the Caribbean Community, based on national sources.

SOURCES

Column 1: determined on the basis of the HPI-1 values in column 2.

Column 2: calculated on the basis of data in columns 3–6; see *Technical note 1* for details.

Column 3: UN 2005b.

Column 4: calculated on the basis of data on adult literacy rates from UNESCO Institute for Statistics 2006a.

Column 5: UN 2006c, based on a joint effort by the United Nations Children's Fund and the World Health Organization.

Column 6: UNICEF 2005.

Columns 7–9: World Bank 2006.

Column 10: calculated on the basis of data in columns 1 and 7.

HPI-1 ranks for 102 developing countries and areas

1 Uruguay	21 Turkey	42 Mongolia	63 Lao People's Dem. Rep.	84 Senegal
2 Chile	22 Brazil	43 Cape Verde	64 Tanzania, U. Rep. of	85 Bangladesh
3 Argentina	23 Suriname	44 Egypt	65 Pakistan	86 Gambia
4 Costa Rica	24 Mauritius	45 Fiji	66 Madagascar	87 Zambia
5 Barbados	25 Peru	46 Algeria	67 Rwanda	88 Zimbabwe
6 Cuba	26 China	47 Myanmar	68 Nepal	89 Lesotho
7 Singapore	27 Dominican Republic	48 Guatemala	69 Equatorial Guinea	90 Benin
8 Occupied Palestinian Territories	28 Bolivia	49 Vanuatu	70 Eritrea	91 Central African Republic
9 Mexico	29 Syrian Arab Republic	50 Gabon	71 Bhutan	92 Guinea-Bissau
10 Colombia	30 Jamaica	51 Congo	72 Togo	93 Botswana
11 Jordan	31 Philippines	52 Djibouti	73 Cambodia	94 Mozambique
12 Panama	32 El Salvador	53 South Africa	74 Haiti	95 Sierra Leone
13 Qatar	33 Viet Nam	54 Sudan	75 Papua New Guinea	96 Guinea
14 Paraguay	34 United Arab Emirates	55 India	76 Nigeria	97 Swaziland
15 Malaysia	35 Iran, Islamic Rep. of	56 Comoros	77 Yemen	98 Ethiopia
16 Venezuela, RB	36 Maldives	57 Namibia	78 Burundi	99 Niger
17 Trinidad and Tobago	37 Honduras	58 Ghana	79 Angola	100 Chad
18 Ecuador	38 Sri Lanka	59 Morocco	80 Congo, Dem. Rep. of the	101 Burkina Faso
19 Thailand	39 Tunisia	60 Kenya	81 Mauritania	102 Mali
20 Lebanon	40 Nicaragua	61 Cameroon	82 Côte d'Ivoire	
	41 Indonesia	62 Uganda	83 Malawi	

Human and income poverty: OECD countries, Central and Eastern Europe and the CIS

HDI rank	Human poverty index (HPI-2) [a]		Probability at birth of not surviving to age 60 [b, †] (% of cohort) 2000–05	Population lacking functional literacy skills [c, †] (% ages 16–65) 1994–2003	Long-term unemployment [†] (% of labour force) 2005	Population below income poverty line (%)			HPI-2 rank minus income poverty rank [d]
	Rank	Value (%)				50% of median income [†] 1994–2002 [e]	$11 a day 1994–95 [e]	$4 a day 1996–99 [e]	
HIGH HUMAN DEVELOPMENT									
1 Norway	2	7.0	8.4	7.9	0.4	6.4	4.3	..	−1
2 Iceland	..	..	6.8	..	0.3 [f]	..	..	..	..
3 Australia	14	12.8	7.7	17.0 [g]	0.9	14.3	17.6	..	−1
4 Ireland	17	16.1	8.7	22.6 [g]	1.5	16.5	..	..	0
5 Sweden	1	6.5	7.2	7.5 [g]	1.0 [f]	6.5	6.3	..	−3
6 Canada	8	10.9	8.1	14.6	0.7	11.4	7.4	..	−3
7 Japan	11	11.7	7.1	.. [h]	1.5	11.8 [i]	..	..	−1
8 United States	16	15.4	11.8	20.0	0.6	17.0	13.6	..	−2
9 Switzerland	7	10.7	7.8	15.9	1.6	7.6	..	..	0
10 Netherlands	3	8.2	8.7	10.5 [g]	2.5	7.3	7.1	..	−3
11 Finland	4	8.2	9.7	10.4 [g]	2.1	5.4	4.8	..	3
12 Luxembourg	9	11.1	9.7	.. [h]	1.2 [j]	6.0	0.3	..	7
13 Belgium	12	12.4	9.4	18.4 [g, k]	4.3	8.0	..	..	4
14 Austria	..	..	9.1	..	1.5	7.7	..	..	..
15 Denmark	5	8.4	10.4	9.6 [g]	1.3	.. [l]	..	..	0
16 France	10	11.4	9.8	.. [h]	4.3	8.0	9.9	..	2
17 Italy	18	29.9	7.8	47.0	4.0	12.7	..	..	4
18 United Kingdom	15	14.8	8.7	21.8 [g]	1.1	12.4	15.7	..	2
19 Spain	13	12.6	8.7	.. [h]	3.0	14.3	..	..	−2
20 New Zealand	..	..	8.9	18.4 [g]	0.3	..	..	..	..
21 Germany	6	10.3	8.8	14.4 [g]	5.0	8.3	7.3	..	−4
23 Israel	..	..	7.7	..	..	15.6	..	..	..
24 Greece	..	..	9.2	..	5.7	14.4	..	..	..
27 Slovenia	..	..	11.8	..	..	8.2	..	<1	..
28 Portugal	..	..	10.3	..	3.6	..	..	..	..
30 Czech Republic	..	..	12.1	..	4.3	4.9	..	<1	..
32 Malta	..	..	7.7	..	..	..	..	..	..
35 Hungary	..	..	18.3	..	3.3	6.7	..	<1	..
37 Poland	..	..	15.1	..	9.3	8.6	..	10	..
40 Estonia	..	..	21.7	..	..	12.4	..	18	..
41 Lithuania	..	..	20.6	..	..	..	..	17	..
42 Slovakia	..	..	14.9	..	11.2	7.0	..	8	..
44 Croatia	..	..	13.1	..	..	..	..	..	..
45 Latvia	..	..	21.5	..	..	..	..	28	..
54 Bulgaria	..	..	16.6	..	..	..	..	22	..
60 Romania	..	..	19.0	..	..	8.1	..	23	..
62 Bosnia and Herzegovina	..	..	13.6	..	..	..	..	..	..

TABLE 4

Human and income poverty: OECD countries, Central and Eastern Europe and the CIS

HDI rank	Human poverty index (HPI-2) [a] Rank	Human poverty index (HPI-2) [a] Value (%)	Probability at birth of not surviving to age 60 [b, †] (% of cohort) 2000–05	Population lacking functional literacy skills [c, †] (% ages 16–65) 1994–2003	Long-term unemployment [†] (% of labour force) 2005	Population below income poverty line (%) 50% of median income [†] 1994–2002 [e]	Population below income poverty line (%) $11 a day 1994–95 [e]	Population below income poverty line (%) $4 a day 1996–99 [e]	HPI-2 rank minus income poverty rank [d]
MEDIUM HUMAN DEVELOPMENT									
65 Russian Federation	..	..	31.6	..	..	18.8	..	53	..
66 Macedonia, TFYR	..	..	13.3	..	..	..	..	..	..
67 Belarus	..	..	26.7	..	..	..	..	..	..
73 Albania	..	..	11.4	..	..	..	..	..	..
77 Ukraine	..	..	31.0	..	..	..	..	25	..
79 Kazakhstan	..	..	32.0	..	..	..	..	62	..
80 Armenia	..	..	18.0	..	..	..	..	..	..
97 Georgia	..	..	18.9	..	..	..	..	..	..
99 Azerbaijan	..	..	24.9	..	..	..	..	..	..
105 Turkmenistan	..	..	32.0	..	..	..	..	..	..
110 Kyrgyzstan	..	..	26.0	..	..	..	..	88	..
113 Uzbekistan	..	..	26.3	..	..	..	..	..	..
114 Moldova, Rep. of	..	..	25.5	..	..	..	..	82	..
122 Tajikistan	..	..	29.0	..	..	..	..	..	..

NOTES

This table includes Israel and Malta, which are not Organisation for Economic Co-operation and Development (OECD) member countries, but excludes the Republic of Korea, Mexico and Turkey, which are. For the human poverty index (HPI-2) and related indicators for these countries, see table 3.

† Denotes indicator used to calculate HPI-2; for details see *Technical note 1*.

a HPI-2 is calculated for selected high-income OECD countries only.

b Data refer to the probability at birth of not surviving to age 60, multiplied by 100.

c Based on scoring at level 1 on the prose literacy scale of the International Adult Literacy Survey. Data refer to the most recent year available during the period specified.

d Income poverty refers to the share of the population living on less than 50% of the median adjusted disposable household income. A positive figure indicates that the country performs better in income poverty than in human poverty, a negative the opposite.

e Data refer to the most recent year available during the period specified.

f Data refer to 2004.

g Based on OECD and Statistics Canada 2000. Data refer to the most recent year available during the period specified.

h For calculating HPI-2, an estimate of 16.4%, the unweighted average of countries with available data, was applied.

i Smeeding 1997.

j Data are based on small sample sizes and should be treated with caution.

k Data refer to Flanders.

l In the absence of a recent estimate for Denmark, and outdated value of 7.2% was used to calculate the HPI-2. Efforts are ongoing to produce a more accurate internationally comparable poverty estimate.

SOURCES

Column 1: determined on the basis of HPI-2 values in column 2.

Column 2: calculated on the basis of data in columns 3–6; see *Technical note 1* for details.

Column 3: calculated on the basis of survival data from UN 2005b.

Column 4: OECD and Statistics Canada 2005, unless otherwise specified.

Column 5: calculated on the basis of data on youth long-term unemployment and labour force from OECD 2006b.

Column 6: LIS 2006.

Column 7: Smeeding, Rainwater and Burtless 2000.

Column 8: Milanovic 2002.

Column 9: calculated on the basis of data in columns 1 and 6.

HPI-2 ranks for 18 selected OECD countries

1	Sweden	7	Switzerland	13	Spain
2	Norway	8	Canada	14	Australia
3	Netherlands	9	Luxembourg	15	United Kingdom
4	Finland	10	France	16	United States
5	Denmark	11	Japan	17	Ireland
6	Germany	12	Belgium	18	Italy

TABLE 5

... to lead a long and healthy life ...

Demographic trends

HDI rank	Total population (millions)			Annual population growth rate (%)		Urban population (% of total) [a]			Population under age 15 (% of total)		Population ages 65 and older (% of total)		Total fertility rate (births per woman)	
	1975	2004	2015 [b]	1975–2004	2004–15 [b]	1975	2004	2015 [b]	2004	2015 [b]	2004	2015 [b]	1970–75 [c]	2000–05 [c]
HIGH HUMAN DEVELOPMENT														
1 Norway	4.0	4.6	4.8	0.5	0.5	68.2	77.3	78.6	19.7	17.5	15.0	17.5	2.2	1.8
2 Iceland	0.2	0.3	0.3	1.0	0.8	86.7	92.7	93.6	22.3	19.4	11.7	14.0	2.8	2.0
3 Australia	13.6	19.9	22.2	1.3	1.0	85.9	88.0	89.9	20.0	17.7	12.6	15.5	2.5	1.7
4 Ireland	3.2	4.1	4.7	0.9	1.2	53.6	60.2	63.8	20.3	20.2	10.9	12.6	3.8	1.9
5 Sweden	8.2	9.0	9.3	0.3	0.3	82.7	84.1	85.1	17.7	16.4	17.1	20.4	1.9	1.6
6 Canada	23.1	32.0	35.1	1.1	0.8	75.6	80.0	81.4	17.9	15.3	13.0	16.2	2.0	1.5
7 Japan	111.5	127.9	128.0	0.5	(.)	56.8	65.7	68.2	14.1	13.3	19.2	26.0	2.1	1.3
8 United States	220.2	295.4	325.7	1.0	0.9	73.7	80.5	83.7	20.9	19.7	12.3	14.1	2.0	2.0
9 Switzerland	6.3	7.2	7.3	0.5	0.1	55.8	74.8	78.8	16.8	14.1	15.7	19.8	1.8	1.4
10 Netherlands	13.7	16.2	16.8	0.6	0.3	63.2	79.6	84.9	18.3	16.4	14.0	17.5	2.1	1.7
11 Finland	4.7	5.2	5.4	0.4	0.2	58.3	61.1	62.7	17.5	15.8	15.7	20.3	1.6	1.7
12 Luxembourg	0.4	0.5	0.5	0.8	1.2	77.3	83.0	82.1	19.0	17.6	13.8	14.3	2.0	1.7
13 Belgium	9.8	10.4	10.5	0.2	0.1	94.5	97.2	97.5	16.9	15.5	17.5	19.4	1.9	1.7
14 Austria	7.6	8.2	8.3	0.3	0.1	65.6	65.9	67.7	15.8	13.4	16.4	19.6	2.0	1.4
15 Denmark	5.1	5.4	5.6	0.2	0.2	82.2	85.5	86.9	18.8	17.0	14.9	18.4	2.0	1.8
16 France	52.7	60.3	62.3	0.5	0.3	72.9	76.5	79.0	18.2	17.6	16.6	19.0	2.3	1.9
17 Italy	55.4	58.0	57.8	0.2	(.)	65.6	67.5	69.5	14.1	13.2	19.7	23.0	2.3	1.3
18 United Kingdom	55.4	59.5	61.4	0.2	0.3	82.7	89.6	90.6	18.2	16.4	15.9	18.1	2.0	1.7
19 Spain	35.6	42.6	44.4	0.6	0.4	69.6	76.6	78.3	14.3	15.3	16.5	18.0	2.9	1.3
20 New Zealand	3.1	4.0	4.3	0.9	0.7	82.8	86.1	87.4	21.7	18.9	12.2	15.0	2.8	2.0
21 Germany	78.7	82.6	82.5	0.2	(.)	72.7	75.1	76.3	14.6	12.9	18.3	20.7	1.6	1.3
22 Hong Kong, China (SAR)	4.4	7.0	7.8	1.6	1.0	89.7	100.0	100.0	14.8	12.7	11.8	14.4	2.9	0.9
23 Israel	3.4	6.6	7.8	2.3	1.6	86.6	91.6	91.9	27.9	25.8	10.1	11.5	3.8	2.9
24 Greece	9.0	11.1	11.2	0.7	0.1	55.3	58.9	61.0	14.4	13.5	18.0	19.3	2.3	1.3
25 Singapore	2.3	4.3	4.8	2.2	1.1	100.0	100.0	100.0	20.2	13.2	8.2	13.3	2.6	1.4
26 Korea, Rep. of	35.3	47.6	49.1	1.0	0.3	48.0	80.6	83.1	19.1	13.9	9.0	13.2	4.3	1.2
27 Slovenia	1.7	2.0	1.9	0.4	−0.1	42.4	50.9	53.3	14.2	13.0	15.4	18.1	2.2	1.2
28 Portugal	9.1	10.4	10.8	0.5	0.3	40.8	57.0	63.6	15.9	15.1	16.9	18.9	2.7	1.5
29 Cyprus	0.6	0.8	0.9	1.0	1.0	47.3	69.2	71.5	20.4	17.2	11.9	14.2	2.5	1.6
30 Czech Republic	10.0	10.2	10.1	0.1	−0.1	63.7	73.6	74.1	15.0	13.4	14.1	18.4	2.2	1.2
31 Barbados	0.2	0.3	0.3	0.3	0.2	40.8	52.1	58.8	19.3	16.7	10.1	11.5	2.7	1.5
32 Malta	0.3	0.4	0.4	0.9	0.4	89.7	95.0	97.2	18.0	15.2	13.3	18.3	2.1	1.5
33 Kuwait	1.0	2.6	3.4	3.3	2.4	89.4	98.3	98.5	24.5	23.2	1.7	3.1	6.9	2.4
34 Brunei Darussalam	0.2	0.4	0.5	2.8	2.0	62.0	73.1	77.6	30.0	25.8	3.1	4.3	5.4	2.5
35 Hungary	10.5	10.1	9.8	−0.1	−0.3	62.2	65.9	70.3	16.0	14.0	15.1	17.5	2.1	1.3
36 Argentina	26.0	38.4	42.7	1.3	1.0	81.0	89.9	91.6	26.7	23.9	10.1	11.1	3.1	2.4
37 Poland	34.0	38.6	38.1	0.4	−0.1	55.3	62.0	64.0	16.8	14.3	12.8	14.9	2.3	1.3
38 Chile	10.4	16.1	17.9	1.5	1.0	78.4	87.3	90.1	25.5	20.9	7.9	10.5	3.6	2.0
39 Bahrain	0.3	0.7	0.9	3.3	1.6	85.0	96.2	98.2	27.5	21.7	3.0	4.4	5.9	2.5
40 Estonia	1.4	1.3	1.3	−0.2	−0.3	67.6	69.1	70.1	15.6	15.7	16.3	17.4	2.2	1.4
41 Lithuania	3.3	3.4	3.3	0.1	−0.4	55.7	66.6	66.8	17.4	13.8	15.2	16.7	2.3	1.3
42 Slovakia	4.7	5.4	5.4	0.5	(.)	46.3	56.2	58.0	17.2	14.0	11.7	14.1	2.5	1.2
43 Uruguay	2.8	3.4	3.7	0.7	0.6	83.4	91.9	93.1	24.4	22.4	13.2	13.8	3.0	2.3
44 Croatia	4.3	4.5	4.5	0.2	−0.2	45.1	56.3	59.5	15.8	13.9	17.0	18.7	2.0	1.3
45 Latvia	2.5	2.3	2.2	−0.2	−0.5	64.2	67.8	68.9	15.2	14.1	16.6	18.3	2.0	1.3
46 Qatar	0.2	0.8	1.0	5.2	2.0	88.9	95.3	96.2	22.2	21.8	1.3	2.0	6.8	3.0
47 Seychelles	0.1	0.1	0.1	1.0	0.9	46.3	52.5	58.2	..	..	..	..	..	..
48 Costa Rica	2.1	4.3	5.0	2.5	1.4	41.3	61.2	66.9	29.0	23.8	5.7	7.4	4.3	2.3
49 United Arab Emirates	0.5	4.3	5.6	7.2	2.4	83.6	76.7	77.4	22.4	19.8	1.1	1.4	6.4	2.5
50 Cuba	9.3	11.2	11.4	0.7	0.2	64.2	75.7	74.7	19.5	16.6	10.5	14.4	3.5	1.6
51 Saint Kitts and Nevis	(.)	(.)	(.)	−0.2	1.1	35.0	32.2	33.5	..	..	..	..	..	..
52 Bahamas	0.2	0.3	0.4	1.8	1.2	71.5	90.1	92.2	28.6	24.7	6.1	8.2	3.4	2.3
53 Mexico	59.3	105.7	119.1	2.0	1.1	62.8	75.7	78.7	31.6	25.5	5.2	7.1	6.6	2.4

TABLE 5

Demographic trends

HDI rank	Total population (millions)			Annual population growth rate (%)		Urban population (% of total) [a]			Population under age 15 (% of total)		Population ages 65 and older (% of total)		Total fertility rate (births per woman)	
	1975	2004	2015 [b]	1975–2004	2004–15 [b]	1975	2004	2015 [b]	2004	2015 [b]	2004	2015 [b]	1970–75 [c]	2000–05 [c]
54 Bulgaria	8.7	7.8	7.2	−0.4	−0.8	57.6	69.8	72.8	14.1	13.1	16.8	18.6	2.2	1.2
55 Tonga	0.1	0.1	0.1	0.4	0.1	20.3	23.8	27.4	36.3	30.7	5.9	6.9	5.5	3.5
56 Oman	0.9	2.5	3.2	3.5	2.0	34.1	71.5	72.3	34.9	30.6	2.5	3.4	7.2	3.8
57 Trinidad and Tobago	1.0	1.3	1.3	0.9	0.3	11.4	11.9	15.8	22.0	20.2	7.2	9.9	3.5	1.6
58 Panama	1.7	3.2	3.8	2.1	1.6	49.0	69.9	77.9	30.6	27.2	5.9	7.5	4.9	2.7
59 Antigua and Barbuda	0.1	0.1	0.1	0.9	1.2	34.2	38.7	44.7	..	..	..	..	..	..
60 Romania	21.2	21.8	20.9	0.1	−0.4	42.8	53.5	56.1	15.9	14.4	14.6	15.5	2.6	1.3
61 Malaysia	12.3	24.9	29.6	2.4	1.6	37.7	66.3	75.4	32.8	27.2	4.5	6.1	5.2	2.9
62 Bosnia and Herzegovina	3.7	3.9	3.9	0.1	(.)	31.3	45.2	51.8	16.9	14.0	13.5	16.7	2.6	1.3
63 Mauritius	0.9	1.2	1.3	1.1	0.8	43.4	42.4	44.1	24.9	21.3	6.5	8.3	3.2	2.0
MEDIUM HUMAN DEVELOPMENT														
64 Libyan Arab Jamahiriya	2.4	5.7	7.0	2.9	1.8	57.3	84.5	87.4	30.4	28.9	4.0	5.6	7.6	3.0
65 Russian Federation	134.2	143.9	136.7	0.2	−0.5	66.9	73.1	72.6	15.7	16.4	13.6	13.3	2.0	1.3
66 Macedonia, TFYR	1.7	2.0	2.1	0.7	0.1	50.6	68.1	75.2	20.1	16.6	10.9	12.9	3.0	1.5
67 Belarus	9.4	9.8	9.2	0.2	−0.6	50.6	71.8	76.7	15.8	14.5	14.6	13.5	2.3	1.2
68 Dominica	0.1	0.1	0.1	0.3	0.9	55.3	72.5	76.4	..	..	..	..	..	..
69 Brazil	108.1	183.9	209.4	1.8	1.2	61.7	83.7	88.2	28.1	25.4	6.0	7.8	4.7	2.3
70 Colombia	25.4	44.9	52.1	2.0	1.3	60.0	72.4	75.7	31.4	26.8	5.0	6.5	5.0	2.6
71 Saint Lucia	0.1	0.2	0.2	1.3	0.8	25.2	27.6	29.0	29.4	25.4	7.2	7.3	5.7	2.2
72 Venezuela, RB	12.7	26.3	31.3	2.5	1.6	75.8	93.0	95.9	31.7	27.8	4.9	6.8	4.9	2.7
73 Albania	2.4	3.1	3.3	0.9	0.6	32.7	44.6	52.8	27.6	23.1	8.1	9.9	4.7	2.3
74 Thailand	41.3	63.7	69.1	1.5	0.7	23.8	32.0	36.2	24.1	21.2	6.9	9.3	5.0	1.9
75 Samoa (Western)	0.2	0.2	0.2	0.7	0.8	21.0	22.3	24.9	40.8	34.2	4.5	5.0	5.7	4.4
76 Saudi Arabia	7.3	24.0	30.8	4.1	2.3	58.4	80.8	83.2	37.8	32.3	2.9	3.5	7.3	4.1
77 Ukraine	49.0	47.0	41.8	−0.1	−1.1	58.4	67.6	70.2	15.4	13.5	15.8	16.4	2.2	1.1
78 Lebanon	2.7	3.5	4.0	1.0	1.0	67.0	86.5	87.9	29.1	24.4	7.3	7.7	4.8	2.3
79 Kazakhstan	14.1	14.8	14.9	0.2	(.)	52.6	57.1	60.3	23.9	21.3	8.3	8.0	3.5	2.0
80 Armenia	2.8	3.0	3.0	0.2	−0.2	63.6	64.2	64.1	21.7	17.4	11.9	11.0	3.0	1.3
81 China	927.8 [d]	1,308.0 [d]	1,393.0 [d]	1.2 [d]	0.6 [d]	17.4	39.5	49.2	22.0	18.5	7.5	9.6	4.9	1.7
82 Peru	15.2	27.6	32.2	2.1	1.4	61.5	72.4	74.9	32.7	27.9	5.2	6.5	6.0	2.9
83 Ecuador	6.9	13.0	15.1	2.2	1.4	42.4	62.3	67.6	32.8	28.1	5.7	7.3	6.0	2.8
84 Philippines	42.0	81.6	96.8	2.3	1.6	35.6	61.9	69.6	35.7	30.0	3.8	4.9	6.0	3.2
85 Grenada	0.1	0.1	0.1	0.4	1.3	32.6	30.6	32.2	..	..	..	..	..	..
86 Jordan	1.9	5.6	7.0	3.6	2.0	57.7	81.9	85.3	37.6	31.7	3.1	4.0	7.8	3.5
87 Tunisia	5.7	10.0	11.1	2.0	1.0	49.9	64.9	69.1	26.7	21.9	6.2	6.8	6.2	2.0
88 Saint Vincent and the Grenadines	0.1	0.1	0.1	0.7	0.4	27.0	45.6	50.0	29.8	26.5	6.5	7.1	5.5	2.3
89 Suriname	0.4	0.4	0.5	0.7	0.5	49.5	73.5	77.4	30.4	26.7	6.3	7.2	5.3	2.6
90 Fiji	0.6	0.8	0.9	1.3	0.6	36.7	50.3	56.1	32.0	27.6	3.8	5.4	4.2	2.9
91 Paraguay	2.7	6.0	7.6	2.8	2.1	39.0	57.9	64.4	38.0	33.9	3.7	4.3	5.7	3.9
92 Turkey	41.2	72.2	82.6	1.9	1.2	41.6	66.8	71.9	29.5	25.8	5.4	6.2	5.3	2.5
93 Sri Lanka	14.0	20.6	22.3	1.3	0.7	19.5	15.2	15.7	24.5	21.4	7.1	9.3	4.1	2.0
94 Dominican Republic	5.1	8.8	10.1	1.9	1.3	45.7	65.9	73.6	33.1	29.5	4.1	5.3	5.6	2.7
95 Belize	0.1	0.3	0.3	2.3	1.8	50.2	48.1	51.2	37.3	31.2	4.3	4.7	6.3	3.2
96 Iran, Islamic Rep. of	33.3	68.8	79.9	2.5	1.4	45.8	66.4	71.9	29.8	25.6	4.5	4.9	6.4	2.1
97 Georgia	4.9	4.5	4.2	−0.3	−0.7	49.5	52.2	53.8	19.5	15.8	14.1	14.4	2.6	1.5
98 Maldives	0.1	0.3	0.4	2.9	2.4	17.3	29.2	34.8	41.3	35.7	3.5	3.3	7.0	4.3
99 Azerbaijan	5.7	8.4	9.1	1.3	0.8	51.9	51.5	52.8	26.8	21.2	6.9	6.7	4.3	1.9
100 Occupied Palestinian Territories	1.3	3.6	5.0	3.6	3.0	59.6	71.5	72.9	45.7	41.6	3.1	3.0	7.7	5.6
101 El Salvador	4.1	6.8	8.0	1.7	1.5	41.5	59.5	63.2	34.3	29.8	5.3	6.2	6.1	2.9
102 Algeria	16.0	32.4	38.1	2.4	1.5	40.3	62.6	69.3	30.4	26.7	4.5	5.0	7.4	2.5
103 Guyana	0.7	0.8	0.7	0.1	−0.1	30.0	28.3	29.4	29.6	24.8	5.1	6.6	4.9	2.3
104 Jamaica	2.0	2.6	2.7	0.9	0.4	44.1	52.8	56.7	31.7	26.7	7.6	8.2	5.0	2.4
105 Turkmenistan	2.5	4.8	5.5	2.2	1.3	47.6	46.0	50.8	32.7	27.0	4.7	4.4	6.2	2.8
106 Cape Verde	0.3	0.5	0.6	2.0	2.2	21.4	56.6	64.3	40.1	35.6	4.3	3.3	7.0	3.8

TABLE 5

HDI rank	Total population (millions)			Annual population growth rate (%)		Urban population (% of total) [a]			Population under age 15 (% of total)		Population ages 65 and older (% of total)		Total fertility rate (births per woman)	
	1975	2004	2015 [b]	1975–2004	2004–15 [b]	1975	2004	2015 [b]	2004	2015 [b]	2004	2015 [b]	1970–75 [c]	2000–05 [c]
107 Syrian Arab Republic	7.5	18.6	23.8	3.1	2.3	45.1	50.5	53.4	37.4	33.2	3.1	3.6	7.5	3.5
108 Indonesia	134.4	220.1	246.8	1.7	1.0	19.3	47.0	58.5	28.6	25.2	5.4	6.4	5.2	2.4
109 Viet Nam	48.0	83.1	95.0	1.9	1.2	18.8	26.0	31.6	30.3	25.0	5.5	5.6	6.7	2.3
110 Kyrgyzstan	3.3	5.2	5.9	1.6	1.1	38.2	35.7	38.1	32.1	27.5	6.1	5.5	4.7	2.7
111 Egypt	39.3	72.6	88.2	2.1	1.8	43.5	42.7	45.4	33.9	31.4	4.7	5.5	5.7	3.3
112 Nicaragua	2.6	5.4	6.6	2.5	1.9	48.9	58.7	63.0	39.5	33.4	3.3	3.9	6.8	3.3
113 Uzbekistan	14.0	26.2	30.7	2.2	1.4	39.1	36.7	38.0	34.0	28.3	4.7	4.4	6.3	2.7
114 Moldova, Rep. of	3.8	4.2	4.1	0.3	−0.2	36.2	46.5	50.0	19.1	15.2	10.0	10.9	2.6	1.2
115 Bolivia	4.8	9.0	10.9	2.2	1.7	41.3	63.7	68.8	38.5	33.5	4.5	5.2	6.5	4.0
116 Mongolia	1.4	2.6	3.0	2.0	1.2	48.7	56.6	58.8	31.3	26.3	3.8	4.1	7.3	2.4
117 Honduras	3.0	7.0	8.8	2.9	2.0	32.1	46.0	51.4	39.7	33.8	3.8	4.5	7.1	3.7
118 Guatemala	6.2	12.3	15.9	2.4	2.3	36.7	46.8	52.0	43.5	39.7	4.3	4.7	6.2	4.6
119 Vanuatu	0.1	0.2	0.3	2.5	1.8	13.4	23.1	28.1	40.4	35.5	3.3	4.0	6.1	4.2
120 Equatorial Guinea	0.2	0.5	0.6	2.7	2.2	27.4	38.9	41.1	44.3	45.6	3.9	3.8	5.7	5.9
121 South Africa	25.9	47.2	47.9	2.1	0.1	48.1	58.8	64.1	32.8	30.2	4.1	6.1	5.5	2.8
122 Tajikistan	3.4	6.4	7.6	2.2	1.5	35.5	24.9	24.6	39.7	33.0	3.8	3.5	6.8	3.8
123 Morocco	17.3	31.0	36.2	2.0	1.4	37.8	58.0	65.0	31.5	28.4	4.8	5.2	6.9	2.8
124 Gabon	0.6	1.4	1.6	2.8	1.5	43.0	83.0	87.7	40.5	35.5	4.4	4.4	5.3	4.0
125 Namibia	0.9	2.0	2.2	2.8	1.0	23.7	34.5	41.1	42.1	34.7	3.4	4.2	6.6	4.0
126 India	620.7	1,087.1	1,260.4	1.9	1.3	21.3	28.5	32.0	32.5	28.0	5.2	6.2	5.4	3.1
127 São Tomé and Principe	0.1	0.2	0.2	2.1	2.1	31.6	57.1	65.8	39.8	36.4	4.3	3.4	6.5	4.1
128 Solomon Islands	0.2	0.5	0.6	3.0	2.2	9.1	16.7	20.5	41.0	36.4	2.4	2.8	7.2	4.3
129 Cambodia	7.1	13.8	17.1	2.3	1.9	10.3	19.1	26.1	37.7	34.1	3.4	4.4	5.5	4.1
130 Myanmar	30.1	50.0	55.0	1.7	0.9	24.0	30.1	37.4	30.1	23.6	4.9	6.4	5.8	2.5
131 Botswana	0.9	1.8	1.7	2.4	−0.4	11.8	56.6	64.6	37.9	34.7	3.2	4.8	6.8	3.2
132 Comoros	0.3	0.8	1.0	3.1	2.5	21.2	36.4	44.0	42.2	38.5	2.7	3.1	7.1	4.9
133 Lao People's Dem. Rep.	3.0	5.8	7.3	2.2	2.1	11.1	20.3	24.9	41.2	37.1	3.6	3.7	6.2	4.8
134 Pakistan	68.3	154.8	193.4	2.8	2.0	26.3	34.5	39.6	38.9	34.1	3.8	4.2	6.6	4.3
135 Bhutan	1.2	2.1	2.7	2.1	2.2	4.6	10.8	14.8	38.9	34.7	4.5	5.1	5.9	4.4
136 Ghana	10.2	21.7	26.6	2.6	1.9	30.1	47.1	55.1	39.5	35.2	3.6	4.3	6.7	4.4
137 Bangladesh	73.2	139.2	168.2	2.2	1.7	9.9	24.7	29.9	35.9	31.4	3.6	4.2	6.2	3.2
138 Nepal	13.5	26.6	32.7	2.3	1.9	4.8	15.3	20.9	39.5	33.9	3.6	4.2	5.8	3.7
139 Papua New Guinea	2.9	5.8	7.0	2.4	1.8	11.9	13.3	15.0	40.7	34.0	2.4	2.7	6.1	4.1
140 Congo	1.5	3.9	5.4	3.2	3.1	43.3	59.8	64.2	47.0	47.4	2.9	2.7	6.3	6.3
141 Sudan	17.1	35.5	44.0	2.5	2.0	18.9	39.8	49.4	39.5	35.6	3.6	4.3	6.7	4.4
142 Timor-Leste	0.7	0.9	1.5	1.0	4.7	14.6	26.1	31.2	41.6	46.7	2.9	3.0	6.2	7.8
143 Madagascar	7.9	18.1	23.8	2.9	2.5	16.3	26.6	30.1	44.2	40.7	3.1	3.3	6.7	5.4
144 Cameroon	7.6	16.0	19.0	2.6	1.6	27.3	53.7	62.7	41.6	37.2	3.7	3.9	6.3	4.6
145 Uganda	10.8	27.8	41.9	3.3	3.7	7.0	12.5	14.5	50.4	50.8	2.5	2.2	7.1	7.1
146 Swaziland	0.5	1.0	1.0	2.3	−0.4	14.0	23.9	27.5	41.6	37.2	3.4	4.6	6.9	4.0
LOW HUMAN DEVELOPMENT														
147 Togo	2.4	6.0	7.8	3.1	2.5	22.8	39.4	47.4	43.7	40.2	3.1	3.4	7.1	5.4
148 Djibouti	0.2	0.8	0.9	4.3	1.6	67.1	85.6	89.6	41.8	37.3	2.8	3.4	7.2	5.1
149 Lesotho	1.1	1.8	1.7	1.6	−0.3	10.8	18.5	22.0	39.0	36.6	5.2	5.8	5.7	3.6
150 Yemen	7.0	20.3	28.5	3.7	3.1	14.8	26.9	31.9	46.7	43.4	2.3	2.4	8.5	6.2
151 Zimbabwe	6.2	12.9	13.8	2.5	0.6	19.9	35.4	40.9	40.5	36.6	3.6	4.1	7.7	3.6
152 Kenya	13.5	33.5	44.2	3.1	2.5	12.9	20.5	24.1	42.9	42.6	2.8	2.8	8.0	5.0
153 Mauritania	1.4	3.0	4.0	2.5	2.6	20.6	40.3	43.1	43.1	41.7	3.4	3.4	6.5	5.8
154 Haiti	4.9	8.4	9.8	1.8	1.3	21.7	38.1	45.5	38.0	34.9	4.0	4.5	5.8	4.0
155 Gambia	0.6	1.5	1.9	3.4	2.2	24.4	53.0	61.8	40.3	36.8	3.7	4.4	6.5	4.7
156 Senegal	5.3	11.4	14.5	2.7	2.2	33.7	41.3	44.7	43.0	38.8	3.1	3.4	7.0	5.0
157 Eritrea	2.1	4.2	5.8	2.4	2.9	13.5	19.0	24.4	44.8	42.6	2.3	2.6	6.5	5.5
158 Rwanda	4.4	8.9	11.3	2.4	2.2	4.0	18.5	28.7	44.1	41.6	2.4	2.6	8.3	5.7
159 Nigeria	58.9	128.7	160.9	2.7	2.0	23.4	47.3	55.9	44.5	41.3	3.0	3.2	6.9	5.8

Human development indicators

TABLE 5

Demographic trends

HDI rank	Total population (millions) 1975	2004	2015 b	Annual population growth rate (%) 1975–2004	2004–15 b	Urban population (% of total) a 1975	2004	2015 b	Population under age 15 (% of total) 2004	2015 b	Population ages 65 and older (% of total) 2004	2015 b	Total fertility rate (births per woman) 1970–75 c	2000–05 c
160 Guinea	4.2	9.2	11.9	2.7	2.3	19.5	32.6	38.1	43.8	42.0	3.5	3.9	6.9	5.9
161 Angola	6.8	15.5	20.9	2.8	2.7	19.1	52.7	59.7	46.6	45.5	2.5	2.4	7.2	6.8
162 Tanzania, U. Rep. of	16.0	37.6	45.6	2.9	1.7	11.2	23.8	28.9	42.9	38.9	3.2	3.7	6.8	5.0
163 Benin	3.2	8.2	11.2	3.2	2.9	21.9	39.7	44.6	44.5	42.0	2.7	3.0	7.1	5.9
164 Côte d'Ivoire	6.6	17.9	21.6	3.4	1.7	32.2	44.6	49.8	42.1	38.2	3.2	3.7	7.4	5.1
165 Zambia	5.2	11.5	13.8	2.8	1.7	34.9	34.9	37.0	46.0	43.7	3.0	3.2	7.8	5.7
166 Malawi	5.2	12.6	16.0	3.0	2.2	7.7	16.7	22.1	47.3	44.9	3.0	3.2	7.4	6.1
167 Congo, Dem. Rep. of the	23.9	55.9	78.0	2.9	3.0	29.5	31.6	38.6	47.2	48.0	2.7	2.6	6.5	6.7
168 Mozambique	10.6	19.4	23.5	2.1	1.7	8.7	33.7	42.4	44.1	41.6	3.3	3.6	6.6	5.5
169 Burundi	3.7	7.3	10.6	2.4	3.4	3.2	9.7	13.5	45.5	46.4	2.8	2.5	6.8	6.8
170 Ethiopia	34.1	75.6	97.2	2.7	2.3	9.5	15.7	19.1	44.8	41.7	2.9	3.2	6.8	5.9
171 Chad	4.2	9.4	12.8	2.8	2.8	15.6	24.8	30.5	47.2	47.7	3.1	2.7	6.7	6.7
172 Central African Republic	2.1	4.0	4.6	2.3	1.4	32.0	37.9	40.4	43.1	40.6	4.0	4.0	5.7	5.0
173 Guinea-Bissau	0.7	1.5	2.1	3.0	3.0	16.0	29.6	31.1	47.4	48.0	3.1	2.8	7.1	7.1
174 Burkina Faso	5.9	12.8	17.7	2.6	2.9	6.4	17.9	22.8	47.4	45.7	2.8	2.6	7.8	6.7
175 Mali	6.2	13.1	18.1	2.6	2.9	16.2	29.9	36.5	48.3	46.7	2.7	2.4	7.6	6.9
176 Sierra Leone	2.9	5.3	6.9	2.1	2.3	21.2	39.9	48.2	42.8	42.8	3.3	3.3	6.5	6.5
177 Niger	5.3	13.5	19.3	3.2	3.2	11.4	16.7	19.3	49.0	47.9	2.0	2.0	8.1	7.9
Developing countries	2,967.1 T	5,093.6 T	5,885.6 T	1.9	1.3	26.5	42.2	48.0	31.2	28.0	5.4	6.5	5.5	2.9
Least developed countries	355.2 T	740.7 T	950.1 T	2.5	2.3	14.9	26.3	31.6	42.0	39.5	3.2	3.5	6.6	5.0
Arab States	144.6 T	310.5 T	386.0 T	2.6	2.0	41.8	54.9	58.9	35.8	32.5	3.8	4.4	6.7	3.7
East Asia and the Pacific	1,310.4 T	1,944.0 T	2,108.9 T	1.4	0.7	20.4	41.9	51.0	24.3	20.7	6.8	8.7	5.0	1.9
Latin America and the Caribbean	318.4 T	548.3 T	628.3 T	1.9	1.2	61.2	76.8	80.4	30.4	26.5	5.9	7.5	5.1	2.6
South Asia	838.7 T	1,528.1 T	1,801.4 T	2.1	1.5	21.2	29.9	33.8	33.6	29.3	4.8	5.7	5.6	3.2
Sub-Saharan Africa	313.1 T	689.6 T	877.4 T	2.7	2.2	21.2	34.3	39.4	43.9	42.0	3.1	3.3	6.8	5.5
Central and Eastern Europe and the CIS	366.6 T	405.3 T	396.8 T	0.3	–0.2	57.3	62.9	63.6	18.6	17.3	12.7	12.9	2.5	1.5
OECD	925.7 T	1,164.8 T	1,233.6 T	0.8	0.5	66.8	75.4	78.1	19.6	17.8	13.6	16.1	2.6	1.8
High-income OECD	765.9 T	922.6 T	968.5 T	0.6	0.4	69.3	76.8	79.4	17.7	16.4	15.2	18.0	2.2	1.6
High human development	1,012.5 T	1,275.0 T	1,350.0 T	0.8	0.5	67.2	75.9	78.7	19.6	17.8	13.5	16.0	2.5	1.7
Medium human development	2,743.2 T	4,433.1 T	4,995.8 T	1.7	1.1	27.7	42.4	48.2	28.8	25.4	6.1	7.2	5.0	2.5
Low human development	255.0 T	571.7 T	737.1 T	2.8	2.3	18.3	32.0	37.6	44.8	42.6	2.9	3.1	7.0	5.8
High income	792.3 T	982.5 T	1,040.9 T	0.7	0.5	69.4	77.4	80.0	18.4	17.0	14.6	17.3	2.3	1.7
Middle income	2,042.9 T	3,043.0 T	3,319.6 T	1.4	0.8	34.7	53.2	60.3	25.4	22.4	7.2	8.6	4.6	2.1
Low income	1,237.0 T	2,361.3 T	2,856.0 T	2.2	1.7	20.7	29.9	34.4	36.8	33.2	4.3	4.9	6.0	3.9
World	4,073.7 T e	6,389.2 T e	7,219.4 T e	1.6	1.1	37.2	48.3	52.8	28.5	25.9	7.3	8.4	4.5	2.7

NOTES

a Because data are based on national definitions of what constitutes a city or metropolitan area, cross-country comparisons should be made with caution.
b Data refer to medium-variant projections.
c Data refer to estimates for the period specified.
d Population estimates include Taiwan, province of China.
e Data refer to the total world population from UN 2005b. The total population of the 177 countries included in the main indicator tables was estimated to be 4,068.1 million in 1975, 6,381 million in 2004 and projected to be 7,210.3 in 2015.

SOURCES

Columns 1–3, 13 and 14: UN 2005b.
Columns 4 and 5: calculated on the basis of data in columns 1 and 2.
Columns 6 and 8: UN 2006e.
Column 7: UN 2006b.
Columns 9 and 10: calculated on the basis of data on population under age 15 and total population from UN 2005b.
Columns 11 and 12: calculated on the basis of data on population ages 65 and older and data on total population from UN 2005b.

TABLE 6

... to lead a long and healthy life ...

Commitment to health: resources, access and services

	Health expenditure			MDG One-year-olds fully immunized		Children with diarrhoea receiving oral rehydration and continued feeding	MDG Contraceptive prevalence rate[a]	MDG Births attended by skilled health personnel	Physicians
	Public (% of GDP)	Private (% of GDP)	Per capita (PPP US$)	Against tuberculosis (%)	Against measles (%)	(% under age 5)	(% of married women ages 15–49)	(%)	(per 100,000 people)
HDI rank	2003	2003	2003	2004	2004	1996–2004[b]	1996–2004[b]	1996–2004[b]	1990–2004[b]
HIGH HUMAN DEVELOPMENT									
1 Norway	8.6	1.7	3,809	..	88	..	..	100 [c]	313
2 Iceland	8.8	1.7	3,110	..	93	..	..	..	362
3 Australia	6.4	3.1	2,874	..	93	..	..	100	247
4 Ireland	5.8	1.5	2,496	90	81	..	..	100	279
5 Sweden	8.0	1.4	2,704	16 [d]	94	..	..	100 [c]	328
6 Canada	6.9	3.0	2,989	..	95	..	75 [e]	98	214
7 Japan	6.4	1.5	2,244	..	99	..	56	100	198
8 United States	6.8	8.4	5,711	..	93	..	76 [e]	99	256
9 Switzerland	6.7	4.8	3,776	..	82	..	82 [e]	..	361
10 Netherlands	6.1	3.7	2,987	..	96	..	79 [e]	100	315
11 Finland	5.7	1.7	2,108	98	97	..	..	100	316
12 Luxembourg	6.2	0.6	3,680	..	91	..	..	100	266
13 Belgium	6.3	3.1	2,828	..	82	..	78 [e]	100 [c]	449
14 Austria	5.1	2.4	2,306	..	74	..	51	100 [e]	338
15 Denmark	7.5	1.5	2,762	..	96	..	..	100 [c]	293
16 France	7.7	2.4	2,902	85	86	..	75 [e]	99 [e]	337
17 Italy	6.3	2.1	2,266	..	84	..	60	..	420
18 United Kingdom	6.9	1.1	2,389	..	81	..	84 [f]	99	230
19 Spain	5.5	2.2	1,853	..	97	..	81 [e]	..	330
20 New Zealand	6.3	1.8	1,893	..	85	..	75 [e]	100 [e]	237
21 Germany	8.7	2.4	3,001	..	92	..	75 [e]	100 [c]	337
22 Hong Kong, China (SAR)	..	..	..	..	..	..	86 [e]	..	..
23 Israel	6.1	2.8	1,911	..	96	..	..	99 [c]	382
24 Greece	5.1	4.8	1,997	88	88	..	..	..	438
25 Singapore	1.6	2.9	1,156	99	94	..	62	100	140
26 Korea, Rep. of	2.8	2.8	1,074	93	99	..	81	100	157
27 Slovenia	6.7	2.1	1,669	98	94	..	74 [e]	100 [c]	225
28 Portugal	6.7	2.9	1,791	83	95	..	..	100 [c]	342
29 Cyprus	3.1	3.3	1,143	..	86	..	..	100	234
30 Czech Republic	6.8	0.8	1,302	99	97	..	72	100	351
31 Barbados	4.8	2.1	1,050	..	98	..	..	98	121
32 Malta	7.4	1.9	1,436	..	87	..	..	98 [e]	318
33 Kuwait	2.7	0.8	567	..	97	..	50	98	153
34 Brunei Darussalam	2.8	0.7	681	99	99	..	..	99	101
35 Hungary	6.1	2.3	1,269	99	99	..	77 [e]	100	333
36 Argentina	4.3	4.6	1,067	99	95	..	..	99	301
37 Poland	4.5	2.0	745	94	97	..	49 [e]	100 [c]	247
38 Chile	3.0	3.1	707	96	95	..	..	100	109
39 Bahrain	2.8	1.3	813	70	99	..	62 [e]	98 [e]	109
40 Estonia	4.1	1.2	682	99	96	..	70 [e]	100	448
41 Lithuania	5.0	1.6	754	99	98	..	47 [e]	100	397
42 Slovakia	5.2	0.7	777	98	98	..	74 [e]	99	318
43 Uruguay	2.7	7.1	824	99	95	..	..	100	365
44 Croatia	6.5	1.3	838	98	96	..	..	100	244
45 Latvia	3.3	3.1	678	99	99	..	48 [e]	100	301
46 Qatar	2.0	0.7	685	99	99	..	43	99	222
47 Seychelles	4.3	1.6	599	99	99	..	..	..	151
48 Costa Rica	5.8	1.5	616	90	88	..	80	98	132
49 United Arab Emirates	2.5	0.8	623	98	94	..	28 [e]	99 [e]	202
50 Cuba	6.3	1.0	251	99	99	..	73	100	591
51 Saint Kitts and Nevis	3.4	1.9	670	89	98	..	..	99	119
52 Bahamas	3.0	3.4	1,220	..	89	..	..	99 [c]	105
53 Mexico	2.9	3.3	582	99	96	..	68	95	198

TABLE 6

Commitment to health: resources, access and services

Human development indicators

HDI rank	Health expenditure Public (% of GDP) 2003	Private (% of GDP) 2003	Per capita (PPP US$) 2003	MDG One-year-olds fully immunized Against tuberculosis (%) 2004	Against measles (%) 2004	Children with diarrhoea receiving oral rehydration and continued feeding (% under age 5) 1996–2004 [b]	MDG Contraceptive prevalence rate [a] (% of married women ages 15–49) 1996–2004 [b]	MDG Births attended by skilled health personnel (%) 1996–2004 [b]	Physicians (per 100,000 people) 1990–2004 [b]
54 Bulgaria	4.1	3.4	573	98	95	..	42	99	356
55 Tonga	5.5	1.0	300	99	99	..	..	95	34
56 Oman	2.7	0.5	419	99	98	..	24 e	95	132
57 Trinidad and Tobago	1.5	2.4	532	..	95	31	38	96	79
58 Panama	5.0	2.6	555	99	99	..	..	93	150
59 Antigua and Barbuda	3.2	1.3	477	..	97	..	..	100	17
60 Romania	3.8	2.3	540	99	97	..	64	99	190
61 Malaysia	2.2	1.6	374	99	95	..	55 e	97	70
62 Bosnia and Herzegovina	4.8	4.7	327	95	88	23	48	100	134
63 Mauritius	2.2	1.5	430	99	98	..	75 e	98	106
MEDIUM HUMAN DEVELOPMENT									
64 Libyan Arab Jamahiriya	2.6	1.5	327	99	99	..	45 e	94 e	129
65 Russian Federation	3.3	2.3	551	96	98	..	..	99	425
66 Macedonia, TFYR	6.0	1.1	389	94	96	..	..	99	219
67 Belarus	3.9	1.6	570	99	99	..	50 e	100	455
68 Dominica	4.5	1.8	320	99	99	..	..	100	50
69 Brazil	3.4	4.2	597	99	99	28	77	96	115
70 Colombia	6.4	1.2	522	92	92	44	77	86	135
71 Saint Lucia	3.4	1.6	294	99	95	..	..	100	517
72 Venezuela, RB	2.0	2.5	231	97	80	51	..	94	194
73 Albania	2.7	3.8	366	97	96	51	75	98	131
74 Thailand	2.0	1.3	260	99	96	..	72	99	37
75 Samoa (Western)	4.3	1.1	209	93	25	..	..	100	70
76 Saudi Arabia	3.0	1.0	578	95	97	..	32	91	137
77 Ukraine	3.8	1.9	305	98	99	..	68	100	295
78 Lebanon	3.0	7.2	730	..	96	..	61	89	325
79 Kazakhstan	2.0	1.5	315	65	99	22	66	99	354
80 Armenia	1.2	4.8	302	96	92	48	61	97	359
81 China	2.0	3.6	278	94	84	..	84	96	106
82 Peru	2.1	2.3	233	91	89	46	69	59	117
83 Ecuador	2.0	3.1	220	99	99	..	66	69	148
84 Philippines	1.4	1.8	174	91	80	76	19	60	58
85 Grenada	4.9	1.8	473	..	74	..	54 e	100	50
86 Jordan	4.2	5.2	440	58	99	44	56	100	203
87 Tunisia	2.5	2.9	409	97	95	..	63	90	134
88 Saint Vincent and the Grenadines	4.1	2.0	384	99	99	..	..	100	87
89 Suriname	3.6	4.3	309	..	86	43	42	85	45
90 Fiji	2.3	1.4	220	93	62	..	..	99	34
91 Paraguay	2.3	5.0	301	82	89	..	73	77	111
92 Turkey	5.4	2.2	528	88	81	19	64	83	135
93 Sri Lanka	1.6	1.9	121	99	96	..	70	96	55
94 Dominican Republic	2.3	4.7	335	97	79	53	70	99	188
95 Belize	2.2	2.3	309	99	95	..	47 e	83	105
96 Iran, Islamic Rep. of	3.1	3.4	498	99	96	..	73	90	45
97 Georgia	1.0	3.0	174	91	86	..	41	96	409
98 Maldives	5.5	0.7	364	98	97	..	42	70	92
99 Azerbaijan	0.9	2.7	140	99	98	40	55	100	355
100 Occupied Palestinian Territories	..	..	..	98	96 c	..	..	97	..
101 El Salvador	3.7	4.4	378	94	93	..	67	92	124
102 Algeria	3.3	0.8	186	98	81	..	64	96	113
103 Guyana	4.0	0.8	283	94	88	40	37	86	48
104 Jamaica	2.7	2.6	216	85	80	21	66	97	85
105 Turkmenistan	2.6	1.3	221	99	97	..	62	97	418
106 Cape Verde	3.4	1.2	185	79	69	..	53	89	49

TABLE 6

	Health expenditure			MDG One-year-olds fully immunized		Children with diarrhoea receiving oral rehydration and continued feeding	MDG Contraceptive prevalence rate[a]	MDG Births attended by skilled health personnel	Physicians
	Public (% of GDP)	Private (% of GDP)	Per capita (PPP US$)	Against tuberculosis (%)	Against measles (%)	(% under age 5)	(% of married women ages 15–49)	(%)	(per 100,000 people)
HDI rank	2003	2003	2003	2004	2004	1996–2004[b]	1996–2004[b]	1996–2004[b]	1990–2004[b]
107 Syrian Arab Republic	2.5	2.6	116	99	98	..	40 [e]	77 [e]	140
108 Indonesia	1.1	2.0	113	82	72	61	60	72	13
109 Viet Nam	1.5	3.9	164	96	97	39	79	85	53
110 Kyrgyzstan	2.2	3.1	161	98	99	16	60	98	251
111 Egypt	2.5	3.3	235	98	97	29	60	69	54
112 Nicaragua	3.7	4.0	208	88	84	49	69	67	37
113 Uzbekistan	2.4	3.1	159	99	98	33	68	96	274
114 Moldova, Rep. of	3.9	3.3	177	96	96	52	62	99	264
115 Bolivia	4.3	2.4	176	93	64	54	58	67	122
116 Mongolia	4.3	2.4	140	95	96	66	67	97	263
117 Honduras	4.0	3.1	184	93	92	..	62	56	57
118 Guatemala	2.1	3.3	235	98	75	22	43	41	90
119 Vanuatu	2.9	1.0	110	63	48	..	..	88	11
120 Equatorial Guinea	1.0	0.5	179	73	51	36	..	65	30
121 South Africa	3.2	5.2	669	97	81	37	56	84	77
122 Tajikistan	0.9	3.5	71	97	89	29	34	71	203
123 Morocco	1.7	3.4	218	95	95	50	63	63	51
124 Gabon	2.9	1.5	255	89	55	44	33	86	29
125 Namibia	4.5	1.9	359	71	70	39	44	76	30
126 India	1.2	3.6	82	73	56	22	48 [g]	43	60
127 São Tomé and Principe	7.2	1.4	93	99	91	44	29	76	49
128 Solomon Islands	4.5	0.3	87	84	72	..	..	85	13
129 Cambodia	2.1	8.8	188	95	80	59	24	32	16
130 Myanmar	0.5	2.3	51	85	78	48	37	57	36
131 Botswana	3.3	2.3	375	99	90	7	40	94	40
132 Comoros	1.5	1.2	25	79	73	31	26	62	15
133 Lao People's Dem. Rep.	1.2	2.0	56	60	36	37	32	19	59
134 Pakistan	0.7	1.7	48	80	67	33 [c]	28	..	74
135 Bhutan	2.6	0.5	59	92	87	..	19 [e]	37	5
136 Ghana	1.4	3.1	98	92	83	40	25	47	15
137 Bangladesh	1.1	2.3	68	95	77	35	58	13	26
138 Nepal	1.5	3.8	64	85	73	43	39	15	21
139 Papua New Guinea	3.0	0.4	132	54	44	..	26	41	5
140 Congo	1.3	0.7	23	85	65	..	..	..	20
141 Sudan	1.9	2.4	54	51	59	38	10 [e]	87 [c]	22
142 Timor-Leste	7.3	2.3	125	72	55	..	10	18	10
143 Madagascar	1.7	1.0	24	72	59	47	27	51	29
144 Cameroon	1.2	3.0	64	83	64	33	26	62	19
145 Uganda	2.2	5.1	75	99	91	29	23	39	8
146 Swaziland	3.3	2.5	324	84	70	24	28	74	16
LOW HUMAN DEVELOPMENT									
147 Togo	1.4	4.2	62	91	70	25	26	61	4
148 Djibouti	3.8	1.9	72	78	60	..	..	61	18
149 Lesotho	4.1	1.1	106	83	70	29	30	60	5
150 Yemen	2.2	3.3	89	63	76	23 [c]	21	27	33
151 Zimbabwe	2.8	5.1	132	95	80	80	54	73	16
152 Kenya	1.7	2.6	65	87	73	33	39	42	14
153 Mauritania	3.2	1.0	59	86	64	28	8	57	11
154 Haiti	2.9	4.6	84	71	54	41	28	24	25
155 Gambia	3.2	4.9	96	95	90	38	10	55	11
156 Senegal	2.1	3.0	58	95	57	33	11	58	6
157 Eritrea	2.0	2.4	50	91	84	54	8	28	5
158 Rwanda	1.6	2.1	32	86	84	16	13	31	5
159 Nigeria	1.3	3.7	51	48	35	28	13	35	28

Human development indicators

TABLE 6

Commitment to health: resources, access and services

		Health expenditure			One-year-olds fully immunized	MDG	Children with diarrhoea receiving oral rehydration and continued feeding	MDG Contraceptive prevalence rate [a]	MDG Births attended by skilled health personnel	Physicians
		Public (% of GDP)	Private (% of GDP)	Per capita (PPP US$)	Against tuberculosis (%)	Against measles (%)	(% under age 5)	(% of married women ages 15–49)	(%)	(per 100,000 people)
HDI rank		2003	2003	2003	2004	2004	1996–2004 [b]	1996–2004 [b]	1996–2004 [b]	1990–2004 [b]
160	Guinea	0.9	4.5	95	71	73	44	6	56	11
161	Angola	2.4	0.4	49	72	64	32	6	45	8
162	Tanzania, U. Rep. of	2.4	1.9	29	91	94	38	25	46	2
163	Benin	1.9	2.5	36	99	85	42	19	66	4
164	Côte d'Ivoire	1.0	2.6	57	51	49	34	15	68	12
165	Zambia	2.8	2.6	51	94	84	48	34	43	12
166	Malawi	3.3	6.0	46	97	80	51	31	61	2
167	Congo, Dem. Rep. of the	0.7	3.3	14	78	64	17	31	61	11
168	Mozambique	2.9	1.8	45	87	77	33	17	48	3
169	Burundi	0.7	2.4	15	84	75	16	16	25	3
170	Ethiopia	3.4	2.5	20	82	71	38	8	6	3
171	Chad	2.6	3.9	51	38	56	50	3	16	4
172	Central African Republic	1.5	2.5	47	70	35	47	28	44	8
173	Guinea-Bissau	2.6	3.0	45	80	80	23	8	35	12
174	Burkina Faso	2.6	3.0	68	99	78	..	14	38	6
175	Mali	2.8	2.0	39	75	75	45	8	41	8
176	Sierra Leone	2.0	1.5	34	83	64	39	4	42	3
177	Niger	2.5	2.2	30	72	74	43	14	16	3
Developing countries		..	..	..	84	74	..	..	59	..
Least developed countries		..	..	..	82	72	..	..	36	..
Arab States		..	..	..	85	86	..	..	72	..
East Asia and the Pacific		..	..	..	92	83	..	..	86	..
Latin America and the Caribbean		..	..	..	96	92	..	..	87	..
South Asia		..	..	..	78	62	..	..	38	..
Sub-Saharan Africa		..	..	..	77	66	..	..	43	..
Central and Eastern Europe and the CIS		..	..	..	96	97	..	..	97	..
OECD		..	..	..	92	92	..	..	97	..
High-income OECD		..	..	..	84	92	..	..	99	..
High human development		..	..	..	95	93	..	..	99	..
Medium human development		..	..	..	86	76	..	..	65	..
Low human development		..	..	..	74	64	..	..	39	..
High income		..	..	..	88	92	..	..	99	..
Middle income		..	..	..	94	87	..	..	87	..
Low income		..	..	..	77	64	..	..	41	..
World		..	..	..	84 [h]	76 [h]	..	..	63 [h]	..

NOTES

a Data usually refer to women ages 15–49 who are married or in union; the actual age range covered may vary across countries.

b Data refer to the most recent year available during the period specified.

c Data are from UNICEF 2005. Data refer to a period other than that specified.

d Data refer to high-risk children only.

e Data refer to a year or period other than that specified, differ from the standard definition or refer to only part of a country.

f Excluding Northern Ireland.

g Excluding the state of Tripura.

h Data are world aggregates from UNICEF 2005.

SOURCES

Columns 1 and 2: calculated on the basis of data on health expenditure from WHO 2006b.

Column 3: WHO 2006b.

Columns 4 and 6: UNICEF 2005.

Columns 5 and 8: UN 2006c, based on a joint effort by the United Nations Children's Fund and the World Health Organization.

Column 7: UN 2006c, based on data from the United Nations Population Fund.

Column 9: WHO 2006c.

Human development indicators

TABLE 7

. . . to lead a long and healthy life . . .

Water, sanitation and nutritional status

	MDG Population with sustainable access to improved sanitation (%)		MDG Population with sustainable access to an improved water source (%)		MDG Population undernourished (% of total)		MDG Children under weight for age (% under age 5)	Children under height for age (% under age 5)	Infants with low birthweight (%)
HDI rank	1990	2004	1990	2004	1990/92 [a]	2001/03 [a]	1996–2004 [b]	1996–2004 [b]	1996–2004 [b]
HIGH HUMAN DEVELOPMENT									
1 Norway	..	..	100	100	..	..	..	..	5
2 Iceland	100	100	100	100	..	..	..	..	4
3 Australia	100	100	100	100	..	..	..	..	7
4 Ireland	..	..	..	..	..	..	..	..	6
5 Sweden	100	100	100	100	..	..	..	..	4
6 Canada	100	100	100	100	..	..	..	..	6
7 Japan	100	100	100	100	..	..	..	6 [c]	8
8 United States	100	100	100	100	..	..	1 [c]	1	8
9 Switzerland	100	100	100	100	..	..	..	..	6
10 Netherlands	100	100	100	100	..	..	..	1 [c]	..
11 Finland	100	100	100	100	..	..	..	..	4
12 Luxembourg	..	..	100	100	..	..	..	..	8
13 Belgium	..	..	..	..	..	..	..	..	8
14 Austria	100	100	100	100	..	..	..	..	7
15 Denmark	..	..	100	100	..	..	..	..	5
16 France	..	..	100	100	..	..	..	..	7
17 Italy	..	..	..	..	..	..	..	3 [c]	6
18 United Kingdom	..	..	100	100	..	..	..	..	8
19 Spain	100	100	100	100	..	..	..	..	6
20 New Zealand	..	..	97	..	..	..	..	..	6
21 Germany	100	100	100	100	..	..	..	..	7
22 Hong Kong, China (SAR)	..	..	..	..	..	..	..	..	..
23 Israel	..	..	100	100	..	..	..	..	8
24 Greece	..	..	..	..	..	..	..	..	8
25 Singapore	100	100	100	100	..	..	14 [d]	2	8
26 Korea, Rep. of	..	..	..	92	<2.5	<2.5	..	..	4
27 Slovenia	..	..	..	..	..	3	..	..	6
28 Portugal	..	..	..	..	..	..	..	..	8
29 Cyprus	100	100	100	100	<2.5	<2.5	..	..	..
30 Czech Republic	99	98	100	100	..	<2.5	1 [c]	2 [c]	7
31 Barbados	100	100	100	100	<2.5	<2.5	6 [d]	7 [c]	10
32 Malta	..	..	100	100	..	..	..	..	6
33 Kuwait	..	..	..	..	24	5	10	3	7
34 Brunei Darussalam	..	..	..	..	4	3	..	..	10
35 Hungary	..	95	99	99	..	<2.5	2 [d]	3 [c]	9
36 Argentina	81	91	94	96	<2.5	<2.5	5	12	7
37 Poland	..	..	..	..	..	<2.5	..	..	6
38 Chile	84	91	90	95	8	4	1	1	5
39 Bahrain	..	..	..	..	..	..	9 [c]	10 [c]	8
40 Estonia	97	97	100	100	..	3	..	..	4
41 Lithuania	..	..	..	..	..	<2.5	..	..	4
42 Slovakia	99	99	100	100	..	6	..	..	7
43 Uruguay	100	100	100	100	7	3	5 [c]	10 [c]	8
44 Croatia	100	100	100	100	..	7	1	1	6
45 Latvia	..	78	99	99	..	3	..	..	5
46 Qatar	100	100	100	100	..	..	6 [c]	8 [c]	10
47 Seychelles	..	..	88	88	14	9	6 [d]	5 [c]	..
48 Costa Rica	..	92	..	97	6	4	5	6	7
49 United Arab Emirates	97	98	100	100	4	<2.5	14 [c]	17 [d]	15
50 Cuba	98	98	..	91	8	<2.5	4 [c]	5	6
51 Saint Kitts and Nevis	95	95	100	100	13	11	..	..	9
52 Bahamas	100	100	..	97	9	7	..	..	7
53 Mexico	58	79	82	97	5	5	8	18	9

TABLE 7

Water, sanitation and nutritional status

HDI rank	MDG Population with sustainable access to improved sanitation (%)		MDG Population with sustainable access to an improved water source (%)		MDG Population undernourished (% of total)		MDG Children under weight for age (% under age 5)	Children under height for age (% under age 5)	Infants with low birthweight (%)
	1990	2004	1990	2004	1990/92 [a]	2001/03 [a]	1996–2004 [b]	1996–2004 [b]	1996–2004 [b]
54 Bulgaria	99	99	99	99	..	9	..	..	10
55 Tonga	96	96	100	100	..	..	..	1 [c]	0
56 Oman	83	..	80	..	..	..	24	10	8
57 Trinidad and Tobago	100	100	92	91	13	11	7 [d]	4	23
58 Panama	71	73	90	90	21	25	7	18	10
59 Antigua and Barbuda	..	95	..	91	..	..	10 [d]	7 [d]	8
60 Romania	..	..	..	57	..	<2.5	6	10	9
61 Malaysia	..	94	98	99	3	3	11	16	10
62 Bosnia and Herzegovina	..	95	97	97	..	9	4	10	4
63 Mauritius	..	94	100	100	6	6	15 [c]	10 [c]	13
MEDIUM HUMAN DEVELOPMENT									
64 Libyan Arab Jamahiriya	97	97	71	..	<2.5	<2.5	5 [c]	15 [c]	7
65 Russian Federation	87	87	94	97	..	3	3	13 [d]	6
66 Macedonia, TFYR	..	..	..	..	..	7	6	7	5
67 Belarus	..	84	100	100	..	3	..	..	5
68 Dominica	..	84	..	97	4	8	5 [d]	6 [d]	10
69 Brazil	71	75	83	90	12	8	6	11	10
70 Colombia	82	86	92	93	17	14	7	14	9
71 Saint Lucia	..	89	98	98	8	5	14 [d]	11 [c]	8
72 Venezuela, RB	..	68	..	83	11	18	4	13	7
73 Albania	..	91	96	96	..	6	14	35	3
74 Thailand	80	99	95	99	30	21	19 [c]	13 [c]	9
75 Samoa (Western)	98	100	91	88	11	4	2	4	4
76 Saudi Arabia	..	..	90	..	4	4	14 [c]	16 [c]	11
77 Ukraine	..	96	..	96	..	3	1	3	5
78 Lebanon	..	98	100	100	<2.5	3	3	12	6
79 Kazakhstan	72	72	87	86	..	8	4	10	8
80 Armenia	..	83	..	92	..	29	3	13	7
81 China	23	44	70	77	16	12	8	14	6
82 Peru	52	63	74	83	42	12	7	25	11
83 Ecuador	63	89	73	94	8	5	12	26	16
84 Philippines	57	72	87	85	26	19	28	32	20
85 Grenada	97	96	..	95	9	7	..	..	9
86 Jordan	93	93	97	97	4	7	4	9	10
87 Tunisia	75	85	81	93	<2.5	<2.5	4	12	7
88 Saint Vincent and the Grenadines	..	..	..	..	22	12	..	..	10
89 Suriname	..	94	..	92	13	10	13	10	13
90 Fiji	68	72	..	47	10	4	8 [c]	3 [c]	10
91 Paraguay	58	80	62	86	18	15	5 [c]	14 [c]	9
92 Turkey	85	88	85	96	<2.5	3	4	16	16
93 Sri Lanka	69	91	68	79	28	22	29	14	22
94 Dominican Republic	52	78	84	95	27	27	5	9	11
95 Belize	..	47	..	91	7	5	6 [c]	..	6
96 Iran, Islamic Rep. of	83	..	92	94	4	4	11	15	7
97 Georgia	97	94	80	82	..	13	3	12	6
98 Maldives	..	59	96	83	17	11	30	25	22
99 Azerbaijan	..	54	68	77	..	10	7	13	11
100 Occupied Palestinian Territories	..	73	..	92	..	16	4	9 [d]	9 [d]
101 El Salvador	51	62	67	84	12	11	10	19	13
102 Algeria	88	92	94	85	5	5	10	19	7
103 Guyana	..	70	..	83	21	9	14	11	12
104 Jamaica	75	80	92	93	14	10	4	4	9
105 Turkmenistan	..	62	..	72	..	8	12	22	6
106 Cape Verde	..	43	..	80	..	..	14 [c]	16 [c]	13

TABLE 7

HDI rank	MDG Population with sustainable access to improved sanitation (%)		MDG Population with sustainable access to an improved water source (%)		MDG Population undernourished (% of total)		MDG Children under weight for age (% under age 5)	Children under height for age (% under age 5)	Infants with low birthweight (%)
	1990	2004	1990	2004	1990/92 [a]	2001/03 [a]	1996–2004 [b]	1996–2004 [b]	1996–2004 [b]
107 Syrian Arab Republic	73	90	80	93	5	4	7	19	6
108 Indonesia	46	55	72	77	9	6	28	42	9
109 Viet Nam	36	61	65	85	31	17	28	37	9
110 Kyrgyzstan	60	59	78	77	..	4	11	25	7
111 Egypt	54	70	94	98	4	3	9	16	12
112 Nicaragua	45	47	70	79	30	27	10	20	12
113 Uzbekistan	51	67	94	82	..	26	8	21	7
114 Moldova, Rep. of	..	68	..	92	..	11	3	10 [d]	5
115 Bolivia	33	46	72	85	28	23	8	27	9
116 Mongolia	..	59	63	62	34	28	13	25	8
117 Honduras	50	69	84	87	23	22	17	29	14
118 Guatemala	58	86	79	95	16	23	23	49	13
119 Vanuatu	..	50	60	60	12	12	20 [d]	20	6
120 Equatorial Guinea	..	53	..	43	..	..	19	39 [d]	13
121 South Africa	69	65	83	88	..	..	12	25	15
122 Tajikistan	..	51	..	59	..	61	..	36	15
123 Morocco	56	73	75	81	6	6	10	18	11
124 Gabon	..	36	..	88	10	5	12	21	14
125 Namibia	24	25	57	87	34	23	24	24	14
126 India	14	33	70	86	25	20	49	45	30
127 São Tomé and Principe	..	25	..	79	18	12	13	29	20 [d]
128 Solomon Islands	..	31	..	70	33	20	21 [d]	27 [c]	13
129 Cambodia	..	17	..	41	43	33	45	45	11
130 Myanmar	24	77	57	78	10	5	32	32	15
131 Botswana	38	42	93	95	23	30	13	23	10
132 Comoros	32	33	93	86	47	62	26	42	25
133 Lao People's Dem. Rep.	..	30	..	51	29	21	40	42	14
134 Pakistan	37	59	83	91	24	23	38	37	19
135 Bhutan	..	70	..	62	..	..	19	40	15
136 Ghana	15	18	55	75	37	12	22	30	11
137 Bangladesh	20	39	72	74	35	30	48	43	30
138 Nepal	11	35	70	90	20	17	48	51	21
139 Papua New Guinea	44	44	39	39	15	13	35 [d]	43 [c]	11
140 Congo	..	27	..	58	54	34	14	28 [c]	..
141 Sudan	33	34	64	70	31	27	17 [c]	43	31
142 Timor-Leste	..	36	..	58	11	8	46	49	10
143 Madagascar	14	34	40	50	35	38	42	48	14
144 Cameroon	48	51	50	66	33	25	18	32	11
145 Uganda	42	43	44	60	24	19	23	39	12
146 Swaziland	..	48	..	62	14	19	10	30	9
LOW HUMAN DEVELOPMENT									
147 Togo	37	35	50	52	33	25	25	22	15
148 Djibouti	79	82	72	73	53	26	18	26	..
149 Lesotho	37	37	..	79	17	12	18	46	14
150 Yemen	32	43	71	67	34	37	46	52	32
151 Zimbabwe	50	53	78	81	45	45	13	27	11
152 Kenya	40	43	45	61	39	31	20	30	11
153 Mauritania	31	34	38	53	15	10	32	35	..
154 Haiti	24	30	47	54	65	47	17	23	21
155 Gambia	..	53	..	82	22	27	17	19	17
156 Senegal	33	57	65	76	23	23	23	25	18
157 Eritrea	7	9	43	60	..	73	40	38	21
158 Rwanda	37	42	59	74	43	36	27	43	9
159 Nigeria	39	44	49	48	13	9	29	38	14

Human development indicators

TABLE 7

Water, sanitation and nutritional status

HDI rank	MDG Population with sustainable access to improved sanitation (%)		MDG Population with sustainable access to an improved water source (%)		MDG Population undernourished (% of total)		MDG Children under weight for age (% under age 5)	Children under height for age (% under age 5)	Infants with low birthweight (%)
	1990	2004	1990	2004	1990/92 [a]	2001/03 [a]	1996–2004 [b]	1996–2004 [b]	1996–2004 [b]
160 Guinea	14	18	44	50	39	24	21	26	12
161 Angola	29	31	36	53	58	38	31	45	12
162 Tanzania, U. Rep. of	47	47	46	62	37	44	22	44	13
163 Benin	12	33	63	67	20	14	23	31	16
164 Côte d'Ivoire	21	37	69	84	18	14	17	25	17
165 Zambia	44	55	50	58	48	47	23	47	12
166 Malawi	47	61	40	73	50	34	22	49	16
167 Congo, Dem. Rep. of the	16	30	43	46	31	72	31	38	12
168 Mozambique	20	32	36	43	66	45	24	41	14
169 Burundi	44	36	69	79	48	67	45	57	16
170 Ethiopia	3	13	23	22	..	46	47	52	15
171 Chad	7	9	19	42	58	33	28	29	17
172 Central African Republic	23	27	52	75	50	45	24	28 [c]	14
173 Guinea-Bissau	..	35	..	59	24	37	25	31	22
174 Burkina Faso	7	13	38	61	21	17	38	39	19
175 Mali	36	46	34	50	29	28	33	38	23
176 Sierra Leone	..	39	..	57	46	50	27	34	23 [d]
177 Niger	7	13	39	46	41	32	40	40	17
Developing countries	33	49	71	79	20	17	..	..	..
Least developed countries	22	37	51	59	34	33	..	..	..
Arab States	61	71	84	86	11	10	..	..	..
East Asia and the Pacific	30	50	72	79	17	12	..	..	..
Latin America and the Caribbean	67	78	83	91	14	10	..	..	..
South Asia	18	37	72	85	25	20	..	..	..
Sub-Saharan Africa	32	37	48	56	31	30	..	..	..
Central and Eastern Europe and the CIS	..	..	93	94	..	..	..	..	..
OECD	94	96	97	99	..	..	..	..	..
High-income OECD	100	100	100	100	..	..	..	..	..
High human development	94	97	98	99	..	..	..	..	..
Medium human development	34	51	74	83	19	15	..	..	..
Low human development	28	35	45	52	32	32	..	..	..
High income	..	..	100	100	..	..	..	..	..
Middle income	46	61	78	84	15	11	..	..	..
Low income	22	38	64	76	27	23	..	..	..
World	49 [e]	59 [e]	78 [e]	83 [e]	20	17	..	..	..

NOTES

a Data refer to the average for the years specified.
b Data refer to the most recent year available during the period specified.
c Data refer to a year or period other than that specified.
d UNICEF 2005. Data refer to a year or period other than that specified, differ from the standard definition or refer to only part of the country.
e Figure is the world aggregate from UN 2006c.

SOURCES

Columns 1–4 and 7: UN 2006c, based on a joint effort by the United Nations Children's Fund and the World Health Organization.
Columns 5 and 6: UN 2006c, based on data from the Food and Agriculture Organization.
Columns 8 and 9: WHO 2006a.

TABLE

8

. . . to lead a long and healthy life . . .

Inequalities in maternal and child health

HDI rank	Survey year	Births attended by skilled health personnel (%)		One-year-olds fully immunized [a] (%)		Children under height for age (% under age 5)		Infant mortality rate [b] (per 1,000 live births)		Under-five mortality rate [b] (per 1,000 live births)	
		Poorest 20%	Richest 20%	Poorest 20%	Richest 20%	Poorest 20%	Richest 20%	Poorest 20%	Richest 20%	Poorest 20%	Richest 20%
MEDIUM HUMAN DEVELOPMENT											
69 Brazil	1996	72	99	57	74	17	2	83	29	99	33
70 Colombia	1995	61	98	58	77	17	5	41	16	52	24
79 Kazakhstan	1999	99	99	69	62	13	4	68	42	82	45 c
80 Armenia	2000	93	100	66	68	16	8	52	27	61	30
82 Peru	2000	13	88	58	81	29	4	64	14	93	18
84 Philippines	1998	21	92	60	87	..	..	49	21	80	29
86 Jordan	1997	91	99	21	17	11	5	35	23	42	25
91 Paraguay	1998	53	98	28	70	15	3	68	30	85	33
92 Turkey	1990	41	98	20	53	17	3	43	16	57	20
94 Dominican Republic	1996	89	98	34	47	14	2	67	23	90	27
105 Turkmenistan	2000	97	98	85	78	17	11	89	58	106	70
108 Indonesia	1997	21	89	43	72	..	..	78	23	109	29
109 Viet Nam	2000	58	100	44	92	..	..	39	14	53	16
110 Kyrgyzstan	1997	96	100	69	73	28	12	83	46	96	49
111 Egypt	2000	31	94	91	92	16	8	76	30	98	34
112 Nicaragua	2001	78	99	64	71	22	4	50	16	64	19
113 Uzbekistan	1996	92	100	81	78	20	16	54	46	70	50
115 Bolivia	1998	20	98	22	31	25	4	107	26	147	32
118 Guatemala	1998	9	92	66	56	30	7	58	39	78	39
121 South Africa	1998	68	98	51	70	..	..	62	17	87	22
123 Morocco	1992	5	78	54	95	23	7	80	35	112	39
124 Gabon	2000	67	97	6	24	21	9	57	36	93	55
125 Namibia	2000	55	97	60	68	18	9	36	23	55	31
126 India	1998	16	84	21	64	25	17	97	38	141	46
129 Cambodia	2000	15	81	29	68	27	14	110	50	155	64
132 Comoros	1996	26	85	40	82	23	18	87	65	129	87 c
134 Pakistan	1990	5	55	23	55	25	17	89	63	125	74
136 Ghana	1998	18	86	50	79	20	9	73	26	139	52
137 Bangladesh	1999	4	42	50	75	..	..	93	58	140	72
138 Nepal	2001	4	45	54	82	33	25	86	53	130	68
143 Madagascar	1997	30	89	22	66	25	25	119	58	195	101
144 Cameroon	1991	32	95	27	64	19	8	104	51	201	82
145 Uganda	2000	20	77	27	43	25	18	106	60	192	106

TABLE 8

Inequalities in maternal and child health

		Survey year	Births attended by skilled health personnel (%)		One-year-olds fully immunized[a] (%)		Children under height for age (% under age 5)		Infant mortality rate[b] (per 1,000 live births)		Under-five mortality rate[b] (per 1,000 live births)	
HDI rank			Poorest 20%	Richest 20%	Poorest 20%	Richest 20%	Poorest 20%	Richest 20%	Poorest 20%	Richest 20%	Poorest 20%	Richest 20%
LOW HUMAN DEVELOPMENT												
147	Togo	1998	25	91	22	52	19	10	84	66	168	97
150	Yemen	1997	7	50	8	56	26	22	109	60	163	73
151	Zimbabwe	1999	57	94	64	64	19	13	59	44	100	62
152	Kenya	1998	23	80	48	60	27	11	96	40	136	61
153	Mauritania	2000	15	93	16	45	18	15	61	62	98	79
154	Haiti	2000	4	70	25	42	18	5	100	97	164	109
156	Senegal	1997	20	86	..	..	..	..	85	45	181	70
157	Eritrea	1995	5	74	25	84	23	15	74	68	152	104
158	Rwanda	2000	17	60	71	79	27	16	139	88	246	154
159	Nigeria	1990	12	70	14	58	22	19	102	69	240	120
160	Guinea	1999	12	82	17	52	19	12	119	70	230	133
162	Tanzania, U. Rep. of	1999	29	83	53	78	29	16	115	92	160	135
163	Benin	1996	34	98	38	74	17	12	119	63	208	110
164	Côte d'Ivoire	1994	17	84	16	64	21	10	117	63	190	97
165	Zambia	2001	20	91	64	80	27	20	115	57	192	92
166	Malawi	2000	43	83	65	81	26	23	132	86	231	149
168	Mozambique	1997	18	82	20	85	22	14	188	95	278	145
170	Ethiopia	2000	1	25	7	34	26	23	93	95	159	147
171	Chad	1996	3	47	4	23	23	18	80	89	171	172
172	Central African Republic	1994	14	82	18	64	22	15	132	54	193	98
174	Burkina Faso	1998	18	75	21	52	21	15	106	77	239	155
175	Mali	2001	8	82	20	56	20	12	137	90	248	148
177	Niger	1998	4	63	5	51	21	21	131	86	282	184

NOTES

This table presents data for developing countries based on data from Demographic and Health Surveys conducted since 1990. Quintiles are defined by socioeconomic status in terms of assets or wealth, rather than income or consumption. For details, see Gwatkin and others 2005.

a Includes tuberculosis (BCG), measles, and diptheria, pertussis and tetanus (DPT) vaccinations.

b Based on births in the 10 years preceding the survey.

c Large sampling error due to small number of cases.

SOURCE

All columns: Gwatkin and others 2005.

TABLE 9

. . . to lead a long and healthy life . . .

Leading global health crises and risks

	HDI rank	HIV prevalence[a] (% ages 15–49) 2005	MDG Condom use at last high-risk sex[b] (% ages 15–24)		MDG Children under age 5		MDG Tuberculosis cases			Prevalence of smoking (% of adults)[f]	
			Women 1998–2004[g]	Men 1998–2004[g]	Using insecticide-treated bednets (%) 1999–2004[g]	With fever treated with antimalarial drugs (%) 1999–2004[g]	Prevalence[c] (per 100,000 people) 2004	Detected under DOTS[d] (%) 2004	Cured under DOTS[e] (%) 2003	Women 2002–04[g]	Men 2002–04[g]
HIGH HUMAN DEVELOPMENT											
1	Norway	0.1 [0.1–0.2]	..	..	..	..	4	46	97	25	27
2	Iceland	0.2 [0.1–0.3]	..	..	..	..	2	57	100	20	25
3	Australia	0.1 [<0.2]	..	..	..	..	6	33	82	16	19
4	Ireland	0.2 [0.1–0.4]	..	..	..	..	9	..	..	26	28
5	Sweden	0.2 [0.1–0.3]	..	..	..	..	3	69	84	18	17
6	Canada	0.3 [0.2–0.5]	..	..	..	..	4	58	35	17	22
7	Japan	<0.1 [<0.2]	..	..	..	..	39	45	76	15	47
8	United States	0.6 [0.4–1.0]	..	..	..	..	4	85	70	19	24
9	Switzerland	0.4 [0.3–0.8]	..	..	..	..	6	..	..	23	27
10	Netherlands	0.2 [0.1–0.4]	..	..	..	..	6	61	86	28	36
11	Finland	0.1 [<0.2]	..	..	..	..	7	..	..	19	26
12	Luxembourg	0.2 [0.1–0.4]	..	..	..	..	9	83	..	26	39
13	Belgium	0.3 [0.2–0.5]	..	..	..	..	10	65	73	25	30
14	Austria	0.3 [0.2–0.5]	..	..	..	..	11	42	68	..	..
15	Denmark	0.2 [0.1–0.4]	..	..	..	..	6	78	84	25	31
16	France	0.4 [0.3–0.8]	..	..	..	..	10	..	..	21	30
17	Italy	0.5 [0.3–0.9]	..	..	..	..	6	58	95	17	31
18	United Kingdom	0.2 [0.1–0.4]	..	..	..	..	9	..	..	25	27
19	Spain	0.6 [0.4–1.0]	..	..	..	..	20	..	..	..	..
20	New Zealand	0.1 [<0.2]	..	..	..	..	11	59	36	22	24
21	Germany	0.1 [0.1–0.2]	..	..	..	..	6	51	71	28	37
22	Hong Kong, China (SAR)	..	..	..	..	..	77	55	78	..	..
23	Israel	[<0.2]	..	..	..	..	7	34	80	18	32
24	Greece	0.2 [0.1–0.3]	..	..	..	..	17	..	..	..	..
25	Singapore	0.3 [0.2–0.7]	..	..	..	..	41	67	77	..	..
26	Korea, Rep. of	<0.1 [<0.2]	..	..	..	..	125	21	82	..	..
27	Slovenia	<0.1 [<0.2]	..	..	..	..	17	66	85	..	..
28	Portugal	0.4 [0.3–0.9]	..	..	..	..	35	78	84	..	..
29	Cyprus	[<0.2]	..	..	..	..	4	69	79	..	..
30	Czech Republic	0.1 [<0.2]	..	..	..	..	11	61	79	20	31
31	Barbados	1.5 [0.8–2.5]	..	..	..	..	12	139	100	..	..
32	Malta	0.1 [0.1–0.2]	..	..	..	..	5	20	100	18	30
33	Kuwait	[<0.2]	..	..	..	..	30	83	62	..	..
34	Brunei Darussalam	<0.1 [<0.2]	..	..	..	..	63	130	60	..	..
35	Hungary	0.1 [<0.2]	..	..	..	..	30	47	48	28	41
36	Argentina	0.6 [0.3–1.9]	..	..	..	..	53	65	66	25	32
37	Poland	0.1 [0.1–0.2]	..	..	..	..	32	56	78	25	40
38	Chile	0.3 [0.2–1.2]	..	..	..	..	16	114	85	37	48
39	Bahrain	[<0.2]	..	..	..	..	50	49	97	..	..
40	Estonia	1.3 [0.6–4.3]	..	..	..	..	49	75	70	18	45
41	Lithuania	0.2 [0.1–0.6]	..	..	..	..	67	89	74	13	44
42	Slovakia	<0.1 [<0.2]	..	..	..	..	23	34	87	..	..
43	Uruguay	0.5 [0.2–6.1]	..	..	..	..	33	86	86	24	35
44	Croatia	<0.1 [<0.2]	..	..	..	..	65	..	..	..	..
45	Latvia	0.8 [0.5–1.3]	..	..	..	..	71	83	74	19	51
46	Qatar	[<0.2]	..	..	..	..	77	35	73	..	..
47	Seychelles	..	..	..	..	..	83	106	100	..	..
48	Costa Rica	0.3 [0.1–3.6]	..	..	..	..	15	153	94	1	17
49	United Arab Emirates	[<0.2]	..	..	..	..	26	17	64	..	..
50	Cuba	0.1 [<0.2]	..	..	..	..	12	90	94	..	..
51	Saint Kitts and Nevis	..	..	..	..	..	15	..	..	..	..
52	Bahamas	3.3 [1.3–4.5]	..	..	..	..	50	68	62	..	..
53	Mexico	0.3 [0.2–0.7]	..	..	..	..	43	71	83	5	13

Human development indicators

TABLE 9

Leading global health crises and risks

HDI rank	HIV prevalence [a] (% ages 15–49) 2005	MDG Condom use at last high-risk sex [b] (% ages 15–24) Women 1998–2004 [g]	MDG Condom use at last high-risk sex [b] (% ages 15–24) Men 1998–2004 [g]	MDG Children under age 5 Using insecticide-treated bednets (%) 1999–2004 [g]	MDG Children under age 5 With fever treated with antimalarial drugs (%) 1999–2004 [g]	MDG Tuberculosis cases Prevalence [c] (per 100,000 people) 2004	MDG Tuberculosis cases Detected under DOTS [d] (%) 2004	MDG Tuberculosis cases Cured under DOTS [e] (%) 2003	Prevalence of smoking (% of adults) [f] Women 2002–04 [g]	Prevalence of smoking (% of adults) [f] Men 2002–04 [g]
54 Bulgaria	<0.1 [<0.2]	..	..	..	..	36	104	91	..	..
55 Tonga	..	..	..	..	..	42	..	..	..	..
56 Oman	[<0.2]	..	..	..	..	12	123	90	..	..
57 Trinidad and Tobago	2.6 [1.4–4.2]	..	..	..	..	12	..	..	..	..
58 Panama	0.9 [0.5–3.7]	..	..	..	..	45	133	74	..	..
59 Antigua and Barbuda	..	..	..	..	..	10	..	..	..	..
60 Romania	<0.1 [<0.2]	..	..	..	..	188	41	80	..	..
61 Malaysia	0.5 [0.2–1.5]	..	..	..	..	133	69	72	2	43
62 Bosnia and Herzegovina	<0.1 [<0.2]	..	..	..	..	53	96	94	30	49
63 Mauritius	0.6 [0.3–1.8]	..	..	..	..	135	33	87	1	32
MEDIUM HUMAN DEVELOPMENT										
64 Libyan Arab Jamahiriya	[<0.2]	..	..	..	..	20	169	62	..	..
65 Russian Federation	1.1 [0.7–1.8]	..	..	..	..	160	13	61	..	..
66 Macedonia, TFYR	<0.1 [<0.2]	..	..	..	..	34	73	84	..	..
67 Belarus	0.3 [0.2–0.8]	..	..	..	..	68	42	73	7	53
68 Dominica	..	..	..	..	..	23	..	..	..	..
69 Brazil	0.5 [0.3–1.6]	..	..	..	..	77	47	83	14	22
70 Colombia	0.6 [0.3–2.5]	30	..	1	..	75	17	83	..	..
71 Saint Lucia	..	..	..	..	..	21	93	89	..	..
72 Venezuela, RB	0.7 [0.3–8.9]	..	..	..	..	52	77	82	..	..
73 Albania	[<0.2]	..	..	..	..	31	34	91	..	..
74 Thailand	1.4 [0.7–2.1]	..	..	..	..	208	71	73	..	..
75 Samoa (Western)	..	..	..	..	..	43	..	..	..	..
76 Saudi Arabia	[<0.2]	..	..	..	..	55	40	79	..	..
77 Ukraine	1.4 [0.8–4.3]	..	..	..	..	151	..	..	..	..
78 Lebanon	0.1 [0.1–0.5]	..	..	..	..	12	82	92	31	42
79 Kazakhstan	0.1 [0.1–3.2]	32	65	..	..	160	79	75	..	..
80 Armenia	0.1 [0.1–0.6]	..	44	..	..	98	44	77	..	..
81 China	0.1 [<0.2]	..	..	..	..	221	63	94	4 [h]	67
82 Peru	0.6 [0.3–1.7]	19	..	..	..	216	83	89	..	..
83 Ecuador	0.3 [0.1–3.5]	..	..	..	..	196	43	84	..	..
84 Philippines	<0.1 [<0.2]	..	..	..	..	463	73	88	8	41
85 Grenada	..	..	..	..	..	8	..	..	..	..
86 Jordan	[<0.2]	..	..	..	..	5	79	87	8	51
87 Tunisia	0.1 [0.1–0.3]	..	..	..	..	24	96	91	2	50
88 Saint Vincent and the Grenadines	..	..	..	..	..	39	33	..	..	..
89 Suriname	1.9 [1.1–3.1]	..	..	3	..	98	..	..	..	..
90 Fiji	0.1 [0.1–0.4]	..	..	..	..	41	58	86	4	26
91 Paraguay	0.4 [0.2–4.6]	..	..	..	..	107	21	85	7	23
92 Turkey	[<0.2]	..	..	..	..	45	3	93	18	49
93 Sri Lanka	<0.1 [<0.2]	..	..	..	..	91	70	81	2	23
94 Dominican Republic	1.1 [0.9–1.3]	29	52	..	..	118	71	81	11	16
95 Belize	2.5 [1.4–4.0]	..	..	..	..	59	60	89	..	..
96 Iran, Islamic Rep. of	0.2 [0.1–0.4]	..	..	..	..	35	58	84	..	..
97 Georgia	0.2 [0.1–2.7]	..	..	..	..	89	79	66	..	..
98 Maldives	[<0.2]	..	..	..	..	57	94	91	..	..
99 Azerbaijan	0.1 [0.1–0.4]	..	..	1	1	90	47	70	..	..
100 Occupied Palestinian Territories	..	..	..	..	..	36	..	80	..	..
101 El Salvador	0.9 [0.5–3.8]	..	..	..	..	74	57	88	..	..
102 Algeria	0.1 [<0.2]	..	..	..	..	54	106	90	(.)	32
103 Guyana	2.4 [1.0–4.9]	..	..	6	3	185	27	57	..	..
104 Jamaica	1.5 [0.8–2.4]	..	..	..	..	9	79	53	..	..
105 Turkmenistan	<0.1 [<0.2]	..	..	..	..	83	38	82	..	..
106 Cape Verde	..	..	..	..	..	314	..	..	..	..

TABLE 9

HDI rank	HIV prevalence[a] (% ages 15–49) 2005	MDG Condom use at last high-risk sex[b] (% ages 15–24) Women 1998–2004[g]	Men 1998–2004[g]	MDG Children under age 5 Using insecticide-treated bednets (%) 1999–2004[g]	With fever treated with antimalarial drugs (%) 1999–2004[g]	MDG Tuberculosis cases Prevalence[c] (per 100,000 people) 2004	Detected under DOTS[d] (%) 2004	Cured under DOTS[e] (%) 2003	Prevalence of smoking (% of adults)[f] Women 2002–04[g]	Men 2002–04[g]
107 Syrian Arab Republic	[<0.2]	..	..	..	..	51	46	88	..	..
108 Indonesia	0.1 [0.1–0.2]	..	68 [j]	..	1	275	53	87	..	..
109 Viet Nam	0.5 [0.3–0.9]	..	..	16	7	232	89	92	2	35
110 Kyrgyzstan	0.1 [0.1–1.7]	..	..	..	..	137	62	85	..	..
111 Egypt	<0.1 [<0.2]	..	..	..	..	35	61	80	..	..
112 Nicaragua	0.2 [0.1–0.6]	17	..	..	2	80	87	84	..	..
113 Uzbekistan	0.2 [0.1–0.7]	..	50	..	..	156	28	81	1	24
114 Moldova, Rep. of	1.1 [0.6–2.6]	44	63	..	..	214	59	65	2	34
115 Bolivia	0.1 [0.1–0.3]	20	37	..	..	290	71	81	..	..
116 Mongolia	<0.1 [<0.2]	..	..	..	..	209	80	88	..	..
117 Honduras	1.5 [0.8–2.4]	..	..	..	..	97	83	87	..	..
118 Guatemala	0.9 [0.5–2.7]	..	..	1	..	107	55	91	..	..
119 Vanuatu	..	..	..	..	..	64	107	56	..	..
120 Equatorial Guinea	3.2 [2.6–3.8]	..	..	1	49	322	82	51	..	..
121 South Africa	18.8 [16.8–20.7]	20	..	..	..	670	83	67	8	23
122 Tajikistan	0.1 [0.1–1.7]	..	..	2	69	277	12	86	..	..
123 Morocco	0.1 [0.1–0.4]	..	..	..	..	105	80	86	(.)	29
124 Gabon	7.9 [5.1–11.5]	33	48	..	..	339	81	34	..	..
125 Namibia	19.6 [8.6–31.7]	48	69	3	14	586	88	63	10	23
126 India	0.9 [0.5–1.5]	51	59	..	..	312	57	86	17	47
127 São Tomé and Principe	..	..	..	23	61	253	..	..	..	..
128 Solomon Islands	..	..	..	..	..	59	123	87	..	..
129 Cambodia	1.6 [0.9–2.6]	..	..	..	..	709	61	93	..	..
130 Myanmar	1.3 [0.7–2.0]	..	..	..	..	180	83	81	12	36
131 Botswana	24.1 [23.0–32.0]	75	88	..	..	553	67	77	..	..
132 Comoros	<0.1 [<0.2]	..	..	9	63	95	39	..	..	..
133 Lao People's Dem. Rep.	0.1 [0.1–0.4]	..	..	18	9	318	55	79	13	59
134 Pakistan	0.1 [0.1–0.2]	..	..	..	..	329	27	75	..	..
135 Bhutan	<0.1 [<0.2]	..	..	..	..	184	35	90	..	..
136 Ghana	2.3 [1.9–2.6]	33	52	5	63	376	37	66	1	7
137 Bangladesh	<0.1 [<0.2]	..	..	..	..	435	44	85	27	55
138 Nepal	0.5 [0.3–1.3]	..	..	..	..	257	67	87	24	49
139 Papua New Guinea	1.8 [0.9–4.4]	..	..	..	..	448	19	58	..	..
140 Congo	5.3 [3.3–7.5]	..	..	..	..	464	65	69	..	..
141 Sudan	1.6 [0.8–2.7]	..	..	(.)	50	370	35	82	..	..
142 Timor-Leste	[<0.2]	..	..	8	47	692	46	81	..	..
143 Madagascar	0.5 [0.2–1.2]	5	12	(.)	61	351	74	71	..	..
144 Cameroon	5.4 [4.9–5.9]	46	57	1.3	66	227	91	..	..	..
145 Uganda	6.7 [5.7–7.6]	53	55	(.)	..	646	43	68	..	..
146 Swaziland	33.4 [21.2–45.3]	..	..	(.)	26	1,120	38	42	3	11
LOW HUMAN DEVELOPMENT										
147 Togo	3.2 [1.9–4.7]	22	41	2	60	718	17	64	..	..
148 Djibouti	3.1 [0.8–6.9]	..	..	..	..	1,137	43	74	..	..
149 Lesotho	23.2 [21.9–24.7]	50	48	..	..	544	86	70	..	..
150 Yemen	[<0.2]	..	..	..	..	144	40	82	..	..
151 Zimbabwe	20.1 [13.3–27.6]	42	69	..	..	673	42	66	2	20
152 Kenya	6.1 [5.2–7.0]	25	47	5	27	888	46	80	1	21
153 Mauritania	0.7 [0.4–2.8]	..	..	4.1	33	502	44	58	..	..
154 Haiti	3.8 [2.2–5.4]	19	30	..	12	387	49	78	6 [h]	..
155 Gambia	2.4 [1.2–4.1]	..	..	15	55	329	66	75	..	..
156 Senegal	0.9 [0.4–1.5]	34	54 [j]	2	36	451	52	70	..	..
157 Eritrea	2.4 [1.3–3.9]	..	81	4	4	437	14	85	..	..
158 Rwanda	3.1 [2.9–3.2]	28	41	5	13	660	29	67	..	..
159 Nigeria	3.9 [2.3–5.6]	24	46	1	34	531	21	59	1	..

Human development indicators

TABLE 9

Leading global health crises and risks

HDI rank	HIV prevalence[a] (% ages 15–49) 2005	MDG Condom use at last high-risk sex[b] (% ages 15–24) Women 1998–2004[g]	Men 1998–2004[g]	MDG Children under age 5 Using insecticide-treated bednets (%) 1999–2004[g]	With fever treated with antimalarial drugs (%) 1999–2004[g]	MDG Tuberculosis cases Prevalence[c] (per 100,000 people) 2004	MDG Detected under DOTS[d] (%) 2004	MDG Cured under DOTS[e] (%) 2003	Prevalence of smoking (% of adults)[f] Women 2002–04[g]	Men 2002–04[g]
160 Guinea	1.5 [1.2–1.8]	42 [h]	27	4	56	410	52	75	..	..
161 Angola	3.7 [2.3–5.3]	..	..	2	63	310	94	68	..	..
162 Tanzania, U. Rep. of	6.5 [5.8–7.2]	42	47	10	58	479	47	81	..	..
163 Benin	1.8 [1.2–2.5]	19	34	7	60	142	82	81	..	..
164 Côte d'Ivoire	7.1 [4.3–9.7]	25	56	1	58	651	38	72	..	..
165 Zambia	17 [15.9–18.1]	35	40	7	52	707	54	75	1	16
166 Malawi	14.1 [6.9–21.4]	35	47	36	18	501	40	73	5	21
167 Congo, Dem. Rep. of the	3.2 [1.8–4.9]	..	..	1	45	551	70	83	..	..
168 Mozambique	16.1 [12.5–20.0]	29	33	..	15	635	46	76	..	..
169 Burundi	3.3 [2.7–3.8]	..	..	1	31	564	29	79	..	..
170 Ethiopia	[0.9–3.5]	17	30	..	3	533	36	70	(.)	6
171 Chad	3.5 [1.7–6.0]	17	25	1	32	566	16	78	..	..
172 Central African Republic	10.7 [4.5–17.2]	..	..	2	69	549	4	59	..	..
173 Guinea-Bissau	3.8 [2.1–6.0]	..	..	7	58	306	75	80	..	..
174 Burkina Faso	2 [1.5–2.5]	54	67	7	50	365	18	66	..	..
175 Mali	1.7 [1.3–2.1]	14	30	8	38	578	19	65	..	..
176 Sierra Leone	1.6 [0.9–2.4]	..	..	2	61	847	36	83	..	..
177 Niger	1.1 [0.5–1.9]	7	30	6	48	288	46	70		
Developing countries	1.1 [1.0–1.4]	..	..	..	..	275	..	..	..	..
Least developed countries	2.7 [2.3–3.1]	..	..	..	..	456	..	..	..	..
Arab States	0.2 [0.2–04]	..	..	..	..	125	..	..	..	..
East Asia and the Pacific	0.2 [0.1–0.3]	..	..	..	..	236	..	..	..	..
Latin America and the Caribbean	0.6 [0.4–1.2]	..	..	..	..	83	..	..	..	..
South Asia	0.7 [0.4–1.1]	..	..	..	..	315	..	..	..	..
Sub-Saharan Africa	6.1 [5.4–6.9]	..	..	..	..	540	..	..	..	..
Central and Eastern Europe and the CIS	0.6 [0.4–1.0]	..	..	..	..	124	..	..	..	..
OECD	0.4 [0.3–0.5]	..	..	..	..	22	..	..	..	..
High-income OECD	0.4 [0.3–0.6]	..	..	..	..	18	..	..	..	..
High human development	0.4 [0.3–0.5]	..	..	..	..	27	..	..	..	..
Medium human development	0.7 [0.6–1.0]	..	..	..	..	245	..	..	..	..
Low human development	4.9 [4.1–5.7]	..	..	..	..	532	..	..	..	..
High income	0.4 [0.3–0.6]	..	..	..	..	19	..	..	..	..
Middle income	0.6 [0.5–0.8]	..	..	..	..	182	..	..	..	..
Low income	1.8 [1.5–2.2]	..	..	..	..	376	..	..	..	..
World	1.0 [0.9–1.2]	..	..	..	..	229	..	..	..	..

NOTES

a Data are point and range estimates based on estimation models developed by the Joint United Nations Programme on HIV/AIDS (UNAIDS). Range estimates are in square brackets.

b Because of data limitations, comparisons across countries should be made with caution. Data for some countries may refer only to part of the country or differ from the standard definition.

c Data refer to all forms of tuberculosis.

d Calculated by dividing the new smear-positive cases of tuberculosis detected under DOTS, the internationally recommended tuberculosis control strategy, by the estimated annual incidence of new smear-positive cases. Values can exceed 100% because of intense case detection in an area with a backlog of chronic cases, overreporting (for example, double counting), overdiagnosis or underestimation of incidence (WHO 2006d).

e Data are the share of new smear-positive cases registered for treatment under the DOTS case detection and treatment strategy that were successfully treated.

f The age range varies among countries, but in most is 18 and older or 15 and older.

g Data refer to the most recent year available during the period specified.

h Data refer to 2005.

SOURCES

Column 1: UNAIDS 2006; aggregates were calculated for the Human Development Report Office by UNAIDS.

Columns 2 and 3: UN 2006c, based on data from a joint effort by UNAIDS, the United Nations Children's Fund (UNICEF) and the World Health Organization (WHO).

Columns 4–8: UN 2006c, based on data from UNICEF and the WHO.

Columns 9 and 10: World Bank 2006, based on data from the WHO and the National Tobacco Information Online System.

TABLE 10

. . . to lead a long and healthy life . . .

Survival: progress and setbacks

	Life expectancy at birth (years)		MDG Infant mortality rate (per 1,000 live births)		MDG Under-five mortality rate (per 1,000 live births)		Probability at birth of surviving to age 65 [a] (% of cohort)		MDG Maternal mortality ratio (per 100,000 live births)	
HDI rank	1970–75 [d]	2000–05 [d]	1970	2004	1970	2004	Female 2000–05 [d]	Male 2000–05 [d]	Reported [b] 1990–2004 [e]	Adjusted [c] 2000
HIGH HUMAN DEVELOPMENT										
1 Norway	74.4	79.3	13	4	15	4	90.6	84.7	6	16
2 Iceland	74.3	80.6	13	2	14	3	91.4	87.4	..	0
3 Australia	71.7	80.2	17	5	20	6	91.5	85.7	..	8
4 Ireland	71.3	77.7	20	5	27	6	89.7	83.1	6	5
5 Sweden	74.7	80.1	11	3	15	4	91.5	86.4	5	2
6 Canada	73.2	79.9	19	5	22	6	90.7	85.0	..	6
7 Japan	73.3	81.9	14	3	21	4	93.3	85.7	8	10
8 United States	71.5	77.3	20	7	26	8	86.7	79.1	8	17
9 Switzerland	73.8	80.5	15	5	18	5	91.9	85.4	5	7
10 Netherlands	74.0	78.3	13	5	15	6	89.7	83.5	7	16
11 Finland	70.7	78.4	13	3	16	4	91.2	80.9	6	6
12 Luxembourg	70.7	78.4	19	5	26	6	89.9	82.6	0	28
13 Belgium	71.4	78.8	21	4	29	5	90.4	82.5	..	10
14 Austria	70.6	78.9	26	5	33	5	91.0	82.4	..	4
15 Denmark	73.6	77.1	14	4	19	5	87.0	81.0	10	5
16 France	72.4	79.4	18	4	24	5	91.2	80.9	10	17
17 Italy	72.1	80.0	30	4	33	5	92.2	84.6	7	5
18 United Kingdom	72.0	78.3	18	5	23	6	89.4	83.6	7	13
19 Spain	72.9	79.5	27	3	34	5	92.8	82.1	6	4
20 New Zealand	71.7	79.0	17	5	20	6	89.1	84.1	15	7
21 Germany	71.0	78.7	22	4	26	5	90.5	82.3	8	8
22 Hong Kong, China (SAR)	72.0	81.5	..	..	..	..	93.7	86.4	..	..
23 Israel	71.6	79.7	24	5	27	6	91.5	85.5	5	17
24 Greece	72.3	78.2	38	4	54	5	91.5	82.0	1	9
25 Singapore	69.5	78.6	22	3	27	3	90.7	84.5	6	30
26 Korea, Rep. of	62.6	76.9	43	5	54	6	90.2	76.9	20	20
27 Slovenia	69.8	76.3	25	4	29	4	88.9	76.1	17	17
28 Portugal	68.0	77.2	53	4	62	5	90.2	79.8	8	5
29 Cyprus	71.4	78.5	29	5	33	5	91.6	84.3	0	47
30 Czech Republic	70.1	75.5	21	4	24	4	88.2	75.2	3	9
31 Barbados	69.4	74.9	40	10	54	12	86.7	74.8	0	95
32 Malta	70.7	78.3	25	5	32	6	90.3	85.4	..	21
33 Kuwait	67.0	76.8	49	10	59	12	87.9	82.7	5	5
34 Brunei Darussalam	68.3	76.3	58	8	78	9	87.9	84.7	0	37
35 Hungary	69.3	72.6	36	7	39	8	83.7	64.7	5	16
36 Argentina	67.1	74.3	59	16	71	18	84.9	72.1	44	82
37 Poland	70.5	74.3	32	7	36	8	87.0	69.7	4	13
38 Chile	63.4	77.9	78	8	98	8	88.5	79.1	17	31
39 Bahrain	63.3	74.2	55	9	82	11	84.6	78.9	46	28
40 Estonia	70.5	71.2	21	6	26	8	83.9	57.2	46	63
41 Lithuania	71.3	72.2	23	8	28	8	85.2	60.5	13	13
42 Slovakia	70.0	74.0	25	6	29	9	86.8	69.3	16	3
43 Uruguay	68.7	75.3	48	15	57	17	85.9	73.3	26	27
44 Croatia	69.6	74.9	34	6	42	7	88.1	73.2	2	8
45 Latvia	70.1	71.4	21	10	26	12	81.9	60.1	25	42
46 Qatar	62.1	72.7	45	18	65	21	81.2	74.0	10	7
47 Seychelles	..	..	46	12	59	14	..	..	57	..
48 Costa Rica	67.9	78.1	62	11	83	13	88.4	81.2	33	43
49 United Arab Emirates	62.2	77.9	61	7	83	8	90.2	85.0	3	54
50 Cuba	70.7	77.2	34	6	43	7	86.2	80.0	34	33
51 Saint Kitts and Nevis	..	..	..	18	..	21	..	..	250	..
52 Bahamas	66.5	69.5	38	10	49	13	73.6	61.4	..	60
53 Mexico	62.4	74.9	79	23	110	28	84.0	75.2	65	83

Human development indicators

TABLE 10

Survival: progress and setbacks

HDI rank		Life expectancy at birth (years)		MDG Infant mortality rate (per 1,000 live births)		MDG Under-five mortality rate (per 1,000 live births)		Probability at birth of surviving to age 65 [a] (% of cohort)		MDG Maternal mortality ratio (per 100,000 live births)	
		1970–75 [d]	2000–05 [d]	1970	2004	1970	2004	Female 2000–05 [d]	Male 2000–05 [d]	Reported [b] 1990–2004 [e]	Adjusted [c] 2000
54	Bulgaria	71.0	72.1	28	12	31	15	84.5	68.2	15	32
55	Tonga	65.6	72.1	40	20	50	25	78.2	73.4	..	..
56	Oman	52.1	74.0	126	10	200	13	84.2	78.8	23	87
57	Trinidad and Tobago	65.9	69.9	49	18	57	20	76.1	64.5	45	160
58	Panama	66.2	74.7	46	19	68	24	85.1	76.3	70	160
59	Antigua and Barbuda	..	..	..	11	..	12	..	..	65	..
60	Romania	69.2	71.3	46	17	57	20	82.9	65.3	31	49
61	Malaysia	63.0	73.0	46	10	70	12	83.5	73.4	30	41
62	Bosnia and Herzegovina	67.5	74.1	60	13	82	15	85.2	74.2	10	31
63	Mauritius	62.9	72.1	64	14	86	15	80.9	66.9	22	24

MEDIUM HUMAN DEVELOPMENT

HDI rank		1970–75 [d]	2000–05 [d]	1970	2004	1970	2004	Female 2000–05 [d]	Male 2000–05 [d]	Reported [b] 1990–2004 [e]	Adjusted [c] 2000
64	Libyan Arab Jamahiriya	52.8	73.4	105	18	160	20	82.5	74.6	77	97
65	Russian Federation	69.7	65.4	29	17	36	21	76.3	44.7	32	67
66	Macedonia, TFYR	67.5	73.7	85	13	119	14	84.6	75.4	7	23
67	Belarus	71.5	68.1	22	9	27	11	79.3	50.6	18	35
68	Dominica	..	..	..	13	..	14	..	..	67	..
69	Brazil	59.5	70.3	95	32	135	34	77.7	62.7	64	260
70	Colombia	61.6	72.2	69	18	108	21	81.0	71.0	78	130
71	Saint Lucia	65.3	72.3	..	13	..	14	77.0	71.3	35	..
72	Venezuela, RB	65.7	72.8	47	16	61	19	82.8	71.7	68	96
73	Albania	67.7	73.7	78	17	109	19	87.6	80.0	23	55
74	Thailand	61.0	69.7	74	18	102	21	80.3	64.5	24	44
75	Samoa (Western)	56.1	70.0	73	25	101	30	78.4	65.5	..	130
76	Saudi Arabia	53.9	71.6	118	21	185	27	81.2	73.4	..	23
77	Ukraine	70.1	66.1	22	14	27	18	76.4	46.6	13	35
78	Lebanon	66.4	71.9	45	27	54	31	81.7	73.0	100	150
79	Kazakhstan	63.2	63.2	..	63	..	73	71.9	48.0	50	210
80	Armenia	70.8	71.4	..	29	..	32	81.7	66.4	9	55
81	China	63.2	71.5	85	26	120	31	81.3	74.2	51	56
82	Peru	55.5	69.8	115	24	178	29	77.1	68.1	190	410
83	Ecuador	58.8	74.2	87	23	140	26	82.6	72.7	80	130
84	Philippines	58.1	70.2	56	26	90	34	78.6	70.1	170	200
85	Grenada	..	..	..	18	..	21	..	..	1	..
86	Jordan	56.5	71.2	77	23	107	27	77.7	71.6	41	41
87	Tunisia	55.6	73.1	135	21	201	25	84.9	75.7	69	120
88	Saint Vincent and the Grenadines	61.6	71.0	..	18	..	22	81.3	70.3	93	..
89	Suriname	64.0	69.0	..	30	..	39	77.3	63.1	150	110
90	Fiji	60.6	67.8	50	16	61	20	72.2	62.0	38	75
91	Paraguay	65.9	70.9	58	21	78	24	79.8	71.3	180	170
92	Turkey	57.0	68.6	150	28	201	32	77.9	67.3	130	70
93	Sri Lanka	63.1	73.9	65	12	100	14	85.6	76.1	92	92
94	Dominican Republic	59.7	67.1	91	27	127	32	75.1	60.8	180	150
95	Belize	67.6	71.9	..	32	..	39	80.9	71.7	140	140
96	Iran, Islamic Rep. of	55.2	70.2	122	32	191	38	79.2	71.7	37	76
97	Georgia	68.2	70.5	..	41	..	45	83.0	66.3	52	32
98	Maldives	51.4	66.3	157	35	255	46	67.5	67.8	140	110
99	Azerbaijan	65.6	66.9	..	75	..	90	76.0	60.3	25	94
100	Occupied Palestinian Territories	56.6	72.4	..	22	..	24	81.4	75.0	..	100
101	El Salvador	58.2	70.7	111	24	162	28	77.7	67.3	170	150
102	Algeria	54.5	71.0	143	35	220	40	78.4	75.2	120	140
103	Guyana	60.0	62.9	..	48	..	64	65.7	54.2	190	170
104	Jamaica	69.0	70.7	49	17	64	20	73.4	67.9	110	87
105	Turkmenistan	59.2	62.4	..	80	..	103	69.8	52.1	14	31
106	Cape Verde	57.5	70.2	..	27	..	36	79.8	67.7	76	150

TABLE 10

HDI rank	Life expectancy at birth (years)		MDG Infant mortality rate (per 1,000 live births)		MDG Under-five mortality rate (per 1,000 live births)		Probability at birth of surviving to age 65[a] (% of cohort)		MDG Maternal mortality ratio (per 100,000 live births)	
	1970–75[d]	2000–05[d]	1970	2004	1970	2004	Female 2000–05[d]	Male 2000–05[d]	Reported[b] 1990–2004[e]	Adjusted[c] 2000
107 Syrian Arab Republic	57.4	73.2	90	15	128	16	83.2	76.3	65	160
108 Indonesia	49.2	66.5	104	30	172	38	72.1	63.8	310	230
109 Viet Nam	50.3	70.4	55	17	87	23	78.4	71.0	170	130
110 Kyrgyzstan	61.2	66.8	104	58	130	68	76.0	58.6	44	110
111 Egypt	52.1	69.6	157	26	235	36	79.3	69.3	84	84
112 Nicaragua	55.2	69.5	113	31	165	38	74.9	66.1	83	230
113 Uzbekistan	63.6	66.5	83	57	101	69	72.9	59.9	34	24
114 Moldova, Rep. of	64.8	67.5	46	23	61	28	74.3	56.5	44	36
115 Bolivia	46.7	63.9	147	54	243	69	68.0	60.0	230	420
116 Mongolia	53.8	63.9	..	41	..	52	67.6	57.9	99	110
117 Honduras	53.9	67.6	116	31	170	41	70.1	63.5	110	110
118 Guatemala	53.7	67.1	115	33	168	45	73.5	59.7	150	240
119 Vanuatu	54.0	68.4	107	32	155	40	75.2	67.6	68	32
120 Equatorial Guinea	40.5	43.5	..	122	..	204	33.0	30.6	..	880
121 South Africa	53.7	49.0	..	54	..	67	38.1	28.9	150	230
122 Tajikistan	60.9	63.5	..	91	..	93	69.4	59.3	45	100
123 Morocco	52.9	69.5	119	38	184	43	78.9	70.3	230	220
124 Gabon	48.7	54.6	..	60	..	91	48.9	45.6	520	420
125 Namibia	53.9	48.6	85	47	135	63	36.7	31.6	270	300
126 India	50.3	63.1	127	62	202	85	67.4	59.2	540	540
127 São Tomé and Principe	56.5	62.9	..	75	..	118	68.6	63.1	100	..
128 Solomon Islands	55.6	62.2	71	34	99	56	62.0	59.0	550	130
129 Cambodia	40.3	56.0	..	97	..	141	61.5	45.0	440	450
130 Myanmar	49.2	60.1	122	76	179	106	63.5	52.7	230	360
131 Botswana	56.1	36.6	99	84	142	116	16.5	13.1	330	100
132 Comoros	48.9	63.0	159	52	215	70	66.5	57.8	520	480
133 Lao People's Dem. Rep.	40.4	54.5	145	65	218	83	53.1	47.8	530	650
134 Pakistan	51.9	62.9	120	80	181	101	65.6	62.7	530	500
135 Bhutan	41.5	62.7	156	67	267	80	65.3	60.2	260	420
136 Ghana	49.9	56.7	111	68	186	112	52.9	50.4	210	540
137 Bangladesh	45.2	62.6	145	56	239	77	63.7	59.3	380	380
138 Nepal	44.0	61.4	165	59	250	76	61.0	57.9	540	740
139 Papua New Guinea	44.7	55.1	106	68	147	93	46.6	41.5	370	300
140 Congo	54.9	51.9	100	81	160	108	43.5	38.6	..	510
141 Sudan	45.1	56.3	104	63	172	91	55.4	49.6	550	590
142 Timor-Leste	40.0	55.2	..	64	..	80	52.7	47.3	..	660
143 Madagascar	44.9	55.3	109	76	180	123	54.1	48.7	470	550
144 Cameroon	45.7	45.8	127	87	215	149	36.1	33.1	430	730
145 Uganda	51.1	46.8	100	80	170	138	34.4	32.9	510	880
146 Swaziland	49.6	33.0	132	108	196	156	12.0	9.3	230	370
LOW HUMAN DEVELOPMENT										
147 Togo	49.8	54.2	128	78	216	140	53.8	45.2	480	570
148 Djibouti	44.4	52.7	..	101	..	126	48.1	42.9	74	730
149 Lesotho	49.8	36.7	128	61	190	82	18.6	11.6	..	550
150 Yemen	39.9	60.3	202	82	303	111	61.0	54.9	370	570
151 Zimbabwe	55.6	37.2	86	79	138	129	15.5	15.7	700	1,100
152 Kenya	53.6	47.0	96	79	156	120	31.8	35.0	410	1,000
153 Mauritania	43.4	52.5	151	78	250	125	50.7	44.5	750	1,000
154 Haiti	48.5	51.5	148	74	221	117	41.3	38.2	520	680
155 Gambia	38.0	55.5	183	89	319	122	54.3	48.7	730	540
156 Senegal	40.1	55.6	164	78	279	137	54.6	49.4	560	690
157 Eritrea	44.3	53.5	143	52	237	82	45.5	35.9	1,000	630
158 Rwanda	44.6	43.6	124	118	209	203	35.5	29.6	1,100	1,400
159 Nigeria	42.8	43.3	140	101	265	197	33.2	31.6	..	800

Human development indicators

TABLE 10

Survival: progress and setbacks

HDI rank	Life expectancy at birth (years)		MDG Infant mortality rate (per 1,000 live births)		MDG Under-five mortality rate (per 1,000 live births)		Probability at birth of surviving to age 65 [a] (% of cohort)		MDG Maternal mortality ratio (per 100,000 live births)	
	1970–75 [d]	2000–05 [d]	1970	2004	1970	2004	Female 2000–05 [d]	Male 2000–05 [d]	Reported [b] 1990–2004 [e]	Adjusted [c] 2000
160 Guinea	39.3	53.6	197	101	345	155	52.6	49.1	530	740
161 Angola	37.9	40.7	180	154	300	260	33.0	27.8	..	1,700
162 Tanzania, U. Rep. of	49.5	46.0	129	78	218	126	35.8	33.4	580	1,500
163 Benin	47.0	53.8	149	90	252	152	52.9	48.4	500	850
164 Côte d'Ivoire	49.8	46.0	158	117	239	194	38.5	34.8	600	690
165 Zambia	50.2	37.4	109	102	181	182	18.5	20.0	730	750
166 Malawi	41.8	39.6	189	110	330	175	24.5	23.2	1,100	1,800
167 Congo, Dem. Rep. of the	46.0	43.1	148	129	245	205	34.4	30.8	1,300	990
168 Mozambique	40.7	41.9	168	104	278	152	30.5	26.7	410	1,000
169 Burundi	44.1	43.5	138	114	233	190	33.1	29.7	..	1,000
170 Ethiopia	43.5	47.6	160	110	239	166	40.7	36.6	870	850
171 Chad	40.6	43.6	..	117	..	200	35.1	31.2	830	1,100
172 Central African Republic	43.5	39.4	145	115	238	193	24.5	21.9	1,100	1,100
173 Guinea-Bissau	36.5	44.6	..	126	..	203	38.8	33.2	910	1,100
174 Burkina Faso	43.8	47.4	166	97	295	192	41.7	37.9	480	1,000
175 Mali	38.0	47.8	225	121	400	219	44.8	40.8	580	1,200
176 Sierra Leone	35.4	40.6	206	165	363	283	36.2	30.7	1,800	2,000
177 Niger	38.4	44.3	197	152	330	259	40.2	37.8	590	1,600
Developing countries	55.6	64.9	109	57	166	83	69.6	62.3	..	..
Least developed countries	44.5	52.0	148	94	240	147	47.9	43.5	..	..
Arab States	52.1	66.9	132	38	202	51	73.3	66.3	..	..
East Asia and the Pacific	60.5	70.4	84	28	122	34	79.2	71.3	..	..
Latin America and the Caribbean	61.1	71.7	86	26	123	31	79.7	68.2	..	..
South Asia	50.1	63.2	128	62	203	84	67.1	60.0	..	..
Sub-Saharan Africa	45.8	46.1	144	103	243	174	37.0	33.8	..	..
Central and Eastern Europe and the CIS	69.0	68.1	37	22	46	26	78.8	55.4	..	..
OECD	70.3	77.6	41	10	52	12	88.4	79.6	..	..
High-income OECD	71.6	78.8	22	5	27	6	89.9	81.8	..	..
High human development	70.6	77.7	34	9	42	10	88.7	79.6	..	..
Medium human development	57.4	66.9	103	45	156	60	73.5	64.5	..	..
Low human development	44.4	45.6	151	106	254	178	36.7	34.0	..	..
High income	71.5	78.6	24	6	30	7	89.7	81.6	..	..
Middle income	62.0	70.0	87	27	126	34	78.7	68.4	..	..
Low income	48.9	58.3	129	77	206	117	58.5	52.6	..	..
World	59.9	67.0	97	51	146	75	73.1	64.5	..	..

NOTES

a Data refer to the probability at birth of surviving to age 65, multiplied by 100.

b Data reported by national authorities.

c Data adjusted based on reviews by the United Nations Children's Fund (UNICEF), World Health Organization (WHO) and United Nations Population Fund to account for well-documented problems of underreporting and misclassifications.

d Data are estimates for the period specified.

e Data refer to the most recent year available during the period specified.

SOURCES

Columns 1, 2, 7 and 8: UN 2005b.

Columns 3–6 and 10: UN 2006c, based on data from a joint effort by UNICEF and the WHO.

Column 9: UNICEF 2005.

Human development indicators

TABLE 11

. . . to acquire knowledge . . .

Commitment to education: public spending

	Public expenditure on education				Current public expenditure on education by level [a] (% of all levels)					
	As % of GDP		As % of total government expenditure		Pre-primary and primary		Secondary		Tertiary	
HDI rank	1991	2002–04 [b]	1991	2002–04 [b]	1991	2002–04 [b]	1991	2002–04 [b]	1991	2002–04 [b]
HIGH HUMAN DEVELOPMENT										
1 Norway	7.1	7.7	14.6	..	38.3 [c]	29.4 [d]	26.9	35.8 [d]	16.5	31.5 [d]
2 Iceland	..	8.0	..	..	..	41.9 [d]	..	33.7 [d]	..	16.2 [d]
3 Australia	4.9	4.8	14.8	..	..	34.7 [d]	..	38.8 [d]	..	24.5 [d]
4 Ireland	5.0	4.3	9.7	..	37.5	32.6 [d]	40.1	35.1 [d]	20.6	26.8 [d]
5 Sweden	7.1	7.0	13.8	..	47.7	..	19.6	..	13.2	..
6 Canada	6.5	5.2	14.2	..	..	..	..	..	..	34.4 [d]
7 Japan	..	3.7	..	..	..	..	..	..	..	..
8 United States	5.1	5.9	12.3	..	..	..	..	..	..	..
9 Switzerland	5.3	5.4	18.8	..	49.5	34.3	25.7	38.7	19.4	24.0
10 Netherlands	5.6	5.3	14.3	..	22.6	34.9	36.9	39.7	31.8	25.3
11 Finland	6.5	6.5	11.9	..	..	26.2 [d]	..	40.5 [d]	..	33.3 [d]
12 Luxembourg	3.0	..	10.8	..	..	..	..	..	..	..
13 Belgium	5.0	6.2	..	..	23.6 [c]	..	41.7	..	16.4	..
14 Austria	5.5	5.5	7.6	..	23.9	27.4	46.2	45.9	19.8	22.5
15 Denmark	6.9	8.4	11.8	..	..	30.5	..	34.8	..	32.8
16 France	5.6	6.0	..	..	26.4	31.9	40.4	49.5	13.8	17.2
17 Italy	3.0	4.9	..	..	34.5	34.5	61.8	46.5	..	18.1
18 United Kingdom	4.8	5.5	..	11.5 [d]	29.7	..	43.8	..	19.6	..
19 Spain	4.3	4.5	..	..	29.4	37.5	44.8	42.8	16.1	19.7
20 New Zealand	6.1	6.9	..	15.1	30.5	28.1 [d]	25.3	41.7 [d]	37.4	24.5 [d]
21 Germany	..	4.8	..	..	..	..	..	..	..	..
22 Hong Kong, China (SAR)	2.8	4.7	17.4	23.3	..	25.0	..	34.9	..	31.6
23 Israel	6.5	7.3	11.4	13.7	..	45.2	..	30.1	..	17.1
24 Greece	2.3	4.3	..	..	33.7	29.0 [d]	45.3	36.8 [d]	19.6	29.9 [d]
25 Singapore	3.1	..	18.2	..	..	..	..	..	..	..
26 Korea, Rep. of	3.8	4.6	25.6	16.1	44.5	35.6 [d]	38.6	40.8 [d]	7.2	14.7 [d]
27 Slovenia	4.8	6.0	16.1	..	43.3	..	37.0	..	17.0	..
28 Portugal	4.6	5.9	..	..	42.9	37.9	35.1	42.2	15.0	16.1
29 Cyprus	3.7	7.4	11.6	..	38.8	36.7	49.7	51.3	3.9	12.0
30 Czech Republic	..	4.6	..	..	..	26.0	..	51.3	..	19.5
31 Barbados	7.8	7.3	22.2	17.3	..	31.9 [d]	..	31.0	..	34.4
32 Malta	4.4	4.6	8.5	..	23.0 [c]	31.6	40.1	47.9	19.0	20.0
33 Kuwait	4.8	8.2	3.4	17.4	..	30.4	..	37.5	..	31.0
34 Brunei Darussalam	3.5	..	..	..	22.4	..	29.6	..	2.0	..
35 Hungary	6.1	6.0	7.8	..	55.4	31.5 [d]	24.6	41.6 [d]	14.9	18.9 [d]
36 Argentina	3.3	3.5	..	14.6	..	43.2 [d]	..	39.2 [d]	..	17.6 [d]
37 Poland	5.2	5.8	14.6	12.8	36.5 [c]	40.5 [d]	..	39.1 [d]	..	18.4 [d]
38 Chile	2.5	3.7	10.0	18.5	..	49.8	..	39.1	..	11.1
39 Bahrain	3.9	..	12.8	..	..	..	..	..	..	..
40 Estonia	..	5.7	..	..	..	32.2	..	40.2	..	20.9
41 Lithuania	5.5	5.2	20.6	..	..	..	..	..	..	23.1
42 Slovakia	5.6	4.4	..	..	..	26.8 [d]	..	50.7 [d]	..	18.8 [d]
43 Uruguay	2.5	2.2	16.6	7.9	36.4 [c]	..	29.3	..	24.4	..
44 Croatia	5.5	4.5	..	10.0	..	32.4 [d]	..	46.2 [d]	..	19.3
45 Latvia	4.1	5.4	16.9	..	..	..	..	..	..	..
46 Qatar	3.5	..	..	..	..	..	..	..	..	..
47 Seychelles	6.5	5.4 [d]	11.6	..	..	39.8 [d]	..	30.0 [d]	..	18.3 [d]
48 Costa Rica	3.4	4.9	21.8	18.5	38.2	65.7	21.6	34.3	36.1	..
49 United Arab Emirates	1.9	1.6 [d]	15.0	22.5 [d]	..	45.2 [d]	..	50.6 [d]	..	2.6 [d]
50 Cuba	9.7	..	10.8	19.4	27.1	41.0	37.2	35.6	15.2	20.6
51 Saint Kitts and Nevis	2.7	4.4 [d]	11.6	12.7	42.7	42.1	56.2	36.5	..	..
52 Bahamas	3.7	..	16.3	..	..	..	..	..	..	..
53 Mexico	3.8	5.8	15.3	..	39.4	49.2	27.6	28.6	16.7	19.6

TABLE 11

Commitment to education: public spending

	Public expenditure on education				Current public expenditure on education by level [a] (% of all levels)					
	As % of GDP		As % of total government expenditure		Pre-primary and primary		Secondary		Tertiary	
HDI rank	1991	2002–04 [b]	1991	2002–04 [b]	1991	2002–04 [b]	1991	2002–04 [b]	1991	2002–04 [b]
54 Bulgaria	5.4	4.2	..	..	70.0	38.2 [d]	..	47.2 [d]	13.8	14.3 [d]
55 Tonga	..	4.8	..	13.5	..	59.1 [c]	..	26.5	..	..
56 Oman	3.4	4.6 [d]	15.8	26.1 [d]	52.3 [c]	43.4 [c, d]	39.7	38.6 [d]	6.6	9.6 [d]
57 Trinidad and Tobago	4.1	4.3 [d]	12.4	..	..	..	..	..	..	..
58 Panama	4.6	3.9 [d]	18.9	8.9 [d]	35.9 [c]	..	22.4	..	20.2	..
59 Antigua and Barbuda	..	3.8	..	..	..	31.9	..	34.8	..	7.0
60 Romania	3.5	3.6	..	..	..	23.2 [d]	..	47.1 [d]	..	17.3 [d]
61 Malaysia	5.1	8.0	18.0	28.0	34.0 [c]	29.3 [d]	34.9	33.2 [d]	19.9	36.5 [d]
62 Bosnia and Herzegovina	..	..	..	..	..	..	..	..	..	..
63 Mauritius	3.8	4.7	11.8	15.7	37.7	31.4	36.4	40.2	16.6	14.0
MEDIUM HUMAN DEVELOPMENT										
64 Libyan Arab Jamahiriya	..	..	..	..	..	..	..	..	..	..
65 Russian Federation	3.6	3.7	..	12.3	..	..	..	..	..	..
66 Macedonia, TFYR	..	3.4	..	..	..	..	..	..	..	..
67 Belarus	5.7	5.8	..	13.0	37.7 [c]	..	..	..	..	..
68 Dominica	..	..	..	..	..	..	..	..	..	..
69 Brazil	..	4.1	..	10.9	..	..	..	..	..	..
70 Colombia	2.4	4.9	14.3	11.7	..	42.2	..	29.1	..	12.9
71 Saint Lucia	..	5.0	..	..	48.1 [c]	47.7	..	33.2	..	..
72 Venezuela, RB	4.5	..	17.0	..	..	..	..	..	..	..
73 Albania	..	2.8 [d]	..	..	..	..	..	..	..	..
74 Thailand	3.1	4.2	20.0	40.0 [e]	56.2	..	21.6	..	14.6	..
75 Samoa (Western)	..	4.3 [d]	..	13.7 [d]	..	..	..	..	..	..
76 Saudi Arabia	5.8	..	17.8	..	..	..	..	..	..	..
77 Ukraine	6.2	4.6	18.9	18.3	..	..	..	..	..	..
78 Lebanon	..	2.6	..	12.7	..	..	..	..	..	26.4
79 Kazakhstan	3.9	2.4	19.1	..	..	..	..	..	..	..
80 Armenia	..	3.2 [d]	..	..	..	..	..	..	..	..
81 China	2.2	..	12.7	..	..	..	..	..	..	..
82 Peru	2.8	3.0	..	17.1	..	44.1	..	28.4	..	15.0
83 Ecuador	3.4	..	17.5	..	..	..	..	..	..	..
84 Philippines	3.0	3.2	10.5	17.2	..	59.5 [d]	..	24.6 [d]	..	13.7 [d]
85 Grenada	4.9	5.2	11.9	12.9	..	40.8 [d]	..	34.7 [d]	..	11.1 [d]
86 Jordan	8.0	..	19.1	..	..	..	..	..	..	..
87 Tunisia	6.0	8.1	14.3	..	..	36.7 [c, d]	..	43.9 [d]	..	19.4
88 Saint Vincent and the Grenadines	5.9	11.1	13.8	20.3	64.1	47.1	31.7	17.4	..	..
89 Suriname	..	..	..	..	59.0 [c]	..	15.2	..	9.1	..
90 Fiji	5.1	6.4	..	20.0	..	40.3	..	33.5	..	16.3
91 Paraguay	1.9	4.3	10.3	10.8	..	54.6	..	28.3	..	16.9
92 Turkey	2.4	3.7	..	..	59.2 [c]	..	29.2	..	-	..
93 Sri Lanka	3.2	..	8.4	..	..	..	..	..	..	..
94 Dominican Republic	..	1.1	..	6.3	..	66.5	..	10.6	..	..
95 Belize	4.6	5.1	18.5	18.1	60.3 [c]	55.3	..	28.2	..	13.2
96 Iran, Islamic Rep. of	4.1	4.8	22.4	17.9	..	24.7	..	35.5	..	14.5
97 Georgia	..	2.9	..	13.1	..	..	..	..	..	..
98 Maldives	7.0	8.1 [d]	16.0 [d]	..	..	..	..	..	..	..
99 Azerbaijan	7.7	3.3 [d]	24.7	19.2	..	25.3 [d]	..	52.6 [d]	..	5.7
100 Occupied Palestinian Territories	..	..	..	..	..	..	..	..	..	..
101 El Salvador	1.8	2.8 [d]	15.2	20.0	..	60.0 [d]	..	23.6 [d]	..	7.0
102 Algeria	5.1	..	22.0	..	..	..	..	..	..	..
103 Guyana	2.2	5.5	6.5	18.4	..	55.9	..	23.0	..	4.1
104 Jamaica	4.5	4.9	12.8	9.5	37.4	36.9 [d]	33.2	42.6 [d]	21.1	19.5 [d]
105 Turkmenistan	3.9	..	19.7	..	..	..	..	..	..	..
106 Cape Verde	3.6	7.3	19.9	20.7	..	44.2 [c]	..	26.3	..	11.6

Human development indicators

TABLE 11

	Public expenditure on education				Current public expenditure on education by level [a] (% of all levels)					
	As % of GDP		As % of total government expenditure		Pre-primary and primary		Secondary		Tertiary	
HDI rank	1991	2002–04 [b]	1991	2002–04 [b]	1991	2002–04 [b]	1991	2002–04 [b]	1991	2002–04 [b]
107 Syrian Arab Republic	3.9	..	14.2	..	..	..	..	..	..	..
108 Indonesia	1.0	0.9	..	9.0 [d]	..	39.3 [d]	..	41.6 [d]	..	19.2 [d]
109 Viet Nam	1.8	..	9.7	..	..	..	..	..	..	..
110 Kyrgyzstan	6.0	4.4 [d]	22.7	..	..	22.6 [d]	..	45.6 [d]	..	18.7
111 Egypt	3.9	..	..	..	..	..	..	..	..	..
112 Nicaragua	3.4	3.1 [d]	12.1	15.0	..	..	..	..	..	..
113 Uzbekistan	9.4	..	17.8	..	..	..	..	..	..	..
114 Moldova, Rep. of	5.3	4.9 [d]	21.6	21.4	..	37.4 [d]	..	52.0 [d]	..	10.6
115 Bolivia	2.4	6.4 [d]	..	18.1	..	49.3	..	25.3	..	22.6
116 Mongolia	11.5	5.6	22.7	..	..	43.3	..	31.9	..	19.4
117 Honduras	3.8	..	..	..	..	..	..	..	..	..
118 Guatemala	1.3	..	13.0	..	..	..	..	..	..	..
119 Vanuatu	4.6	9.6	18.8	..	..	..	..	..	..	..
120 Equatorial Guinea	..	0.6 [d]	..	..	..	..	..	..	..	..
121 South Africa	5.9	5.4	..	18.1	75.6 [c]	40.5	..	36.1	21.5	13.9
122 Tajikistan	..	2.8	24.4	16.9	..	29.5 [d]	..	49.7 [d]	..	5.6
123 Morocco	5.0	6.3	26.3	27.8	35.0 [c]	40.5 [c]	48.7	44.5	16.3	14.7
124 Gabon	..	..	..	..	..	..	..	..	..	..
125 Namibia	7.9	7.2	..	..	..	..	..	..	..	..
126 India	3.7	3.3	12.2	10.7	..	..	..	..	..	..
127 São Tomé and Principe	..	..	..	..	..	..	..	..	..	..
128 Solomon Islands	3.8	..	7.9	..	56.5	..	29.8	..	13.7	..
129 Cambodia	..	2.0	..	..	..	..	..	..	..	..
130 Myanmar	..	..	..	..	..	..	..	..	..	..
131 Botswana	6.2	..	17.0	..	..	..	..	..	..	..
132 Comoros	..	3.9	..	24.1	..	..	..	..	..	..
133 Lao People's Dem. Rep.	..	2.3	..	11.0 [d]	..	58.5	..	23.9	..	9.8
134 Pakistan	2.6	2.0	7.4	..	..	..	..	..	..	..
135 Bhutan	..	..	..	..	..	..	..	..	..	..
136 Ghana	..	..	..	..	..	39.2 [e]	..	37.4 [e]	..	18.0 [e]
137 Bangladesh	1.5	2.2	10.3	15.5	..	39.0 [c]	..	49.5	..	11.5
138 Nepal	2.0	3.4	8.5	14.9	..	53.4 [d]	..	27.5	..	12.4
139 Papua New Guinea	..	..	..	..	..	..	..	..	..	..
140 Congo	7.4	3.2 [d]	..	..	..	41.1 [d]	..	30.6 [d]	..	26.5 [d]
141 Sudan	6.0	..	2.8	..	..	..	..	..	..	..
142 Timor-Leste	..	..	..	..	..	..	..	..	..	..
143 Madagascar	2.5	3.3	..	18.2	..	..	..	..	..	..
144 Cameroon	3.2	3.8	19.6	17.2	..	..	..	..	..	10.9
145 Uganda	1.5	5.2 [d]	11.5	18.3 [d]	..	61.9 [c, d]	..	19.9 [d]	..	12.1 [d]
146 Swaziland	5.8	6.2	19.5	..	31.1 [c]	37.7 [d]	..	28.0 [d]	..	26.6
LOW HUMAN DEVELOPMENT										
147 Togo	..	2.6	..	13.6	..	..	..	..	..	17.3
148 Djibouti	3.5	6.1	11.1	20.5	53.4 [c]	..	21.1	..	13.9	..
149 Lesotho	6.2	9.0 [d]	12.2	..	..	50.8 [c, d]	..	25.6 [d]	..	19.7 [d]
150 Yemen	..	..	..	..	..	..	..	..	..	..
151 Zimbabwe	7.7	..	..	..	54.1 [c]	..	28.6	..	-	..
152 Kenya	6.7	7.0	17.0	29.2	49.1 [c]	64.1	..	25.2	..	10.8
153 Mauritania	4.6	3.4 [d]	13.9	..	..	54.3 [c]	..	32.6	..	4.3
154 Haiti	1.4	..	20.0	..	53.1	..	19.0	..	9.1	..
155 Gambia	3.8	1.9 [d]	14.6	8.9	41.6 [c]	..	21.2	..	17.8	..
156 Senegal	3.9	4.0	26.9	..	43.0 [c]	44.7	..	15.6	..	22.9
157 Eritrea	..	3.8	..	..	..	32.5 [c]	..	14.7	..	31.2
158 Rwanda	..	..	..	..	..	..	..	..	..	..
159 Nigeria	0.9	..	..	..	..	..	..	..	..	..

Human development indicators

TABLE 11

Commitment to education: public spending

		Public expenditure on education				Current public expenditure on education by level [a] (% of all levels)					
		As % of GDP		As % of total government expenditure		Pre-primary and primary		Secondary		Tertiary	
HDI rank		1991	2002–04 [b]	1991	2002–04 [b]	1991	2002–04 [b]	1991	2002–04 [b]	1991	2002–04 [b]
160	Guinea	2.0	..	25.7	..	..	..	..	..	..	..
161	Angola	..	..	..	..	..	..	..	..	..	..
162	Tanzania, U. Rep. of	2.8	..	11.4	..	..	..	..	..	..	..
163	Benin	..	3.3 [d]	..	..	..	..	..	..	..	..
164	Côte d'Ivoire	..	..	..	..	..	..	..	..	..	..
165	Zambia	2.8	2.8	7.1	14.8	..	63.5 [c]	..	13.4	..	18.2
166	Malawi	3.2	6.0	11.1	..	44.7 [c]	62.7 [c]	..	10.2	..	..
167	Congo, Dem. Rep. of the	..	..	..	..	..	..	..	..	..	..
168	Mozambique	..	..	..	..	..	..	..	..	..	..
169	Burundi	3.5	5.2	17.7	13.0	43.0 [c]	44.4	28.1	31.7	27.2	23.9
170	Ethiopia	3.4	4.6 [d]	9.4	..	53.9	..	28.1	..	..	..
171	Chad	1.6	..	..	..	47.1	..	20.9	..	8.2	..
172	Central African Republic	2.2	..	..	..	54.5 [c]	..	16.7	..	23.7	..
173	Guinea-Bissau	..	..	..	..	..	..	..	..	..	..
174	Burkina Faso	2.6	..	..	..	..	..	..	..	..	..
175	Mali	..	..	..	..	..	..	..	..	..	..
176	Sierra Leone	..	..	..	..	..	..	..	..	..	..
177	Niger	3.3	2.3	18.6	..	..	..	..	..	..	..

NOTES

In 2006 the United Nations Educational, Scientific and Cultural Organization (UNESCO) Institute for Statistics changed its convention for citing the reference year in which the academic or financial year ends—from 2003/04, for example, to 2004. Data for some countries may refer to national or UNESCO Institute for Statistics estimates. As a result of limitations in the data and metholodogical changes, comparisons of education expenditure data across countries and over time must be made with caution. For detailed notes on the data see www.uis.unesco.org.

a Expenditures by level may not sum to 100 as a result of rounding or the omission of the categories expenditures in postsecondary education and expenditures not allocated by level.

b Data refer to the most recent year available during the period specified.

c Data refer to primary school expenditure only.

d Data refer to a UNESCO Institute for Statistics estimate when national estimate is not available.

e Data refer to 2005.

SOURCES

Columns 1–5 and 7–10: UNESCO Institute for Statistics 2006b.

Column 6: calculated on the basis of data on public expenditure on education by pre-primary and primary levels from UNESCO Institute for Statistics 2006b.

TABLE 12

. . . to acquire knowledge . . .

Literacy and enrolment

HDI rank	Adult literacy rate [a] (% ages 15 and older)		MDG Youth literacy rate [a] (% ages 15–24)		MDG Net primary enrolment ratio [b] (%)		Net secondary enrolment ratio [b, c] (%)		MDG Children reaching grade 5 [d] (% of grade 1 students)		Tertiary students in science, engineering, manufacturing and construction (% of tertiary students)
	1990	2004	1990	2004	1991 [e]	2004 [e]	1991 [e]	2004 [e]	1991 [e]	2003 [e]	1999–2004 [e, f]
HIGH HUMAN DEVELOPMENT											
1 Norway	..	..	..	..	100	99	88	96	101	100	17
2 Iceland	..	..	..	..	101 [g]	99 [g]	..	86 [g]	..	100 [h]	17
3 Australia	..	..	..	..	99	96	79 [g]	85 [g]	99	86 [g]	23
4 Ireland	..	..	..	..	90	96	80	87	101	100	23 [i]
5 Sweden	..	..	..	..	100	99	85	98	102		30
6 Canada	..	..	..	..	98	99 [g, j]	89	94 [k]	97		20 [i]
7 Japan	..	..	..	..	100	100	97	100 [g]	100		20
8 United States	..	..	..	..	97	92	85	90	..	..	..
9 Switzerland	..	..	..	..	84	94	80	83	..	..	..
10 Netherlands	..	..	..	..	95	99	84	89	..	100	16
11 Finland	..	..	..	..	98 [g]	99	93	94	101	100	38
12 Luxembourg	..	..	..	..	..	91	..	79	..	92 [g, h]	..
13 Belgium	..	..	..	..	96	99	87	97 [g, l]	91		21
14 Austria	..	..	..	..	88 [g]	..	..	..	..	..	25
15 Denmark	..	..	..	..	98	100	87	92	94	100 [m]	19
16 France	..	..	..	..	101	99	..	96	96	98 [k]	..
17 Italy	97.7	98.4	99.8	99.8	103 [g]	99	..	92	..	96 [i]	24
18 United Kingdom	..	..	..	..	100 [g]	99	81	95	..	..	..
19 Spain	96.3	..	99.6	..	103	99	..	97	..	..	31
20 New Zealand	..	..	..	..	98	99	85	95	..	..	19
21 Germany	..	..	..	..	..	..	..	..	..	..	..
22 Hong Kong, China (SAR)	..	..	98.2	..	..	93 [n]	..	78 [n]	101	100	30 [i, n]
23 Israel	91.4	97.1	98.7	99.8	92 [g]	98	..	89	..	100	30
24 Greece	94.9	96.0	99.5	98.9	95	99	83	87	101		32
25 Singapore	88.8	92.5	99.0	99.5	..	..	..	..	..	..	..
26 Korea, Rep. of	..	..	99.8	..	104	100	86	88	99	100	41
27 Slovenia	99.6	..	99.8	..	96 [g]	98	..	95	..	..	22
28 Portugal	87.2	..	99.5	..	98	99	..	82 [l]	..	..	29
29 Cyprus	94.3	96.8	99.7	99.8	87	96 [n]	69	93 [n]	101	99	17
30 Czech Republic	..	..	..	..	87 [g]	..	..	..	..	98	30
31 Barbados	99.4	..	99.8	..	80 [g]	97	..	95	..	97	..
32 Malta	88.4	87.9 [o]	97.5	96.0 [o]	97	94	78	88	103	99 [h]	15
33 Kuwait	76.7	93.3	87.5	99.7	49 [g]	86 [g]	..	78 [g, h]	..	..	..
34 Brunei Darussalam	85.5	92.7	97.9	98.9	92	..	71	..	..	93 [m]	8
35 Hungary	99.1	..	99.7	..	91	89	75	91 [g]	98	..	19
36 Argentina	95.7	97.2	98.2	98.9	..	99 [l]	..	79	..	84 [h]	19
37 Poland	99.6	..	99.8	..	97	97	76	90	98	100	20
38 Chile	94.0	95.7	98.1	99.0	89	..	55	..	92	99	29
39 Bahrain	82.1	86.5	95.6	97.0	99	97	85	90	89	100	21
40 Estonia	99.8	99.8	99.8	99.8	100 [g]	94	..	90	..	99	22
41 Lithuania	99.3	99.6	99.8	99.7	..	89	..	93	..	..	26
42 Slovakia	..	..	..	..	..	..	..	..	..	..	26
43 Uruguay	96.5	..	98.7	..	91	..	..	..	97	88 [h]	..
44 Croatia	96.9	98.1	99.6	99.6	79	87 [l]	63 [g]	85 [l]	..	..	24
45 Latvia	99.8	99.7	99.8	99.8	92 [g]	..	..	..	..	..	17
46 Qatar	77.0	89.0	90.3	95.9	89	95	70	87	64	..	19
47 Seychelles	..	91.8	..	99.1	..	96 [n]	..	93 [n]	93	99 [h]	..
48 Costa Rica	93.9	94.9	97.4	97.6	87	..	38	..	84	92 [g]	23
49 United Arab Emirates	71.0	..	84.7	..	103	71	60	62	80	95	..
50 Cuba	95.1	99.8	99.3	100.0	93	96	70	87	92	98	..
51 Saint Kitts and Nevis	..	..	..	..	..	94 [n]	..	98 [n]	..	87 [m]	..
52 Bahamas	..	..	96.5	..	90 [g]	84	..	74	84		..
53 Mexico	87.3	91.0	95.2	97.6	98	98	44	64	80	93	33

TABLE 12

Literacy and enrolment

		Adult literacy rate [a] (% ages 15 and older)		MDG Youth literacy rate [a] (% ages 15–24)		MDG Net primary enrolment ratio [b] (%)		Net secondary enrolment ratio [b, c] (%)		MDG Children reaching grade 5 [d] (% of grade 1 students)		Tertiary students in science, engineering, manufacturing and construction (% of tertiary students)
HDI rank		1990	2004	1990	2004	1991 [e]	2004 [e]	1991 [e]	2004 [e]	1991 [e]	2003 [e]	1999–2004 [e, f]
54	Bulgaria	97.2	98.2	99.4	98.2	86	95	63	88	91	..	27
55	Tonga	..	98.9 [o]	..	99.3 [o]	..	96 [i]	..	68 [g]	..	92 [m]	..
56	Oman	54.7	81.4	85.6	97.3	69	78	..	75	97	98	14
57	Trinidad and Tobago	96.8	..	99.6	..	91	92 [n]	..	72 [g]	..	100 [n]	..
58	Panama	89.0	91.9	95.3	96.1	..	98	..	64	..	84 [g]	21
59	Antigua and Barbuda	..	..	..	..	..	..	..	..	..	..	..
60	Romania	97.1	97.3	99.3	97.8	81 [g]	92	..	81	..	..	26
61	Malaysia	80.7	88.7	94.8	97.2	..	93 [l]	..	76 [l]	97	98 [h]	40
62	Bosnia and Herzegovina	..	96.7	..	99.8	..	..	..	..	..	..	..
63	Mauritius	79.8	84.4	91.1	94.5	91	95	..	80 [g]	97	99 [i]	26
MEDIUM HUMAN DEVELOPMENT												
64	Libyan Arab Jamahiriya	68.1	..	91.0	..	96 [g]	..	..	..	..	..	31
65	Russian Federation	99.2	99.4	99.8	99.7	99 [g]	91 [g]	..	..	..	..	..
66	Macedonia, TFYR	..	96.1	..	98.7	94	92	..	81 [g, h]	..	..	..
67	Belarus	99.5	99.6 [o]	99.8	99.8 [o]	86 [g]	90	..	87	..	..	..
68	Dominica	..	..	..	..	..	88 [n]	..	90 [g]	75	84	..
69	Brazil	82.0	88.6	91.8	96.8	85	93 [l]	17	76 [l]	73	..	16
70	Colombia	88.4	92.8	94.9	98.0	69	83	34	55 [g]	76	77 [g]	32
71	Saint Lucia	..	..	..	..	95 [g]	98	..	71 [g]	96	90	..
72	Venezuela, RB	88.9	93.0	96.0	97.2	87	92	18	61	86	91	..
73	Albania	77.0	98.7	94.8	99.4	95 [g]	96 [l]	..	74 [l]	..	..	11
74	Thailand	92.4	92.6	98.1	98.0	76 [g]	..	..	..	..	..	..
75	Samoa (Western)	98.0	..	99.0	..	..	90 [g]	..	66 [g]	..	94 [m]	14
76	Saudi Arabia	66.2	79.4	85.4	95.9	59	59 [h]	31	52 [g]	83	94	14
77	Ukraine	99.4	99.4	99.8	99.8	80 [g]	82	..	84	..	..	..
78	Lebanon	80.3	..	92.1	..	73 [g]	93	..	..	..	98	26
79	Kazakhstan	98.8	99.5 [o]	99.8	99.8 [o]	89 [g]	93	..	92	..	..	..
80	Armenia	97.5	99.4	99.5	99.8	..	94	..	89	..	..	7 [i]
81	China	78.3	90.9	95.3	98.9	97	..	..	..	86	..	..
82	Peru	85.5	87.7	94.5	96.8	..	97	..	69	..	90	..
83	Ecuador	87.6	91.0	95.5	96.4	98 [g]	98 [g]	..	52	..	76 [g]	..
84	Philippines	91.7	92.6	97.3	95.1	96 [g]	94	..	61	..	75	25
85	Grenada	..	..	..	..	..	84 [n]	..	78 [g]	..	79 [h]	..
86	Jordan	81.5	89.9	96.7	99.1	94	91	..	81	..	99	27
87	Tunisia	59.1	74.3	84.1	94.3	94	97	..	67 [g, h]	86	97	..
88	Saint Vincent and the Grenadines	..	..	..	..	..	94 [g]	..	62	..	88 [g, h]	..
89	Suriname	..	89.6	..	94.9	81 [g]	92 [g, l]	..	63 [g, l]	..	..	19
90	Fiji	88.6	..	97.8	..	..	96	..	83 [g]	87	99	..
91	Paraguay	90.3	..	95.6	..	94	..	26	..	74	82 [h]	..
92	Turkey	77.9	87.4	92.7	95.6	89	89 [g]	42	..	98	95 [g]	..
93	Sri Lanka	88.7	90.7	95.1	95.6	..	97 [g]	..	..	92	..	..
94	Dominican Republic	79.4	87.0	87.5	94.2	57 [g]	86	..	49 [g]	..	59	..
95	Belize	89.1	..	96.0	..	94 [g]	95	31	71 [g]	67	91 [m]	9 [i]
96	Iran, Islamic Rep. of	63.2	77.0	86.3	..	92 [g]	89	..	78	90	88 [h]	38
97	Georgia	..	..	..	..	97 [g]	93	..	81	..	..	28
98	Maldives	94.8	96.3	98.1	98.2	..	90 [h]	..	51 [g, h]	..	..	..
99	Azerbaijan	..	98.8 [o]	..	99.9 [o]	89	84	..	77	..	..	..
100	Occupied Palestinian Territories	..	92.4	..	99.0	..	86	..	89	..	..	18
101	El Salvador	72.4	..	83.8	..	..	92 [g]	..	48 [g, l]	58	73 [g]	23
102	Algeria	52.9	69.9	77.3	90.1	89	97	53	66 [g]	95	96	18 [i]
103	Guyana	97.2	..	99.8	..	89	..	67	..	..	64 [g, j]	22
104	Jamaica	82.2	79.9 [o, p]	91.2	..	96	91	64	79	..	90 [h]	..
105	Turkmenistan	..	98.8 [o]	..	99.8 [o]	..	..	..	..	..	..	..
106	Cape Verde	63.8	..	81.5	..	91 [g]	92	..	55	..	91	..

TABLE 12

HDI rank		Adult literacy rate [a] (% ages 15 and older)		MDG Youth literacy rate [a] (% ages 15–24)		MDG Net primary enrolment ratio [b] (%)		Net secondary enrolment ratio [b, c] (%)		MDG Children reaching grade 5 [d] (% of grade 1 students)		Tertiary students in science, engineering, manufacturing and construction (% of tertiary students)
		1990	2004	1990	2004	1991 [e]	2004 [e]	1991 [e]	2004 [e]	1991 [e]	2003 [e]	1999–2004 [e, f]
107	Syrian Arab Republic	64.8	79.6	79.9	92.2	91	95 [h]	43	58	96	92 [j]	..
108	Indonesia	79.5	90.4	95.0	98.7	97	94	39	57	84	92	..
109	Viet Nam	90.4	90.3 [o]	94.1	93.9 [o]	90 [g]	93 [g, h]	..	65 [g, h]	..	87 [g, h]	..
110	Kyrgyzstan	..	98.7 [o]	..	99.7 [o]	92 [g]	90	..	..	..	..	14
111	Egypt	47.1	71.4	61.3	84.9	84 [g]	95 [g]	..	79 [g, h]	..	99 [g]	..
112	Nicaragua	62.7	76.7	68.2	86.2	73	88	..	41	44	59 [g]	..
113	Uzbekistan	98.7	..	99.6	..	78 [g]	..	..	..	..	..	..
114	Moldova, Rep. of	97.5	98.4	99.8	99.5	89 [g]	86 [n]	..	77 [n]	..	..	..
115	Bolivia	78.1	86.7	92.6	97.3	..	95 [g]	..	74 [g]	..	86 [g]	..
116	Mongolia	97.8	97.8	98.9	97.7	90 [g]	84	..	82	..	..	24
117	Honduras	68.1	80.0	79.7	88.9	89 [g]	91	21	..	..	..	23
118	Guatemala	61.0	69.1	73.4	82.2	..	93	..	34 [g]	..	78 [g]	19 [i]
119	Vanuatu	..	74.0 [o]	..	..	..	94	17	39 [g]	..	72 [k]	..
120	Equatorial Guinea	73.3	87.0	92.7	94.9	91 [g]	85 [h]	..	24 [g, j]	..	33 [g, j]	..
121	South Africa	81.2	82.4 [o]	88.5	93.9 [o]	90	89 [l]	45	62 [g, m]	..	84 [h]	19
122	Tajikistan	98.2	99.5	99.8	99.8	77 [g]	97	..	79	..	..	..
123	Morocco	38.7	52.3	55.3	70.5	56	86	..	35 [g, l]	75	76	18
124	Gabon	..	..	..	..	85 [g]	77 [g, j]	..	..	..	69 [g, h]	..
125	Namibia	74.9	85.0	87.4	92.3	..	74 [l]	..	37 [l]	62	88 [g, h]	12
126	India	49.3	61.0	64.3	76.4	..	90 [g]	..	..	..	79	22
127	São Tomé and Principe	..	..	..	..	..	98	..	26	..	66	..
128	Solomon Islands	..	..	..	..	..	80	..	26 [g, l]	88	..	..
129	Cambodia	62.0	73.6	73.5	83.4	69 [g]	98	..	26 [g]	..	60	19
130	Myanmar	80.7	89.9	88.2	94.5	98 [g]	87	..	37	..	69	42
131	Botswana	68.1	81.2	83.3	94.0	83	82 [g]	35	61 [g]	84	91 [g]	19
132	Comoros	53.8	..	56.7	..	57 [g]	55 [m, n]	..	..	..	63	11
133	Lao People's Dem. Rep.	56.5	68.7	70.1	78.5	63 [g]	84	..	37	..	63	11 [i]
134	Pakistan	35.4	49.9	47.4	65.5	33 [g]	66 [n]	..	..	..	70 [q]	..
135	Bhutan	..	..	..	..	..	..	..	..	..	91 [m]	..
136	Ghana	58.5	57.9	81.8	70.7	54 [g]	58	..	36 [g]	80	63 [h]	26
137	Bangladesh	34.2	..	42.0	..	..	94 [n]	..	48 [l]	..	65	13
138	Nepal	30.4	48.6	46.6	70.1	..	78 [l, n]	..	..	51	67 [g]	..
139	Papua New Guinea	56.6	57.3	68.6	66.7	..	..	..	..	69	68 [g, h]	..
140	Congo	67.1	..	92.5	..	79 [g]	..	..	..	60	66 [h]	11 [i]
141	Sudan	45.8	60.9 [r]	65.0	77.2 [r]	40 [g]	43 [g, m]	..	..	94	92	..
142	Timor-Leste	..	..	..	..	..	..	..	20 [g, j]	..	..	..
143	Madagascar	58.0	70.7	72.2	70.2	64 [g]	89	..	11 [g, k]	21	57	20
144	Cameroon	57.9	67.9	81.1	..	74 [g]	..	..	..	..	64 [g, h]	23 [n]
145	Uganda	56.1	66.8	70.1	76.6	..	..	..	15	36	64 [j]	..
146	Swaziland	71.6	79.6	85.1	88.4	77 [g]	77 [l]	31	29 [l]	77	77 [h]	9
LOW HUMAN DEVELOPMENT												
147	Togo	44.2	53.2	63.5	74.4	64	79	15	22 [g, m]	48	76	..
148	Djibouti	..	..	73.2	..	29	33	..	19 [g]	87	88 [g, j]	22
149	Lesotho	78.0	82.2	87.2	..	71	86	15	23	66	63	6 [i]
150	Yemen	32.7	..	50.0	..	51 [g]	75 [g]	..	34 [g, m]	..	73 [g]	..
151	Zimbabwe	80.7	..	93.9	..	..	82 [l]	..	34 [l]	76	70 [g, h]	..
152	Kenya	70.8	73.6	89.8	80.3	..	76	..	40 [g]	77	75 [n]	29
153	Mauritania	34.8	51.2	45.8	61.3	35 [g]	74	..	14 [g]	75	82	10 [g]
154	Haiti	39.7	..	54.8	..	22	..	..	..	..	..	..
155	Gambia	..	..	42.2	..	48 [g]	75 [g]	..	45 [g]	..	78	21
156	Senegal	28.4	39.3	40.1	49.1	43 [g]	66	..	15	85	78	37
157	Eritrea	..	..	60.9	..	16 [g]	48	..	24	..	80	..
158	Rwanda	53.3	64.9	72.7	77.6	66	73	7	..	60	46	..
159	Nigeria	48.7	..	73.6	..	58 [g]	60 [g]	..	27 [g]	89	36	..

Human development indicators

TABLE 12

Literacy and enrolment

HDI rank	Adult literacy rate[a] (% ages 15 and older) 1990	2004	MDG Youth literacy rate[a] (% ages 15–24) 1990	2004	MDG Net primary enrolment ratio[b] (%) 1991[e]	2004[e]	Net secondary enrolment ratio[b,c] (%) 1991[e]	2004[e]	MDG Children reaching grade 5[d] (% of grade 1 students) 1991[e]	2003[e]	Tertiary students in science, engineering, manufacturing and construction (% of tertiary students) 1999–2004[e,f]
160 Guinea	..	29.5	..	46.6	27 g	64	..	21 g	59	82	34
161 Angola	..	67.4	..	72.2	50 g	..	..	..	..	..	18
162 Tanzania, U. Rep. of	62.9	69.4	83.1	78.4	49	86	..	..	81 g	88	..
163 Benin	26.4	34.7	40.4	45.3	41 g	83	..	17 g,j	55	69	25
164 Côte d'Ivoire	38.5	48.7	52.6	60.7	45	56 l,n	..	20 g,h	73	88 g,m	..
165 Zambia	68.2	68.0 o	81.2	69.5 o	..	80	..	24 g	..	98 j	..
166 Malawi	51.8	64.1 o	63.2	76.0 o	48	95	..	25	64	44 j	33
167 Congo, Dem. Rep. of the	47.5	67.2	68.9	70.4	54	..	..	..	55	..	..
168 Mozambique	33.5	..	48.8	..	43	71	..	4	34	49 j	24
169 Burundi	37.0	59.3	51.6	73.3	53 g	57	..	..	62	63	10 i
170 Ethiopia	28.6	..	43.0	..	22 g	46	..	25 g	18	..	19
171 Chad	27.7	25.7	48.0	37.6	35 g	57 g,l	..	11 g,l	51 g	46 g	..
172 Central African Republic	33.2	48.6	52.1	58.5	52	..	..	..	23	..	..
173 Guinea-Bissau	..	..	44.1	..	38 g	45 g,j	..	9 g,j	..	..	..
174 Burkina Faso	..	21.8	..	31.2	29	40	..	10 g	70	76	..
175 Mali	18.8	19.0 o	27.6	24.2 o	21 g	46	5 g	..	70 g	79	..
176 Sierra Leone	..	35.1	..	47.6	43 g	..	..	..	..	..	8
177 Niger	11.4	28.7	17.0	36.5	22	39	5	7	62	74	..
Developing countries	68.8	78.9	83.0	87.4	..	..	..	..	..	..	..
Least developed countries	52.4	63.7	66.9	71.9	..	..	..	..	..	..	..
Arab States	49.8	69.9	66.4	85.3	..	..	..	..	..	..	..
East Asia and the Pacific	79.7	90.7	95.0	97.8	..	..	..	..	..	..	..
Latin America and the Caribbean	85.6	90.2	93.3	96.7	..	..	..	..	..	..	..
South Asia	49.1	60.9	62.7	75.1	..	..	..	..	..	..	..
Sub-Saharan Africa	55.5	63.3	70.7	71.1	..	..	..	..	..	..	..
Central and Eastern Europe and the CIS	98.7	99.2	99.7	99.6	..	..	..	..	..	..	..
OECD	..	..	..	..	..	..	..	..	..	..	..
High-income OECD	..	..	..	..	..	..	..	..	..	..	..
High human development	..	..	..	..	..	..	..	..	..	..	..
Medium human development	71.2	80.5	84.2	88.9	..	..	..	..	..	..	..
Low human development	48.1	57.9	65.1	65.9	..	..	..	..	..	..	..
High income	..	..	..	..	..	..	..	..	..	..	..
Middle income	81.0	89.9	93.5	96.9	..	..	..	..	..	..	..
Low income	51.6	62.3	65.9	75.2	..	..	..	..	..	..	..
World	..	..	..	..	..	..	..	..	..	..	..

NOTES

a Data for 1990 refer to estimates produced by the United Nations Educational, Scientific and Cultural Organization (UNESCO) Institute for Statistics based on data before 1990; data for 2004 refer to national literacy estimates from censuses or surveys conducted between 2000 and 2005, unless otherwise specified. Due to differences in methodology and timeliness of underlying data, comparisons across countries and over time should be made with caution. For more details, see www. uis.unesco.org.

b The net enrolment ratio is the ratio of enrolled children of the official age for the education level indicated to the total population of that age. Net enrolment ratios exceeding 100% reflect discrepancies between these two data sets.

c Enrolment ratios are based on the new International Standard Classification of Education, adopted in 1997 (UNESCO 1997), and so may not be strictly comparable with those for earlier years.

d Calculated on the basis of survival rates that may exceed 100% due to fluctuations in enrolment. Where such results are published, they should be interpreted as the country having a survival rate approaching 100%.

e In 2006 the UNESCO Institute for Statistics changed its convention for citing the reference year of education data to the calendar year in which the academic or financial year ends—from 2003/04, for example, to 2004. Data for some countries may refer to national or UNESCO Institute for Statistics estimates.

f Data refer to the most recent year available during the period specified.

g Preliminary UNESCO Institute for Statistics estimate, subject to further revision.

h Data refer to the 2002 school year.

i Figure should be treated with caution because the reported number of enrolled pupils in the "Not known or unspecified" category represents more than 10% of total enrolment.

j Data refer to the 2001 school year.

k Data refer to the 1999 school year.

l Data refer to the 2003 school year.

m Data refer to the 2000 school year.

n National estimates.

o Data refer to the most recent year available between 1995 and 1999.

p Data are based on a literacy assessment.

q Data refer to the 2004 school year.

r Estimates are based primarily on information for Northern Sudan.

SOURCES

Columns 1–4: UNESCO Institute for Statistics 2006a.
Columns 5–10: UNESCO Institute for Statistics 2006c.
Column 11: UNESCO Institute for Statistics 2006d.

Human development indicators

TABLE 13

... to acquire knowledge ...

Technology: diffusion and creation

HDI rank	MDG Telephone mainlines[a] (per 1,000 people)		MDG Cellular subscribers[a] (per 1,000 people)		MDG Internet users (per 1,000 people)		Patents granted to residents (per million people)	Receipts of royalties and licence fees (US$ per person)	Research and development (R&D) expenditures (% of GDP)	Researchers in R&D (per million people)
	1990	2004	1990	2004	1990	2004	2004	2004	2000–03[b]	1990–2003[b]
HIGH HUMAN DEVELOPMENT										
1 Norway	503	669	46	861	7	390	..	52.6	1.7	4,587
2 Iceland	512	652	39	998	0	772	14	5.8	3.1	6,807
3 Australia	456	541	11	818	6	646	26	23.6	1.6	3,670
4 Ireland	280	496	7	929	0	265	80	54.2	1.1	2,674
5 Sweden	683	708	54	1,034	6	756	275	384.0	4.0	5,416
6 Canada	550	..	21	469	4	626	35	94.5	1.9	3,597
7 Japan	441	460	7	716	(.)	587	874	122.7	3.1	5,287
8 United States	545	606	21	617	8	630	281	178.2	2.6	4,484
9 Switzerland	587	710	19	849	6	474	..	..	2.6	3,601
10 Netherlands	464	483	5	910	3	614	116	259.2	1.8	2,482
11 Finland	535	453	52	954	4	629	222	162.3	3.5	7,992
12 Luxembourg	481	..	2	..	0	597	..	355.7	1.8	4,301
13 Belgium	393	456	4	876	(.)	403	..	..	2.3	3,478
14 Austria	418	460	10	978	1	477	95	20.9	2.2	2,968
15 Denmark	566	643	29	956	1	696	28	..	2.5	5,016
16 France	495	561	5	738	1	414	156	84.1	2.2	3,213
17 Italy	394	451	5	1,090	(.)	501	..	13.3	1.2	1,213
18 United Kingdom	441	563	19	1,021	1	628	64	202.1	1.9	2,706
19 Spain	325	416	1	905	(.)	336	39	11.4	1.1	2,195
20 New Zealand	426	443	16	745	0	788	156	24.7	1.2	3,405
21 Germany	401	661	3	864	1	500	156	61.7	2.5	3,261
22 Hong Kong, China (SAR)	434	549	23	1,184	0	506	5	49.5 [c]	0.6	1,564
23 Israel	349	441	3	1,057	1	471	..	74.7	4.9	1,613
24 Greece	389	466	0	999	0	177	29	2.9	0.6	1,413
25 Singapore	346	440	17	910	0	571	75	52.4	2.2	4,745
26 Korea, Rep. of	310	542	2	761	(.)	657	738	37.6	2.6	3,187
27 Slovenia	211	..	0	951	0	476	115	6.0	1.5	2,543
28 Portugal	240	404	1	981	0	281	10	3.9	0.9	1,949
29 Cyprus	361	507	5	776	0	361	..	21.4	0.3	563
30 Czech Republic	157	338	0	1,054	0	470	29	5.6	1.3	1,594
31 Barbados	281	505	0	744	0	558	..	8.6	..	..
32 Malta	356	..	0	..	0	750	..	(.)	0.3	694
33 Kuwait	156	202	10	813	0	244	..	0.0	0.2	69
34 Brunei Darussalam	136	..	7	..	0	153	..	..	..	274
35 Hungary	96	354	(.)	863	0	267	15	54.5	0.9	1,472
36 Argentina	93	227	(.)	352	0	133	..	1.5	0.4	720
37 Poland	86	..	0	605	0	236	20	0.7	0.6	1,581
38 Chile	66	206	1	593	0	267	..	3.0	0.6	444
39 Bahrain	191	268	10	908	0	213	..	..	..	..
40 Estonia	204	329	0	931	0	497	4	3.0	0.8	2,523
41 Lithuania	211	239	0	996	0	282	18	0.2	0.7	2,136
42 Slovakia	135	232	0	794	0	423	7	9.2 [c]	0.6	1,984
43 Uruguay	134	291	0	174	0	198	1	0.0	0.3	366
44 Croatia	172	425	(.)	640	0	293	6	8.9	1.1	1,296
45 Latvia	232	273	0	664	0	350	38	3.5	0.4	1,434
46 Qatar	197	246	8	631	0	212	..	..	..	19
47 Seychelles	124	253	0	589	0	239	..	..	..	19
48 Costa Rica	92	316	0	217	0	235	..	0.1	0.4	368
49 United Arab Emirates	224	275	19	853	0	321	..	..	..	..
50 Cuba	32	68	0	7	0	13	4	..	0.6	537
51 Saint Kitts and Nevis	231	532	0	213	0	..	..	..	..	..
52 Bahamas	274	439	8	584	0	292	..	0.0 [c]	..	..
53 Mexico	64	174	1	370	0	135	2	0.9	0.4	268

Human development indicators

TABLE 13

Technology: diffusion and creation

HDI rank		MDG Telephone mainlines[a] (per 1,000 people)		MDG Cellular subscribers[a] (per 1,000 people)		MDG Internet users (per 1,000 people)		Patents granted to residents (per million people)	Receipts of royalties and licence fees (US$ per person)	Research and development (R&D) expenditures (% of GDP)	Researchers in R&D (per million people)
		1990	2004	1990	2004	1990	2004	2004	2004	2000–03[b]	1990–2003[b]
54	Bulgaria	250	357	0	609	0	283	11	0.9	0.5	1,263
55	Tonga	46	..	0	..	0	29	..	..	..	..
56	Oman	57	95	1	318	0	97	..	..	..	..
57	Trinidad and Tobago	136	247	0	498	0	123	..	..	0.1	399
58	Panama	90	118	0	270	0	94	..	0.0	0.3	97
59	Antigua and Barbuda	254	474	0	674	0	250	..	..	..	..
60	Romania	102	202	0	471	0	208	43	0.4	0.4	976
61	Malaysia	89	179	5	587	0	397	..	0.8 [c]	0.7	299
62	Bosnia and Herzegovina	..	..	0	..	0	58	(.)	..	..	..
63	Mauritius	53	287	2	413	0	146	..	0.1	0.4	201
MEDIUM HUMAN DEVELOPMENT											
64	Libyan Arab Jamahiriya	51	..	0	..	0	36	..	0.0	..	361
65	Russian Federation	140	..	0	517	0	111	133	1.6	1.3	3,319
66	Macedonia, TFYR	150	308	0	..	0	78	11	1.5	0.3	..
67	Belarus	154	329	0	249	0	163	76	0.2	0.6	1,871
68	Dominica	161	293	0	585	0	259	..	..	..	..
69	Brazil	63	230	(.)	357	0	120	..	0.6	1.0	344
70	Colombia	69	195	0	232	0	80	..	0.2	0.2	109
71	Saint Lucia	127	..	0	568	0	336	..	..	..	483
72	Venezuela, RB	75	128	(.)	322	0	89	..	0.0	0.3	236
73	Albania	12	90	0	64	0	24	..	1.7 [c]	..	..
74	Thailand	24	107	1	430	0	109	..	0.2	0.2	286
75	Samoa (Western)	25	..	0	..	0	33	..	..	..	..
76	Saudi Arabia	75	154	1	383	0	66	..	0.0	..	..
77	Ukraine	135	256	0	289	0	79	..	0.9	1.2	1,774
78	Lebanon	144	178	0	251	0	169	..	..	..	..
79	Kazakhstan	82	167	0	184	0	27	..	(.)	0.2	629
80	Armenia	158	192	0	67	0	50	48	..	0.3	1,537
81	China	6	241	(.)	258	0	73	..	0.2	1.3	663
82	Peru	26	74	(.)	148	0	117	(.)	0.1	0.1	226
83	Ecuador	48	124	0	348	0	48	..	0.0	0.1	50
84	Philippines	10	42	0	404	0	54	(.)	0.1	..	..
85	Grenada	162	309	2	410	0	76	..	..	..	..
86	Jordan	78	113	(.)	293	0	110	..	..	..	1,927
87	Tunisia	37	121	(.)	359	0	84	..	1.8	0.6	1,013
88	Saint Vincent and the Grenadines	120	161	0	481	0	68	..	..	0.2	179
89	Suriname	91	182	0	477	0	67	..	..	..	..
90	Fiji	59	..	0	..	0	73	..	..	..	..
91	Paraguay	27	50	0	294	0	25	..	32.2	0.1	79
92	Turkey	122	267	1	484	0	142	..	0.0	0.7	341
93	Sri Lanka	7	51	(.)	114	0	14	..	..	..	..
94	Dominican Republic	48	107	(.)	289	0	91	..	0.0	..	..
95	Belize	92	119	0	346	0	124	..	0.0	..	..
96	Iran, Islamic Rep. of	40	..	0	64	0	82	18	..	..	467
97	Georgia	99	151	0	186	0	39	..	1.7	0.3	2,600
98	Maldives	29	98	0	353	0	59	..	20.4	..	..
99	Azerbaijan	87	118	0	215	0	49	..	..	0.3	1,236
100	Occupied Palestinian Territories	..	102	0	278	0	46	..	..	..	..
101	El Salvador	24	131	0	271	0	87	..	(.)	..	47
102	Algeria	32	71	(.)	145	0	26	1	..	..	..
103	Guyana	22	137	0	192	0	193	..	44.9	..	..
104	Jamaica	44	189	0	832	0	403	..	3.7	0.1	..
105	Turkmenistan	60	..	0	..	0	8	..	..	..	..
106	Cape Verde	23	148	0	133	0	50	..	0.2 [c]	..	127

TABLE 13

HDI rank		MDG Telephone mainlines [a] (per 1,000 people)		MDG Cellular subscribers [a] (per 1,000 people)		MDG Internet users (per 1,000 people)		Patents granted to residents (per million people)	Receipts of royalties and licence fees (US$ per person)	Research and development (R&D) expenditures (% of GDP)	Researchers in R&D (per million people)
		1990	2004	1990	2004	1990	2004	2004	2004	2000–03 [b]	1990–2003 [b]
107	Syrian Arab Republic	39	143	0	126	0	43	..	..	..	29
108	Indonesia	6	46	(.)	138	0	67	..	1.0	..	..
109	Viet Nam	1	70	0	60	0	71	..	..	..	..
110	Kyrgyzstan	71	..	0	59	0	52	..	0.9	0.2	406
111	Egypt	29	130	(.)	105	0	54	..	1.4	0.2	..
112	Nicaragua	12	40	0	137	0	23	..	0.0	(.)	44
113	Uzbekistan	68	..	0	21	0	34	3	..	..	..
114	Moldova, Rep. of	106	205	0	187	0	96	57	0.5	..	172
115	Bolivia	27	69	0	200	0	39	..	0.2	0.3	120
116	Mongolia	32	..	0	..	0	80	32	..	0.3	681
117	Honduras	18	53	0	100	0	32	..	0.0	(.)	78
118	Guatemala	21	92	(.)	258	0	61	..	(.)	..	..
119	Vanuatu	17	33	0	51	0	36	..	..	..	..
120	Equatorial Guinea	4	..	0	113	0	10	..	..	..	..
121	South Africa	94	..	(.)	428	0	78	..	1.0	0.8	307
122	Tajikistan	45	..	0	..	0	1	2	0.2	..	..
123	Morocco	17	44	(.)	313	0	117	..	0.5	0.6	782
124	Gabon	22	28	0	359	0	29	..	..	..	..
125	Namibia	38	64	0	142	0	37	..	0.0 c	..	..
126	India	6	41	0	44	0	32	1	(.) c	0.8	119
127	São Tomé and Principe	19	..	0	..	0	131	..	..	..	..
128	Solomon Islands	15	..	0	..	0	6	..	..	..	..
129	Cambodia	(.)	..	0	..	0	3	..	..	..	..
130	Myanmar	2	8	0	2	0	1	..	0.0 c	..	..
131	Botswana	18	77	0	319	0	34	..	1.9 c	..	..
132	Comoros	8	..	0	..	0	14	..	..	..	..
133	Lao People's Dem.Rep.	2	13	0	35	0	4	..	..	..	..
134	Pakistan	8	30	(.)	33	0	13	..	0.1	0.2	86
135	Bhutan	3	33	0	20	0	22	..	..	..	..
136	Ghana	3	14	0	78	0	17	..	0.0	..	..
137	Bangladesh	2	6	0	31	0	2	..	(.)	..	..
138	Nepal	3	15	0	7	0	7	..	..	0.7	59
139	Papua New Guinea	7	12	0	7	0	29	..	..	..	..
140	Congo	6	4	0	99	0	9	..	..	..	30
141	Sudan	2	29	0	30	0	32	..	..	0.3	263
142	Timor-Leste	..	..	..	..	..	..	..	..	..	..
143	Madagascar	3	..	0	18	0	5	(.)	0.1 c	0.1	15
144	Cameroon	3	7	0	96	0	10	..	..	..	..
145	Uganda	2	3	0	42	0	7	..	0.2	0.8	24
146	Swaziland	18	..	0	101	0	32	..	(.)	..	..
LOW HUMAN DEVELOPMENT											
147	Togo	3	..	0	..	0	37	..	0.0 c	..	..
148	Djibouti	10	14	0	..	0	12	..	..	..	..
149	Lesotho	8	21	0	88	0	24	..	9.5	(.)	42
150	Yemen	10	39	0	53	0	9	..	..	..	..
151	Zimbabwe	12	25	0	31	0	63	..	..	..	..
152	Kenya	7	9	0	76	0	45	..	0.5	..	..
153	Mauritania	3	..	0	175	0	5	..	..	..	..
154	Haiti	7	17	0	48	0	59	..	0.0 c	..	..
155	Gambia	7	..	0	118	0	33	..	..	..	..
156	Senegal	6	..	0	90	0	42	..	0.0 c	..	..
157	Eritrea	..	9	0	5	0	12	..	..	..	..
158	Rwanda	1	3	0	16	0	4	..	0.0	..	..
159	Nigeria	3	8	0	71	0	14	..	..	..	..

Human development indicators

TABLE 13

Technology: diffusion and creation

HDI rank	MDG Telephone mainlines[a] (per 1,000 people)		MDG Cellular subscribers[a] (per 1,000 people)		MDG Internet users (per 1,000 people)		Patents granted to residents (per million people)	Receipts of royalties and licence fees (US$ per person)	Research and development (R&D) expenditures (% of GDP)	Researchers in R&D (per million people)
	1990	2004	1990	2004	1990	2004	2004	2004	2000–03[b]	1990–2003[b]
160 Guinea	2	..	0	..	0	5	..	0.0	..	251
161 Angola	7	6	0	48	0	11	..	14.6	..	..
162 Tanzania, U. Rep. of	3	..	0	44	0	9	..	..	..	..
163 Benin	3	9	0	..	0	12	..	(.)[c]	..	..
164 Côte d'Ivoire	6	13	0	86	0	17	..	0.0	..	..
165 Zambia	8	8	0	26	0	20	..	..	..	51
166 Malawi	3	7	0	18	0	4	..	..	..	..
167 Congo, Dem. Rep. of the	1	(.)	0	37	0	..	..	..	..	..
168 Mozambique	4	..	0	36	0	7	..	(.)	..	..
169 Burundi	1	..	0	..	0	3	..	0.0[c]	..	..
170 Ethiopia	2	..	0	3	0	2	..	(.)	..	..
171 Chad	1	1	0	13	0	6	..	..	..	..
172 Central African Republic	2	3	0	15	0	2	..	..	..	..
173 Guinea-Bissau	6	..	0	..	0	17	..	..	..	..
174 Burkina Faso	2	6	0	31	0	4	..	..	..	17
175 Mali	1	6	0	30	0	4	..	0.0[c]	..	..
176 Sierra Leone	3	5	0	22	0	2	..	0.2	..	..
177 Niger	1	2	0	11	0	2	..	..	..	..
Developing countries	21	122	(.)	175	(.)	64	..	0.7	1.1	416
Least developed countries	3	9	0	28	0	8	..	0.4		
Arab States	34	91	(.)	169	0	55	..	0.4		
East Asia and the Pacific	18	199	(.)	262	(.)	91	..	1.3	1.7	740
Latin America and the Caribbean	61	179	(.)	319	0	115	..	1.0	0.6	306
South Asia	7	35	(.)	42	0	29	..	(.)	0.7	132
Sub-Saharan Africa	10	..	(.)	77	0	19	..	0.5		
Central and Eastern Europe and the CIS	125	..	(.)	455	0	139	75	2.5	1.0	2,204
OECD	390	491	10	714	3	484	266	92.4	2.5	3,108
High-income OECD	462	551	12	770	3	563	318	115.6	2.5	3,748
High human development	369	469	10	703	2	470	250	85.1	2.5	2,968
Medium human development	24	128	(.)	184	0	59	..	0.3	0.9	523
Low human development	4	9	0	45	0	15	..	0.5		
High income	450	536	12	766	3	545	..	109.3	2.5	3,702
Middle income	40	192	(.)	294	0	92	..	0.8	0.9	772
Low income	6	30	(.)	42	0	24	..	(.)	0.7	
World	98	190	2	276	1	138	..	17.3	2.4	1,153

NOTES

a Telephone mainlines and cellular subscribers combined form an indicator for Millennium Development Goal 8; see *Index to Millennium Development Goal Indicators in the indicator tables.*

b Data refer to the most recent year available during the period specified.

c Data refer to 2003.

SOURCES

Columns 1–6, 9 and 10: World Bank 2006; aggregates calculated for the Human Development Report Office by the World Bank.

Column 7: calculated on the basis of data on patents from WIPO 2006 and data on population from UN 2005b.

Column 8: calculated on the basis of data on royalties and license fees from World Bank 2006 and data on population from UN 2005b.

TABLE 14

... to have access to the resources needed for a decent standard of living ...

Economic performance

		GDP		GDP per capita		GDP per capita				Average annual change in consumer price index	
		US$ billions	PPP US$ billions	US$	PPP US$	Annual growth rate (%)		Highest value during 1975–2004 (PPP US$)	Year of highest value	(%)	
HDI rank		2004	2004	2004	2004	1975–2004	1990–2004			1990–2004	2003–04
HIGH HUMAN DEVELOPMENT											
1	Norway	250.1	176.5	54,465	38,454	2.6	2.5	38,454	2004	2.2	0.5
2	Iceland	12.2	9.7	41,893	33,051	1.7	2.0	33,051	2004	3.2	2.8
3	Australia	637.3	610.0	31,690	30,331	2.1	2.5	30,747	1997	2.4	2.3
4	Ireland	181.6	158.0	44,644	38,827	5.2	7.3	38,827	2004	2.8	2.2
5	Sweden	346.4	265.6	38,525	29,541	1.7	1.8	29,541	2004	1.7	0.4
6	Canada	978.0	999.6	30,586	31,263	1.6	2.1	31,263	2004	1.9	1.8
7	Japan	4,622.8	3,737.3	36,182	29,251	2.3	0.8	29,251	2004	0.3	(.)
8	United States	11,711.8	11,651.1 [a]	39,883	39,676 [a]	2.0	1.9	39,676	2004	2.6	2.7
9	Switzerland	357.5	244.1	48,385	33,040	1.0	0.2	34,304	2002	1.3	0.8
10	Netherlands	579.0	517.6	35,560	31,789	1.9	2.1	31,899	2002	2.6	1.3
11	Finland	185.9	156.6	35,562	29,951	2.0	2.2	29,951	2004	1.6	0.2
12	Luxembourg	31.9	31.7	70,295	69,961	4.1	5.4	69,961	2004	2.0	2.2
13	Belgium	352.3	324.1	33,807	31,096	1.8	1.7	31,096	2004	1.9	2.1
14	Austria	292.3	263.8	35,766	32,276	2.1	2.0	32,276	2004	2.0	2.1
15	Denmark	241.4	172.5	44,673	31,914	1.6	1.7	31,914	2004	2.2	1.2
16	France	2,046.6	1,769.2	33,896	29,300	1.8	1.7	29,300	2004	1.6	2.1
17	Italy	1,677.8	1,622.4	29,143	28,180	2.0	1.3	28,180	2004	3.2	2.2
18	United Kingdom	2,124.4	1,845.2	35,485	30,821	2.1	2.2	30,821	2004	2.7	3.0
19	Spain	1,039.9	1,069.3	24,360	25,047	2.2	2.3	25,047	2004	3.4	3.0
20	New Zealand	98.9	95.1	24,364	23,413	1.2	2.1	23,413	2004	1.9	2.3
21	Germany	2,740.6	2,335.5	33,212	28,303	2.1	1.5	28,303	2004	1.7	1.7
22	Hong Kong, China (SAR)	163.0	212.1	23,684	30,822	4.1	2.0	30,822	2004	3.0	−0.4
23	Israel	116.9	165.7	17,194	24,382	1.9	1.6	25,959	2000	7.1	−0.4
24	Greece	205.2	245.5	18,560	22,205	1.2	2.6	22,205	2004	6.8	2.9
25	Singapore	106.8	119.1	25,191	28,077	4.7	3.8	28,077	2004	1.3	1.7
26	Korea, Rep. of	679.7	985.6	14,136	20,499	6.0	4.5	20,499	2004	4.4	3.6
27	Slovenia	32.2	41.8	16,115	20,939	..	3.6	20,939 [b]	2004	9.7	3.6
28	Portugal	167.7	206.1	15,970	19,629	2.7	2.1	20,117	2001	3.9	2.4
29	Cyprus	15.4	18.8	18,668	22,805	4.5	3.0	22,805	2004	3.3	2.3
30	Czech Republic	107.0	198.3	10,475	19,408	..	2.7	19,408 [b]	2004	5.6	2.8
31	Barbados	2.8	..	10,401	..	..	..	..	..	2.2	1.4
32	Malta	5.3	7.6	13,256	18,879	4.6	3.6	19,864	2000	2.8	2.8
33	Kuwait	55.7	47.7 [c]	22,654	19,384 [c]	−0.8	−0.4	30,205 [b]	1975	1.8	1.2
34	Brunei Darussalam	..	..	..	..	..	..	..	..	..	..
35	Hungary	100.7	169.9	9,962	16,814	1.4	3.1	16,814	2004	15.9	6.8
36	Argentina	153.0	510.3	3,988	13,298	0.4	1.3	14,097	1998	7.1	4.4
37	Poland	242.3	495.4	6,346	12,974	..	4.0	12,974 [b]	2004	17.5	3.6
38	Chile	94.1	175.3	5,836	10,874	3.9	3.7	10,874	2004	6.7	1.1
39	Bahrain	11.0	14.9	15,384	20,758	1.2	2.2	20,758 [b]	2004	0.4	..
40	Estonia	11.2	19.6	8,331	14,555	2.1	4.3	14,555 [b]	2004	13.3	3.0
41	Lithuania	22.3	45.0	6,480	13,107	..	1.4	13,107 [b]	2004	16.7	1.2
42	Slovakia	41.1	78.7	7,635	14,623	0.9	2.7	14,623 [b]	2004	8.1	7.5
43	Uruguay	13.2	32.4	3,842	9,421	1.1	0.8	10,126	1998	23.9	9.2
44	Croatia	34.3	54.2	7,724	12,191	..	2.5	12,191 [b]	2004	19.7	2.1
45	Latvia	13.6	27.0	5,868	11,653	0.3	2.8	11,653	2004	17.0	6.2
46	Qatar	20.4 [d]	..	27,857 [d]	..	..	..	..	..	2.6	6.8
47	Seychelles	0.7	1.4	8,411	16,652	2.8	2.1	19,539	2000	2.5	3.8
48	Costa Rica	18.5	40.3 [c]	4,349	9,481 [c]	1.3	2.5	9,820	1999	13.7	12.3
49	United Arab Emirates	104.2	103.9 [c]	24,121	24,056 [c]	−2.8	−0.5	48,529	1975	..	..
50	Cuba	..	..	..	..	..	..	..	..	..	..
51	Saint Kitts and Nevis	0.4	0.6 [d]	8,447	12,702 [d]	5.6	4.0	12,702 [b]	2003	3.1	2.3
52	Bahamas	5.3 [d]	5.5 [e]	16,728 [d]	17,843 [e]	1.0	0.2	18,726 [b]	1989	2.0	0.5
53	Mexico	676.5	1,017.5	6,518	9,803	0.9	1.3	9,843	2000	15.7	4.7

Human development indicators

TABLE 14

Economic performance

		GDP		GDP per capita		GDP per capita				Average annual change in consumer price index (%)	
						Annual growth rate (%)		Highest value during 1975–2004	Year of highest value		
HDI rank		US$ billions 2004	PPP US$ billions 2004	US$ 2004	PPP US$ 2004	1975–2004	1990–2004	(PPP US$)		1990–2004	2003–04
54	Bulgaria	24.1	62.7	3,109	8,078	0.6	0.7	8,078 b	2004	75.1	6.3
55	Tonga	0.2	0.8 c	2,084	7,870 c	2.0	2.1	7,870 b	2004	4.8	11.0
56	Oman	24.3	38.7	9,584	15,259	2.3	1.9	15,259	2004	0.1	0.4
57	Trinidad and Tobago	12.5	15.9	9,640	12,182	0.3	3.3	12,182	2004	5.1	3.7
58	Panama	13.7	23.1	4,325	7,278	1.1	2.2	7,278	2004	1.1	0.4
59	Antigua and Barbuda	0.9	1.0	10,794	12,586	3.9	1.5	12,586 b	2004	..	..
60	Romania	73.2	183.9	3,374	8,480	..	1.4	8,480 b	2004	72.3	11.9
61	Malaysia	118.3	255.8	4,753	10,276	4.1	3.5	10,276	2004	3.0	1.5
62	Bosnia and Herzegovina	8.5	27.5	2,183	7,032	..	12.0	7,032 b	2004	..	..
63	Mauritius	6.0	14.8	4,889	12,027	4.4	3.9	12,027 b	2004	6.3	4.7
MEDIUM HUMAN DEVELOPMENT											
64	Libyan Arab Jamahiriya	29.1	..	5,073	..	..	..	..	..	1.9	−2.2
65	Russian Federation	581.4	1,424.4	4,042	9,902	−1.2	−0.6	11,407 b	1989	59.4	10.9
66	Macedonia, TFYR	5.4	13.4	2,637	6,610	..	−0.4	7,607 b	1990	6.3	−0.4
67	Belarus	22.9	68.5	2,330	6,970	..	1.6	6,970 b	2004	163.7	18.1
68	Dominica	0.3	0.4	3,794	5,643	3.4	1.4	6,454 b	2000	1.6	2.3
69	Brazil	604.0	1,507.1	3,284	8,195	0.7	1.2	8,195	2004	98.3	6.6
70	Colombia	97.7	325.9 c	2,176	7,256 c	1.4	0.5	7,256	2004	16.1	5.9
71	Saint Lucia	0.8	1.0	4,663	6,324	3.7	0.4	6,324 b	2004	2.5	4.7
72	Venezuela, RB	110.1	157.9	4,214	6,043	−0.9	−1.2	8,255	1977	39.3	21.8
73	Albania	7.6	15.5	2,439	4,978	1.3	4.8	4,978 b	2004	17.3	2.3
74	Thailand	161.7	515.3	2,539	8,090	5.0	2.6	8,090	2004	3.9	2.8
75	Samoa (Western)	0.4	1.0	2,042	5,613	1.5	4.9	5,640 b	2002	3.8	16.3
76	Saudi Arabia	250.6	331.1 c	10,462	13,825 c	−2.3	−0.1	25,314	1977	0.5	0.3
77	Ukraine	64.8	303.4	1,366	6,394	−4.5	−3.2	9,959 b	1989	73.3	9.0
78	Lebanon	21.8	20.7	6,149	5,837	5.0	3.7	5,837 b	2004	..	..
79	Kazakhstan	40.7	111.6	2,717	7,440	..	1.7	7,440 b	2004	33.6	6.9
80	Armenia	3.1	12.4	1,017	4,101	..	2.7	4,101 b	2004	31.4	8.1
81	China	1,931.7	7,642.3 f	1,490	5,896 f	8.4	8.9	5,896	2004	5.5	4.0
82	Peru	68.6	156.5	2,490	5,678	−0.5	2.1	5,999	1981	16.6	3.7
83	Ecuador	30.3	51.7	2,322	3,963	0.3	0.2	3,963	2004	36.0	2.7
84	Philippines	84.6	376.6	1,036	4,614	(.)	0.9	4,689	1982	6.7	6.0
85	Grenada	0.4	0.8	4,135	8,021	2.9	3.1	8,241 b	2003	2.0	..
86	Jordan	11.5	25.5	2,117	4,688	0.5	0.5	5,339	1987	2.8	3.4
87	Tunisia	28.2	77.2	2,838	7,768	2.3	3.2	7,768	2004	3.8	3.6
88	Saint Vincent and the Grenadines	0.4	0.8	3,412	6,398	3.5	1.6	6,398	2004	1.8	2.9
89	Suriname	1.1	..	2,484	..	..	..	..	..	67.7	..
90	Fiji	2.6	5.1	3,125	6,066	1.0	1.4	6,066 b	2004	3.1	2.8
91	Paraguay	7.3	29.0 c	1,220	4,813 c	0.4	−0.8	5,670	1981	11.5	4.3
92	Turkey	302.8	556.1	4,221	7,753	1.8	1.6	7,753	2004	68.4	8.6
93	Sri Lanka	20.1	85.2	1,033	4,390	3.3	3.8	4,390	2004	9.5	7.6
94	Dominican Republic	18.7	65.3 c	2,130	7,449 c	2.3	4.2	7,449	2004	9.8	51.5
95	Belize	1.1	1.9	3,870	6,747	3.2	2.6	6,895	2002	1.7	3.1
96	Iran, Islamic Rep. of	163.4	504.2	2,439	7,525	−0.1	2.3	8,679	1976	22.0	14.8
97	Georgia	5.2	12.8	1,151	2,844	−4.2	−1.0	6,514	1985	13.9	5.7
98	Maldives	0.8	..	2,345	..	..	..	..	..	4.6	6.4
99	Azerbaijan	8.5	34.5	1,026	4,153	..	5.5	4,153 b	2004	76.8	6.7
100	Occupied Palestinian Territories	3.5 d	..	1,026 d	..	..	..	..	..	..	..
101	El Salvador	15.8	34.1 c	2,340	5,041 c	0.2	1.8	5,544	1978	6.2	4.5
102	Algeria	84.6	213.7 c	2,616	6,603 c	0.1	0.9	6,603	2004	11.6	3.6
103	Guyana	0.8	3.3 c	1,047	4,439 c	0.8	1.5	4,624	1997	5.6	4.7
104	Jamaica	8.9	11.0	3,352	4,163	0.6	−0.1	4,270	1991	17.3	13.6
105	Turkmenistan	6.2	20.9 g	1,294	4,584 g	..	−4.4	6,585 b	1988	..	..
106	Cape Verde	0.9	2.8 c	1,915	5,727 c	3.0	3.5	5,727 b	2004	4.2	−1.9

TABLE 14

	GDP		GDP per capita		GDP per capita				Average annual change in consumer price index	
					Annual growth rate (%)		Highest value during 1975–2004	Year of highest value	(%)	
HDI rank	US$ billions 2004	PPP US$ billions 2004	US$ 2004	PPP US$ 2004	1975–2004	1990–2004	(PPP US$)		1990–2004	2003–04
107 Syrian Arab Republic	24.0	67.1	1,293	3,610	1.1	1.5	3,772	1998	4.9	..
108 Indonesia	257.6	785.2	1,184	3,609	4.1	1.8	3,609	2004	13.5	6.2
109 Viet Nam	45.2	225.5	550	2,745	5.6	5.5	2,745 [b]	2004	3.0	7.8
110 Kyrgyzstan	2.2	9.9	433	1,935	−2.3	−1.3	2,658 [b]	1990	14.7	4.1
111 Egypt	78.8	305.9	1,085	4,211	2.6	2.5	4,211	2004	6.8	11.3
112 Nicaragua	4.6	19.5 [c]	847	3,634 [c]	−2.3	0.1	7,429	1977	20.4	8.4
113 Uzbekistan	12.0	49.0	456	1,869	..	1.3	1,869 [b]	2004	..	..
114 Moldova, Rep. of	2.6	7.3	615	1,729	−6.1	−5.3	4,168 [b]	1989	17.0	12.5
115 Bolivia	8.8	24.5	974	2,720	(.)	1.2	2,763	1977	6.6	4.4
116 Mongolia	1.6	5.2	641	2,056	0.9	2.4	2,056 [b]	2004	26.3	8.2
117 Honduras	7.4	20.3 [c]	1,046	2,876 [c]	0.2	0.2	2,933	1979	15.7	8.1
118 Guatemala	27.5	53.0 [c]	2,233	4,313 [c]	0.4	1.3	4,327	2002	8.8	7.4
119 Vanuatu	0.3	0.6 [c]	1,526	3,051 [c]	−0.2	−0.2	3,978 [b]	1984	2.7	1.4
120 Equatorial Guinea	3.2	9.4 [c, g]	6,572	20,510 [c, g]	17.0	30.4	20,510 [b]	2001	..	..
121 South Africa	212.8	509.3 [c]	4,675	11,192 [c]	−0.5	0.6	12,038	1981	7.7	1.4
122 Tajikistan	2.1	7.7	322	1,202	−6.8	−4.8	2,851 [b]	1988	..	..
123 Morocco	50.0	128.5	1,678	4,309	1.4	1.1	4,309	2004	2.9	1.0
124 Gabon	7.2	9.0	5,306	6,623	−1.1	−0.1	12,107	1976	3.3	0.4
125 Namibia	5.7	14.9 [c]	2,843	7,418 [c]	−0.8	1.3	8,939 [b]	1980	..	4.1
126 India	691.2	3,389.7 [c]	640	3,139 [c]	3.4	4.0	3,139	2004	7.5	3.8
127 São Tomé and Principe	0.1	..	407	..	..	..	..	..	..	..
128 Solomon Islands	0.3	0.8 [c]	554	1,814 [c]	1.0	−2.7	2,778	1996	9.8	7.1
129 Cambodia	4.9	33.4 [c]	354	2,423 [c]	..	5.0	2,423 [b]	2004	4.0	3.9
130 Myanmar	..	..	..	..	..	..	..	..	25.7	4.5
131 Botswana	9.0	17.6	5,073	9,945	5.7	4.2	9,945	2004	9.4	6.9
132 Comoros	0.4	1.1 [c]	623	1,943 [c]	−0.7	−0.5	2,263 [b]	1985	..	..
133 Lao People's Dem. Rep.	2.5	11.3	423	1,954	3.6	4.2	1,954 [b]	2004	29.0	10.5
134 Pakistan	96.1	338.4	632	2,225	2.9	1.6	2,225	2004	7.7	7.4
135 Bhutan	0.7	..	751	..	..	..	..	..	7.3	4.6
136 Ghana	8.9	48.5 [c]	409	2,240 [c]	0.6	1.9	2,240	2004	26.3	12.6
137 Bangladesh	56.6	260.4	406	1,870	1.7	2.5	1,870	2004	4.9	3.2
138 Nepal	6.7	39.6	252	1,490	2.0	2.1	1,490	2004	7.0	2.8
139 Papua New Guinea	3.9	14.7 [c]	677	2,543 [c]	0.6	0.5	2,891	1994	10.3	2.1
140 Congo	4.3	3.8	1,118	978	1.2	−0.2	1,355	1996	6.7	2.4
141 Sudan	21.1	69.2 [c]	594	1,949 [c]	1.6	3.4	1,949	2004	46.1	8.5
142 Timor-Leste	0.3	..	367	..	..	..	..	..	..	..
143 Madagascar	4.4	15.5	241	857	−1.6	−1.1	1,356	1975	15.1	13.8
144 Cameroon	14.4	34.9	897	2,174	−0.6	0.5	2,913	1986	5.5	..
145 Uganda	6.8	41.1 [c]	245	1,478 [c]	2.5	3.5	1,478 [b]	2004	7.4	3.3
146 Swaziland	2.4	6.3	2,140	5,638	2.1	2.1	5,638	2004	9.2	..
LOW HUMAN DEVELOPMENT										
147 Togo	2.1	9.2 [c]	344	1,536 [c]	−1.1	(.)	2,218	1980	6.1	0.4
148 Djibouti	0.7	1.6 [c]	851	1,993 [c]	..	−1.9	2,413 [b]	1995	..	..
149 Lesotho	1.3	4.7 [c]	730	2,619 [c]	4.7	4.5	2,619	2004	8.7	..
150 Yemen	12.8	17.9	631	879	..	1.7	879 [b]	2004	20.8	..
151 Zimbabwe	4.7	26.7	363	2,065	−0.3	−1.9	3,224	1998	36.1	..
152 Kenya	16.1	38.1	481	1,140	(.)	−0.6	1,247	1990	12.0	11.6
153 Mauritania	1.5	5.8 [c]	515	1,940 [c]	0.2	1.2	1,967	2001	5.6	10.4
154 Haiti	3.5	15.7 [c, d]	420	1,892 [c, d]	−2.3	−2.2	3,423	1980	19.7	22.8
155 Gambia	0.4	2.9 [c]	281	1,991 [c]	(.)	0.2	2,137	1986	4.8	14.2
156 Senegal	7.8	19.5	683	1,713	−0.1	0.9	1,725	1976	3.9	0.5
157 Eritrea	0.9	4.1 [c]	219	977 [c]	..	0.6	1,246 [b]	1997	..	..
158 Rwanda	1.8	11.2 [c]	208	1,263 [c]	−0.4	−0.1	1,451	1983	11.7	12.0
159 Nigeria	72.1	148.6	560	1,154	0.2	0.8	1,154	2004	24.5	15.0

Human development indicators

TABLE 14

Economic performance

	GDP		GDP per capita		GDP per capita				Average annual change in consumer price index	
	US$ billions	PPP US$ billions	US$	PPP US$	Annual growth rate (%)		Highest value during 1975–2004	Year of highest value	(%)	
HDI rank	2004	2004	2004	2004	1975–2004	1990–2004	(PPP US$)		1990–2004	2003–04
160 Guinea	3.9	20.1	421	2,180	0.7	1.0	2,197 b	2002	..	..
161 Angola	19.5	33.8 c	1,258	2,180 c	−0.7	−1.2	2,764 b	1992	446.2	37.3
162 Tanzania, U. Rep. of	10.9	25.4	288	674	0.8	1.1	674 b	2004	14.9	(.)
163 Benin	4.1	8.9	498	1,091	0.4	1.4	1,099	2003	6.0	0.9
164 Côte d'Ivoire	15.5	27.7	866	1,551	−2.1	−1.1	2,977	1978	5.6	1.4
165 Zambia	5.4	10.8	471	943	−2.0	−1.1	1,557	1976	42.4	18.0
166 Malawi	1.9	8.1	149	646	−0.4	0.9	733	1979	29.7	11.4
167 Congo, Dem. Rep. of the	6.6	39.4 c	119	705 c	−4.8	−6.0	2,469	1975	496.4	4.1
168 Mozambique	6.1	24.0 c	313	1,237 c	2.6	4.2	1,237 b	2004	23.4	12.7
169 Burundi	0.7	4.9 c	90	677 c	−0.8	−2.5	933	1991	13.9	12.6
170 Ethiopia	8.0	52.9 c	114	756 c	−0.2	1.5	776 b	1983	4.0	3.3
171 Chad	4.2	19.7 c	447	2,090 c	0.7	2.1	2,090	2004	5.6	−5.4
172 Central African Republic	1.3	4.4 c	328	1,094 c	−1.5	−0.6	1,761	1977	4.1	−2.1
173 Guinea-Bissau	0.3	1.1 c	182	722 c	−0.3	−2.6	1,106	1997	22.1	0.9
174 Burkina Faso	4.8	15.0 c	376	1,169 c	0.9	1.3	1,169	2004	4.3	−0.4
175 Mali	4.9	13.1	371	998	0.2	2.5	998	2004	4.0	−3.1
176 Sierra Leone	1.1	3.0	202	561	−3.1	−5.5	1,151	1982	20.9	14.2
177 Niger	3.1	10.5 c	228	779 c	−1.8	−0.7	1,322	1979	4.6	0.3
Developing countries	8,346.5 T	24,127.9 T	1,685	4,775	2.4	3.0	..	..	..	..
Least developed countries	257.3 T	990.7 T	355	1,350	0.6	1.6	..	..	..	..
Arab States	852.2 T	1,755.0 T	3,054	5,680	0.3	1.3	..	..	..	..
East Asia and the Pacific	3,608.4 T	11,327.5 T	1,921	5,872	6.1	5.8	..	..	..	..
Latin America and the Caribbean	2,028.0 T	4,350.2 T	3,755	7,964	0.6	1.1	..	..	..	..
South Asia	1,041.3 T	4,650.6 T	697	3,072	2.5	3.3	..	..	..	..
Sub-Saharan Africa	498.5 T	1,327.5 T	731	1,946	−0.6	0.3	..	..	..	..
Central and Eastern Europe and the CIS	1,499.1 T	3,545.0 T	3,722	8,802	..	0.9	..	..	..	..
OECD	33,031.8 T	32,007.9 T	28,453	27,571	2.0	1.8	..	..	..	..
High-income OECD	31,561.5 T	29,492.0 T	34,249	32,003	2.2	1.9	..	..	..	..
High human development	34,046.5 T	33,777.4 T	26,999	26,568	2.0	1.8	..	..	..	..
Medium human development	6,520.2 T	21,564.7 T	1,494	4,901	2.2	2.9	..	..	..	..
Low human development	227.8 T	630.0 T	402	1,113	−0.7	0.2	..	..	..	..
High income	32,590.4 T	30,746.4 T	33,266	31,331	2.1	1.8	..	..	..	..
Middle income	7,155.3 T	20,386.4 T	2,388	6,756	2.0	2.8	..	..	..	..
Low income	1,236.6 T	5,381.4 T	538	2,297	2.0	2.7	..	..	..	..
World	40,850.4 T	55,970.3 T	6,588	8,833	1.4	1.4	..	..	..	..

NOTES

a In theory, for the United States the value of GDP in purchasing power parity (PPP) US dollars should be the same as that in US dollars, but practical issues arising in the calculation of the PPP US dollar GDP prevent this.

b Data refer to a period shorter than that specified.

c Estimates are based on regression.

d Data refer to 2003.

e Data refer to 2002.

f Estimate based on a bilateral comparison between China and the United States (Ruoen and Kai 1995).

g Data refer to 2001.

SOURCES

Columns 1–4: World Bank 2006; aggregates calculated for the Human Development Report Office by the World Bank.

Columns 5 and 6: World Bank 2006; aggregates calculated for the Human Development Report Office by the World Bank using the least squares method.

Columns 7 and 8: based on GDP per capita (PPP US$) time series from World Bank 2006.

Columns 9 and 10: calculated on the basis of data on the consumer price index from World Bank 2006.

TABLE 15

... to have access to the resources needed for a decent standard of living ...

Inequality in income or expenditure

HDI rank	Survey year	MDG Share of income or expenditure (%)				Inequality measures		
		Poorest 10%	Poorest 20%	Richest 20%	Richest 10%	Richest 10% to poorest 10%[a]	Richest 20% to poorest 20%[a]	Gini index[b]
HIGH HUMAN DEVELOPMENT								
1 Norway	2000[c]	3.9	9.6	37.2	23.4	6.1	3.9	25.8
2 Iceland	..	..	..	..	..	..	..	..
3 Australia	1994[c]	2.0	5.9	41.3	25.4	12.5	7.0	35.2
4 Ireland	2000[c]	2.9	7.4	42.0	27.2	9.4	5.6	34.3
5 Sweden	2000[c]	3.6	9.1	36.6	22.2	6.2	4.0	25.0
6 Canada	2000[c]	2.6	7.2	39.9	24.8	9.4	5.5	32.6
7 Japan	1993[c]	4.8	10.6	35.7	21.7	4.5	3.4	24.9
8 United States	2000[c]	1.9	5.4	45.8	29.9	15.9	8.4	40.8
9 Switzerland	2000[c]	2.9	7.6	41.3	25.9	9.0	5.5	33.7
10 Netherlands	1999[c]	2.5	7.6	38.7	22.9	9.2	5.1	30.9
11 Finland	2000[c]	4.0	9.6	36.7	22.6	5.6	3.8	26.9
12 Luxembourg	..	..	..	..	..	..	..	..
13 Belgium	2000[c]	3.4	8.5	41.4	28.1	8.2	4.9	33.0
14 Austria	2000[c]	3.3	8.6	37.8	23.0	6.9	4.4	29.1
15 Denmark	1997[c]	2.6	8.3	35.8	21.3	8.1	4.3	24.7
16 France	1995[c]	2.8	7.2	40.2	25.1	9.1	5.6	32.7
17 Italy	2000[c]	2.3	6.5	42.0	26.8	11.6	6.5	36.0
18 United Kingdom	1999[c]	2.1	6.1	44.0	28.5	13.8	7.2	36.0
19 Spain	2000[c]	2.6	7.0	42.0	26.6	10.3	6.0	34.7
20 New Zealand	1997[c]	2.2	6.4	43.8	27.8	12.5	6.8	36.2
21 Germany	2000[c]	3.2	8.5	36.9	22.1	6.9	4.3	28.3
22 Hong Kong, China (SAR)	1996[c]	2.0	5.3	50.7	34.9	17.8	9.7	43.4
23 Israel	2001[c]	2.1	5.7	44.9	28.8	13.4	7.9	39.2
24 Greece	2000[c]	2.5	6.7	41.5	26.0	10.2	6.2	34.3
25 Singapore	1998[c]	1.9	5.0	49.0	32.8	17.7	9.7	42.5
26 Korea, Rep. of	1998[c]	2.9	7.9	37.5	22.5	7.8	4.7	31.6
27 Slovenia	1998–99[c]	3.6	9.1	35.7	21.4	5.9	3.9	28.4
28 Portugal	1997[c]	2.0	5.8	45.9	29.8	15.0	8.0	38.5
29 Cyprus	..	..	..	..	..	..	..	..
30 Czech Republic	1996[c]	4.3	10.3	35.9	22.4	5.2	3.5	25.4
31 Barbados	..	..	..	..	..	..	..	..
32 Malta	..	..	..	..	..	..	..	..
33 Kuwait	..	..	..	..	..	..	..	..
34 Brunei Darussalam	..	..	..	..	..	..	..	..
35 Hungary	2002[d]	4.0	9.5	36.5	22.2	5.5	3.8	26.9
36 Argentina	2003[c, e]	1.1	3.2	56.8	39.6	34.5	17.6	52.8
37 Poland	2002[d]	3.1	7.5	42.2	27.0	8.8	5.6	34.5
38 Chile	2000[c]	1.2	3.3	62.2	47.0	40.6	18.7	57.1
39 Bahrain	..	..	..	..	..	..	..	..
40 Estonia	2003[d]	2.5	6.7	42.8	27.6	10.8	6.4	35.8
41 Lithuania	2003[d]	2.7	6.8	43.2	27.7	10.4	6.3	36.0
42 Slovakia	1996[c]	3.1	8.8	34.8	20.9	6.7	4.0	25.8
43 Uruguay	2003[c, e]	1.9	5.0	50.5	34.0	17.9	10.2	44.9
44 Croatia	2001[d]	3.4	8.3	39.6	24.5	7.3	4.8	29.0
45 Latvia	2003[d]	2.5	6.6	44.7	29.1	11.6	6.8	37.7
46 Qatar	..	..	..	..	..	..	..	..
47 Seychelles	..	..	..	..	..	..	..	..
48 Costa Rica	2001[c]	1.3	3.9	54.8	38.4	30.0	14.2	49.9
49 United Arab Emirates	..	..	..	..	..	..	..	..
50 Cuba	..	..	..	..	..	..	..	..
51 Saint Kitts and Nevis	..	..	..	..	..	..	..	..
52 Bahamas	..	..	..	..	..	..	..	..
53 Mexico	2002[d]	1.6	4.3	55.1	39.4	24.6	12.8	49.5

Human development indicators

TABLE 15

Inequality in income or expenditure

HDI rank	Survey year	MDG Share of income or expenditure (%)				Inequality measures		
		Poorest 10%	Poorest 20%	Richest 20%	Richest 10%	Richest 10% to poorest 10% [a]	Richest 20% to poorest 20% [a]	Gini index [b]
54 Bulgaria	2003 [d]	3.4	8.7	38.3	23.9	7.0	4.4	29.2
55 Tonga	..	..	..	..	..	..	..	..
56 Oman	..	..	..	..	..	..	..	..
57 Trinidad and Tobago	1992 [c]	2.1	5.5	45.9	29.9	14.4	8.3	40.3
58 Panama	2002 [c]	0.8	2.5	60.3	43.6	54.7	23.9	56.4
59 Antigua and Barbuda	..	..	..	..	..	..	..	..
60 Romania	2003 [d]	3.3	8.1	39.2	24.4	7.5	4.9	31.0
61 Malaysia	1997 [c]	1.7	4.4	54.3	38.4	22.1	12.4	49.2
62 Bosnia and Herzegovina	2001 [d]	3.9	9.5	35.8	21.4	5.4	3.8	26.2
63 Mauritius	..	..	..	..	..	..	..	..
MEDIUM HUMAN DEVELOPMENT								
64 Libyan Arab Jamahiriya	..	..	..	..	..	..	..	..
65 Russian Federation	2002 [d]	2.4	6.1	46.6	30.6	12.7	7.6	39.9
66 Macedonia, TFYR	2003 [d]	2.4	6.1	45.5	29.6	12.5	7.5	39.0
67 Belarus	2002 [d]	3.4	8.5	38.3	23.5	6.9	4.5	29.7
68 Dominica	..	..	..	..	..	..	..	..
69 Brazil	2003 [c]	0.8	2.6	62.1	45.8	57.8	23.7	58.0
70 Colombia	2003 [c]	0.7	2.5	62.7	46.9	63.8	25.3	58.6
71 Saint Lucia	..	..	..	..	..	..	..	..
72 Venezuela, RB	2000 [c]	1.6	4.7	49.3	32.8	20.4	10.6	44.1
73 Albania	2002 [d]	3.8	9.1	37.4	22.4	5.9	4.1	28.2
74 Thailand	2002 [d]	2.7	6.3	49.0	33.4	12.6	7.7	42.0
75 Samoa (Western)	..	..	..	..	..	..	..	..
76 Saudi Arabia	..	..	..	..	..	..	..	..
77 Ukraine	2003 [d]	3.9	9.2	37.5	23.0	5.9	4.1	28.1
78 Lebanon	..	..	..	..	..	..	..	..
79 Kazakhstan	2003 [d]	3.0	7.4	41.5	25.9	8.5	5.6	33.9
80 Armenia	2003 [d]	3.6	8.5	42.8	29.0	8.0	5.0	33.8
81 China	2001 [d]	1.8	4.7	50.0	33.1	18.4	10.7	44.7
82 Peru	2002 [c]	1.1	3.2	58.7	43.2	40.5	18.6	54.6
83 Ecuador	1998 [d]	0.9	3.3	58.0	41.6	44.9	17.3	43.7
84 Philippines	2000 [d]	2.2	5.4	52.3	36.3	16.5	9.7	46.1
85 Grenada	..	..	..	..	..	..	..	..
86 Jordan	2002–03 [d]	2.7	6.7	46.3	30.6	11.3	6.9	38.8
87 Tunisia	2000 [d]	2.3	6.0	47.3	31.5	13.4	7.9	39.8
88 Saint Vincent and the Grenadines	..	..	..	..	..	..	..	..
89 Suriname	..	..	..	..	..	..	..	..
90 Fiji	..	..	..	..	..	..	..	..
91 Paraguay	2002 [c]	0.6	2.2	61.3	45.4	73.4	27.8	57.8
92 Turkey	2003 [d]	2.0	5.3	49.7	34.1	16.8	9.3	43.6
93 Sri Lanka	1999–00 [d]	3.4	8.3	42.2	27.8	8.1	5.1	33.2
94 Dominican Republic	2003 [c]	1.4	3.9	56.8	41.3	30.0	14.4	51.7
95 Belize	..	..	..	..	..	..	..	..
96 Iran, Islamic Rep. of	1998 [d]	2.0	5.1	49.9	33.7	17.2	9.7	43.0
97 Georgia	2003 [d]	2.0	5.6	46.4	30.3	15.4	8.3	40.4
98 Maldives	..	..	..	..	..	..	..	..
99 Azerbaijan	2002 [d]	5.4	12.2	31.1	18.0	3.3	2.6	19.0
100 Occupied Palestinian Territories	..	..	..	..	..	..	..	..
101 El Salvador	2002 [c]	0.7	2.7	55.9	38.8	57.5	20.9	52.4
102 Algeria	1995 [d]	2.8	7.0	42.6	26.8	9.6	6.1	35.3
103 Guyana	..	..	..	..	..	..	..	..
104 Jamaica	2000 [d]	2.7	6.7	46.0	30.3	11.4	6.9	37.9
105 Turkmenistan	1998 [d]	2.6	6.1	47.5	31.7	12.3	7.7	40.8
106 Cape Verde	..	..	..	..	..	..	..	..

TABLE 15

HDI rank	Survey year	MDG Share of income or expenditure (%)				Inequality measures		
		Poorest 10%	Poorest 20%	Richest 20%	Richest 10%	Richest 10% to poorest 10% [a]	Richest 20% to poorest 20% [a]	Gini index [b]
107 Syrian Arab Republic	..	..	..	..	..	..	..	..
108 Indonesia	2002 [d]	3.6	8.4	43.3	28.5	7.8	5.2	34.3
109 Viet Nam	2002 [d]	3.2	7.5	45.4	29.9	9.4	6.0	37.0
110 Kyrgyzstan	2003 [d]	3.8	8.9	39.4	24.3	6.4	4.4	30.3
111 Egypt	1999–00 [d]	3.7	8.6	43.6	29.5	8.0	5.1	34.4
112 Nicaragua	2001 [d]	2.2	5.6	49.3	33.8	15.5	8.8	43.1
113 Uzbekistan	2000 [d]	3.6	9.2	36.3	22.0	6.1	4.0	26.8
114 Moldova, Rep. of	2003 [d]	3.2	7.8	41.4	26.4	8.2	5.3	33.2
115 Bolivia	2002 [c]	0.3	1.5	63.0	47.2	168.1	42.3	60.1
116 Mongolia	1998 [d]	2.1	5.6	51.2	37.0	17.8	9.1	30.3
117 Honduras	2003 [c]	1.2	3.4	58.3	42.2	34.2	17.2	53.8
118 Guatemala	2002 [c]	0.9	2.9	59.5	43.4	48.2	20.3	55.1
119 Vanuatu	..	..	..	..	..	..	..	..
120 Equatorial Guinea	..	..	..	..	..	..	..	..
121 South Africa	2000 [d]	1.4	3.5	62.2	44.7	33.1	17.9	57.8
122 Tajikistan	2003 [d]	3.3	7.9	40.8	25.6	7.8	5.2	32.6
123 Morocco	1998–99 [d]	2.6	6.5	46.6	30.9	11.7	7.2	39.5
124 Gabon	..	..	..	..	..	..	..	..
125 Namibia	1993 [c]	0.5	1.4	78.7	64.5	128.8	56.1	74.3
126 India	1999–00 [d]	3.9	8.9	43.3	28.5	7.3	4.9	32.5
127 São Tomé and Principe	..	..	..	..	..	..	..	..
128 Solomon Islands	..	..	..	..	..	..	..	..
129 Cambodia	1997 [d]	2.9	6.9	47.6	33.8	11.6	6.9	40.4
130 Myanmar	..	..	..	..	..	..	..	..
131 Botswana	1993 [d]	0.7	2.2	70.3	56.6	77.6	31.5	63.0
132 Comoros	..	..	..	..	..	..	..	..
133 Lao People's Dem. Rep.	2002 [d]	3.4	8.1	43.3	28.5	8.3	5.4	34.6
134 Pakistan	2002 [d]	4.0	9.3	40.3	26.3	6.5	4.3	30.6
135 Bhutan	..	..	..	..	..	..	..	..
136 Ghana	1998–99 [d]	2.1	5.6	46.6	30.0	14.1	8.4	40.8
137 Bangladesh	2000 [d]	3.9	9.0	41.3	26.7	6.8	4.6	31.8
138 Nepal	2003–04 [d]	2.6	6.0	54.6	40.6	15.8	9.1	47.2
139 Papua New Guinea	1996 [d]	1.7	4.5	56.5	40.5	23.8	12.6	50.9
140 Congo	..	..	..	..	..	..	..	..
141 Sudan	..	..	..	..	..	..	..	..
142 Timor-Leste	..	..	..	..	..	..	..	..
143 Madagascar	2001 [d]	1.9	4.9	53.5	36.6	19.2	11.0	47.5
144 Cameroon	2001 [d]	2.3	5.6	50.9	35.4	15.7	9.1	44.6
145 Uganda	1999 [d]	2.3	5.9	49.7	34.9	14.9	8.4	43.0
146 Swaziland	1994 [c]	1.0	2.7	64.4	50.2	49.7	23.8	60.9
LOW HUMAN DEVELOPMENT								
147 Togo	..	..	..	..	..	..	..	..
148 Djibouti	..	..	..	..	..	..	..	..
149 Lesotho	1995 [d]	0.5	1.5	66.5	48.3	105.0	44.2	63.2
150 Yemen	1998 [d]	3.0	7.4	41.2	25.9	8.6	5.6	33.4
151 Zimbabwe	1995 [d]	1.8	4.6	55.7	40.3	22.0	12.0	50.1
152 Kenya	1997 [d]	2.5	6.0	49.1	33.9	13.6	8.2	42.5
153 Mauritania	2000 [d]	2.5	6.2	45.7	29.5	12.0	7.4	39.0
154 Haiti	2001 [c]	0.7	2.4	63.4	47.7	71.7	26.6	59.2
155 Gambia	1998 [d]	1.8	4.8	53.4	37.0	20.2	11.2	50.2
156 Senegal	1995 [d]	2.6	6.4	48.2	33.5	12.8	7.5	41.3
157 Eritrea	..	..	..	..	..	..	..	..
158 Rwanda	1983–85 [d]	4.2	9.7	39.1	24.2	5.8	4.0	28.9
159 Nigeria	2003 [d]	1.9	5.0	49.2	33.2	17.8	9.7	43.7

Human development indicators

TABLE **15**

Inequality in income or expenditure

			MDG Share of income or expenditure (%)				Inequality measures		
HDI rank		Survey year	Poorest 10%	Poorest 20%	Richest 20%	Richest 10%	Richest 10% to poorest 10% [a]	Richest 20% to poorest 20% [a]	Gini index [b]
160	Guinea	1994 d	2.6	6.4	47.2	32.0	12.3	7.3	40.3
161	Angola	..	..	..	..	..	..	..	..
162	Tanzania, U. Rep. of	2000–01 d	2.9	7.3	42.4	26.9	9.2	5.8	34.6
163	Benin	2003 d	3.1	7.4	44.5	29.0	9.4	6.0	36.5
164	Côte d'Ivoire	2002 d	2.0	5.2	50.7	34.0	16.6	9.7	44.6
165	Zambia	2002–03 d	2.4	6.1	48.8	33.7	13.9	8.0	42.1
166	Malawi	1997 d	1.9	4.9	56.1	42.2	22.7	11.6	50.3
167	Congo, Dem. Rep. of the	..	..	..	..	..	..	..	..
168	Mozambique	1996–97 d	2.5	6.5	46.5	31.7	12.5	7.2	39.6
169	Burundi	1998 d	1.7	5.1	48.0	32.8	19.3	9.5	42.4
170	Ethiopia	1999–00 d	3.9	9.1	39.4	25.5	6.6	4.3	30.0
171	Chad	..	..	..	..	..	..	..	..
172	Central African Republic	1993 d	0.7	2.0	65.0	47.7	69.2	32.7	61.3
173	Guinea-Bissau	1993 d	2.1	5.2	53.4	39.3	19.0	10.3	47.0
174	Burkina Faso	2003 d	2.8	6.9	47.2	32.2	11.6	6.9	39.5
175	Mali	1994 d	1.8	4.6	56.2	40.4	23.1	12.2	50.5
176	Sierra Leone	1989 d	0.5	1.1	63.4	43.6	87.2	57.6	62.9
177	Niger	1995 d	0.8	2.6	53.3	35.4	46.0	20.7	50.5

NOTES

Because the underlying household surveys differ in method and in the type of data collected, the distribution data are not strictly comparable across countries.

a Data show the ratio of the income or expenditure share of the richest group to that of the poorest. Because of rounding, results may differ from ratios calculated using the income or expenditure shares in columns 2–5.

b A value of 0 represents perfect equality, and a value of 100 perfect inequality.

c Data refer to income shares by percentiles of population, ranked by per capita income.

d Data refer to expenditure shares by percentiles of population, ranked by per capita expenditure.

e Data refer to urban areas only.

SOURCES

Columns 1–5 and 8: World Bank 2006.
Columns 6 and 7: calculated on the basis of data on income or expenditure from World Bank 2006.

TABLE 16

The structure of trade

HDI rank		Imports of goods and services (% of GDP)		Exports of goods and services (% of GDP)		Primary exports (% of merchandise exports)		Manufactured exports (% of merchandise exports)		High-technology exports (% of manufactured exports)		Terms of trade (1980=100)[a]
		1990	2004	1990	2004	1990	2004	1990	2004	1990	2004	2004
HIGH HUMAN DEVELOPMENT												
1	Norway	34	30	40	44	67	77	32	19	12	18	130
2	Iceland	33	43	35	37	91	82	8	17	10	6	..
3	Australia	17	21 [b]	17	18 [b]	71	58	26	25	12	14	96
4	Ireland	52	65	57	80	26	10	70	86	41	34	94
5	Sweden	29	38	30	46	16	14	83	81	13	17	98
6	Canada	26	34 [b]	26	38 [b]	36	35	59	60	14	14	99
7	Japan	9	10 [b]	10	12 [b]	3	3	96	93	24	24	116
8	United States	11	14 [b]	10	10 [b]	21	14	75	82	34	32	112
9	Switzerland	34	37 [b]	36	44 [b]	6	7	94	93	12	22	..
10	Netherlands	51	60	54	65	37	30	59	70	16	29	99
11	Finland	24	32	23	37	17	16	83	83	8	21	99
12	Luxembourg	100	125	104	146	..	13	..	86	..	10	..
13	Belgium	69	81	71	84	19	18	77	81	..	8	..
14	Austria	37	46	38	51	12	15	88	84	8	12	..
15	Denmark	31	38	36	43	35	31	60	66	15	20	110
16	France	23	26	21	26	23	17	77	83	16	19	..
17	Italy	20	26	20	27	11	11	88	88	8	8	132
18	United Kingdom	27	28	24	25	19	18	79	76	24	24	99
19	Spain	20	29	16	26	24	21	75	77	6	7	121
20	New Zealand	27	29 [b]	27	29 [b]	72	65	26	31	10	14	121
21	Germany	25	33	25	38	10	9	89	84	11	17	112
22	Hong Kong, China (SAR)	124	184	132	193	7	3	92	96	..	32	99
23	Israel	45	49	35	44	13	5	87	94	10	19	118
24	Greece	28	29	18	21	46	38	54	59	2	11	79
25	Singapore	..	..	..	..	27	13	72	84	40	59	70
26	Korea, Rep. of	29	40	28	44	6	8	94	92	18	33	75
27	Slovenia	79	61	91	60	..	10	..	90	..	6	..
28	Portugal	39	38	33	31	19	15	80	85	4	9	..
29	Cyprus	57	..	52	..	42	35	58	65	8	22	..
30	Czech Republic	43	72	45	72	..	10	..	90	..	13	..
31	Barbados	52	54 [b]	49	49 [b]	55	47	43	52	..	15	..
32	Malta	99	83	85	76	7	9	93	90	44	58	..
33	Kuwait	58	33	45	60	94	..	6	..	3	..	..
34	Brunei Darussalam	..	..	..	..	97	88 [b]	3	12 [b]	..	5 [b]	..
35	Hungary	29	68	31	64	35	11	63	88	..	29	84
36	Argentina	5	18	10	25	71	70	29	29	..	8	103
37	Poland	22	41	29	39	..	19	..	81	..	3	459
38	Chile	31	30	35	36	87	86	11	13	5	5	47
39	Bahrain	95	64	116	82	54	90	45	10	..	3	..
40	Estonia	..	86	..	78	..	22	..	77	..	14	..
41	Lithuania	61	61	52	54	..	42	..	58	..	5	..
42	Slovakia	36	79	27	77	..	14	..	86	..	5	..
43	Uruguay	18	28	24	30	61	68	39	32	..	2	77
44	Croatia	..	56	..	47	..	27	..	72	..	13	..
45	Latvia	49	60	48	44	..	36	..	61	..	5	..
46	Qatar	..	..	..	..	82	87	18	13	..	1	..
47	Seychelles	67	96	62	94	74	93	26	6	..	10	..
48	Costa Rica	41	49	35	46	66	37	27	63	..	37	125
49	United Arab Emirates	41	65	66	82	..	..	..	..	..	..	..
50	Cuba	..	..	..	..	..	..	..	..	..	..	..
51	Saint Kitts and Nevis	83	63	52	50	..	18 [b]	..	82 [b]	..	1 [b]	..
52	Bahamas	..	..	..	..	..	..	..	..	..	..	..
53	Mexico	20	32	19	30	56	20	43	80	8	21	32

Human development indicators

TABLE 16

The structure of trade

HDI rank		Imports of goods and services (% of GDP)		Exports of goods and services (% of GDP)		Primary exports (% of merchandise exports)		Manufactured exports (% of merchandise exports)		High-technology exports (% of manufactured exports)		Terms of trade (1980=100)[a]
		1990	2004	1990	2004	1990	2004	1990	2004	1990	2004	2004
54	Bulgaria	37	69	33	58	..	33	..	62	..	4	..
55	Tonga	65	..	34	..	..	..	24	..	..	..	..
56	Oman	28	43	47	57	94	87	5	12	2	1	..
57	Trinidad and Tobago	29	48	45	60	73	65 [b]	27	35 [b]	..	1 [b]	..
58	Panama	79	65	87	63	78	90	21	10	..	2	81
59	Antigua and Barbuda	87	69 [c]	89	61 [c]	..	..	..	..	..	..	..
60	Romania	26	46	17	37	26	17	73	82	2	3	..
61	Malaysia	72	100	75	121	46	23	54	76	38	55	138
62	Bosnia and Herzegovina	..	55	..	26	..	..	..	..	..	..	..
63	Mauritius	71	56	64	56	34	28	66	71	1	4	96
MEDIUM HUMAN DEVELOPMENT												
64	Libyan Arab Jamahiriya	31	36 [c]	40	47 [c]	..	..	..	..	..	..	..
65	Russian Federation	18	22	18	35	..	62	..	21	..	9	..
66	Macedonia, TFYR	36	61	26	40	..	23	..	77	..	1	..
67	Belarus	44	74	46	68	..	39	..	60	..	3	..
68	Dominica	81	61	55	48	65	42	35	58	..	8	..
69	Brazil	7	13	8	18	47	46	52	54	7	12	149
70	Colombia	15	22	21	21	74	62	25	38	..	6	83
71	Saint Lucia	84	69 [b]	73	56 [b]	68	71	32	28	..	20	..
72	Venezuela, RB	20	20	39	36	90	88	10	12	4	3	70
73	Albania	23	43	15	21	..	18	..	82	..	1	..
74	Thailand	42	66	34	71	36	22 [b]	63	75 [b]	21	30 [b]	61
75	Samoa (Western)	..	48	..	26	90	23	10	77	..	(.)	..
76	Saudi Arabia	32	25	41	53	92	88 [c]	8	12 [c]	..	2 [c]	..
77	Ukraine	29	54	28	61	..	32 [c]	..	67 [c]	..	5 [c]	..
78	Lebanon	100	41	18	21	..	31 [b]	..	68 [b]	..	2 [b]	..
79	Kazakhstan	..	46	..	55	..	84	..	16	..	2	..
80	Armenia	46	53	35	39	..	38	..	62	..	1	..
81	China	16	31	19	34	27	8	72	91	..	30	78
82	Peru	14	18	16	21	82	80	18	20	..	2	45
83	Ecuador	32	29	33	27	98	91	2	9	(.)	7	51
84	Philippines	33	51	28	52	31	10	38	55	..	64	84
85	Grenada	63	71 [b]	42	(.)	66	54 [b]	34	46 [b]	..	5 [b]	..
86	Jordan	93	80	62	48	44	28	56	72	7	5	99
87	Tunisia	51	48	44	45	31	22	69	78	2	5	80
88	Saint Vincent and the Grenadines	77	66	66	43	..	81	..	19	..	8	..
89	Suriname	44	64 [b]	42	28 [b]	26	..	74	..	..	..	..
90	Fiji	67	..	62	..	64	55	35	45	12	1	..
91	Paraguay	39	37	33	36	..	87	10	13	(.)	7	164 [b]
92	Turkey	18	35	13	29	32	15	68	85	1	2	94
93	Sri Lanka	38	45	29	36	42	26	54	74	1	1	119
94	Dominican Republic	44	49	34	50	..	..	..	..	..	..	54
95	Belize	60	65 [b]	62	52 [b]	..	86 [b]	15	13 [b]	..	3 [b]	..
96	Iran, Islamic Rep. of	24	30	22	32	..	91 [b]	..	9 [b]	..	2 [b]	..
97	Georgia	46	47	40	31	..	63	..	37	..	38	..
98	Maldives	64	83	24	95	..	74	..	26	..	1	..
99	Azerbaijan	39	74	44	50	..	89	..	10	..	2	..
100	Occupied Palestinian Territories	..	49 [b]	..	10 [b]	..	..	..	..	..	..	..
101	El Salvador	31	44	19	27	62	40	38	60	..	4	97
102	Algeria	25	26	23	40	97	98	3	2	..	1	75
103	Guyana	80	106	63	96	..	70	..	30	..	(.)	..
104	Jamaica	52	58	48	41	30	35 [c]	70	65 [c]	..	(.) [c]	..
105	Turkmenistan	..	57	..	66	..	..	..	..	..	..	..
106	Cape Verde	44	64	13	31	..	..	..	88 [b]	..	..	91

Human development indicators

TABLE 16

HDI rank	Imports of goods and services (% of GDP)		Exports of goods and services (% of GDP)		Primary exports (% of merchandise exports)		Manufactured exports (% of merchandise exports)		High-technology exports (% of manufactured exports)		Terms of trade (1980=100)[a]
	1990	2004	1990	2004	1990	2004	1990	2004	1990	2004	2004
107 Syrian Arab Republic	28	34	28	35	64	87	36	11	..	1	..
108 Indonesia	24	27	25	31	65	44	35	56	1	16	..
109 Viet Nam	45	74 [c]	36	66	..	46 [b]	..	53 [b]	..	6 [b]	..
110 Kyrgyzstan	50	53	29	43	..	57	..	43	..	2 [b]	..
111 Egypt	33	29	20	29	57	64	42	31	..	1	50
112 Nicaragua	46	54	25	26	92	89	8	11	..	6	56
113 Uzbekistan	48	33	29	40	..	..	..	..	..	..	..
114 Moldova, Rep. of	51	82	48	51	..	64	..	36	..	4	..
115 Bolivia	24	26	23	31	95	86	5	14	..	9	58
116 Mongolia	53	87	24	75	..	62 [b]	..	38 [b]	..	(.) [b]	..
117 Honduras	40	54 [b]	36	37 [b]	91	73 [b]	9	27 [b]	..	2 [b]	79
118 Guatemala	25	32	21	18	76	58	24	42	..	7	70
119 Vanuatu	77	..	49	..	..	..	13	..	20	..	..
120 Equatorial Guinea	70	..	32	..	..	..	..	..	..	..	..
121 South Africa	19	27	24	27	..	42	..	58	..	6	95
122 Tajikistan	35	65	28	46	..	..	..	..	..	..	..
123 Morocco	32	39	26	33	48	31	52	69	..	10	109
124 Gabon	31	40	46	61	..	93	..	7	..	15	41
125 Namibia	67	45	52	46	..	58 [b]	..	41 [b]	..	3 [b]	87
126 India	9	23	7	19	28	26	70	73	2	5	106
127 São Tomé and Principe	72	95	14	39	..	..	..	..	..	..	..
128 Solomon Islands	73	44 [b]	47	42 [b]	..	..	..	..	..	..	..
129 Cambodia	13	76	6	65	..	3	..	97	..	(.)	..
130 Myanmar	5	..	3	..	..	..	..	..	..	..	..
131 Botswana	50	32	55	40	..	..	..	..	..	..	110
132 Comoros	35	31	14	16	..	..	..	..	..	..	52
133 Lao People's Dem. Rep.	25	42	12	29	..	..	..	..	..	..	..
134 Pakistan	23	15	16	16	21	15	79	85	(.)	1	65
135 Bhutan	32	43 [c]	28	22 [c]	..	..	..	..	..	..	..
136 Ghana	26	54	17	35	..	85 [b]	..	14 [b]	..	4 [b]	59
137 Bangladesh	14	21	6	15	..	10	77	90	(.)	(.)	64
138 Nepal	22	31	11	17	..	26 [b]	83	74 [b]	..	(.) [b]	..
139 Papua New Guinea	49	60 [b]	41	71 [b]	89	94 [b]	10	6 [b]	..	39 [b]	..
140 Congo	46	57	54	84	..	..	..	..	..	..	125
141 Sudan	..	21	..	18	..	98 [b]	..	2 [b]	..	(.) [b]	..
142 Timor-Leste	..	..	..	..	..	..	..	..	..	..	..
143 Madagascar	28	48	17	32	85	76	14	22	8	1	99
144 Cameroon	17	26	20	26	91	95	9	5	3	1	140
145 Uganda	19	28	7	14	..	85	..	15	..	13	..
146 Swaziland	87	92	75	84	..	23 [c]	..	76 [c]	..	1 [c]	94
LOW HUMAN DEVELOPMENT											
147 Togo	45	47	33	34	89	53	9	47	..	(.)	25
148 Djibouti	..	..	..	..	44	..	8	..	..	..	..
149 Lesotho	122	105	17	48	..	..	..	..	..	..	69
150 Yemen	20	34	14	25	..	97	..	3	..	13	..
151 Zimbabwe	23	44	23	36	68	72	31	28	2	1	123
152 Kenya	31	32	26	26	70	79	30	21	4	3	91
153 Mauritania	61	70	46	29	..	..	..	..	..	..	131
154 Haiti	20	47 [b]	18	16 [b]	15	..	85	..	14	..	39
155 Gambia	72	52	60	42	..	73 [b]	..	27 [b]	..	3 [b]	63
156 Senegal	30	40	25	28	77	61	23	39	..	6	60
157 Eritrea	..	86	..	13	..	..	..	..	..	..	..
158 Rwanda	14	27	6	10	..	90 [b]	..	10 [b]	..	25 [b]	156
159 Nigeria	29	37	43	55	..	98 [b]	..	2 [b]	..	2 [b]	68

Human development indicators

TABLE 16

The structure of trade

HDI rank	Imports of goods and services (% of GDP)		Exports of goods and services (% of GDP)		Primary exports (% of merchandise exports)		Manufactured exports (% of merchandise exports)		High-technology exports (% of manufactured exports)		Terms of trade (1980=100) [a]
	1990	2004	1990	2004	1990	2004	1990	2004	1990	2004	2004
160 Guinea	31	23	31	21	..	75 c	..	25 c	..	(.) c	..
161 Angola	21	55	39	71	100	..	(.)	..	..	..	..
162 Tanzania, U. Rep. of	37	29	13	19	..	80	..	20	..	2	..
163 Benin	26	26	14	15	..	91 c	..	9 c	..	2 c	108
164 Côte d'Ivoire	27	38	32	48	..	78 b	..	20 b	..	8 b	60
165 Zambia	37	27	36	20	..	90	..	10	..	1	53
166 Malawi	33	49	24	27	93	84	7	16	4	2	50
167 Congo, Dem. Rep. of the	29	22 c	30	19 c	..	..	..	..	..	..	112
168 Mozambique	36	38	8	30	..	96 c	..	3 c	..	9 c	39
169 Burundi	28	25	8	9	..	95	..	5	..	6	36
170 Ethiopia	12	40	8	19	..	89 b	..	11 b	..	(.) b	..
171 Chad	28	36	13	52	..	..	..	..	..	..	93
172 Central African Republic	28	16	15	11	..	63 b	..	37 b	..	(.) b	38
173 Guinea-Bissau	37	49	10	35	..	..	..	..	..	..	75
174 Burkina Faso	24	23	11	9	..	92	..	8	..	10	150
175 Mali	34	36	17	28	..	..	2	..	..	..	97 b
176 Sierra Leone	24	39	22	23	..	..	..	7 c	..	31 c	..
177 Niger	22	26	15	16	..	91 b	..	8 b	..	3 b	57
Developing countries	24	36	25	39	38	22	59	74	..	24	..
Least developed countries	22	32	13	23	84	66	..	..	..	..	..
Arab States	38	36	38	48	73	75	..	..	..	..	..
East Asia and the Pacific	33	52	34	56	23	11	73	86	..	33	..
Latin America and the Caribbean	15	23	17	26	65	46	36	56	7	13	..
South Asia	13	23	11	21	27	24	71	76	..	4	..
Sub-Saharan Africa	26	34	27	33	73	70	..	32 b	..	4	..
Central and Eastern Europe and the CIS	28	44	29	46	32	13	..	55	..	10	..
OECD	18 b	22 b	17	21 b	20	17	77	80	18	18	..
High-income OECD	18 b	21 b	17	20 b	19	17	78	80	19	18	..
High human development	19 b	23 b	19	23 b	20	17	76	80	18	19	..
Medium human development	19	29	19	31	49	25	50	60	..	17	..
Low human development	29	37	27	36	74	71	..	8 b	..	3	..
High income	19 b	22 b	18	22 b	19	16	77	80	18	19	..
Middle income	21	32	22	35	53	26	50	64	..	20	..
Low income	17	27	13	24	38	30	..	50 b	..	4	..
World	19 b	24 b	19	24 b	23	18	72	77	18	19	..

NOTES

a The ratio of the export price index to the import price index measured relative to the base year 1980. A value of more than 100 means that the price of exports has risen relative to the price of imports.
b Data refer to 2003.
c Data refer to 2002.

SOURCES

Columns 1–10: World Bank 2006, based on data from United Nations Conference on Trade and Development; aggregates calculated for the Human Development Report Office by the World Bank.
Column 11: calculated on the basis of data on terms of trade from World Bank 2006.

Human development indicators

TABLE 17

... to have access to the resources needed for a decent standard of living ...

Rich country responsibilities: aid

| | | MDG Net official development assistance (ODA) disbursed | | | MDG ODA per capita of donor country | | MDG ODA to least developed countries[b] | | MDG ODA to basic social services[c] | | MDG Untied bilateral ODA | |
| | | Total[a] (US$ millions) | As % of GNI | | (2004 US$) | | (% of total) | | (% of total allocable by sector) | | (% of total) | |
HDI rank		2004	1990[d]	2004	1990	2004	1990	2004	1995/96[e]	2003/04[e]	1990	2004
HIGH HUMAN DEVELOPMENT												
1	Norway	2,199	1.17	0.87	396	477	44	38	10.7	18.0	61	100
3	Australia	1,460	0.34	0.25	70	73	18	24	5.9	15.8	33	77
4	Ireland	607	0.16	0.39	26	152	37	53	0.5	28.9	..	100
5	Sweden	2,722	0.91	0.78	257	302	39	28	14.2	16.0	87	87
6	Canada	2,599	0.44	0.27	103	81	30	27	8.9	29.0	47	57
7	Japan	8,922	0.31	0.19	94	70	19	19	2.0	5.4	89	94
8	United States	19,705	0.21	0.17	61	67	22	23	19.0	19.1	..	..
9	Switzerland	1,545	0.32	0.41	149	210	43	26	6.5	8.4	78	97
10	Netherlands	4,204	0.92	0.73	244	258	33	35	11.7	18.1	56	87
11	Finland	680	0.65	0.37	174	130	38	25	8.9	15.3	31	..
12	Luxembourg	236	0.21	0.83	101	524	39	37	..	20.7	..	..
13	Belgium	1,463	0.46	0.41	120	141	41	44	9.2	14.7	..	93
14	Austria	678	0.11	0.23	28	83	63	25	2.6	12.6	32	52
15	Denmark	2,037	0.94	0.85	305	377	39	36	13.1	23.6	..	89
16	France	8,473	0.60	0.41	160	137	33	37	..	10.0	64	94
17	Italy	2,462	0.31	0.15	75	43	41	32	7.3	18.4	22	..
18	United Kingdom	7,883	0.27	0.36	70	131	32	38	24.4	31.8	..	100
19	Spain	2,437	0.20	0.24	33	56	20	17	8.3	13.8	..	68
20	New Zealand	212	0.23	0.23	41	52	19	31	1.7	19.1	100	81
21	Germany	7,534	0.42	0.28	124	91	28	31	8.8	12.7	62	92
24	Greece	465	..	0.23	..	42	..	14	19.3	20.6	..	23
28	Portugal	1,031	0.24	0.63	25	100	70	85	4.2	2.8	..	99
DAC		79,553 T	0.33	0.26	91	91	29	30	8.1	16.0	..	..

NOTES

This table presents data for members of the Development Assistance Committee (DAC) of the Organisation for Economic Co-operation and Development (OECD).

a Some non-DAC countries and areas also provide ODA. According to OECD-DAC 2006b, net ODA disbursed in 2004 by Czech Republic, Hungary, Iceland, Israel, Republic of Korea, Kuwait, Poland, Saudi Arabia, Slovakia, Turkey, United Arab Emirates and other small donors, including Estonia, Latvia and Lithuania, totaled $3,741 million. China also provides aid but does not disclose the amount.

b Includes imputed multilateral flows that make allowance for contributions through multilateral organizations. These are calculated using the geographic distribution of disbursements for the year specified.

c Data refer to the share of sector-allocable ODA; they exclude technical cooperation and administrative costs.

d Data for individual countries (but not the DAC average) include forgiveness of non-ODA claims.

e Data refer to the average for the years specified.

SOURCE

All columns: OECD-DAC 2006a.

TABLE 18

. . . to have access to the resources needed for a decent standard of living . . .

Flows of aid, private capital and debt

		Official development assistance (ODA) received [a] (net disbursements)				Net foreign direct investment inflows [b] (% of GDP)		Other private flows [b, c] (% of GDP)		Total debt service As % of GDP		MDG As % of exports of goods, services and net income from abroad	
		Total (US$ millions)	Per capita (US$)	As % of GDP									
HDI rank		2004	2004	1990	2004	1990	2004	1990	2004	1990	2004	1990	2004
HIGH HUMAN DEVELOPMENT													
22	Hong Kong, China (SAR)	7.0 d	1.0 d	0.1	(.) d	..	20.9	..	..	..	..	..	..
23	Israel	478.9 d	72.6 d	2.6	0.4 d	0.3	1.4	..	..	..	..	..	..
25	Singapore	9.2 d	2.2 d	(.)	(.) d	15.1	15.0	..	..	..	..	..	..
26	Korea, Rep. of	−67.6 d	−1.4 d	(.)	(.) d	0.3	1.2	..	..	..	..	..	..
27	Slovenia	62.2 d	31.6 d	..	0.2 d	..	2.6	..	..	..	..	..	..
29	Cyprus	60.0 d	72.6 d	0.7	0.4 d	2.3	7.2	..	..	..	..	..	..
30	Czech Republic	279.8 d	27.4 d	(.)	0.3 d	0.2	4.2	..	2.6	..	7.8	..	3.0
31	Barbados	29.1	108.2	0.2	1.0	0.6	1.8	−0.8	−0.4	8.2	3.1	14.6	5.5
32	Malta	6.2 d	15.5 d	0.2	0.1 d	..	..	..	..	..	..	..	..
33	Kuwait	2.6 d	1.0 d	(.)	(.) d	0.0	(.)	..	..	..	..	..	..
34	Brunei Darussalam	0.8 d	2.1 d	..	.. d	..	..	..	..	..	..	..	..
35	Hungary	302.7 d	29.9 d	0.2	0.3 d	1.9	4.6	−1.4	12.3	12.8	17.0	33.4	4.9
36	Argentina	91.2	2.4	0.1	0.1	1.3	2.7	−1.5	−1.0	4.4	8.1	34.7	18.8
37	Poland	1,524.8 d	39.5 d	2.2	0.6 d	0.2	5.2	(.)	2.1	1.6	14.3	4.4	4.9
38	Chile	49.1	3.0	0.3	0.1	2.2	8.1	5.1	0.4	9.1	10.2	18.1	4.1
39	Bahrain	103.9	145.1	3.2	0.9	..	..	..	..	..	..	..	..
40	Estonia	136.4 d	102.2 d	..	1.2 d	..	9.3	..	23.2	..	12.9	..	0.7
41	Lithuania	252.2 d	73.3 d	..	1.1 d	..	3.5	..	5.8	..	7.9	..	6.3
42	Slovakia	235.2 d	43.5 d	(.)	0.6 d	..	2.7	..	2.6	..	12.3	..	6.9 e
43	Uruguay	22.0	6.4	0.6	0.2	0.4	2.4	−2.1	−2.3	10.6	11.7	35.2	31.6
44	Croatia	120.8	26.6	..	0.4	..	3.6	..	11.4	..	15.4	..	8.7
45	Latvia	164.6 d	71.0 d	..	1.2 d	..	5.1	..	12.2	..	10.1	..	5.8
46	Qatar	2.4 d	3.1 d	(.)	.. d	..	..	..	..	..	..	..	..
47	Seychelles	10.3	129.4	9.8	1.5	5.4	5.3	−1.7	9.5	5.9	7.4	7.8	7.8
48	Costa Rica	13.5	3.2	4.0	0.1	2.9	3.4	−2.5	0.2	8.8	3.7	22.0	6.5
49	United Arab Emirates	5.7 d	1.3 d	(.)	(.) d	..	..	..	..	..	..	..	..
50	Cuba	90.5	8.0	..	..	..	..	..	..	..	..	..	..
51	Saint Kitts and Nevis	−0.1	−2.6	5.1	(.)	30.8	15.5	−0.3	−2.3	1.9	11.8	3.4	24.5 f
52	Bahamas	4.8 d	15.0 d	0.1	.. d	−0.6	3.6 e	..	..	..	..	..	..
53	Mexico	121.1	1.1	0.1	(.)	1.0	2.6	2.7	−0.6	4.3	7.6	18.3	11.9
54	Bulgaria	622.4 d	80.0 d	0.1	2.6 d	(.)	8.3	..	4.4	..	10.2	18.6	11.2
55	Tonga	19.3	188.9	26.2	9.1	0.2	0.0	−0.1	0.0	1.7	1.4	3.4	5.8 f
56	Oman	54.9	21.7	0.5	0.2	1.2	−0.1	−3.4	0.5	6.3	4.1	12.0	3.2
57	Trinidad and Tobago	−0.8	−0.6	0.4	(.)	2.2	8.0	−3.5	−1.2	8.9	3.2	15.6	3.3 e
58	Panama	37.7	11.9	1.9	0.3	2.6	7.4	−0.1	5.7	6.5	10.2	4.1	11.2
59	Antigua and Barbuda	1.7	20.5	1.2	0.2	..	..	..	..	..	..	..	..
60	Romania	915.7 d	42.0 d	0.6	1.3 d	(.)	7.4	(.)	5.6	(.)	6.5	0.0	8.4
61	Malaysia	289.5	11.6	1.1	0.2	5.3	3.9	−4.2	3.7	9.8	7.8	10.6	4.7 e
62	Bosnia and Herzegovina	671.0	171.6	..	7.9	..	7.2	..	0.5	..	2.1	..	4.2
63	Mauritius	37.9	30.8	3.7	0.6	1.7	0.2	1.9	−0.3	6.5	4.3	7.3	5.4
MEDIUM HUMAN DEVELOPMENT													
64	Libyan Arab Jamahiriya	17.6 d	3.1 d	0.1	0.1 d	..	..	..	..	..	..	..	..
65	Russian Federation	1,313.1 d	9.1 d	(.)	0.2 d	..	2.1	..	1.9	..	3.6	..	6.1
66	Macedonia, TFYR	248.4	122.3	..	4.6	..	2.9	..	0.8	..	4.6	..	6.5
67	Belarus	46.2 d	4.7 d	..	0.2 d	..	0.7	..	−0.3	..	1.4	..	1.5
68	Dominica	29.2	372.1	11.9	10.8	7.8	6.8	−0.3	0.0	3.5	6.8	6.0	9.1 f
69	Brazil	285.1	1.6	(.)	(.)	0.2	3.0	−0.1	−0.4	1.8	8.9	18.5	23.2
70	Colombia	509.0	11.3	0.2	0.5	1.2	3.1	−0.4	−1.2	9.7	7.9	34.5	18.5
71	Saint Lucia	−21.5	−134.8	3.1	−2.8	11.3	14.6	−0.2	−0.1	1.6	3.5	2.1	5.5 f
72	Venezuela, RB	48.6	1.8	0.2	(.)	1.0	1.4	−1.2	0.6	10.6	6.0	19.6	10.5
73	Albania	362.5	116.5	0.5	4.8	0.0	5.6	..	0.4	..	1.0	0.9	3.8 e
74	Thailand	−1.8	(.)	0.9	(.)	2.9	0.9	2.3	0.3	6.2	7.7	11.4	4.1
75	Samoa (Western)	30.8	167.4	42.6	8.2	0.0	0.1	0.0	0.0	4.9	5.6	10.6	..

TABLE 18

		Official development assistance (ODA) received [a] (net disbursements)				Net foreign direct investment inflows [b] (% of GDP)		Other private flows [b, c] (% of GDP)		Total debt service As % of GDP		MDG As % of exports of goods, services and net income from abroad	
		Total (US$ millions)	Per capita (US$)	As % of GDP									
HDI rank		2004	2004	1990	2004	1990	2004	1990	2004	1990	2004	1990	2004
76	Saudi Arabia	32.3	1.3	(.)	(.)	..	..	..	..	..	..	..	..
77	Ukraine	360.1 [d]	7.7 [d]	0.4	0.6 [d]	..	2.6	..	5.1	..	6.6	..	4.8
78	Lebanon	264.8	74.8	8.9	1.2	0.2	1.3	0.2	11.9	3.5	20.0	..	..
79	Kazakhstan	265.0	17.9	..	0.7	..	10.1	..	20.0	..	21.5	..	3.8
80	Armenia	254.1	84.0	..	8.3	0.2	7.1	..	(.)	..	3.5	..	7.4
81	China	1,661.1	1.3	0.6	0.1	1.0	2.8	1.3	1.0	2.0	1.2	10.6	1.2
82	Peru	487.4	17.7	1.5	0.7	0.2	2.6	0.1	1.8	1.8	4.0	7.3	16.3
83	Ecuador	160.5	12.3	1.6	0.5	1.2	3.8	0.6	2.0	10.5	12.3	31.0	21.8
84	Philippines	462.8	5.7	2.9	0.5	1.2	0.6	0.2	2.4	8.1	13.7	25.6	16.0
85	Grenada	15.4	150.4	6.3	3.5	5.9	9.7	0.1	8.6	1.5	6.7	3.1	15.3 [f]
86	Jordan	581.4	104.5	22.1	5.0	0.9	5.4	5.3	−1.2	15.6	6.1	22.1	10.4
87	Tunisia	327.7	32.8	3.2	1.2	0.6	2.1	−1.6	1.6	11.6	7.2	25.6	13.8
88	Saint Vincent and the Grenadines	10.5	88.3	7.8	2.6	4.0	13.8	0.0	6.0	2.2	5.2	3.1	6.7 [f]
89	Suriname	23.9	53.5	15.5	2.2	..	..	..	..	..	..	..	..
90	Fiji	63.9	76.0	3.8	2.4	6.9	−0.4	−1.2	−0.1	7.9	0.6	9.0	..
91	Paraguay	0.3	(.)	1.1	(.)	1.5	1.3	−0.2	−1.8	6.2	6.8	11.5	9.5
92	Turkey	257.0	3.6	0.8	0.1	0.5	0.9	0.8	3.1	4.9	11.2	29.9	19.5
93	Sri Lanka	519.1	25.2	9.1	2.6	0.5	1.2	0.1	−0.3	4.8	3.8	14.8	8.8
94	Dominican Republic	86.9	9.9	1.4	0.5	1.9	3.5	(.)	2.2	3.3	4.0	10.7	7.4
95	Belize	7.4	27.9	7.4	0.7	4.1	11.7	0.5	−5.2	4.4	30.4	7.0	64.2
96	Iran, Islamic Rep. of	189.4	2.8	0.1	0.1	−0.3	0.3	(.)	0.4	0.5	1.2	1.3	..
97	Georgia	315.4	69.8	..	6.1	..	9.6	..	1.2	..	4.2	..	10.7
98	Maldives	27.9	87.0	9.8	3.7	2.8	2.0	0.5	2.6	4.1	4.3	4.0	4.5
99	Azerbaijan	175.6	21.0	..	2.1	..	41.7	..	1.4	..	2.8	..	3.2
100	Occupied Palestinian Territories	1,136.4	316.8	..	..	..	..	..	..	..	..	..	..
101	El Salvador	211.5	31.3	7.2	1.3	(.)	2.9	0.1	1.6	4.3	3.9	18.2	12.5
102	Algeria	312.6	9.7	0.2	0.4	0.1	1.0	−0.7	−0.6	14.2	6.8	63.7	..
103	Guyana	144.6	192.7	42.6	18.4	2.0	3.8	−4.1	−0.1	74.5	6.2	..	5.9 [g, h]
104	Jamaica	75.4	28.6	5.9	0.9	3.0	6.8	−1.0	7.9	14.4	9.4	27.0	19.0
105	Turkmenistan	37.2	7.8	..	0.6	..	..	..	..	..	..	..	..
106	Cape Verde	139.8	282.4	31.8	14.7	0.1	2.2	(.)	−0.5	1.7	2.7	8.9	6.7 [e]
107	Syrian Arab Republic	110.2	5.9	5.6	0.5	0.6	1.1	−0.1	(.)	9.7	1.4	20.3	2.5
108	Indonesia	84.1	0.4	1.5	(.)	1.0	0.4	1.6	0.5	8.7	7.9	25.6	12.7
109	Viet Nam	1,830.3	22.0	2.9	4.0	2.8	3.6	0.0	(.)	2.7	1.7	..	5.9 [f]
110	Kyrgyzstan	258.2	49.6	..	11.7	..	3.5	..	−2.4	..	7.3	..	6.2
111	Egypt	1,457.7	20.1	12.6	1.8	1.7	1.6	−0.2	−0.3	7.1	2.9	23.7	6.8
112	Nicaragua	1,232.4	229.2	32.9	27.1	0.1	5.5	2.0	0.6	1.6	2.8	2.3	4.6 [g, h]
113	Uzbekistan	245.5	9.4	..	2.1	..	1.2	..	−1.3	..	7.1	..	..
114	Moldova, Rep. of	117.9	28.0	..	4.5	..	3.1	..	−1.2	..	9.6	..	7.4
115	Bolivia	766.6	85.1	11.2	8.7	0.6	1.3	−0.5	(.)	7.9	5.9	33.5	12.6 [g, h]
116	Mongolia	261.9	100.2	..	16.2	..	5.8	..	(.)	..	2.5	0.3	2.8
117	Honduras	641.7	91.0	14.7	8.7	1.4	4.0	1.0	2.2	12.8	4.5	33.0	6.5 [g, h]
118	Guatemala	218.4	17.8	2.6	0.8	0.6	0.6	−0.1	1.3	3.0	2.0	12.6	10.2
119	Vanuatu	37.8	182.2	33.0	11.9	8.6	6.9	−0.1	0.0	1.6	1.1	1.6	1.2 [e]
120	Equatorial Guinea	29.7	60.3	46.0	0.9	8.3	51.4	0.0	0.0	3.9	0.2	11.5	..
121	South Africa	617.3	13.1	..	0.3	−0.1	0.3	..	3.4	..	1.8	0.0	2.4
122	Tajikistan	240.9	37.5	..	11.6	..	13.1	..	−1.2	..	4.9	..	5.9
123	Morocco	705.9	22.8	4.1	1.4	0.6	1.5	1.2	(.)	7.0	6.0	27.9	15.2
124	Gabon	37.8	27.7	2.2	0.5	1.2	4.5	0.5	−0.3	3.0	3.1	4.8	10.8 [e]
125	Namibia	179.1	89.1	5.2	3.1	..	..	0.5	1.8	2.6	2.8	29.3	19.5 [e]
126	India	691.2	0.6	0.4	0.1	0.1	0.8	..	..	4.9	15.4	28.7	11.6 [f, g, i]
127	São Tomé and Principe	33.4	218.5	95.0	53.7	0.0	86.7	−0.2	0.0	4.9	15.4	28.7	11.6 [f, g, i]
128	Solomon Islands	122.2	262.3	21.7	47.3	4.7	−1.9	−1.5	−3.0	5.5	6.4	11.3	..
129	Cambodia	478.3	34.7	3.7	9.8	..	2.7	0.0	0.0	2.7	0.6	..	0.8

Human development indicators

TABLE 18

Flows of aid, private capital and debt

		Official development assistance (ODA) received [a] (net disbursements)				Net foreign direct investment inflows [b] (% of GDP)		Other private flows [b, c] (% of GDP)		MDG Total debt service			
		Total (US$ millions)	Per capita (US$)	As % of GDP						As % of GDP		As % of exports of goods, services and net income from abroad	
HDI rank		2004	2004	1990	2004	1990	2004	1990	2004	1990	2004	1990	2004
130	Myanmar	121.1	2.4	..	..	..	..	..	..	..	..	18.2	3.3 [g, j]
131	Botswana	39.0	22.1	3.9	0.4	2.5	0.5	−0.5	0.1	2.8	0.5	4.3	1.2 [e]
132	Comoros	24.5	31.5	17.3	6.7	0.1	0.5	0.0	0.0	0.4	0.9	2.5	.. [g, j]
133	Lao People's Dem. Rep.	269.6	46.5	17.4	11.0	0.7	0.7	0.0	0.0	1.1	2.2	8.5	.. [g, j]
134	Pakistan	1,421.0	9.2	2.8	1.5	0.6	1.2	−0.2	0.2	4.8	4.5	22.9	22.8
135	Bhutan	78.0	36.9	16.5	11.6	0.6	0.1	−0.9	0.0	1.8	1.8	..	..
136	Ghana	1,357.6	62.7	9.6	15.3	0.3	1.6	−0.4	0.3	6.2	2.7	36.0	5.6 [g, h]
137	Bangladesh	1,404.1	10.1	7.0	2.5	(.)	0.8	0.2	(.)	2.5	1.2	34.8	6.9
138	Nepal	427.3	16.1	11.7	6.4	0.2	0.0	−0.4	(.)	1.9	1.7	15.2	8.9
139	Papua New Guinea	266.3	46.1	12.8	6.8	4.8	0.7	1.5	−5.5	17.2	12.1	18.4	..
140	Congo	116.0	29.9	7.8	2.7	0.8	0.0	−3.6	0.0	19.0	8.1	32.2	14.7 [e, g, i]
141	Sudan	882.3	24.8	6.2	4.2	−0.2	7.2	0.0	0.3	0.4	1.5	4.8	8.1 [g, j]
142	Timor-Leste	152.8	172.2	..	45.1	..	..	..	..	..	..	..	..
143	Madagascar	1,235.8	68.2	12.9	28.3	0.7	1.0	−0.5	(.)	7.2	1.8	44.4	4.4 [e, g, h]
144	Cameroon	761.5	47.5	4.0	5.3	−1.0	(.)	−0.1	0.2	4.6	4.5	13.1	7.1 [g, i]
145	Uganda	1,159.0	41.7	15.5	17.0	−0.1	3.3	0.4	0.1	3.4	1.5	78.6	10.0 [g, h]
146	Swaziland	116.5	112.7	6.1	4.9	3.4	2.9	−0.5	0.7	5.3	1.8	5.6	1.7
LOW HUMAN DEVELOPMENT													
147	Togo	61.4	10.3	16.0	3.0	1.1	2.9	0.3	0.1	5.3	1.0	11.5	2.1 [e, g, j]
148	Djibouti	64.1	82.3	46.4	9.7	(.)	5.0	−0.1	0.0	3.6	2.7	..	..
149	Lesotho	102.1	56.8	23.0	7.8	2.8	9.4	(.)	−0.7	3.8	4.0	4.2	4.6
150	Yemen	251.9	12.4	8.4	2.0	−2.7	1.1	3.3	1.7	3.5	1.7	7.1	4.3
151	Zimbabwe	186.5	14.4	3.9	4.0	−0.1	1.3	1.1	0.2	5.4	2.0	19.4	..
152	Kenya	635.1	19.0	13.8	3.9	0.7	0.3	0.8	−0.7	9.2	2.3	28.6	7.7
153	Mauritania	179.8	60.3	23.3	11.7	0.7	19.6	−0.1	(.)	14.3	3.7	28.8	9.6 [g, h]
154	Haiti	242.7	28.9	5.9	6.9	0.3	0.2	0.0	0.0	1.2	3.8	9.0	10.7 [e]
155	Gambia	62.8	42.5	31.3	15.1	4.5	14.5	−2.4	0.0	11.9	8.1	21.8	23.2 [g, i]
156	Senegal	1,051.5	92.4	14.4	13.5	1.0	0.9	−0.2	1.2	5.7	4.3	18.3	7.6 [e, g, h]
157	Eritrea	259.5	61.3	..	28.1	..	3.2	..	0.0	..	2.1	..	..
158	Rwanda	467.5	52.6	11.3	25.3	0.3	0.4	−0.1	0.0	0.8	1.3	10.7	9.8 [g, h]
159	Nigeria	573.4	4.5	0.9	0.8	2.1	2.6	−0.4	−0.2	11.7	3.3	22.3	8.8
160	Guinea	279.3	30.3	10.4	7.2	0.6	2.6	−0.7	0.0	6.0	4.4	19.6	7.5 [g, i]
161	Angola	1,144.1	73.9	2.6	5.9	−3.3	7.4	5.6	6.6	3.2	10.5	7.1	14.8
162	Tanzania, U. Rep. of	1,746.0	46.4	27.5	16.1	(.)	2.3	0.1	(.)	4.2	1.1	31.3	6.4 [g, h]
163	Benin	378.0	46.2	14.5	9.3	3.4	1.5	(.)	(.)	2.1	1.6	9.2	7.6 [e, g, h]
164	Côte d'Ivoire	153.6	8.6	6.4	1.0	0.4	1.1	0.1	−0.9	11.7	3.5	19.1	4.8 [g, k]
165	Zambia	1,081.0	94.2	14.6	20.0	6.2	6.2	−0.3	−0.4	6.1	7.9	14.5	18.2 [g, h]
166	Malawi	476.1	37.8	26.8	25.3	1.2	0.9	0.1	−0.1	7.1	3.2	28.0	13.5 [f, g, i]
167	Congo, Dem. Rep. of the	1,815.0	32.5	9.6	27.4	−0.2	0.0	−0.1	−0.1	3.7	1.8	..	4.8 [g, i]
168	Mozambique	1,228.4	63.2	40.7	20.2	0.4	4.0	1.0	−0.4	3.2	1.4	17.3	3.2 [g, h]
169	Burundi	350.7	48.2	23.3	53.4	0.1	0.5	−0.5	−0.7	3.7	13.4	41.7	119.4 [e, g, i]
170	Ethiopia	1,823.1	24.1	11.8	22.8	0.1	6.8	−0.7	0.9	2.7	1.2	37.6	6.3 [g, h]
171	Chad	318.9	33.8	18.0	7.6	0.5	11.3	(.)	0.0	0.7	1.1	3.8	1.8 [g, i]
172	Central African Republic	104.5	26.2	16.8	8.0	0.1	−1.0	(.)	−0.3	2.0	1.4	12.5	.. [g, j]
173	Guinea-Bissau	76.2	49.5	52.7	27.2	0.8	1.8	(.)	0.0	3.4	16.0	22.1	5.5 [g, h]
174	Burkina Faso	610.0	47.6	10.6	12.6	(.)	0.0	(.)	0.0	1.1	1.2	7.8	9.1 [g, h]
175	Mali	567.4	43.2	19.9	11.7	0.2	3.7	(.)	(.)	2.8	2.1	14.7	6.4 [e, g, h]
176	Sierra Leone	359.7	67.4	9.4	33.4	4.9	2.4	0.6	0.0	3.3	2.5	10.1	10.2 [g, i]
177	Niger	536.1	39.7	16.0	17.4	1.7	0.0	0.4	−0.2	4.0	1.6	6.6	4.6 [e, g, h]

TABLE 18

HDI rank	Official development assistance (ODA) received [a] (net disbursements) Total (US$ millions) 2004	Per capita (US$) 2004	As % of GDP 1990	As % of GDP 2004	Net foreign direct investment inflows [b] (% of GDP) 1990	(% of GDP) 2004	Other private flows [b, c] (% of GDP) 1990	(% of GDP) 2004	MDG Total debt service As % of GDP 1990	As % of GDP 2004	As % of exports of goods, services and net income from abroad 1990	...2004
Developing countries	53,287.0 T	10.5	1.4	0.5	0.9	2.7	0.5	0.7	4.4	4.9	15.6	7.0
Least developed countries	24,755.6 T	33.4	12.0	9.6	0.3	3.8	0.5	0.6	3.1	2.6	16.8	8.7
Arab States	11,163.2 T	35.9	2.7	0.6	0.5	1.5	..	..	..	..	21.3	8.5
East Asia and the Pacific	6,490.1 T	3.3	0.7	0.2	1.7	3.4	..	..	..	..	9.9	2.6
Latin America and the Caribbean	5,635.4 T	10.3	0.4	0.3	0.8	3.0	0.5	−0.2	4.0	7.8	20.6	14.6
South Asia	6,947.8 T	4.5	1.1	0.5	(.)	0.7	0.3	1.3	2.3	2.6	22.8	14.7
Sub-Saharan Africa	22,733.6 T	33.0	..	..	0.4	2.0	..	..	..	..	10.5	5.8
Central and Eastern Europe and the CIS	10,697.9 T	26.4	..	..	..	4.0	..	..	..	..	..	..
OECD	.. T	..	..	..	1.0	1.3	..	..	..	..	..	..
High-income OECD	.. T	..	..	..	1.0	1.3	..	..	..	..	..	..
High human development	.. T	..	..	..	1.0	1.5	..	..	..	..	..	..
Medium human development	31,704.9 T	7.2	1.1	0.4	0.6	2.1	0.5	0.9	4.1	4.4	..	..
Low human development	17,186.5 T	30.1	9.8	7.5	0.6	2.9	0.5	0.4	6.6	3.5	19.4	8.8
High income	.. T	..	..	..	1.0	1.4	..	..	..	..	..	..
Middle income	29,785.7 T	9.8	0.8	0.3	0.8	2.8	0.5	1.0	4.6	6.0	..	..
Low income	33,954.4 T	14.4	4.0	2.5	0.4	1.4	0.3	1.0	3.8	2.8	22.2	9.7
World	64,470.0 T	11.7	..	..	1.0	1.6	..	..	..	..	..	..

NOTES

This table presents data for countries included in Parts I and II of the Development Assistance Committee's (DAC) list of aid recipients (OECD-DAC 2006b). The denominator conventionally used when comparing official development assistance and total debt service to the size of the economy is GNI, not GDP (see *Definitions of statistical terms*). GDP is used here, however, to allow comparability throughout the table. With few exceptions the denominators produce similar results.

a ODA receipts are total net ODA flows from DAC countries as well as Czech Republic, Hungary, Iceland, Israel, Republic of Korea, Kuwait, Poland, Saudi Arabia, Slovakia, Turkey, United Arab Emirates, other small donors, including Estonia, Latvia and Lithuania, and concessional lending from multilateral organizations. A negative value indicates that repayments of ODA loans exceed the amount of ODA received.

b A negative value indicates that the capital flowing out of the country exceeds that flowing in.
c Other private flows combine non-debt-creating portfolio equity investment flows, portfolio debt flows and bank and trade-related lending.
d Data refer to official aid.
e Data refer to 2003.
f Data refer to 2002.
g Country included in the Heavily Indebted Poor Countries (HIPCs) Debt Initiative.
h Completion point reached under the Enhanced HIPC Initiative.
i Decision point reached under the Enhanced HIPC Initiative.
j Country still to be considered under the Enhanced HIPC Initiative.
k Decision point reached under the original HIPC Initiative but not under the Enhanced HIPC Initiative.

SOURCES
Columns 1–4: OECD-DAC 2006c.
Columns 5 and 6: World Bank 2006; aggregates calculated for the Human Development Report Office by the World Bank.
Columns 7 and 8: calculated on the basis of data on portfolio investment, bank- and trade-related lending and GDP data from World Bank 2006.
Columns 9 and 10: calculated on the basis of data on debt service and GDP from World Bank 2006.
Columns 11 and 12: UN 2006c, based on a joint effort by the International Monetary Fund and the World Bank.

Human development indicators

TABLE 19

... to have access to the resources needed for a decent standard of living ...

Priorities in public spending

HDI rank	Public expenditure on health (% of GDP) 2003–04 [c]	Public expenditure on education (% of GDP) 1991 [d]		Military expenditure [a] (% of GDP) 1990		Total debt service [b] (% of GDP) 1990	
		1991 [d]	2002–04 [c]	1990	2004	1990	2004
HIGH HUMAN DEVELOPMENT							
1 Norway	8.6	7.1	7.7	2.9	2.0	..	..
2 Iceland	8.8	..	8.0	0.0	0.0	..	..
3 Australia	6.4	4.9	4.8	2.1	1.9	..	..
4 Ireland	5.8	5.0	4.3	1.2	0.7	..	..
5 Sweden	8.0	7.1	7.0	2.6	1.6	..	..
6 Canada	6.9	6.5	5.2	2.0	1.1	..	..
7 Japan	6.4	..	3.7	0.9	1.0	..	..
8 United States	6.8	5.1	5.9	5.3	4.0	..	..
9 Switzerland	6.7	5.3	5.4	1.8	1.0	..	..
10 Netherlands	6.1	5.6	5.3	2.5	1.7	..	..
11 Finland	5.7	6.5	6.5	1.6	1.2	..	..
12 Luxembourg	6.2	3.0	..	0.9	0.9	..	..
13 Belgium	6.3	5.0	6.2	2.4	1.3	..	..
14 Austria	5.1	5.5	5.5	1.0	0.8	..	..
15 Denmark	7.5	6.9	8.4	2.0	1.5	..	..
16 France	7.7	5.6	6.0	3.4	2.6	..	..
17 Italy	6.3	3.0	4.9	2.1	2.0	..	..
18 United Kingdom	6.9	4.8	5.5	3.9	2.8	..	..
19 Spain	5.5	4.3	4.5	1.8	1.1	..	..
20 New Zealand	6.3	6.1	6.9	1.8	1.0	..	..
21 Germany	8.7	..	4.8	2.8 [e]	1.4	..	..
22 Hong Kong, China (SAR)	..	2.8	4.7	..	..	..	..
23 Israel	6.1	6.5	7.3	12.4	8.7	..	..
24 Greece	5.1	2.3	4.3	4.5	4.2	..	..
25 Singapore	1.6	3.1	..	4.9	4.7	..	..
26 Korea, Rep. of	2.8	3.8	4.6	3.7	2.4	..	..
27 Slovenia	6.7	4.8	6.0	..	1.6	..	..
28 Portugal	6.7	4.6	5.9	2.7	2.3	..	..
29 Cyprus	3.1	3.7	7.4	5.0	1.5	..	..
30 Czech Republic	6.8	..	4.6	..	1.8	..	7.8
31 Barbados	4.8	7.8	7.3	0.8	..	8.2	3.1
32 Malta	7.4	4.4	4.6	0.9	0.8	..	..
33 Kuwait	2.7	4.8	8.2	48.5	7.9	..	..
34 Brunei Darussalam	2.8	3.5	..	..	..	..	..
35 Hungary	6.1	6.1	6.0	2.8	1.5	12.8	17.0
36 Argentina	4.3	3.3	3.5	1.2	1.1	4.4	8.1
37 Poland	4.5	5.2	5.8	2.8	2.0	1.6	14.3
38 Chile	3.0	2.5	3.7	4.3	3.9	9.1	10.2
39 Bahrain	2.8	3.9	..	5.1	4.4	..	..
40 Estonia	4.1	..	5.7	0.0	1.8	..	12.9
41 Lithuania	5.0	5.5	5.2	..	1.7	..	7.9
42 Slovakia	5.2	5.6	4.4	..	1.7	..	12.3
43 Uruguay	2.7	2.5	2.2	3.1	1.2	10.6	11.7
44 Croatia	6.5	5.5	4.5	..	1.7	..	15.4
45 Latvia	3.3	4.1	5.4	..	1.7	..	10.1
46 Qatar	2.0	3.5	..	..	..	..	..
47 Seychelles	4.3	6.5	5.4 [f]	4.0	2.3	5.9	7.4
48 Costa Rica	5.8	3.4	4.9	0.0	0.0	8.8	3.7
49 United Arab Emirates	2.5	1.9	1.6 [f]	6.2	2.4	..	..
50 Cuba	6.3	9.7	..	..	..	..	..
51 Saint Kitts and Nevis	3.4	2.7	4.4 [f]	..	..	1.9	11.8
52 Bahamas	3.0	3.7	..	0.6	0.7	..	..
53 Mexico	2.9	3.8	5.8	0.4	0.4	4.3	7.6

TABLE 19

HDI rank	Public expenditure on health (% of GDP) 2003–04 [c]	Public expenditure on education (% of GDP) 1991 [d]	2002–04 [c]	Military expenditure [a] (% of GDP) 1990	2004	Total debt service [b] (% of GDP) 1990	2004
54 Bulgaria	4.1	5.4	4.2	3.5	2.4	..	10.2
55 Tonga	5.5	..	4.8	..	..	1.7	1.4
56 Oman	2.7	3.4	4.6 [f]	16.5	12.0	6.3	4.1
57 Trinidad and Tobago	1.5	4.1	4.3 [f]	..	..	8.9	3.2
58 Panama	5.0	4.6	3.9 [f]	1.3	0.0	6.5	10.2
59 Antigua and Barbuda	3.2	..	3.8	..	..	..	..
60 Romania	3.8	3.5	3.6	4.6	2.1	(.)	6.5
61 Malaysia	2.2	5.1	8.0	2.6	2.3	9.8	7.8
62 Bosnia and Herzegovina	4.8	..	..	..	2.5	..	2.1
63 Mauritius	2.2	3.8	4.7	0.3	0.2	6.5	4.3
MEDIUM HUMAN DEVELOPMENT							
64 Libyan Arab Jamahiriya	2.6	..	..	..	2.0	..	..
65 Russian Federation	3.3	3.6	3.7	12.3	3.9	..	3.6
66 Macedonia, TFYR	6.0	..	3.4	..	2.6	..	4.6
67 Belarus	3.9	5.7	5.8	..	1.4	..	1.4
68 Dominica	4.5	..	..	..	..	3.5	6.8
69 Brazil	3.4	..	4.1	2.5	1.5	1.8	8.9
70 Colombia	6.4	2.4	4.9	2.2	3.8	9.7	7.9
71 Saint Lucia	3.4	..	5.0	..	..	1.6	3.5
72 Venezuela, RB	2.0	4.5	..	..	1.2	10.6	6.0
73 Albania	2.7	..	2.8 [f]	5.9	1.2	..	1.0
74 Thailand	2.0	3.1	4.2	2.6	1.2	6.2	7.7
75 Samoa (Western)	4.3	..	4.3 [f]	..	..	4.9	5.6
76 Saudi Arabia	3.0	5.8	..	15.6	8.3	..	..
77 Ukraine	3.8	6.2	4.6	..	2.6	..	6.6
78 Lebanon	3.0	..	2.6	7.6	3.8	3.5	20.0
79 Kazakhstan	2.0	3.9	2.4	..	1.0	..	21.5
80 Armenia	1.2	..	3.2 [f]	..	2.6	..	3.5
81 China	2.0	2.2	..	2.7	2.4	2.0	1.2
82 Peru	2.1	2.8	3.0	0.1	1.2	1.8	4.0
83 Ecuador	2.0	3.4	..	1.9	2.4	10.5	12.3
84 Philippines	1.4	3.0	3.2	1.4	0.9	8.1	13.7
85 Grenada	4.9	4.9	5.2	..	..	1.5	6.7
86 Jordan	4.2	8.0	..	9.9	8.2	15.6	6.1
87 Tunisia	2.5	6.0	8.1	2.0	1.5	11.6	7.2
88 Saint Vincent and the Grenadines	4.1	5.9	11.1	..	..	2.2	5.2
89 Suriname	3.6	..	..	..	..	..	..
90 Fiji	2.3	5.1	6.4	2.3	1.2	7.9	0.6
91 Paraguay	2.3	1.9	4.3	1.0	0.7	6.2	6.8
92 Turkey	5.4	2.4	3.7	3.5	3.1	4.9	11.2
93 Sri Lanka	1.6	3.2	..	2.1	2.8	4.8	3.8
94 Dominican Republic	2.3	..	1.1	0.6	0.5	3.3	4.0
95 Belize	2.2	4.6	5.1	1.2	..	4.4	30.4
96 Iran, Islamic Rep. of	3.1	4.1	4.8	2.9	4.5	0.5	1.2
97 Georgia	1.0	..	2.9	..	1.4	..	4.2
98 Maldives	5.5	7.0	8.1 [f]	..	..	4.1	4.3
99 Azerbaijan	0.9	7.7	3.3 [f]	..	1.8	..	2.8
100 Occupied Palestinian Territories	..	..	..	..	..	..	..
101 El Salvador	3.7	1.8	2.8 [f]	2.0	0.7	4.3	3.9
102 Algeria	3.3	5.1	..	1.5	3.4	14.2	6.8
103 Guyana	4.0	2.2	5.5	0.9	..	74.5	6.2
104 Jamaica	2.7	4.5	4.9	0.6	0.7	14.4	9.4
105 Turkmenistan	2.6	3.9	..	..	..	..	..
106 Cape Verde	3.4	3.6	7.3	0.0	0.7	1.7	2.7

Human development indicators

TABLE 19

Priorities in public spending

HDI rank	Public expenditure on health (% of GDP) 2003–04[c]	Public expenditure on education (% of GDP) 1991[d]	Public expenditure on education (% of GDP) 2002–04[c]	Military expenditure[a] (% of GDP) 1990	Military expenditure[a] (% of GDP) 2004	Total debt service[b] (% of GDP) 1990	Total debt service[b] (% of GDP) 2004
107 Syrian Arab Republic	2.5	3.9	..	6.9	6.6	9.7	1.4
108 Indonesia	1.1	1.0	0.9	1.8	1.1	8.7	7.9
109 Viet Nam	1.5	1.8	..	7.9	..	2.7	1.7
110 Kyrgyzstan	2.2	6.0	4.4[f]	..	2.9	..	7.3
111 Egypt	2.5	3.9	..	4.5	2.8	7.1	2.9
112 Nicaragua	3.7	3.4	3.1[f]	10.6	0.7	1.6	2.8
113 Uzbekistan	2.4	9.4	..	..	..	..	7.1
114 Moldova, Rep. of	3.9	5.3	4.9[f]	..	0.4	..	9.6
115 Bolivia	4.3	2.4	6.4[f]	2.4	2.0	7.9	5.9
116 Mongolia	4.3	11.5	5.6	5.7	2.0	..	2.5
117 Honduras	4.0	3.8	..	..	0.7	12.8	4.5
118 Guatemala	2.1	1.3	..	1.5	0.4	3.0	2.0
119 Vanuatu	2.9	4.6	9.6	..	..	1.6	1.1
120 Equatorial Guinea	1.0	..	0.6[f]	..	..	3.9	0.2
121 South Africa	3.2	5.9	5.4	3.8	1.4	..	1.8
122 Tajikistan	0.9	..	2.8	..	2.2	..	4.9
123 Morocco	1.7	5.0	6.3	4.1	4.5	7.0	6.0
124 Gabon	2.9	..	..	..	1.7	3.0	3.1
125 Namibia	4.5	7.9	7.2	..	3.1	..	..
126 India	1.2	3.7	3.3	3.2	3.0	2.6	2.8
127 São Tomé and Principe	7.2	..	..	..	..	4.9	15.4
128 Solomon Islands	4.5	3.8	..	..	..	5.5	6.4
129 Cambodia	2.1	..	2.0	3.1	2.2	2.7	0.6
130 Myanmar	0.5	..	..	3.4	..	..	..
131 Botswana	3.3	6.2	..	4.1	3.8	2.8	0.5
132 Comoros	1.5	..	3.9	..	..	0.4	0.9
133 Lao People's Dem. Rep.	1.2	..	2.3	..	..	1.1	2.2
134 Pakistan	0.7	2.6	2.0	5.8	3.4	4.8	4.5
135 Bhutan	2.6	..	..	..	..	1.8	1.8
136 Ghana	1.4	..	..	0.4	0.8	6.2	2.7
137 Bangladesh	1.1	1.5	2.2	1.0	1.2	2.5	1.2
138 Nepal	1.5	2.0	3.4	0.9	1.7	1.9	1.7
139 Papua New Guinea	3.0	..	..	2.1	0.6	17.2	12.1
140 Congo	1.3	7.4	3.2[f]	..	..	19.0	8.1
141 Sudan	1.9	6.0	..	3.5	0.0	0.4	1.5
142 Timor-Leste	7.3	..	..	..	..	..	..
143 Madagascar	1.7	2.5	3.3	1.2	..	7.2	1.8
144 Cameroon	1.2	3.2	3.8	1.5	1.4	4.6	4.5
145 Uganda	2.2	1.5	5.2[f]	3.1	2.3	3.4	1.5
146 Swaziland	3.3	5.8	6.2	1.9	..	5.3	1.8
LOW HUMAN DEVELOPMENT							
147 Togo	1.4	..	2.6	3.1	1.6	5.3	1.0
148 Djibouti	3.8	3.5	6.1	5.9	..	3.6	2.7
149 Lesotho	4.1	6.2	9.0[f]	4.5	2.3	3.8	4.0
150 Yemen	2.2	..	..	7.9	6.3	3.5	1.7
151 Zimbabwe	2.8	7.7	..	4.4	..	5.4	2.0
152 Kenya	1.7	6.7	7.0	2.9	1.6	9.2	2.3
153 Mauritania	3.2	4.6	3.4[f]	3.8	1.4	14.3	3.7
154 Haiti	2.9	1.4	..	0.1	..	1.2	3.8
155 Gambia	3.2	3.8	1.9[f]	1.2	0.4	11.9	8.1
156 Senegal	2.1	3.9	4.0	2.0	1.4	5.7	4.3
157 Eritrea	2.0	..	3.8	..	..	..	2.1
158 Rwanda	1.6	..	..	3.7	2.2	0.8	1.3
159 Nigeria	1.3	0.9	..	0.9	1.0	11.7	3.3

TABLE 19

HDI rank	Public expenditure on health (% of GDP) 2003–04 [c]	Public expenditure on education (% of GDP)		Military expenditure [a] (% of GDP)		Total debt service [b] (% of GDP)	
		1991 [d]	2002–04 [c]	1990	2004	1990	2004
160 Guinea	0.9	2.0	..	..	..	6.0	4.4
161 Angola	2.4	..	..	2.7	4.2	3.2	10.5
162 Tanzania, U. Rep. of	2.4	2.8	..	..	1.1	4.2	1.1
163 Benin	1.9	..	3.3 [f]	1.8	..	2.1	1.6
164 Côte d'Ivoire	1.0	..	..	1.3	..	11.7	3.5
165 Zambia	2.8	2.8	2.8	3.7	..	6.1	7.9
166 Malawi	3.3	3.2	6.0	1.3	..	7.1	3.2
167 Congo, Dem. Rep. of the	0.7	..	..	..	3.0	3.7	1.8
168 Mozambique	2.9	..	..	5.9	1.3	3.2	1.4
169 Burundi	0.7	3.5	5.2	3.4	6.3	3.7	13.4
170 Ethiopia	3.4	3.4	4.6 [f]	8.5	..	2.7	1.2
171 Chad	2.6	1.6	..	..	1.0	0.7	1.1
172 Central African Republic	1.5	2.2	..	..	1.2	2.0	1.4
173 Guinea-Bissau	2.6	..	..	..	..	3.4	16.0
174 Burkina Faso	2.6	2.6	..	3.0	1.3	1.1	1.2
175 Mali	2.8	..	..	2.1	1.9	2.8	2.1
176 Sierra Leone	2.0	..	..	1.4	1.2	3.3	2.5
177 Niger	2.5	3.3	2.3	..	1.1	4.0	1.6

NOTES

a Because of limitations in the data, comparisons across countries should be made with caution. For detailed notes on the data see SIPRI 2006a.

b For aggregates, see table 18.

c Data refer to the most recent year available during the period specified.

d Data may not be comparable across countries because of differences in methods of data collection.

e Data refer to the Federal Republic of Germany before reunification.

f Data refer to United Nations Educational, Scientific and Cultural Organization Institute for Statistics estimate when national estimate is not available.

SOURCES

Column 1: calculated on the basis of data on health expenditure from WHO 2006b.

Columns 2 and 3: UNESCO Institute for Statistics 2006b.

Columns 4 and 5: SIPRI 2006c.

Columns 6 and 7: calculated on the basis of data on GDP and total debt service from World Bank 2006.

TABLE **20**

... to have access to the resources needed for a decent standard of living ...

Unemployment in OECD countries

| | | Unemployed people (thousands) | Unemployment rate | | | MDG Youth unemployment rate | | Long-term unemployment (% of total unemployment) | |
| | | | Total (% of labour force) | Average annual (% of labour force) | Female (% of male rate) | Total (% of labour force ages 15–24) [a] | Female (% of male rate) | Women | Men |
HDI rank		2005	2005	1995–2005	2005	2005	2005	2005	2005
HIGH HUMAN DEVELOPMENT									
1	Norway	111.2	4.6	4.1	91	12.0	92	8.5	10.4
2	Iceland	4.2	2.5	3.1	99	7.2	70	14.0 [b]	8.8 [b]
3	Australia	535.0	5.1	6.9	106	10.8	95	14.9	20.2
4	Ireland	86.4	4.3	6.8	82	8.3	80	21.1	42.4
5	Sweden	252.4	5.6	5.9	100	26.2	104	16.4 [b]	20.9 [b]
6	Canada	1,175.8	6.8	8.0	91	12.4	75	9.1	10.1
7	Japan	2,902.0	4.4	4.4	94	8.7	74	22.6	40.3
8	United States	7,598.8	5.1	5.1	100	11.3	82	10.8	12.6
9	Switzerland	179.2	4.1	3.4	131	8.8	108	40.4	37.1
10	Netherlands	539.5	6.2	4.5	99	9.7	91	35.0	44.7
11	Finland	225.0	8.6	10.8	105	19.9	93	21.9	27.9
12	Luxembourg	9.8	4.6	3.3	167	13.7	138	20.3	33.6
13	Belgium	387.4	8.4	8.3	122	19.9	93	52.7	50.4
14	Austria	252.7	5.8	5.4	118	7.8	83	26.5 [b]	28.6 [b]
15	Denmark	142.3	4.9	5.1	133	7.9	159	22.7	29.7
16	France	2,742.2	10.0	10.4	121	22.8	115	43.2	41.8
17	Italy	1,858.0	7.7	10.2	162	24.0	128	53.8	50.5
18	United Kingdom	1,438.7	4.8	6.0	82	11.8	75	16.9	26.2
19	Spain	1,895.0	9.1	12.9	172	19.7	140	36.0	28.2
20	New Zealand	77.3	3.6	5.6	117	9.4	108	6.2	12.6
21	Germany	3,987.2	9.3	8.0	96	14.2	88	54.4	53.8
24	Greece	492.0	10.6	10.7	259	25.3	199	59.6	43.1
26	Korea, Rep. of	891.3	3.8	3.9	86	10.2	73	0.4	1.0
28	Portugal	412.0	7.5	5.8	129	16.1	140	49.9	47.1
30	Czech Republic	412.7	8.0	7.0	151	19.3	99	54.2	52.9
35	Hungary	296.1	7.1	7.4	107	19.4	97	44.2	47.9
37	Poland	3,020.2	17.8	15.6	115	37.8	107	53.1	51.3
42	Slovakia	432.6	16.4	15.8	112	29.9	93	67.4	68.7
53	Mexico	1,575.2	3.6	3.1	105	6.6	121	2.6	2.3
MEDIUM HUMAN DEVELOPMENT									
92	Turkey	2,526.4	10.0	8.2	101	19.3	100	47.4	36.9
OECD		36,458.5 T	6.5	6.6	108	13.3	94	33.0	32.9

NOTES
a The age range may be 16–24 for some countries.
b Data refer to 2004.

SOURCES
Columns 1–3 and 5: OECD 2006a.
Columns 4 and 6: calculated on the basis of data on male and female unemployment rates from OECD 2006c.
Columns 7 and 8: OECD 2006b.

Human development indicators

TABLE 21
. . . while preserving it for future generations . . .

Energy and the environment

HDI rank		Traditional fuel consumption (% of total energy requirements) 2003	Electricity consumption per capita (kilowatt-hours)		MDG GDP per unit of energy use (2000 PPP US$ per kg of oil equivalent)		MDG Carbon dioxide emissions Per capita (metric tons)		Share of world total [b] (%)	Ratification of environmental treaties [a] Cartagena Protocol on Biosafety	Framework Convention on Climate Change	Kyoto Protocol to the Framework Convention on Climate Change	Convention on Biological Diversity
			1980	2003	1980	2003	1980	2003	2003				
HIGH HUMAN DEVELOPMENT													
1	Norway	6.1 c, d	22,400 c	25,295 c	4.5	6.8	8.2 e	9.9 e	0.2 e	●	●	●	●
2	Iceland	0.0	13,838	29,412	3.1	2.5	8.2	7.6	(.)	○	●	●	●
3	Australia	7.1	6,599	11,446	3.6	4.8	13.9	18.0	1.4		●	○	●
4	Ireland	1.0	3,106	6,660	4.2	9.3	7.7	10.3	0.2	●	●	●	●
5	Sweden	20.4	11,700	16,603	3.7	4.6	8.6	5.9	0.2	●	●	●	●
6	Canada	4.3	14,243	18,329	2.5	3.4	17.2	17.9	2.3	○	●	●	●
7	Japan	1.2	4,944	8,212	5.7	6.5	7.9	9.7	4.9	●	●	●	●
8	United States	3.1	10,336	14,057	2.8	4.5	20.1 f	19.8 f	23.0 f		●	○	○
9	Switzerland	5.8 g	5,878 g	8,701 g	7.8	8.1	6.5	5.6	0.2	●	●	●	●
10	Netherlands	1.4	4,560	7,026	4.2	5.8	10.9	8.7	0.6	●	●	●	●
11	Finland	22.0	8,372	17,111	3.2	3.7	11.9	13.0	0.3	●	●	●	●
12	Luxembourg	1.2	10,879	16,348	2.4	6.5	29.1	22.0	(.)	●	●	●	●
13	Belgium	1.5	5,177	8,791	4.0	4.9	13.3	8.3	0.3	●	●	●	●
14	Austria	13.2	4,988	8,527	6.1	7.2	6.9	8.6	0.3	●	●	●	●
15	Denmark	11.8	5,059	7,138	5.2	7.5	12.3	10.1	0.2	●	●	●	●
16	France	4.6 h	4,633 h	8,319 h	4.9	5.9	9.0 h	6.2 h	1.5 h	●	●	●	●
17	Italy	1.8 i	3,364 i	5,943 i	7.4	8.2	6.6 i	7.7 i	1.8 i	●	●	●	●
18	United Kingdom	0.6	5,022	6,755	4.8	7.1	10.5	9.4	2.2	●	●	●	●
19	Spain	3.7	2,906	6,325	7.4	7.0	5.3	7.3	1.2	●	●	●	●
20	New Zealand	4.5	7,270	10,453	5.0	4.8	5.6	8.8	0.1	●	●	●	●
21	Germany	2.7	..	7,258	3.7	6.1	..	9.8	3.2	●	●	●	●
22	Hong Kong, China (SAR)	0.4 d	2,449	6,103	11.1	10.9	3.3	5.5	0.2				
23	Israel	0.0	3,187	6,843	7.0	7.1	5.6	10.6	0.3		●	●	●
24	Greece	3.9	2,413	5,497	8.7	7.3	5.4	8.7	0.4	●	●	●	●
25	Singapore	0.2	2,836	8,087	3.9	4.5	12.5	11.3	0.2		●	●	●
26	Korea, Rep. of	1.8 d	1,051	7,338	4.5	4.2	3.3	9.6	1.8	○	●	●	●
27	Slovenia	7.5	..	7,109	..	5.2	..	7.8	0.1	●	●	●	●
28	Portugal	12.8	1,750	4,770	10.1	7.2	2.8	5.6	0.2	●	●	●	●
29	Cyprus	1.1	1,692	5,656	5.7	6.3	5.2	8.9	(.)	●	●	●	●
30	Czech Republic	3.0	..	6,567	..	3.9	..	11.4	0.5	●	●	●	●
31	Barbados	6.3	1,333	3,226	..	..	2.7	4.4	(.)	●	●	●	●
32	Malta	0.0	1,627	5,632	6.7	7.7	3.1	6.2	(.)		●	●	●
33	Kuwait	0.0 i	6,849	16,379	1.8	1.8	19.7 i	31.1 i	0.3 i		●	●	●
34	Brunei Darussalam	1.1	2,430	9,133	..	..	35.6	12.7	(.)		●	●	●
35	Hungary	5.0	2,920	4,051	3.7	5.6	7.7	5.7	0.2	●	●	●	●
36	Argentina	4.1	1,413	2,543	7.9	7.2	3.8	3.4	0.5	○	●	●	●
37	Poland	5.7	3,419	3,702	..	4.6	12.8	7.9	1.2	●	●	●	●
38	Chile	11.5	1,054	3,092	5.4	5.9	2.5	3.7	0.2	○	●	●	●
39	Bahrain	..	4,784	11,274	1.6	1.8	22.6	31.0	0.1		●	●	●
40	Estonia	17.1	..	6,094	..	3.4	..	13.6	0.1	●	●	●	●
41	Lithuania	13.0	..	3,453	..	4.3	..	3.7	0.1	●	●	●	●
42	Slovakia	2.2	..	5,377	..	3.7	..	7.0	0.1	●	●	●	●
43	Uruguay	23.1	1,163	2,310	8.5	10.5	2.0	1.3	(.)	○	●	●	●
44	Croatia	6.2	..	3,733	..	5.6	..	5.3	0.1	●	●	○	●
45	Latvia	46.5	..	2,835	..	5.3	..	2.9	(.)	●	●	●	●
46	Qatar	0.0	10,616	19,374	..	..	57.2	63.1	0.2		●	●	●
47	Seychelles	..	794	2,716 d	..	..	1.5	6.9	(.)	○	●	●	●
48	Costa Rica	29.6	964	1,764	10.2	9.9	1.1	1.5	(.)	●	●	●	●
49	United Arab Emirates	0.0	6,204	15,878	6.5	2.2	36.4	33.6	0.5	●	●	●	●
50	Cuba	17.7	1,029	1,407	..	..	3.2	2.3	0.1	●	●	●	●
51	Saint Kitts and Nevis	..	..	3,256	..	..	..	3.0	(.)	●	●	●	●
52	Bahamas	..	4,062	6,700	..	..	38.1	6.0	(.)	●	●	●	●
53	Mexico	13.0	999	2,108	5.5	5.6	4.2	4.0	1.7	●	●	●	●

Human development indicators

TABLE 21

Energy and the environment

HDI rank		Traditional fuel consumption (% of total energy requirements) 2003	Electricity consumption per capita (kilowatt-hours) 1980	2003	MDG GDP per unit of energy use (2000 PPP US$ per kg of oil equivalent) 1980	2003	MDG Carbon dioxide emissions Per capita (metric tons) 1980	2003	Share of world total [b] (%) 2003	Ratification of environmental treaties [a] Cartagena Protocol on Biosafety	Framework Convention on Climate Change	Kyoto Protocol to the Framework Convention on Climate Change	Convention on Biological Diversity
54	Bulgaria	6.5	4,371	4,735	1.6	2.8	8.5	5.6	0.2	●	●		●
55	Tonga	0.0[d]	109	356[d]	..	..	0.4	1.1	(.)	●	●		●
56	Oman	0.0	847	3,817	8.5	2.8	5.0	12.9	0.1	●	●	●	●
57	Trinidad and Tobago	0.6	1,900	4,925	2.7	1.2	15.4	22.1	0.1	●	●	●	●
58	Panama	28.5	930	1,733	7.3	7.6	1.8	1.9	(.)	●	●	●	●
59	Antigua and Barbuda	..	984	1,603[d]	..	..	2.2	5.0	(.)	●	●	●	●
60	Romania	12.4	3,061	2,441	..	4.0	8.7	4.2	0.4	●	●	●	●
61	Malaysia	6.5[d]	740	3,196	4.5	3.9	2.0	6.4	0.6	●	●	●	●
62	Bosnia and Herzegovina	7.9	..	2,636	..	5.3	..	4.9	0.1		●	●	●
63	Mauritius	25.5	482	1,683	..	..	0.6	2.6	(.)	●	●	●	●
MEDIUM HUMAN DEVELOPMENT													
64	Libyan Arab Jamahiriya	1.7	1,588	3,347	..	..	8.9	8.9	0.2	●	●		●
65	Russian Federation	2.7	..	6,303	..	1.9	..	10.3	5.9		●	●	●
66	Macedonia, TFYR	9.7	..	3,794	..	..	..	5.2	(.)	●	●	●	●
67	Belarus	5.5	..	3,388	..	2.2	..	6.4	0.2	●	●	●	●
68	Dominica	..	149	1,243[d]	..	..	0.5	1.8	(.)	●	●	●	●
69	Brazil	29.1	1,145	2,246	7.5	6.9	1.5	1.6	1.2	●	●	●	●
70	Colombia	15.8	726	1,045	7.4	10.1	1.4	1.3	0.2	●	●	●	●
71	Saint Lucia	..	504	1,851[d]	..	..	0.9	2.1	(.)	●	●	●	●
72	Venezuela, RB	2.5	2,379	3,510	2.9	2.3	5.8	5.6	0.6	●	●	●	●
73	Albania	6.3	1,204	1,743	..	6.4	1.8	1.0	(.)	●	●	●	●
74	Thailand	17.7	340	1,896[d]	5.1	5.0	0.9	3.9	1.0	●	●	●	●
75	Samoa (Western)	..	252	613[d]	..	..	0.6	0.8	(.)	●	●	●	●
76	Saudi Arabia	(.)[j]	1,969	6,749	6.6	2.2	17.3[j]	13.0[j]	1.2[j]	●	●	●	●
77	Ukraine	1.6	..	3,683	..	1.9	..	6.6	1.3		●		●
78	Lebanon	0.4	1,056	2,829	..	3.0	2.3	5.4	0.1		●		●
79	Kazakhstan	0.2	..	4,114	..	1.9	..	10.7	0.6	●	●	○	●
80	Armenia	1.1	..	1,375	..	5.2	..	1.1	(.)	●	●	●	●
81	China	4.6	307	1,440	1.3	4.5	1.5	3.2	16.5	●	●	●	●
82	Peru	24.7	579	868	7.9	11.3	1.4	1.0	0.1	●	●	●	●
83	Ecuador	18.7	423	950	5.2	4.9	1.7	1.8	0.1	●	●	●	●
84	Philippines	33.2	373	655	9.8	7.8	0.8	1.0	0.3	○	●	●	●
85	Grenada	0.0	281	1,628	..	..	0.5	2.2	(.)	●	●	●	●
86	Jordan	1.3	366	1,524	5.5	4.0	2.1	3.2	0.1	●	●	●	●
87	Tunisia	8.6	434	1,200	6.9	8.1	1.5	2.1	0.1	●	●	●	●
88	Saint Vincent and the Grenadines	..	276	940[d]	..	..	0.4	1.6	(.)	●	●	●	●
89	Suriname	3.3	4,442	3,537	..	..	6.7	5.1	(.)		●		●
90	Fiji	36.0[d]	489	627[d]	..	..	1.2	1.3	(.)	●	●	●	●
91	Paraguay	55.0	233	1,113	7.3	6.4	0.5	0.7	(.)	●	●	●	●
92	Turkey	9.1	554	1,979	5.9	6.0	1.7	3.1	0.9	●	●		●
93	Sri Lanka	60.4	113	407	5.8	8.8	0.2	0.5	(.)	●	●	●	●
94	Dominican Republic	26.9	582	1,532	6.5	7.4	1.1	2.5	0.1	●	●	●	●
95	Belize	25.0[d]	370	708[d]	..	..	1.3	3.0	(.)	●	●	●	●
96	Iran, Islamic Rep. of	0.7	570	2,304	4.9	3.2	3.0	5.6	1.5	●	●	●	●
97	Georgia	23.9	..	1,566	..	4.1	..	0.8	(.)	●	●	●	●
98	Maldives	0.0	25	490	..	..	0.3	1.4	(.)	●	●	●	●
99	Azerbaijan	0.0	..	2,815	..	2.3	..	3.5	0.1	●	●	●	●
100	Occupied Palestinian Territories	..	..	..	..	..	..	..	..				
101	El Salvador	46.3	336	663	7.6	6.9	0.5	1.0	(.)	●	●	●	●
102	Algeria	6.4	381	929	8.5	5.6	3.5	5.1	0.7	●	●	●	●
103	Guyana	43.6	545	1,172[d]	..	..	2.3	2.2	(.)	●	●	●	●
104	Jamaica	17.0	834	2,696	2.9	2.5	4.0	4.1	(.)	○	●	●	●
105	Turkmenistan	0.0	..	1,999	..	..	..	9.2	0.2		●	●	●
106	Cape Verde	0.0[d]	55	100[d]	..	..	0.4	0.3	(.)	●	●	●	●

TABLE 21

HDI rank		Traditional fuel consumption (% of total energy requirements) 2003	Electricity consumption per capita (kilowatt-hours) 1980	Electricity consumption per capita (kilowatt-hours) 2003	MDG GDP per unit of energy use (2000 PPP US$ per kg of oil equivalent) 1980	MDG GDP per unit of energy use 2003	MDG Carbon dioxide emissions Per capita (metric tons) 1980	Per capita 2003	Share of world total[b] (%) 2003	Cartagena Protocol on Biosafety	Framework Convention on Climate Change	Kyoto Protocol to the Framework Convention on Climate Change	Convention on Biological Diversity
107	Syrian Arab Republic	0.0	433	1,683	4.7	3.4	2.2	2.7	0.2	●	●	●	●
108	Indonesia	15.9	94	498	3.9	4.3	0.6	1.4	1.2	●	●	●	●
109	Viet Nam	23.3	78	503 d	..	4.4	0.3	0.9	0.3	●	●	●	●
110	Kyrgyzstan	0.0	..	2,417	..	3.2	..	1.0	(.)	●	●	●	●
111	Egypt	9.4 d	433	1,340 d	6.4	5.1	1.0	2.0	0.6	●	●	●	●
112	Nicaragua	69.3	363	492	8.7	5.5	0.7	0.7	(.)	●	●	●	●
113	Uzbekistan	0.0	..	1,890	..	0.8	..	4.8	0.5	●	●	●	●
114	Moldova, Rep. of	2.1	..	1,900	..	1.9	..	1.7	(.)	●	●	●	●
115	Bolivia	18.8	292	481	5.4	4.9	0.8	0.9	(.)	●	●	●	●
116	Mongolia	2.2	1,119	1,273	..	..	4.1	3.1	(.)	●	●	●	●
117	Honduras	63.6	259	694	5.0	4.9	0.6	0.9	(.)	○	●	●	●
118	Guatemala	72.1	245	501	7.0	6.5	0.6	0.9	(.)	●	●	●	●
119	Vanuatu	50.0 d	171	208 d	..	..	0.5	0.4	(.)		●	●	●
120	Equatorial Guinea	57.1	83	51 d	..	..	0.3	0.3	(.)		●	●	●
121	South Africa	11.6 k	3,181 k	4,595 k	4.5	3.9	7.2	7.8	1.4	●	●	●	●
122	Tajikistan	..	..	2,645	..	2.1	..	0.7	(.)	●	●	●	●
123	Morocco	6.1	254	649	11.3	10.2	0.8	1.2	0.2	○	●	●	●
124	Gabon	65.8	766	1,229	3.5	4.9	8.9	0.9	(.)		●	●	●
125	Namibia	..l	..l	..l	..	9.9	..	1.2	(.)	●	●	●	●
126	India	19.8	173	594	3.3	5.3	0.5	1.2	5.1	●	●	●	●
127	São Tomé and Principe	..	96	102 d	..	..	0.4	0.6	(.)		●	●	●
128	Solomon Islands	50.0 d	93	69 d	..	..	0.4	0.4	(.)	●	●	●	●
129	Cambodia	92.2	15	9 d	..	..	(.)	(.)	(.)	●	●	●	●
130	Myanmar	83.9	44	126	..	..	0.1	0.2	(.)	○	●	●	●
131	Botswana	..l	..l	..l	..	..	0.9	2.3	(.)	●	●	●	●
132	Comoros	..	26	32 d	..	..	0.1	0.1	(.)		●	●	●
133	Lao People's Dem. Rep.	78.4	68	135 d	..	..	0.1	0.2	(.)	●	●	●	●
134	Pakistan	23.5	176	493	3.5	4.2	0.4	0.8	0.5	○	●	●	●
135	Bhutan	87.8	17	218 d	..	..	(.)	0.2	(.)	●	●	●	●
136	Ghana	84.7	450	285	4.8	5.0	0.2	0.4	(.)	●	●	●	●
137	Bangladesh	51.5	30	145	10.8	10.4	0.1	0.3	0.1	●	●	●	●
138	Nepal	93.2	17	91	2.7	4.0	(.)	0.1	(.)	○	●	●	●
139	Papua New Guinea	62.2	406	251 d	..	..	0.6	0.4	(.)	●	●	●	●
140	Congo	69.0	98	206	1.6	3.3	0.2	0.4	(.)		●	●	●
141	Sudan	86.5	47	101	2.5	3.7	0.2	0.3	(.)	●	●	●	●
142	Timor-Leste	..	..	301 d	..	..	..	0.2	(.)				
143	Madagascar	81.9	49	50 d	..	..	0.2	0.1	(.)	●	●	●	●
144	Cameroon	86.3	168	226	5.3	4.6	0.4	0.2	(.)	●	●	●	●
145	Uganda	93.5	28	59 d	..	..	0.1	0.1	(.)	●	●	●	●
146	Swaziland	..l	..l	..l	..	..	0.8	0.9	(.)		●	●	●
LOW HUMAN DEVELOPMENT													
147	Togo	84.4	74	91	6.4	3.2	0.2	0.4	(.)	●	●	●	●
148	Djibouti	..	416	455 d	..	..	0.9	0.5	(.)	●	●	●	●
149	Lesotho	..l	..l	..l	..	..	..	..	..	●	●	●	●
150	Yemen	4.0	..	212	..	2.8	..	0.9	0.1	●	●	●	●
151	Zimbabwe	67.2	1,020	998	2.8	2.6	1.3	0.9	(.)	●	●	●	●
152	Kenya	83.1	109	154	1.8	2.1	0.4	0.3	(.)	●	●	●	●
153	Mauritania	35.8 d	60	60 d	..	..	0.4	0.9	(.)	●	●	●	●
154	Haiti	79.5	58	61	8.2	6.4	0.1	0.2	(.)	○	●	●	●
155	Gambia	66.7	70	101 d	..	..	0.2	0.2	(.)	●	●	●	●
156	Senegal	70.9	115	192 d	4.3	5.2	0.6	0.4	(.)	●	●	●	●
157	Eritrea	85.2	..	62	..	..	..	0.2	(.)	●	●	●	●
158	Rwanda	84.7	32	39 d	..	..	0.1	0.1	(.)	●	●	●	●
159	Nigeria	82.9	108	162	1.3	1.3	1.0	0.4	0.2	●	●	●	●

Human development indicators

TABLE 21

Energy and the environment

		Traditional fuel consumption (% of total energy requirements)	Electricity consumption per capita (kilowatt-hours)		MDG GDP per unit of energy use (2000 PPP US$ per kg of oil equivalent)		MDG Carbon dioxide emissions			Ratification of environmental treaties [a]			
							Per capita (metric tons)		Share of world total [b] (%)	Cartagena Protocol on Biosafety	Framework Convention on Climate Change	Kyoto Protocol to the Framework Convention on Climate Change	Convention on Biological Diversity
HDI rank		2003	1980	2003	1980	2003	1980	2003	2003				
160	Guinea	87.1	85	89 d	..	..	0.2	0.1	(.)	○	●	●	●
161	Angola	74.4	214	178	..	3.1	0.7	0.6	(.)		●		●
162	Tanzania, U. Rep. of	94.4	41	78	..	1.3	0.1	0.1	(.)	●	●	●	●
163	Benin	81.3	37	82	2.4	3.5	0.1	0.3	(.)	●	●	●	●
164	Côte d'Ivoire	75.5	220	209	5.2	3.8	0.7	0.3	(.)		●	●	●
165	Zambia	87.2	1,125	631	1.5	1.4	0.6	0.2	(.)	●	●	●	●
166	Malawi	82.9	66	77 d	..	..	0.1	0.1	(.)	○	●	●	●
167	Congo, Dem. Rep. of the	97.2	161	86	6.0	2.1	0.1	(.)	(.)	●	●	●	●
168	Mozambique	90.9	364	399	1.0	2.5	0.3	0.1	(.)	●	●	●	●
169	Burundi	95.7	12	23 d	..	..	(.)	(.)	(.)		●	●	●
170	Ethiopia	96.5	..	33	..	2.1	(.)	0.1	(.)	●	●	●	●
171	Chad	98.6	10	11 d	..	..	(.)	(.)	(.)	○	●		●
172	Central African Republic	83.3	29	35 d	..	..	(.)	0.1	(.)	○	●		●
173	Guinea-Bissau	50.0	18	45 d	..	..	0.2	0.2	(.)		●	●	●
174	Burkina Faso	83.3	16	32 d	..	..	0.1	0.1	(.)	●	●	●	●
175	Mali	86.7	15	38 d	..	..	0.1	(.)	(.)	●	●	●	●
176	Sierra Leone	91.2	62	49 d	..	..	0.2	0.1	(.)		●		●
177	Niger	85.6	..	40 d	..	..	0.1	0.1	(.)	●	●	●	●
	Developing countries	26.3	388	1,157	3.7	4.7	1.3	2.2	42.7	..	..	..	..
	Least developed countries	78.3	83	114	..	3.8	0.1	0.2	0.5	..	..	..	..
	Arab States	16.9	626	1,977	5.8	3.5	3.2	4.4	4.8	..	..	..	..
	East Asia and the Pacific	11.4	329	1,418	2.1	4.6	1.4	2.9	22.5	..	..	..	..
	Latin America and the Caribbean	23.3	1,019	1,932	6.4	6.2	2.4	2.4	5.2	..	..	..	..
	South Asia	24.8	171	598	3.8	5.0	0.5	1.2	7.2	..	..	..	..
	Sub-Saharan Africa	81.2	434	522	3.2	2.7	1.0	0.8	2.1	..	..	..	..
	Central and Eastern Europe and the CIS	4.1	3,284	3,432	..	2.5	10.1	6.2	12.2	..	..	..	..
	OECD	4.6	5,761	8,777	3.9	5.3	10.9	11.2	51.1	..	..	..	..
	High-income OECD	3.2	6,698	10,483	3.8	5.3	12.1	13.1	46.5	..	..	..	..
	High human development	4.9	5,532	8,502	3.9	5.2	10.7	11.1	54.7	..	..	..	..
	Medium human development	18.4	341	1,100	3.5	4.2	1.2	2.1	43.7	..	..	..	..
	Low human development	83.7	162	165	2.2	1.9	0.4	0.2	0.6	..	..	..	..
	High income	3.1	6,559	10,331	3.9	5.2	12.2	13.1	49.7	..	..	..	..
	Middle income	10.5	615	1,593	3.7	4.2	2.1	3.1	42.7	..	..	..	..
	Low income	44.0	174	414	3.2	4.2	0.5	0.8	7.6	..	..	..	..
	World	21.7 m	1,573	2,490	3.8	4.7	3.4	3.7	100.0	..	..	..	..

● Ratification, acceptance, approval, accession or succession.
○ Signature.

NOTES

a Information is as of 28 August 2006. The Cartagena Protocol on Biosafety was signed in Cartagena in 2000, the United Nations Framework Convention on Climate Change in New York in 1992, the Kyoto Protocol to the United Nations Framework Convention on Climate Change in Kyoto in 1997 and the Convention on Biological Diversity in Rio de Janeiro in 1992.

b The world total includes carbon dioxide emissions not included in national totals, such as those from bunker fuels and oxidation of nonfuel hydrocarbon products, and emissions by countries not shown in the main indicator tables. These emissions amount to approximately 0.2% of the world total. Thus the shares listed for individual countries in this table do not sum to 100%.

c Includes Svalbard and Jan Mayen Islands.
d Data are estimates produced by the United Nations, Department of Economic and Social Affairs, Statistics Division.
e Preliminary data.
f Based on natural gas data.
g Includes Liechtenstein.
h Includes Monaco.
i Includes San Marino.
j Includes part of the Neutral Zone.
k Data refer to the South African Customs Union, which includes Botswana, Lesotho, Namibia and Swaziland.
l Included in data for South Africa.
m Figure is the aggregate from UN 2006a.

SOURCES

Column 1: calculated on the basis of data on traditional fuel consumption and total energy requirements from UN 2006a.
Columns 2 and 3: UN 2006f.
Columns 4 and 5: World Bank 2006, based on data from the International Energy Agency.
Columns 6–8: UN 2006c, based on data from the Carbon Dioxide Information Analysis Center.
Columns 9–12: UN 2006d.

TABLE 22

... protecting personal security ...

Refugees and armaments

HDI rank		Internally displaced people[a] (thousands) 2005[e]	Refugees By country of asylum (thousands) 2005[e]	Refugees By country of origin[c] (thousands) 2005[e]	Conventional arms transfers[b] (1990 prices) Imports (US$ millions) 1995	Imports (US$ millions) 2005	Exports US$ millions 2005	Exports Share[d] (%) 2001–05	Total armed forces Thousands 2006	Total armed forces Index (1985=100) 2006
HIGH HUMAN DEVELOPMENT										
1	Norway	..	43	0	83	9	13	(.)	26	70
2	Iceland	..	0	0	..	..	0	0	0	..
3	Australia	..	65	0	147	396	50	(.)	53	75
4	Ireland	..	7	0	0	4	..	..	10	73
5	Sweden	..	75	0	95	104	592	2	28	43
6	Canada	..	147	0	339	112	365	2	62	75
7	Japan	..	2	0	877	250	0	0	260	107
8	United States	..	379	1	415	387	7,101	30	1,546	72
9	Switzerland	..	48	0	93	144	74	(.)	4	20
10	Netherlands	..	118	0	46	129	840	2	53	50
11	Finland	..	12	0	159	77	22	(.)	28	77
12	Luxembourg	..	2	0	0	0	..	..	1	129
13	Belgium	..	15	0	16	0	173	(.)	37	40
14	Austria	..	21	0	23	21	3	(.)	40	73
15	Denmark	..	44	0	127	78	2	(.)	21	71
16	France	..	137	0	43	3	2,399	9	255	55
17	Italy	..	21	0	315	224	827	2	191	50
18	United Kingdom	..	293	0	633	94	791	4	217	65
19	Spain	..	5	0	363	281	113	1	147	46
20	New Zealand	..	5	0	7	8	0	(.)	9	73
21	Germany	..	700	0	252	216	1,855	6	285	60
22	Hong Kong, China (SAR)	..	2	0	..	..	..	..	..	..
23	Israel	150–300[f]	1	1	265	1,422	160	2	168	118
24	Greece	..	2	0	870	1,114	0	(.)	164	81
25	Singapore	..	0	0	237	423	3	(.)	73	133
26	Korea, Rep. of	..	0	0	1,674	544	38	(.)	688	115
27	Slovenia	..	0	0	19	2	..	..	7	..
28	Portugal	..	0	0	18	406	0	0	45	62
29	Cyprus	210	1	0	33	0	0	0	10	100
30	Czech Republic	..	2	4	0	630	10	(.)	22	11
31	Barbados	..	..	0	..	..	..	..	1	61
32	Malta	..	2	0	0	18	0	(.)	2	250
33	Kuwait	..	2	0	631	55	0	0	16	133
34	Brunei Darussalam	..	..	0	0	0	..	..	7	171
35	Hungary	..	8	4	24	12	70	(.)	32	30
36	Argentina	..	3	1	70	67	0	(.)	71	66
37	Poland	..	5	20	125	96	124	(.)	142	45
38	Chile	..	1	1	468	456	0	(.)	78	77
39	Bahrain	..	0	0	49	0	0	(.)	11	393
40	Estonia	..	0	1	18	10	0	0	5	..
41	Lithuania	..	1	1	4	9	0	(.)	14	..
42	Slovakia	..	0	1	220	0	0	(.)	20	..
43	Uruguay	..	0	0	8	18	0	0	24	75
44	Croatia	5	3	119	22	0	0	0	21	..
45	Latvia	..	0	2	16	7	0	0	5	..
46	Qatar	..	0	0	11	0	0	0	12	200
47	Seychelles	..	..	0	0	0	..	..	(.)	17
48	Costa Rica	..	11	0	0	0	..	..	0	..
49	United Arab Emirates	..	0	0	426	2,381	10	(.)	51	119
50	Cuba	..	1	19	0	0	..	..	49	30
51	Saint Kitts and Nevis	..	..	0	..	..	..	..	..	..
52	Bahamas	..	..	0	0	0	..	..	1	172
53	Mexico	10–12	3	2	45	35	..	..	193	149

Human development indicators

TABLE 22

Refugees and armaments

		Internally displaced people [a] (thousands)	Refugees		Conventional arms transfers [b] (1990 prices)					Total armed forces	
			By country of asylum (thousands)	By country of origin [c] (thousands)	Imports (US$ millions)		Exports			Thousands	Index (1985=100)
							US$ millions	Share [d] (%)			
HDI rank		2005 [e]	2005 [e]	2005 [e]	1995	2005	2005	2001–05		2006	2006
54	Bulgaria	..	4	4	0	158	0	(.)		51	34
55	Tonga	..	..	0	0	0	..	..		..	..
56	Oman	..	0	0	157	98	0	0		42	144
57	Trinidad and Tobago	..	..	0	0	0	..	..		3	143
58	Panama	..	2	0	0	0	..	..		0	0
59	Antigua and Barbuda	..	..	0	..	..	..	..		(.)	170
60	Romania	..	2	11	0	579	17	(.)		97	51
61	Malaysia	..	34	0	898	467	0	0		110	100
62	Bosnia and Herzegovina	183	11	110	0	0	0	(.)		12	..
63	Mauritius	..	0	0	0	0	..	..		0	0
MEDIUM HUMAN DEVELOPMENT											
64	Libyan Arab Jamahiriya	..	12	2	0	0	0	(.)		76	104
65	Russian Federation	265	2	103	40	0	5,771	31		1,027	19
66	Macedonia, TFYR	1	1	9	0	0	..	..		11	..
67	Belarus	..	1	9	0	0	0	1		73	..
68	Dominica	..	..	0	..	..	..	..		..	..
69	Brazil	..	3	0	237	142	62	(.)		287	104
70	Colombia	1,706–3,663 [g]	0	60	37	11	..	..		207	313
71	Saint Lucia	..	..	0	..	..	..	..		..	..
72	Venezuela, RB	..	0	3	0	7	0	(.)		82	167
73	Albania	..	0	13	24	31	..	..		22	54
74	Thailand	..	117	0	558	98	0	(.)		307	130
75	Samoa (Western)	..	..	0	..	..	..	..		..	..
76	Saudi Arabia	..	241	0	975	470	36	(.)		200	320
77	Ukraine	..	2	84	..	..	188	2		188	..
78	Lebanon	68–600	1	18	34	1	0	(.)		72	414
79	Kazakhstan	..	7	4	99	68	0	(.)		66	..
80	Armenia	8	220	14	49	0	..	..		48	..
81	China	..	299	124	523	2,697	129	2		2,255	58
82	Peru	60	1	5	32	368	0	(.)		80	63
83	Ecuador	..	10	1	10	33	..	..		47	111
84	Philippines	60	0	0	36	38	..	..		106	92
85	Grenada	..	..	0	..	..	..	..		..	..
86	Jordan	..	1	2	19	23	15	(.)		101	144
87	Tunisia	..	0	3	42	156	..	..		35	100
88	Saint Vincent and the Grenadines	..	..	0	..	..	..	..		..	..
89	Suriname	..	0	0	0	0	..	..		2	100
90	Fiji	..	..	1	12	0	..	..		4	148
91	Paraguay	..	0	0	0	1	..	..		10	69
92	Turkey	356–1,000+	2	170	1,562	746	28	(.)		515	82
93	Sri Lanka	325	0	108	49	8	..	..		111	514
94	Dominican Republic	..	..	0	0	0	..	..		25	113
95	Belize	..	1	0	0	0	..	..		1	167
96	Iran, Islamic Rep. of	..	716	99	373	403	0	(.)		545	89
97	Georgia	240	2	7	0	0	0	(.)		11	..
98	Maldives	..	..	0	0	0	..	..		..	..
99	Azerbaijan	558	3	234	0	0	..	..		67	..
100	Occupied Palestinian Territories	21–50 [h]	0	350	1	0	..	..		0	..
101	El Salvador	..	0	4	3	0	..	..		16	38
102	Algeria	1,000 [i]	94	12	346	149	..	..		138	81
103	Guyana	..	..	0	0	0	..	..		1	15
104	Jamaica	..	..	0	0	0	..	..		3	143
105	Turkmenistan	..	12	1	0	0	..	..		26	..
106	Cape Verde	..	..	0	0	0	..	..		1	13

TABLE 22

	Internally displaced people [a] (thousands) 2005 [e]	Refugees By country of asylum (thousands) 2005 [e]	Refugees By country of origin [c] (thousands) 2005 [e]	Conventional arms transfers [b] (1990 prices) Imports (US$ millions) 1995	Imports 2005	Exports US$ millions 2005	Exports Share [d] (%) 2001–05	Total armed forces Thousands 2006	Index (1985=100) 2006
HDI rank									
107 Syrian Arab Republic	305	26	16	43	0	0	0	308	77
108 Indonesia	342–600	0	34	339	19	8	(.)	302	109
109 Viet Nam	..	2	357	270	291	..	..	455	44
110 Kyrgyzstan		3	3	0	3	0	(.)	13	..
111 Egypt	..	89	6	1,700	596	0	(.)	469	105
112 Nicaragua	..	0	1	0	0	0	0	14	22
113 Uzbekistan	3	44	8	0	0	0	1	55	..
114 Moldova, Rep. of	..	0	12	6	0	4	(.)	7	..
115 Bolivia	..	1	0	1	9	..	..	33	120
116 Mongolia	..	0	1	..	..	..	..	9	27
117 Honduras	..	0	1	0	0	..	..	12	72
118 Guatemala	242	0	3	3	0	..	..	29	91
119 Vanuatu	..	..	..	..	..	..	..	..	..
120 Equatorial Guinea	..	0	0	0	0	..	..	1	45
121 South Africa	..	30	0	38	606	39	(.)	56	53
122 Tajikistan	..	1	55	0	0	..	..	8	..
123 Morocco	..	0	3	30	32	..	..	201	135
124 Gabon	..	9	0	0	0	..	..	5	208
125 Namibia	..	5	1	4	0	..	..	9	..
126 India	600	139	16	943	1,471	0	(.)	1,325	105
127 São Tomé and Principe		0	0	..	..	..	..	..	..
128 Solomon Islands	..	..	0	0	0	..	..	..	..
129 Cambodia	..	0	18	0	0	0	0	124	354
130 Myanmar	540 [f]	0	165	216	20	..	..	376	202
131 Botswana	..	3	0	7	0	..	..	9	225
132 Comoros	..	0	0	..	..	..	..	..	..
133 Lao People's Dem. Rep.	..	0	24	0	0	..	..	29	54
134 Pakistan	20 [f]	1,085	30	316	161	9	(.)	619	128
135 Bhutan	..	..	107	0	0	..	..	..	..
136 Ghana	..	54	18	0	0	..	..	7	46
137 Bangladesh	500	21	7	121	27	..	..	126	138
138 Nepal	100–200	126	2	1	0	..	..	69	276
139 Papua New Guinea	..	10	0	0	0	..	..	3	94
140 Congo	100–147	66	24	0	0	..	..	10	115
141 Sudan	5,355	147	693	3	0	..	..	105	186
142 Timor-Leste	..	0	0	..	..	..	..	1	..
143 Madagascar	..	0	0	0	0	..	..	14	66
144 Cameroon	..	52	9	0	0	..	..	23	315
145 Uganda	1,740 [f]	257	34	38	0	..	..	45	225
146 Swaziland	..	1	0	0	0	..	..	..	..
LOW HUMAN DEVELOPMENT									
147 Togo	3	9	51	3	0	..	..	9	250
148 Djibouti	..	10	1	3	0	..	..	10	333
149 Lesotho	..	0	0	0	0	..	..	2	100
150 Yemen	..	82	1	124	289	..	..	67	105
151 Zimbabwe	570	14	11	0	0	..	..	29	71
152 Kenya	382	251	5	0	25	..	..	24	175
153 Mauritania	..	1	32	1	0	..	..	16	188
154 Haiti	..	0	14	..	..	..	..	0	0
155 Gambia	..	7	2	0	0	..	..	1	160
156 Senegal	64	21	9	2	0	..	..	14	139
157 Eritrea	51	4	144	3	276	0	0	202	..
158 Rwanda	..	45	100	0	0	..	..	51	981
159 Nigeria	..	9	22	2	0	0	0	79	84

Human development indicators

TABLE 22

Refugees and armaments

	Internally displaced people[a] (thousands)	Refugees By country of asylum (thousands)	Refugees By country of origin[c] (thousands)	Conventional arms transfers[b] (1990 prices) Imports (US$ millions)		Exports US$ millions	Exports Share[d] (%)	Total armed forces Thousands	Total armed forces Index (1985=100)
HDI rank	2005[e]	2005[e]	2005[e]	1995	2005	2005	2001–05	2006	2006
160 Guinea	82	64	6	0	0	..	..	10	101
161 Angola	62	14	216	1	22	0	(.)	108	218
162 Tanzania, U. Rep. of	..	549	2	0	0	..	..	27	67
163 Benin	..	30	0	0	0	..	..	5	111
164 Côte d'Ivoire	800[f]	42	18	2	0	..	..	17	129
165 Zambia	..	156	0	0	0	0	0	15	93
166 Malawi	..	4	0	0	0	0	0	5	94
167 Congo, Dem. Rep. of the	1,664	204	431	0	14	..	..	65	135
168 Mozambique	..	2	0	0	0	..	..	11	70
169 Burundi	117	21	439	0	0	..	..	51	981
170 Ethiopia	150–265	101	65	0	0	..	..	183	84
171 Chad	55–65	275	48	1	0	..	..	30	246
172 Central African Republic	..	25	43	0	0	..	..	3	130
173 Guinea-Bissau	..	8	1	0	0	..	..	9	105
174 Burkina Faso	..	1	1	0	19	..	..	11	275
175 Mali	..	11	1	0	0	..	..	7	143
176 Sierra Leone	..	60	40	15	0	..	..	13	419
177 Niger	..	0	1	0	0	..	..	5	227
Developing countries	..	5,761	..	..	..	..	..	13,909 T	89
Least developed countries	..	2,265	..	..	..	..	..	1,862 T	159
Arab States	..	755	..	..	..	..	..	2,141 T	79
East Asia and the Pacific	..	464	..	..	..	..	..	5,955 T	80
Latin America and the Caribbean	..	37	..	..	..	..	..	1,269 T	94
South Asia	..	2,087	..	..	..	..	..	2,822 T	111
Sub-Saharan Africa	..	2,415	..	..	..	..	..	1,197 T	142
Central and Eastern Europe and the CIS	..	482	..	..	..	..	..	2,115 T	32
OECD	..	2,161	..	..	..	..	..	5,094 T	70
High-income OECD	..	2,141	..	..	..	..	..	4,170 T	71
High human development	..	2,240	..	..	..	..	..	5,520 T	71
Medium human development	..	3,919	..	..	..	..	..	11,637 T	69
Low human development	..	2,020	..	..	..	..	..	1,079 T	151
High income	..	2,390	..	..	..	..	..	4,728 T	76
Middle income	..	1,984	..	..	..	..	..	9,402 T	58
Low income	..	4,013	..	..	..	..	..	5,546 T	111
World	23,700 T	8,387 T	..	21,085 T[j]	21,965 T[j]	21,961 T[j]	..	19,676 T	72

NOTES

a Estimates maintained by the Internal Displacement Monitoring Centre based on various sources. Estimates are associated with high levels of uncertainty.

b Data are as of 10 May 2006. Figures are trend indicator values, which are an indicator only of the volume of international arms transfers, not of the actual financial value of such transfers. Published reports of arms transfers provide partial information, as not all transfers are fully reported. The estimates presented are conservative and may understate actual transfers of conventional weapons.

c The country of origin for many refugees is unavailable or unreported. These data may therefore be underestimates.

d Calculated using the 2001–05 totals for all countries and nonstate actors with exports of major conventional weapons as defined in SIPRI 2006b.

e Data refer to the end of 2005 unless otherwise specified.

f Estimate excludes certain parts of the country or some groups of internally displaced people.

g Lower estimate is cumulative since 1994. Higher figure is cumulative since 1985.

h Lower estimate includes only internally displaced people evicted mainly by dwelling demolitions since 2000. Higher figure is cumulative since 1967.

i Figure is cumulative since 1992.

j Data refer to the total volume of arms transfers and include all countries and nonstate actors with transfers of major conventional weapons as defined in SIPRI 2006a.

SOURCES

Column 1: Internal Displacement Monitoring Centre 2006.
Columns 2 and 3: UNHCR 2006.
Columns 4–6: SIPRI 2006b.
Column 7: calculated on the basis of data on arms transfers from SIPRI 2006b.
Column 8: IISS 2006.
Column 9: calculated on the basis of data on armed forces from IISS 2006.

Human development indicators

TABLE

23

. . . protecting personal security . . .

Victims of crime

| | | Population victimized by crime [a] | | | | | |
| | | (% of total) | | | | | |
	Year [b]	Total crime [c]	Property crime [d]	Robbery	Sexual assault [e]	Assault	Bribery (corruption) [f]
NATIONAL							
Australia	1999	30.1	13.9	1.2	1.0	2.4	0.3
Austria	1995	18.8	3.1	0.2	1.2	0.8	0.7
Belgium	1999	21.4	7.7	1.0	0.3	1.2	0.3
Canada	1999	23.8	10.4	0.9	0.8	2.3	0.4
Denmark	1999	23.0	7.6	0.7	0.4	1.4	0.3
England and Wales	1999	26.4	12.2	1.2	0.9	2.8	0.1
Finland	1999	19.1	4.4	0.6	1.1	2.1	0.2
France	1999	21.4	8.7	1.1	0.7	1.4	1.3
Italy	1991	24.6	12.7	1.3	0.6	0.2	..
Japan	1999	15.2	3.4	0.1	0.1	0.1	(.)
Malta	1996	23.1	10.9	0.4	0.1	1.1	4.0
Netherlands	1999	25.2	7.4	0.8	0.8	1.0	0.4
New Zealand	1991	29.4	14.8	0.7	1.3	2.4	..
Northern Ireland	1999	15.0	6.2	0.1	0.1	2.1	0.2
Poland	1999	22.7	9.0	1.8	0.2	1.1	5.1
Portugal	1999	15.5	7.5	1.1	0.2	0.4	1.4
Scotland	1999	23.2	7.6	0.7	0.3	3.0	..
Slovenia	2000	21.2	7.7	1.1	0.8	1.1	2.1
Sweden	1999	24.7	8.4	0.9	1.1	1.2	0.1
Switzerland	1999	18.2	4.5	0.7	0.6	1.0	0.2 [g]
United States	1999	21.1	10.0	0.6	0.4	1.2	0.2
MAJOR CITY							
Asunción (Paraguay)	1995	34.4	16.7	6.3	1.7	0.9	13.3
Baku (Azerbaijan)	1999	8.3	2.4	1.6	0.0	0.4	20.8
Beijing (China)	1991	19.0	2.2	0.5	0.6	0.6	..
Bishkek (Kyrgyzstan)	1995	27.8	11.3	1.6	2.2	2.1	19.3
Bogotá (Colombia)	1996	54.6	27.0	11.5	4.8	2.5	19.5
Bratislava (Slovakia)	1996	36.0	20.8	1.2	0.4	0.5	13.5
Bucharest (Romania)	1999	25.4	10.8	1.8	0.4	0.6	19.2
Budapest (Hungary)	1999	32.1	15.6	1.8	0.9	0.8	9.8
Buenos Aires (Argentina)	1995	61.1	30.8	6.4	6.4	2.3	30.2
Cairo (Egypt)	1991	28.7	12.1	2.2	1.8	1.1	..
Dar es Salaam (Tanzania, U. Rep. of)	1991	..	23.1	8.2	6.1	1.7	..
Gaborone (Botswana)	1996	31.7	19.7	2.0	0.7	3.2	2.8
Jakarta (Indonesia)	1995	20.9	9.4	0.7	1.3	0.5	29.9
Johannesburg (South Africa)	1995	38.0	18.3	4.7	2.7	4.6	6.9
Kampala (Uganda)	1995	40.9	20.6	2.3	5.1	1.7	19.5
Kiev (Ukraine)	1999	29.1	8.9	2.5	1.2	1.5	16.2
La Paz (Bolivia)	1995	39.8	18.1	5.8	1.5	2.0	24.4
Manila (Philippines)	1995	10.6	3.3	1.5	0.1	0.1	4.3
Maputo (Mozambique)	2001	40.6	29.3	7.6	2.2	3.2	30.5
Minsk (Belarus)	1999	23.6	11.1	1.4	1.4	1.3	20.6
Moscow (Russian Federation)	1999	26.3	10.9	2.4	1.2	1.1	16.6
Mumbai (India)	1995	31.8	6.7	1.3	3.5	0.8	22.9
New Delhi (India)	1995	30.5	6.1	1.0	1.7	0.8	21.0
Prague (Czech Republic)	1999	34.1	21.6	0.5	0.9	1.1	5.7
Riga (Latvia)	1999	26.5	9.4	2.8	0.5	1.9	14.3
Rio de Janeiro (Brazil)	1995	44.0	14.7	12.2	7.5	3.4	17.1
San José (Costa Rica)	1995	40.4	21.7	8.9	3.5	1.7	9.2
Skopje (Macedonia, TFYR)	1995	21.1	9.4	1.1	0.3	0.7	7.4
Sofia (Bulgaria)	1999	27.2	16.1	1.5	0.1	0.6	16.4
Tallinn (Estonia)	1999	41.2	22.5	6.3	3.3	3.7	9.3
Tbjlisi (Georgia)	1999	23.6	11.1	1.8	0.4	0.9	16.6

Human development indicators

TABLE

23

Victims of crime

	Year[b]	Population victimized by crime[a] (% of total)					
		Total crime[c]	Property crime[d]	Robbery	Sexual assault[e]	Assault	Bribery (corruption)[f]
Tirana (Albania)	1999	31.7	11.2	2.9	1.2	0.7	59.1
Tunis (Tunisia)	1991	37.5	20.1	5.4	1.5	0.4	..
Ulaanbaatar (Mongolia)	1999	41.8	20.0	4.5	1.4	2.1	21.3
Vilnius (Lithuania)	1999	31.0	17.8	3.2	2.0	1.4	22.9
Zagreb (Croatia)	1999	14.3	4.4	0.5	0.8	0.5	9.5

NOTES

a Data refer to victimization as reported in the International Crime Victims Survey.

b Surveys were conducted in 1992, 1995, 1996–97 and 2000–01. Data are for the year preceding the survey.

c Data refer to people victimized by 1 or more of 11 crimes recorded in the survey: robbery, burglary, attempted burglary, car theft, car vandalism, bicycle theft, sexual assault, theft from car, theft of personal property, assault and threats, and theft of motorcycle or moped.

d Includes car theft, theft from car, burglary with entry and attempted burglary.

e Data refer to women only.

f Data refer to people who have been asked or expected to pay a bribe by a government official.

g Data refer to 1995.

SOURCE

All columns: UNODC 2004.

TABLE 24

Gender-related development index

HDI rank		Gender-related development index (GDI)		Life expectancy at birth (years) 2004		Adult literacy rate [a] (% ages 15 and older) 2004		Combined gross enrolment ratio for primary, secondary and tertiary schools (%) 2004 [b]		Estimated earned income [c] (PPP US$) 2004		HDI rank minus GDI rank [d]
		Rank	Value	Female	Male	Female	Male	Female	Male	Female	Male	
HIGH HUMAN DEVELOPMENT												
1	Norway	1	0.962	82.0	77.1	.. [e]	.. [e]	105	96	33,034	43,950	0
2	Iceland	2	0.958	82.7	79.0	.. [e]	.. [e]	102 [f]	91 [f]	27,496	38,603	0
3	Australia	3	0.956	83.0	77.9	.. [e]	.. [e]	114	112	24,966	35,832	0
4	Ireland	4	0.951	80.5	75.4	.. [e]	.. [e]	101	97	26,160	51,633	0
5	Sweden	5	0.949	82.5	78.1	.. [e]	.. [e]	102	91	26,408	32,724	0
6	Canada	7	0.947	82.6	77.6	.. [e]	.. [e]	96 [f,g]	90 [f,g]	24,277 [h]	38,374 [h]	−1
7	Japan	13	0.942	85.6	78.6	.. [e]	.. [e]	84	86	18,130	40,885	−5
8	United States	8	0.946	80.2	74.8	.. [e]	.. [e]	97	89	30,581 [h]	49,075 [h]	1
9	Switzerland	10	0.944	83.4	77.8	.. [e]	.. [e]	83	88	25,314	41,258	0
10	Netherlands	9	0.945	81.2	75.8	.. [e]	.. [e]	98	99	24,652	39,035	2
11	Finland	11	0.943	81.9	75.3	.. [e]	.. [e]	104	97	24,862	35,263	1
12	Luxembourg	6	0.949	81.6	75.3	.. [e]	.. [e]	89 [i]	88 [i]	45,938 [j]	94,696 [j]	1
13	Belgium	12	0.943	82.1	75.9	.. [e]	.. [e]	96	93	24,123	38,338	1
14	Austria	17	0.937	82.0	76.2	.. [e]	.. [e]	92	90	20,032	45,095	−3
15	Denmark	15	0.940	79.6	75.0	.. [e]	.. [e]	106	97	27,048	36,882	0
16	France	14	0.940	83.1	76.0	.. [e]	.. [e]	95	91	23,015	35,922	2
17	Italy	18	0.934	83.2	77.1	98.0 [e]	98.8 [e]	92	87	18,070 [h]	38,902 [h]	−1
18	United Kingdom	16	0.938	80.8	76.2	.. [e]	.. [e]	96 [f]	90 [f]	24,448	37,506	2
19	Spain	19	0.933	83.3	76.0	.. [e]	.. [e]	99	93	16,751 [h]	33,648 [h]	0
20	New Zealand	20	0.932	81.5	77.0	.. [e]	.. [e]	105	95	19,264	27,711	0
21	Germany	21	0.928	81.7	75.9	.. [e]	.. [e]	88 [f]	89 [f]	20,851	36,114	0
22	Hong Kong, China (SAR)	..	..	84.8	78.9	..	..	74	79	20,637	42,166	..
23	Israel	22	0.925	82.0	77.8	95.9	98.5	92	87	19,165 [h]	29,714 [h]	0
24	Greece	23	0.917	81.0	75.7	94.2 [e]	97.8 [e]	96	91	15,728	28,837	0
25	Singapore	..	..	80.8	77.0	88.6	96.6	..	..	18,905	37,125	..
26	Korea, Rep. of	25	0.905	80.9	73.7	.. [e]	.. [e]	88	101	12,912	28,036	−1
27	Slovenia	24	0.908	80.2	72.9	.. [e]	.. [e]	100	91	15,992 [h]	26,129 [h]	1
28	Portugal	26	0.902	80.8	74.1	.. [e]	.. [e]	93	86	14,635	24,971	0
29	Cyprus	27	0.900	81.2	76.2	95.1	98.6	79	78	17,012	28,891	0
30	Czech Republic	28	0.881	78.9	72.5	.. [e]	.. [e]	82	81	13,141	26,017	0
31	Barbados	..	..	78.6	71.7	..	..	94 [g]	84 [g]	..	..	..
32	Malta	29	0.869	80.9	76.1	89.2 [k]	86.4 [k]	81	82	12,226	25,644	0
33	Kuwait	31	0.864	79.7	75.4	91.0	94.4	79 [f]	69 [f]	9,623 [h]	25,847 [h]	−1
34	Brunei Darussalam	..	..	79.1	74.5	90.2	95.2	78 [f]	76 [f]	..	..	..
35	Hungary	30	0.867	77.1	68.9	.. [e]	.. [e]	90	85	13,311	20,666	1
36	Argentina	32	0.859	78.4	70.9	97.2	97.2	94 [g]	85 [g]	9,258 [h]	17,518 [h]	0
37	Poland	33	0.859	78.6	70.5	.. [e]	.. [e]	90	82	9,746 [h]	16,400 [h]	0
38	Chile	37	0.850	81.1	75.1	95.6	95.8	80	82	6,134 [h]	15,715 [h]	−3
39	Bahrain	38	0.849	76.0	73.2	83.6	88.6	89 [f]	82 [f]	9,654	29,107	−3
40	Estonia	34	0.856	77.2	65.8	99.8 [e]	99.8 [e]	98	86	11,377 [h]	18,285 [h]	2
41	Lithuania	35	0.856	78.0	66.9	99.6 [e]	99.6 [e]	96	87	10,839	15,699	2
42	Slovakia	36	0.853	78.1	70.3	.. [e]	.. [e]	78	75	10,856 [h]	18,617 [h]	2
43	Uruguay	39	0.847	79.2	71.9	.. [l]	.. [m]	95 [f,g]	84 [f,g]	6,764 [h]	12,240 [h]	0
44	Croatia	40	0.844	78.6	71.6	97.1	99.3	75 [g]	72 [g]	9,872	14,690	0
45	Latvia	41	0.843	77.2	66.1	99.7 [e]	99.8 [e]	97	84	9,530	14,171	0
46	Qatar	..	..	76.2	71.4	88.6	89.1	82	71	..	..	..
47	Seychelles	..	..	..	..	92.3	91.4	82	77	..	..	..
48	Costa Rica	42	0.831	80.8	76.0	95.1	94.7	69 [f,g]	67 [f,g]	5,969	12,878	0
49	United Arab Emirates	43	0.829	81.1	76.7	.. [l]	.. [m]	68 [f,g]	54 [f,g]	7,630 [h]	31,788 [h]	0
50	Cuba	..	..	79.5	75.8	99.8 [e]	99.8 [e]	81 [g]	79 [g]	..	..	..
51	Saint Kitts and Nevis	..	..	..	..	..	..	81	78	..	..	..
52	Bahamas	..	..	73.4	67.1	..	..	66 [f]	65 [f]	14,414 [h]	20,459 [h]	..
53	Mexico	45	0.812	77.8	72.8	89.6	92.4	76	75	5,594	14,202	−1

Human development indicators

TABLE 24

Gender-related development index

HDI rank		Gender-related development index (GDI)		Life expectancy at birth (years) 2004		Adult literacy rate [a] (% ages 15 and older) 2004		Combined gross enrolment ratio for primary, secondary and tertiary schools (%) 2004 [b]		Estimated earned income [c] (PPP US$) 2004		HDI rank minus GDI rank [d]
		Rank	Value	Female	Male	Female	Male	Female	Male	Female	Male	
54	Bulgaria	44	0.814	75.8	69.1	97.7	98.7	81	81	6,406	9,855	1
55	Tonga	46	0.809	73.7	71.1	99.0 [k]	98.8 [k]	81 [f]	79 [f]	5,026 [h]	10,606 [h]	0
56	Oman	57	0.785	76.0	73.1	73.5	86.8	68 [f]	69 [f]	4,273 [h]	23,676 [h]	−10
57	Trinidad and Tobago	48	0.805	72.8	67.0	.. [l]	.. [m]	68	66	7,766 [h]	16,711 [h]	0
58	Panama	47	0.806	77.6	72.5	91.2	92.5	83	76	5,219	9,300	2
59	Antigua and Barbuda	..	..	..	..	..	..	..	..	..	..	..
60	Romania	49	0.804	75.2	68.0	96.3	98.4	77	73	6,723	10,325	1
61	Malaysia	51	0.795	75.8	71.1	85.4	92.0	76 [g]	70 [g]	5,391	15,015	0
62	Bosnia and Herzegovina	..	..	77.0	71.5	94.4	99.0	..	..	5,568 [h]	8,582 [h]	..
63	Mauritius	53	0.792	75.8	69.0	80.5	88.4	74 [f]	75 [f]	6,948 [h]	17,173 [h]	−1
MEDIUM HUMAN DEVELOPMENT												
64	Libyan Arab Jamahiriya	..	..	76.4	71.8	..	..	98 [f, g]	91 [f, g]	..	..	..
65	Russian Federation	50	0.795	72.0	58.9	99.2 [e]	99.7 [e]	92 [f]	84 [f]	7,735 [h]	12,401 [h]	3
66	Macedonia, TFYR	54	0.791	76.5	71.5	94.1	98.2	71	69	4,286 [h]	8,943 [h]	0
67	Belarus	52	0.793	74.1	62.5	99.4 [e, k]	99.8 [e, k]	90	86	5,510 [h]	8,632 [h]	3
68	Dominica	..	..	..	..	..	..	84	81	..	..	..
69	Brazil	55	0.789	74.8	67.0	88.8	88.4	88 [g]	84 [g]	6,004	10,447	1
70	Colombia	56	0.787	75.6	69.6	92.7	92.9	74	71	5,356	9,202	1
71	Saint Lucia	..	..	74.1	71.0	..	..	80	72	4,308 [h]	8,399 [h]	..
72	Venezuela, RB	60	0.780	76.1	70.2	92.7	93.3	76 [f, g]	73 [f, g]	4,083 [h]	7,982 [h]	−2
73	Albania	59	0.780	76.9	71.1	98.3	99.2	67 [g]	69 [g]	3,487 [h]	6,492 [h]	0
74	Thailand	58	0.781	74.0	66.7	90.5	94.9	74	73	6,036	10,214	2
75	Samoa (Western)	63	0.770	73.9	67.5	.. [l]	.. [m]	76 [f]	72 [f]	3,046 [h]	7,980 [h]	−2
76	Saudi Arabia	72	0.744	74.2	70.3	69.3	87.1	58 [f]	59 [f]	3,486 [h]	22,617 [h]	−10
77	Ukraine	62	0.771	72.4	60.1	99.2 [e]	99.7 [e]	87	83	4,535	8,583	1
78	Lebanon	..	..	74.4	70.1	..	..	85	82	2,786 [h]	9,011 [h]	..
79	Kazakhstan	61	0.772	69.1	58.0	99.3 [e, k]	99.8 [e, k]	93	89	5,799	9,222	3
80	Armenia	65	0.765	74.8	68.1	99.2 [e]	99.7 [e]	77	71	3,222 [h]	5,105 [h]	0
81	China	64	0.765	73.7	70.2	86.5	95.1	70 [f]	71 [f]	4,561 [h]	7,159 [h]	2
82	Peru	67	0.759	72.9	67.8	82.1	93.5	88 [f]	85 [f]	3,294	8,036	0
83	Ecuador	..	..	77.5	71.6	89.7	92.3	..	..	2,796 [h]	5,123 [h]	..
84	Philippines	66	0.761	72.8	68.6	92.7	92.5	84	79	3,449	5,763	2
85	Grenada	..	..	..	..	..	..	75 [f]	71 [f]	..	..	..
86	Jordan	69	0.747	73.2	70.2	84.7	95.1	80	78	2,143	7,038	0
87	Tunisia	73	0.744	75.6	71.4	65.3	83.4	77 [f]	74 [f]	3,421 [h]	12,046 [h]	−3
88	Saint Vincent and the Grenadines	..	..	74.1	68.5	..	..	67	68	4,300 [h]	8,513 [h]	..
89	Suriname	..	..	72.7	66.1	87.2	92.0	77 [f, g]	68 [f, g]	..	..	..
90	Fiji	..	..	70.3	65.9	..	..	76 [f]	74 [f]	3,921 [h]	8,142 [h]	..
91	Paraguay	..	..	73.5	68.9	..	..	70 [f, g]	69 [f, g]	2,789	6,806	..
92	Turkey	71	0.745	71.3	66.6	79.6	95.3	63	75	4,038	11,408	0
93	Sri Lanka	68	0.749	77.0	71.7	89.1	92.3	64 [f, g]	63 [f, g]	2,561	6,158	4
94	Dominican Republic	70	0.745	71.3	64.1	87.2	86.8	78 [f]	70 [f]	4,376 [h]	10,461 [h]	3
95	Belize	..	..	74.4	69.5	..	..	81	81	3,760 [h]	9,674 [h]	..
96	Iran, Islamic Rep. of	74	0.736	72.3	69.2	70.4	83.5	70 [f]	74 [f]	4,122 [h]	10,830 [h]	0
97	Georgia	..	..	74.4	66.6	..	..	76	75	1,561	4,273	..
98	Maldives	..	..	66.6	67.4	96.4	96.2	69 [f]	68 [f]	..	..	..
99	Azerbaijan	75	0.733	70.6	63.3	98.2 [k]	99.5 [k]	67	69	3,262 [h]	5,096 [h]	0
100	Occupied Palestinian Territories	..	..	74.2	71.1	88.0	96.7	83 [f]	80 [f]	..	..	..
101	El Salvador	76	0.725	74.1	68.0	.. [l]	.. [m]	69 [f]	70 [f]	3,077	7,074	0
102	Algeria	79	0.713	72.7	70.1	60.1	79.6	73	73	3,259 [h]	9,888 [h]	−2
103	Guyana	..	..	66.7	60.6	..	..	78 [f, g]	78 [f, g]	2,615 [h]	6,375 [h]	..
104	Jamaica	77	0.721	72.5	69.0	85.9 [k]	74.1 [k]	79 [f]	75 [f]	3,027 [h]	5,327 [h]	1
105	Turkmenistan	..	..	66.9	58.4	98.3 [k]	99.3 [k]	..	..	3,425 [h]	5,385 [h]	..
106	Cape Verde	78	0.714	73.5	67.3	.. [l]	.. [m]	67	67	3,045 [h]	8,641 [h]	1

TABLE 24

HDI rank	Gender-related development index (GDI) Rank	Value	Life expectancy at birth (years) 2004 Female	Male	Adult literacy rate[a] (% ages 15 and older) 2004 Female	Male	Combined gross enrolment ratio for primary, secondary and tertiary schools (%) 2004[b] Female	Male	Estimated earned income[c] (PPP US$) 2004 Female	Male	HDI rank minus GDI rank[d]
107 Syrian Arab Republic	82	0.702	75.4	71.8	73.6	86.0	60[f]	65[f]	1,794[h]	5,402[h]	−2
108 Indonesia	81	0.704	69.2	65.3	86.8	94.0	67	70	2,257[h]	4,963[h]	0
109 Viet Nam	80	0.708	72.9	68.8	86.9[k]	93.9[k]	61[f]	65[f]	2,271[h]	3,220[h]	2
110 Kyrgyzstan	83	0.701	71.3	62.9	98.1[k]	99.3[k]	80	77	1,422[h]	2,464[h]	0
111 Egypt	..	..	72.4	68.0	59.4	83.0	..	..	1,588	6,817	..
112 Nicaragua	88	0.684	72.4	67.6	76.6	76.8	71[f]	69[f]	1,747[h]	5,524[h]	−4
113 Uzbekistan	84	0.694	69.9	63.4	..[l]	..[m]	72[f]	75[f]	1,398[h]	2,346[h]	1
114 Moldova, Rep. of	85	0.692	71.7	64.4	97.7	99.1	73	68	1,349[h]	2,143[h]	1
115 Bolivia	86	0.687	66.5	62.3	80.7	93.1	83[f]	89[f]	1,983[h]	3,462[h]	1
116 Mongolia	87	0.685	66.5	62.5	97.5	98.0	83	72	1,379[h]	2,730[h]	1
117 Honduras	89	0.676	70.2	66.1	80.2	79.8	74[f]	68[f]	1,771[h]	3,964[h]	0
118 Guatemala	90	0.659	71.3	63.9	63.3	75.4	63[f]	69[f]	2,130[h]	6,604[h]	0
119 Vanuatu	..	..	70.9	67.2	..	..	61[f]	66[f]	2,468[h]	3,612[h]	..
120 Equatorial Guinea	93	0.639	43.3	42.3	80.5	93.4	52[f, g]	64[f, g]	11,491[h]	26,967[h]	−2
121 South Africa	92	0.646	48.2	45.7	80.9[k]	84.1[k]	77[g]	76[g]	7,014[h]	15,521[h]	0
122 Tajikistan	91	0.648	66.4	61.2	99.2[e]	99.7[e]	65	77	876[h]	1,530[h]	2
123 Morocco	95	0.615	72.2	67.8	39.6	65.7	54	62	1,742[h]	6,907[h]	−1
124 Gabon	..	..	54.7	53.4	..	..	68[f, g]	72[f, g]	4,814[h]	8,449[h]	..
125 Namibia	94	0.622	47.5	46.8	83.5	86.8	69[g]	66[g]	5,416[h]	9,455[h]	1
126 India	96	0.591	65.3	62.1	47.8	73.4	58[f]	66[f]	1,471[h]	4,723[h]	0
127 São Tomé and Principe	..	..	64.2	62.1	..	..	63	64	..	..	..
128 Solomon Islands	..	..	63.3	61.9	..	..	45[f, g]	49[f, g]	1,202[h]	2,387[h]	..
129 Cambodia	97	0.578	60.1	52.7	64.1	84.7	55[f, g]	65[f, g]	2,077[h]	2,793[h]	0
130 Myanmar	..	..	63.5	57.8	86.4	93.9	50[f]	48[f]	..	..	..
131 Botswana	98	0.555	34.8	34.9	81.8	80.4	72[f]	69[f]	5,322	14,738	0
132 Comoros	99	0.550	65.8	61.5	..[l]	..[m]	42[f]	50[f]	1,306[h]	2,576[h]	0
133 Lao People's Dem. Rep.	100	0.545	56.3	53.8	60.9	77.0	55	66	1,328[h]	2,579[h]	0
134 Pakistan	105	0.513	63.6	63.2	36.0	63.0	32	44	977[h]	3,403[h]	−4
135 Bhutan	..	..	64.6	62.2	..	..	..	..	..	..	..
136 Ghana	101	0.528	57.4	56.5	49.8	66.4	44[f]	50[f]	1,860[h]	2,611[h]	1
137 Bangladesh	102	0.524	64.2	62.5	..[l]	..[m]	58[g]	56[g]	1,170[h]	2,540[h]	1
138 Nepal	106	0.513	62.4	61.6	34.9	62.7	52[g]	62[g]	995[h]	1,993[h]	−2
139 Papua New Guinea	103	0.521	56.3	55.2	50.9	63.4	38[f, g]	43[f, g]	2,127[h]	2,934[h]	2
140 Congo	104	0.519	53.5	51.0	..[l]	..[m]	49[f]	55[f]	652[h]	1,310[h]	2
141 Sudan	110	0.492	58.0	55.1	51.8[n]	71.1[n]	34[f]	39[f]	778[h]	3,105[h]	−3
142 Timor-Leste	..	..	57.1	54.9	..	..	..	..	..	..	..
143 Madagascar	107	0.507	56.9	54.3	65.3	76.5	55[f]	58[f]	704[h]	1,012[h]	1
144 Cameroon	109	0.497	46.2	45.1	59.8	77.0	56[f]	69[f]	1,435[h]	2,921[h]	0
145 Uganda	108	0.498	48.8	47.9	57.7	76.8	65	67	1,216[h]	1,741[h]	2
146 Swaziland	114	0.479	31.3	31.3	78.3	80.9	57[f, g]	59[f, g]	2,576	8,936	−3
LOW HUMAN DEVELOPMENT											
147 Togo	116	0.476	56.4	52.6	38.5	68.7	46[f]	64[f]	927[h]	2,159[h]	−4
148 Djibouti	..	..	54.1	51.8	..	..	21	27	1,305[h]	2,681[h]	..
149 Lesotho	112	0.486	36.2	34.0	90.3	73.7	66[f]	65[f]	1,848[h]	3,506[h]	1
150 Yemen	117	0.462	62.4	59.7	..[l]	..[m]	42[f]	68[f]	397[h]	1,346[h]	−3
151 Zimbabwe	113	0.483	36.0	37.2	..[l]	..[m]	51[f, g]	54[f, g]	1,527[h]	2,613[h]	2
152 Kenya	111	0.487	46.5	48.5	70.2	77.7	58[f]	62[f]	1,037	1,242	5
153 Mauritania	115	0.478	54.7	51.5	43.4	59.5	44	47	1,295[h]	2,601[h]	2
154 Haiti	..	..	52.7	51.3	..	..	..	..	1,283[h]	2,465[h]	..
155 Gambia	..	..	57.5	54.7	..	..	50[f]	51[f]	1,378[h]	2,615[h]	..
156 Senegal	118	0.451	57.2	54.8	29.2	51.1	36[f]	41[f]	1,200[h]	2,243[h]	0
157 Eritrea	..	..	56.1	52.3	..	..	29	41	557	1,414	..
158 Rwanda	119	0.449	45.8	42.6	59.8	71.4	52	52	1,083[h]	1,454[h]	0
159 Nigeria	120	0.443	43.5	43.2	..[l]	..[m]	50[f]	60[f]	669[h]	1,628[h]	0

Human development indicators

TABLE 24

Gender-related development index

HDI rank	Gender-related development index (GDI)		Life expectancy at birth (years) 2004		Adult literacy rate [a] (% ages 15 and older) 2004		Combined gross enrolment ratio for primary, secondary and tertiary schools (%) 2004 [b]		Estimated earned income [c] (PPP US$) 2004		HDI rank minus GDI rank [d]
	Rank	Value	Female	Male	Female	Male	Female	Male	Female	Male	
160 Guinea	121	0.434	54.2	53.6	18.1	42.6	35	49	1,764 [h]	2,576 [h]	0
161 Angola	122	0.431	42.5	39.6	54.2	82.9	24 [f, g]	28 [f, g]	1,670 [h]	2,706 [h]	0
162 Tanzania, U. Rep. of	123	0.426	46.2	45.6	62.2	77.5	47 [f]	49 [f]	569 [h]	781 [h]	0
163 Benin	124	0.412	55.0	53.5	23.3	47.9	41 [f]	58 [f]	702 [h]	1,475 [h]	0
164 Côte d'Ivoire	125	0.401	46.7	45.2	38.6	60.8	32 [f, g]	47 [f, g]	749 [h]	2,324 [h]	0
165 Zambia	126	0.396	37.1	38.2	59.8 [k]	76.3 [k]	52 [f]	56 [f]	670 [h]	1,216 [h]	0
166 Malawi	127	0.394	39.6	40.0	54.0 [k]	74.9 [k]	64 [f]	65 [f]	547 [h]	747 [h]	0
167 Congo, Dem. Rep. of the	130	0.378	44.5	42.5	54.1	80.9	24 [f, g]	30 [f, g]	482 [h]	931 [h]	−2
168 Mozambique	128	0.387	42.3	41.0	.. [l]	.. [m]	44	53	1,110 [h]	1,372 [h]	1
169 Burundi	129	0.380	44.9	43.0	52.2	67.3	32	40	594 [h]	765 [h]	1
170 Ethiopia	..	..	48.8	46.8	..	..	30	42	570 [h]	944 [h]	..
171 Chad	131	0.350	44.7	42.6	12.8	40.8	25 [f]	44 [f]	1,644 [h]	2,545 [h]	0
172 Central African Republic	132	0.336	39.8	38.4	33.5	64.8	23 [f, g]	36 [f, g]	836 [h]	1,367 [h]	0
173 Guinea-Bissau	..	..	46.2	43.4	..	..	29 [f, g]	45 [f, g]	487 [h]	963 [h]	..
174 Burkina Faso	133	0.335	48.6	47.2	15.2	29.4	23 [f]	30 [f]	930 [h]	1,405 [h]	0
175 Mali	134	0.329	48.7	47.4	11.9 [k]	26.7 [k]	30 [f]	40 [f]	800 [h]	1,197 [h]	0
176 Sierra Leone	135	0.317	42.4	39.6	24.4	46.9	55 [f]	75 [f]	353 [h]	775 [h]	0
177 Niger	136	0.292	44.7	44.6	15.1	42.9	18	25	560 [h]	989 [h]	0

NOTES

a Data refer to national literacy estimates from censuses or surveys conducted between 2000 and 2005, unless otherwise specified. Due to differences in methodology and timeliness of underlying data, comparisons across countries and over time should be made with caution. For more details, see www.uis.unesco.org.

b In 2006 the United Nations Educational, Scientific and Cultural Organization (UNESCO) Institute for Statistics changed its convention for citing the reference year of education data to the calendar year in which the academic or financial year ends—from 2003/04, for example, to 2004. Data for some countries may refer to national or UNESCO Institute for Statistics estimates. For details, see www.uis.unesco.org. Because data are from different sources, comparisons across countries should be made with caution.

c Because of the lack of gender-disaggregated income data, female and male earned income are crudely estimated on the basis of data on the ratio of the female nonagricultural wage to the male nonagricultural wage, the female and male shares

of the economically active population, the total female and male population and GDP per capita in purchasing power parity terms in US dollars (see Technical note 1). Estimates are based on data for the most recent year available during 1991–2004, unless otherwise specified.

d The HDI ranks used in this calculation are recalculated for the 136 countries with a GDI value. A positive figure indicates that the GDI rank is higher than the HDI rank, a negative the opposite.

e For the purposes of calculating the GDI, a value of 99.0% was applied.

f Preliminary UNESCO Institute for Statistics estimate, subject to further revision.

g Data refer to a year other than that specified.

h No wage data are available. For the purposes of calculating the estimated female and male earned income, a value of 0.75 was used for the ratio of the female nonagricultural wage to the male nonagricultural wage.

i Statec 2006.

j For the purposes of calculating the GDI, a value of $40,000 (PPP US$) was applied.

k Data refer to the most recent year available between 1995 and 1999.

l In the absence of recent data, estimates from UNESCO Institute for Statistics 2005, based on outdated census or survey information, were used and should be interpreted with caution: Bangladesh 33.1, Cape Verde 70.8, Comoros 49.7, Congo 80.8, El Salvador 78.8, Mozambique 35.6, Nigeria 64.2, Samoa (Western) 98.4, Trinidad and Tobago 98.3, United Arab Emirates 82.7, Uruguay 98.4, Uzbekistan 99.1, Yemen 33.4 and Zimbabwe 86.3.

m In the absence of recent data, estimates from UNESCO Institute for Statistics 2005, based on outdated census or survey information, were used and should be interpreted with caution: Bangladesh 51.7, Cape Verde 86.6, Comoros 63.9, Congo 91.2, El Salvador 83.6, Mozambique 65.7, Nigeria 96.9, Samoa (Western) 98.9, Trinidad and Tobago 99.2, United Arab Emirates 76.8, Uruguay 97.5, Uzbekistan 99.6, Yemen 72.5 and Zimbabwe 93.8.

n Data refer to a year or period other than that specified, differ from the standard definition or refer to only part of a country.

SOURCES

Column 1: determined on the basis of the GDI values in column 2.

Column 2: calculated on the basis of data in columns 3–10; see Technical note 1 for details.

Columns 3 and 4: UN 2005a, unless otherwise specified.

Columns 5 and 6: UNESCO Institute for Statistics 2006a, unless otherwise specified.

Columns 7 and 8: UNESCO Institute for Statistics 2006c, unless otherwise specified.

Columns 9 and 10: calculated on the basis of data on GDP per capita (PPP US$) and population from World Bank 2006, unless otherwise specified; data on wages from ILO 2006b; data on the economically active population from ILO 2005a.

Column 11: calculated on the basis of the recalculated HDI ranks and the GDI ranks in column 1.

GDI ranks for 136 countries

1	Norway	25	Korea, Rep. of	48	Trinidad and Tobago	71	Turkey	94	Namibia
2	Iceland	26	Portugal	49	Romania	72	Saudi Arabia	95	Morocco
3	Australia	27	Cyprus	50	Russian Federation	73	Tunisia	96	India
4	Ireland	28	Czech Republic	51	Malaysia	74	Iran, Islamic Rep. of	97	Cambodia
5	Sweden	29	Malta	52	Belarus	75	Azerbaijan	98	Botswana
6	Luxembourg	30	Hungary	53	Mauritius	76	El Salvador	99	Comoros
7	Canada	31	Kuwait	54	Macedonia, TFYR	77	Jamaica	100	Lao People's Dem. Rep.
8	United States	32	Argentina	55	Brazil	78	Cape Verde	101	Ghana
9	Netherlands	33	Poland	56	Colombia	79	Algeria	102	Bangladesh
10	Switzerland	34	Estonia	57	Oman	80	Viet Nam	103	Papua New Guinea
11	Finland	35	Lithuania	58	Thailand	81	Indonesia	104	Congo
12	Belgium	36	Slovakia	59	Albania	82	Syrian Arab Republic	105	Pakistan
13	Japan	37	Chile	60	Venezuela, RB	83	Kyrgyzstan	106	Nepal
14	France	38	Bahrain	61	Kazakhstan	84	Uzbekistan	107	Madagascar
15	Denmark	39	Uruguay	62	Ukraine	85	Moldova, Rep. of	108	Uganda
16	United Kingdom	40	Croatia	63	Samoa (Western)	86	Bolivia	109	Cameroon
17	Austria	41	Latvia	64	China	87	Mongolia	110	Sudan
18	Italy	42	Costa Rica	65	Armenia	88	Nicaragua	111	Kenya
19	Spain	43	United Arab Emirates	66	Philippines	89	Honduras	112	Lesotho
20	New Zealand	44	Bulgaria	67	Peru	90	Guatemala	113	Zimbabwe
21	Germany	45	Mexico	68	Sri Lanka	91	Tajikistan	114	Swaziland
22	Israel	46	Tonga	69	Jordan	92	South Africa	115	Mauritania
23	Greece	47	Panama	70	Dominican Republic	93	Equatorial Guinea	116	Togo
24	Slovenia								

117	Yemen
118	Senegal
119	Rwanda
120	Nigeria
121	Guinea
122	Angola
123	Tanzania, U. Rep. of
124	Benin
125	Côte d'Ivoire
126	Zambia
127	Malawi
128	Mozambique
129	Burundi
130	Congo, Dem. Rep. of the
131	Chad
132	Central African Republic
133	Burkina Faso
134	Mali
135	Sierra Leone
136	Niger

TABLE 25

... and achieving equality for all women and men

Gender empowerment measure

HDI rank	Gender empowerment measure (GEM) Rank	Value	Seats in parliament held by women [a] (% of total)	Female legislators, senior officials and managers [b] (% of total)	Female professional and technical workers [b] (% of total)	Ratio of estimated female to male earned income [c]
HIGH HUMAN DEVELOPMENT						
1 Norway	1	0.932	37.9	29	50	0.75
2 Iceland	3	0.866	33.3	29	55	0.71
3 Australia	8	0.833	28.3	37	55	0.70
4 Ireland	17	0.753	14.2	29	51	0.51
5 Sweden	2	0.883	45.3	31	51	0.81
6 Canada	11	0.810	24.3	36	56	0.63
7 Japan	42	0.557	10.7	10	46	0.44
8 United States	12	0.808	15.0	42	55	0.62
9 Switzerland	14	0.797	24.8	27	46	0.61
10 Netherlands	7	0.844	34.2	26	48	0.63
11 Finland	6	0.853	37.5	28	54	0.71
12 Luxembourg	..	..	23.3	..	..	0.49
13 Belgium	5	0.855	35.7	30	48	0.63
14 Austria	10	0.815	32.2	28	46	0.44
15 Denmark	4	0.861	36.9	25	52	0.73
16 France	..	..	13.9	..	..	0.64
17 Italy	24	0.653	16.1	21	45	0.46
18 United Kingdom	16	0.755	18.5	33	46	0.65
19 Spain	15	0.776	30.5	32	47	0.50
20 New Zealand	13	0.797	32.2	36	52	0.70
21 Germany	9	0.816	30.5	35	50	0.58
22 Hong Kong, China (SAR)	..	..	..	27	40	0.49
23 Israel	23	0.656	14.2	29	54	0.64
24 Greece	29	0.614	13.0	27	49	0.55
25 Singapore	18	0.707	18.9	26	45	0.51
26 Korea, Rep. of	53	0.502	13.4	7	38	0.46
27 Slovenia	32	0.603	10.8	34	57	0.61
28 Portugal	20	0.681	21.3	32	52	0.59
29 Cyprus	38	0.584	14.3	15	45	0.59
30 Czech Republic	28	0.615	15.7	28	52	0.51
31 Barbados	..	..	17.6	43	52	..
32 Malta	58	0.493	9.2	16	39	0.48
33 Kuwait	..	..	1.5	..	..	0.37
34 Brunei Darussalam	..	..	..[d]	..	..	..
35 Hungary	41	0.560	10.4	34	61	0.64
36 Argentina	19	0.697	36.5	25	55	0.53
37 Poland	30	0.610	19.1	34	61	0.59
38 Chile	52	0.506	12.7	24	52	0.39
39 Bahrain	..	..	7.5	..	..	0.33
40 Estonia	31	0.608	18.8	35	67	0.62
41 Lithuania	25	0.635	22.0	42	68	0.69
42 Slovakia	34	0.599	16.7	32	61	0.58
43 Uruguay	50	0.513	10.8	35	53	0.55
44 Croatia	33	0.602	21.7	23	52	0.67
45 Latvia	27	0.621	21.0	42	64	0.67
46 Qatar	..	..	0.0	..	..	..
47 Seychelles	..	..	29.4	..	..	..
48 Costa Rica	21	0.675	38.6	26	40	0.46
49 United Arab Emirates	70	0.353	0.0	8	25	0.24
50 Cuba	..	..	36.0	..	..	..
51 Saint Kitts and Nevis	..	..	0.0	..	..	..
52 Bahamas	..	..	26.8	40	..	0.70
53 Mexico	35	0.597	25.0	25	42	0.39

Human development indicators

TABLE 25

Gender empowerment measure

HDI rank	Gender empowerment measure (GEM)		Seats in parliament held by women[a] (% of total)	Female legislators, senior officials and managers[b] (% of total)	Female professional and technical workers[b] (% of total)	Ratio of estimated female to male earned income[c]
	Rank	Value				
54 Bulgaria	37	0.595	22.1	33	61	0.65
55 Tonga	..	..	3.3			0.47
56 Oman	..	..	7.8			0.18
57 Trinidad and Tobago	22	0.660	25.4	38	54	0.46
58 Panama	40	0.568	16.7	39	51	0.56
59 Antigua and Barbuda	..	..	13.9	..	..	
60 Romania	59	0.492	10.7	29	57	0.65
61 Malaysia	55	0.500	13.1	23	40	0.36
62 Bosnia and Herzegovina	..	..	12.3	..	..	0.65
63 Mauritius	..	..	17.1	..	..	0.40
MEDIUM HUMAN DEVELOPMENT						
64 Libyan Arab Jamahiriya	..	..	4.7	..	..	..
65 Russian Federation	62	0.482	8.0	38	64	0.62
66 Macedonia, TFYR	43	0.554	19.2	28	53	0.48
67 Belarus	..	..	29.8	..	..	0.64
68 Dominica	..	..	12.9	..	..	..
69 Brazil	61	0.486	9.1	34	53	0.57
70 Colombia	51	0.506	10.8[e]	38	50	0.58
71 Saint Lucia	..	..	17.2	..	..	0.51
72 Venezuela, RB	46	0.532	18.0	27	61	0.51
73 Albania	..	..	7.1	..	..	0.54
74 Thailand	60	0.486	10.7	28	53	0.59
75 Samoa (Western)	..	..	4.1	..	..	0.38
76 Saudi Arabia	74	0.242	0.0	31	6	0.15
77 Ukraine	63	0.455	7.1	43	60	0.53
78 Lebanon	..	..	4.7	..	..	0.31
79 Kazakhstan	..	..	8.6	..	..	0.63
80 Armenia	..	..	5.3	..	..	0.63
81 China	..	..	20.3	..	..	0.64
82 Peru	39	0.580	29.0	19	44	0.41
83 Ecuador	49	0.524	16.0	34	49	0.55
84 Philippines	45	0.533	15.8	58	61	0.60
85 Grenada	..	..	28.6	..	..	..
86 Jordan	..	..	7.9	..	..	0.30
87 Tunisia	..	..	19.3	..	..	0.28
88 Saint Vincent and the Grenadines	..	..	18.2	..	..	0.51
89 Suriname	..	..	25.5	28	51	..
90 Fiji	..	..	11.7	..	..	0.48
91 Paraguay	..	..	9.6	..	..	0.41
92 Turkey	72	0.289	4.4	7	31	0.35
93 Sri Lanka	69	0.372	4.9	21	46	0.42
94 Dominican Republic	..	..	15.4[e]	..	50	0.42
95 Belize	57	0.495	11.9	31	52	0.39
96 Iran, Islamic Rep. of	71	0.326	4.1	13	33	0.38
97 Georgia	64	0.407	9.4	26	63	0.37
98 Maldives	..	..	12.0	15	40	..
99 Azerbaijan	..	..	12.3	..	..	0.64
100 Occupied Palestinian Territories	..	..	..	11	35	..
101 El Salvador	48	0.529	16.7	33	45	0.43
102 Algeria	..	..	5.3	..	..	0.33
103 Guyana	..	..	30.8	..	..	0.41
104 Jamaica	..	..	13.6	..	..	0.57
105 Turkmenistan	..	..	16.0	..	..	0.64
106 Cape Verde	..	..	15.3	..	..	0.35

TABLE 25

HDI rank	Gender empowerment measure (GEM)		Seats in parliament held by women[a] (% of total)	Female legislators, senior officials and managers[b] (% of total)	Female professional and technical workers[b] (% of total)	Ratio of estimated female to male earned income[c]
	Rank	**Value**				
107 Syrian Arab Republic	..	..	12.0	..	..	0.33
108 Indonesia	..	..	11.3	..	..	0.45
109 Viet Nam	..	..	27.3	..	..	0.71
110 Kyrgyzstan	..	..	0.0	..	..	0.58
111 Egypt	73	0.262	3.8	9	30	0.23
112 Nicaragua	..	..	20.7	..	..	0.32
113 Uzbekistan	..	..	16.4	..	..	0.60
114 Moldova, Rep. of	44	0.544	21.8	39	66	0.63
115 Bolivia	56	0.499	14.6	36	40	0.57
116 Mongolia	65	0.388	6.6	30	66	0.51
117 Honduras	47	0.530	23.4	22	36	0.45
118 Guatemala	..	..	8.2	..	..	0.32
119 Vanuatu	..	..	3.8	..	..	0.68
120 Equatorial Guinea	..	..	18.0	..	..	0.43
121 South Africa	..	..	32.8[f]	..	..	0.45
122 Tajikistan	..	..	19.6	..	..	0.57
123 Morocco	..	..	6.4	..	..	0.25
124 Gabon	..	..	11.9	..	..	0.57
125 Namibia	26	0.623	26.9	30	55	0.57
126 India	..	..	9.2	..	..	0.31
127 São Tomé and Principe	..	..	7.3	..	..	..
128 Solomon Islands	..	..	0.0	..	..	0.50
129 Cambodia	68	0.373	11.4	14	33	0.74
130 Myanmar	..	..	..[g]	..	..	..
131 Botswana	54	0.501	11.1	31	53	0.36
132 Comoros	..	..	3.0	..	..	0.51
133 Lao People's Dem. Rep.	..	..	22.9	..	..	0.52
134 Pakistan	66	0.377	20.4	2	26	0.29
135 Bhutan	..	..	9.3	..	..	..
136 Ghana	..	..	10.9	..	..	0.71
137 Bangladesh	67	0.374	14.8[h]	23	12	0.46
138 Nepal	..	..	6.7	..	..	0.50
139 Papua New Guinea	..	..	0.9	..	..	0.73
140 Congo	..	..	10.1	..	..	0.50
141 Sudan	..	..	13.6	..	..	0.25
142 Timor-Leste	..	..	25.3[i]	..	..	..
143 Madagascar	..	..	8.4	..	..	0.70
144 Cameroon	..	..	8.9	..	..	0.49
145 Uganda	..	..	28.8	..	..	0.70
146 Swaziland	..	..	16.8	..	..	0.29
LOW HUMAN DEVELOPMENT						
147 Togo	..	..	8.6	..	..	0.43
148 Djibouti	..	..	10.8	..	..	0.49
149 Lesotho	..	..	17.0	..	..	0.53
150 Yemen	75	0.128	0.7	4	15	0.30
151 Zimbabwe	..	..	20.8	..	..	0.58
152 Kenya	..	..	7.3	..	..	0.83
153 Mauritania	..	..	..[j]	..	..	0.50
154 Haiti	..	..	6.2	..	..	0.52
155 Gambia	..	..	13.2	..	..	0.53
156 Senegal	..	..	19.2	..	..	0.53
157 Eritrea	..	..	22.0	..	..	0.39
158 Rwanda	..	..	45.3	..	..	0.74
159 Nigeria	..	..	5.8	..	..	0.41

Human development indicators

TABLE

25

Gender empowerment measure

HDI rank	Gender empowerment measure (GEM)		Seats in parliament held by women [a] (% of total)	Female legislators, senior officials and managers [b] (% of total)	Female professional and technical workers [b] (% of total)	Ratio of estimated female to male earned income [c]
	Rank	Value				
160 Guinea	..	..	19.3	..	..	0.68
161 Angola	..	..	15.0	..	..	0.62
162 Tanzania, U. Rep. of	36	0.597	30.4	49	32	0.73
163 Benin	..	..	7.2	..	..	0.48
164 Côte d'Ivoire	..	..	8.5	..	..	0.32
165 Zambia	..	..	12.7	..	..	0.55
166 Malawi	..	..	13.6	..	..	0.73
167 Congo, Dem. Rep. of the	..	..	10.2	..	..	0.52
168 Mozambique	..	..	34.8	..	..	0.81
169 Burundi	..	..	31.7	..	..	0.78
170 Ethiopia	..	..	21.4	..	..	0.60
171 Chad	..	..	6.5	..	..	0.65
172 Central African Republic	..	..	10.5	..	..	0.61
173 Guinea-Bissau	..	..	14.0	..	..	0.51
174 Burkina Faso	..	..	11.7	..	..	0.66
175 Mali	..	..	10.2	..	..	0.67
176 Sierra Leone	..	..	14.5	..	..	0.45
177 Niger	..	..	12.4	..	..	0.57

NOTES

a Data are as of 31 May 2006, unless otherwise specified. Where there are lower and upper houses, data refer to the weighted average of women's shares of seats in both houses.

b Data refer to the most recent year available during 1992–2004. Estimates for countries that have implemented the recent International Standard Classification of Occupations (ISCO-88) are not strictly comparable with those for countries using the previous classification (ISCO-68).

c Calculated on the basis of data in columns 9 and 10 in table 24. Estimates are based on data for the most recent year available during 1991–2004.

d Does not currently have a parliament.

e Data are as of 1 March 2005.

f Does not include the 36 special rotating delegates appointed on an ad hoc basis. The shares given

are therefore calculated on the basis of the 54 permanent seats.

g The parliament elected in 1990 has never been convened nor authorized to sit, and many of its members were detained or forced into exile.

h In 2004 the number of seats in parliament was raised from 300 to 345, with the additional 45 seats reserved for women and filled in September and October 2005.

i The purpose of elections held on 30 August 2001 was to elect members of the Constituent Assembly of Timor-Leste. This body became the National Parliament on 20 May 2002, the date on which the country became independent, without any new elections.

j The Parliament of Mauritania was suspended following a coup d'etat in August 2005.

SOURCES

Column 1: determined on the basis of GEM values in column 2.

Column 2: calculated on the basis of data in columns 3–6; see *Technical note 1* for details.

Column 3: calculated on the basis of data on parliamentary seats from IPU 2006a, 2006c.

Columns 4 and 5: calculated on the basis of occupational data from ILO 2006b.

Column 6: calculated on the basis of data in columns 9 and 10 of table 24.

TABLE 26

... and achieving equality for all women and men

Gender inequality in education

		Adult literacy [a]		MDG Youth literacy [a]		MDG Net primary enrolment [b, c]		MDG Net secondary enrolment [b, c]		MDG Gross tertiary enrolment [c, d]	
HDI rank		Female rate (% ages 15 and older) 2004	Female rate as % of male rate 2004	Female rate (% ages 15–24) 2004	Female rate as % of male rate 2004	Female ratio (%) 2004[f]	Ratio of female to male[e] 2004[f]	Female ratio (%) 2004[f]	Ratio of female to male[e] 2004[f]	Female ratio (%) 2004[f]	Ratio of female to male[e] 2004[f]
HIGH HUMAN DEVELOPMENT											
1	Norway	..	..	..	..	99	1.00	97	1.01	98	1.54
2	Iceland	..	..	..	..	98 [g]	0.98 [g]	88 [g]	1.04 [g]	79 [g]	1.78 [g]
3	Australia	..	..	..	..	96	1.01	86 [g]	1.01 [g]	80	1.23
4	Ireland	..	..	..	..	96	1.00	89	1.06	66	1.28
5	Sweden	..	..	..	..	99	1.00	100	1.03	102	1.55
6	Canada	..	..	..	..	100 [g, h]	1.00 [g, h]	94 [i]	0.99 [i]	70 [j]	1.36 [j]
7	Japan	..	..	..	..	100	1.00	100 [g, k]	1.01 [g, k]	51	0.89
8	United States	..	..	..	..	91	0.96	91	1.02	96	1.39
9	Switzerland	..	..	..	..	94	1.00	80	0.93	42	0.80
10	Netherlands	..	..	..	..	98	0.99	90	1.01	62	1.08
11	Finland	..	..	..	..	99	1.00	94	1.01	98	1.20
12	Luxembourg	..	..	..	..	91	1.00	82	1.07	13 [g]	1.18 [g]
13	Belgium	..	..	..	..	99	1.00	97 [g, l]	1.01 [g, l]	69	1.21
14	Austria	..	..	..	..	..	..	..	..	54	1.19
15	Denmark	..	..	..	..	100	1.00	94	1.03	87	1.42
16	France	..	..	..	..	99	1.00	97	1.02	63	1.28
17	Italy	98.0	99	99.8	100	99	1.00	93	1.02	72	1.34
18	United Kingdom	..	..	..	..	99	1.00	97	1.03	70	1.37
19	Spain	..	..	..	..	99	0.99	99	1.04	72	1.22
20	New Zealand	..	..	..	..	99	1.00	96	1.03	74	1.41
21	Germany	..	..	..	..	..	..	..	..	..	..
22	Hong Kong, China (SAR)	..	..	..	..	90 [m]	0.95 [m]	77 [m]	0.97 [m]	32	0.97
23	Israel	95.9	97	99.6	100	98	1.01	89	1.00	65	1.33
24	Greece	94.2	96	99.0	100	99	0.99	88	1.04	86	1.17
25	Singapore	88.6	92	99.6	100	..	..	..	..	..	..
26	Korea, Rep. of	..	..	..	..	99	0.99	88	1.00	67	0.61
27	Slovenia	..	..	..	..	98	1.00	95	1.00	86	1.38
28	Portugal	..	..	..	..	99	0.99	87 [l]	1.11 [l]	65	1.32
29	Cyprus	95.1	96	99.8	100	96 [m]	1.00 [m]	95 [m]	1.03 [m]	36 [m]	0.98 [m]
30	Czech Republic	..	..	..	..	..	..	..	..	45	1.10
31	Barbados	..	..	..	..	97	0.99	98	1.05	54 [h]	2.47 [h]
32	Malta	89.2 [n]	103 [n]	97.8 [n]	104 [n]	94	1.00	90	1.06	30	1.33
33	Kuwait	91.0	96	99.8	100	87 [g]	1.03 [g]	80 [g, j]	1.05 [g, j]	33 [g]	2.72 [g]
34	Brunei Darussalam	90.2	95	98.9	100	..	..	..	..	17 [g]	1.74 [g]
35	Hungary	..	..	..	..	88	0.99	90 [g]	0.99 [g]	70	1.40
36	Argentina	97.2	100	99.1	100	98 [l]	0.99 [l]	82 [l]	1.07 [l]	77 [l]	1.51 [l]
37	Poland	..	..	..	..	98	1.00	92	1.03	72	1.41
38	Chile	95.6	100	99.2	100	..	..	..	..	42	0.95
39	Bahrain	83.6	94	97.3	100	97	1.01	93	1.07	45 [g]	1.84 [g]
40	Estonia	99.8	100	99.8	100	94	1.00	91	1.03	82	1.68
41	Lithuania	99.6	100	99.7	100	89	1.00	93	1.01	89	1.55
42	Slovakia	..	..	..	..	..	..	..	..	40	1.22
43	Uruguay	..	..	..	..	..	..	..	..	53 [g, l]	2.04 [g, l]
44	Croatia	97.1	98	99.7	100	87 [l]	0.99 [l]	86 [l]	1.02 [l]	42 [l]	1.19 [l]
45	Latvia	99.7	100	99.8	100	..	..	..	..	94	1.72
46	Qatar	88.6	99	97.5	103	94	0.99	86	0.98	34	3.67
47	Seychelles	92.3	101	99.4	101	97 [m]	1.01 [m]	96 [m]	1.07 [m]	..	..
48	Costa Rica	95.1	100	98.0	101	..	..	..	..	28	1.26
49	United Arab Emirates	..	..	..	..	70	0.97	64	1.06	40 [g, l]	3.24 [g, l]
50	Cuba	99.8	100	100.0	100	95	0.97	87	1.02	38 [l]	1.34 [l]
51	Saint Kitts and Nevis	..	..	..	..	98 [m]	1.08 [m]	97 [m]	0.97 [m]	..	..
52	Bahamas	..	..	..	..	85	1.02	78	1.12	..	..
53	Mexico	89.6	97	97.6	100	98	1.00	65	1.03	23	0.98

Human development indicators

TABLE 26

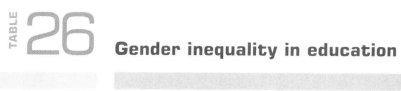

Gender inequality in education

		Adult literacy[a]		Youth literacy[a]		MDG Net primary enrolment[b, c]		MDG Net secondary enrolment[b, c]		MDG Gross tertiary enrolment[c, d]	
		Female rate (% ages 15 and older)	Female rate as % of male rate	Female rate (% ages 15–24)	Female rate as % of male rate	Female ratio (%)	Ratio of female to male[e]	Female ratio (%)	Ratio of female to male[e]	Female ratio (%)	Ratio of female to male[e]
HDI rank		2004	2004	2004	2004	2004[f]	2004[f]	2004[f]	2004[f]	2004[f]	2004[f]
54	Bulgaria	97.7	99	98.1	100	95	0.99	87	0.98	44	1.16
55	Tonga	99.0[n]	100[n]	99.4[n]	100[n]	89[i]	0.97[i]	75[g]	1.23[g]	8[g]	1.67[g]
56	Oman	73.5	85	96.7	99	79	1.02	75	1.01	15	1.38
57	Trinidad and Tobago	..	..	..	..	92[m]	0.99[m]	74[g]	1.06[g]	13	1.27
58	Panama	91.2	99	95.6	99	98	0.99	67	1.10	57	1.59
59	Antigua and Barbuda	..	..	..	..	..	..	..	..	..	..
60	Romania	96.3	98	97.8	100	92	0.99	82	1.03	45	1.26
61	Malaysia	85.4	93	97.3	100	93[l]	1.00[l]	81[l]	1.14[l]	38[l]	1.41[l]
62	Bosnia and Herzegovina	94.4	95	99.8	100	..	..	..	..	..	..
63	Mauritius	80.5	91	95.4	102	96	1.02	80[g]	1.00[g]	20	1.39
MEDIUM HUMAN DEVELOPMENT											
64	Libyan Arab Jamahiriya	..	..	..	..	..	..	..	..	59[g,l]	1.09[g,l]
65	Russian Federation	99.2	100	99.8	100	92[g]	1.01[g]	..	..	79[g]	1.36[g]
66	Macedonia, TFYR	94.1	96	98.5	99	92	1.00	80[g,j]	0.97[g,j]	33	1.39
67	Belarus	99.4[n]	100[n]	99.8[n]	100[n]	88[g]	0.97[g]	88[g]	1.01[g]	71	1.39
68	Dominica	..	..	..	..	88[m]	1.01[m]	92[g]	1.03[g]	..	..
69	Brazil	88.8	100	97.9	102	..	..	78[l]	1.07[l]	25[l]	1.32[l]
70	Colombia	92.7	100	98.4	101	84	1.01	58[g]	1.11[g]	28	1.09
71	Saint Lucia	..	..	..	..	96	0.97	74[g]	1.09[g]	22	3.43
72	Venezuela, RB	92.7	99	98.1	102	92	1.01	66	1.15	41[g,l]	1.07[g,l]
73	Albania	98.3	99	99.5	100	95[l]	0.99[l]	73[l]	0.98[l]	20[l]	1.57[l]
74	Thailand	90.5	95	97.8	100	..	..	..	..	44	1.17
75	Samoa (Western)	..	..	..	..	91[g]	1.00[g]	70[g]	1.14[g]	7[g,h]	0.94[g,h]
76	Saudi Arabia	69.3	80	93.7	96	57[j]	0.92[j]	51[g]	0.96[g]	33	1.50
77	Ukraine	99.2	99	99.8	100	82[m]	1.00[m]	84[m]	1.00[m]	71[m]	1.19[m]
78	Lebanon	..	..	..	..	93	0.99	..	..	50	1.12
79	Kazakhstan	99.3[n]	100[n]	99.9[n]	100[n]	92	0.99	92	0.99	56	1.38
80	Armenia	99.2	99	99.9	100	96	1.04	90	1.03	29	1.21
81	China	86.5	91	98.5	99	..	..	..	..	17[g]	0.84[g]
82	Peru	82.1	88	95.7	98	97	1.00	69	1.00	34[g]	1.03[g]
83	Ecuador	89.7	97	96.5	100	98[g]	1.01[g]	53	1.01	..	..
84	Philippines	92.7	100	95.7	101	95	1.02	67	1.20	32	1.28
85	Grenada	..	..	..	..	84[m]	0.99[m]	82[g]	1.10[g]	..	..
86	Jordan	84.7	89	98.9	100	92	1.02	82	1.02	41	1.10
87	Tunisia	65.3	78	92.2	96	98	1.00	69[g,j]	1.04[g,j]	33	1.36
88	Saint Vincent and the Grenadines	..	..	..	..	93[g]	0.97[g]	63	1.02	..	..
89	Suriname	87.2	95	94.1	98	96[g,l]	1.07[g,l]	74[g,l]	1.38[g,l]	15[j]	1.62[j]
90	Fiji	..	..	..	..	96	0.99	85[g]	1.06[g]	17	1.20
91	Paraguay	..	..	..	..	..	..	..	..	28[g,l]	1.37[g,l]
92	Turkey	79.6	84	93.3	95	87[g]	0.95[g]	..	..	24	0.73
93	Sri Lanka	89.1	97	96.1	101	98[g,l]	1.00[g,l]	..	..	..	..
94	Dominican Republic	87.2	100	95.4	103	87	1.02	54[g]	1.21[g]	41[g]	1.64[g]
95	Belize	..	..	..	..	96	1.01	73[g]	1.05[g]	4	2.47
96	Iran, Islamic Rep. of	70.4	84	..	..	88	0.99	76	0.94	24	1.10
97	Georgia	..	..	..	..	93	0.99	81	1.00	42	1.03
98	Maldives	96.4	100	98.3	100	90[j]	1.01[j]	55[g,j]	1.15[g,j]	(.)[g]	3.00[g]
99	Azerbaijan	98.2[n]	99[n]	99.9[n]	100[n]	83	0.98	76	0.98	14	0.87
100	Occupied Palestinian Territories	88.0	91	98.8	100	86	1.00	92	1.05	39	1.03
101	El Salvador	..	..	..	..	93[g]	1.00[g]	49[g,l]	1.03[g,l]	20	1.22
102	Algeria	60.1	76	86.1	92	95	0.98	68[g]	1.05[g]	20	1.09
103	Guyana	..	..	..	..	..	..	..	..	12	1.94
104	Jamaica	85.9[n]	116[n]	..	..	91	1.01	81	1.03	26[g,l]	2.29[g,l]
105	Turkmenistan	98.3[n]	99[n]	99.8[n]	100[n]	..	..	..	..	..	..
106	Cape Verde	..	..	..	..	91	0.99	58	1.12	6	1.09

TABLE 26

HDI rank		Adult literacy [a] — Female rate (% ages 15 and older) 2004	Adult literacy [a] — Female rate as % of male rate 2004	MDG Youth literacy [a] — Female rate (% ages 15–24) 2004	Youth literacy [a] — Female rate as % of male rate 2004	MDG Net primary enrolment [b,c] — Female ratio (%) 2004 [f]	Net primary enrolment — Ratio of female to male [e] 2004 [f]	MDG Net secondary enrolment [b,c] — Female ratio (%) 2004 [f]	Net secondary enrolment — Ratio of female to male [e] 2004 [f]	MDG Gross tertiary enrolment [c,d] — Female ratio (%) 2004 [f]	Gross tertiary enrolment — Ratio of female to male [e] 2004 [f]
107	Syrian Arab Republic	73.6	86	90.2	96	92 [j]	0.95 [j]	56	0.93	..	..
108	Indonesia	86.8	92	98.5	100	93	0.98	57	0.99	15	0.79
109	Viet Nam	86.9 [n]	93 [n]	93.6 [n]	99 [n]	92 [g,h]	0.94 [g,h]	..	..	9 [g]	0.77 [g]
110	Kyrgyzstan	98.1 [n]	99 [n]	99.7 [n]	100 [n]	90	0.99	..	..	43	1.19
111	Egypt	59.4	71	78.9	88	94 [g]	0.97 [g]	77 [g,j]	0.94 [g,j]	..	..
112	Nicaragua	76.6	100	88.8	106	87	0.99	43	1.13	19 [g,l]	1.11 [g,l]
113	Uzbekistan	..	..	..	..	..	..	..	..	14 [g]	0.79 [g]
114	Moldova, Rep. of	97.7	99	99.5	100	86 [m]	0.99 [m]	79 [m]	1.04 [m]	43 [m]	1.36 [m]
115	Bolivia	80.7	87	96.1	98	96 [g]	1.01 [g]	73 [g]	0.99 [g]	..	..
116	Mongolia	97.5	100	98.4	101	85	1.01	88	1.14	49	1.64
117	Honduras	80.2	101	90.9	105	92	1.02	..	..	20 [g]	1.46 [g]
118	Guatemala	63.3	84	78.4	91	91	0.95	32 [g]	0.92 [g]	8 [g,l]	0.72 [g,l]
119	Vanuatu	..	..	..	..	93	0.98	36 [g]	0.86 [g]	4 [g]	0.57 [g]
120	Equatorial Guinea	80.5	86	94.9	100	78 [j]	0.85 [j]	18 [g,h]	0.59 [g,h]	2 [k]	0.43 [k]
121	South Africa	80.9 [n]	96 [n]	94.3 [n]	101 [n]	89 [l]	1.01 [l]	65 [g,k]	1.12 [g,k]	17 [l]	1.17 [l]
122	Tajikistan	99.2	100	99.8	100	95	0.96	73	0.85	8	0.33
123	Morocco	39.6	60	60.5	75	83	0.94	32 [g,l]	0.86 [g,l]	10	0.87
124	Gabon	..	..	..	..	77 [g,h]	0.99 [g,h]	..	..	5 [i]	0.53 [i]
125	Namibia	83.5	96	93.5	103	77 [l]	1.08 [l]	43 [l]	1.35 [l]	7 [l]	1.14 [l]
126	India	47.8	65	67.7	80	87 [g]	0.94 [g]	..	..	9	0.66
127	São Tomé and Principe	..	..	..	..	98	0.99	27	1.08	..	..
128	Solomon Islands	..	..	..	..	79	0.99	24 [g,l]	0.86 [g,l]	..	..
129	Cambodia	64.1	76	78.9	90	96	0.96	22 [g]	0.73 [g]	2	0.45
130	Myanmar	86.4	92	93.4	98	87	1.01	36	0.95	15 [g,h]	1.77 [g,h]
131	Botswana	81.8	102	95.6	104	83 [g]	1.03 [g]	64 [g]	1.11 [g]	6	0.85
132	Comoros	..	..	..	..	51 [k,m]	0.85 [k,m]	..	..	2 [g]	0.77 [g]
133	Lao People's Dem. Rep.	60.9	79	74.7	90	82	0.94	34	0.85	5	0.63
134	Pakistan	36.0	57	54.7	72	56 [m]	0.73 [m]	..	..	3	0.80
135	Bhutan	..	..	..	..	..	..	..	..	..	..
136	Ghana	49.8	75	65.5	86	58 [g]	1.01 [g]	33 [g]	0.86 [g]	2	0.48
137	Bangladesh	..	..	..	..	95 [m]	1.03 [m]	51 [l]	1.11 [l]	4 [l]	0.50 [l]
138	Nepal	34.9	56	60.1	75	73 [l,m]	0.87 [l,m]	..	..	3	0.41
139	Papua New Guinea	50.9	80	64.1	93	..	..	..	..	2 [g,i]	0.56 [g,i]
140	Congo	..	..	..	..	..	..	..	..	1 [g,l]	0.18 [g,l]
141	Sudan	51.8	73	71.4	84	39 [g,k]	0.83 [g,k]	..	..	6 [g,k]	0.92 [g,k]
142	Timor-Leste	..	..	..	..	..	..	..	..	12 [j,m]	1.48 [j,m]
143	Madagascar	65.3	85	68.2	94	89	1.00	11 [g,i]	1.03 [g,i]	2	0.89
144	Cameroon	59.8	78	..	..	..	..	..	..	4 [g]	0.63 [g]
145	Uganda	57.7	75	71.2	86	..	..	14	0.90	3	0.62
146	Swaziland	78.3	97	89.8	103	77 [l]	1.01 [l]	32 [l]	1.24 [l]	5	1.08
LOW HUMAN DEVELOPMENT											
147	Togo	38.5	56	63.6	76	72	0.85	14 [g,k]	0.48 [g,k]	1 [g,h]	0.20 [g,h]
148	Djibouti	..	..	..	..	29	0.80	15 [g]	0.70 [g]	1	0.82
149	Lesotho	90.3	123	..	..	89	1.06	28	1.54	3 [l]	1.50 [l]
150	Yemen	..	..	..	..	63 [g]	0.73 [g]	21 [g,k]	0.46 [g,k]	5	0.38
151	Zimbabwe	..	..	..	..	82 [l]	1.01 [l]	33 [l]	0.93 [l]	3 [l]	0.62 [l]
152	Kenya	70.2	90	80.7	101	77	1.00	40 [g]	1.01 [g]	2	0.61
153	Mauritania	43.4	73	55.5	82	74	0.99	13 [g]	0.82 [g]	2	0.30
154	Haiti	..	..	..	..	..	..	..	..	..	..
155	Gambia	..	..	..	..	77 [g]	1.06 [g]	41 [g]	0.83 [g]	1	0.26
156	Senegal	29.2	57	41.0	70	65	0.95	13	0.72	..	0.15
157	Eritrea	..	..	..	..	44	0.85	18	0.63	(.)	0.15
158	Rwanda	59.8	84	76.9	98	75	1.05	..	..	2	0.62
159	Nigeria	..	..	..	..	57 [g]	0.89 [g]	25 [g]	0.83 [g]	7	0.55

TABLE 26

Gender inequality in education

HDI rank	Adult literacy [a] Female rate (% ages 15 and older) 2004	Adult literacy [a] Female rate as % of male rate 2004	Youth literacy [a] Female rate (% ages 15–24) 2004	Youth literacy [a] Female rate as % of male rate 2004	MDG Net primary enrolment [b,c] Female ratio (%) 2004[f]	MDG Net primary enrolment [b,c] Ratio of female to male[e] 2004[f]	MDG Net secondary enrolment [b,c] Female ratio (%) 2004[f]	MDG Net secondary enrolment [b,c] Ratio of female to male[e] 2004[f]	MDG Gross tertiary enrolment [c,d] Female ratio (%) 2004[f]	MDG Gross tertiary enrolment [c,d] Ratio of female to male[e] 2004[f]
160 Guinea	18.1	43	33.7	57	58	0.84	14[g]	0.51[g]	1	0.19
161 Angola	54.2	65	63.2	75	..	..	..	..	1[g,l]	0.70[g,l]
162 Tanzania, U. Rep. of	62.2	80	76.2	94	85	0.98	..	..	1	0.41
163 Benin	23.3	49	33.2	56	72	0.78	11[g,h]	0.49[g,h]	1[g,h]	0.25[g,h]
164 Côte d'Ivoire	38.6	63	52.1	74	50[l,m]	0.80[l,m]	15[g,j]	0.57[g,j]	3[i]	0.36[i]
165 Zambia	59.8[n]	78[n]	66.2[n]	91[n]	80	1.00	21[g]	0.78[g]	2[g,k]	0.47[g,k]
166 Malawi	54.0[n]	72[n]	70.7[n]	86[n]	98	1.05	23	0.86	(.)	0.60
167 Congo, Dem. Rep. of the	54.1	67	63.1	81	..	..	..	..	..	..
168 Mozambique	..	..	..	..	67	0.90	4	0.78	1	0.44
169 Burundi	52.2	78	70.4	92	54	0.89	..	..	1	0.38
170 Ethiopia	..	..	..	..	44	0.89	19[g]	0.61[g]	1	0.35
171 Chad	12.8	31	23.2	42	46[g,l]	0.68[g,l]	5[g,l]	0.33[g,l]	(.)[g,h]	0.14[g,h]
172 Central African Republic	33.5	52	46.9	67	..	..	..	..	1[k]	0.19[k]
173 Guinea-Bissau	..	..	..	..	38[g,h]	0.71[g,h]	6[g,h]	0.55[g,h]	(.)[g,h]	0.17[g,h]
174 Burkina Faso	15.2	52	24.8	65	35	0.77	6[g,h]	0.55[g,h]	(.)[g,h]	0.17[g,h]
175 Mali	11.9[n]	44[n]	16.9[n]	52[n]	43	0.85	8[g]	0.68[g]	1[g]	0.31[g]
176 Sierra Leone	24.4	52	37.2	63	..	..	..	..	1	0.46
177 Niger	15.1	35	23.2	44	32	0.71	5	0.67	1[g,j]	0.39[g,j]
Developing countries	71.7	84	83.0	92	..	..	..	..	(.)	0.36
Least developed countries	50.4	72	61.6	82	..	..	..	..	..	..
Arab States	59.7	74	80.4	89	..	..	..	..	..	..
East Asia and the Pacific	..	..	..	..	..	..	..	..	..	..
Latin America and the Caribbean	89.5	98	97.1	101	..	..	..	..	..	..
South Asia	47.7	66	65.3	79	..	..	..	..	..	..
Sub-Saharan Africa	53.2	76	64.0	86	..	..	..	..	..	..
Central and Eastern Europe and the CIS	98.7	99	99.6	100	..	..	..	..	..	..
OECD	..	..	..	..	..	..	..	..	..	..
High-income OECD	..	..	..	..	..	..	..	..	..	..
High human development	..	..	..	..	..	..	..	..	..	..
Medium human development	74.4	86	85.6	93	..	..	..	..	..	..
Low human development	46.1	70	57.5	82	..	..	..	..	..	..
High income	..	..	..	..	..	..	..	..	..	..
Middle income	86.4	93	96.2	99	..	..	..	..	..	..
Low income	50.2	69	66.6	82	..	..	..	..	..	..
World	74.4	86	84.2	..	..	..	..	..	..	..

NOTES

a Data refer to national literacy estimates from censuses or surveys conducted between 2000 and 2005, unless otherwise specified. Due to differences in methodology and timeliness of underlying data, comparisons across countries and over time should be made with caution. For more details, see www.uis.unesco.org.

b The net enrolment ratio is the ratio of enrolled children of the official age for the education level indicated to the total population at that age. Net enrolment ratios exceeding 100% reflect discrepancies between these two data sets.

c Data for some countries may refer to national or United Nations Educational, Scientific and Cultural Organization (UNESCO) Institute for Statistics estimates. For details, see www.uis.unesco.org. Because data are from different sources, comparisons across countries should be made with caution.

d Tertiary enrolment is generally calculated as a gross ratio.

e Calculated as the ratio of the female enrolment ratio to the male enrolment ratio.

f In 2006 the UNESCO Institute for Statistics changed its convention for citing the reference year of education data to the calendar year in which the academic or financial year ends—from 2003/04, for example, to 2004.

g Preliminary UNESCO Institute for Statistics estimate, subject to further revision.

h Data refer to the 2001 school year.

i Data refer to the 1999 school year.

j Data refer to the 2002 school year.

k Data refer to the 2000 school year.

l Data refer to the 2003 school year.

m National estimate.

n Data refer to a year between 1995 and 1999.

SOURCES

Columns 1 and 3: UNESCO Institute for Statistics 2006a.

Column 2: calculated on the basis of data on adult literacy rates from UNESCO Institute for Statistics 2006a.

Column 4: calculated on the basis of data on youth literacy rates from UNESCO Institute for Statistics 2006a.

Columns 5, 7 and 9: UNESCO Institute for Statistics 2006c.

Columns 6, 8 and 10: calculated on the basis of data on net enrolment rates from UNESCO Institute for Statistics 2006c.

TABLE 27

... and achieving equality for all women and men

Gender inequality in economic activity

		Female economic activity (ages 15 and older)			Employment by economic activity [a] (%)						Contributing family workers (%)	
					Agriculture		Industry		Services			
		Rate (%)	Index (1990=100)	As % of male rate	Women	Men	Women	Men	Women	Men	Women	Men
HDI rank		2004	2004	2004	1995–2003 [b]	1995–2003 [b]	1995–2003 [b]	1995–2003 [b]	1995–2003 [b]	1995–2003 [b]	1995–2004 [b]	1995–2004 [b]
HIGH HUMAN DEVELOPMENT												
1	Norway	63.1	111	87	2	6	9	33	88	58	43	57
2	Iceland	70.9	105	87	3	12	10	33	85	54	50	50
3	Australia	56.1	108	79	3	6	10	30	87	64	59	41
4	Ireland	51.9	146	72	2	11	14	39	83	50	53	47
5	Sweden	58.8	93	87	1	3	11	36	88	61	55	55
6	Canada	60.2	104	83	2	4	11	33	87	64	66	34
7	Japan	48.5	97	65	5	5	21	37	73	57	80	20
8	United States	59.6	105	81	1	3	12	32	87	65	64	36
9	Switzerland	60.1	115	79	3	5	13	36	84	59	62	38
10	Netherlands	55.8	128	76	2	4	9	31	86	64	79	21
11	Finland	56.9	98	86	4	7	14	40	82	53	36	55
12	Luxembourg	44.1	122	68	..	..	..	..	..	..	..	..
13	Belgium	43.4	119	72	1	3	10	36	82	58	85	15
14	Austria	49.3	114	75	6	5	14	43	80	52	68	32
15	Denmark	59.4	96	84	2	5	14	36	85	59	86	14
16	France	48.2	105	79	1	2	13	34	86	64	..	..
17	Italy	37.0	103	61	5	6	20	39	75	55	54	46
18	United Kingdom	55.0	104	79	1	2	11	36	88	62	60	40
19	Spain	44.2	130	65	5	8	15	42	81	51	64	36
20	New Zealand	59.8	112	81	6	12	12	32	82	56	68	32
21	Germany	50.4	114	76	2	3	18	44	80	52	76	24
22	Hong Kong, China (SAR)	52.9	112	74	(.)	(.)	10	27	90	73	86	14
23	Israel	49.7	121	84	..	..	..	..	..	..	71	29
24	Greece	42.7	119	66	18	15	12	30	70	56	68	32
25	Singapore	50.8	101	66	(.)	(.)	18	31	81	69	76	24
26	Korea, Rep. of	50.1	106	68	12	9	19	34	70	57	89	11
27	Slovenia	53.4	99	80	10	10	29	46	61	43	58	42
28	Portugal	55.2	112	79	14	12	23	44	63	44	65	35
29	Cyprus	53.0	111	74	4	5	13	31	83	58	81	19
30	Czech Republic	51.7	85	76	3	6	28	50	68	44	74	26
31	Barbados	64.6	109	83	4	5	10	29	63	49	..	..
32	Malta	32.5	153	47	1	3	21	36	78	61	..	..
33	Kuwait	48.0	138	56	..	..	..	..	..	..	..	..
34	Brunei Darussalam	44.3	99	56	..	..	..	..	..	..	..	..
35	Hungary	42.1	91	73	4	9	26	42	71	49	71	29
36	Argentina	52.2	136	68	(.)	1	12	30	87	69	60	40
37	Poland	47.9	84	78	19	19	18	40	63	40	60	40
38	Chile	36.4	113	51	..	..	..	..	..	..	54	46
39	Bahrain	29.2	104	33	..	..	..	..	..	..	..	..
40	Estonia	52.2	81	80	4	10	23	42	73	48	50	50
41	Lithuania	51.8	87	81	12	20	21	34	67	45	62	38
42	Slovakia	51.9	87	76	4	8	26	48	71	44	74	26
43	Uruguay	55.7	122	71	2	6	14	32	85	62	64	37
44	Croatia	44.7	96	74	15	16	21	37	63	47	73	27
45	Latvia	49.1	78	77	12	18	16	35	72	47	56	45
46	Qatar	35.7	121	40	..	..	..	..	..	..	..	..
47	Seychelles	..	..	..	..	..	..	..	..	..	..	..
48	Costa Rica	43.7	133	54	4	22	15	27	80	51	50	50
49	United Arab Emirates	37.4	149	41	(.)	9	14	36	86	55	..	..
50	Cuba	43.8	112	59	..	..	..	..	..	..	..	..
51	Saint Kitts and Nevis	..	..	..	..	..	..	..	..	..	..	..
52	Bahamas	64.5	105	91	1	6	5	24	93	69	..	..
53	Mexico	39.9	115	49	6	24	22	28	72	48	51	49

TABLE 27

Gender inequality in economic activity

		Female economic activity (ages 15 and older)			Employment by economic activity [a] (%)						Contributing family workers (%)	
					Agriculture		Industry		Services			
		Rate (%) 2004	Index (1990=100) 2004	As % of male rate 2004	Women 1995–2003 [b]	Men 1995–2003 [b]	Women 1995–2003 [b]	Men 1995–2003 [b]	Women 1995–2003 [b]	Men 1995–2003 [b]	Women 1995–2004 [b]	Men 1995–2004 [b]
HDI rank												
54	Bulgaria	41.9	70	79	..	..	..	..	..	..	65	35
55	Tonga	46.3	126	62	..	..	..	..	..	..	..	..
56	Oman	21.9	145	27	..	..	..	..	..	..	..	..
57	Trinidad and Tobago	46.6	112	61	3	11	13	36	84	53	72	28
58	Panama	49.9	129	63	6	29	10	20	85	51	42	58
59	Antigua and Barbuda	..	..	..	..	..	..	..	..	..	..	..
60	Romania	50.7	95	80	45	40	22	30	33	30	70	30
61	Malaysia	46.1	105	56	14	21	29	34	57	45	71	29
62	Bosnia and Herzegovina	57.9	96	85	..	..	..	..	..	..	..	..
63	Mauritius	42.2	101	53	13	15	43	39	45	46	75	25
MEDIUM HUMAN DEVELOPMENT												
64	Libyan Arab Jamahiriya	30.8	161	39	..	..	..	..	..	..	..	..
65	Russian Federation	54.3	90	80	8	15	23	36	69	49	7	22
66	Macedonia, TFYR	40.9	85	63	..	..	..	..	..	..	..	..
67	Belarus	52.5	87	82	..	..	..	..	..	..	..	..
68	Dominica	..	..	..	14	31	10	24	72	40	51	49
69	Brazil	56.3	127	70	16	24	10	27	74	49	55	45
70	Colombia	60.5	133	75	7	33	17	19	76	48	60	40
71	Saint Lucia	53.4	113	67	16	27	14	24	71	49	68	32
72	Venezuela, RB	55.9	148	67	2	15	12	28	86	57	..	..
73	Albania	49.4	85	69	..	..	..	..	..	..	..	..
74	Thailand	65.4	87	81	48	50	17	20	35	30	64	36
75	Samoa (Western)	39.6	101	51	..	..	..	..	..	..	..	..
76	Saudi Arabia	17.3	116	22	..	..	..	..	..	..	..	..
77	Ukraine	49.9	87	79	17	22	22	39	55	33	50	50
78	Lebanon	31.7	100	40	..	..	..	..	..	..	..	..
79	Kazakhstan	65.0	106	87	..	..	..	..	..	..	54	46
80	Armenia	48.1	67	79	..	..	..	..	..	..	..	..
81	China	69.2	95	84	..	..	..	..	..	..	..	..
82	Peru	58.2	124	71	6	11	10	24	84	65	66	34
83	Ecuador	58.9	181	72	4	10	16	30	79	60	67	33
84	Philippines	53.8	114	65	25	45	12	18	63	37	56	44
85	Grenada	..	..	..	10	17	12	32	77	46	..	..
86	Jordan	27.0	153	35	..	..	..	..	..	..	..	..
87	Tunisia	27.9	134	37	..	..	..	..	..	..	..	..
88	Saint Vincent and the Grenadines	53.5	120	67	..	..	..	..	..	..	..	..
89	Suriname	33.1	91	52	2	8	1	22	97	64	45	55
90	Fiji	51.4	105	63	..	..	..	..	..	..	..	..
91	Paraguay	64.2	124	76	20	39	10	21	69	40	..	..
92	Turkey	27.8	81	36	56	24	15	28	29	48	67	33
93	Sri Lanka	35.0	78	45	49	38	22	23	27	37	70	30
94	Dominican Republic	45.5	125	55	2	21	17	26	81	53	23	77
95	Belize	42.4	133	52	6	37	12	19	81	44	32	68
96	Iran, Islamic Rep. of	37.2	173	50	..	..	..	..	..	..	46	54
97	Georgia	51.1	74	67	53	53	6	12	41	35	65	35
98	Maldives	46.1	229	64	5	18	24	16	39	55	57	43
99	Azerbaijan	59.6	94	81	43	37	7	14	50	49	..	..
100	Occupied Palestinian Territories	10.3	112	15	26	9	11	32	62	58	52	48
101	El Salvador	46.7	92	61	4	34	22	25	74	42	41	59
102	Algeria	34.8	154	44	..	..	..	..	..	..	29	71
103	Guyana	43.3	119	53	..	..	..	..	..	..	..	..
104	Jamaica	54.8	84	73	10	30	9	26	81	45	77	23
105	Turkmenistan	60.4	94	83	..	..	..	..	..	..	..	..
106	Cape Verde	34.1	82	44	..	..	..	..	..	..	..	..

TABLE 27

		Female economic activity (ages 15 and older)			Employment by economic activity [a] (%)						Contributing family workers (%)	
					Agriculture		Industry		Services			
HDI rank		Rate (%) 2004	Index (1990=100) 2004	As % of male rate 2004	Women 1995–2003 [b]	Men 1995–2003 [b]	Women 1995–2003 [b]	Men 1995–2003 [b]	Women 1995–2003 [b]	Men 1995–2003 [b]	Women 1995–2004 [b]	Men 1995–2004 [b]
107	Syrian Arab Republic	38.0	133	44	..	..	..	..	..	..	..	..
108	Indonesia	50.7	101	60	..	..	..	..	..	..	..	..
109	Viet Nam	72.4	98	93	..	..	..	..	..	..	71	29
110	Kyrgyzstan	55.1	94	74	53	52	8	14	38	34	65	35
111	Egypt	20.1	76	28	39	27	7	25	54	48	40	60
112	Nicaragua	35.5	100	41	..	..	..	..	..	..	..	..
113	Uzbekistan	56.2	94	78	..	..	..	..	..	..	..	..
114	Moldova, Rep. of	56.6	92	81	50	52	10	18	40	31	75	25
115	Bolivia	62.1	128	74	3	6	14	39	82	55	63	37
116	Mongolia	53.9	97	66	..	..	..	..	..	..	70	30
117	Honduras	52.2	156	59	..	..	..	..	..	..	25	75
118	Guatemala	33.7	115	41	18	50	23	18	56	27	39	61
119	Vanuatu	79.3	100	90	..	..	..	..	..	..	..	..
120	Equatorial Guinea	50.5	105	56	..	..	..	..	..	..	..	..
121	South Africa	46.4	85	59	9	12	14	33	75	50	62	38
122	Tajikistan	46.5	89	74	..	..	..	..	..	..	..	..
123	Morocco	26.7	109	33	6	6	40	32	54	63	19	81
124	Gabon	61.5	99	75	..	..	..	..	..	..	..	..
125	Namibia	47.0	96	74	29	33	7	17	63	49	59	41
126	India	34.0	94	41	..	..	..	..	..	..	..	..
127	São Tomé and Principe	29.6	80	40	..	..	..	..	..	..	..	..
128	Solomon Islands	54.4	97	66	..	..	..	..	..	..	..	..
129	Cambodia	74.4	96	93	..	..	..	..	..	..	64	36
130	Myanmar	68.2	99	79	..	..	..	..	..	..	..	..
131	Botswana	45.7	80	67	17	22	14	26	67	51	36	64
132	Comoros	57.8	92	66	..	..	..	..	..	..	..	..
133	Lao People's Dem. Rep.	54.0	101	67	..	..	..	..	..	..	..	..
134	Pakistan	32.0	115	38	73	44	9	20	18	36	33	67
135	Bhutan	44.3	127	55	..	..	..	..	..	..	..	..
136	Ghana	70.5	92	94	..	..	..	..	..	..	..	..
137	Bangladesh	52.9	84	61	77	53	9	11	12	30	58	42
138	Nepal	49.7	103	63	..	..	..	..	..	..	..	..
139	Papua New Guinea	71.8	100	97	..	..	..	..	..	..	..	..
140	Congo	56.4	98	65	..	..	..	..	..	..	..	..
141	Sudan	23.7	86	33	..	..	..	..	..	..	..	..
142	Timor-Leste	53.5	107	66	..	..	..	..	..	..	..	..
143	Madagascar	78.9	100	92	..	..	..	..	..	..	63	37
144	Cameroon	51.8	93	64	..	..	..	..	..	..	73	27
145	Uganda	79.7	99	92	..	..	..	..	..	..	..	..
146	Swaziland	31.5	83	43	..	..	..	..	..	..	..	..
LOW HUMAN DEVELOPMENT												
147	Togo	50.5	94	56	..	..	..	..	..	..	..	..
148	Djibouti	53.1	95	64	..	..	..	..	..	..	..	..
149	Lesotho	46.3	82	64	..	..	..	..	..	..	..	..
150	Yemen	29.4	107	39	88	43	3	14	9	43	26	74
151	Zimbabwe	64.2	92	77	..	..	..	..	..	..	..	..
152	Kenya	69.3	93	78	16	20	10	23	75	57	..	..
153	Mauritania	54.3	97	65	..	..	..	..	..	..	..	..
154	Haiti	55.2	96	67	37	63	6	15	57	23	..	..
155	Gambia	59.3	95	69	..	..	..	..	..	..	..	..
156	Senegal	56.5	92	68	..	..	..	..	..	..	..	..
157	Eritrea	58.2	95	65	..	..	..	..	..	..	..	..
158	Rwanda	80.4	94	95	..	..	..	..	..	..	53	47
159	Nigeria	45.6	95	54	2	4	11	30	87	67	..	..

Human development indicators

TABLE 27

Gender inequality in economic activity

		Female economic activity (ages 15 and older)			Employment by economic activity[a] (%)						Contributing family workers (%)	
					Agriculture		Industry		Services			
		Rate (%)	Index (1990=100)	As % of male rate	Women	Men	Women	Men	Women	Men	Women	Men
HDI rank		2004	2004	2004	1995–2003[b]	1995–2003[b]	1995–2003[b]	1995–2003[b]	1995–2003[b]	1995–2003[b]	1995–2004[b]	1995–2004[b]
160	Guinea	79.4	100	90	..	..	..	..	..	..	..	..
161	Angola	73.8	100	81	..	..	..	..	..	..	..	..
162	Tanzania, U. Rep. of	86.0	97	95	..	..	..	..	..	..	..	..
163	Benin	54.0	93	63	..	..	..	..	..	..	..	..
164	Côte d'Ivoire	39.0	90	44	..	..	..	..	..	..	..	..
165	Zambia	66.1	100	73	..	..	..	..	..	..	..	..
166	Malawi	85.2	100	95	..	..	..	..	..	..	43	57
167	Congo, Dem. Rep. of the	61.2	101	68	..	..	..	..	..	..	..	..
168	Mozambique	84.7	96	102	..	..	..	..	..	..	..	..
169	Burundi	91.8	101	99	..	..	..	..	..	..	..	..
170	Ethiopia	70.9	98	79	..	..	..	..	..	..	59	41
171	Chad	65.5	102	84	..	..	..	..	..	..	..	..
172	Central African Republic	70.4	99	79	..	..	..	..	..	..	..	..
173	Guinea-Bissau	60.9	105	66	..	..	..	..	..	..	..	..
174	Burkina Faso	77.6	101	87	..	..	..	..	..	..	..	..
175	Mali	72.4	100	85	..	..	..	..	..	..	..	..
176	Sierra Leone	56.0	105	60	..	..	..	..	..	..	..	..
177	Niger	71.2	101	75	..	..	..	..	..	..	..	..
Developing countries		52.4	97	64	..	..	..	..	..	..	..	..
Least developed countries		61.8	95	72	..	..	..	..	..	..	..	..
Arab States		26.4	105	34	..	..	..	..	..	..	..	..
East Asia and the Pacific		65.4	96	79	..	..	..	..	..	..	..	..
Latin America and the Caribbean		51.4	125	64	..	..	..	..	..	..	..	..
South Asia		36.0	96	44	..	..	..	..	..	..	..	..
Sub-Saharan Africa		63.0	96	73	..	..	..	..	..	..	..	..
Central and Eastern Europe and the CIS		52.4	89	79	..	..	..	..	..	..	..	..
OECD		50.1	104	71	..	..	..	..	..	..	..	..
High-income OECD		52.7	106	75	..	..	..	..	..	..	..	..
High human development		50.8	105	72	..	..	..	..	..	..	..	..
Medium human development		52.3	95	65	..	..	..	..	..	..	..	..
Low human development		62.6	97	72	..	..	..	..	..	..	..	..
High income		52.0	106	74	..	..	..	..	..	..	..	..
Middle income		57.1	97	72	..	..	..	..	..	..	..	..
Low income		45.7	96	55	..	..	..	..	..	..	..	..
World		52.5	98	67	..	..	..	..	..	..	..	..

NOTES

Because of limitations in the data, comparisons of labour statistics over time and across countries should be made with caution. For detailed notes on the data, see ILO 2005a, 2005b, 2006b.

a The percentage shares of employment by economic activity may not sum to 100 because of rounding or the omission of activities not classified.

b Data refer to the most recent year available during the period specified.

SOURCES

Column 1: ILO 2005a.

Columns 2 and 3: calculated on the basis of data on the economically active rates from ILO 2005a.

Columns 4–9: ILO 2005b.

Columns 10 and 11: calculated on the basis of data on contributing family workers from ILO 2006b.

TABLE 28

... and achieving equality for all women and men

Gender, work and time allocation

	Year[a]	Total work time (hours and minutes per day)		Female work time (% of male)	Time allocation (%)					
					Total work time		Time spent by women		Time spent by men	
		Women	Men		Market activities[b]	Nonmarket activities	Market activities[b]	Nonmarket activities	Market activities[b]	Nonmarket activities
SELECTED DEVELOPING COUNTRIES										
URBAN AREAS										
Colombia	1983	6h 39m	5h 56m	112	49	51	24	76	77	23
Indonesia	1992	6h 38m	6h 6m	109	60	40	35	65	86	14
Kenya	1986	9h 50m	9h 32m	103	46	54	41	59	79	21
Nepal	1978	9h 39m	9h 14m	105	58	42	25	75	67	33
Uruguay[c]	2002	7h 20m	6h 56m	115	49	51	33	67	68	32
Venezuela, RB	1983	7h 20m	6h 56m	106	59	41	30	70	87	13
RURAL AREAS										
Bangladesh	1990	9h 5m	8h 16m	110	52	48	35	65	70	30
Guatemala	1977	11h 18m	9h 39m	117	59	41	37	63	84	16
Kenya	1988	11h 16m	8h 20m	135	56	44	42	58	76	24
Nepal	1978	10h 41m	9h 7m	117	56	44	46	54	67	33
Highlands	1978	11h 32m	9h 46m	118	59	41	52	48	66	34
Mountains	1978	10h 49m	8h 54m	122	56	44	48	52	65	35
Rural Hills	1978	9h 43m	8h 40m	112	52	48	37	63	70	30
Philippines	1975–77	9h 6m	7h 32m	121	73	27	29	71	84	16
NATIONAL										
Benin[c]	1998	7h 55m	5h 30m	144	69	31	59	41	81	19
India[d]	2000	7h 37m	6h 31m	117	61	39	35	65	92	8
Madagascar[c]	2001	7h 15m	6h 24m	113	68	32	51	49	67	33
Mauritius[c]	2003	6h 33m	6h 9m	107	54	46	30	70	80	20
Mongolia[d]	2000	9h 5m	8h 21m	109	61	39	49	51	75	25
South Africa[d]	2000	5h 32m	4h 33m	122	51	49	35	65	70	30
SELECTED OECD COUNTRIES[e]										
Australia	1997	7h 15m	6h 58m	104	46	54	30	70	62	38
Austria[f]	1992	7h 18m	6h 33m	111	49	51	31	69	71	29
Canada	1998	7h 0m	7h 9m	98	53	47	41	59	65	35
Denmark[f]	1987	7h 29m	7h 38m	98	68	32	58	42	79	21
Finland[f]	1987–88	7h 10m	6h 50m	105	51	49	39	61	64	36
France	1999	6h 31m	6h 3m	108	46	54	33	67	60	40
Germany[f]	1991–92	7h 20m	7h 21m	100	44	56	30	70	61	39
Hungary	1999	7h 12m	7h 25m	97	51	49	41	59	60	40
Israel[f]	1991–92	6h 15m	6h 17m	99	51	49	29	71	74	26
Italy[f]	1988–89	7h 50m	6h 7m	128	45	55	22	78	77	23
Japan	1996	6h 33m	6h 3m	108	66	34	43	57	93	7
Korea, Rep. of	1999	7h 11m	6h 13m	116	64	36	45	55	88	12
Latvia	1996	8h 55m	8h 1m	111	46	54	35	65	58	42
Mexico[c]	2002	8h 10m	6h 25m	127	46	54	23	77	78	22
Netherlands	1995	5h 8m	5h 15m	98	48	52	27	73	69	31
New Zealand	1999	7h 0m	6h 57m	101	46	54	32	68	60	40
Norway[f]	1990–91	7h 25m	6h 52m	108	50	50	38	62	64	36
United Kingdom[f]	1985	6h 53m	6h 51m	100	51	49	37	63	68	32
United States[f]	1985	7h 33m	7h 8m	106	50	50	37	63	63	37

NOTES

Data are estimates based on time use surveys available at the time of publication. Time use data have also been collected in other countries, including Chad, Cuba, the Dominican Republic, Ecuador, the Lao People's Democratic Republic, Mali, Morocco, Nicaragua, Nigeria, Oman, Thailand and Viet Nam.

a Surveys before 1993 are not strictly comparable with those for later years.

b Refers to market-oriented production activities as defined by the 1993 revised UN System of National Accounts.

c Charmes 2006.

d Classifications of market and nonmarket activities are not strictly based on the 1993 revised UN System of National Accounts, so comparisons between countries and areas must be made with caution.

e Includes Israel and Latvia although they are not OECD countries.

f Goldschmidt-Clermont and Pagnossin-Aligisakis 1995.

SOURCE

All columns: for urban and rural areas in selected developing countries, Harvey 1995; for national studies in selected developing countries, UN 2002; for OECD countries and Latvia, Harvey 2001, unless otherwise specified.

TABLE

29

. . . and achieving equality for all women and men

Women's political participation

		Year women received right [a]		Year first woman elected (E) or appointed (A) to parliament	Women in government at ministerial level (% of total) [b] 2005	MDG Seats in parliament held by women (% of total) [c]		
						Lower or single house		Upper house or senate
HDI rank		To vote	To stand for election			1990	2006	2006
HIGH HUMAN DEVELOPMENT								
1	Norway	1913	1907, 1913	1911 A	44.4	36	37.9	—
2	Iceland	1915, 1920	1915, 1920	1922 E	27.3	21	33.3	—
3	Australia	1902, 1962	1902, 1962	1943 E	20.0	6	24.7	35.5
4	Ireland	1918, 1928	1918, 1928	1918 E	21.4	8	13.3	16.7
5	Sweden	1919, 1921	1919, 1921	1921 E	52.4	38	45.3	—
6	Canada	1917, 1960	1920, 1960	1921 E	23.1	13	20.8	35.0
7	Japan	1945, 1947	1945, 1947	1946 E	12.5	1	9.0	14.0
8	United States	1920, 1965	1788 [d]	1917 E	14.3	7	15.2	14.0
9	Switzerland	1971	1971	1971 E	14.3	14	25.0	23.9
10	Netherlands	1919	1917	1918 E	36.0	21	36.7	29.3
11	Finland	1906	1906	1907 E	47.1	32	37.5	—
12	Luxembourg	1919	1919	1919 E	14.3	13	23.3	—
13	Belgium	1919, 1948	1921	1921 A	21.4	9	34.7	38.0
14	Austria	1918	1918	1919 E	35.3	12	33.9	27.4
15	Denmark	1915	1915	1918 E	33.3	31	36.9	—
16	France	1944	1944	1945 E	17.6	7	12.2	16.9
17	Italy	1945	1945	1946 E	8.3	13	17.3	13.7
18	United Kingdom	1918, 1928	1918, 1928	1918 E	28.6	6	19.7	17.5
19	Spain	1931	1931	1931 E	50.0	15	36.0	23.2
20	New Zealand	1893	1919	1933 E	23.1	14	32.2	—
21	Germany	1918	1918	1919 E	46.2	..	31.8	18.8
22	Hong Kong, China (SAR)	..	..	..	..	..	..	..
23	Israel	1948	1948	1949 E	16.7	7	14.2	—
24	Greece	1952	1952	1952 E	5.6	7	13.0	—
25	Singapore	1947	1947	1963 E	0	5	18.9	—
26	Korea, Rep. of	1948	1948	1948 E	5.6	2	13.4	—
27	Slovenia	1946	1946	1992 E [e]	6.3	..	12.2	7.5
28	Portugal	1931, 1976	1931, 1976	1934 E+A	16.7	8	21.3	—
29	Cyprus	1960	1960	1963 E	0	2	14.3	—
30	Czech Republic	1920	1920	1992 E [e]	11.1	..	17.0	12.3
31	Barbados	1950	1950	1966 A	29.4	4	13.3	23.8
32	Malta	1947	1947	1966 E	15.4	3	9.2	—
33	Kuwait	2005	2005	2005 A	0	..	1.5	—
34	Brunei Darussalam	—	—	—	9.1	.. [f]	.. [f]	.. [f]
35	Hungary	1918, 1945	1918, 1945	1945 E	11.8	21	10.4	—
36	Argentina	1947	1947	1951 E	8.3	6	35.0	41.7
37	Poland	1918	1918	1919 E	5.9	14	20.4	13.0
38	Chile	1949	1949	1951 E	16.7	..	15.0	5.3
39	Bahrain	1973, 2002	1973, 2002	2002 A	8.7	..	0.0	15.0
40	Estonia	1918	1918	1919 E	15.4	..	18.8	—
41	Lithuania	1919	1919	1920 A	15.4	..	22.0	—
42	Slovakia	1920	1920	1992 E [e]	0	..	16.7	—
43	Uruguay	1932	1932	1942 E	0	6	11.1	9.7
44	Croatia	1945	1945	1992 E [e]	33.3	..	21.7	—
45	Latvia	1918	1918	..	23.5	..	21.0	—
46	Qatar	2003 [g]	..	..	7.7	..	0.0	—
47	Seychelles	1948	1948	1976 E+A	12.5	16	29.4	—
48	Costa Rica	1949	1949	1953 E	25.0	11	38.6	—
49	United Arab Emirates	—	—		5.6	0	0.0	—
50	Cuba	1934	1934	1940 E	16.2	34	36.0	—
51	Saint Kitts and Nevis	1951	1951	1984 E	0	7	0.0	—
52	Bahamas	1961, 1964	1961, 1964	1977 A	26.7	4	20.0	43.8
53	Mexico	1947	1953	1952 A	9.4	12	25.8	21.9

Human development indicators

TABLE 29

		Year women received right [a]		Year first woman elected (E) or appointed (A) to parliament	Women in government at ministerial level (% of total) [b] 2005	MDG Seats in parliament held by women (% of total) [c]		
						Lower or single house		Upper house or senate
HDI rank		To vote	To stand for election			1990	2006	2006
54	Bulgaria	1937, 1945	1945	1945 E	23.8	21	22.1	—
55	Tonga	1960	1960	1993 E	..	0	3.3	—
56	Oman	1994, 2003	1994, 2003	..	10.0	..	2.4	15.5
57	Trinidad and Tobago	1946	1946	1962 E+A	18.2	17	19.4	32.3
58	Panama	1941, 1946	1941, 1946	1946 E	14.3	8	16.7	—
59	Antigua and Barbuda	1951	1951	1984 A	15.4	0	10.5	17.6
60	Romania	1929, 1946	1929, 1946	1946 E	12.5	34	11.2	9.5
61	Malaysia	1957	1957	1959 E	9.1	5	9.1	25.7
62	Bosnia and Herzegovina	1946	1946	1990 E [e]	11.1	..	16.7	0.0
63	Mauritius	1956	1956	1975 E	8.0	7	17.1	—
MEDIUM HUMAN DEVELOPMENT								
64	Libyan Arab Jamahiriya	1964	1964	..	..	..	4.7	—
65	Russian Federation	1918	1918	1993 E [e]	0	..	9.8	3.4
66	Macedonia, TFYR	1946	1946	1990 E [e]	16.7	..	19.2	—
67	Belarus	1919	1919	1990 E [e]	10.0	..	29.1	31.0
68	Dominica	1951	1951	1980 E	0	10	12.9	—
69	Brazil	1932	1932	1933 E	11.4	5	8.6	12.3
70	Colombia	1954	1954	1954 A	35.7	5	12.0 [h]	8.8 [h]
71	Saint Lucia	1951	1951	1979 A	8.3	0	5.6	36.4
72	Venezuela, RB	1946	1946	1948 E	13.6	10	18.0	—
73	Albania	1920	1920	1945 E	5.3	29	7.1	—
74	Thailand	1932	1932	1947 A	7.7	3	10.8	10.5
75	Samoa (Western)	1948, 1990	1948, 1990	1976 A	7.7	0	4.1	—
76	Saudi Arabia	—	—	—	0	..	0.0	—
77	Ukraine	1919	1919	1990 E [e]	5.6	..	7.1	—
78	Lebanon	1952	1952	1963	6.9	0	4.7	—
79	Kazakhstan	1924, 1993	1924, 1993	1990 E [e]	17.6	..	10.4	5.1
80	Armenia	1918	1918	1990 E [e]	0	36	5.3	—
81	China	1949	1949	1954 E	6.3	21	20.3	—
82	Peru	1955	1955	1956 E	11.8	6	29	—
83	Ecuador	1929	1929	1956 E	14.3	5	16.0	—
84	Philippines	1937	1937	1941 E	25.0	9	15.7	16.7
85	Grenada	1951	1951	1976 E+A	40.0	..	26.7	30.8
86	Jordan	1974	1974	1989 A	10.7	0	5.5	12.7
87	Tunisia	1959	1959	1959 E	7.1	4	22.8	13.4
88	Saint Vincent and the Grenadines	1951	1951	1979 E	20.0	10	18.2	—
89	Suriname	1948	1948	1963 E	11.8	8	25.5	—
90	Fiji	1963	1963	1970 A	9.1	..	11.3	12.5
91	Paraguay	1961	1961	1963 E	30.8	6	10.0	8.9
92	Turkey	1930	1934	1935 A	4.3	1	4.4	—
93	Sri Lanka	1931	1931	1947 E	10.3	5	4.9	—
94	Dominican Republic	1942	1942	1942 E	14.3	8	17.3 [h]	6.3 [h]
95	Belize	1954	1954	1984 E+A	6.3	0	6.7	25.0
96	Iran, Islamic Rep. of	1963	1963	1963 E+A	6.7	2	4.1	—
97	Georgia	1918, 1921	1918, 1921	1992 E [e]	22.2	..	9.4	—
98	Maldives	1932	1932	1979 E	11.8	6	12.0	—
99	Azerbaijan	1918	1918	1990 E [e]	15.0	..	12.3	—
100	Occupied Palestinian Territories	..	..	..	..	..	..	..
101	El Salvador	1939	1961	1961 E	35.3	12	16.7	—
102	Algeria	1944, 1962	1962	1962 A	10.5	2	6.2	2.8
103	Guyana	1953	1945	1953 E	22.2	37	30.8	—
104	Jamaica	1944	1944	1944 E	17.6	5	11.7	19.0
105	Turkmenistan	1927	1927	1990 E [e]	9.5	26	16.0	—
106	Cape Verde	1975	1975	1975 E	18.8	12	15.3	—

TABLE 29

Women's political participation

HDI rank	Year women received right [a] — To vote	To stand for election	Year first woman elected (E) or appointed (A) to parliament	Women in government at ministerial level (% of total) [b] 2005	MDG Seats in parliament held by women (% of total) [c] — Lower or single house 1990	Lower or single house 2006	Upper house or senate 2006
107 Syrian Arab Republic	1949, 1953	1953	1973 E	6.3	9	12.0	—
108 Indonesia	1945	1945	1950 A	10.8	12	11.3	—
109 Viet Nam	1946	1946	1946 E	11.5	18	27.3	—
110 Kyrgyzstan	1918	1918	1990 E [e]	12.5	..	0.0	—
111 Egypt	1956	1956	1957 E	5.9	4	2.0	6.8
112 Nicaragua	1955	1955	1972 E	14.3	15	20.7	—
113 Uzbekistan	1938	1938	1990 E [e]	3.6	..	17.5	15.0
114 Moldova, Rep. of	1924, 1993	1924, 1993	1990 E	11.1	..	21.8	—
115 Bolivia	1938, 1952	1938, 1952	1966 E	6.7	9	16.9	3.7
116 Mongolia	1924	1924	1951 E	5.9	25	6.6	—
117 Honduras	1955	1955	1957 E	14.3	10	23.4	—
118 Guatemala	1946	1946, 1965	1956 E	25.0	7	8.2	—
119 Vanuatu	1975, 1980	1975, 1980	1987 E	8.3	4	3.8	—
120 Equatorial Guinea	1963	1963	1968 E	4.5	13	18.0	—
121 South Africa	1930, 1994	1930, 1994	1933 E	41.4	3	32.8	33.3 [l]
122 Tajikistan	1924	1924	1990 E [e]	3.1	..	17.5	23.5
123 Morocco	1963	1963	1993 E	5.9	0	10.8	1.1
124 Gabon	1956	1956	1961 E	11.8	13	9.2	15.4
125 Namibia	1989	1989	1989 E	19.0	7	26.9	26.9
126 India	1935, 1950	1935, 1950	1952 E	3.4	5	8.3	11.2
127 São Tomé and Principe	1975	1975	1975 E	14.3	12	7.3	—
128 Solomon Islands	1974	1974	1993 E	0	0	0.0	—
129 Cambodia	1955	1955	1958 E	7.1	..	9.8	14.8
130 Myanmar	1935	1946	1947 E	..	.. [j]	.. [j]	.. [j]
131 Botswana	1965	1965	1979 E	26.7	5	11.1	—
132 Comoros	1956	1956	1993 E	..	0	3.0	—
133 Lao People's Dem. Rep.	1958	1958	1958 E	0	6	22.9	—
134 Pakistan	1935, 1947	1935, 1947	1973 E [e]	5.6	10	21.3	17.0
135 Bhutan	1953	1953	1975 E	0	2	9.3	—
136 Ghana	1954	1954	1960	11.8	..	10.9	—
137 Bangladesh	1935, 1972	1935, 1972	1973 E	8.3	10	14.8 [k]	—
138 Nepal	1951	1951	1952 A	7.4	6	5.9	16.7
139 Papua New Guinea	1964	1963	1977 E	..	0	0.9	—
140 Congo	1947, 1961	1963	1963 E	14.7	14	8.5	13.3
141 Sudan	1964	1964	1964 E	2.6	..	14.7	4.0
142 Timor-Leste	..	..	..	22.2	..	25.3 [l]	—
143 Madagascar	1959	1959	1965 E	5.9	7	6.9	11.1
144 Cameroon	1946	1946	1960 E	11.1	14	8.9	—
145 Uganda	1962	1962	1962 E	23.4	12	28.8 [m]	—
146 Swaziland	1968	1968	1972 E+A	13.3	4	10.8	30.0
LOW HUMAN DEVELOPMENT							
147 Togo	1945	1945	1961 E	20.0	5	8.6	—
148 Djibouti	1946	1986	2003 E	5.3	0	10.8	—
149 Lesotho	1965	1965	1965 A	27.8	..	11.7	36.4
150 Yemen	1967, 1970	1967, 1970	1990 E [e]	2.9	4	0.3	1.8
151 Zimbabwe	1919, 1957	1919, 1978	1980 E+A	14.7	11	16.0	31.8
152 Kenya	1919, 1963	1919, 1963	1969 E+A	10.3	1	7.3	—
153 Mauritania	1961	1961	1975 E	9.1	..	.. [n]	.. [n]
154 Haiti	1957	1957	1961 E	25.0	..	4.0 [m]	13.8
155 Gambia	1960	1960	1982 E	20.0	8	13.2	—
156 Senegal	1945	1945	1963 E	20.6	13	19.2	—
157 Eritrea	1955	1955	1994 E	17.6	..	22.0	—
158 Rwanda	1961	1961	1981 E	35.7	17	48.8	34.6
159 Nigeria	1958	1958	..	10.0	..	6.4	3.7

TABLE 29

HDI rank	Year women received right [a] — To vote	To stand for election	Year first woman elected (E) or appointed (A) to parliament	Women in government at ministerial level (% of total) [b] 2005	MDG Seats in parliament held by women (% of total) [c] — Lower or single house 1990	Lower or single house 2006	Upper house or senate 2006
160 Guinea	1958	1958	1963 E	15.4	..	19.3	—
161 Angola	1975	1975	1980 E	5.7	15	15.0	—
162 Tanzania, U. Rep. of	1959	1959	..	15.4	..	30.4	—
163 Benin	1956	1956	1979 E	19.0	3	7.2	—
164 Côte d'Ivoire	1952	1952	1965 E	17.1	6	8.5	—
165 Zambia	1962	1962	1964 E+A	25.0	7	12.7	—
166 Malawi	1961	1961	1964 E	14.3	10	13.6	—
167 Congo, Dem. Rep. of the	1967	1970	1970 E	12.5	5	12.0	2.5
168 Mozambique	1975	1975	1977 E	13.0	16	34.8	—
169 Burundi	1961	1961	1982 E	10.7	..	30.5	34.7
170 Ethiopia	1955	1955	1957 E	5.9	..	21.9	18.8
171 Chad	1958	1958	1962 E	11.5	..	6.5	—
172 Central African Republic	1986	1986	1987 E	10.0	4	10.5	—
173 Guinea-Bissau	1977	1977	1972 A	37.5	20	14.0	—
174 Burkina Faso	1958	1958	1978 E	14.8	..	11.7	—
175 Mali	1956	1956	1959 E	18.5	..	10.2	—
176 Sierra Leone	1961	1961	..	13.0	..	14.5	—
177 Niger	1948	1948	1989 E	23.1	5	12.4	—
OTHERS [o]							
Afghanistan	1963	1963	1965 E	10.0	4	27.3	22.5
Andorra	1970	1973	1993 E	33.3	..	28.6	—
Iraq	1980	1980	1980 E	18.8	11	25.5	—
Kiribati	1967	1967	1990 E	0	0	4.8	—
Korea, Dem. Rep.	1946	1946	1948 E	..	21	20.1	—
Liberia	1946	1946	..	13.6	..	12.5	16.7
Liechtenstein	1984	1984	1986 E	20.0	4	24.0	—
Marshall Islands	1979	1979	1991 E	0	..	3.0	—
Micronesia, Fed. Sts.	1979	1979	..	..	..	0.0	—
Monaco	1962	1962	1963 E	0	11	20.8	—
Montenegro	.. [p]	.. [p]	..	..	..	12.5	—
Nauru	1968	1968	1986 E	0	6	0.0	—
Palau	1979	1979	..	12.5	..	0.0	0.0
San Marino	1959	1973	1974 E	12.5	12	16.7	—
Serbia	.. [p]	.. [p]	..	..	..	12.0	—
Somalia	1956	1956	1979 E	..	4	7.8	—
Tuvalu	1967	1967	1989 E	0	8	0.0	—

NOTES

a Data refer to the year in which the right to vote or stand for national election on a universal and equal basis was recognized. Where two years are shown, the first refers to the first partial recognition of the right to vote or stand for election. In some countries, women were granted the right to vote or stand at local elections before obtaining these rights for national elections. Data on local election rights are not included in this table.

b Data are as of 1 January 2005. The total includes deputy prime ministers and ministers. Prime ministers who hold ministerial portfolios and vice-presidents and heads of ministerial-level departments or agencies who exercise a ministerial function in the government structure are also included.

c Data are as of 31 May 2006 unless otherwise specified. The percentage was calculated using as a reference the number of total seats filled in parliament at that time.

d No information is available on the year all women received the right to stand for election. However, the constitution does not mention gender with regard to this right.

e Refers to the year women were elected to the current parliamentary system.

f Brunei Darussalam does not currently have a parliament.

g According to the new constitution approved in 2003, women are granted suffrage. To date no elections have been held.

h Data are as of 1 March 2005.

i Does not include the 36 special rotating delegates appointed on an ad hoc basis. The shares given are therefore calculated on the basis of the 54 permanent seats.

j The parliament elected in 1990 has never been convened nor authorized to sit, and many of its members were detained or forced into exile.

k In 2004 the number of seats in parliament was raised from 300 to 345, with the additional 45 seats reserved for women and filled in September and October 2005.

l Elections were held on 30 August 2001 to elect members of the Constituent Assembly. This body became the National Parliament on 20 May 2002, the date on which the country became independent, without new elections.

m IPU 2006a.

n The parliament was suspended following a coup d'etat in August 2005.

o UN member states not included in the main indicator tables.

p Serbia and Montenegro separated into two independent states in June 2006. Women received the right to vote and to stand for elections in 1946, when Serbia and Montenegro were part of the former Yugoslavia.

SOURCES

Columns 1–3: IPU 2006b.
Column 4: IPU 2005.
Column 5: UN 2006c, based on data from the Inter-Parliamentary Union.
Columns 6 and 7: IPU 2006c.

Human development indicators

TABLE **30**

Human and labour rights instruments

Status of major international human rights instruments

HDI rank	International Convention on the Prevention and Punishment of the Crime of Genocide 1948	International Convention on the Elimination of All Forms of Racial Discrimination 1965	International Covenant on Civil and Political Rights 1966	International Covenant on Economic, Social and Cultural Rights 1966	Convention on the Elimination of All Forms of Discrimination against Women 1979	Convention against Torture and Other Cruel, Inhuman or Degrading Treatment or Punishment 1984	Convention on the Rights of the Child 1989
HIGH HUMAN DEVELOPMENT							
1 Norway	●	●	●	●	●	●	●
2 Iceland	●	●	●	●	●	●	●
3 Australia	●	●	●	●	●	●	●
4 Ireland	●	●	●	●	●	●	●
5 Sweden	●	●	●	●	●	●	●
6 Canada	●	●	●	●	●	●	●
7 Japan		●	●	●	●	●	●
8 United States	●	●	●	○	○	●	○
9 Switzerland	●	●	●	●	●	●	●
10 Netherlands	●	●	●	●	●	●	●
11 Finland	●	●	●	●	●	●	●
12 Luxembourg	●	●	●	●	●	●	●
13 Belgium	●	●	●	●	●	●	●
14 Austria	●	●	●	●	●	●	●
15 Denmark	●	●	●	●	●	●	●
16 France	●	●	●	●	●	●	●
17 Italy	●	●	●	●	●	●	●
18 United Kingdom	●	●	●	●	●	●	●
19 Spain	●	●	●	●	●	●	●
20 New Zealand	●	●	●	●	●	●	●
21 Germany	●	●	●	●	●	●	●
23 Israel	●	●	●	●	●	●	●
24 Greece	●	●	●	●	●	●	●
25 Singapore	●				●		●
26 Korea, Rep. of		●	●	●	●	●	●
27 Slovenia	●	●	●	●	●	●	●
28 Portugal	●	●	●	●	●	●	●
29 Cyprus	●	●	●	●	●	●	●
30 Czech Republic	●	●	●	●	●	●	●
31 Barbados	●		●	●	●	●	●
32 Malta		●	●	●	●	●	●
33 Kuwait	●	●	●	●	●	●	●
34 Brunei Darussalam					●		●
35 Hungary	●	●	●	●	●	●	●
36 Argentina	●	●	●	●	●	●	●
37 Poland	●	●	●	●	●	●	●
38 Chile	●	●	●	●	●	●	●
39 Bahrain	●	●			●	●	●
40 Estonia	●	●	●	●	●	●	●
41 Lithuania	●	●	●	●	●	●	●
42 Slovakia	●	●	●	●	●	●	●
43 Uruguay	●	●	●	●	●	●	●
44 Croatia	●	●	●	●	●	●	●
45 Latvia	●	●	●	●	●		●
46 Qatar		●				●	●
47 Seychelles	●	●	●	●	●	●	●
48 Costa Rica	●	●	●	●	●	●	●
49 United Arab Emirates	●	●			●		●
50 Cuba	●	●			●	●	●
51 Saint Kitts and Nevis					●		●
52 Bahamas	●	●			●		●
53 Mexico	●	●	●	●	●	●	●
54 Bulgaria	●	●	●	●	●	●	●

Human development indicators

TABLE 30

HDI rank	International Convention on the Prevention and Punishment of the Crime of Genocide 1948	International Convention on the Elimination of All Forms of Racial Discrimination 1965	International Covenant on Civil and Political Rights 1966	International Covenant on Economic, Social and Cultural Rights 1966	Convention on the Elimination of All Forms of Discrimination against Women 1979	Convention against Torture and Other Cruel, Inhuman or Degrading Treatment or Punishment 1984	Convention on the Rights of the Child 1989
55 Tonga	●	●					●
56 Oman		●			●		●
57 Trinidad and Tobago	●	●	●	●	●		●
58 Panama	●	●	●	●	●	●	●
59 Antigua and Barbuda	●	●			●	●	●
60 Romania	●	●	●	●	●	●	●
61 Malaysia	●				●		●
62 Bosnia and Herzegovina	●	●	●	●	●	●	●
63 Mauritius		●	●	●	●	●	●
MEDIUM HUMAN DEVELOPMENT							
64 Libyan Arab Jamahiriya	●	●	●	●	●	●	●
65 Russian Federation	●	●	●	●	●	●	●
66 Macedonia, TFYR	●	●	●	●	●	●	●
67 Belarus	●	●	●	●	●	●	●
68 Dominica			●	●	●		●
69 Brazil	●	●	●	●	●	●	●
70 Colombia	●	●	●	●	●	●	●
71 Saint Lucia		●			●		●
72 Venezuela, RB	●	●	●	●	●	●	●
73 Albania	●	●	●	●	●	●	●
74 Thailand			●	●	●		●
75 Samoa (Western)					●		●
76 Saudi Arabia	●	●			●	●	●
77 Ukraine	●	●	●	●	●	●	●
78 Lebanon	●	●	●	●	●	●	●
79 Kazakhstan	●	●	●	●	●	●	●
80 Armenia	●	●	●	●	●	●	●
81 China	●	●	○	●	●	●	●
82 Peru	●	●	●	●	●	●	●
83 Ecuador	●	●	●	●	●	●	●
84 Philippines	●	●	●	●	●	●	●
85 Grenada		○	●	●	●		●
86 Jordan	●	●	●	●	●	●	●
87 Tunisia	●	●	●	●	●	●	●
88 Saint Vincent and the Grenadines	●	●	●	●	●	●	●
89 Suriname		●	●	●	●		●
90 Fiji	●	●			●		●
91 Paraguay	●	●	●	●	●	●	●
92 Turkey	●	●	●	●	●	●	●
93 Sri Lanka	●	●	●	●	●	●	●
94 Dominican Republic	○	●	●	●	●	○	●
95 Belize	●	●	●	○	●	●	●
96 Iran, Islamic Rep. of	●	●	●	●			●
97 Georgia	●	●	●	●	●	●	●
98 Maldives	●	●	●	●	●	●	●
99 Azerbaijan	●	●	●	●	●	●	●
101 El Salvador	●	●	●	●	●	●	●
102 Algeria	●	●	●	●	●	●	●
103 Guyana		●	●	●	●	●	●
104 Jamaica	●	●	●	●	●		●
105 Turkmenistan		●	●	●	●	●	●
106 Cape Verde		●	●	●	●	●	●
107 Syrian Arab Republic	●	●	●	●	●	●	●
108 Indonesia		●			●	●	●

Human development indicators

TABLE 30

Status of major international human rights instruments

HDI rank	International Convention on the Prevention and Punishment of the Crime of Genocide 1948	International Convention on the Elimination of All Forms of Racial Discrimination 1965	International Covenant on Civil and Political Rights 1966	International Covenant on Economic, Social and Cultural Rights 1966	Convention on the Elimination of All Forms of Discrimination against Women 1979	Convention against Torture and Other Cruel, Inhuman or Degrading Treatment or Punishment 1984	Convention on the Rights of the Child 1989
109 Viet Nam	●	●	●	●	●		●
110 Kyrgyzstan	●	●	●	●	●	●	●
111 Egypt	●	●	●	●	●	●	●
112 Nicaragua	●	●	●	●	●	●	●
113 Uzbekistan	●	●	●	●	●	●	●
114 Moldova, Rep. of	●	●	●	●	●	●	●
115 Bolivia	●	●	●	●	●	●	●
116 Mongolia	●	●	●	●	●	●	●
117 Honduras	●	●	●	●	●	●	●
118 Guatemala	●	●	●	●	●	●	●
119 Vanuatu					●		●
120 Equatorial Guinea		●	●	●	●	●	●
121 South Africa	●	●	●	○	●	●	●
122 Tajikistan		●	●	●	●	●	●
123 Morocco	●	●	●	●	●	●	●
124 Gabon	●	●	●	●	●	●	●
125 Namibia	●	●	●	●	●	●	●
126 India	●	●	●	●	●	○	●
127 São Tomé and Principe	○	○	○	○	●	○	●
128 Solomon Islands		●		●	●		●
129 Cambodia	●	●	●	●	●		●
130 Myanmar	●				●		●
131 Botswana		●	●		●	●	●
132 Comoros	●	●			●	○	●
133 Lao People's Dem. Rep.	●	●	○	○	●		●
134 Pakistan	●	●		○	●		●
135 Bhutan		○			●		●
136 Ghana	●	●	●	●	●	●	●
137 Bangladesh	●	●	●	●	●	●	●
138 Nepal	●	●	●	●	●	●	●
139 Papua New Guinea		●	●	●	●		●
140 Congo		●	●	●	●	●	●
141 Sudan	●	●	●	●		○	●
142 Timor-Leste		●	●	●	●	●	●
143 Madagascar		●	●	●	●	●	●
144 Cameroon		●	●	●	●	●	●
145 Uganda	●	●	●	●	●	●	●
146 Swaziland		●	●	●	●	●	●
LOW HUMAN DEVELOPMENT							
147 Togo	●	●	●	●	●	●	●
148 Djibouti		○	●	●	●	●	●
149 Lesotho	●	●	●	●	●	●	●
150 Yemen	●	●	●	●	●	●	●
151 Zimbabwe	●	●	●	●	●		●
152 Kenya		●	●	●	●	●	●
153 Mauritania		●	●	●	●	●	●
154 Haiti	●	●	●		●		●
155 Gambia	●	●	●	●	●	○	●
156 Senegal	●	●	●	●	●	●	●
157 Eritrea		●	●	●	●		●
158 Rwanda	●	●	●	●	●		●
159 Nigeria		●	●	●	●	●	●
160 Guinea	●	●	●	●	●	●	●
161 Angola			●	●	●		●

Human development indicators

TABLE 30

HDI rank	International Convention on the Prevention and Punishment of the Crime of Genocide 1948	International Convention on the Elimination of All Forms of Racial Discrimination 1965	International Covenant on Civil and Political Rights 1966	International Covenant on Economic, Social and Cultural Rights 1966	Convention on the Elimination of All Forms of Discrimination against Women 1979	Convention against Torture and Other Cruel, Inhuman or Degrading Treatment or Punishment 1984	Convention on the Rights of the Child 1989
162 Tanzania, U. Rep. of	●	●	●	●	●		●
163 Benin		●	●	●	●	●	●
164 Côte d'Ivoire	●	●	●	●	●	●	●
165 Zambia		●	●	●	●	●	●
166 Malawi		●	●	●	●	●	●
167 Congo, Dem. Rep. of the	●	●	●	●	●	●	●
168 Mozambique	●	●	●	●	●	●	●
169 Burundi	●	●	●	●	●	●	●
170 Ethiopia	●	●	●	●	●	●	●
171 Chad		●	●	●	●	●	●
172 Central African Republic		●	●	●	●		●
173 Guinea-Bissau		○	○	●	●	○	●
174 Burkina Faso	●	●	●	●	●	●	●
175 Mali	●	●	●	●	●	●	●
176 Sierra Leone		●	●	●	●	●	●
177 Niger		●	●	●	●	●	●
OTHERS [a]							
Afghanistan	●	●	●	●	●	●	●
Andorra		○	○		●	○	●
Iraq	●	●	●	●	●		●
Kiribati					●		●
Korea, Dem. Rep.	●		●	●	●		●
Liberia	●	●	●	●	●	●	●
Liechtenstein	●	●	●	●	●	●	●
Marshall Islands					●		●
Micronesia, Fed. Sts.					●		●
Monaco	●	●	●	●	●	●	●
Montenegro [c]	○						
Nauru		○	○			○	●
Palau							●
San Marino		●	●	●	●	○	●
Serbia [c]	●	●	●	●	●	●	●
Somalia		●	●	●		●	○
Tuvalu					●		●
Total state parties [b]	138	170	156	153	183	141	192
Signatures not yet followed by ratification	2	7	6	6	1	10	2

● Ratification, accession or succession.
○ Signature not yet followed by ratification.

NOTES

The table includes states that have signed or ratified at least one of the seven human rights instruments. Information is as of 28 August 2006.

a Countries or areas, in addition to the 177 countries or areas included in the main indicator tables, that have signed or ratified at least one of the seven human rights instruments.

b Refers to ratification, accession or succession.

c Following the separation of Serbia and Montenegro into two independent states in June 2006, all treaty actions (such as ratification or signature) continue in force for the Republic of Serbia. As of 28 August 2006, the UN Secretary-General had not received notification from the Republic of Montenegro with regard to the treaties reported in this table, unless otherwise specified.

SOURCE
All columns: UN 2006d.

Human development indicators

TABLE 31

Human and labour rights instruments

Status of fundamental labour rights conventions

HDI rank	Freedom of association and collective bargaining		Elimination of forced and compulsory labour		Elimination of discrimination in respect of employment and occupation		Abolition of child labour	
	Convention 87 [a]	Convention 98 [b]	Convention 29 [c]	Convention 105 [d]	Convention 100 [e]	Convention 111 [f]	Convention 138 [g]	Convention 182 [h]
HIGH HUMAN DEVELOPMENT								
1 Norway	●	●	●	●	●	●	●	●
2 Iceland	●	●	●	●	●	●	●	●
3 Australia	●	●	●	●	●	●		●
4 Ireland	●	●	●	●	●	●	●	●
5 Sweden	●	●	●	●	●	●	●	●
6 Canada	●			●	●	●		●
7 Japan	●	●	●		●		●	●
8 United States				●				●
9 Switzerland	●	●	●	●	●	●	●	●
10 Netherlands	●	●	●	●	●	●	●	●
11 Finland	●	●	●	●	●	●	●	●
12 Luxembourg	●	●	●	●	●	●	●	●
13 Belgium	●	●	●	●	●	●	●	●
14 Austria	●	●	●	●	●	●	●	●
15 Denmark	●	●	●	●	●	●	●	●
16 France	●	●	●	●	●	●	●	●
17 Italy	●	●	●	●	●	●	●	●
18 United Kingdom	●	●	●	●	●	●	●	●
19 Spain	●	●	●	●	●	●	●	●
20 New Zealand		●	●	●	●	●		●
21 Germany	●	●	●	●	●	●	●	●
23 Israel	●	●	●	●	●	●	●	●
24 Greece	●	●	●	●	●	●	●	●
25 Singapore	●	●	●	▽			●	●
26 Korea, Rep. of					●	●	●	●
27 Slovenia	●	●	●	●	●	●	●	●
28 Portugal	●	●	●	●	●	●	●	●
29 Cyprus	●	●	●	●	●	●	●	●
30 Czech Republic	●	●	●	●	●	●	●	●
31 Barbados	●	●	●	●	●	●	●	●
32 Malta	●	●	●	●	●	●	●	●
33 Kuwait	●		●	●		●	●	●
34 Brunei Darussalam								
35 Hungary	●	●	●	●	●	●	●	●
36 Argentina	●	●	●	●	●	●	●	●
37 Poland	●	●	●	●	●	●	●	●
38 Chile	●	●	●	●	●	●	●	●
39 Bahrain			●	●		●		●
40 Estonia	●	●	●	●	●			●
41 Lithuania	●	●	●	●	●	●	●	●
42 Slovakia	●	●	●	●	●	●		●
43 Uruguay	●	●	●		●	●		●
44 Croatia	●	●	●	●	●	●	●	●
45 Latvia	●	●	●	●	●		●	●
46 Qatar			●			●	●	●
47 Seychelles	●	●	●	●	●	●		●
48 Costa Rica	●	●	●	●	●	●	●	●
49 United Arab Emirates			●	●	●	●	●	●
50 Cuba	●	●	●	●	●	●	●	
51 Saint Kitts and Nevis	●	●	●	●	●	●	●	●
52 Bahamas	●	●	●	●	●	●	●	●
53 Mexico	●		●	●	●	●		●
54 Bulgaria	●	●	●	●	●	●	●	●

Human development indicators

TABLE
31

HDI rank	Freedom of association and collective bargaining		Elimination of forced and compulsory labour		Elimination of discrimination in respect of employment and occupation		Abolition of child labour	
	Convention 87[a]	Convention 98[b]	Convention 29[c]	Convention 105[d]	Convention 100[e]	Convention 111[f]	Convention 138[g]	Convention 182[h]
55 Tonga								
56 Oman			●	●			●	●
57 Trinidad and Tobago	●	●	●	●	●	●	●	●
58 Panama	●	●	●	●	●	●	●	●
59 Antigua and Barbuda	●	●	●	●	●	●	●	●
60 Romania	●	●	●	●	●	●	●	●
61 Malaysia		●	●	◆	●		●	●
62 Bosnia and Herzegovina	●	●	●	●	●	●	●	●
63 Mauritius	●	●	●	●	●	●		●
MEDIUM HUMAN DEVELOPMENT								
64 Libyan Arab Jamahiriya	●	●	●	●	●	●	●	●
65 Russian Federation	●	●	●	●	●	●	●	●
66 Macedonia, TFYR	●	●	●	●	●	●	●	●
67 Belarus	●	●	●	●	●	●	●	●
68 Dominica	●		●	●	●	●	●	●
69 Brazil		●	●	●	●	●	●	●
70 Colombia	●	●	●	●	●	●	●	●
71 Saint Lucia	●	●	●	●	●	●		●
72 Venezuela, RB	●	●	●	●	●	●	●	●
73 Albania	●	●	●	●	●	●	●	●
74 Thailand			●	●	●		●	
75 Samoa (Western)								
76 Saudi Arabia			●	●	●	●	●	●
77 Ukraine	●	●	●	●	●	●	●	●
78 Lebanon		●	●	●	●	●	●	●
79 Kazakhstan	●	●	●	●	●	●	●	●
80 Armenia	●	●	●	●	●	●	●	●
81 China					●	●	●	●
82 Peru	●	●	●	●	●	●	●	●
83 Ecuador	●	●	●	●	●	●	●	●
84 Philippines	●	●	●	●	●	●	●	●
85 Grenada	●	●	●	●	●	●		●
86 Jordan		●	●	●	●	●	●	●
87 Tunisia	●	●	●	●	●	●	●	●
88 Saint Vincent and the Grenadines	●	●	●	●	●	●	●	●
89 Suriname	●	●	●	●				●
90 Fiji	●	●	●	●	●	●	●	●
91 Paraguay	●	●	●	●	●	●	●	●
92 Turkey	●	●	●	●	●	●	●	●
93 Sri Lanka	●	●	●	●	●	●	●	●
94 Dominican Republic	●	●	●	●	●	●	●	●
95 Belize	●	●	●	●	●	●	●	●
96 Iran, Islamic Rep. of			●	●	●	●		●
97 Georgia	●	●	●	●	●	●	●	●
98 Maldives								
99 Azerbaijan	●	●	●	●	●	●	●	●
101 El Salvador			●	●	●	●	●	●
102 Algeria	●	●	●	●	●	●	●	●
103 Guyana	●	●	●	●	●	●	●	●
104 Jamaica	●	●	●	●	●	●	●	●
105 Turkmenistan	●	●	●	●	●	●		
106 Cape Verde	●	●	●	●	●	●		●
107 Syrian Arab Republic	●	●	●	●	●	●	●	●
108 Indonesia	●	●	●	●	●	●		●

Human development indicators

TABLE **31**

Status of fundamental labour rights conventions

HDI rank	Freedom of association and collective bargaining		Elimination of forced and compulsory labour		Elimination of discrimination in respect of employment and occupation		Abolition of child labour	
	Convention 87[a]	Convention 98[b]	Convention 29[c]	Convention 105[d]	Convention 100[e]	Convention 111[f]	Convention 138[g]	Convention 182[h]
109 Viet Nam					●	●	●	●
110 Kyrgyzstan	●	●	●	●	●	●	●	●
111 Egypt	●	●	●	●	●	●	●	●
112 Nicaragua	●	●	●	●	●	●	●	●
113 Uzbekistan		●	●	●	●	●		●
114 Moldova, Rep. of	●	●	●	●	●	●	●	●
115 Bolivia	●	●	●		●	●	●	●
116 Mongolia	●	●	●		●	●	●	●
117 Honduras	●	●	●	●	●	●	●	●
118 Guatemala	●	●	●	●	●	●	●	●
119 Vanuatu					●	●		
120 Equatorial Guinea	●	●	●	●	●	●	●	●
121 South Africa	●	●	●	●	●	●	●	●
122 Tajikistan	●	●	●	●	●	●	●	●
123 Morocco		●	●	●	●	●	●	●
124 Gabon	●		●	●	●	●		●
125 Namibia	●	●	●	●		●	●	●
126 India			●	●	●	●		
127 São Tomé and Principe	●	●	●		●		●	●
128 Solomon Islands			●					
129 Cambodia	●	●	●		●	●	●	●
130 Myanmar	●		●					
131 Botswana	●	●	●	●	●	●	●	●
132 Comoros	●	●	●	●	●	●	●	●
133 Lao People's Dem. Rep.			●	●	●	●	●	●
134 Pakistan	●	●	●	●	●	●		●
135 Bhutan								
136 Ghana	●	●	●	●	●	●		
137 Bangladesh	●	●	●	●	●	●		●
138 Nepal		●	●	●	●	●	●	●
139 Papua New Guinea	●	●	●	●	●	●	●	●
140 Congo	●	●	●	●	●	●		●
141 Sudan		●	●	●	●	●	●	●
142 Timor-Leste								
143 Madagascar	●	●	●		●	●	●	●
144 Cameroon	●	●	●	●	●	●	●	●
145 Uganda	●	●	●	●	●	●	●	●
146 Swaziland	●	●	●	●	●	●	●	●
LOW HUMAN DEVELOPMENT								
147 Togo	●	●	●	●	●	●	●	●
148 Djibouti	●	●	●	●	●	●	●	●
149 Lesotho	●	●	●	●	●	●	●	●
150 Yemen	●	●	●	●	●	●	●	●
151 Zimbabwe	●	●	●	●	●	●	●	●
152 Kenya		●	●	●	●	●	●	●
153 Mauritania	●	●	●	●	●	●	●	●
154 Haiti	●	●	●	●	●	●		●
155 Gambia	●	●	●	●	●	●	●	●
156 Senegal	●	●	●	●	●	●	●	●
157 Eritrea	●	●	●	●	●	●	●	
158 Rwanda	●	●	●	●	●	●	●	●
159 Nigeria	●	●	●	●	●	●	●	●
160 Guinea	●	●	●	●	●	●	●	●
161 Angola	●	●	●	●	●	●	●	●

Human development indicators

TABLE 31

HDI rank	Freedom of association and collective bargaining		Elimination of forced and compulsory labour		Elimination of discrimination in respect of employment and occupation		Abolition of child labour	
	Convention 87[a]	Convention 98[b]	Convention 29[c]	Convention 105[d]	Convention 100[e]	Convention 111[f]	Convention 138[g]	Convention 182[h]
162 Tanzania, U. Rep. of	●	●	●	●	●	●	●	●
163 Benin	●	●	●	●	●	●	●	●
164 Côte d'Ivoire	●	●	●	●	●	●	●	●
165 Zambia	●	●	●	●	●	●	●	●
166 Malawi	●	●	●	●	●	●	●	●
167 Congo, Dem. Rep. of the	●	●	●	●	●	●	●	●
168 Mozambique	●	●	●	●	●	●	●	●
169 Burundi	●	●	●	●	●	●	●	●
170 Ethiopia	●	●	●	●	●	●	●	●
171 Chad	●	●	●	●	●	●	●	●
172 Central African Republic	●	●	●	●	●	●	●	●
173 Guinea-Bissau		●	●	●	●	●		
174 Burkina Faso	●	●	●	●	●	●	●	●
175 Mali	●	●	●	●	●	●	●	●
176 Sierra Leone	●	●	●	●	●	●	●	●
177 Niger	●	●	●	●	●	●	●	●
OTHERS[i]								
Afghanistan				●	●	●		
Iraq		●	●	●	●	●	●	●
Kiribati	●	●	●					
Liberia	●	●	●			●	●	●
Montenegro[j]								
San Marino	●	●	●	●	●	●	●	●
Serbia[j]	●	●	●	●	●	●	●	●
Somalia			●	●		●		
Total ratifications	145	154	169	163	163	165	147	161

● Convention ratified.
▼ Convention denounced.

NOTES

Table includes UN member states. Information is as of 28 August 2006.

a Freedom of Association and Protection of the Right to Organize Convention (1948).
b Right to Organize and Collective Bargaining Convention (1949).
c Forced Labour Convention (1930).
d Abolition of Forced Labour Convention (1957).
e Equal Remuneration Convention (1951).
f Discrimination (Employment and Occupation) Convention (1958).
g Minimum Age Convention (1973).
h Worst Forms of Child Labour Convention (1999).
i Countries or areas, in addition to the 177 countries or areas included in the main indicator tables, that are members of the International Labour Organization (ILO).
j Following the separation of Serbia and Montenegro into two independent states in June 2006, all conventions ratified by Serbia and Montenegro continue in force for the Republic of Serbia. As of 28 August 2006, the ILO had not received notification from the Republic of Montenegro with regard to the conventions reported in this table.

SOURCE
All columns: ILO 2006a.

Human development indicators

Calculating the human development indices

The diagrams here summarize how the five human development indices used in the *Human Development Report* are constructed, highlighting both their similarities and their differences. The text on the following pages provides a detailed explanation.

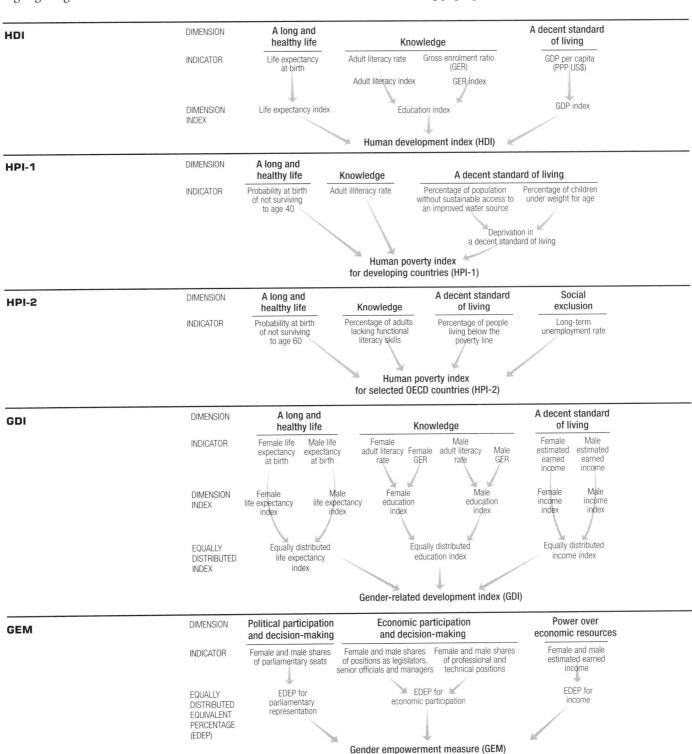

The human development index (HDI)

The HDI is a summary measure of human development. It measures the average achievements in a country in three basic dimensions of human development:

- A long and healthy life, as measured by life expectancy at birth.
- Knowledge, as measured by the adult literacy rate (with two-thirds weight) and the combined primary, secondary and tertiary gross enrolment ratio (with one-third weight).
- A decent standard of living, as measured by GDP per capita in purchasing power parity (PPP) terms in US dollars.

Before the HDI itself is calculated, an index needs to be created for each of these dimensions. To calculate these indices—the life expectancy, education and GDP indices—minimum and maximum values (goalposts) are chosen for each underlying indicator.

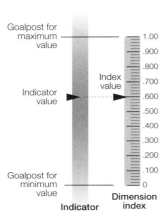

Performance in each dimension is expressed as a value between 0 and 1 by applying the following general formula:

$$\text{Dimension index} = \frac{\text{actual value} - \text{minimum value}}{\text{maximum value} - \text{minimum value}}$$

The HDI is then calculated as a simple average of the dimension indices. The box at right illustrates the calculation of the HDI for a sample country.

Goalposts for calculating the HDI

Indicator	Maximum value	Minimum value
Life expectancy at birth (years)	85	25
Adult literacy rate (%)	100	0
Combined gross enrolment ratio (%)	100	0
GDP per capita (PPP US$)	40,000	100

Calculating the HDI

This illustration of the calculation of the HDI uses data for Brazil.

1. Calculating the life expectancy index

The life expectancy index measures the relative achievement of a country in life expectancy at birth. For Brazil, with a life expectancy of 70.8 years in 2004, the life expectancy index is 0.764.

$$\text{Life expectancy index} = \frac{70.8 - 25}{85 - 25} = \mathbf{0.764}$$

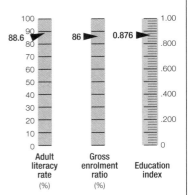

2. Calculating the education index

The education index measures a country's relative achievement in both adult literacy and combined primary, secondary and tertiary gross enrolment. First, an index for adult literacy and one for combined gross enrolment are calculated. Then these two indices are combined to create the education index, with two-thirds weight given to adult literacy and one-third weight to combined gross enrolment. For Brazil, with an adult literacy rate of 88.6% in 2004 and a combined gross enrolment ratio of 86% in 2004, the education index is 0.876.

$$\text{Adult literacy index} = \frac{88.6 - 0}{100 - 0} = 0.886$$

$$\text{Gross enrolment index} = \frac{86 - 0}{100 - 0} = 0.857$$

$$\text{Education index} = 2/3 \text{ (adult literacy index)} + 1/3 \text{ (gross enrolment index)}$$
$$= 2/3 \text{ (0.886)} + 1/3 \text{ (0.857)} = \mathbf{0.876}$$

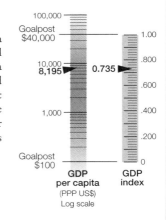

3. Calculating the GDP index

The GDP index is calculated using adjusted GDP per capita (PPP US$). In the HDI income serves as a surrogate for all the dimensions of human development not reflected in a long and healthy life and in knowledge. Income is adjusted because achieving a respectable level of human development does not require unlimited income. Accordingly, the logarithm of income is used. For Brazil, with a GDP per capita of $8,195 (PPP US$) in 2004, the GDP index is 0.735.

$$\text{GDP index} = \frac{\log (8,195) - \log (100)}{\log (40,000) - \log (100)} = \mathbf{0.735}$$

4. Calculating the HDI

Once the dimension indices have been calculated, determining the HDI is straightforward. It is a simple average of the three dimension indices.

$$\text{HDI} = 1/3 \text{ (life expectancy index)} + 1/3 \text{ (education index)}$$
$$+ 1/3 \text{ (GDP index)}$$
$$= 1/3 \text{ (0.764)} + 1/3 \text{ (0.876)} + 1/3 \text{ (0.735)} = \mathbf{0.792}$$

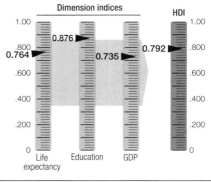

The human poverty index for developing countries (HPI-1)

While the HDI measures average achievement, the HPI-1 measures *deprivations* in the three basic dimensions of human development captured in the HDI:

- A long and healthy life—vulnerability to death at a relatively early age, as measured by the probability at birth of not surviving to age 40.
- Knowledge—exclusion from the world of reading and communications, as measured by the adult illiteracy rate.
- A decent standard of living—lack of access to overall economic provisioning, as measured by the unweighted average of two indicators, the percentage of the population without sustainable access to an improved water source and the percentage of children under weight for age.

Calculating the HPI-1 is more straightforward than calculating the HDI. The indicators used to measure the deprivations are already normalized between 0 and 100 (because they are expressed as percentages), so there is no need to create dimension indices as for the HDI.

Originally, the measure of deprivation in a decent standard of living also included an indicator of access to health services. But because reliable data on access to health services are lacking for recent years, in this year's Report deprivation in a decent standard of living is measured by two rather than three indicators—the percentage of the population without sustainable access to an improved water source and the percentage of children under weight for age.

The human poverty index for selected OECD countries (HPI-2)

The HPI-2 measures deprivations in the same dimensions as the HPI-1 and also captures social exclusion. Thus it reflects deprivations in four dimensions:

- A long and healthy life—vulnerability to death at a relatively early age, as measured by the probability at birth of not surviving to age 60.
- Knowledge—exclusion from the world of reading and communications, as measured by the percentage of adults (ages 16–65) lacking functional literacy skills.
- A decent standard of living—as measured by the percentage of people living below the income poverty line (50% of the median adjusted household disposable income).
- Social exclusion—as measured by the rate of long-term unemployment (12 months or more).

Calculating the HPI-1

1. Measuring deprivation in a decent standard of living

An unweighted average of two indicators is used to measure deprivation in a decent standard of living.

Unweighted average = 1/2 (population without sustainable access to an improved water source)
+ 1/2 (children under weight for age)

A sample calculation: Namibia

Percentage of population without sustainable access to an improved water source = 13%
Percentage of children under weight for age = 24%

Unweighted average = 1/2 (13) + 1/2 (24) = 18.5%

2. Calculating the HPI-1

The formula for calculating the HPI-1 is as follows:

$$\text{HPI-1} = [1/3\,(P_1^{\alpha} + P_2^{\alpha} + P_3^{\alpha})]^{1/\alpha}$$

Where:

P_1 = Probability at birth of not surviving to age 40 (times 100)
P_2 = Adult illiteracy rate
P_3 = Unweighted average of population without sustainable access to an improved water source and children under weight for age
α = 3

A sample calculation: Namibia

P_1 = 45.4%
P_2 = 15.0%
P_3 = 18.5%

$$\text{HPI-1} = [1/3\,(45.4^3 + 15.0^3 + 18.5^3)]^{1/3} = \mathbf{32.5}$$

Calculating the HPI-2

The formula for calculating the HPI-2 is as follows:

$$\text{HPI-2} = [1/4\,(P_1^{\alpha} + P_2^{\alpha} + P_3^{\alpha} + P_4^{\alpha})]^{1/\alpha}$$

Where:

P_1 = Probability at birth of not surviving to age 60 (times 100)
P_2 = Percentage of adults lacking functional literacy skills
P_3 = Percentage of population below income poverty line (50% of median adjusted household disposable income)
P_4 = Rate of long-term unemployment (lasting 12 months or more)
α = 3

A sample calculation: Australia

P_1 = 7.7%
P_2 = 17.0%
P_3 = 14.3%
P_4 = 0.9%

$$\text{HPI-2} = [1/4\,(7.7^3 + 17.0^3 + 14.3^3 + 0.9^3)]^{1/3} = \mathbf{12.8}$$

Why α = 3 in calculating the HPI-1 and HPI-2

The value of α has an important impact on the value of the HPI. If $\alpha = 1$, the HPI is the average of its dimensions. As α rises, greater weight is given to the dimension in which there is the most deprivation. Thus as α increases towards infinity, the HPI will tend towards the value of the dimension in which deprivation is greatest (for Namibia, the example used for calculating the HPI-1, it would be 45.4, equal to the probability at birth of not surviving to age 40).

In this Report the value 3 is used to give additional but not overwhelming weight to areas of more acute deprivation. For a detailed analysis of the HPI's mathematical formulation, see Sudhir Anand and Amartya Sen's "Concepts of Human Development and Poverty: A Multidimensional Perspective" and the technical note in *Human Development Report 1997* (see the list of selected readings at the end of this technical note).

The gender-related development index (GDI)

While the HDI measures average achievement, the GDI adjusts the average achievement to reflect the *inequalities* between men and women in the following dimensions:

- A long and healthy life, as measured by life expectancy at birth.
- Knowledge, as measured by the adult literacy rate and the combined primary, secondary and tertiary gross enrolment ratio.
- A decent standard of living, as measured by estimated earned income (PPP US$).

The calculation of the GDI involves three steps. First, female and male indices in each dimension are calculated according to this general formula:

$$\text{Dimension index} = \frac{\text{actual value} - \text{minimum value}}{\text{maximum value} - \text{minimum value}}$$

Second, the female and male indices in each dimension are combined in a way that penalizes differences in achievement between men and women. The resulting index, referred to as the equally distributed index, is calculated according to this general formula:

Equally distributed index
= {[female population share (female index$^{1-\epsilon}$)]
+ [male population share (male index$^{1-\epsilon}$)]}$^{1/1-\epsilon}$

ϵ measures the aversion to inequality. In the GDI ϵ = 2. Thus the general equation becomes:

Equally distributed index
= {[female population share (female index^{-1})]
+ [male population share (male index^{-1})]}$^{-1}$

which gives the harmonic mean of the female and male indices.

Third, the GDI is calculated by combining the three equally distributed indices in an unweighted average.

Goalposts for calculating the GDI

Indicator	Maximum value	Minimum value
Female life expectancy at birth (years)	87.5	27.5
Male life expectancy at birth (years)	82.5	22.5
Adult literacy rate (%)	100	0
Combined gross enrolment ratio (%)	100	0
Estimated earned income (PPP US$)	40,000	100

Note: The maximum and minimum values (goalposts) for life expectancy are five years higher for women to take into account their longer life expectancy.

Calculating the GDI

This illustration of the calculation of the GDI uses data for Thailand.

1. Calculating the equally distributed life expectancy index
The first step is to calculate separate indices for female and male achievements in life expectancy, using the general formula for dimension indices.

FEMALE
Life expectancy: 74.0 years

$$\text{Life expectancy index} = \frac{74.0 - 27.5}{87.5 - 27.5} = 0.776$$

MALE
Life expectancy: 66.7 years

$$\text{Life expectancy index} = \frac{66.7 - 22.5}{82.5 - 22.5} = 0.737$$

Next, the female and male indices are combined to create the equally distributed life expectancy index, using the general formula for equally distributed indices.

FEMALE
Population share: 0.509
Life expectancy index: 0.776

MALE
Population share: 0.491
Life expectancy index: 0.737

Equally distributed life expectancy index = {[0.509 (0.776^{-1})] + [0.491 (0.737^{-1})]}$^{-1}$ = **0.756**

2. Calculating the equally distributed education index
First, indices for the adult literacy rate and the combined primary, secondary and tertiary gross enrolment ratio are calculated separately for females and males. Calculating these indices is straightforward, since the indicators used are already normalized between 0 and 100.

FEMALE
Adult literacy rate: 90.5%
Adult literacy index: 0.905
Gross enrolment ratio: 74.0%
Gross enrolment index: 0.740

MALE
Adult literacy rate: 94.9%
Adult literacy index: 0.949
Gross enrolment ratio: 73.4%
Gross enrolment index: 0.734

Second, the education index, which gives two-thirds weight to the adult literacy index and one-third weight to the gross enrolment index, is computed separately for females and males.

Education index = 2/3 (adult literacy index) + 1/3 (gross enrolment index)

Female education index = 2/3 (0.905) + 1/3 (0.740) = 0.850

Male education index = 2/3 (0.949) + 1/3 (0.734) = 0.877

Finally, the female and male education indices are combined to create the equally distributed education index.

FEMALE
Population share: 0.509
Education index: 0.850

MALE
Population share: 0.491
Education index: 0.877

Equally distributed education index = {[0.509 (0.850^{-1})] + [0.491 (0.877^{-1})]}$^{-1}$ = **0.863**

3. Calculating the equally distributed income index
First, female and male earned income (PPP US$) are estimated (for details on this calculation, see the addendum to this technical note). Then the income index is calculated for each gender. As for the HDI, income is adjusted by taking the logarithm of estimated earned income (PPP US$):

$$\text{Income index} = \frac{\log (\text{actual value}) - \log (\text{minimum value})}{\log (\text{maximum value}) - \log (\text{minimum value})}$$

FEMALE
Estimated earned income (PPP US$): 6,036

$$\text{Income index} = \frac{\log (6,036) - \log (100)}{\log (40,000) - \log (100)} = 0.684$$

MALE
Estimated earned income (PPP US$): 10,214

$$\text{Income index} = \frac{\log (10,214) - \log (100)}{\log (40,000) - \log (100)} = 0.772$$

Calculating the GDI continues on next page

Calculating the GDI (continued)

Second, the female and male income indices are combined to create the equally distributed income index:

FEMALE
Population share: 0.509
Income index: 0.684

MALE
Population share: 0.491
Income index: 0.772

Equally distributed income index = $\{[0.509 \, (0.684^{-1})] + [0.491 \, (0.772^{-1})]\}^{-1}$ = **0.725**

4. Calculating the GDI

Calculating the GDI is straightforward. It is simply the unweighted average of the three component indices—the equally distributed life expectancy index, the equally distributed education index and the equally distributed income index.

GDI = 1/3 (life expectancy index) + 1/3 (education index) + 1/3 (income index)
= 1/3 (0.756) + 1/3 (0.863) + 1/3 (0.725) = **0.781**

Why $\epsilon = 2$ in calculating the GDI

The value of ϵ is the size of the penalty for gender inequality. The larger the value, the more heavily a society is penalized for having inequalities.

If $\epsilon = 0$, gender inequality is not penalized (in this case the GDI would have the same value as the HDI). As ϵ increases towards infinity, more and more weight is given to the lesser achieving group.

The value 2 is used in calculating the GDI (as well as the GEM). This value places a moderate penalty on gender inequality in achievement.

For a detailed analysis of the GDI's mathematical formulation, see Sudhir Anand and Amartya Sen's "Gender Inequality in Human Development: Theories and Measurement," Kalpana Bardhan and Stephan Klasen's "UNDP's Gender-Related Indices: A Critical Review" and the technical notes in *Human Development Report 1995* and *Human Development Report 1999* (see the list of selected readings at the end of this technical note).

The gender empowerment measure (GEM)

Focusing on women's opportunities rather than their capabilities, the GEM captures gender inequality in three key areas:

- Political participation and decision-making power, as measured by women's and men's percentage shares of parliamentary seats.
- Economic participation and decision-making power, as measured by two indicators—women's and men's percentage shares of positions as legislators, senior officials and managers and women's and men's percentage shares of professional and technical positions.
- Power over economic resources, as measured by women's and men's estimated earned income (PPP US$).

For each of these three dimensions, an equally distributed equivalent percentage (EDEP) is calculated, as a population-weighted average, according to the following general formula:

$$EDEP = \{[\text{female population share (female index}^{1-\epsilon})] + [\text{male population share (male index}^{1-\epsilon})]\}^{1/1-\epsilon}$$

ϵ measures the aversion to inequality. In the GEM (as in the GDI) $\epsilon = 2$, which places a moderate penalty on inequality. The formula is thus:

$$EDEP = \{[\text{female population share (female index}^{-1})] + [\text{male population share (male index}^{-1})]\}^{-1}$$

For political and economic participation and decision-making, the EDEP is then indexed by dividing it by 50. The rationale for this indexation: in an ideal society, with equal empowerment of the sexes, the GEM variables would equal 50%—that is, women's share would equal men's share for each variable.

Where a male or female index value is zero, the EDEP according to the above formula is not defined. However, the limit of EDEP, when the index tends towards zero, is zero. Accordingly, in these cases the value of the EDEP is set to zero.

Finally, the GEM is calculated as a simple average of the three indexed EDEPs.

Calculating the GEM

This illustration of the calculation of the GEM uses data for Argentina.

1. Calculating the EDEP for parliamentary representation

The EDEP for parliamentary representation measures the relative empowerment of women in terms of their political participation. The EDEP is calculated using the female and male shares of the population and female and male percentage shares of parliamentary seats according to the general formula.

FEMALE
Population share: 0.511
Parliamentary share: 36.5%

MALE
Population share: 0.489
Parliamentary share: 63.5%

EDEP for parliamentary representation = $\{[0.511 (36.5^{-1})] + [0.489 (63.5^{-1})]\}^{-1} = 46.07$

Then this initial EDEP is indexed to an ideal value of 50%.

Indexed EDEP for parliamentary representation = $\dfrac{46.07}{50} = \mathbf{0.921}$

2. Calculating the EDEP for economic participation

Using the general formula, an EDEP is calculated for women's and men's percentage shares of positions as legislators, senior officials and managers, and another for women's and men's percentage shares of professional and technical positions. The simple average of the two measures gives the EDEP for economic participation.

FEMALE
Population share: 0.511
Percentage share of positions as legislators, senior officials and managers: 25.4%
Percentage share of professional and technical positions: 54.7%

MALE
Population share: 0.489
Percentage share of positions as legislators, senior officials and managers: 74.6%
Percentage share of professional and technical positions: 45.3%

EDEP for positions as legislators, senior officials and managers = $\{[0.511 (25.4^{-1})] + [0.489 (74.6^{-1})]\}^{-1} = 37.46$

Indexed EDEP for positions as legislators, senior officials and managers = $\dfrac{37.46}{50} = 0.749$

EDEP for professional and technical positions = $\{[0.511 (54.7^{-1})] + [0.489 (45.3^{-1})]\}^{-1} = 49.67$

Indexed EDEP for professional and technical positions = $\dfrac{49.67}{50} = 0.993$

The two indexed EDEPs are averaged to create the EDEP for economic participation:

EDEP for economic participation = $\dfrac{0.749 + 0.993}{2} = \mathbf{0.871}$

3. Calculating the EDEP for income

Earned income (PPP US$) is estimated for women and men separately and then indexed to goalposts as for the HDI and the GDI. For the GEM, however, the income index is based on unadjusted values, not the logarithm of estimated earned income. (For details on the estimation of earned income for men and women, see the addendum to this technical note.)

FEMALE
Population share: 0.511
Estimated earned income (PPP US$): 9,258
Income index = $\dfrac{9,258 - 100}{40,000 - 100} = 0.230$

MALE
Population share: 0.489
Estimated earned income (PPP US$): 17,518
Income index = $\dfrac{17,518 - 100}{40,000 - 100} = 0.437$

The female and male indices are then combined to create the equally distributed index:

EDEP for income = $\{[0.511 (0.230^{-1})] + [0.489 (0.437^{-1})]\}^{-1} = \mathbf{0.299}$

4. Calculating the GEM

Once the EDEP has been calculated for the three dimensions of the GEM, determining the GEM is straightforward. It is a simple average of the three EDEP indices.

GEM = $\dfrac{0.921 + 0.871 + 0.299}{3} = \mathbf{0.697}$

Female and male earned income

Despite the importance of having gender-disaggregated data on income, direct measures are unavailable. For this Report crude estimates of female and male earned income have therefore been derived.

Income can be seen in two ways: as a resource for consumption and as earnings by individuals. The use measure is difficult to disaggregate between men and women because they share resources within a family unit. By contrast, earnings are separable because different members of a family tend to have separate earned incomes.

The income measure used in the GDI and the GEM indicates a person's capacity to earn income. It is used in the GDI to capture the disparities between men and women in command over resources and in the GEM to capture women's economic independence. (For conceptual and methodological issues relating to this approach, see Sudhir Anand and Amartya Sen's "Gender Inequality in Human Development" and, in *Human Development Report 1995,* chapter 3 and technical notes 1 and 2; see the list of selected readings at the end of this technical note.)

Female and male earned income (PPP US$) are estimated using the following data:

- Ratio of the female nonagricultural wage to the male nonagricultural wage.
- Male and female shares of the economically active population.
- Total female and male population.
- GDP per capita (PPP US$).

Key

W_f / W_m = ratio of female nonagricultural wage to male nonagricultural wage
EA_f = female share of economically active population
EA_m = male share of economically active population
S_f = female share of wage bill
Y = total GDP (PPP US$)
N_f = total female population
N_m = total male population
Y_f = estimated female earned income (PPP US$)
Y_m = estimated male earned income (PPP US$)

Note

Calculations based on data in the technical note may yield results that differ from those in the indicator tables because of rounding.

Estimating female and male earned income

This illustration of the estimation of female and male earned income uses 2004 data for the Netherlands.

1. Calculating total GDP (PPP US$)
Total GDP (PPP US$) is calculated by multiplying the total population by GDP per capita (PPP US$).

Total population: 16,282 (thousand)
GDP per capita (PPP US$): 31,789
Total GDP (PPP US$) = 16,282 (31,789) = 517,586,944 (thousand)

2. Calculating the female share of the wage bill
Because data on wages in rural areas and in the informal sector are rare, the Report has used nonagricultural wages and assumed that the ratio of female wages to male wages in the nonagricultural sector applies to the rest of the economy. The female share of the wage bill is calculated using the ratio of the female nonagricultural wage to the male nonagricultural wage and the female and male percentage shares of the economically active population. Where data on the wage ratio are not available, a value of 75% is used.

Ratio of female to male nonagricultural wage (W_f/W_m) = 0.815
Female percentage share of economically active population (EA_f) = 44.0%
Male percentage share of economically active population (EA_m) = 56.0%

$$\text{Female share of wage bill } (S_f) = \frac{W_f/W_m\,(EA_f)}{[W_f/W_m\,(EA_f)] + EA_m} = \frac{0.815\,(44.0)}{[0.815\,(44.0)] + 56.0} = \mathbf{0.391}$$

3. Calculating female and male earned income (PPP US$)
An assumption has to be made that the female share of the wage bill is equal to the female share of GDP.

Female share of wage bill (S_f) = 0.391
Total GDP (PPP US$) ($Y$) = 517,586,944 (thousand)
Female population (N_f) = 8,202 (thousand)

$$\text{Estimated female earned income (PPP US\$) } (Y_f) = \frac{S_f(Y)}{N_f} = \frac{0.391\,(517,586,944)}{8,202} = \mathbf{24,652}$$

Male population (N_m) = 8,080 (thousand)

$$\text{Estimated male earned income (PPP US\$) } (Y_m) = \frac{Y - S_f(Y)}{N_m} = \frac{517,586,944 - [0.391\,(517,586,944)]}{8,080} = \mathbf{39,035}$$

Selected readings

Anand, Sudhir, and Amartya Sen. 1994. "Human Development Index: Methodology and Measurement." Occasional Paper 12. United Nations Development Programme, Human Development Report Office, New York. *(HDI)*

———. 1995. "Gender Inequality in Human Development: Theories and Measurement." Occasional Paper 19. United Nations Development Programme, Human Development Report Office, New York. *(GDI, GEM)*

———. 1997. "Concepts of Human Development and Poverty: A Multi-dimensional Perspective." In United Nations Development Programme, *Human Development Report 1997 Papers: Poverty and Human Development.* New York. *(HPI-1, HPI-2)*

Bardhan, Kalpana, and Stephan Klasen. 1999. "UNDP's Gender-Related Indices: A Critical Review." *World Development* 27 (6): 985–1010. *(GDI, GEM)*

United Nations Development Programme. 1995. *Human Development Report 1995.* New York: Oxford University Press. Technical notes 1 and 2 and chapter 3. *(GDI, GEM)*

———. 1997. *Human Development Report 1997.* New York: Oxford University Press. Technical note 1 and chapter 1. *(HPI-1, HPI-2)*

———. 1999. *Human Development Report 1999.* New York: Oxford University Press. Technical note. *(HDI, GDI)*

A human development index by income groups

The human development index (HDI) provides a composite snapshot of the national average of three important indicators of human well-being (see *Technical note 1*). But it does not capture variations around the average linked to inequality. This year's Report presents for the first time an HDI by income quintiles. The new measure, intended both to address a major human development issue and to stimulate discussion, points to large inequalities between rich and poor in many countries.

The HDI by income quintiles disaggregates performance by income quintile for 15 countries. Full details of the methodology used are in a background paper prepared for this year's Report (Grimm and others 2006). This technical note provides a brief summary.

Methodology

Construction of the HDI by income quintiles follows the same procedure as for the standard HDI. Life expectancy, school enrolment, literacy and income per capita data from household surveys are used to calculate the three dimension indices—health, education and income—by income quintile.

Data for the index are drawn from a variety of sources. For developing countries household income surveys are used to calculate the education and gross domestic product (GDP) indices for each quintile, and Demographic and Health Surveys are used to calculate the life expectancy index. Because the two data sets do not cover the same households, the information from the surveys is linked by approximating income for households in the Demographic and Health Surveys using variables that are available in both sets of surveys. The correlation between household income per capita and a set of household characteristics available in both surveys is estimated and used to generate a proxy for the income of households in the Demographic and Health Surveys. These characteristics include household structure, education and age of the household head, area of residence, housing characteristics and the like.

For the two developed countries in the study, Finland and the United States, GDP and education data are from the Luxembourg Income Study, and income and life expectancy data are from published empirical work.

Data for the construction of the index are derived as follows.

Life expectancy
Calculations are based on infant mortality data from Demographic and Health Surveys. Infant mortality has proven a reliable proxy for overall mortality patterns and thus for life expectancy. Infant mortality rates for each income quintile are applied to Ledermann model life tables (a tool for estimating life expectancy based on the historical relationship between life expectancy and infant mortality).

The education index
The education index is based on adult literacy and school enrolment data. Adult literacy data are available directly from the household income surveys for each income quintile. To calculate the quintile-specific gross enrolment index, the combined gross enrolment ratio for each quintile is calculated. Each individual ages

The work on the human development index by income group was undertaken by Michael Grimm, Kenneth Harttgen, Stephan Klasen and Mark Misselhorn, with inputs from Teresa Munzi and Tim Smeeding from the Luxembourg Income Study team.

5–23 attending school or university, whether general or vocational, is considered enrolled. The quintile-specific gross enrolment index is then calculated using the same minimum and maximum values that are used in calculating the standard HDI.

GDP index

The GDP index is calculated using the income variable from the household income survey. For conceptual reasons and because of measurement errors, mean income per capita calculated from the household income surveys can be very different from GDP per capita from national accounts data, which are used to calculate the GDP index in the standard HDI. To eliminate differences in national price levels, household income per capita calculated from the household income surveys is expressed in US dollars in purchasing power parity (PPP) terms using conversion factors based on price data from the latest International Comparison Program surveys provided by the World Bank. This income per capita is then rescaled using the ratio between the household income variable and GDP per capita expressed in PPP (taken from the standard HDI).

Finally, these data are rescaled to the same average as that of the standard HDI for the relevant year. The HDI by income quintiles is then calculated according to the standard formula (see *Technical note 1*):

$$\frac{\text{Life expectancy index} + \text{education index} + \text{GDP index}}{3} = \frac{\text{Human}}{\text{development}}\ \text{index}$$

This calculation is carried out for each quintile.

Issues for discussion

The HDI by income quintiles exercise provides a simple, intuitive and transparent approach for measuring important human development disparities within countries. It provides a useful composite indicator for tracking inequalities in income and wider inequalities in opportunity linked to health and education. However, the use of the HDI model to examine national inequalities raises a number of conceptual and methodological problems.

Consider first the relationship between income and the other indicators. The HDI by income quintiles measures annual incomes, which fluctuate considerably due to shocks and to lifecycle developments. Taking an annual average snapshot of the income of a household in, say, the poorest quintile can obscure very large dynamic changes over time. This produces additional methodological problems, not least because linking more stable health and education outcomes to fluctuating incomes can bias the results.

Data quality in the household surveys presents another set of problems. These problems are addressed here by the simplifying assumptions outlined above and explained in more detail in Grimm and others (2006). But aligning demographic and health survey and household income survey data is inherently problematic, and other approaches are possible. For developed countries, data quality is a less immediate problem. But cross-country comparisons remain difficult. In the case of Finland and the United States the assessment of life expectancy by income groups is based on data for the early 1990s linked to current incomes. However, data constraints mean that the income measure differs from that used for the other two components. In addition, Luxembourg Income Study data do not contain enrolment data, which must then be proxied by attainment data.

One final concern relates to the scale of inequality. In proportionate terms, differences between the rich and poor are much larger in the income dimension than in the health and education dimension. Arguably, smaller differences in health and education might, however, be just as important from a human development point of view and should therefore attract a greater weight in the HDI by income quintiles than they currently have. These are broader methodological issues inherent in such composite indices that will be investigated in future Reports.

Measuring risk in lack of access to water and sanitation

Access to water and sanitation is a matter of life and death. But what are the parameters of risk associated with not having access? Given the scale of illness and death associated with the problem, that question has received surprisingly little attention.

Chapter 1 sets out the results of a research exercise looking at the risks associated with deprivation in access to water and sanitation. The approach borrows from analytical techniques used in medical and economic research to examine the relationship between behaviour or treatment and health outcomes. It focuses on the association between access to specific types of water and sanitation infrastructure and changes in the risk of illness or premature death. More specifically, the exercise captures how access to water and sanitation affects the risk of neonatal (0–1 months) and post-neonatal (1–12 months) mortality, as well as the risk of diarrhoea, the leading water-related cause of death in children.

Data

Data for the research are derived from Demographic and Health Surveys, which collect information on a wide set of socioeconomic variables at the individual, household and community levels and are usually conducted every five years to allow comparison over time. Each survey sample consists of 5,000–30,000 households. The samples are not longitudinal by design, but they are representative at the national, urban and rural levels. Although Demographic and Health Surveys' primary focus is women ages 15–49, they also collect information on several demographic indicators for all members of the household, including children.

Some 22 surveys from 18 countries were used to construct the data set (table 1). Surveys conducted in or since 2000 were used in most cases to include the most recent information available. For the analysis here, children were the primary unit of analysis.

Methodology

The methodology follows a two-step approach. First, the elements that affect the chance of survival in different stages of life were identified, disentangling the effects of individual, household and community characteristics that contribute to mortality and illness. For neonatal mortality the main variable was defined as a discrete indicator with two values: zero if the child is alive and one if the child died during the first month of life. For diarrhoea a discrete outcome approach was used, with a one indicating a diarrhoeal episode within the two weeks

Table 1	Country coverage	
Country	**Year**	**Sample size**
Bangladesh	1999–2000	6,368
Benin	2001	5,349
Cameroon	2004	8,125
Egypt	1995	12,135
	2000	11,467
Ethiopia	2000	10,873
Gabon	2000	4,405
Ghana	2003	3,844
Guatemala	1998–99	4,943
Haiti	2000	6,685
Indonesia	2002–03	16,206
Mali	2001	13,097
Morocco	2003–04	6,180
Nepal	2001	6,931
Nicaragua	2001	6,986
Peru	1996	17,549
	2000	13,697
Uganda	2000–01	7,113
Viet Nam	1997	1,775
	2002	1,317
Zambia	2001–02	6,877
Zimbabwe	1999	3,643

prior to the interview. A logit model was then estimated in both cases (box 1).

A different model and different outcome variable were used to estimate the impact of specific elements on post-neonatal survival. All children older than one month were included, with the outcome variable indicating the occurrence of death between the 2nd and 11th months of life. A Cox proportional hazard model was then used to estimate the chances of survival.

At each step a set of control variables was used to identify the effects of specific characteristics. The control variables include individual variables (such as the sex of the child, birth intervals and whether the child was breastfed), household variables (such as type of dwelling, education of the mother and wealth of the household as measured by an asset index) and community-level variables (such as urban or rural, region of residence and so on). A regression analysis was then conducted to isolate the specific risks associated with each type of sanitation and water facility, using the absence of water and sanitation infrastructure as the reference scenario.

Typically, the wealth of households is measured by a standard asset index, which measures possessions such as vehicles and televisions as well as access to water and sanitation. Since the main interest of the study is the effect of water and sanitation infrastructure on health outcomes, an asset index that excludes these variables was constructed. Following standard procedures, eight household assets were included to calculate the first principal component, which was then used to construct a standardized index. This index was then used to divide households into wealth quintiles.

Finally, the robustness of the research was further tested. In particular, the mortality study was expanded using propensity score matching to check for endogeneity of the outcome variable or unobserved characteristics that may be correlated with access to water and sanitation.

Most of the results are shown and discussed in chapter 1. For further details, refer to the background papers prepared for this year's Report by Fuentes, Pfütze and Seck.[1]

Note

1   Fuentes, Pfütze and Seck 2006a, 2006b.

Box 1   **Technical model for measuring risk**

Two basic statistical methods were used to capture the risk underlying access to water and sanitation.

For neonatal mortality and incidence of diarrhoea, a standard logit model was used. Logit estimations are used when the outcome variable has two possible values (thus logits are often referred to as binary models). The two possible outcomes are labelled as failure ($Y = 0$) or success ($Y = 1$).

Parameters in logit estimations can be interpreted as the change in probability associated with a unit increase in the independent variables. The resulting parameters thus show the change in probability of the event conditional on the individual, household and community characteristics.

Formally, in the logit model the dependant variable Y_i is assumed to follow a Bernoulli distribution conditional on the vector of explanatory variable $\boldsymbol{X}_i$. The probability of success is written as

$$P(Y_i = 1 \mid x_i) = \Lambda(x_i\beta) \text{ and } P(Y_i = 0 \mid x_i) = 1 - \Lambda(x_i\beta)$$

with $\Lambda(z) = (1 + \exp^{-z})^{-1}$ being the cumulative distribution function of the logistic model.

The conditional density can be written as

$$f(y_i \mid x_i) = \Lambda(x_i\beta)^{y_i}[1 - \Lambda(x_i\beta)]^{1-y_i}.$$

The log likelihood function becomes

$$l(\beta) = \sum_{i=1}^{n} \log f(y_i \mid x_i) = \sum_{y_i=1} \log \Lambda(x_i\beta) + \sum_{y_i=0} \log[1 - \Lambda(x_i\beta)].$$

The maximum likelihood estimate $\hat{\beta}$ of β is the value that maximizes the log likelihood function $l(\beta)$.

For the determinant factors in post-neonatal mortality a more elaborate estimation framework is needed because of the problem of censored observations. The data used do not contain observations for the entire period of analysis for all children. For example, a child who is four months old at the time of the interview and dies at the age of five months will not be recorded by the survey as a death; this characteristic creates a bias that needs to be corrected. One way to address this problem is to restrict the sample to children who were at least 12 months old at the time of the interview. However, this would eliminate a considerable number of observations. Instead, a hazard model is used to account for censoring issues. Based on the extensive literature on mortality, a Cox proportional hazard model is applied. The model is a semi-parametric estimation, given that the underlying hazard rate is not modelled by some functional form. This model has only one requisite structural assumption: the effect of the covariates on the relative hazard rate must be constant over the period under consideration.

Formally, the (conditional) hazard function of the Cox model given a k-dimensional vector of covariates ($\boldsymbol{X}$) can be written as

$$\lambda(t \mid X) = \lambda_0(t) \exp(\beta'X),$$

where $\beta' = (\beta_1, \beta_2, ..., \beta_k)'$ is the vector of parameters (proportional change in the hazard function) and $\lambda_0(t)$ is the baseline hazard function.

The parameters β' can be estimated without estimating $\lambda_0(t)$ using maximum likelihood. If i denotes the index of ordered failure times $t_i, i = (1, 2, ..., N)$, d_i the number of observations that fail at t_i, D_i the set of observations at t_i and R_i the risk set, the partial log likelihood function can be written as

$$l(\beta) = \sum_{i=1}^{N} d_i [\beta'X_i - \ln \sum_{j \in R_i} \exp(\beta'X_j)].$$

Definitions of statistical terms

Armed forces, total Strategic, land, naval, air, command, administrative and support forces. Also included are paramilitary forces such as the gendarmerie, customs service and border guard, if these are trained in military tactics.

Arms transfers, conventional Refers to the voluntary transfer by the supplier (and thus excludes captured weapons and weapons obtained through defectors) of weapons with a military purpose destined for the armed forces, paramilitary forces or intelligence agencies of another country. These include major conventional weapons or systems in six categories: ships, aircraft, missiles, artillery, armoured vehicles and guidance and radar systems (excluded are trucks, services, ammunition, small arms, support items, components and component technology and towed or naval artillery under 100-millimetre calibre).

Births attended by skilled health personnel The percentage of deliveries attended by personnel (including doctors, nurses and midwives) trained to give the necessary care, supervision and advice to women during pregnancy, labour and the postpartum period; to conduct deliveries on their own; and to care for newborns.

Birthweight, infants with low The percentage of infants with a birthweight of less than 2,500 grams.

Carbon dioxide emissions Anthropogenic (human originated) carbon dioxide emissions stemming from the burning of fossil fuels, gas flaring and the production of cement. Emissions are calculated from data on the consumption of solid, liquid and gaseous fuels; gas flaring; and the production of cement.

Cellular subscribers (also referred to as cellular mobile subscribers) Subscribers to an automatic public mobile telephone service that provides access to the public switched telephone network using cellular technology. Systems can be analogue or digital.

Children reaching grade 5 The percentage of children starting primary school who eventually attain grade 5 (grade 4 if the duration of primary school is four years). The estimates are based on the reconstructed cohort method, which uses data on enrolment and repeaters for two consecutive years.

Children under age five with diarrhoea receiving oral rehydration and continued feeding The percentage of children (ages 0–4) with diarrhoea in the two weeks preceding the survey who received either oral

rehydration therapy (oral rehydration solutions or recommended homemade fluids) or increased fluids and continued feeding.

Condom use at last high-risk sex The percentage of men and women who have had sex with a nonmarital, noncohabiting partner in the last 12 months and who say they used a condom the last time they did so.

Consumer price index, average annual change in Reflects changes in the cost to the average consumer of acquiring a basket of goods and services that may be fixed or may change at specified intervals.

Contraceptive prevalence rate The percentage of married women (including women in union) ages 15–49 who are using, or whose partners are using, any form of contraception, whether modern or traditional.

Contributing family worker Defined according to the 1993 International Classification by Status in Employment (ICSE) as a person who works without pay in an economic enterprise operated by a related person living in the same household.

Crime, people victimized by The percentage of the population who perceive that they have been victimized by certain types of crime in the preceding year, based on responses to the International Crime Victims Survey.

Debt service, total The sum of principal repayments and interest actually paid in foreign currency, goods or services on long-term debt (having a maturity of more than one year), interest paid on short-term debt and repayments to the International Monetary Fund.

Earned income (PPP US$), estimated Roughly derived on the basis of the ratio of the female nonagricultural wage to the male nonagricultural wage, the female and male shares of the economically active population, total female and male population and GDP per capita (in purchasing power parity terms in US dollars; see *PPP*). For details on this estimation, see *Technical note 1*.

Earned income, ratio of estimated female to male The ratio of estimated female earned income to estimated male earned income. See *earned income (PPP US$), estimated*.

Economic activity rate, female The share of the female population ages 15 and older who supply, or are available to supply, labour for the production of goods and services.

Education expenditure, current public Spending on goods and services that are consumed within the current year and that would need to be renewed the following year, including such expenditures as staff salaries and benefits, contracted or purchased services, books and teaching materials, welfare services, furniture and equipment, minor repairs, fuel, insurance, rents, telecommunications and travel.

Education expenditure, public Includes both capital expenditures (spending on construction, renovation, major repairs and purchases of heavy equipment or vehicles) and current expenditures. See *education expenditure, current public*.

Education index One of the three indices on which the human development index is built. It is based on the adult literacy rate and the combined gross enrolment ratio for primary, secondary and tertiary schools. See *literacy rate, adult*, and *enrolment ratio, gross combined, for primary, secondary and tertiary schools*. For details on how the index is calculated, see *Technical note 1*.

Education levels Categorized as pre-primary, primary, secondary or tertiary in accordance with the International Standard Classification of Education (ISCED). *Pre-primary education* (ISCED level 0) is provided at such schools as kindergartens and nursery and infant schools and is intended for children not old enough to enter school at the primary level. *Primary education* (ISCED level 1) provides the basic elements of education at such establishments as primary and elementary schools. *Secondary education* (ISCED levels 2 and 3) is based on at least four years of previous instruction at the first level and provides general or specialized instruction, or both, at such institutions as middle schools, secondary schools, high schools, teacher training schools at this level and vocational or technical schools. *Tertiary education* (ISCED levels 5–7) refers to education at such institutions as universities, teachers colleges and higher level professional schools—requiring as a minimum condition of admission the successful completion of education at the second level or evidence of the attainment of an equivalent level of knowledge.

Electricity consumption per capita Refers to gross production in per capita terms and includes consumption by station auxiliaries and any losses in transformers that are considered integral parts of the station. Also included is total electric energy produced by pumping installations without deduction of electric energy absorbed by pumping.

Employment by economic activity, female Female employment in industry, agriculture or services as defined according to the International Standard Industrial Classification (ISIC) system (revisions 2 and 3). *Industry* refers to mining and quarrying, manufacturing, construction and public utilities (gas, water and electricity). *Agriculture* refers to activities in agriculture, hunting, forestry and fishing. *Services* refer to

wholesale and retail trade; restaurants and hotels; transport, storage and communications; finance, insurance, real estate and business services; and community, social and personal services.

Energy use, GDP per unit of The ratio of GDP (in 2000 PPP US$) to commercial energy use, measured in kilograms of oil equivalent. This ratio provides a measure of energy efficiency by showing comparable and consistent estimates of real GDP across countries relative to physical inputs (units of energy use). See *GDP (gross domestic product)* and *PPP (purchasing power parity)*.

Enrolment ratio, gross The number of students enrolled in a level of education, regardless of age, as a percentage of the population of official school age for that level. The gross enrolment ratio can be greater than 100% as a result of grade repetition and entry at ages younger or older than the typical age at that grade level. See *education levels*.

Enrolment ratio, gross combined, for primary, secondary and tertiary schools The number of students enrolled in primary, secondary and tertiary levels of education, regardless of age, as a percentage of the population of official school age for the three levels. See *education levels* and *enrolment ratio, gross*.

Enrolment ratio, net The number of students enrolled in a level of education who are of official school age for that level, as a percentage of the population of official school age for that level. See *education levels*.

Environmental treaties, ratification of After signing a treaty, a country must ratify it, often with the approval of its legislature. Such process implies not only an expression of interest as indicated by the signature, but also the transformation of the treaty's principles and obligations into national law.

Exports, high-technology Exports of products with a high intensity of research and development. They include high-technology products such as in aerospace, computers, pharmaceuticals, scientific instruments and electrical machinery.

Exports, manufactured Defined according to the Standard International Trade Classification to include exports of chemicals, basic manufactures, machinery and transport equipment and other miscellaneous manufactured goods.

Exports of goods and services The value of all goods and other market services provided to the rest of the world. Included is the value of merchandise, freight, insurance, transport, travel, royalties, licence fees and other services, such as communication, construction, financial, information, business, personal and government services. Excluded are labour and property income and transfer payments.

Exports, primary Defined according to the Standard International Trade Classification to include exports of food, agricultural raw materials, fuels and ores and metals.

Fertility rate, total The number of children that would be born to each woman if she were to live to the end of her child-bearing years and bear children at each age in accordance with prevailing age-specific fertility rates.

Foreign direct investment, net inflows of Net inflows of investment to acquire a lasting management interest (10% or more of voting stock) in an enterprise operating in an economy other than that of the investor. It is the sum of equity capital, reinvestment of earnings, other long-term capital and short-term capital.

Fuel consumption, traditional Estimated consumption of fuel wood, charcoal, bagasse (sugar cane waste), and animal and vegetable wastes.

GDP (gross domestic product) The sum of value added by all resident producers in the economy plus any product taxes (less subsidies) not included in the valuation of output. It is calculated without making deductions for depreciation of fabricated capital assets or for depletion and degradation of natural resources. Value added is the net output of an industry after adding up all outputs and subtracting intermediate inputs.

GDP (US$) Gross domestic product converted to US dollars using the average official exchange rate reported by the International Monetary Fund. An alternative conversion factor is applied if the official exchange rate is judged to diverge by an exceptionally large margin from the rate effectively applied to transactions in foreign currencies and traded products. See *GDP (gross domestic product)*.

GDP index One of the three indices on which the human development index is built. It is based on gross domestic product per capita (in purchasing power parity terms in US dollars; see *PPP*). For details on how the index is calculated, see *Technical note 1*.

GDP per capita (PPP US$) Gross domestic product (in purchasing power parity terms in US dollars) divided by midyear population. See *GDP (gross domestic product), PPP (purchasing power parity)* and *population, total*.

GDP per capita (US$) Gross domestic product in US dollar terms divided by midyear population. See *GDP (US$)* and *population, total*.

GDP per capita annual growth rate Least squares annual growth rate, calculated from constant price GDP per capita in local currency units.

Gender empowerment measure (GEM) A composite index measuring gender inequality in three basic dimensions of empowerment—economic participation and decision-making, political participation, and decision-making and power over economic resources. For details on how the index is calculated, see *Technical note 1*.

Gender-related development index (GDI) A composite index measuring average achievement in the three basic dimensions captured in the human development index—a long and healthy life, knowledge and a decent standard of living—adjusted to account for inequalities

between men and women. For details on how the index is calculated, see *Technical note 1*.

Gini index Measures the extent to which the distribution of income (or consumption) among individuals or households within a country deviates from a perfectly equal distribution. A Lorenz curve plots the cumulative percentages of total income received against the cumulative number of recipients, starting with the poorest individual or household. The Gini index measures the area between the Lorenz curve and a hypothetical line of absolute equality, expressed as a percentage of the maximum area under the line. A value of 0 represents perfect equality, a value of 100 perfect inequality.

GNI (gross national income) The sum of value added by all resident producers in the economy plus any product taxes (less subsidies) not included in the valuation of output plus net receipts of primary income (compensation of employees and property income) from abroad. Value added is the net output of an industry after adding up all outputs and subtracting intermediate inputs. Data are in current US dollars converted using the *World Bank Atlas* method.

Health expenditure per capita (PPP US$) The sum of public and private expenditure (in purchasing power parity terms in US dollars), divided by the population. Health expenditure includes the provision of health services (preventive and curative), family planning activities, nutrition activities and emergency aid designated for health, but excludes the provision of water and sanitation. See *health expenditure, private; health expenditure, public;* and *PPP (purchasing power parity)*.

Health expenditure, private Direct household (out of pocket) spending, private insurance, spending by nonprofit institutions serving households and direct service payments by private corporations. Together with public health expenditure, it makes up total health expenditure. See *health expenditure per capita (PPP US$)* and *health expenditure, public*.

Health expenditure, public Current and capital spending from government (central and local) budgets, external borrowings and grants (including donations from international agencies and nongovernmental organizations) and social (or compulsory) health insurance funds. Together with private health expenditure, it makes up total health expenditure. See *health expenditure per capita (PPP US$)* and *health expenditure, private*.

HIPC completion point The date at which a country included in the Debt Initiative for Heavily Indebted Poor Countries (HIPCs) successfully completes the key structural reforms agreed on at the HIPC decision point, including developing and implementing a poverty reduction strategy. The country then receives the bulk of its debt relief under the HIPC Initiative without further policy conditions.

HIPC decision point The date at which a heavily indebted poor country (HIPC) with an established track record of good performance under adjustment programmes supported by the International Monetary

Fund and the World Bank commits, under the Debt Initiative for Heavily Indebted Poor Countries, to undertake additional reforms and to develop and implement a poverty reduction strategy.

HIV prevalence The percentage of people ages 15–49 who are infected with HIV.

Human development index (HDI) A composite index measuring average achievement in three basic dimensions of human development—a long and healthy life, knowledge and a decent standard of living. For details on how the index is calculated, see *Technical note 1*.

Human poverty index (HPI-1) for developing countries A composite index measuring deprivations in the three basic dimensions captured in the human development index—a long and healthy life, knowledge and a decent standard of living. For details on how the index is calculated, see *Technical note 1*.

Human poverty index (HPI-2) for selected high-income OECD countries A composite index measuring deprivations in the three basic dimensions captured in the human development index— a long and healthy life, knowledge and a decent standard of living—and also capturing social exclusion. For details on how the index is calculated, see *Technical note 1*.

Illiteracy rate, adult Calculated as 100 minus the adult literacy rate. See *literacy rate, adult*.

Immunization, one-year-olds fully immunized against measles or tuberculosis One-year-olds injected with an antigen or a serum containing specific antibodies against measles or tuberculosis.

Imports of goods and services The value of all goods and other market services received from the rest of the world. Included is the value of merchandise, freight, insurance, transport, travel, royalties, licence fees and other services, such as communication, construction, financial, information, business, personal and government services. Excluded are labour and property income and transfer payments.

Income poverty line, population below The percentage of the population living below the specified poverty line:
- $1 a day—at 1985 international prices (equivalent to $1.08 at 1993 international prices), adjusted for purchasing power parity.
- $2 a day—at 1985 international prices (equivalent to $2.15 at 1993 international prices), adjusted for purchasing power parity.
- $4 a day—at 1990 international prices, adjusted for purchasing power parity.
- $11 a day (per person for a family of three)—at 1994 international prices, adjusted for purchasing power parity.
- National poverty line—the poverty line deemed appropriate for a country by its authorities. National estimates are based on population-weighted subgroup estimates from household surveys.

- 50% of median income—50% of the median adjusted disposable household income. See *PPP (purchasing power parity)*.

Income or consumption, shares of The shares of income or consumption accruing to subgroups of population indicated by deciles or quintiles, based on national household surveys covering various years. Consumption surveys produce results showing lower levels of inequality between poor and rich than do income surveys, as poor people generally consume a greater share of their income. Because data come from surveys covering different years and using different methodologies, comparisons between countries must be made with caution.

Infant mortality rate See *mortality rate, infant*.

Internally displaced people People or groups of people who have been forced or obliged to flee or to leave their homes or places of habitual residence, in particular as a result of or to avoid the effects of armed conflict, situations of generalized violence, violations of human rights or natural or human-made disasters, and who have not crossed an internationally recognized state border

Internet users People with access to the worldwide network.

Labour force All people employed (including people above a specified age who, during the reference period, were in paid employment, at work, self-employed or with a job but not at work) and unemployed (including people above a specified age who, during the reference period, were without work, currently available for work and seeking work).

Legislators, senior officials and managers, female Women's share of positions defined according to the International Standard Classification of Occupations (ISCO-88) to include legislators, senior government officials, traditional chiefs and heads of villages, senior officials of special-interest organizations, corporate managers, directors and chief executives, production and operations department managers and other department and general managers.

Life expectancy at birth The number of years a newborn infant would live if prevailing patterns of age-specific mortality rates at the time of birth were to stay the same throughout the child's life.

Life expectancy index One of the three indices on which the human development index is built. For details on how the index is calculated, see *Technical note 1*.

Literacy rate, adult The percentage of people ages 15 and older who can, with understanding, both read and write a short, simple statement related to their everyday life.

Literacy rate, youth The percentage of people ages 15–24 who can, with understanding, both read and write a short, simple statement related to their everyday life.

Literacy skills, functional, people lacking The share of the population ages 16–65 scoring at level 1 on the prose literacy scale of the International Adult Literacy Survey. Most tasks at this level require the reader to locate a piece of information in the text that is identical to or synonymous with the information given in the directive.

Malaria prevention, children under age five The percentage of children under age five sleeping under insecticide-treated bednets.

Malaria treatment, children under age five with fever The percentage of children under age five who were ill with fever in the two weeks before the survey and received antimalarial drugs.

Market activities Defined according to the 1993 revised UN System of National Accounts to include employment in establishments, primary production not in establishments, services for income and other production of goods not in establishments. See *nonmarket activities* and *work time, total*.

Mortality rate, infant The probability of dying between birth and exactly one year of age, expressed per 1,000 live births.

Mortality rate, under-five The probability of dying between birth and exactly five years of age, expressed per 1,000 live births.

Mortality ratio, maternal The annual number of female deaths from pregnancy-related causes per 100,000 live births.

Mortality ratio, maternal adjusted Maternal mortality ratio adjusted to account for well documented problems of underreporting and misclassification of maternal deaths, as well as estimates for countries with no data. See *mortality ratio, maternal*.

Mortality ratio, maternal reported Maternal mortality ratio as reported by national authorities. See *mortality ratio, maternal*.

Medium-variant projection Population projections by the United Nations Population Division assuming medium-fertility path, normal mortality and normal international migration. Each assumption implies projected trends in fertility, mortality and net migration levels, depending on the specific demographic characteristics and relevant policies of each country or group of countries. In addition, for the countries highly affected by the HIV/AIDS epidemic, the impact of HIV/AIDS is included in the projection. The United Nations Population Division also publishes low- and high-variant projections. For more information, see http://esa.un.org/unpp/assumptions.html.

Military expenditure All expenditures of the defence ministry and other ministries on recruiting and training military personnel as well as on construction and purchase of military supplies and equipment. Military assistance is included in the expenditures of the donor country.

Nonmarket activities Defined according to the 1993 revised UN System of National Accounts to include household maintenance (cleaning, laundry and meal preparation and cleanup), management and shopping for own household; care for children, the sick, the elderly and the disabled in own household; and community services. See *market activities* and *work time, total*.

Official aid Grants or loans that meet the same standards as for official development assistance (ODA) except that recipient countries do not qualify as recipients of ODA. These countries are identified in part II of the Development Assistance Committee (DAC) list of recipient countries, which includes more advanced countries of Central and Eastern Europe, the countries of the former Soviet Union and certain advanced developing countries and territories. See *official development assistance (ODA), net*.

Official development assistance (ODA), net Disbursements of loans made on concessional terms (net of repayments of principal) and grants by official agencies of the members of the Development Assistance Committee (DAC), by multilateral institutions and by non-DAC countries to promote economic development and welfare in countries and territories in part I of the DAC list of aid recipients. It includes loans with a grant element of at least 25% (calculated at a discount rate of 10%).

Official development assistance (ODA), per capita of donor country Official development assistance granted by a specific country divided by the country's total population. See *official development assistance (ODA), net*.

Official development assistance (ODA) to basic social services ODA directed to basic social services, which include basic education (primary education, early childhood education and basic life skills for youth and adults), basic health (including basic health care, basic health infrastructure, basic nutrition, infectious disease control, health education and health personnel development) and population policies and programmes and reproductive health (population policy and administrative management; reproductive health care; family planning; control of sexually transmitted diseases, including HIV/AIDS; and personnel development for population and reproductive health). Aid to water supply and sanitation is included only if it has a poverty focus.

Official development assistance (ODA) to least developed countries See *official development assistance (ODA), net* and country classifications for least developed countries.

Official development assistance (ODA), untied Bilateral ODA for which the associated goods and services may be fully and freely procured in substantially all countries and that is given by one country to another.

Patents granted to residents Refers to documents issued by a government office that describe an invention and create a legal situation in which the patented invention can normally be exploited (made, used, sold, imported) only by or with the authorization of the patentee. The protection of inventions is generally limited to 20 years from the filing date of the application for the grant of a patent.

Physicians Includes graduates of a faculty or school of medicine who are working in any medical field (including teaching, research and practice).

Population growth rate, annual Refers to the average annual exponential growth rate for the period indicated. See *population, total.*

Population, total Refers to the de facto population, which includes all people actually present in a given area at a given time.

Population, urban The midyear population of areas classified as urban according to the criteria used by each country, as reported to the United Nations. See *population, total.*

PPP (purchasing power parity) A rate of exchange that accounts for price differences across countries, allowing international comparisons of real output and incomes. At the PPP US$ rate (as used in this Report), PPP US$1 has the same purchasing power in the domestic economy as $1 has in the United States.

Private flows, other A category combining non-debt-creating portfolio equity investment flows (the sum of country funds, depository receipts and direct purchases of shares by foreign investors), portfolio debt flows (bond issues purchased by foreign investors) and bank and trade-related lending (commercial bank lending and other commercial credits).

Probability at birth of not surviving to a specified age Calculated as 1 minus the probability of surviving to a specified age for a given cohort. See *probability at birth of surviving to a specified age.*

Probability at birth of surviving to a specified age The probability of a newborn infant surviving to a specified age if subject to prevailing patterns of age-specific mortality rates.

Professional and technical workers, female Women's share of positions defined according to the International Standard Classification of Occupations (ISCO-88) to include physical, mathematical and engineering science professionals (and associate professionals), life science and health professionals (and associate professionals), teaching professionals (and associate professionals) and other professionals and associate professionals.

Refugees People who have fled their country because of a well founded fear of persecution for reasons of their race, religion, nationality, political opinion or membership in a particular social group and who cannot or do not want to return. *Country of asylum* is the country in which a refugee has filed a claim of asylum but has not yet received a decision or is otherwise registered as an asylum seeker. *Country of origin* refers to the claimant's nationality or country of citizenship.

Research and development expenditures Current and capital expenditures (including overhead) on creative, systematic activity intended to increase the stock of knowledge. Included are fundamental and applied research and experimental development work leading to new devices, products or processes.

Researchers in R&D People trained to work in any field of science who are engaged in professional research and development (R&D) activity. Most such jobs require the completion of tertiary education.

Royalties and licence fees, receipts of Receipts by residents from nonresidents for the authorized use of intangible, nonproduced, nonfinancial assets and proprietary rights (such as patents, trademarks, copyrights, franchises and industrial processes) and for the use, through licensing agreements, of produced originals of prototypes (such as films and manuscripts). Data are based on the balance of payments.

Sanitation facilities, improved, population with sustainable access to The percentage of the population with access to adequate excreta disposal facilities, such as a connection to a sewer or septic tank system, a pour-flush latrine, a simple pit latrine or a ventilated improved pit latrine. An excreta disposal system is considered adequate if it is private or shared (but not public) and if it can effectively prevent human, animal and insect contact with excreta.

Science, math and engineering, tertiary students in The share of tertiary students enrolled in natural sciences; engineering; mathematics and computer sciences; architecture and town planning; transport and communications; trade, craft and industrial programmes; and agriculture, forestry and fisheries. See *education levels.*

Seats in parliament held by women Refers to seats held by women in a lower or single house or an upper house or senate, where relevant.

Smoking, prevalence among adults of The percentage of men and women who smoke cigarettes.

Telephone mainlines Telephone lines connecting a customer's equipment to the public switched telephone network.

Tenure, households with access to secure Households that own or are purchasing their homes, are renting privately or are in social housing or subtenancy.

Terms of trade The ratio of the export price index to the import price index measured relative to a base year. A value of more than 100 means that the price of exports has risen relative to the price of imports.

Tuberculosis cases, prevalence The total number of tuberculosis cases reported to the World Health Organization. A tuberculosis case is defined as a patient in whom tuberculosis has been bacteriologically confirmed or diagnosed by a clinician.

Tuberculosis cases cured under DOTS The percentage of estimated new infectious tuberculosis cases cured under DOTS, the internationally recommended tuberculosis control strategy.

Tuberculosis cases detected under DOTS The percentage of estimated new infectious tuberculosis cases detected (diagnosed in a given period) under DOTS, the internationally recommended tuberculosis control strategy.

Under-five mortality rate See *mortality rate, under-five.*

Under height for age, children under age five Includes moderate and severe stunting, defined as more than two standard deviations below the median height for age of the reference population.

Under weight for age, children under age five Includes moderate underweight, defined as more than two standard deviations below the median weight for age of the reference population, and severe underweight, defined as more than three standard deviations below the median weight.

Undernourished people People whose food intake is chronically insufficient to meet their minimum energy requirements.

Unemployment Refers to all people above a specified age who are not in paid employment or self-employed, but are available for work and have taken specific steps to seek paid employment or self-employment.

Unemployment, long-term Unemployment lasting 12 months or longer. See *unemployment.*

Unemployment rate The unemployed divided by the labour force (those employed plus the unemployed). See *unemployment* and *labour force.*

Unemployment rate, youth Refers to unemployment between the ages of 15 or 16 and 24, depending on the national definition. See *unemployment.*

Water source, improved, population without sustainable access to Calculated as 100 minus the percentage of the population with sustainable access to an improved water source. Unimproved sources include vendors, bottled water, tanker trucks and unprotected wells and springs. See *water source, improved, population with sustainable access to.*

Water source, improved, population with sustainable access to The share of the population with reasonable access to any of the following types of water supply for drinking: household connections, public standpipes, boreholes, protected dug wells, protected springs and rainwater collection. *Reasonable access* is defined as the availability of at least 20 litres a person per day from a source within 1 kilometre of the user's dwelling.

Women in government at ministerial level Includes deputy prime ministers and ministers. Prime ministers were included when they held ministerial portfolios. Vice-presidents and heads of ministerial-level departments or agencies were also included when exercising a ministerial function in the government structure.

Work time, total Time spent on market and nonmarket activities as defined according to the 1993 revised UN System of National Accounts. See *market activities* and *nonmarket activities.*

Statistical references

Charmes, Jacques. 2006. Correspondence on time use. June. Paris.

Fuentes, Ricardo, Tobias Pfütze, and Papa Seck. 2006a. "Does Access to Water and Sanitation Affect Child Survival? A Five Country Analysis." Background paper for *Human Development Report 2006*. United Nations Development Programme, Human Development Report Office, New York.

———. 2006b. "A Logistic Analysis of Diarrhea Incidence and Access to Water and Sanitation." Background paper for *Human Development Report 2006*. United Nations Development Programme, Human Development Report Office, New York.

Goldschmidt-Clermont, Luisella, and Elisabetta Pagnossin-Aligisakis. 1995. "Measures of Unrecorded Economic Activities in Fourteen Countries." Background paper for *Human Development Report 1995*. United Nations Development Programme, Human Development Report Office, New York.

Grimm, M., K. Harttgen, S. Klasen and M. Misselhorn. 2006. "A Human Development Index by Income Groups." Background paper for *Human Development Report 2006*. United Nations Development Programme, Human Development Report Office, New York.

Gwatkin, Davidson, Shea Rutstein, Kiersten Johnson, Eldaw Abdalla Suliman, Adam Wagstaff, and Agbessi Amouzou. 2005. *Socioeconomic Differences in Health, Nutrition, and Population*. Second edition. Washington, D.C.: World Bank.

Harvey, Andrew S. 1995. "Market and Non-Market Productive Activity in Less Developed and Developing Countries: Lessons from Time Use." Background paper for *Human Development Report 1995*. United Nations Development Programme, Human Development Report Office, New York.

———. 2001. "National Time Use Data on Market and Non-Market Work by Both Women and Men." Background paper for *Human Development Report 2001*. United Nations Development Programme, Human Development Report Office, New York.

Heston, Alan, Robert Summers, and Bettina Aten. 2001. Correspondence on data from the Penn World Table 6.0. March. Philadelphia, Penn.

———. 2002. "Penn World Tables Version 6.1." University of Pennsylvania, Center for International Comparisons, Philadelphia. [http://pwt.econ.upenn.edu/]. Accessed March 2005.

IBGE (Brazilian Institute for Geography and Statistics). 2005. Pesquisa Nacional por Amostra de Domicílios 2004. Brasilia. [http://www.ibge.gov.br/home/estatistica/populacao/trabalhoerendimento/pnad2004/sintesepnad2004.pdf]. Accessed August 2006.

IISS (International Institute for Strategic Studies). 2006. *The Military Balance 2005–2006*. London: Routledge, Taylor and Francis Group.

ILO (International Labour Organization). 2005a. *Estimates and Projections of the Economically Active Population, 1980–2020*. Fifth edition, revision 2. Database. Geneva.

———. 2005b. *Key Indicators of the Labour Market*. Fourth edition. CD-ROM. Geneva. [www.ilo.org/kilm/]. Accessed April 2006.

———. 2006a. *Database on International Labour Standards (ILOLEX)*. Geneva. [www.ilo.org/ilolex/english/docs/declworld.htm]. Accessed August 2006.

———. 2006b. *LABORSTA Database*. Geneva. [http://laborsta.ilo.org]. Accessed April 2006.

Internal Displacement Monitoring Centre. 2006. "Global Statistics." Geneva. [www.internal-displacement.org]. Accessed May 2006.

IPU (Inter-Parliamentary Union). 2005. Correspondence on women in government at the ministerial level. March. Geneva.

———. 2006a. Correspondence on women in national parliaments. May. Geneva.

———. 2006b. Correspondence on year women received the right to vote and to stand for election and year first woman was elected or appointed to parliament. July. Geneva.

———. 2006c. *Parline Database*. Geneva. [www.ipu.org]. Accessed July 2006.

Kennedy, John F. 1962. Remarks in Pueblo, Colorado, August 17. *The Public Papers of the Presidents of the United States*. Washington, DC: National Archives and Records Administration.

LIS (Luxembourg Income Study). 2006. "Relative Poverty Rates for the Total Population, Children and the Elderly." Luxembourg. [www.lisproject.org/keyfigures/povertytable.htm]. Accessed May 2006.

Milanovic, Branko. 2002. Correspondence on income, inequality and poverty during the transition from planned to market economy. March. World Bank, Washington, D.C.

OECD-DAC (Organisation for Economic Co-operation and Development, Development Assistance Committee). 2006a. Correspondence on official development assistance disbursed. May. Paris.

———. 2006b. DAC Journal: Development Cooperation 2006 Report. Paris.

———. 2006c. *DAC Online*. Database. Paris.

OECD (Organisation for Economic Co-operation and Development). 2006a. Correspondence on employment rates. May. Paris.

———. 2006b. Correspondence on long-term unemployment rates. May. Paris.

———. 2006c. Correspondence on unemployment rates. May. Paris.

OECD (Organisation for Economic Co-operation and Development) and Statistics Canada. 2000. *Literacy in the Information Age: Final Report on the IALS*. Paris.

———. 2005. *Learning a Living by Earning Skills: First Results of the Adult Literacy and Life Skills Survey*. Paris.

Ruoen, Ren, and Chen Kai. 1995. "China's GDP in U.S. Dollars Based on Purchasing Power Parity." Policy Research Working Paper 1415. World Bank, Washington, D.C.

Sen, Amartya. 1999. *Development as Freedom*. New York: Oxford University Press.

SIPRI (Stockholm International Peace Research Institute). 2006a. *SIPRI Yearbook: Armaments, Disarmaments and International Security*. Oxford, U.K.: Oxford University Press.

———. 2006b. Correspondence on arms transfers. March. Stockholm.

———. 2006c. Correspondence on military expenditure data. May. Stockholm.

Smeeding, Timothy M. 1997. "Financial Poverty in Developed Countries: The Evidence from the Luxembourg Income Study." Background paper for *Human Development Report 1997*. United Nations Development Programme, Human Development Report Office, New York.

Smeeding, Timothy M., Lee Rainwater, and Gary Burtless. 2000. "United States Poverty in a Cross-National Context." In Sheldon H. Danziger and Robert H. Haveman, eds., *Understanding Poverty*. New York: Russell Sage Foundation; and Cambridge, Mass.: Harvard University Press.

Statec. 2006. Correspondence on gross enrolment ratio for Luxembourg. May. Luxembourg.

UN (United Nations). 2002. Correspondence on time use surveys. Department of Economic and Social Affairs. Statistics Division. February. New York.

————. 2005a. Correspondence on life expectancy at birth. Department of Economic and Social Affairs, Population Division. March. New York.

————. 2005b. *World Population Prospects 1950–2050: The 2004 Revision*. Database. Department of Economic and Social Affairs, Population Division. New York.

————. 2006a. Correspondence on traditional fuel use. Department of Economic and Social Affairs, Statistics Division. March. New York.

————. 2006b. Correspondence on urban population. Department of Economic and Social Affairs, Population Division. New York.

————. 2006c. Millennium Indicators Database. Department of Economic and Social Affairs, Statistics Division, New York. [http://mdgs.un.org]. Accessed July 2006.

————. 2006d. "Multilateral Treaties Deposited with the Secretary-General." New York. [http://untreaty.un.org]. Accessed August 2006.

————. 2006e. *World Urbanization Prospects: The 2005 Revision*. Department of Economic and Social Affairs, Population Division. New York.

————. 2006f. Correspondence on energy consumption. Department of Economic and Social Affairs, Statistics Division. March. New York.

UNAIDS (Joint United Nations Programme on HIV/AIDS). 2006. Correspondence on HIV prevalence. May. Geneva.

UNDP (United Nations Development Programme). 2005a. *Bosnia and Herzegovina Human Development Report 2005*. Sarajevo.

————. 2005b. *Ethnic and Cultural Diversity: Citizenship in a Plural State*. National Human Development Report for Guatemala. Guatemala City.

————. 2005c. *Linking Industrialization with Human Development*. National Human Development Report for Kenya. Nairobi.

————. 2005d. *Towards Human Development with Equity*. National Human Development Report for China. Beijing.

UNESCO (United Nations Educational, Scientific and Cultural Organization). 1997. "International Standard Classification of Education 1997." Paris. [www.uis.unesco.org/TEMPLATE/pdf/isced/ISCED_A.pdf]. Accessed May 2006.

UNESCO (United Nations Educational, Scientific and Cultural Organization) Institute for Statistics. 1999. *Statistical Yearbook*. Montreal.

————. 2003. Correspondence on adult and youth literacy rates. March. Montreal.

————. 2005. Correspondence on adult and youth literacy rates. March. Montreal.

————. 2006a. Correspondence on adult and youth literacy rates. April. Montreal.

————. 2006b. Correspondence on education expenditure data. May. Montreal.

————. 2006c. Correspondence on gross and net enrolment ratios and children reaching grade 5. May. Montreal.

————. 2006d. Correspondence on students in science, engineering, manufacturing and construction. May. Montreal.

UNHCR (Office of the United Nations High Commissioner for Refugees). 2006. Correspondence on refugees by country of asylum and country of origin. May. Geneva.

UNICEF (United Nations Children's Fund). 2004. *State of the World's Children 2005*. New York.

————. 2005. *State of the World's Children 2006*. New York.

UNODC (United Nations Office on Drugs and Crime). 2004. Correspondence on data on crime victims. March. Vienna.

UN-OHRLLS (United Nations Office of the High Representative for the Least Developed Countries, Landlocked Developing Countries and Small Island Developing States). 2006. "List of Least Developed Countries." [www.un.org/special-rep/ohrlls/ldc/list.htm]. Accessed June 2006.

WHO (World Health Organization). 2006a. "Core Health Indicators." Geneva. [www3.who.int/whosis/core/core_select.cfm]. June 2006.

————. 2006b. Correspondence on health expenditure. May. Geneva.

————. 2006c. *World Health Statistics 2006*. Geneva.

————. 2006d. *Global Tuberculosis Control: WHO Report 2006*. Geneva. [www.who.int/tb/publications/global_report/en/index.html]. Accessed July 2006.

WIPO (World Intellectual Property Organization). 2006. "Patents Granted by Office (1985 to 2004)." Geneva. [http://wipo.int/ipstats/en/statistics/patents/source/granted_national_table.csv]. Accessed May 2006.

World Bank. 2003. *World Development Indicators 2003*. CD-ROM. Washington, D.C.

————. 2005. *World Development Indicators 2005*. CD-ROM. Washington, D.C.

————. 2006. *World Development Indicators 2006*. CD-ROM. Washington, D.C.

Classification of countries

Countries in the human development aggregates

High human development (HDI 0.800 and above)

Antigua and Barbuda	Seychelles
Argentina	Singapore
Australia	Slovakia
Austria	Slovenia
Bahamas	Spain
Bahrain	Sweden
Barbados	Switzerland
Belgium	Tonga
Bosnia and Herzegovina	Trinidad and Tobago
Brunei Darussalam	United Arab Emirates
Bulgaria	United Kingdom
Canada	United States
Chile	Uruguay
Costa Rica	(63 countries or areas)
Croatia	
Cuba	
Cyprus	
Czech Republic	
Denmark	
Estonia	
Finland	
France	
Germany	
Greece	
Hong Kong, China (SAR)	
Hungary	
Iceland	
Ireland	
Israel	
Italy	
Japan	
Korea, Rep. of	
Kuwait	
Latvia	
Lithuania	
Luxembourg	
Malaysia	
Malta	
Mauritius	
Mexico	
Netherlands	
New Zealand	
Norway	
Oman	
Panama	
Poland	
Portugal	
Qatar	
Romania	
Saint Kitts and Nevis	

Medium human development (HDI 0.500–0.799)

Albania	Nepal
Algeria	Nicaragua
Armenia	Occupied Palestinian
Azerbaijan	Territories
Bangladesh	Pakistan
Belarus	Papua New Guinea
Belize	Paraguay
Bhutan	Peru
Bolivia	Philippines
Botswana	Russian Federation
Brazil	Saint Lucia
Cambodia	Saint Vincent and the
Cameroon	Grenadines
Cape Verde	Samoa (Western)
China	São Tomé and Principe
Colombia	Saudi Arabia
Comoros	Solomon Islands
Congo	South Africa
Dominica	Sri Lanka
Dominican Republic	Sudan
Ecuador	Suriname
Egypt	Swaziland
El Salvador	Syrian Arab Republic
Equatorial Guinea	Tajikistan
Fiji	Thailand
Gabon	Timor-Leste
Georgia	Tunisia
Ghana	Turkey
Grenada	Turkmenistan
Guatemala	Uganda
Guyana	Ukraine
Honduras	Uzbekistan
India	Vanuatu
Indonesia	Venezuela, RB
Iran, Islamic Rep. of	Viet Nam
Jamaica	(83 countries or areas)
Jordan	
Kazakhstan	
Kyrgyzstan	
Lao People's Dem. Rep.	
Lebanon	
Libyan Arab Jamahiriya	
Macedonia, TFYR	
Madagascar	
Maldives	
Moldova, Rep. of	
Mongolia	
Morocco	
Myanmar	
Namibia	

Low human development (HDI below 0.500)

Angola	
Benin	
Burkina Faso	
Burundi	
Central African Republic	
Chad	
Congo, Dem. Rep. of the	
Côte d'Ivoire	
Djibouti	
Eritrea	
Ethiopia	
Gambia	
Guinea	
Guinea-Bissau	
Haiti	
Kenya	
Lesotho	
Malawi	
Mali	
Mauritania	
Mozambique	
Niger	
Nigeria	
Rwanda	
Senegal	
Sierra Leone	
Tanzania, U. Rep. of	
Togo	
Yemen	
Zambia	
Zimbabwe	
(31 countries or areas)	

Note: The following UN member countries are not included in the human development aggregates because the HDI cannot be computed for them: Afghanistan, Andorra, Iraq, Kiribati, the Democratic Republic of Korea, Liberia, Liechtenstein, Marshall Islands, the Federated States of Micronesia, Montenegro, Monaco, Nauru, Palau, San Marino, Serbia, Somalia and Tuvalu.

Countries in the income aggregates

High income (GNI per capita of $10,066 or more in 2004)

Andorra
Australia
Austria
Bahamas
Bahrain
Belgium
Brunei Darussalam
Canada
Cyprus
Denmark
Finland
France
Germany
Greece
Hong Kong, China (SAR)
Iceland
Ireland
Israel
Italy
Japan
Korea, Rep. of
Kuwait
Liechtenstein
Luxembourg
Malta
Monaco
Netherlands
New Zealand
Norway
Portugal
Qatar
San Marino
Saudi Arabia
Singapore
Slovenia
Spain
Sweden
Switzerland
United Arab Emirates
United Kingdom
United States
(41 countries or areas)

Middle income (GNI per capita of $826–$10,065 in 2004)

Albania
Algeria
Angola
Antigua and Barbuda
Argentina
Armenia
Azerbaijan
Barbados
Belarus
Belize
Bolivia
Bosnia and Herzegovina
Botswana
Brazil
Bulgaria
Cape Verde
Chile
China
Colombia
Costa Rica
Croatia
Cuba
Czech Republic
Djibouti
Dominica
Dominican Republic
Ecuador
Egypt
El Salvador
Equatorial Guinea
Estonia
Fiji
Gabon
Georgia
Grenada
Guatemala
Guyana
Honduras
Hungary
Indonesia
Iran, Islamic Rep. of
Iraq
Jamaica
Jordan
Kazakhstan
Kiribati
Latvia
Lebanon
Libyan Arab Jamahiriya
Lithuania

Macedonia, TFYR
Malaysia
Maldives
Marshall Islands
Mauritius
Mexico
Micronesia, Fed. Sts.
Montenegro [a]
Morocco
Namibia
Northern Mariana Islands
Occupied Palestinian
  Territories
Oman
Palau
Panama
Paraguay
Peru
Philippines
Poland
Romania
Russian Federation
Saint Kitts and Nevis
Saint Lucia
Saint Vincent and the
  Grenadines
Samoa (Western)
Serbia [a]
Seychelles
Slovakia
South Africa
Sri Lanka
Suriname
Swaziland
Syrian Arab Republic
Thailand
Tonga
Trinidad and Tobago
Tunisia
Turkey
Turkmenistan
Ukraine
Uruguay
Vanuatu
Venezuela, RB
(93 countries or areas)

Low income (GNI per capita of $825 or less in 2004)

Afghanistan
Bangladesh
Benin
Bhutan
Burkina Faso
Burundi
Cambodia
Cameroon
Central African Republic
Chad
Comoros
Congo
Congo, Dem. Rep. of the
Côte d'Ivoire
Eritrea
Ethiopia
Gambia
Ghana
Guinea
Guinea-Bissau
Haiti
India
Kenya
Korea, Dem. Rep.
Kyrgyzstan
Lao People's Dem. Rep.
Lesotho
Liberia
Madagascar
Malawi
Mali
Mauritania
Moldova, Rep. of
Mongolia
Mozambique
Myanmar
Nepal
Nicaragua
Niger
Nigeria
Pakistan
Papua New Guinea
Rwanda
São Tomé and Principe
Senegal
Sierra Leone
Solomon Islands
Somalia
Sudan
Tajikistan

Tanzania, U. Rep. of
Timor-Leste
Togo
Uganda
Uzbekistan
Viet Nam
Yemen
Zambia
Zimbabwe
(59 countries or areas)

Note: Income aggregates use World Bank classification (effective 1 July 2005) based on gross national income (GNI) per capita. They include the following countries or areas that are not UN member states and therefore not included in the HDI tables: high income, Aruba, Bermuda, Cayman Islands, Faeroe Islands, French Polynesia, Greenland, Guam, Isle of Man, Macao, China (SAR), Netherlands Antilles, New Caledonia, Puerto Rico and Virgin Islands (U.S.); middle income, American Samoa. These countries or areas are included in the aggregates by income level. UN member countries Nauru and Tuvalu are not included because of lack of data.

a The income classification and aggregates based on it refer to Serbia and Montenegro before it separated into two independent states in June 2006.

Countries in the major world aggregates

Developing countries

Afghanistan
Algeria
Angola
Antigua and Barbuda
Argentina
Bahamas
Bahrain
Bangladesh
Barbados
Belize
Benin
Bhutan
Bolivia
Botswana
Brazil
Brunei Darussalam
Burkina Faso
Burundi
Cambodia
Cameroon
Cape Verde
Central African Republic
Chad
Chile
China
Colombia
Comoros
Congo
Congo, Dem. Rep. of the
Costa Rica
Côte d'Ivoire
Cuba
Cyprus
Djibouti
Dominica
Dominican Republic
Ecuador
Egypt
El Salvador
Equatorial Guinea
Eritrea
Ethiopia
Fiji
Gabon
Gambia
Ghana
Grenada
Guatemala
Guinea
Guinea-Bissau

Guyana
Haiti
Honduras
Hong Kong, China (SAR)
India
Indonesia
Iran, Islamic Rep. of
Iraq
Jamaica
Jordan
Kenya
Kiribati
Korea, Dem. Rep.
Korea, Rep. of
Kuwait
Lao People's Dem. Rep.
Lebanon
Lesotho
Liberia
Libyan Arab Jamahiriya
Madagascar
Malawi
Malaysia
Maldives
Mali
Marshall Islands
Mauritania
Mauritius
Mexico
Micronesia, Fed. Sts.
Mongolia
Morocco
Mozambique
Myanmar
Namibia
Nauru
Nepal
Nicaragua
Niger
Nigeria
Occupied Palestinian
    Territories
Oman
Pakistan
Palau
Panama
Papua New Guinea
Paraguay
Peru
Philippines

Qatar
Rwanda
Saint Kitts and Nevis
Saint Lucia
Saint Vincent and the
    Grenadines
Samoa (Western)
São Tomé and Principe
Saudi Arabia
Senegal
Seychelles
Sierra Leone
Singapore
Solomon Islands
Somalia
South Africa
Sri Lanka
Sudan
Suriname
Swaziland
Syrian Arab Republic
Tanzania, U. Rep. of
Thailand
Timor-Leste
Togo
Tonga
Trinidad and Tobago
Tunisia
Turkey
Tuvalu
Uganda
United Arab Emirates
Uruguay
Vanuatu
Venezuela, RB
Viet Nam
Yemen
Zambia
Zimbabwe
(137 countries or areas)

Least developed countries [a]

Afghanistan
Angola
Bangladesh
Benin
Bhutan
Burkina Faso
Burundi

Cambodia
Cape Verde
Central African Republic
Chad
Comoros
Congo, Dem. Rep. of the
Djibouti
Equatorial Guinea
Eritrea
Ethiopia
Gambia
Guinea
Guinea-Bissau
Haiti
Kiribati
Lao People's Dem. Rep.
Lesotho
Liberia
Madagascar
Malawi
Maldives
Mali
Mauritania
Mozambique
Myanmar
Nepal
Niger
Rwanda
Samoa (Western)
São Tomé and Principe
Senegal
Sierra Leone
Solomon Islands
Somalia
Sudan
Tanzania, U. Rep. of
Timor-Leste
Togo
Tuvalu
Uganda
Vanuatu
Yemen
Zambia
(50 countries or areas)

Central and Eastern Europe and the Commonwealth of Independent States (CIS)

Albania
Armenia
Azerbaijan
Belarus
Bosnia and Herzegovina
Bulgaria
Croatia
Czech Republic
Estonia
Georgia
Hungary
Kazakhstan
Kyrgyzstan
Latvia
Lithuania
Macedonia, TFYR
Moldova, Rep. of
Montenegro [b]
Poland
Romania
Russian Federation
Serbia [b]
Slovakia
Slovenia
Tajikistan
Turkmenistan
Ukraine
Uzbekistan
(28 countries or areas)

Organisation for Economic Co-operation and Development (OECD)

Australia
Austria
Belgium
Canada
Czech Republic
Denmark
Finland
France
Germany
Greece
Hungary

Iceland
Ireland
Italy
Japan
Korea, Rep. of
Luxembourg
Mexico
Netherlands
New Zealand
Norway
Poland
Portugal
Slovakia
Spain
Sweden
Switzerland
Turkey
United Kingdom
United States
(30 countries or areas)

High-income OECD countries

Australia
Austria
Belgium
Canada
Denmark
Finland
France
Germany
Greece
Iceland
Ireland
Italy
Japan
Korea, Rep. of
Luxembourg
Netherlands
New Zealand
Norway
Portugal
Spain
Sweden
Switzerland
United Kingdom
United States
(24 countries or areas)

a UN classification based on UN-OHRLLS 2006.
b Regional aggregates are based on data for Serbia and Montenegro before it separated into two independent states in June 2006.

Developing countries in the regional aggregates

Arab States
Algeria
Bahrain
Djibouti
Egypt
Iraq
Jordan
Kuwait
Lebanon
Libyan Arab Jamahiriya
Morocco
Occupied Palestinian
  Territories
Oman
Qatar
Saudi Arabia
Somalia
Sudan
Syrian Arab Republic
Tunisia
United Arab Emirates
Yemen
(20 countries or areas)

East Asia and the Pacific
Brunei Darussalam
Cambodia
China
Fiji
Hong Kong, China (SAR)
Indonesia
Kiribati
Korea, Dem. Rep.
Korea, Rep. of
Lao People's Dem. Rep.
Malaysia
Marshall Islands
Micronesia, Fed. Sts.
Mongolia
Myanmar
Nauru
Palau
Papua New Guinea
Philippines
Samoa (Western)
Singapore
Solomon Islands
Thailand
Timor-Leste
Tonga
Tuvalu
Vanuatu
Viet Nam
(28 countries or areas)

South Asia
Afghanistan
Bangladesh
Bhutan
India
Iran, Islamic Rep. of
Maldives
Nepal
Pakistan
Sri Lanka
(9 countries or areas)

Latin America and the Caribbean
Antigua and Barbuda
Argentina
Bahamas
Barbados
Belize
Bolivia
Brazil
Chile
Colombia
Costa Rica
Cuba
Dominica
Dominican Republic
Ecuador
El Salvador
Grenada
Guatemala
Guyana
Haiti
Honduras
Jamaica
Mexico
Nicaragua
Panama
Paraguay
Peru
Saint Kitts and Nevis
Saint Lucia
Saint Vincent and the
  Grenadines
Suriname
Trinidad and Tobago
Uruguay
Venezuela, RB
(33 countries or areas)

Southern Europe
Cyprus
Turkey
(2 countries or areas)

Sub-Saharan Africa
Angola
Benin
Botswana
Burkina Faso
Burundi
Cameroon
Cape Verde
Central African Republic
Chad
Comoros
Congo
Congo, Dem. Rep. of the
Côte d'Ivoire
Equatorial Guinea
Eritrea
Ethiopia
Gabon
Gambia
Ghana
Guinea
Guinea-Bissau
Kenya
Lesotho
Liberia
Madagascar
Malawi
Mali
Mauritania
Mauritius
Mozambique
Namibia
Niger
Nigeria
Rwanda
São Tomé and Principe
Senegal
Seychelles
Sierra Leone
South Africa
Swaziland
Tanzania, U. Rep. of
Togo
Uganda
Zambia
Zimbabwe
(45 countries or areas)

Index to indicators

Goals and targets from the Millennium Declaration	Indicators for measuring progress	Indicator table
Goal 1 Eradicate extreme poverty and hunger		
Target 1 Halve, between 1990 and 2015, the proportion of people whose income is less than $1 a day	1. Proportion of population below $1 (PPP) a day 2. Poverty gap ratio (incidence × depth of poverty) 3. Share of poorest quintile in national consumption	3 15
Target 2 Halve, between 1990 and 2015, the proportion of people who suffer from hunger	4. Prevalence of underweight children under five years of age 5. Proportion of population below minimum level of dietary energy consumption	3, 7 1a[a], 7[a]
Goal 2 Achieve universal primary education		
Target 3 Ensure that, by 2015, children everywhere, boys and girls alike, will be able to complete a full course of primary schooling	6. Net enrolment ratio in primary education 7. Proportion of pupils starting grade 1 who reach grade 5 8. Literacy rate of 15- to 24-year-olds	1a, 12 12 12
Goal 3 Promote gender equality and empower women		
Target 4 Eliminate gender disparity in primary and secondary education, preferably by 2005, and in all levels of education no later than 2015	9. Ratio of girls to boys in primary, secondary and tertiary education 10. Ratio of literate women to men ages 15–24 11. Share of women in wage employment in the non-agricultural sector[b] 12. Proportion of seats held by women in national parliaments	26[c] 26[d] 29
Goal 4 Reduce child mortality		
Target 5 Reduce by two-thirds, between 1990 and 2015, the under-five mortality rate	13. Under-five mortality rate 14. Infant mortality rate 15. Proportion of one-year-old children immunized against measles	1a, 10 10 6
Goal 5 Improve maternal health		
Target 6. Reduce by three-quarters, between 1990 and 2015, the maternal mortality ratio	16. Maternal mortality ratio 17. Proportion of births attended by skilled health personnel	10 6
Goal 6 Combat HIV/AIDS, malaria and other diseases		
Target 7 Have halted by 2015 and begun to reverse the spread of HIV/AIDS	18. HIV prevalence among pregnant women 15–24[e] 19. Condom use rate of the contraceptive prevalence rate 19a. Condom use at last high-risk sex 19b. Percentage of 15- to 24-year-olds with comprehensive correct knowledge of HIV/AIDS 19c. Contraceptive prevalence rate 20. Ratio of school attendance of orphans to school attendance of non-orphans ages 10–14	 9 6
Target 8 Have halted by 2015 and begun to reverse the incidence of malaria and other major diseases	21. Prevalence and death rates associated with malaria 22. Proportion of population in malaria-risk areas using effective malaria prevention and treatment measures 23. Prevalence and death rates associated with tuberculosis 24. Proportion of tuberculosis cases detected and cured under directly observed treatment short course (DOTS)	 9[f] 9[g] 9
Goal 7 Ensure environmental sustainability		
Target 9 Integrate the principles of sustainable development into country policies and programmes and reverse the loss of environmental resources	25. Proportion of land area covered by forest 26. Ratio of area protected to maintain biological diversity to surface area 27. Energy use (kilograms of oil equivalent) per $1 GDP (PPP) 28. Carbon dioxide emissions per capita and consumption of ozone-depleting chlorofluorocarbons (CFCs) 29. Proportion of population using solid fuels	 21[h] 21[i]
Target 10 Halve, by 2015, the proportion of people without sustainable access to safe drinking water and sanitation	30. Proportion of population with sustainable access to an improved water source, urban and rural 31. Proportion of population with access to improved sanitation, urban and rural	1a[j], 7[j] 7[k]

(continued on next page)

Goals and targets from the Millennium Declaration	Indicators for measuring progress	Indicator table
Target 11 By 2020, to have achieved a significant improvement in the lives of at least 100 million slum dwellers	32. Proportion of households with access to secure tenure	

Goal 8 Develop a global partnership for development

Goals and targets from the Millennium Declaration	Indicators for measuring progress	Indicator table
Target 12 Develop further an open, rule-based, predictable, non-discriminatory trading and financial system. Includes a commitment to good governance, development, and poverty reduction—both nationally and internationally	*Official development assistance (ODA)* 33. Net ODA, total and to least developed countries, as a percentage of OECD/DAC donors' gross national income (GNI) 34. Proportion of total bilateral, sector-allocable ODA of OECD/DAC donors to basic social services (basic education, primary health care, nutrition, safe water and sanitation) 35. Proportion of bilateral ODA of OECD/DAC donors that is untied	17 l 17
Target 13 Address the special needs of the least developed countries. Includes: tariff- and quota-free access for least-developed countries' exports; enhanced programme of debt relief for HIPCs and cancellation of official bilateral debt; and more generous ODA for countries committed to poverty reduction	36. ODA received in landlocked countries as proportion of their gross national incomes 37. ODA received in small island developing states as proportion of their gross national incomes *Market access* 38. Proportion of total developed country imports (by value and excluding arms) from developing countries and from the least developed countries, admitted free of duties	17
Target 14 Address the special needs of landlocked countries and small island developing states	39. Average tariffs imposed by developed countries on agricultural products and textiles and clothing from developing countries	
Target 15 Deal comprehensively with the debt problems of developing countries through national and international measures in order to make debt sustainable in the long term	40. Agricultural support estimate for OECD countries as a percentage of their gross domestic product 41. Proportion of ODA provided to help build trade capacity *Debt sustainability* 42. Total number of countries that have reached their HIPC decision points and number that have reached their HIPC completion points (cumulative) 43. Debt relief committed under HIPC Debt Initiative 44. Debt service as a percentage of exports of goods and services	18
Target 16 In cooperation with developing countries, develop and implement strategies for decent and productive work for youth	45. Unemployment rate of 15- to 24-year-olds, male and female and total	20 m
Target 17 In cooperation with pharmaceutical companies, provide access to affordable essential drugs in developing countries	46. Proportion of population with access to affordable essential drugs on a sustainable basis	
Target 18 In cooperation with the private sector, make available the benefits of new technologies, especially information and communications	47. Telephone lines and cellular subscribers per 100 people 48a. Personal computers in use per 100 people 48b. Internet users per 100 people	13 n 13

a Tables 1a and 7 present this indicator as undernourished people as a percentage of total population.
b Table 27 includes data on female employment by economic activity.
c Table presents female (net or gross) enrolment ratio as a percentage of male ratio for primary, secondary and tertiary education levels separately.
d Table presents data on female youth literacy data as a percentage of male rate.
e Tables 1a and 9 present HIV prevalence among people ages 15–49.
f Table includes data on children under age five using insecticide-treated bed nets, and children under age five with fever treated with antimalarial drugs.
g Table includes data on tuberculosis cases per 100,000 people.
h Table presents this indicator as GDP per unit of energy use (2000 PPP US$ per kilogram of oil equivalent).
i Table includes data on carbon dioxide emissions per capita.
j Tables 1a and 7 include data on population with sustainable access to an improved water source for urban and rural combined.
k Table includes data on population with sustainable access to improved sanitation for urban and rural combined.
l Table includes data on official development assistance (ODA) to least developed countries as a percentage of total ODA.
m Table includes data on unemployment rate of 15- to 24-year-olds as total and female rate as a percentage of male rate for OECD countries only.
n Table presents telephone lines and cellular subscribers separately.